Education and Cultural Process

Third Edition

Education and Cultural Process

Anthropological Approaches

Third Edition

edited by

George D. Spindler

Stanford University

WAVELAND

PRESS, INC.

Long Grove, Illinois

For information about this book, contact:
    Waveland Press, Inc.
    4180 IL Route 83, Suite 101
    Long Grove, IL 60047-9580
    (847) 634-0081
    info@waveland.com
    www.waveland.com

This book is dedicated to Louise Schaubel Spindler.

Your radiant smile, your loving personality, your care and concern for others, and your keen intellect—always curious about the next bend in the river, the next page of a book, or the next interview or observation—will be sorely missed by all who knew you.

Deceased March 24, 1997

Contents

Preface   xi

PART I: HISTORY   1

Preview   2

1 Theory, Research, and Application in Educational
   Anthropology   4
Elizabeth M. Eddy

2 Educational Anthropology: Early History and Educationist
   Contributors   26
Rosalie Ford

PART II: APPROACHES TO THE STUDY OF SCHOOLS   47

Preview   48

3 Ethnography: An Anthropological View   50
George and *Louise Spindler*

4 Cultural Process and Ethnography:
   An Anthropological Perspective   56
George and *Louise Spindler*

5 The Teacher as an Enemy   77
Harry F. Wolcott

PART III: EDUCATION AND CULTURAL PROCESS
               IN THE UNITED STATES   93

Preview   94

6 Why Have Minority Groups in North America
   Been Disadvantaged by Their Schools?   96
George D. Spindler

7 Achieving School Failure 1972–1997   110
Raymond P. McDermott

8 Racing in Place: Middle Class Work in Success/Failure   136
Hervé Varenne, Shelley Goldman and *Raymond P. McDermott*

9 Education in Communitarian Societies—The Old Order
Amish and the Hutterian Brethren   158
John A. Hostetler

10 The Bauer County Fair: Community Celebration as Context for
Youth Experiences of Learning and Belonging   179
Maureen K. Porter

11 Teaching and Learning through Mien Culture: A Case Study in
Community-School Relations   215
Lorie Hammond

12 Beth Anne: A Case Study of Culturally Defined Adjustment
and Teacher Perceptions   246
George D. Spindler

13 Playing by the Rules   262
Margaret A. Gibson

**PART IV: CULTURAL PROCESS IN EDUCATION
VIEWED TRANSCULTURALLY**   **271**

Preview   272

14 The Transmission of Culture   275
George D. Spindler

15 The Anthropology of Learning   310
Harry F. Wolcott

16 Instruction and Affect in Hopi Cultural Continuity   339
Dorothy Eggan

17 Contrasts between Prepubertal and Postpubertal Education   362
C. W. M. Hart

18 Some Discontinuities in the Enculturation
of Mistassini Cree Children   383
Peter S. Sindell

19 The Display of Cultural Knowledge in Cultural Transmission:
Models of Participation from the Pacific Island of Kosrae   393
Vera S. Michalchik

PART V: TRANSCULTURAL COMPARISONS   **427**

Preview   428

20 Day Care Teachers and Children in the United States and Japan: Ethnography, Reflexive Interviewing and Cultural Dialogue   430
Mariko Fujita and *Toshiyuki Sano*

21 Does Formalism Spell Failure?: Values and Pedagogies in Cross-Cultural Perspective   454
Victoria J. Baker

22 Crosscultural, Comparative, Reflective Interviewing in Schoenhausen and Roseville   472
George and *Louise Spindler*

PART VI: TEACHING CULTURE   **495**

Preview   496

23 Transcultural Sensitization   498
George D. Spindler

24 Anthropology in a Zuni High School Classroom: The Zuni-Stanford Program   513
Clifford Barnett and *John Rick*

25 Teaching Culture   536
George and *Louise Spindler*

26 Class Discussion: Comparing Hutterite Education and an Inner City School   548
Mica Pollock

Finis   558

Preface

This book is intended as a text in the anthropology of education, for courses and seminars that utilize anthropological materials and perspectives in the analysis of educative processes. These courses and seminars are offered to both the upper-level undergraduate and the first- or second-year graduate student. Some are given in schools of education, others in departments of anthropology. Many are listed in both. This book may also be used as a text or collateral reading in the cultural foundations of education, the sociology of education, in teacher training and curricular courses, and in other foundation areas such as philosophy, history, and psychology, as well as in applied anthropology and cultural dynamics courses that are in part concerned with education. It must therefore serve a wide range of interest and expertise. It is designed with this diverse audience in mind.

This volume first appeared in 1955 as *Education and Anthropology* (Stanford University Press). That book was an edited version of a four-day conference seminar in Carmel Valley, California, supported by the Carnegie Foundation and organized by George and Louise Spindler. Although there were important antecedents to this conference (as a reading of Part I of this book will demonstrate), it is often touted as the origin of the field of educational anthropology. Twelve prominent anthropologists and as many prominent educators exchanged papers and views on topics that still concern us today. One chapter from that volume, C.W.M. Hart's classic paper on prepubertal and postpubertal education, survives in the present volume forty-three years later. *Education and Culture: Anthropological Approaches* was published by Holt, Rinehart and Winston in 1963 under George Spindler's editorship. The first edition of *Education and Cultural Process* was published by Holt, Rinehart and Winston in 1974. The second edition of that book was published in 1987 by Waveland Press, as is the present volume—the 1997 third edition—which contains twelve new chapters representing significant recent developments and issues in the field.

Each of the parts of this volume are arranged around certain themes. Part I represents the history of the field from two different points of view, one of them anthropological and the other one educationist. They overlap considerably, but still the emphasis is different.

Part II is concerned with approaches to the study of schools. Chapters 3 and 4 are explicitly about ethnographic approaches. Chapter 5 concerns a condition many teachers encounter in the course of their professional activity that affects both their ability to teach and their ability to do ethnography of their own classrooms.

Part III addresses education and cultural process in the United States. Its topics range widely, including chapters on minority groups and their circumstances in American society and American schools; characteristic features of American schools, such as emphasis on competition; education in communitarian societies, such as the old-order Amish; and the incorporation of Mien culture (a Southeast Asian culture) with a science curriculum in the elementary schools.

Part IV addresses cultural process in education viewed transculturally. The focus is on nonliterate, non-Western cultures such as the Hopi, the Tiwi, the Mistassini Cree, and a formerly nonliterate culture on the Pacific Island of Kosrae.

Part V concerns transcultural comparisons, including a chapter comparing Japanese and American day-care centers and another chapter making a cross-cultural comparison of schooling in Germany and in Wisconsin. Another chapter contrasts the formalistic teaching methods characteristic of schools in developing countries and the progressive, mainstream Western concepts of a proper education.

Part VI, Teaching Culture, includes a report of an experiment in teaching anthropology in a Zuni Native American high school, a chapter on teaching cultures using case studies, and a class discussion comparing Hutterite education with an inner-city school education. The reader will find the approach in this book anthropological but eclectic. The wide range of problems should stir the imagination of everyone who considers what the authors have to say.

Those familiar with the previous edition of this volume will notice the absence of a section of readings devoted to nonhuman primate learning. Due to space limitations I have foregone the inclusion of contributions on this important area. As a replacement we recommend William McGrew's *Gombe: Wild Chimpanzees in Western Tanzania* (Harcourt Brace, 1998). This study of chimpanzee culture describes all phases of chimpanzee learning, including social learning.

Fundamental to the anthropological approach is the transcultural perspective—a special feature of anthropology and of this book. Although there is only one section explicitly devoted to cultural process in education viewed transculturally, every section displays the influence of this perspective. From the anthropological point of view, "transcultural" is easily converted to "multicultural." The world is diverse, and so must be our approaches to understanding it.

Our colleagues Ray McDermott and Fred Erickson recently conducted interview sessions with Louise and myself dealing with our practice of ethnography since 1948. The uncut, unedited video, *A Life with Ethnography*, offers frank and revealing discussions, with special attention given to our work in schools and with the problems we see in education. It is our hope that instructors will find this to be a useful companion to this latest edition of *Education and Cultural Process*, as well as an important tool for stimulating classroom discussions. For more information, write to me c/o Ethnographics, Box 38, Calistoga, CA 94515.

In the editorial previews I often refer to "we." By this I mean George and Louise Spindler. Since most of our chapters and the thinking behind the previews are joint products, this seems appropriate.

G.D.S.
Calistoga, CA 1997

Acknowledgments

Thanks are due all of the authors, without whom, obviously, there would be no book. Special thanks are due Gayle Zawilla of Waveland Press, who worked through the myriad details involved in a volume of this kind, and who kept the project on track. Thanks also to Ona Ondre of Stanford University, who saw to it that my dictations were transcribed quickly and accurately, and to Tom Curtin, who saw the virtue in a revision and encouraged me to do it. I appreciate everyone's goodwill and good help during a time of bereavement for me after the sudden death of my partner and sweetheart.

George Spindler, Editor

Part I

HISTORY

Preview

The two chapters of Part I include an overview of the history of the field—one chapter from an anthropological perspective and another from an educationist point of view, providing useful background for the rest of the book. The anthropologist, Elizabeth Eddy, obtained her Ph.D. in cultural anthropology but has worked in and around education for many years. The educationist, Rosalie Ford, obtained her Ph.D. in the social foundations of education and also studied anthropology during this time. She obtained a master's degree in anthropology but worked in education and within public schools for many years. She currently works for the City of Springfield, Massachusetts, School Department, with at-risk children. Early in her career she taught Hispanic children in a rural area in New Mexico and African-American youngsters in Kansas City, Missouri. It is interesting to see not only how these two chapters overlap but also the ways in which their emphases diverge. Some of the contributions cited by one author are not cited by the other. One acquires a feeling for the contributions of the educationist to the development of an educational anthropology that is usually lacking in anthropologically oriented overviews.

It is important for us to know that educational anthropology is not an upstart field of recent interest without roots in the mainstream of anthropological and educationist inquiry and thought. Although there may be some tendency in contemporary work to detach educational anthropology from the rest of the discipline, the history of our subdiscipline is embedded in the history of anthropology—and, if we have a future, will continue to be so but at the same time will relate effectively to the concerns of educators and the processes of education.

There is a tendency for fellow anthropologists to think of educational anthropology as applied anthropology. It is true that there is a strong ameliorationist orientation in our field, but educational anthropology is—and must be—more than applied anthropology. I do not mean to suggest that an applied label is demeaning. Far from it. However, applying anthropological concepts, perspectives, methods of research, guiding models and paradigms, and interpretive principles to processes of education, both in our own society and abroad, requires that theory and practice be joined. We cannot be guided solely by the demands of our society for the solution of immediate educational problems. We must maintain a disciplinary posture and approach the study of problems in a disciplinary manner with appropriate tools. This is easier said than done in the present context in which we work. Anthropology is changing. Some would say it is fractionating, falling apart, but this is not our point of view. This volume will show us how anthropology produces a fairly coherent interpretive framework for the analysis of educational process. In any event, the conceptual structuring of the field is a primary concern.

                                                                    The Editor

1

Theory, Research, and Application in Educational Anthropology

University of Florida

Educational anthropology, usually referred to as anthropology and education, has developed within the context of the rise of anthropology as a profession. The transition of anthropology from an avocation pursued by the independently wealthy or those who made their living in other fields into a profession that provides a livelihood for its practitioners did not occur until the early years of the twentieth century. The process of professionalization required the establishment of the discipline within reputable universities, the anthropological training of students who subsequently would support themselves by work in this field, and the increased production of scientific research and publications that were sufficiently technical to be comprehensible primarily to fellow practitioners.[1]

Substantial growth in the number of professional anthropologists is a post-World War II phenomenon. In the United States, the postwar years were accompanied by unprecedented changes in the funding of anthropologists and their careers, intense expansion of specialization within the discipline, and a proliferation of professional associations and journals organized by and for specialized interest groups.

Educational anthropologists represent one of many interest groups but, unlike some specialists, their historical roots date from the late nineteenth century when anthropology emerges as a science. An important reason for the long history of anthropological interest in education is that the process of professionalization was intertwined inevitably with the promotion of the discipline as a legitimate and needed new area of scientific teaching within institutions of higher education. Yet as early as the late 1800s, a few anthropologists were concerned with the practice of education outside the academy. It was then that the

Source: Reproduced with minor revisions by permission of the American Anthropological Association from *Anthropology and Education Quarterly* 16:2 (summer 1985). Not for further reproduction.

potential contributions of anthropology to pedagogy, the school curriculum, and an understanding of the culture of childhood were first recognized (Barnes and Barnes 1896; Chamberlain 1896; Fletcher 1888; Stevenson 1887; Vandewalker 1898). Prior to World War I the fullest and most widely known statement along these lines was that of Maria Montessori, whose *Pedagogical Anthropology* was published in the United States in 1913.

The early beginnings of educational anthropology are important, but contemporary educational anthropology is primarily the outgrowth of social and cultural anthropology as it developed during the 1920s. For this reason, the focus here is on significant relationships between the growth of professionalism in anthropology and the development of educational anthropology as an area of specialization within the discipline during the past 70 years. The historical trends in educational anthropology throughout this period will be divided into two time periods: the formative years, 1925–1954; the institutionalization and specialization years, 1955 to the present.

I argue later in the chapter that the Conference on Anthropology and Education convened at Stanford in 1954 and the formal organization of the Council on Anthropology and Education in 1970 marked major turning points in the history of educational anthropology. Each event culminated previous developments and inaugurated new ones in the field. But these events also mirrored important shifts in professional anthropology as a whole. The changes represented more than the replacement of older theories and research methodologies with newer ones. In addition, they reflected important changes in the sources of economic support for anthropological work, modifications in the relationship of anthropology to applied problems, and more elaborated definitions of the meaning of professionalism.

The factual material and analysis presented here are preliminary at best. A history of educational anthropology has yet to be written, and the history of anthropology itself is only beginning to be documented adequately.[2] Thus the pages to follow provide but a sketch of a much longer story that requires extensive scholarly endeavor and documentation before it can be told fully.

The Formative Years: 1925–1954

An examination of the Roberts and Akinsanya chronological bibliographies on anthropological studies of childhood and anthropology and education reveals a remarkable array of anthropologists who engaged in research related to formalized systems of education and the enculturation of the child during the years between 1925 and 1954 (1976:375–412; see also Roberts, n.d.). The roster reads like a *Who's*

Who of American and British founders of modern anthropology. Luminaries include Gregory Bateson, Ruth Benedict, Franz Boas, John Dollard, John Embree, E. E. Evans-Pritchard, Raymond Firth, Meyer Fortes, John Gillin, Alexander Goldenweiser, Felix Keesing, Melville Herskovits, H. Ian Hogbin, Ralph Linton, Bronislaw Malinowski, Margaret Mead, Siegfried Nadel, Morris Opler, Hortense Powdermaker, Paul Radin, Robert Redfield, Audrey Richards, Edward Sapir, Laura Thompson, W. Lloyd Warner, Mark Hanna Watkins, Camilla Wedgewood, John Whiting, Monica Wilson, and others.

With the exception of Boas and Malinowski, these notables began their careers after anthropology had broken with nineteenth-century unilinear evolution and the extreme diffusionist theories of Grafton Elliot Smith, W. J. Perry, and Fritz Graebner. In England, the publication in 1922 of Malinowski's *Argonauts of the Western Pacific* and Radcliffe-Brown's *The Andaman Islanders* ushered in "practical" or "applied" anthropology, the terms subsequently used by Malinowski (1929) and Radcliffe-Brown (1930), respectively, to denote the emergence of social anthropology as a new branch of the discipline. For both Malinowski and Radcliffe-Brown, there was a close relationship between theoretical and practical applied anthropology. Oriented toward the study of human behavior and institutions in the contemporary world, they argued that the scientific knowledge produced by this type of study would be capable of application by those concerned with the practical problems of planning administrative and educational policies for native populations in the British colonies.

In the United States, Franz Boas' choice of the study of adolescence among a primitive people for Margaret Mead's fieldwork in 1925 marked a similar transition of the discipline into the study of a new set of problems related to the modern world. In *Coming of Age in Samoa* (1928), Mead argued the value of comparing American civilization with "simpler" societies in order to illuminate our own methods of education. By the mid-1930s the study of culture and personality was well established in American anthropology. Mead and other leaders in this field gave considerable attention to the practical relevance of their work to educational problems.

On both sides of the Atlantic, the internal intellectual developments that foreshadowed the florescence of modern social and cultural anthropology were influenced significantly by a transformation in the institutional framework within which the discipline developed after 1920. The major changes were modification in the economic base for funding anthropological research, the growth of an interdisciplinary movement in the social sciences, and the academic expansion of anthropology within universities (Stocking 1976:9–13). These changes were interrelated and greatly facilitated by the liberal funding provided by American foundations for the development of the social sciences, including British social anthropology and the redirection of cultural anthropology in the United States.

The Rockefeller Foundation played the major role by making the support of the social sciences the chief objective of the Laura Spelman Rockefeller Memorial Fund. These monies provided unprecedented funding for the creation of facilities for social science research both at home and abroad and the fellowship monies for the training of able persons working in the social sciences. Important roles also were played by the Carnegie, Phelps-Stokes, Julius Rosenwald, Macy, and other philanthropic agencies. The foundations were instrumental in bringing together anthropologists and other social scientists for the investigation of practical social problems related to topics such as race, immigration, the development of colonial peoples, the consequences of intercultural contact, and the impact of social change. They fostered the international exchange of scholars, which, in the case of anthropology, brought Malinowski, Radcliffe-Brown, and others to American universities as lecturers who diffused new ideas and perspectives into the American version of the discipline.[3]

Within American universities, the linkage of anthropology to the social sciences was expressed organizationally in the formation of new departments in combination with sociology during the 1930s—a common practice until well after World War II. In England, the London School of Economics was already a model of an interdisciplinary college devoted to teaching and research in the social sciences and had been so since its founding by Sydney and Beatrice Webb in 1895. It was there that Malinowski received his training in ethnology prior to World War I and conducted his world-renowned seminars during the 1920s and 1930s.

At this time, anthropology was a young science, and those who entered it typically came by a roundabout way after professional training and experience in other fields. Many of the leaders were the offspring of professionals in other disciplines. For some, interdisciplinary growth and development occurred as a consequence of marriage. For example, Malinowski was the son of an eminent linguist who had done work in Polish ethnography and folklore. Malinowski himself received a doctorate in physics and mathematics at the University of Cracow before beginning postgraduate work at the London School of Economics in 1910 (Firth 1981:101). Margaret Mead was the daughter of an economist father and sociologist mother and completed an M.A. in psychology before entering the graduate program in anthropology at Columbia. Her first husband, Luther Cressman, was a graduate student in sociology and an ordained Episcopal clergyman at the time of their marriage. Her second and third husbands, Reo Fortune and Gregory Bateson, were British-trained social anthropologists (Mead 1972:passim). Meyer Fortes, a native of South Africa, held a Ph.D. in psychology and had professional experience in the first Child Guidance Clinic established in England before undertaking postgraduate training in anthropology under Malinowski, Firth, and Seligman at the London School of Economics in the 1930s (Fortes 1978:2–3). Others in this period represented similar anticipatory socialization patterns that undoubtedly influenced their later professional contributions to anthropology as a social science and to work in interdisciplinary groups.

In summary, the formative years of educational anthropology occurred within the context of disciplinary developments in theory and research methodology that advanced anthropological studies of contemporary peoples in a rapidly changing world. A foundation-based economic support system gave high priority to the development of the social sciences because of their potential contribution to a scientific approach to the management of critical social problems. Within anthropology, the Rockefeller and other foundations were supportive especially of those who were leaders in the new social anthropology in Britain and the redirection of cultural anthropology in the United States. The foundations specifically fostered interdisciplinary relationships among social scientists and between them and those in other professions who were engaged in what a later generation would call the administration and delivery of human services. A major result of these trends was the definition of the social sciences as applied sciences. Thus, to be a modern social and cultural anthropologist during these years also was to be an applied anthropologist. Many who entered the profession at this time brought past experiences congruent with these trends, and a remarkable number of them gave attention to educational processes and problems.

The Ethnography of Childhood
as Applied Anthropology

The application of anthropology to education during this period emphasized several themes. At the theoretical level, anthropologists challenged Freud, Piaget, Watson, and others who generalized about human development and behavior and ignored data about cross-cultural variations that anthropologists were beginning to assemble. During the 1920s and 1930s the eugenics movement was strong, and anthropologists actively refuted those who claimed that human behavior was determined biologically. These debates over theory were more than academic. At the time, they were major controversies over conceptions about the intellectual nature of the child, and they had important implications for educational policy.

Between the mid-1920s and the mid-1950s, anthropological research related to child development increased rapidly, not only in then remote parts of the world such as Africa and Oceania, but also in the United States. During the 1930s, for example, American anthropologists participated in the work of several commissions established by the Progressive Education Association with the support of funds from the General Education Board (Rockefeller Foundation) and the Carnegie Corporation. Their activities included the development of proposals and materials for revising the social studies curriculum in secondary schools, and the initiation of intensive studies of adolescents, their school life, and the communities in which they lived. In addition, anthropologists participated in the 1934 Hanover Conference on Human Relations that carried forward inquiries into the enculturation and socialization of the child that began with the Seminar on the Impact of Culture on Personality in 1930 at Yale under the direction of Edward Sapir and John Dollard. The Hanover Conference formulated an unpublished outline that guided investigations and educational programs such as those of the Progressive Education Association (Frank 1955).

The application of fieldwork methodologies to the study of American communities began in the late 1920s and produced classic studies which revealed that within American society there are diversities of enculturation and participation in formal educational systems related to differences in race, ethnicity, and social class (Davis, Gartner, and Gardner 1941; Dollard 1937; Drake and Cayton 1945; Gillin 1948; Hollingshead 1949; Johnson 1941; Lynd and Lynd 1929, 1937; Warner 1942; Warner and Lunt 1941; Warner, Havighurst, and Loeb 1944; West 1945). During the 1930s, a few American anthropologists also were involved with the educational problems of Native Americans. As employees of the Bureau of Indian Affairs, they wrote historical and ethnographic texts for use in Native American schools and developed orthographies for use in bilingual school texts (Kennard and MacGregor 1958:832–35).

Along with professionals trained in psychology, psychiatry, and medicine, anthropologists participated in a six-year cooperative social action research program on Native American personality, education, and administration. This program was initiated in 1941 by the United States Department of the Interior and Commissioner of Indian Affairs John Collier. It was established first in cooperation with the Committee on Human Development at the University of Chicago and later with the Society for Applied Anthropology. An interdisciplinary study of 1,000 Native American children in 12 reservations representing 5 tribes, the project was oriented toward the collection of scientific data that later became the basis for preparing recommendations to improve federal policies in Native American administration and educational programs (Kennard and MacGregor 1953:835; Thompson 1951). After World War II, the application of ethnographic studies of children to federal policies continued to be a major concern among some anthropologists who joined with other social scientists and played an influential role in the 1954 U.S. Supreme Court *Brown v. Board of Education of Topeka* decision (Kluger 1976:passim).

The involvement of anthropologists with matters of public policy related to education was not confined to the United States. In England during the 1920s, intensive efforts of a small but extraordinarily influential group of leading missionaries, educators, members of Parliament, colonial officers, and others succeeded in attracting the active participation of the Phelps-Stokes Fund and the Carnegie Corporation in seeking better solutions to the problems of education in Africa.[4] These and other philanthropic organizations long had been engaged in attempts to improve schooling for blacks in the South, and the British sought models based on this experience that might be relevant to African education in rural areas. Under the leadership of Thomas Jesse Jones, an American sociologist who had conducted a survey of African-American education in the South (Jones 1917) and was the educational director of the fund, the Phelps-Stokes Fund supported two major surveys of African education. The first Phelps-Stokes Commission visited West and South Africa in 1920–21; three years later, the second Commission went to East, Central, and South Africa (Jones 1922–1925).

In 1923 an Advisory Committee on Native Education in Tropical Africa was established in London by the Secretary of State for the Colonies. This committee was instrumental in fostering greater political concern with African education and supportive of developing innovative approaches based on scientific knowledge. One consequence of these activities was that in 1925 the Carnegie Foundation made the first of many grants to African education and provided funds to the Kenya Education Department for the development of a Jeanes school to train supervisors for village schools. (The name "Jeanes" was taken from the name attached to itinerant supervisors of rural black schools in the American South because initial monies used to support this program there had been provided by the privately endowed Jeanes Fund in the United States.)

Philanthropic American efforts in African education during the 1930s and 1940s were extensive and represented what was then considered to be the best thought on educating the "backward races" as well as an exportation to Africa of the philosophy of industrial and vocational education that had been instituted at Tuskegee, the Hampton

Institute, and other southern schools. Even at the time, the philosophy was controversial within American education, and later historical events demonstrated clearly that it appraised inadequately the educational needs and aspirations of both Africans and African Americans. Yet during the interwar years, the programs often were innovative and brought educational resources to Africa and to the South that otherwise would not have been forthcoming.

Those who were instrumental in turning British attention to the problem of education in Africa during the early 1920s later became key figures in the founding of the International Institute of African Languages and Cultures in 1926. Assisted by grants from the Laura Spelman Rockefeller Memorial Fund, and subsequently from the Rockefeller Foundation, the Institute was based in London but represented an international effort on the part of missionaries, linguists, government officials, educators, and others to achieve a scientifically based understanding of Africa and its native peoples and institutions. From the beginning, both Seligman and Malinowski played an important role in the Institute, but it was the latter who became the more extensively involved in developing the Institute's anthropological research program by training the first generation of anthropologists to undertake modern ethnographic field studies in Africa. Nearly all the early studies on childhood development in African societies are a direct result of Malinowski's working relationships with the Institute and his training of anthropologists, missionaries, educators, and others in ethnographic field methods.[5]

Similar to developments in the United States, what began as ethnographies of childhood and the effects of culture and other environmental factors on children was applied to educational problems, especially those that resulted from culture contact. Malinowski himself traveled to South Africa in 1934 to address the New Education Fellowship, an international conference on progressive education attended by anthropologists, educators, and missionaries who were committed deeply to the need of Western educators to take indigenous native systems of education into account when formulating educational policies (Malinowski 1936). Further, upon his return to England, Malinowski became involved directly in the support of modifications in a particular school in South Africa so that changes could occur that would apply anthropological data to the formal educational system. The theme was echoed in the pages of *Africa*, the official journal of the Institute, by Malinowski's students and by others writing throughout the 1930s and 1940s.

During the same summer of 1934, while Malinowski was in Africa, Radcliffe-Brown was in New Haven giving lectures on comparative sociology. The occasion was a conference titled "Education and Culture

Contacts" convened at Yale under the leadership of Charles Loram, who then chaired the Department of Culture Contacts and Race Relations in the Yale Institute of Human Relations. Funded by the Carnegie Corporation, the conference participants included directors of education, inspectors of schools, missionaries, government officials, social workers, and foundation representatives from the West Indies, India, the Philippines, Great Britain, China, and the United States. The major theme was the need to adapt education to individual and community needs rather than to transfer Western educational practices wholesale (Heyman 1970:126–29). Two years later, in 1936, Felix Keesing organized a five-week study conference at the University of Hawaii that brought together 66 educators and social scientists from 27 nations to examine problems of education and adjustment among peoples of the Pacific (Keesing 1937).

After the war, Margaret Mead helped organize a 1949 conference on "The Educational Problems of Special Cultural Groups" at Teachers College in New York. Sponsored by Teachers College, the Carnegie Corporation, and the General Education Board, this conference was attended by colonial educators from the British Africa territories and American educators from the South in order to discuss the education of blacks in the United States and Africa. In terms of Anglo-American relations, this conference represents a turning point. It marked the end of the era in which attempts were made to apply the experience of African-American education in the South to the problems of African education (Heyman 1970:135–48).

The Stanford Conference, 1954

This summary of selected highlights in the history of educational anthropology between the 1920s and the late 1940s is sufficient to reveal the primary trends in the field at this time. The major research focus was on studies of childhood and youth in a wide variety of societies, including the United States. These data often, but not always, were gathered within the context of broadly based ethnographies or community studies in which data about children and educational processes were only a portion of the total data collected. In the United States, the rise of "culture and personality" as a widely recognized area of scientific inquiry promoted the growth of interest in cross-cultural studies of childhood. In Britain, the impetus came from those who foresaw the strategic importance of education in a rapidly changing empire. Both at home and abroad, American foundations and a few government officials were instrumental in nurturing an emphasis on interdisciplinary collaboration and the application of research to public policy in education.

Anthropological contributions to education during the 1930s and 1940s were impressive. However, as Margaret Mead later observed, the interplay between anthropology and education had been largely "dependent upon personalities rather than any on-going institutionalized process of any sort" (quoted in Spindler 1955:29). The occasion of her remark was the 1954 Stanford Conference on Education and Anthropology, which partially summarized prior developments in the field but also set new directions for the future. A recent retrospective article by Spindler summarizes four major concerns that were thematic throughout the conference: "the search for a philosophical as well as a theoretical articulation of education and anthropology; the necessity for sociocultural contextualization of the educative process; the relation of education to 'culturally phrased' phases of the life cycle; the nature of intercultural understanding and learning" (Spindler 1984:4).

Cast in an exploratory framework, the conference was designed explicitly to address the frontiers of the relationships between the two fields rather than to evaluate what had been done in the past. At the time of the conference, there was no such thing as "educational anthropology" and, as Spindler notes, the conference did not aim to create it (Spindler 1955:5). The status of the field was evident in the then recent compendium *Anthropology Today* (1953) edited by Kroeber, which did not include education in the index despite the attention given to the role of anthropologists in the educational programs of the Bureau of Indian Affairs (Kennard and MacGregor 1953:834–35) and UNESCO (Metraux 1953:886–90) and the inclusion of an article by Mary Hass titled "The Application of Linquistics to Language Teaching" (1953).

The Stanford Conference was funded by the Carnegie Corporation and coordinated by George Spindler, who had accepted a joint appointment as Associate Professor in the School of Education and in the Department of Sociology and Anthropology at Stanford after receiving his Ph.D. in anthropology, sociology, and psychology at UCLA in 1952. Half of the 22 participants were from Stanford. Anthropologists and educators were represented evenly, and the anthropologists included scholars long associated with the field, such as John Gillin, Margaret Mead, and Felix Keesing; and other comparative newcomers, such as Spindler himself, Bernard Siegel, C. W. M. Hart, Jules Henry, Dorothy Lee, Cora DuBois, and Solon Kimball, who in 1953 had accepted a position at Teachers College, Columbia, as Professor of Anthropology in the Department of Philosophy and the Social Sciences. Anthropological respectability was given to the conference by the presence of Alfred Kroeber, then Professor Emeritus at Berkeley. Moreover, the American Anthropological Association co-sponsored the conference, together with the Stanford School of Education and Department of Sociology and Anthropology.

In several respects, the Stanford conference foreshadowed the institutionalization of the relationship between anthropology and education that was to come in the years ahead. Early in the conference both Mead and Keesing commented on the need for institutionalization if the anthropological work of the past was not simply to return to mainstream anthropology. Mead's summary of the conference made the point forcefully:

> [T]his conference has raised the question rather seriously as to whether the communication is between *anthropology* and *education* as such. I mean, can someone defined as pure anthropologist who has no experience in education, who has not primarily studied education in primitive societies, who is not interested in teaching . . . engage in a very profitable form of communication except at the book-reading source material level? . . . So there's a possibility that the communication will have to proceed majorly [sic] either from anthropologists who have taken an active interest in education—an acting professional interest—or educators who've taken an active interest in anthropology . . . And educators should be very careful when they want an anthropologist to cooperate with them, either to expose such anthropologists to a couple of years of internship in the situation where they want them to cooperate, or get anthropologists who have really worked in a field that is relevant, and not order them from the supermarket. . . . (quoted in Spindler 1955:272)

The issues raised by Mead and Keesing presaged the developments in the professionalization of the field described in the remainder of this chapter.

Institutionalization and Specialization: 1955 to the Present

The institutionalization of the relationships between anthropology and education may be seen best against the backdrop of the vast changes in anthropology that occurred after World War II. American isolationism was broken by the war, resulting in the expansion of American influence throughout the world. Educational subsidies provided to veterans made it possible for large numbers of them to return to college and university campuses. Unprecedented numbers of students began to take anthropology courses and to enter graduate programs in the field. The numbers increased as the postwar "baby-boom" generation entered colleges and universities in the 1960s. The 1950s and 1960s were times of intense educational activity and growth in the discipline.

Nourished by rapidly growing student enrollments at all levels and profuse public funding for higher education, anthropologists devoted primary attention to the building of anthropology within the academy.

Dozens of departments were founded where none had existed before, or anthropology severed joint departmental relationships with sociology. Major efforts were made to initiate new graduate programs and to expand old ones so that properly trained anthropologists could fill a demand for teachers of anthropology that far exceeded the supply.

The importance given to teaching in the early 1960s was evident especially in the Educational Resources in Anthropology (ERA) project at Berkeley. Supported by the Course Content Improvement Section of the National Science Foundation, the project sponsored a series of symposia throughout the country on the teaching of anthropology in colleges and universities. In 1963 these papers and additional materials concerned with basic resources for teaching anthropology were published in two volumes by the American Anthropological Association (Mandelbaum, Lasker, and Albert 1963a, 1963b). The volume titled *The Teaching of Anthropology* covered topics related to teaching in all major subfields, including applied anthropology. Attention was given to the undergraduate and graduate curriculum and to interdisciplinary relations in teaching anthropology as part of the curriculum in humanities, biological sciences, and social sciences, or in professional schools and colleges. The articles on this latter topic included one authored by Kimball on "Teaching Anthropology in Professional Education" (Mandelbaum, Lasker, and Albert 1963a:493–502).

The postwar years of academic expansion saw considerable change in the areal and theoretical interests of anthropologists. The earlier leaders of modern anthropology had pioneered anthropological research on a global scale. What had been done by a handful of innovators during the prewar years now became common as anthropologists in training went to foreign settings all over the world to experience fieldwork as a rite of passage into the profession. A changed institutional and economic framework now linked anthropology to interdisciplinary area centers backed by the Social Science Research Council, the Ford Foundation, and the newly established anthropology units of the Smithsonian Institute, National Science Foundation, and the National Institute of Mental Health. Funding from these and other sources, the rise of modern transportation, and the growth of graduate training made it possible for American anthropologists and their students to turn away from the study of cultural diversity at home in favor of study abroad.

Diversity in areal specialization was accompanied by diversity in theoretical interests. No longer dominated by the models of structural functionalism introduced by Malinowski and Radcliffe-Brown and the culture-personality paradigms of Mead and others, contemporary sociocultural anthropology is noteworthy for theoretical diversity, eclecticism, and debate. Further, a wide variety of methodological tools currently are used to collect data and test theory in field settings.

Concomitantly, increased specialization within the discipline is a major trend in professional training and in the professional activities of teaching, publication, and association.

The professionalization of anthropologists that occurred during the halcyon era after World War II was directed toward academic models of professional practice that gave little heed to the application of anthropology to political, economic, or social problems. The development of career roles outside the academy was neglected by a new generation of leaders who themselves had not experienced postdoctoral unemployment and assumed naively that academic expansion would continue indefinitely. The rise of new anthropological theory frequently was intertwined with overt and often unknowledgeable attacks on the motivations or political sympathies of those who earlier had done applied work in the complex settings of the modern world. For all of these reasons, applied anthropology was downgraded or discarded as an area of mainstream anthropological training and interest.

Today the situation is quite different than it was during the 1950s and 1960s. The dramatic postwar expansion of higher education has ended, and doctoral students in anthropology no longer assume that their professional careers will be spent within academe. Of necessity, there is renewed interest in applied anthropology and the practice of anthropology in nonacademic settings. New professional publications, networks, and associations are emerging that define nonacademic employment as a valid anthropological career line. Young anthropologists pioneering in this direction are gradually becoming visible within the profession of anthropology as a whole.[6]

In brief, the post-World War II history of educational anthropology has developed within the milieu of rapid expansion and diversification within the discipline. Although foundations continue to support anthropological research, the major funding comes from governmental sources at the federal and state levels. Anthropology is widely accepted as a discipline at nearly all major universities in the country. At the undergraduate level, the teaching of anthropology occurs in most junior colleges and four-year colleges and is an important basis of support for graduate programs within universities. Despite the successful expansion of anthropology in the academic world, the discipline has been slow to develop career opportunities for anthropologists elsewhere. There are signs that new types of career lines may be emerging currently as one consequence of the end of the abnormal growth period in higher education during the decades after World War II.

Educational Anthropology as Specialized Anthropology

The growth of anthropology as a separate field within higher education was paralleled by its expansion into professional colleges of education. As noted, George Spindler and Solon Kimball were appointed to leading positions in colleges of education in the early 1950s. Although they were not the first anthropologists to teach anthropology to educators, their appointments signaled the beginning of concerted efforts to train graduate students who would be specialists in the field of educational anthropology. Specialized training currently exists at several universities, including Harvard, Stanford, Teachers College (Columbia), and the Universities of California (Berkeley), Florida, Georgia, Oregon, Minnesota, Pennsylvania, Pittsburgh, the State University of New York at Buffalo, and Michigan State.

During the 1950s and 1960s, the teaching of anthropology also increased at the precollegiate level. This was an era when a new social studies movement emerged in which the social sciences gained a larger share of the curriculum. Most social sciences obtained a foothold prior to the war, but anthropology did not make its first appearance until the post-World War II period (Dynneson 1975). For this reason, several anthropologists became involved in presenting the case for anthropology at the precollegiate level, with special attention given to the social studies curriculum. John Chilcott, Solon Kimball, Dorothy Lee, Margaret Mead, and Robert Redfield are among the contributors to educational journals on this topic.[7]

As anthropology began to be taught more widely in professional colleges of education and schools, there were obvious needs for appropriate teaching materials. Anthropology received its first federal support for curriculum development and discipline-oriented teacher training in the early 1960s. Throughout that decade, curriculum development became a conspicuous activity of educational anthropologists.

In 1962 NSF extended support to the Anthropology Curriculum Study Project (ACSP) and at about the same time began to support the Education Development Center's anthropologically oriented curriculum development project, *Man: A Course of Study*. In 1964 the U.S. Office of Education initiated support for the University of Minnesota's Project Social Studies, which also was oriented strongly toward anthropology (Dynneson 1975).

In 1963, a curriculum development project of another type was initiated at Hunter College. Funded by the U.S. Office of Youth Development and Juvenile Delinquency, and known as the Teacher Resources in Urban Education Project (Project TRUE), this program employed several anthropologists and others to develop curricular materials for the training of teachers working in inner-city schools. Many of the materials developed by anthropologists were based on data collected within the schools or from extended interviews with beginning teachers (Eddy 1967, 1969; Fuchs 1966, 1969; Moore 1967). Others were based on extensive reviews of the literature (Roberts 1967, 1971).

Additional curricular materials that could be used in the anthropological training of educators were developed in the late 1960s by George and Louise Spindler, who served as editors of a series of *Case Studies in Education and Culture* published by Holt, Rinehart and Winston, and by Solon Kimball, who edited the *Anthropology and Education Series* published by Teachers College Press.[8] Like many of the Project TRUE materials, the volumes in these series usually were based on field research. Finally, in 1963, George Spindler edited a collection of articles titled *Education and Culture,* which could be used as an introductory text, and in 1965 George Kneller published *Educational Anthropology,* which treated the basic concepts of culture and personality as well as problems of education in American public schools.

In part, the curriculum development efforts of the 1960s were a response to renewed federal efforts to improve the teaching of science in a post-Sputnik age. But they were also an attempt to demonstrate the relevance of anthropology to contemporary educational problems. The 1960s were years of turmoil in American cities and the deprivation and poverty of millions of Americans in urban slums and encapsulated rural areas came to the forefront of national attention. In particular, the failure of formal schooling to meet the needs of African Americans, Hispanics, Native Americans, and other minorities became dramatically evident. There was a spate of attacks upon formal schooling, and it was within this context that curriculum development activities in anthropology and education occurred.

In the mid-1960s, the federal government began to encourage more widespread anthropological research within American schools. The Culture of Schools program was initiated in 1965 under Stanley Diamond at Syracuse University. Developed at the request of Francis A. J. Ianni, then Deputy Commissioner for Research in the United States Office of Education, the program was designed not merely to apply prior knowledge but to promote collaboration between experienced anthropologists and other behavioral scientists in order to develop the foundations for research in American mass education. After a year and a half, the program was transferred to the sponsorship of the American Anthropological Association, while maintaining the support of the Office of Education (Wax, Diamond, and Gearing 1971:x). The result was the Program in Anthropology and Education directed by Fred Gearing.

Under both programs, a series of conferences was organized through the years 1966–1968. At the time, only a small number of anthropologists had engaged in research and writing germane to the social organization and cultural role of formal schooling in America. However, there were others who had undertaken recent research in educational systems abroad or had participated actively in precollegiate curriculum development or the training of educators in colleges of education. Still others were beginning to examine the application of sociolinguistics to the problems of cross-cultural communication in schools. The conferences brought together representatives from all of these groups, several others whose research training and interests were in fields outside of anthropology, and a few who were involved directly in action programs oriented toward educational reform.

The Culture of Schools program and the Program in Anthropology and Education were instrumental in the establishment of national visibility for what rapidly was becoming the next generation of educational anthropologists. By the end of the 1960s, the institutionalization of educational anthropology as a legitimate specialization within the discipline almost was complete. The field was established in schools of education, the journals of professional educators, federally-sponsored conferences, the social studies curriculum, funded research projects, and some of the professional anthropological journals and meetings. Those trained in this specialty were beginning to be accepted as fellows of the American Anthropological Association and as members of educational professional associations. The organizational expression of the professionalization process came in 1968 at the annual meeting of the American Anthropological Association in Seattle when, after a series of informal meetings, an ad hoc Group on Anthropology and Education was founded. The work of this group laid the groundwork for the formal organization of the Council on Anthropology and Education (CAE) in 1970.

The Council on Anthropology and Education

The emergence of CAE in 1970, the immediate initiation of a CAE *Newsletter,* and the subsequent evolution of the *Newsletter* into the journal *Anthropology and Education Quarterly* in 1977, culminated a long series of research and other activities that began in the 1920s and led to the formation of an area of professional specialization in the discipline (Chilcott 1984; Singleton 1984). As noted, the Culture of Schools program and the Program in Anthropology and Education played a vital role in the professionalization process. The first eight and two subsequent presidents of CAE and three of the four editors of the

Newsletter and *Quarterly* also were active participants in at least one of the conferences sponsored by these programs.

Scientific and practical problems germane to education, which, in varying degrees, engaged nearly all of the leaders of modern anthropology during the 1930s and 1940s, are currently of interest to only a segment of those who pursue anthropological careers. Nevertheless, the most recent published bibliography in the field of anthropology and education (Rosenstiel 1977) lists 3,434 annotated entries; elsewhere, Robert (n.d.) has reported that more than half of the known publications have appeared since 1965. Moreover, the paid membership of CAE was 812 in December 1996 (American Anthropological Association 1982:5).

In several respects, CAE as an organization reflects a remarkable continuity with the leaders of modern anthropology who first drew attention to the importance of education in the contemporary world. First, there is the emphasis on anthropology as a discipline concerned with cross-cultural and comparative studies of contemporary peoples. Second, there is a reaffirmation of American society as a multicultural society and an important field of anthropological inquiry. Third, there is the reaffirmation of the view that anthropology should be concerned with child development and learning in all of the various ways and environments in which they occur. Fourth, there is the insistence that ethnographic studies of learning and teaching systems have implications for educational policy. Finally, there is the recognition that education today occurs within the context of sweeping cultural, social, political, economic, and technological change.

Just as the 1954 Stanford Conference had done, so also the 1970 founding of CAE foreshadowed important new developments during the years that followed. These include the noteworthy contributions of cognitive and sociolinguistic research to communication processes in classrooms and other educational settings, the gradual incorporation of ethnographic methods into educational research, the increased attention to education within developing countries, and the recent emergence of a nucleus of educational anthropologists who are working productively in nonacademic positions. It also may be that the council form of organizing diverse interest groups eventually will become a model for professional association within the discipline as a whole.

A Look Ahead

Our era is one in which able young people continue to want to become anthropologists, notwithstanding the paucity of academic career positions. In the 1930s and 1940s, these factors combined to produce a remarkably talented group of leaders who laid the foundation for a modern anthropology in which theory, research, and application were viewed as interrelated aspects of scientific development in the discipline. It was not until the late 1950s that anthropology became characterized widely as an exclusively academic endeavor by a rising new generation of leaders who failed to envision the temporary nature of academic expansion and lacked understanding of the contribution of applied research in the building of science.

The founders of contemporary social and cultural anthropology defined it as applied anthropology. Congruently, those who engaged in research related to education typically did so within a professional milieu that emphasized the application of their studies to major educational problems at home and abroad. Within both anthropology and educational anthropology, this professional orientation eroded during the postwar years, largely due to the disciplinary focus on the building of academic departments and careers. Applied anthropology continued to develop, but it was comprised primarily of activities that sometimes engaged anthropologists who were employed securely in academic positions.

The advent of diminished career opportunities within the academy and new federal research funding priorities and accountability have combined to create a situation during the 1980s that has fostered the revival of concerted efforts to integrate theory, research, and application. On the cutting edge of this revival are a young generation of anthropologists who are carrying anthropology forward into the corporations, government agencies, human services professions, and other institutions and organizations seeking anthropological contributions to the amelioration of nonacademic problems. These anthropologists define their work as *practicing anthropology,* and they are in the process of attempting to develop new types of anthropological careers. They represent still another stage in the development of anthropology as a profession.

If the past is prologue to the future, we may anticipate that educational anthropology will once again be at the forefront of the discipline by incorporating the research and activities of practicing educational anthropologists into the profession of anthropology. This renewal of the practice of anthropology in nonacademic settings is the opportunity of the present and the hope of the future if educational anthropology, and indeed the discipline itself, is to realize its full contribution to the twenty-first century.

Notes

[1] Langham (1981:245) recently has schematized the criteria for professionalism in science as follows: (1) rigorous training by component practitioners of the discipline; (2) earning a living on the basis of one's contributions to the subject; (3) the propagation of one's scientific contributions by training students who will

earn their living from the subject; (4) the utilization or establishment of whatever institutions are necessary to fulfill the second and third criteria; (5) the production of scientific contributions that are sufficiently technical as to be understandable only to a group of fellow practitioners which therefore functions as the exclusive judge and audience for one's work.

[2] To the best of my knowledge, the most extensive work in the history of educational anthropology is being done by Joan I. Roberts, who is preparing a book on this topic. My article has benefitted from her unpublished manuscript titled "Anthropology and Education."

[3] Comments about the role of American foundations in the building of the social sciences are based on my own current, archival research on the history of applied anthropology in Britain, reading of secondary sources, and discussions with Lawrence Kelly. The impact of American foundations on anthropology at the London School of Economics is thoroughly presented by Fisher (1977).

[4] See Berman (1970) and Heyman (1970) for full accounts of the role of the Phelps-Stokes Fund and the Carnegie Corporation in African education at this time.

[5] The importance of Malinowski in developing anthropology and education has been grossly overlooked in America. My statements about his contributions are based on archival materials at the London School of Economics that I only have begun to analyze.

[6] These include the Society for Applied Anthropology publication *Practicing Anthropology;* in founding of the Society of Professional Anthropologists (SOPA) in Tucson, AZ in 1974; and the establishment of similar organizations in other major cities. A directory of practicing anthropologists (American Anthropological Association 1981) lists 353 names, but it is estimated that there are approximately 1,300 anthropologists in nonacademic employment (American Anthropological Association 1982:5). As part of the current reorganization of the American Anthropological Association, a Practicing Anthropology Unit is in the process of formation.

[7] See Dwyer-Schick (1976) for an annotated bibliography of publications related to the study and teaching of anthropology.

[8] Both series have been reviewed recently in the *Anthropology and Education Quarterly.* See Eddy 1983; Spindler and Spindler 1983.

References

American Anthropological Association, 1981. *Directory of Practicing Anthropologists.* Washington, DC: American Anthropological Association.

_____, 1982. *Anthropology Newsletter* 23:5. Washington, DC: American Anthropological Association.

Barnes, Earl, and Mary S. Barnes, 1986. *Education Among the Aztecs.* Stanford, CA: Leland Stanford Jr. University, Studies in Education 2:73–80.

Berman, Edward Henry, 1970. *Education in Africa and America: A History of the Phelps-Stokes Fund, 1911–1945.* Unpublished doctoral dissertation, Teachers College, Columbia University.

Chamberlain, Alexander, 1986. *Child and Childhood in Folk Thought.* New York: Macmillan.

Chilcott, John, 1984. From Newsletter to Quarterly, 1973–1976. *Anthropology and Education Quarterly* 15:67–69.

Davis, Allison, Burleigh B. Gartner, and Mary R. Gardner, 1941. *Deep South: A Social Anthropological Study of Caste and Class.* University of Chicago Press.

Dollard, John, 1937. *Caste and Class in a Southern Town.* New York: Harper and Brothers.

Drake, St. Clair, and Horace R. Cayton, 1945. *Black Metropolis: A Study of Negro Life in a Northern City.* New York: Harcourt Brace.

Dwyer-Schick, Susan, 1976. *The Study and Teaching of Anthropology: An Annotated Bibliography.* Athens, GA: Anthropology Curriculum Project, Publication No. 76-1.

Dynesson, Thomas, 1975. *Pre-collegiate Anthropology: Trends and Materials.* Athens, GA: Anthropology Curriculum Project, Publication No. 75-1.

Eddy, Elizabeth M., 1967. *Walk the White Line: A Profile of Urban Education.* Garden City, NY: Doubleday.

_____, 1969. *Becoming a Teacher: The Passage to Professional Status.* New York: Teachers College Press.

_____, 1983. Review Essay: *The Anthropology and Education Series,* Solon T. Kimball, gen. ed. *Anthropology and Education Quarterly* 14:141–47.

Firth, Sir Raymond, 1981. Bronislaw Malinowski. In *Totems and Teachers: Perspectives on the History of Anthropology,* Sydel Silverman, ed., pp. 101–37. New York: Columbia University Press.

Fisher, Donald, 1977. *The Impact of American Foundations on the Development of British University Education, 1900–1939.* Unpublished doctoral dissertation, University of California, Berkeley.

Fletcher, Alice C., 1888. Glimpses of Child-Life Among the Omaha Indians. *Journal of American Folklore* 1:115–23.

Fortes, Meyer, 1978. An Anthropologist's Apprenticeship. In *Annual Review of Anthropology,* Vol. 8, B. J. Siegel, A. R. Beals, and Stephen A. Tyler, eds. pp. 1–30. Palo Alto, CA: Annual Reviews.

Frank, Lawrence K., 1955. Preface. In *Education and Anthropology,* G. D. Spindler, ed., pp. vii–xi. Stanford University Press.

Fuchs, Estelle S., 1966. *Pickets at the Gates.* New York: Free Press.

_____, 1969. *Teachers Talk: Views from Inside City Schools.* Garden City, NY: Doubleday.

Gillin, John P., 1948. The Old Order Amish of Pennsylvania. In *The Ways of Men,* John P. Gillin, ed., pp. 209–20. New York: Appleton-Century-Crofts.

Haas, Mary R., 1953. The Application of Linguistics to Teaching. In *Anthropology Today,* Alfred Kroeber, ed., pp. 807–18. University of Chicago Press.

Heyman, Richard D., 1970. *The Role of Carnegie Corporation in African Education, 1925–1960.* Unpublished doctoral dissertation, Teachers College, Columbia University.

Hollingshead, August B., 1949. *Elmtown's Youth.* New York: John Wiley.

Johnson, Charles S., 1941. *Growing Up in the Black Belt: Negro Youth in the Rural South.* Washington, DC: American Council on Education.

Jones, Thomas J., 1917. *Negro Education, A Survey of the Private and Higher Schools for Colored People in the United States.* 2 volumes. Washington, DC: Government Printing Office.

_____, 1922. *Education in Africa: A Study of West, South and Equatorial Africa by the African Education Commission.* New York: Phelps-Stokes Fund.

_____, *Education in East Africa: A Study of East Central and South Africa by the Second African Education Commission.* Under the auspices of the Phelps-Stokes Fund, in cooperation with the International Education Board. London: Edinburgh House.

Keesing, Felix, 1937. *Education in Pacific Countries.* Kelley and Walsh.

Kennard, Edward A., and Gordon MacGregor, 1953. Applied Anthropology in Government: United States. In *Anthropology Today,* Alfred Kroeber, ed., pp. 832–40. University of Chicago Press.

Kimball, Solon T., 1963. Teaching Anthropology in Professional Education. In *The Teaching of Anthropology,* D. Mandelbaum, G. Lasker, and E. Albert, eds., pp. 493–502. Washington, DC: American Anthropological Association.

Kluger, Richard, 1976. *Simple Justice: This History of Brown v. Board of Education and Black America's Struggle for Equality.* New York: Alfred Knopf.

Kneller, George F., 1965. *Educational Anthropology: An Introduction.* New York: John Wiley.

Kroeber, Alfred, ed., 1953. *Anthropology Today: An Encyclopedic Inventory.* University of Chicago Press.

Langham, Ian, 1981. *The Building of British Social Anthropology.* Boston: D. Reidel.

Lynd, Robert S. and Helen Lynd, 1929. *Middletown.* New York: Harcourt Brace.

_____, 1937. *Middletown in Transition.* New York: Harcourt Brace.

Malinowski, Bronislaw [1922], 1984. *Argonauts of the Western Pacific.* Prospect Heights, IL: Waveland Press.

_____, 1929. Practical Anthropology. *Africa* 2:23–38.

_____, 1936. Native Education and Culture Contact. *International Review of Missions* 25:480–517.

Mandelbaum, David G., Gabriel W. Lasker, and Ethel M. Albert, eds., 1963a. *The Teaching of Anthropology.* Washington, DC: American Anthropological Association.

_____, 1963b. *Resources for the Teaching of Anthropology.* Washington, DC: American Anthropological Association.

Mead, Margaret, 1928. *Coming of Age in Samoa.* New York: William Morrow.

_____, 1972. *Blackberry Winter.* New York: William Morrow.

Metraux, Alfred, 1953. Applied Anthropology in Government: United Nations. In *Anthropology Today,* Alfred Kroeber, ed., pp. 880–94. University of Chicago Press.

Montessori, Maria, 1913. *Pedagogical Anthropology.* New York: Frederick A. Stokes.

Moore, G. Alexander, 1967. *Realities of the Urban Classroom: Observations in Elementary Schools.* Garden City, NY: Doubleday.

Radcliffe-Brown, A. R., 1922. *The Andaman Islanders* Cambridge: University Press.

_____, 1930. Applied Anthropology. In *Report of the Twentieth Meeting of the Australian and New Zealand Association for the Advancement of Science,* pp. 267–80. Reprinted in *Research in Economic Anthropology,* Vol. 3, 1980, G. Dalton, ed., pp. 123–34. Greenwich, CT: JAI Press.

Roberts, Joan I., 1967. *School Children in the Urban Slum.* New York: Free Press.

_____, 1971. *The Scene of the Battle: Group Behavior and Urban Classrooms.* New York: Doubleday.

_____, n.d. *Anthropology and Education.* Unpublished manuscript.

Roberts, Joan I., and Sherrie K. Akinsanya, 1976. *Educational Patterns and Cultural Configurations.* New York: David McKay.

Rosenstiel, Annette, 1977. *Education and Anthropology: An Annotated Bibliography.* New York: Garland.

Singleton, John, 1984. *Origins of the AEQ: Rituals, Myths, and Cultural Transmission. Anthropology and Education Quarterly* 15:11–16.

Spindler, George D., 1984. Roots Revisited: Three Decades of Perspective. *Anthropology and Education Quarterly* 15:3–10.

_____, ed., 1955. *Education and Anthropology.* Stanford, CA: Stanford University Press.

_____, 1963. *Education and Culture.* New York: Holt, Rinehart and Winston.

Spindler, George D., and Louise Spindler, 1983. Review Essay: The Case Studies in Education and Culture From Cradle to Grave. *Anthropology and Education Quarterly* 14:72–80.

Stevenson, Matilda C., 1887. *Religious Life of the Zuni Child.* Washington, DC: U.S. Bureau of American Ethnology, Fifth Annual Report, 1883–84.

Stocking, George W., Jr., 1976. Ideas and Institutions in American Anthropology: Thoughts Toward a History of the Interwar Years. In *Selected Papers from the American Anthropologist, 1921–1945*, G. W. Stocking, Jr., ed., pp. 1–50. Washington, DC: American Anthropological Association.

Thompson, Laura, 1951. *Personality and Government: Findings and Recommendations of the Indian Administration Research.* Mexico, D.F.: Ediciones del Instituto Indigenista Interamericano.

Vandewalker, Nina, 1898. Some Demands of Education Upon Anthropology. *American Journal of Sociology* 4(1):69–78.

Warner, William Lloyd, 1942. Educative Effects of Social Status. In *Environment and Education: Symposium*, Ernest W. Burgess, W. Lloyd Warner, Franz Alexander, and Margaret Mead, eds., pp. 16–28. University of Chicago Press.

Warner, William Lloyd, and Paul Lunt, 1941. *The Social Life of a Modern Community.* New Haven: Yale University Press.

Warner, William Lloyd, Robert J. Havighurst, and Martin B. Loeb, 1944. *Who Shall Be Educated?* New York: Harper and Brothers.

Wax, Murray L., Stanley Diamond, and Fred O. Gearing, 1971. *Anthropological Perspectives on Education.* New York: Basic Books.

West, James, 1945. *Plainville, U.S.A.* New York: Columbia University Press.

2
Educational Anthropology
Early History and Educationist Contributions

Rosalie Ford

Early History

In the United States the linkage between education and anthropology might be said to have begun just about a hundred years ago. Nearly sixty years would pass, however, before this linkage would develop into a legitimate discipline known as Educational Anthropology.[1] As the eminent American anthropologist, Franz Boas, said, "Sciences do not grow up according to definitions. They are the result of historical development" (899:94). The historical development of a discipline often reveals, even in its primary stages, its future direction. Primary stages of an emerging discipline are frequently characterized by seemingly isolated units which actually constitute a totality when viewed from a historical perspective.

A distinctive feature of education by the late nineteenth century was its eclectic stance. It had already allied itself with sociology, psychology, and the scientific method of direct, inductive inquiry (Barnes 1902:3; Monroe 1923:747–59); and indications, however primitive and sporadic, of a relationship with anthropology also began to emerge. Both educators and anthropologists began to comment on the cultural aspects of education; and these comments constituted, in the United States, the origins of a rapport between the two disciplines.[2]

Earl Barnes (1861–1935)

Earl Barnes, a professor of education at Stanford University, was an early proponent of a relationship between education and anthropology. He sought a more holistic treatment of the history of education and maintained:

> It is a spiritual understanding of trends and tendencies in human affairs that we need, and this can come only through the study of what the Ger-

Source: Written especially for *Education and Cultural Process*, 3rd Edition.

mans call *Culturgeschichte* [sic], which is a combination of our older history with anthropology and sociology, and with something more. (1896:393)

He went on to say:

> It is a pity . . . that we could not illustrate more perfectly the bearing of anthropology and sociology upon all of this work. But these are subjects only just now coming to the front and demanding recognition . . . If I am not a very bad prophet, this history of civilization, this genetic study of the developing soul in all its possibilities, is to be a foundation study in our new professional normal schools and in the departments of pedagogy now forming in all of our colleges and universities. (ibid., 395)

Nina Vandewalker (1857–1934)

As principal of the Kindergarten Department at Milwaukee Wisconsin State Normal School, Nina Vandewalker proposed extraordinarily advanced views regarding the interconnection of education and anthropology. As early as 1898 she devoted an entire eleven-page article to the linkage between both of these disciplines. The article, entitled "Some Demands of Education upon Anthropology," appeared in *The American Journal of Sociology*. This was an early ex professo treatment of the projected union between education and anthropology:

> If education thus looks to sociology for insight, it recognizes that sociology itself finds that insight in no small degree in anthropology, and that many questions of both practical and theoretical import can only be solved, if solved at all, by the help of that science. The question of parallelism between the development of the individual and that of the race . . . the relation of motor activity to intellectual development in the individual and in the race, with its consequences for education; the function of play in development, and its bearing upon the educational process--all these must be considered from the anthropological standpoint as well as from the psychological, as has been the case hitherto . . . anthropology is coming to have an increasing significance for education. (1898:69–70)

As a kindergarten specialist, Vandewalker was particularly interested in child development. She indicated that anthropological research, for the most part, has been restricted "to the phenomena of adult life," and she urged anthropology to provide education with an "anthropological history of childhood, as well as "reliable and interesting material" for pupils on child life in other cultures. She insisted that anthropology provide education with "principles of interpretation" and that the data be "so arranged as to show their educational significance."

Vandewalker's farsightedness and conviction of the advantages of a relationship between the two disciplines was further evidenced in the closing remarks of her article:

The services that anthropology can render the educational cause are . . . many and varied. Education can no longer be isolated; it is identifying itself more and more closely with the general movements of the time. In this movement anthropology is destined to play an increasingly important part. If the peculiar character of the present educational need will in any degree stimulate anthropological research; if it can give it a new direction and focus, if it can create a wider interest in it on the part of the general public, it can in part repay the services it hopes to receive at the hand of that science. (ibid., 78)

Edgar Hewett (1865–1946)

Bridging the two fields of education and anthropology, Edgar Hewett's professional career may be viewed as a kind of paradigm of EA. He successfully incorporated his experience of nineteen years in education and nearly forty years in anthropology into an inseparable union between the two disciplines. His life rather presciently signified a new direction and focus in the research interests of future anthropologists and educators.

Hewett's career in education began as a teacher in rural schools (1884–1886). He then became a professor of literature and history at Tarkio College, Missouri (1886–1887), superintendent of schools in Fairfax, Missouri, and Florence, Colorado (1889–1892), superintendent of the training department of Colorado State Normal School (1894–1898), and finally, president of New Mexico Normal University in Las Vegas (1898–1903). At thirty-eight years of age, Hewett turned to professional archeological research. He became a student in 1903 at the University of Geneva, which awarded him the degree of Doctor of Science five years later.

During this period, he published two articles on the relationship between education and anthropology. In the first of these articles, Hewett proposed a scientific approach to education based on the study of man and culture: "To culture history we must go for the verification of a great body of educational theory." Recognizing that the anthropological data being utilized in educational curriculum was not its "most authentic material," he acknowledged that "the difficulty seems to lie in the existing state of anthropological science":

The science needs closer definition by the masters, and its literature must be brought to a state that will place it in closer relations with education, through the schools of pedagogy, normal schools and teachers' institutes. A joint meeting of the two national societies . . . might contribute to the progress of both. (1904:575)

In a more lengthy article, Hewett reiterated the necessity for a scientific approach to education and emphasized the dependence of education on the "contributory sciences of biology, psychology, sociology, and anthropology." He maintained that the phenomena of these sciences are so "interdependent that they cannot be separated" and stressed culture as a "vital" factor to be considered in the development of any "educational policy" (1905:1–16).

The next forty years of Edgar Hewett's life were marked by distinguished achievements as an archeologist/anthropologist. Some of these accomplishments were: Director of American Research for the Archeological Institute of America (1906–1946), founder and director of the School of American Archeology (now the School of American Research) (1907–1946), founder and director of the Museum of New Mexico (1909–1946), director of exhibits in science and art at the Panama-California Exposition in San Diego (1911–1916), founder and director of the San Diego Museum (1917–1929), professor of anthropology at the State Teachers' College in San Diego (1922–1927), lecturer at the American Schools of Oriental Research in Jerusalem and Baghdad (1923), professor of archeology and anthropology at the University of Southern California (1932–?), and professor of archeology and anthropology at the University of New Mexico in Albuquerque (1927–1940).

Maria Montessori (1870–1952)

Maria Montessori, an Italian physician and educator, is perhaps best known for the scientific method of education she promoted for young children. Her method of education gained much recognition in the United States in the early twentieth century, particularly after her two visits to this country in 1913 and 1915.

A less publicized phase of Montessori's career was her tenure as professor of anthropology at the University of Rome from 1904–1908. In that capacity, she delivered lectures on "pedagogical anthropology" which were later compiled and published (unfortunately without a bibliography) in 1913 under the same title. In the preface to this work, Montessori disclaimed originality for the concept, indicating that "for some time past much has been said in Italy regarding Pedagogical Anthropology." She later credited its beginnings in 1886 to her former teacher, Guiseppe Sergi, "to whom we owe that practical extension of anthropology that leads us straight into the field of pedagogy" (see Riccardi, 1880).

Nonetheless, Montessori was another early advocate of the linkage between education and anthropology whose approach reflected her professional expertise in medicine, psychology, and physical anthropology. She viewed "pedagogical anthropology"as an efficient vehicle for a scientific approach to education and indicated its dependence on contributory sciences:

The new development of pedagogy . . . goes under the name of scientific: in order to educate, it is essential to know those who are to be educated. . . . the naturalistic method must lead us to the study of separate subjects, to a description of them as individuals, and their classification on a basis of characteristics in common; and since the child must be studied not by himself alone, but also in relation to the factors of his origin and his individual evolution—since every one of us represents the effect of multifold causes—it follows that the etiological side of the pedagogical branch of modern anthropology, like all its other branches, necessarily invades the fields of biology and at the same time of sociology. (1913:17)

Bronislaw Malinowski (1884–1942)

Bronislaw Malinowski, a native of Poland and one of the world's foremost anthropologists, was a visiting professor at Yale University from 1939 to 1942. He was not, at that time, a newcomer to the United States. His first visit to this country was in 1926, when he taught for a short time at the University of California. Seven years later he delivered the Messenger lectures at Cornell University, and in 1936 he was awarded the honorary degree of Doctor of Science at the Harvard Tercentenary celebration, which he attended as a professor from the University of London.

In a style that differed quite markedly from earlier writers cited, Malinowski approached the linkage of education and anthropology from a distinctly practical standpoint. He communicated their interrelatedness in two addresses he delivered at a conference organized by the New Education Fellowship in South Africa in 1934. These addresses were later published as one article under the title, "Native Education and Cultural Contact."

In this article Malinowski broadened the definition of education, differentiated it from schooling, and perceived it as an integrative process. He noted the "breakdown of tribal life and cultural continuity" when schooling is "mechanically thrust into a culture where education has gone on for ages without the institution of professional schooling." Although Malinowski was speaking of the cultural impact of Western-European schooling on African tribal education, he pointed out that "the contact of race is a world-wide problem and its implications cannot be discussed with regard to one part of the world alone":

> Schooling of unblushingly European type, which even to us has now become almost obsolete, has been pressed upon native races all the world over by missionaries and enthusiastic educationists, by governments and by economic enterprise. And here, perhaps, is a topic on which the anthropologist has something to say. His very subject-matter, "culture," in its relation to "race," has been completely left out of account. . . .
>
> . . . Culture, that is, the body of material appliances, types of social groupings, customs, beliefs and moral values, is a reality which must be

taken into consideration by every one who frames an educational policy. (1936:481–82)[3]

Malinowski, aware of the potency of education as an "agent of social change," proposed that there be "education experts well trained in anthropology" and urged anthropologists to study the cultural institution of education, since:

> Education must exist in every culture, because everywhere the continuance of tradition has to be preserved by being handed on from one generation to another. In simple cultures there is no schooling; education takes place partly in the domestic milieu through the personal influence of the parents on the children. Everywhere, however, there are some agencies, customs, initiation ceremonies and even social groups more specially connected with training. Again, apprenticeship to technical tasks can either be accomplished through parents or nearest kindred, or given by skilled specialists, or else by the very playmates of the child. These factors combine in such a variety of ways that the anthropologist cannot remain satisfied with a mere enumeration. He has to study the problem afresh in every tribe. (ibid., 507)

Lyman Bryson (1888–1959)

Lyman Bryson was a professor of education at Teachers College, Columbia University, from 1935 to 1953. Earlier in his career, from 1925 to 1932, he lectured on political science, anthropology, and literature at San Diego State Teachers College and was director of the San Diego Museum of Anthropology and Archeology from 1928 to 1930.

On the occasion of an anniversary volume honoring Edgar Hewett, Bryson contributed an article, "Anthropology and Education," in which he viewed education as a cultural institution. He discussed its dual role in maintaining culture and in effecting change. He noted that "anthropologists have been especially aware of the importance of this agency in providing continuity in social structure." Yet, with the exception of Hewett, "few American anthropologists have made contributions to the theory or practice of the education by which our own society is maintained" (1939).

He thus urged anthropologists to make their scientific findings more available not only to teachers but to the general public as well. He deemed this interaction essential in society's "struggle for existence and for rational change," and recommended practical avenues by which anthropological findings could have a wider audience:

> It is my suggestion that this process of applying the findings of the science to help in the solution of public problems could be better accomplished by . . . two channels of communication to the public mind. The first is through adult education in which the museum plays a worthy

role, the second is by making the study of anthropology a part of the training of teachers for secondary and elementary schools. (ibid., 107–8)

Annette Rosenstiel (1911–)

Annette Rosenstiel, a contemporary anthropologist and educator, was inspired by the practical approach of Lyman Bryson to education and anthropology. She directed attention to Bronislaw Malinowski as an anthropologist who realized that education was a "vital integrative phase of primitive life." In 1954, she not only proposed a linkage between the two fields but suggested that they be used as a new inter-disciplinary approach in the analysis of culture. She called this approach educational anthropology and was the first to coin this term.

Rosenstiel stressed that education "is more than 'socialization'," and as such "requires more than just a knowledge of the psychological processes involved in the learning process itself." She insisted that an understanding of "education in either primitive or civilized society involves a recognition of the fact that, in its broadest sense, education may be considered as 'identified with the process of cultural renewal.'" She pointed out that:

> Little or no effort has been made by anthropologists in the United States to foster the knowledge and use of educational concepts in their integra-tive sense for the benefits that might accrue to anthropology and educa-tion alike. They have in the main explained education away as "existing in all cultures," or as an automatic vehicle for cultural transmission. Its true importance is therefore not generally recognized. (1954:29)

Rosenstiel asserted that "it is futile to attempt to explain the basic culture of a people or its reaction to change "without first understanding the principles underlying the educational system of a people," since this system permeates every aspect of community life. She proposed that anthropologists have "some training in education" since they "will need to know how to study education in process, and to differentiate its func-tion."

Rosenstiel offered some explanation for the latent collaboration between both disciplines[4] and called for "the creation of a new interdis-ciplinary field":

> Past efforts by Malinowski and others to point up and accentuate the need for a broader view of education, and a redefinition of its use, not only for the sake of the continuing indigenous culture in cases of culture contact, but also for that of more complex cultures as well, appear to have been fruitless. One of the main difficulties may have been the fact that for the most part anthropologists have taken education for granted, and educators in their turn have left the principles and techniques of anthropology pretty much to the anthropologist. The time has now come for the formulation of a new approach. By making available to both

fields the principles and methodology of each, it may be possible to focus attention upon each individual problem and seek a solution in keeping with the principles of both disciplines. The author suggests that this new, interdisciplinary approach be known as *Educational Anthropology*. (ibid., 33–34)

George Spindler (1920–)

George Spindler, Professor Emeritus of the department of anthropology at Stanford University, also held a joint appointment in the School of Education as early as 1950. He was one of the earliest major anthropologists to become convinced of the validity of "education" as a focus for anthropological inquiry and has been involved in such investigations for over forty years. He has authored numerous publications as well as edited seven volumes and seventeen case studies on the subject which clearly reflect the emergence of a new discipline.

The first of these volumes, *Education and Anthropology*, was published in 1955. It contains a number of papers and discussions which were delivered at the first conference between anthropologists and educators in the United States. The conference, composed of twenty-four participants, was held June 9–14, 1954, at a site not far from Stanford University. It was conducted under the joint auspices of the School of Education and Department of Anthropology of Stanford University and the American Anthropological Association. As coordinator of the conference and editor of its results, Spindler explained in the Foreword to *Education and Anthropology* that the participants in this exploratory seminar were

. . . less interested in what had been done, and its evaluation, than we were in the frontiers of the relationships between these two broad disciplines and their concepts, data, methods, and problems. . . . (1955:v)

Nearly ten years after this conference, *Education and Culture: Anthropological Approaches* was published in 1963. It contains twenty-five articles, most of which examine education as a process of cultural transmission both in the United States and in cross-cultural contexts. (Updated versions of some articles that appeared in the earlier volume are included in this text.) Spindler's overview of education and anthropology was reprinted with extensive revision, and he pointed out that:

Now attention shifts to the contribution of anthropology as a frame of reference for analysis of the educative process. This is a different kind of utilization of the resources of anthropology. . . . (1963:57)

By the 1970s, the terms "anthropology of education" and EA were used interchangeably in the field. In a 1971 article entitled "Prospects in Anthropology and Education," Spindler observed that:

The Anthropology of Education (or Educational Anthropology, if you wish) has passed through its first stage of growth where the potential relevance of anthropological concepts to educators and to the analysis of educational problems has been discovered, and, in general granted. . . .

Another large area that needs substantial work is what might be called a systematic comparative discipline of educational anthropology. (*CAE Newsletter* 2(1):1)

In compliance with this trend, the third volume, *Education and Cultural Process: Towards an Anthropology of Education*, was published in 1974. It was originally intended as a revision of the 1963 text, but Spindler indicated that it was indeed a "new book representing significant contemporary concerns of those anthropologists now producing an anthropology of education." He noted that:

Education and Cultural Process does not sample everything in contemporary educational anthropology. The field is expanding rapidly and going in many different directions. . . . There are not only many specific areas of contemporary educational anthropology that can be represented in any single volume only tangentially, if at all, but there are also many people whose work cannot be represented. I have chosen as a strategy to favor papers written specifically for this volume or written for professional meetings but not published. This has automatically eliminated works from some of the most significant contributors to an educational anthropology. (1974:viii)

The fourth volume, published in 1982, solidified the discipline of EA. Focusing on an aspect within the field, Spindler entitled the text *Doing the Ethnography of Schooling* and subtitled the book *Educational Anthropology in Action*. In discussing the diversity of topics within EA, Spindler asserted that "cultural transmission has been the most influential model in this volume," saying that "this model seemed most important when those few of us who were interested started formulating the purposes of educational anthropology some 30 years ago" (1982:311).

The fifth volume edited by Spindler, *Education and Cultural Process: Anthropological Approaches Second Edition* is a revision of the 1974 text and was published in 1987. It contains twenty-eight articles, half of which appeared in the first edition and "represent established areas" in the discipline. The other fourteen essays are new and "represent significant recent developments and issues" in EA. In the preview to Part I of this book, Spindler stated that:

My purpose as one of the founders[5] of the field has been to give the anthropology of education a focus by defining our special area to be cultural transmission. I go further now in claiming that we are primarily concerned, as a discipline, with intentional intervention in the learning process. The reason why children don't learn everything . . . is that all societies intervene, literally interfere, with what children are learning at critical points throughout the entire developmental process. These interventions—from weaning and toilet training to kindergarten to instruction in high school, occupational training, to the rituals of death—never teach what they are intended to teach—for human beings never learn only one thing at a time. Concomitant learning always takes place. In internally consistent cultural systems the concomitant and intended learning will be at least congruent. In internally inconsistent or disintegrating cultural systems the intended and concomitant will often be at odds . . . If we are to attend to the learning of culture rather than or in addition to the transmission of culture as a focus of anthropology of education . . . we must appraise the models of learning that psychologists have developed, for psychology has a long history of attention to learning. (1987:3)[6]

Interpretive Ethnography of Education At Home and Abroad was also published in 1987 and edited by George Spindler with his wife, Louise. Seventeen of the nineteen articles were written specifically for the book. The articles discuss the nature of ethnography; ethnographic fieldwork of schools in Germany, France, England and China; and ethnographic fieldwork among immigrant, minority and mainstream school populations in this country.

The Spindlers indicate that:

. . . Although organized and written from the perspective of educational anthropology, this book is aimed at a wider and more general audience. . . .

Social historians of education will find kinship with the writings of ethnographers of education, for history and ethnography have always been convergent in interests and even in methods. Comparative educationists will find materials and analysis of direct relevance to them, for this book is about education "at home and abroad." Sociologists of education will find the approaches in these chapters congenial, and will encounter significant additions to their understanding of shared problems. Educational psychologists will find this book challenging, for it is consistent in offering cultural rather than psychological explanations for observed phenomena. Philosophers of education will discover a new way of looking at familiar issues. And practitioners of education—administrators, teachers, consultants, supervisors, learning specialists—will find parallels to the situations in which they work and be informed by the ways in which the various authors have gone about the study and analysis of these situations. With these relevancies and applications in mind, it is appropriate to describe this volume as a significant contribution to the social and cultural foundations of education. (1987:xi–xii)

The most recent volume edited by George and Louise Spindler, *Pathways to Cultural Awareness: Cultural Therapy with Teachers and Students*, was published in 1994. The ten essays in this book are "innovative, pioneering" attempts by EA practitioners to help teachers and students develop positive relationships in the school culture and subsequently have "a more productive environment for social behavior and learning." In the preface to this work, the Spindlers indicate that:

> It is important to understand that we are not fabricating a new way of making students conform to the school, to the classroom, or to the teacher. . . . such a preconception would be fatal to understanding the complex and subtle issues and processes that the contributors to this volume are discussing. (1994:xii–xiii)

In addition to these seven volumes, the Spindlers were asked to review their *Case Studies in Education and Culture* series. In 1964, in their capacity as editors for the well received *Case Studies in Cultural Anthropology*,[7] it occurred to them

> . . . that a similar series focusing on education in a variety of cultures would be useful and would help determine the shape of the then-emerging educational anthropology. (Spindler and Spindler 1983:73)

In 1967, with George and Louise Spindler as general editors, five publications introduced the *Case Studies in Education and Culture* series. These ethnographies investigated the relationship between education and culture in a Japanese junior high, a rural German village, among Kpelle children in Liberia, among Indian youngsters in a one-room village in British Columbia, and in a residential school in the Yukon Territory of northwest Canada. It was

> . . . not an accident that four of the first five volumes were authored by our former graduate students. . . . We knew about their fieldwork and were sure of their training. (ibid., 73)

Over the next several years, the series published ethnographic accounts that researched the relationship between education and culture among the Dusun of Borneo; in a Philippine barrio; amidst diverse African cultures in Ghana, Niger, Malawi; and in a "Western-type" school attended by Muslim children in northeastern Nigeria.

In the United States and Mexico, the case studies focused on education among African American and Puerto Rican youngsters in Harlem, the Alaskan Eskimo, children in an Amish school, the role of an elementary principal in a suburban school, pre-school language patterns of African Americans in a southern Louisiana county, and the education of Native American children in the Chiapas Highlands of Mexico.

Despite the fact that these seventeen case studies were among the most widely used texts in EA (Maring and DeCicco, 1982:342–43), unfortunately the series was discontinued in 1973. Spindler and Spindler attributed the early demise of the series to the cost factor, limited circulation within and outside the field, lack of familiarity with the case study approach by anthropologists and educators, anthropology's resistance to EA, and the fact that the very idea itself may well have been way "ahead of its time."[8]

Theodore Brameld (1904–1987)

Theodore Brameld, a highly regarded educational philosopher, was a participant in the first seminar-conference of educators and anthropologists in 1954. He referred to this symposium as an Educational Anthropology Conference in an article entitled "Education and Culture: A Needed Partnership." In this same publication, he discussed education as a universal phenomenon and noted its meager treatment as a cultural institution by many educators and anthropologists. Attributing this negligence to the "habits of specialization and complacency" in "contemporary Western culture," Brameld stated that the

> possibility that each might learn from the other, if for no other reason than that culture and education vitally depend on each other in actual experience, has apparently seldom occurred to either one. (1955:61)

Admitting it was not his province to advise the anthropologist how to effectuate an interdisciplinary partnership, Brameld instead suggested avenues to the educator which might strengthen cooperation between the two disciplines:

> His first obligation . . . is to take inventory of the most pervasive and fundamental issues confronting education when that institution is viewed not so much from within as from without—that is, in the perspective of the culture of which it is an indigenous and potent agent. With this inventory at hand, his task is to come to grips with the premises and postulates—that is to say, the theory—of culture itself. This is an obligation which thus compels him to rediscover and reassess as much as he can of the central findings of the cultural expert both in the way of positive principles and in the way of problems still awaiting resolution. His third and final task is then to relate the first and second tasks to each other through the medium of proposals for educational experimentation at the level of action. (ibid., 111)

In 1957, two years after this article was published, Brameld authored *Cultural Foundations of Education: An Interdisciplinary Exploration*. He wrote this text with three groups in mind: educators, social scientists, and philosophers. Its aim was to "utilize philosophy as a bridge connecting the theory of education as a central institution of organized human life and the nature of culture as a central concept of the social sciences."

In the preface to this book, Brameld maintained that "education will attain the status of a profession" only when it broadens its base to include the "most authoritative experience and knowledge available from all relevant fields of human achievement." Citing psychology as the main scientific discipline that has received wide recognition and is the "most common requirement" in teacher-training institutions, he pointed out that efforts to "counterbalance" this "over-emphasis" have been made in foundations of education departments. He maintained that:

> Increasing numbers of teachers' colleges are establishing courses that try to provide substantial knowledge of the natural world, of the behavioral sciences, of literature and other fine arts, together with critical interpretation of the assumptions, conflicts, and aims of modern civilization.

> This important shift is far from achieved, however. . . . Educational sociology, philosophy, and similar fields are still regarded as of subordinate importance if they are studied directly at all. . . . Without question, the new field of educational anthropology is ignored by a still larger number. One may doubt whether the average prospective teacher, through no fault of his own, could clearly define anthropology, much less demonstrate familiarity with its subject matter or its significance for his professional work. (1957:xv–xvi)

As a visiting professor of educational philosophy at the University of Puerto Rico (1955–1958), Brameld conducted an EA case study in three subcultures of Puerto Rico. Its aim was to "experiment with a fusion of three disciplines—philosophy, education, and anthropology," and the study was "systemically built upon a theory of culture developed in the previously cited text. It explored the variance between expressed ideology and metacultural beliefs, it and examined the role of education in narrowing the "gap between the explicit and implicit culture."[9]

In 1967, as a professor of educational foundations at Boston University's School of Education, Brameld conducted field experiences for students in EA. He returned to Puerto Rico with sixteen participants, six of whose studies appeared in the December 1967 issue of the *Journal of Education*, published by Boston University's School of Education. This issue, devoted exclusively to this project, examined the following aspects of Puerto Rican culture: adult education, family life, religion and education, nativism, the cooperative movement, and music. As editor of this issue and instructor in this "living-laboratory approach," Brameld acknowledged that his motive in providing field experience was

> not intended to emulate those of professional anthropologists . . . The intent of our own field experiences is . . . to introduce professional educators to some of the techniques by which anthropology approaches, examines, and interprets cultural experience, with particular regard for that important feature of such experience known as education. (1967:4)

In addition to the Puerto Rican experience, Brameld researched culture and education in two small communities in Japan, the results of which he published in 1968. He hinted at the aim of this investigation, while at the same time he displayed his personal conviction and steadfast commitment to an EA:

> That culture and education, broadly rather than narrowly understood, constitute a partnership has long been recognized as an indubitable fact of human evolution. But recognition can hardly be regarded as equivalent to searching penetration. Neither theoretical formulations nor research studies that could contribute fundamentally to the meaning and practical relevance of this partnership are as yet plentiful. Anthropology, the science of culture, has more often than not circumvented systematic treatments of education, while education, in turn, has been derelict in its concern for the significance of culture. To be sure, educational anthropology has begun to emerge as a new specialization, but it is rarely regarded as respectable by the typical anthropologist. As for the typical educationist, he has yet to make its acquaintance. (1968:xvi)

While this observation of Brameld was undoubtedly true in the late 1960s, it is, fortunately, less and less true with every passing year. The transcendent and more important point, furthermore, is that the linkage between anthropology and education has, in fact, produced between the years 1896 and 1954 a valuable and new specialization which has come to be known as EA.[10]

Status

The present status of EA seems to be that it is, at least formally, more under the auspices of anthropology than of education.

Nearly twenty years after the first U.S. conference between anthropologists and educators, the Council on Anthropology and Education (CAE) was formed in 1968. It is composed of representatives from both disciplines who apply anthropological knowledge to educational research and development. As of 1996, it had 921 members (*Encyclopedia of Associations*, 31st ed.). The formation of CAE was a result of:

> . . . anthropological interests in educational problems, practices, and institutions. These interests . . . can be traced back to articles by Edgar L. Hewett, published in 1904–5 by the *American Anthropologist*. Activities during the last several years of CAE members in organizing symposia presentations for the American Anthropological Association, the American Educational Research Association, and other professional associations identified with anthropology or education carry out Hewett's original recommendation that anthropologists and educational researchers work together in the areas of their common interests. (*CAE Newsletter* 1(1):1)

CAE is separately incorporated within the American Anthropological Association and holds its annual meetings in conjunction with the Association. It has its own Board of Directors, as well as twelve Standing Committees. The business office of CAE is at the American Anthropological Association in Arlington, Virginia.[11]

The reference group for researchers whose focus is the application of anthropology to educational research and development has been a subject of discussion among CAE members (see *CAE Newsletter* 4(1):11–16). John Singleton, a former CAE president and then chairman of the International and Development Education Program at the University of Pittsburgh, offered this perspective:

> I should note . . . that Foster is not familiar with many of our education and anthropology undertakings and is probably constrained by his own experiences in educational sociology and comparative education to expect that educational anthropology is seeking to become a "discipline" in its own right rather than an integral extension and application of our anthropological disciplines. I know of no one in our field who has taken this position. Our disciplinary reference group is, and should continue to be, anthropology at large. Obviously we must also relate to the professional field of education. (1973:17)[12]

CAE publishes a scholarly journal whose title has changed several times since its beginnings in 1970. From 1970 to 1973, it was called the *Council on Anthropology and Education Newsletter* (volumes 1–4); from 1974 to 1976, it was published as the *Council on Anthropology and Education Quarterly* (volumes 5–7); and from 1977 to the present it has been entitled *Anthropology and Education Quarterly*. It is presently published by the Council on Anthropology and Education business office in Arlington, Virginia, through the American Anthropological Association. The 1971–1975 *New Serial Titles* (1:617) of the Library of Congress lists eight university libraries in the United States that received this journal, while its 1981–1985 *New Serial Titles* (1:689) indicated that some thirty-three university libraries in this country subscribed to the *Anthropology and Education Quarterly*. As might be expected, the *New Serial Titles* no longer includes this entry. However, the OCLC Database (a worldwide library catalogue system) lists some 292 libraries in the United States that have catalogued this title as of August 23, 1996.

In compliance with the trends of our times, the Educational Resources Information Center (ERIC), a national information system for the dissemination of educational literature, added the term, EA, as a descriptor to its bibliographic databased system in June, 1973.[13] James Houston, a lexicographer for ERIC Reference Facility, offered the following explanation for the inclusion of this new descriptor:

Educational Anthropology was added to the ERIC Thesaurus in 1973 by the ERIC Clearinghouse for Social Studies/Social Science Education, one of 16 subject-area clearinghouses in the ERIC system. Changes in the Thesaurus reflect usages of concepts in the literature of the database. ERIC indexes, working primarily at the clearinghouse level of the ERIC network, are encouraged to recommend Thesaurus changes whenever existing Descriptors cannot adequately describe a document or whenever an existing broad Descriptor is found to be used significantly for a more specific concept. The latter situation was the case with *Educational Anthropology*. Its addition to the Thesaurus allows indexing precision for many documents while permitting the broader *Anthropology* to be reserved for indexing other anthropological contexts.[14]

Although earlier editions of the *Council on Anthropology and Education Newsletter* make mention of EA courses offered in both education and anthropology departments, this is no longer the case (*CAE Newsletters* 3(2):5–7; 3(3)15–17; 4(2):36–38; 4(3):14–16; *CAE Quarterly* 5(1): 30–32; Herzog 1972–74). Eddy, however, notes that:

> Specialized training (in EA) currently exists at several universities, including Harvard, Stanford, Teachers College (Columbia), and the Universities of Florida, Georgia, Oregon, Minnesota, Pennsylvania, Pittsburgh, the State University of New York at Buffalo, and Michigan State. (1985:95)

Notes

[1] Educational Anthropology is hereafter generally referred to as EA. Piddington's concept of education is basic to the entire article:
> Every culture has some system of education, using the term in its widest sense—some means by which the traditions of the people, their practical knowledge and techniques, their language and their codes of morals and good behavior are transmitted from generation to generation. (1950:18)

[2] Rosenstiel (1954:28–36); Spindler (1963:53–83); Roberts (1976:1–13) and Eddy (1985:83–92) have proved to be invaluable sources on several of the figures examined in this section. Helpful information was also obtained from the chronological bibliography of Roberts and Akinsanya (1976:375–404) and the annotated bibliography of Rosenstiel (1977). The individuals included in this section are meant to be representative not exhaustive. They were selected on the basis of their chronology in the emergence of the field and their explicit remarks regarding a linkage between both disciplines.

[3] See also Rosensteil (1954).

[4] For a brief overview of the historical emphasis of American and European anthropologists which, in effect, delayed the emergence of EA, see Marcelo M. Suárez-Orozco, "Learning Culture: The Spindlers' Contributions to the Making of American Anthropology," in *The Psychoanalytic Study of Society*, Vol. 17 (1992), Boyer and Boyer, eds., pp. 52–53 (Hillsdale, NJ: The Atlantic Press).

[5] Spindler has been referred to as a father or grandfather of EA (see Spindler, 1982:21; 1987:vi). On this same point, Suárez-Orozco (see note 4) writes that

> The Spindlers have devoted a substantial portion of their productive intellectual lives to exploring (and teaching others to explore) how cultures maintain themselves through formal education. In the process of elaborating on this concern, they have almost single-handedly given birth to the modern field of anthropology and education. . . . (1992:48)

[6]Regarding the relationship of psychology to EA, see De Vos with Vaughn, "The Interpersonal Self: A Level of Psychocultural Analysis," *The Psychoanalytic Study of Society*, Vol. 17 (NJ: The Atlantic Press, 1992), in which they indicate that

> In our psychocultural research presently conducted in the Institute for Personality Assessment and Research at Berkeley, we have been more specifically investigating the saliency of achievement motivation as related to the study of the "self" in society. One aspect of our research has been devoted to the analysis of fantasy by systematic quantitative methods useful in categorizing all basic interpersonal concerns. The immediate focus of our direct research has been in examining the attitudes of adolescent youth related to school performance and to future occupational interests. Here again, we come in our work close to the abiding research interests of the Spindlers, who have been leaders in developing the field of educational anthropology. Education and psychology are branches of social science examining how knowledge and behavior are passed on from one generation to the next. The "school" as a social institution is concerned with secondary socialization, which consciously operates to implement the teachings of the primary family and community. (1992:100)

In agreement with this position, Suárez-Orozco (see note 4) maintains that

> The field of educational anthropology as we know it today is a relatively new specialization within the broader subfield of sociocultural anthropology. The study of the anthropology of education grew in the shadow of its older cousins, psychological anthropology and anthropological linguistics. Psychological anthropology has been influencing the field of anthropology and education most notably through the work of George De Vos, and George and Louise Spindler.
>
> Any history of anthropology and education must, therefore, fully consider the impact of psychological anthropology via its empirical studies of socialization as a form of what the Spindlers call "cultural transmission." Additionally, the field of linguistic anthropology, particularly the study of the relationships between language, cognition, and society, has also made singular contributions to the field of anthropology and education. (1992:51)

See also Barbara Rogoff and Pablo Chavejay, "What's Become of Research on the Cultural Basis of Cognitive Development?," *American Psychologist* 50 (1995): 859–77; Hugh Mehan, "Language and Schooling," in *Interpretive Ethnography of Schooling at Home and Abroad*, Spindler and Spindler, eds. (Mahwah, NJ: Lawrence Erlbaum, 1987).

[7]Suárez-Orozco (1992:46) indicates that the Spindlers, since 1960, had been and still are the series editors for the *Case Studies in Cultural Anthropology*. This series, also published by Holt, Rinehart and Winston, has generated some 147 titles.

[8]See Spindler, *Case Studies* (1974:542–44) for a complete listing and succinct description of each of the seventeen studies. See also Jean Dresden Grambs, "Extended Review: Case Studies in Education and Culture," *Educational Studies* 4(2)(1973): 61–65 for an extended review on sixteen of the case studies.

[9]Brameld defines metacultural as

> . . . attitudes and beliefs [that] lie beneath the surface of daily experience.

They are absorbed into the "bloodstream" of the people with little awareness that the absorption is occurring steadily from the earliest to the latest years of every normal person. (1958:197)

[10] For a more comprehensive treatment of the historical development of EA, see Spindler (1963:53–83); and Roberts (1976:1–13); see also J. U. Ogbu, "Anthropology and Education," in *The International Encyclopedia of Education*, Husen and Postlethwaite, eds., pp. 276–81 (New York: Pergamon Press, 1985); Brameld and Sullivan, "Anthropology and Education." *Review of Educational Research* 31 (1961): 79–79; William Shunk and Bernice Goldstein, "Anthropology and Education," *Review of Educational Research* 34 (1964): 71–84; Harry Wolcott, *A Kwakiutl Village and School* (New York: Holt Rinehart and Winston, 1967); and Nancy Modiano, *Educational Anthropology: An Overview* (Paper presented at the Annual Meeting of the American Educational Research Association, 1970).

[11] For the gradual organizational affiliation of CAE within the American Anthropological Association, see the following *CAE Newsletters*: 1(1)(May 1970): 2; 1(2)(Oct. 1970): 1; 2(1)(Feb. 1971): 15–16; 4(1)(Feb. 1973) :20.

[12] Some points need further comment. First, Singleton was referring to Philip Foster's (1972:480–82) review of *Anthropological Perspectives on Education* in which Foster discussed the issue of a "distinctive field that can be termed 'anthropology of education'." Secondly, Singleton's statement that no one expects EA "to become a discipline in its own right" suggests that he was unaware of Rosenstiel's (1954:28–36) position.

[13] As compared to educational sociology and educational psychology which were included as descriptors when the database was established in 1966.

[14] Personal communication, James Houston to author, July 8, 1982.

References

Barnes, Earl, ed. 1896–97. *Studies in Education, Vol. 1*. Stanford: Leland Stanford Jr. University.

_____, ed., 1902. *Studies in Education, Vol. 2*. Philadelphia, PA: independently published.

Boas, Franz, 1899. Advances in Methods of Teaching. *Science* 9:93–96.

Brameld, Theodore, 1955. Culture and Education: A Needed Partnership. *The Journal of Higher Education* 26:59 68, 111.

_____, 1957. *Cultural Foundations of Education*. Westport: Greenwood Press.

_____, 1958. Explicit and Implicit Culture in Puerto Rico: A Case Study in Educational Anthropology. *Harvard Educational Review* 28:197–213.

_____, ed., 1967. A Venture in Educational Anthropology. *Journal of Education* 150:3–52.

_____, 1968. *Japan: Culture, Education, and Change in Two Communities*. New York: Holt, Rinehart and Winston.

Bryson, Lyman, 1939. Anthropology and Education. In *So Live the Works of Men*, Donald Brand and Fred Harvey, eds., pp. 107–15. Albuquerque: University of New Mexico.

CAE Newsletters 1(1)(May 1970): 2; 1(2)(Oct. 1970): 1; 2(1)(Feb. 1971): 15 16; 4(1)(Feb. 1973) :20.

Eddy, Elizabeth M., 1985. Theory, Research and Application in Educational Anthropology. *Anthropology and Education Quarterly* 16(2): 83–104.

Encyclopedia of Associations, 31st ed., 1996. S.v. "Council on Anthropology and Education." Detroit, MI: Gale Research.

Foster, Philip, 1972. Review of *Anthropological Perspectives on Education*, Murray Wax, Stanley Diamond, and Fred Gearing, eds., *American Journal of Sociology* 78:480–82.

Herzog, John, ed., 1972–1974. Courses in Anthropology and Education. *Council on Anthropology and Education Newsletter* Vol. 4, No. 2 (July 1973): 36–38.

Hewett, Edgar, 1904. Anthropology and Education. *American Anthropologist* 6:574–75.

_____1905. Ethnic Factors in Education. *American Anthropologist* 7:1–16.

Malinowski, Bronislaw, 1936. Native Education and Culture Contact. *International Review of Missions* 25:480–515.

Maring, Joel M., and Gabriel DeCicco, 1982. Anthropology and Education Questionnaire: A Report. *Anthropology and Education Quarterly* 13(4): 335–47.

Monroe, Paul, 1923. *A Text-Book in the History of Education*. Norwood Press, 1905. Reprinted in 1923. New York: The Macmillan Company.

Montessori, Maria, 1913. *Pedagogical Anthropology*, translated by Frederic Taber Cooper. New York: Frederick A. Stokes Company.

New Serial Titles 1971–1975 Cumulation, Vol. 1, 1976. Washington, DC: Library of Congress.

New Serial Titles 1981–1985 Cumulation, Vol. 1, 1986 , Washington, DC: Library of Congress.

Piddington, Ralph, 1950. *An Introduction to Social Anthropology*. London: Oliver and Boyd.

Riccardi, Paolo, 1880, *L'Attenzione in Bapporto alla Pedagogia*, Part One, Chapters 1 and 2, entitled "Lo Studio dell' Uomo degli Uomine," pp. 3–12 and "Antropologia e Pedagogia," pp. 13–22. Modena: Toschi.

Roberts, Joan, 1976. An Overview of Anthropology and Education: Introduction. In *Educational Patterns and Cultural Configurations*, Joan Roberts and Sherrie Akinsanya, eds., pp. 1–13. New York: David McKay Company.

Roberts, Joan, and Sherrie Akinsanya, 1987. Bibliography on Anthropology and Education. In *Educational Patterns and Cultural Configurations: The Anthropology of Education*, Roberts and Akinsanya, eds., pp. 375–404. New York: David McKay Company.

Rosenstiel, Annette, 1954. Educational Anthropology: A New Approach to Cultural Analysis. *Harvard Educational Review* 24:2–36.

Singleton, John, 1973. Perspectives for the CAE. *Council on Anthropology and Education Newsletter* 4(1): 16–19.

Spindler, George, ed., 1955. *Education and Anthropology*. Stanford: Stanford University Press.

_____, 1963. *Education and Culture*. New York: Holt, Rinehart and Winston.

_____, 1971. Prospects in Anthropology and Education. *Council on Anthropology and Education Newsletter* 2(1): 1–2.

_____, 1974. *Education and Cultural Process*. New York: Holt, Rinehart and Winston.

_____, 1982. *Doing the Ethnography of Schooling: Educational Anthropology in Action*. New York: Holt, Rinehart and Winston.

_____, 1987. *Education and Cultural Process: Anthropological Approaches*, 2d ed. Prospect Heights, IL: Waveland Press.

Spindler, George, and Louise Spindler, 1983. Review Essay: The Case Studies in Education and Culture From Cradle to Grave. *Anthropology and Education Quarterly* 14(1): 73–80.

_____, gen. eds., 1987. *Interpretive Ethnography of Education at Home and Abroad*. Mahwah, NJ: Lawrence Erlbaum.

_____, 1994. *Pathways to Cultural Awareness Cultural Therapy with Teachers and Students*. Thousand Oaks, CA: Corwin Press.

Vandewalker, Nina, 1898. Some Demands of Education upon Anthropology. *The American Journal of Sociology* 4:69–78.

Part II

APPROACHES TO THE STUDY OF SCHOOLS

Preview

All of the chapters in this volume are in some degree a product of ethnographic fieldwork. The three chapters in Part II provide insight into what kind of an approach anthropologists are likely to use when they gather data on educational process. However, readers should be forewarned: Anthropology as a discipline is so divided within itself that all anthropologists will not agree that what is said within these chapters falls within their definition of ethnography. Ethnography is one kind of qualitative method. Qualitative approaches to the study of schooling have become very popular among educators during the past decade. This popularity has carried ethnography along with it to the extent that the term "ethnography" is often mistakenly used in education to describe any study that does not use quantitative methods and that has a qualitative flair to it.

This indiscriminate use of the ethnographic label does harm to ethnography and to anthropology, and it is misleading to educators. The three chapters of Part II are genuinely anthropological. They use models of social structure and culture that issue from anthropology, and they use methods of research that are clearly those of anthropologists doing fieldwork. Harry Wolcott, for example, lived in the study community for at least one year and was a participant observer in the school in that community. Wolcott was the teacher in the school about which he writes. He describes himself as "enemy," an unusual self-description for a teacher to adopt. In making this declaration he focuses on the problem of the intrusive mainstream teacher in a minority community. Teachers in many schools in the United States will recognize his situation and resonate to his problems, if not to his solutions.

The contributions by Louise Spindler and myself are of quite a different nature than the one by Harry Wolcott. We are not describing our fieldwork in a specific community; rather, we are providing a brief introduction to the rationale for doing ethnography. In chapter 3 we describe what it is we think we study in schools—a part of the dialogue that describes the national whole—and we describe, albeit briefly, what we do to study it. Space limitations in this book preclude taking the points we raise further, for our concern is less with method than with substance. Interested readers may wish to explore *Doing the Ethnography of Schooling* (edited by G. Spindler, Holt, Rinehart and Winston, 1982, reprinted by Waveland Press, 1987) and *Interpretive Ethnography of Schooling at Home and Abroad* (edited by George and Louise Spindler, Lawrence Erlbaum Associates, 1987). Some readers will object to the criteria of a good ethnography listed in chapter 4. Some readers would even deny the possibility of there being a "good ethnography" or of there being any ethnography at all. This is obviously not our position. We think that disciplined ethnographic inquiry can produce useful interpretive, descriptive, analyses of complex processes such as those involved in education. Let the readers judge for themselves.

The Editor

3

Ethnography
An Anthropological View

George and Louise Spindler
Stanford University

In the brief compass of these few pages we state what we think ethnography is and what ethnographers study. We are doing so because ethnography has recently become a popular approach to the study of schools, play groups, bars, business establishments—any place where people gather. Anthropologists have "come home" to do their field research more than they did only a few years ago as remote tribesmen and traditional peasants have become less numerous and less accessible.[1] This popularity has been a mixed blessing, for false hopes are raised, particularly in education, partly because many people, who are quite innocent of anthropology as a discipline and who have only vague notions of cultural process, claim to be doing ethnography. We have nothing against anyone doing qualitative field site evaluation, participant or nonparticipant observation, descriptive journalism, or anything else if it is well done. It will produce some tangible result and may be useful, but it should not be called ethnography unless it is, and it is not ethnography unless it uses some model of cultural process in both the gathering and interpretation of data.[2] This gives us great latitude, but there are boundaries. We will explore these boundaries briefly.

What Do Ethnographers Study?

Culture, cultural process, cultural knowledge, appear in various guises. We need to define what we study when we study culture. As we do so, we will also be talking about how we study it. By "we" we mean the authors in the company of many, but not all, anthropologists.

We often refer to an "American" culture.[3] Objections are immediately raised. America is multicultural. America is too diverse to be

Source: Reprinted by permission from *Educational Horizons*, Vol. 63, pp. 154–57 (1985).

called a culture. We say there is an American culture not because we have standardized drug stores, kitchens, cars, and clothing, though uniformities in these things do contribute to some uniformities that are cultural. We certainly do not claim that there is an American culture because we are composed of at least twenty-four ethnic groups, six social classes, males and females, fourteen major religious groupings and countless sects, many degrees of left and right and extreme factions in both contingents, gays and straights, drug users and abstainers, and hillbillies and city slickers. We claim that there is an American culture because since prerevolutionary times we have been dialoguing about freedom and constraint, equality and difference, cooperation and competition, independence and conformity, sociability and individuality, Puritanism and free love, materialism and altruism, hard work and getting by, and achievement and failure. We express the dialogue in great and small institutions, political campaigns, expenditures of billions of dollars, schools and libraries, personnel management, business practices, sales pitches, production goals, foreign policy, etc. It is not because we are all the same, or that we agree on most important matters, that there is an American culture. It is that somehow we agreed to worry, argue, fight, emulate, and agree or disagree about the same pivotal concerns. Call them values, value orientations, cultural foci, themes, whatever. They are pivotal,[4] and they are arranged in oppositional pairs. That is the nature of culture, according to anthropological structuralists.[5] This is the dialogue of American culture. It gives meaning to our lives and actions as Americans. There are other dialogues that give meaning to our personal lives.

Within any social setting and any social scene within a setting, whether great or small, social actors are carrying on a culturally constructed dialogue. This dialogue is expressed in behavior, words, symbols, and in the application of cultural knowledge to make instrumental activities and social situations "work" for one. We learn the dialogue as children and continue learning it all of our lives as our circumstances change. This is the phenomenon we study as ethnographers—the dialogue of action and interaction. We observe behavior and interview, in varying degrees of formality, any "native" (student, teacher, boss, housewife, chief) who will talk with us. When we are in classrooms, we observe the action and talk to students, teachers, principals, counselors, parents, and janitors. We observe, formulate questions, ask them, observe some more, and so on until the patterns of behavior and native explanations for them coalesce into repetitive sequences and configurations. We try to determine how teaching and learning are supported and constrained by understandings, many of them implicit, that govern the interaction of teachers and students.[6] The dialogue of everyday classroom interaction around what is to be taught, how much of it is to be learned, and how the teaching and learning will be conducted is what we try to record and eventually interpret.

In a Nutshell

We think of culture as a continuing dialogue that revolves around pivotal areas of concern in a given community. The dialogue is produced as social actors apply their acquired cultural knowledge so that it works in social situations—they make sense and enhance, or at least maintain, self-esteem. Neither the knowledge nor the situations replicate themselves through time, but both exhibit continuity. The dialogue occurs at several levels simultaneously—from the most explicit and obvious to the tacit and sometimes very hidden.

What Is Education?

We see education as cultural transmission, and of course cultural transmission requires cultural learnings, so learning and transmission are never separated except by convention.[7] Further, we see that aspect of cultural transmission in which we are most interested—education in the broad sense, schooling in the narrower sense (including initiations, rites of passage, apprenticeships, as well as schools)—as a calculated intervention in the learning process. We are not interested in all learning that takes place as children grow into adults, get older, and finally die. We are interested in the learning that takes place as a result of calculated intervention. It is our unique subject matter as educational anthropologists, and without a unique subject matter there is no discipline.

Within the focus that we think is useful, there are surface phenomena—the manifest, overt, cultural content—and then there are the tacit agreements that make the dialogue of intervention possible. In our long-term study of the Schoenhausen Grundschule[8] and in our recent work in the Roseville, Wisconsin, school and community,[9] we find that the implicit, tacit, and hidden levels of culture are most important. They are what explain puzzling persistences that are there over time under a surface level of change, sometimes even apparently dramatic change. And they are what explain, most satisfactorily, some startling differences in classroom management and student-teacher behavior between the German and American schools. Many models for research and analysis used by both social scientists and educators do not permit the study of the very processes we have discovered are the most important—those aspects of the continuing dialogue between students and teachers that are hidden beneath the surface of behavior.

Good Ethnography

We think that *good* ethnography is necessary in order to understand what goes on as education occurs. We have stated what we consider to be the criteria for a good ethnography in *Doing the Ethnography of Schooling*[10] and updated in chapter 4.

We search for clues to the relationship between forms and levels of cultural knowledge and observable behaviors as the dialogue of intervention and response takes place. The search must follow the clues wherever they lead and cannot be predetermined by a schedule of categories of observation or rating scales. Ethnographic study requires direct observation, it requires being immersed in the field situation, and it requires constant interviewing in all degrees of formality and casualness. From this interviewing, backed by observation, one is able to collect and elicit the native view(s) of reality and the native ascription of meaning to events, intentions, and consequences.

Eventually we must face the task of interpretation and cultural translation. The native view of reality must be directly represented in this interpretation but it can rarely stand on its own. We must translate it into the vernacular of the readers, natives in another cultural system, caught up in a different dialogue. And we must apply some concepts, models, paradigms, and theories from our professional discipline in order to give our findings wider applicability and, of course, to communicate with our fellow professional natives. As we have said, our persuasion is toward culture and a special canting of it that we have termed *dialogue.*

Our orientation is ideographic and case-study oriented. Ideographic research is widely regarded as incapable of producing generalizations. We take issue with this and feel that through grounded, case-oriented, open (that is, not predetermined) ethnographic investigation, generalizations can be formulated most effectively. They may be tested, to be sure, with nomothetic methods employing refined statistical models,[11] and often such methods also produce hypotheses for testing.

There is nothing in what we have said that precludes the use of quantitative data and inferential statistics as a part of an overall research program. We have collected and analyzed such data in every one of our four major research projects.[12] Careful use of statistics defines relationships and parameters in a most valuable way that helps define what must be explored with direct observation and interviewing and, conversely, makes possible the extension of generalizations initially derived ideographically.

Concepts Precede Method

There is much more that should be said about ethnographic methods.[13] Not all anthropologists will agree that what we study is the continuing dialogue that holds a given nation, community, or group together or tears it apart. It is what we believe we study, though we have not always called it that. We feel that whether we phrase our object of study as culturally constructed dialogue or simply as culture is relatively unimportant, though to us the former seems less static and more processual than the latter. In any event, what we are after is what the native knows and uses in interaction with others in the situations and instrumental relationships his society provides for him. We want to discover meanings and relationships. The power of this position is great and as yet largely unexploited. Education, business, and government would find it very useful if they employed researchers with the *right stuff*, and the right stuff from our point of view requires training and discipline in cultural interpretation as well as research techniques.

We do not think that this power is going to be exploited quickly in any of its potential sectors of operation. Despite some thirty-five years of intensive work, five major texts in educational anthropology, and the teaching of more than three thousand graduate students in professional education at Stanford and Wisconsin, we do not feel that we have made a significant dent in the educationist consciousness. Perhaps the sudden popularity of ethnography as a method will result in consciousness-raising, but it will not unless the conceptual structure is carried along with the method.

Notes

[1] Donald Messerschmidt, ed., *Anthropologists at Home in North America: Methods and Issues in the Study of One's Own Society* (New York: Cambridge Univ. Press, 1981).

[2] Harry Wolcott, "The Anthropology of Learning," in *Anthropology and Education Quarterly* 13 (1982): 83–108.

[3] George and Louise Spindler, "Anthropologists View American Culture," in *Annual Review of Anthropology*, edited by B. Siegel, et al. (Palo Alto, CA: Annual Reviews Inc., 1983); Marvin Harris, *America Now: The Anthropology of a Changing Culture* (New York: Simon & Schuster, 1981); and Richard Merelman, *Making Something of Ourselves* (Berkeley: Univ. of California Press, 1984).

[4] George and Louise Spindler, "Anthropologists View American Culture." *(Annual Review of Anthropology*, 72, 49–78, 1983).

[5] Richard Merelman, *Making Something of Ourselves*.

[6] Reba Page, "Lower-Track Classes at a College-preparatory High School: A Caricature of Educational Encounters," in *Toward an Interpretive Ethnography of Education*, edited by G. Spindler.

[7] Harry Wolcott, "The Anthropology of Learning," *Anthropology and Education Quarterly* 13 (1982): 83–108; and George and Louise Spindler, "Do Anthropologists Need Learning Theory?" *Anthropology and Education Quarterly* 13 (1982): 109–24.

[8] George D. Spindler, "Schooling in Schoenhausen: A Study of Cultural Transmission and Instrumental Adaptation in an Urbanizing German Village," in *Education and Cultural Process: Toward an Anthropology of Education,* edited by G. Spindler, 230–73 (New York: Holt, Rinehart & Winston, 1974); and George and Louise Spindler, "Roger Harker and Schoenhausen: From the Familiar to the Strange and Back Again," in *Doing the Ethnography of Schooling: Educational Anthropology in Action,* edited by G. Spindler (New York: Holt, Rinehart & Winston, 1982), reprinted in 1988 (Prospect Heights, IL: Waveland Press, Inc.).

[9] George and Louise Spindler, "Schoenhausen Revisited and the Rediscovery of Culture," in *Toward an Interpretive Ethnography of Education.* (New Jersey: Lawrence Erlbaum Assoc. Inc. 1987).

[10] George Spindler, "The Criteria for a Good Ethnography of Schooling," in *Doing the Ethnography of Schooling.*

[11] George Spindler, ed., *The Making of Psychological Anthropology* (Berkeley: Univ. of California Press, 1978), 31–32; and Weston LaBarre in ibid., 270–75.

[12] Louise Spindler, "Researching the Psychology of Culture Change and Urbanization," in *The Making of Psychological Anthropology.*

[13] See Also Michael H. Agar, *The Professional Stranger: An Informal Introduction to Ethnography* (New York: Academic Press, 1980); Frederick Erickson. "What Makes School Ethnography 'Ethnographic'?" *Anthropology and Education Quarterly* 15 (1984):51–66; James Spradley, *The Ethnographic Interview* (New York: Holt, Rinehart & Winston, 1979); James Spradley, Participant Observation (New York: Holt, Rinehart & Winston, 1980); and Harry Wolcott, ed., "Teaching Fieldwork to Educational Researchers: A Symposium," *Anthropology and Education Quarterly* 14(1983): 3.

4

Cultural Process and Ethnography

An Anthropological Perspective

George and Louise Spindler
Stanford University

This essay is divided into two parts: (1) a brief analysis of the changes over time in the ethnography of education as exemplified by six collections edited by George Spindler or by George and Louise Spindler from 1955 to 1987; and (2) a discussion of the ingredients for a good ethnography of schooling.

The mandate by the editors has allowed us the freedom to draw from our own work as an example of "classic" (editors' term) educational ethnography. We are not so sure about the "classic" properties of our studies, nor are we convinced that our approach is "traditional" (editors' term). What we are sure of is that we are going to write about what we have done over the past 40 years as anthropologists deeply interested in the educational process. We have changed and developed over time, and we are doing some of the same things now that we were doing in the 1950s, but a lot that we weren't. Though we will avoid an autobiographical stance, there is unavoidably a personal element in all of this that we hope will be useful and not merely evidence of egotism.

Changes Exemplified in Six Collections, 1955–1987

George Spindler began working in the schools as an anthropologist on a research project directed by Dr. Robert Bush, School of Education, Stanford University, in 1950. This project included case studies of teachers, children, and administrators and was responsible for bringing him (G.S.) into a lifelong relationship with education. *Education and Anthropology* appeared in 1955. His next edited collection,

Abridged version of a longer article of the same name, in *The Handbook of Qualitative Research in Education*, Margaret Le Compte, Wendy Millroy and Judith Preissle, eds. Academic Press (1992).

Education and Culture: Anthropological Approaches, appeared in 1963 and combined a mix of reprints from the 1955 volume and new ones. The third volume appeared in 1974, *Education and Cultural Process: Toward an Anthropology of Education. Doing the Ethnography of Schooling: Educational Anthropology in Action* appeared in 1982, and *Interpretive Ethnography of Education at Home and Abroad*, edited by both Spindlers, appeared in 1987. *Education and Cultural Process* appeared in the second edition in 1987, and *Doing the Ethnography of Schooling* was reprinted with a new Foreword in 1988. Together these volumes constitute a record of the development of the field of educational anthropology and of educational ethnography as construed by cultural anthropologists. Because most of the articles are not written by the Spindlers, they afford a reasonably good cross-section of changes in the field.

Education and Anthropology

The conference that resulted in *Education and Anthropology* (Spindler, 1955a) was held from June 9 to 14, 1954, with Carnegie Foundation support, in a Carmel Valley hideaway and brought twelve cultural anthropologists and as many professional educators into a face-to-face situation for four days. They discussed papers prepared by George Spindler, Bernard Siegel, John Gillin, Solon Kimball, Cora DuBois, C. W. M. Hart, Dorothy Lee, Jules Henry, and Theodore Brameld. Margaret Mead prepared a summary entitled "The Anthropologist and the School as a Field" and Alfred Kroeber commented on the conference as a whole. This conference and the volume issuing from it have often been cited as the beginning of educational anthropology and the ethnography of education. This is not entirely accurate because various workers such as Solon Kimball, Jules Henry, and Margaret Mead were in the field before the conference and, in fact, the "anthropology of education" can be said to have started with Edgar Hewett in 1904 in an article in *American Anthropologist.* The appearance of this volume did, however, provide a substantial platform for the launching of serious anthropological research in the schools and credited the anthropology of education as a legitimate subdiscipline. Although the book was published forty-two years ago, this legitimation both in education and in departments of anthropology has been slow to develop. It is probably correct to say that most professionals working as educational anthropologists feel themselves to be quite marginal in both disciplinary contexts even today.

Ethnography is listed only once in the index for *Education and Anthropology*, and that was in the context of the overview by George Spindler of the use of cross-cultural materials furnished by ethnography, not from the ethnography of education as such. In many cases throughout the volume, ethnography was clearly taken for granted as a source of information, both on other cultures and on our own. However, no one thought of "educational ethnography" or "the ethnography of schooling" as *special fields*. The emphasis throughout the book was on concepts and problems: models for the analysis of the educative process in American communities, the school in the context of the community, learning intercultural understanding, contrasting prepubertal and postpubertal education, discrepancies in the teaching of American culture, education and communications theory, the meeting of educational and anthropological theory, roles for anthropologists and educators, the school as a field of study for the anthropologist, and the educational consequences of the Supreme Court 1954 decision on segregation—*Brown v. the Board of Education.*

It all seemed so clear then. Anthropologists learned about culture by studying the cultures of others. They could put the insights thus gained in interpretations of education and schooling to use in their own (and other) societies. In this way, anthropology furnished the materials for a cultural critique. Education was seen as cultural transmission and as a major instrument in cultural survival, but the learning of culture, the school and the social structure, the exercise of power, the effect of culturally based values on teacher perceptions, the informal transmission of values, the roles of the school administrator and teacher, and American culture as a specific context for schooling were all considered relevant. There was a frank and unselfconscious eclecticism in both concept and method. There was also a clear, implicit understanding of what anthropology was and, thus, what it might do for, with, and in education. The volume is worth reading for the information it provides about the platform from which we have launched ourselves as well as for the feeling of both security *and* excitement that was in the air at the time.

Education and Culture

The term "ethnography" is not listed in the index of *Education and Culture: Anthropological Approaches* (1963). In the overview article by George Spindler, the anthropologist is not described as an ethnographer but rather as a consultant, as a researcher in education whose "greatest contribution" is the holistic approach to research and analysis, and as a teacher—making explicit the cultural assumptions of educators. Ethnography, however, serves as the implicit data base for studies carried out and written about by the authors. Jules Henry writes on attitude organization in elementary school classrooms and spontaneity and creativity in suburban classrooms. Dorothy Eggan writes on instruction and affect in Hopi cultural continuity (see chapter 16). George Spindler analyzes personality, the sociocultural system, and education among the Menomini. Melford Spiro describes education in a communal village in Israel. Jack Fischer considers Japanese schools for the natives of Truk (Caroline Islands). And Bernard Siegel writes about social structures, social change, and education in rural Japan. But no one talked about "ethnography" as such. It was taken for granted. The *problem* was the focus. All of the articles in this volume make for good reading. They are neither tedious, hung up on methodology, nor bound to single cases, except where appropriate. They are intellectually freewheeling and methodologically true to form. These studies employ structured and unstructured interview techniques, questionnaires, psychological tests, socioeconomic inventories, census reports, sociometric techniques, value-projective techniques—the whole range of procedures used in the social and behavioral sciences. Our field has always been methodologically eclectic. But underlying all of these usages is the constant attention to the flow of life around the participant-observer, the anthropologist, that gives meaning to the results of the specialized techniques. This basic approach to research in the field is very apparent in most of the chapters in *Education and Culture*. Jules Henry's two chapters are models for what needs to be done in the application of anthropology to the analysis of educational processes in our own society. The fact that the commitment to direct observation is more apparent in the papers that deal with educational process in non-Western societies than with those at home is an indication that anthropologists had only begun their work in our own society.

A quotation from the introductory chapter in *Education and Culture* by George Spindler indicated what, apparently, needed to be done in the future. "Probably the most substantial contribution that anthropology could make to education would be the building of a body of case materials based on direct observation in a variety of educational situations, but most of this work remains to be done." In the future volumes edited by the Spindlers, this development becomes clear.

Education and Cultural Process

Education and Cultural Process: Toward an Anthropology of Education (1974) is a departure from the first two books, both of which were essentially essay collections taking ethnography for granted but with some exceptions not presenting much direct ethnographic observation. In the 1974 collection, ethnographic case studies are clearly the focus. John Singleton, in his paper on education as cultural transmission, distinguishes participant observation from other observational procedures and applies "these research perspectives to what I like to call 'educational ethnography'." He describes Harry Wolcott's (1973) study of an elementary school principal, Richard King's (1968) study of a Native American residential school in the Yukon, and Gary Rosenfeld's (1971) study of a slum school in Harlem as outstanding examples of this application. Singleton might well have added his own *Nichu,* a case study of a Japanese elementary school (1967), as another good example as well as Richard Warren's (1971) study of education in Rebhausen, a German village. (Wolcott, King, Singleton, and Warren were all Spindler Ph.D.s in the emerging education and anthropology program at Stanford University.) Of twenty-seven papers in this volume, twelve are explicitly ethnographic and focus on single cases. Of these twelve, only McDermott (on achieving school failure) (see chapter 7 for an updated version of this article), Spindler (on a case study of culturally defined adjustment and teacher perceptions), Schwartz and Merten (on the meaning of a sorority initiation ritual), and Wolcott (on the elementary school principal) report on schools in our own society.

The 1974 volume is clearly cross-cultural in character and pays more attention to other cultures than to our own. This may be one of the reasons why educators have been slow to accept the work by anthropologists of education as relevant to their concerns. Why worry about some other culture when you have so many problems in your own? Therein lies a dilemma. Anthropology without its cross-cultural perspective becomes a kind of poor sociology. Whatever insights anthropologists have been able to bring to the analysis of educational process have been derived in significant degree from a cross-cultural perspective. Much of the current work in educational anthropology lacks this explicit reference to a cross-cultural perspective and, in our opinion, is the poorer for it.

Education and Cultural Process (1974) contains the first explicitly "ethnographic" section ("Approaches to the Study of Schools and Classrooms," Part IV) on ethnographic method. The four papers in this section diverge in various ways but have in common a concern for the role of the researcher-ethnographer. Richard King characterizes his role as that of "significant friend," and Harry Wolcott his role as "enemy" (see chapter 5). Both characterizations must be seen in the context of their articles to make full sense. But the concern with the role of the researcher indicates a growing awareness of the effect of researcher and situation on the results of any study involving human beings. This interaction is critical in the study of schooling for the anthropologist-ethnographer and is particularly conspicuous in the small community of the school and the classroom.

Doing the Ethnography of Schooling

Our next edited volume, *Doing the Ethnography of Schooling: Educational Anthropology in Action* (1982), is explicitly ethnographic throughout. Of the fifteen papers in the book, twelve are based on ethnographic research in school sites. Heath describes the problems of white teachers with black children in Trackton. Erickson and Mohatt describe participant structure in two classrooms of Native American students. Varenne describes the symbolic expression of social interaction among American senior high school students. Gearing and Epstein do an ethnographic probe into the hidden curriculum in a working-class school. Hanna describes public social policy and the children's world in a desegregated magnet school. Finnan describes children's spontaneous play in an American school. Warren analyzes ethnic identity in two schools, one of them in the United States, the other in Mexico. Hart analyzes the social organization of reading in an elementary school.

This collection was developed in part as a response to a condition that had developed as educational ethnography became a fad. The book begins with a quote from a California State Department of Education official: "Anything anyone wants to do that has no clear problem, no methodology, and no theory, is likely to be called 'ethnography' around here." One of the major purposes of the volume was to show that anthropological educational ethnography did have clear problems and that it had both methodology and theory. The papers speak for themselves and, on the whole, successfully counter this negative perception.

One of the significant themes that emerges in the papers in this volume is the attention to the "hidden" curriculum, to the covert, tacit or implicit cultural patterns that affect behavior and communication particularly in face-to-face social interaction, and that are largely outside the consciousness of the actor. This focus is clear in most of the papers, although not a primary preoccupation in all. Some analysts refer this orientation to the influence of a paralinguistic model. The editorial commentary draws attention to the fact that covert culture, hidden postulates, dynamic themes, and the like were a primary preoccupation on the part of many anthropologists of the 1940s and that they did not draw from a paralinguistic model.

Interpretive Ethnography of Education

The next collection, *Interpretive Ethnography of Education at Home and Abroad* (1987b) includes nineteen papers, fourteen of which are based on direct ethnographic evidence from single cases. Another three are about ethnographic methods, one of which, by Solon Kimball, is reprinted from the 1955 conference volume. The other two are by George and Louise Spindler on teaching and learning how to do the ethnography of education and by Harry Wolcott on ethnographic intent, in which he tells us both what ethnography is and what it is not. The editors take a strong position on education as cultural transmission. To quote from their first chapter:

We see education as cultural transmission, and of course cultural transmission requires cultural learning, so learning and transmission are
separated only by convention. Further, we see that aspect of cultural
transmission in which we are most interested—education in the broad
sense, schooling in the narrower sense (including initiations, rites of
passage, apprenticeships, as well as schools) as *calculated interventions* in the learning process. We are not interested in all learning that
takes place as children grow into adults, get older, and finally die. We
are interested in the learning that takes place, whether intended or
unanticipated, as a result of calculated intervention. It is our unique
subject matter as educational anthropologists, and, without a unique
subject matter as well as a methodology, there is no discipline.

In retrospect, this statement seems to eliminate learning that is
not a result of calculated intervention from the purview of anthropologist-ethnographers. It could reduce the anthroethnographers' attention
to learning in peer groups or to the concomitant learning that is tangential to calculated intervention. This would be an unfortunate effect.

The rationale for the emphasis on cultural transmission is that
this focus exploits anthropological expertise on sociocultural structure
and process and a focus on learning puts the focus on the individual.
It is all too easy to slip into a "blame the victim" interpretation if one
emphasizes the individual learner and not the context and circumstances of learning. We have not yet found the proper position between
these two possible polar positions—cultural transmission as calculated
intervention and learning as individualized process. Theory in educational anthropology is still in a fairly raw state, although there is quite
a bit of it. We will undoubtedly eventually work out this problem.

Interpretive Ethnography of Education continues to recognize the
importance of comparative and cross-cultural work in the ethnography
of education with papers on Schoenhausen (Germany) (see chapter 22)
by the Spindlers; a first-grade class in a French school, by Katherine
Anderson-Levitt; interethnic images in multicultural England, by Paul
Yates; and a paper on Chinese education in a village setting, by Norman
Chance.

In 1955, and even in 1963, we could take for granted that the
cross-cultural perspective was basic to the whole structure of the discipline. Today we have to make a self-conscious, purposeful attempt to
get such material included in a collection or any other publications
directed largely at educational ethnography. The contents of the quarterly *Anthropology and Education* indicate this to be the case as well.
Few articles have been published in it over the past five years with an
explicit cross-cultural frame of reference. The implications of this for
the future of the anthropology of education and educational ethnography are significant. If anthropology does not contribute a cross-cultural
perspective, then what does it contribute? Because ethnography has

become a household word in most of the social science disciplines, it needs a distinguishing criterion for its anthropological subtype to avoid the possibility that we may simply disappear as a recognizable subdiscipline. Some feel this is happening to cultural anthropology as a whole. If so, it is not surprising that this may happen to educational anthropology. It will be one of the developments to watch over the next several years.

Other notable developments in the ethnography of education appearing in *Interpretive Ethnography of Education* include explicit attention by David Fetterman to evaluation done ethnographically; the appearance of the cultural knowledge framework, drawn initially from ethnoscience and cognitive anthropology, in a paper by Katherine Anderson-Levitt; the distinctions between voluntary and involuntary minorities and their responses to schooling in articles by John Ogbu and Margaret Gibson; the emphasis on transitions between home and school and the participation structures encountered in each in a paper by Concha Delgado-Gaitan; a focus on gender differences in the emergence of sexist behavior in four children's groups by Ruth Goodenough; the combination of attention to participation structures and hidden curriculum in an article by Reba Page on lower-track classes at a college preparatory high school; and the problems attendant to computer literacy as related to curricula by Susan Jungck. One has a clear sense that educational ethnography is reaching out into new areas and beginning to formulate some fairly clear theoretical paradigms.

Education and Cultural Process: Anthropological Approaches

The last volume to be included in this review is the second edition of *Education and Cultural Process: Anthropological Approaches.* There is a thirteen-year separation between the first edition of this volume (1974) and the new one (1987). It adds fourteen new papers on a wide range of topics, including the anthropology of learning and the relevance of learning theory to an anthropology of education; the historical roots of the subdiscipline; the relationships between anthropologists and educational institutions; primate behavior and the transition to human status; ethnography within a systematic methodological framework; the new immigrants and their patterns of academic success; controlled cross-cultural comparisons of schooling; comparative cognitive development in two countries; a comparative analysis of social bias in schooling; and the teaching of anthropology. The difference between *Education and Cultural Process* in both of its editions and the other collections is consistent in that both editions are about the relationships of anthropology to education and do not focus primarily on ethnography as a research tool. There seems to be a constant struggle between these two orientations. The "ethnography of education" framework has tended to supplant as well as supplement the broader concerns of all anthropology of education. The discipline has tended to become more case-centered and more exclusively ethnographic in contrast to other methods (such as surveys, questionnaires, archival research, and psychological tests) than anthropology itself has ever been.

The most important tension in theory represented in the 1987 edition of *Education and Cultural Process* is that between the cultural transmission focus and the learning of culture or cultural acquisition position referred to above. The dialogue is fairly well represented in a paper by Harry Wolcott on the anthropology of learning (see chapter 15) and a paper by George Spindler on cultural transmission in this volume (see chapter 24); however, much remains to be said. A further contribution to the emerging debate is furnished by George and Louise Spindler in "Do Anthropologists Need Learning Theory?" (included in *Education and Cultural Process*, 2/E). The article makes some move toward a combination of cultural transmission and cultural acquisition. In our course titled "Cultural Transmission," offered at Stanford since 1954, we have dealt with such concepts as concomitant learning, incidental learning, unintended learning, and latent learning. These concepts all take as a basic assumption that cultural transmission as intentional intervention is the starting point for analysis.

We acknowledge the credibility of the position taken by Wolcott and others who would start from the other end of the continuum between cultural transmission and the acquisition of culture, but we are concerned that starting thus will result in loss of the unique perspective that anthropology has furnished on the ways in which societies, using their cultural resources, organize the conditions and purposes of learning so that some things are learned and others are not. The situation is complicated by the fact that what is *not* to be learned through intentional interference may be precisely that content which is included in the list of processes previously provided here, such as concomitant learning, and that these kinds of learning provide much of the impetus for sociocultural change because they are "subversive" in their relationship to explicit mandated learning. The relationships between the purposeful organization of educational resources as in cultural transmission and the forms and processes of learning, including forms of "resistance to learning," will constitute, we believe, an important arena for significant theoretical debate in our subdiscipline. A careful, sensitive ethnography of teaching and learning will be of the greatest significance in the development of systematic theory in the arena defined by cultural transmission and in the acquisition of culture by the individual.

The conclusion we draw from this review of these collections is that educational ethnography is alive and well, moving energetically, but without a great deal of consistent theoretical guidance in many directions. It has moved from a position of being taken for granted to a position where it tends to dominate the discipline for which it is a research tool. The emphasis on method will probably subside as stronger problem orientations and theoretical concerns reemerge in the field.

With this we proceed now to the second part of this chapter, which is intended as a somewhat informal and rather personal statement of what we think we do as ethnographers in schools and in other educational institutions or communities.

Toward a Good Ethnography of Schooling

In this section, we are concerned with ethnography as a distinctive approach to the study of education-related phenomena. The list of features characterizing a "good" ethnography is intended to be broadly applicable. Nevertheless, without a doubt there will be colleagues who will find some features objectionable and will want to add others. We do not regard the list as cast in stone.

Direct Observation

The requirement for direct, prolonged, on-the-spot observation cannot be avoided or reduced. It is the guts of the ethnographic approach. This does not always mean *participant* observation. While participant observation is frequently possible in traditional anthropological fieldwork, it is particularly difficult for most adults in such situations as classrooms, playgroups, and other characteristic settings in the ethnography of schooling. One can participate in the teacher role, but it is difficult to participate as a child. Nevertheless, it is often desirable to go as far as one can to assume the role of the child. For example, in George Spindler's first study, in 1968, of the elementary school in Schoenhausen (reported in *Education and Cultural Process*; see Spindler, 1974b), he tried to do the work assignments the third and fourth graders were doing in class, while he was also doing ethnography. This effort did help him to gain rapport with the children. They did their best to help him succeed as a pupil. He found it impossible at times to do ethnography and finish his lessons, so usually opted for doing the former. But he continued to go on hikes, climb towers, and eat lunch with the children. It was all useful—not so much because it made him empathic or gave him special insights into how it was to be a German child in the third grade but, rather, because it made him less threatening and more familiar. In their later restudies (Spindler 1974b; Spindler and Spindler 1982, 1987a,c) of the Schoenhausen school, the Spindlers participated less and observed more. They didn't know the children as well but knew more about their behavior; they had more *data.* Of course the presence of two observers (of both sexes) helped. This in itself is important. The Spindlers now had much more data on girls, which George Spindler did not obtain the first time around, and knew much more about teachers, because they were all female (except for the Rektor) and the women related better to the Spindlers as a couple than to G.S. as a lone man.

It is clear that the *role* of the ethnographer must vary from site to site. Kinds and intensity of participation that are appropriate, sex roles, obtrusiveness (participants may be more obtrusive than passive observers), and multiplicity of demands on the ethnographer all vary greatly. There are no hard-and-fast rules. A *sense* of what is appropriate and of what will probably work can be conveyed by training if the individual being trained already has well-developed sensitivities abut social interaction, self-other relations, and obtrusiveness. Some people, who may be good people in numerous ways, do not possess these sensitivities and should not be ethnographers.

Above all else is the requirement that the ethnographer observe *directly.* No matter what instruments, coding devices, recording devices or techniques are used, the primary obligation is for the ethnographer to be there when the action takes place and to change that action as little as possible by his or her presence.

Sufficient Time on the Site

There is no hard-and-fast rule regarding what constitutes sufficient time on the site. Significant discoveries can be made in two weeks or less of ethnographic observation, but the *validity* of ethnographic observation is based on observation *in situ* that lasts long enough to permit the ethnographer to see things happen not once but repeatedly. Of course some things such as an earthquake, murder, fire, or mass hysteria are likely to occur only once during one's fieldwork, if at all, in which case one must do the best one can. But most of the things we are interested in happen again and again. We must observe these happenings often enough so that finally we learn nothing significant by their reoccurrence. A researcher knows when that point has been reached. Then one should observe still longer, to be sure that one's sense of that point in time is neither premature nor the result of fatigue.

In the traditional anthropological fieldwork situation, we usually think of a year as being a reasonable, although a trifle truncated, period of time to execute the study of a complex community or phenomenon. Most well-received studies have taken longer than that. When George Spindler published his first ethnography on Menomini acculturation in

1955 (Spindler, 1955b), he had worked for a total of nineteen months with the Menomini over a six-year period. His German case study, *Burgbach: Urbanization and Identity in a German Village* (1973), is based on intermittent work over a twelve-year period and the field studies of many students attending Stanford in Germany. Louise Spindler's (1962) *Menomini Woman and Culture Change* is based on intermittent fieldwork from 1948 to 1954. George Spindler's first case study of a single teacher in a fifth-grade classroom in a California school took six months, with two afternoon-long visits, on the average, each week. The first Schoenhausen publication (Spindler, 1974b) was based directly on six weeks of very intensive fieldwork in 1968, but the Spindlers had researched the area (Remstal, Germany) previously in 1960 and 1967.

In contrast to the time required for a community study, if we had to state a desirable time for an adequate study of a single classroom, or even a significant segment of a single classroom (such as a reading group), we would say three months, with observation continuing for a significant portion of every school day. It would be better if this three-month period were spread over an entire school year, because some things just do not happen during a three-month period. Every one of the papers submitted for *Doing the Ethnography of Schooling* and *Interpretive Ethnography of Education* is based on at least nine months of direct observation. Some of them are based on observation over a five- or ten-year period.

It must be emphasized that the relatively long periods of fieldwork mentioned here are for in-depth studies of significant and complex relationships where time is not limited by external conditions. Validity in ethnographic studies largely depends on an adequate period of study. At the same time, it is useless to deny that much of significance can be learned in short periods of time. Policy decisions usually have to be made on the basis of inadequate knowledge. A short-term ethnography may be better than no ethnography at all. But again, *validity* is not to be expected of short-term ethnography. This apparently is not generally understood. There are serious, or apparently to-be-taken-as-serious, ethnographic reports that are based on as little as two weeks of "ethnographic" study. Two weeks of reconnaissance can tell us a lot about the topography we would need to explore in-depth for a "real" ethnographic study, but two weeks is not sufficient time in which to do a serious cultural ethnography.

Volume of Recorded Data

Once upon a time, a prominent anthropologist stated at a national-level meeting of social scientists convened to discuss methodology and field equipment, "Just give us a pad of paper and a pencil and enough time. . . ." We have gone well beyond this and now use video cameras, tape recorders, film cameras, time-lapse photography, and various eliciting instruments and coding devices. However, we cannot let technical devices do our work for us. What such devices collect are data that can be analyzed (and reanalyzed) later.

There is no technological substitute for the alert individual observer, with all senses unstopped and sensitivities working at top efficiency. Of course this "turned on" observer is not simply collecting data impartially. A model of possible relationships exists in the mind of the ethnographer. And yet, there is no substitute for this observer, because only the human observer can be alert to divergences and subtleties that may prove to be more important than the data produced by any predetermined categories of observation or any instrument. True, the observer can keep on observing what is collected with tapes and visual devices long after the action is over, but these devices are so selective, so focused, that the *observer-in-situ* will often pick up what the camera or recorder leaves out. We have found it essential in our work with the Blood, Menomini, and Cree and in schools in Germany and America to collect as much visual and auditory material as possible but to always have a human observer turned on. A worthwhile field trip is usually marked by a high volume of collected data—both extensive field notes and extensive recorded material. Each of the ethnographically based papers for our edited volumes represents only a fraction of the data collected for each project.

The good ethnographer is also a good collector of artifacts, products, documents—anything that can conceivably be related to the object of study. We tried to scoop up anything and everything we could from teachers and students in the German classroom and in Roseville, and if we couldn't take it with us, we'd take a picture of it. One collects documents, such as lesson plans, books, directives from higher echelons, newspaper articles, letters to the principal, texts of speeches, and student products such as artwork and essays. More of this kind of material probably exists than any reasonable researcher will ever get around to analyzing because things for which one initially sees no use within a year after the field study is finished often suddenly appear important ten or twenty years later. In ethnography, one is always dogged with the realization that what is happening will never happen again. The categories of happenings repeat themselves endlessly in human affairs, yet each event is unique.

The Evolving Character of Ethnographic Study

At least in the initial stages of a project, the ethnographer should not work out specific hypotheses, coded instruments, or even highly specific categories of observation. The reason for this is to avoid predetermining what is observed and what is elicited from informants. The problem that one thinks one is going to study is usually not the one actually studied. This does not mean that the ethnographer enters the field *in vacuo*. It is precisely our point, as anthropological ethnographers, that ethnography is not merely a technique; it is a style of inquiry to which certain techniques (direct passive observation, participant observation, ethnographic interview, etc.) are germane, but more importantly, it is a research process that starts with certain models of significant relationships. This model, for anthropological inquiry, is sociocultural and usually addresses cultural knowledge and social interaction in which cultural knowledge is used by actors (who may become informants but are often simply observed acting) to, as Ray McDermott has said, "make sense and feel good."

However, having stated that the ethnographer usually will not have the research problem and hypotheses all worked out beforehand, one is immediately assailed by doubts. Sometimes this is not true, and no hard-and-fast rule can be applied indiscriminately. The situation is usually something like this: The anthropologist gets interested in a problem *area*, such as reading competence and social context; school experience as mediating traditional versus modernization requirements; sex-role differentiation in textbook content and its interpretation in classroom behavior; styles of verbal interaction between white teachers and black children; play behavior as related to social class, ethnicity, and gender; and so forth. As a rule, the specific problem, with related hypotheses, is developed as the fieldwork proceeds. The ethnographer knows something interesting is going on out there and tries to relate to it. Eventually, the observations begin to fall into categories and be governed by models. Of course, this creates a predisposition to certain foci and sensitivities, but not as concretely or as narrowly as when everything possible is worked out beforehand. The model or frame of reference in anthropological ethnography is usually broad enough to encompass a wide range of phenomena. The important criterion is that the ethnographer should proceed in the initial stages of investigation with as open a mind as possible, attending to a wide variety of possible relationships. Soon one begins to formulate hypotheses, more often resembling serious hunches than formal hypotheses, that are explored and tested by continued, repetitive observation and data elicitation.

Instrumentation

Recorded observations and recorded elicited data (such as interviews) are the base grist for the ethnographic mill. Although there is nothing wrong with using instruments such as questionnaires, they are rarely used in the first stages of work. When instruments are employed, usually they should only be used in the following circumstances: (1)

When the investigator already knows what is important to find out. In such a case, a "survey" procedure can be used in which responses are collected efficiently from a relatively large sample of respondents. (2) When the instruments are developed specifically for the field site and the focus of inquiry is judged significant in that site. This means that if instruments are used in an ethnographic study they will usually be generated during the specific research study by the ethnographer. This has been the case for our instrumental activities inventory (Spindler and Spindler, 1965, 1989), values projection technique (C. Spindler, 1977; Spindler, Spindler, Trueba, and Williams, 1990), the expressive autobiographical interview (1970), and the various interpersonal rating scales used in the Roger Harker case study (Spindler et al., 1990). Their form will be determined by the information collected to date. Nevertheless, their results will be viewed with a certain suspicion and must continually be checked against one's direct observations and directly elicited information.

Quantification

By nature, ethnographic data are qualitative, but this does not mean they are inexact, ambiguous, or intuitive (although intuition is important in fieldwork and in data analysis—one must just know when one is being intuitive). The observations collected by Shirley Heath on white teachers questioning black children are very precise, as are the data collected by Susan Phillips on teaching procedures in law school classes and by Fred Gearing and Joseph Epstein on "learning to wait" to learn to read (all in *Doing the Ethnography of Schooling*). Concepts such as "climate," "atmosphere," and "ethos" often seem to be judged proper subjects for ethnographic inquiry, whereas "hardware" questions must be turned over to quantifiers. This is a profound misconception. No research procedure is more rigorous than ethnography.

There is nothing wrong with quantification, when it is necessary, and many ethnographers find it essential once they attempt to make statements about the distribution of phenomena beyond the relatively small group or single institution or social segment in which they are working. We (G.S. and L.S.) almost always report our research in published form with fairly substantial quantification and some form of inferential nonparametric statistics. Most of our colleagues who publish on the ethnography of schooling neither report quantified data nor describe them statistically. Quantification is not the beginning point, nor is it the ultimate goal. There are many phenomena that are better tested out in relation to a hypothesis by doing another, or several, ethnographic probes in different sites than by using instruments that will permit surveys of larger samples and produce data appropriate for quantification and statistical analysis. Instrumentation and quantification are simply procedures employed to extend and to reinforce certain kinds of data, interpretations, and test hypotheses across samples. Both must be kept in their place. One must avoid their premature or overly extensive use as a security mechanism (see Devereux, 1967).

Object of Study

Our reading of ethnographic work in the schools suggests to us that some people doing ethnography do not know what they are doing it for except that it is "qualitative" and "descriptive" and that these are suddenly deemed desirable methodological attributes. Our aims in compiling the collection of work by anthropological ethnographers in *Doing the Ethnography of Schooling* and *Interpretive Ethnography of Education* were to define not only methods and techniques of research, but also the shape of intellectual goals.

A reasonable statement of intellectual purpose for ethnographic research will go something like this: The object of ethnographic research by anthropologists is to discover the cultural knowledge that people hold in their minds, how it is employed in social interaction, and the consequences of its employment. We assume that, although elements and patterns of cultural knowledge are shared in some degree by persons of the same age, sex, social status, etc., within the framework of a given cultural tradition, no two individuals have exactly the same cultural knowledge. When persons interacting in a given social setting are of different age, sex, etc. (i.e., white adult female middle-class teacher and black lower-class male and female children), their cultural knowledge will be disparate in many interactive scenes. This disparateness produces unanticipated consequences in social interaction that stabilize as tacit rules and expectations. These rules and expectations are held differently by different actors in any given setting but, to some extent, are shared (e.g., white teachers ask dumb questions; black children are slow to respond verbally) and ramify into other sectors of behavior (e.g., vandalism, impertinence, negativism).

For each social setting (i.e., classroom) in which various scenes (e.g., reading, "meddlin," going to the bathroom) are studied, there is the prior (native) cultural knowledge held by each of the various actors; the action itself; the emerging, stabilizing rules, expectations, and some understandings that are tacit. Together these constitute a "classroom" or "school" culture.

The complexity of the relationships described earlier define as insufficient the position taken by some anthroethnographers—that the object of study is simply to elicit and report the emic knowledge of the native. It is imperative to discover what the native does not know explicitly (the tacit or implicit culture) and to examine the interaction of persons as actors in social settings. Knowing what natives know is not enough. We start with the emic position, the view of and the knowledge of the native, and work our way our to the etic, interpretive position. It is the interpretive product, however, that usually gets us into trouble with the natives when they read it. An interpretation is a cultural translation influenced, at least, and transformed, at worst, by our theories and models. These theories and models are always extraneous to the cultural knowledge of the native and, right or wrong, will be regarded with suspicion if not outright rejected.

Selective Holism and Contextualization

One often reads that ethnography is "holistic." This ascribed quality derives from the time when one ethnographer alone in a remote village or with a small band would try to record and report on everything from kinship to canoes. Of course, no one ever succeeded in reporting "everything," but there is no denying that traditional ethnographies often include an amazing range of notes and queries on a multitude of things (to borrow from the title of the first known manual for anthropological fieldworkers). Holism is still a desirable ideal if we can reduce its operational meaning to the pursuit of relationships beyond the immediate focus of our research to other relevant contexts. If we study social relationships in a reading group in a fourth-grade classroom, we may also need to study social relationships in the classroom, school, home, and community. We may also find ourselves studying the physical environment of reacting, the value contexts of reading in American culture, and the use of information dissemination techniques that can serve as substitutes for reading. We allow ourselves to go wherever our expanding attention takes us as we try to describe and interpret a complex of relationships at the core of our attention.

One form of contextualization that is frequently neglected in ethnographic study is historical time. Most ethnography is synchronic, expressive of the here and now. Studies conducted intermittently over a period of years help correct this. We worked in the Schoenhausen Grundschule intermittently since 1968, and we found that our understanding of the school expanded each time we studied it. Time produced new data that put the previously collected information in a different perspective.

Whose Ethnography Is It Anyway?

It should be clear that we are trying to define the criteria for a good *anthropological* ethnography of schooling. In doing so, we do not mean to deny doing ethnography to others. Psychologists, sociologists, historians, and various nondenominational inquirers are doing and will continue to do ethnography. Nevertheless, ethnography originated, and persists, as the field arm of cultural anthropology. Its emerging character definition will be greatly influenced by this origin and continuing status within anthropology. Ethnography is presently suffering from overuse, without specification, as a household word in the social sciences and, particularly, in education. This will eventually damage the reputation of this kind of research and erode its potential utility to social scientists, teachers, and policymakers. We are attempting to define the criteria of good anthropological ethnography and clarify its limitations as well as its assets. We must know what it can and cannot do if we want ethnography to assume a place as one of the credible methodologies in the study of the educative process.

Criteria for a Good Ethnography

Given the preceding observations, we posit the following as reasonable criteria for a good ethnography of education.

Criterion I. Observations are contextualized, both in the immediate setting in which behavior is observed and in further contexts beyond that setting, as relevant.

Criterion II. Hypotheses emerge *in situ* as the study continues in the setting selected for observation. Judgment on what may be significant to study in-depth is deferred until the orienting phase of the field study has been completed.

Criterion III. Observation is prolonged and repetitive. Chains of events are observed more than once to establish the reliability of observations.

Criterion IV. The native view of reality is attended through inferences from observation and through the various forms of ethnographic inquiry (including interviews and other eliciting procedures); however, in the ethnography itself, places are made from which native voices may be "heard." Cultural translations are reduced to the minimum, commensurate with effective communication.

Criterion V. Sociocultural knowledge held by social participants makes social behavior and communication sensible. Therefore, a major part of the ethnographic task is to elicit that knowledge from informant participants.

Criterion VI. Instruments, codes, schedules, questionnaires, agenda for interviews, and so forth should be generated *in situ*, as a result of observation and ethnographic inquiry.

Criterion VII. A transcultural, comparative perspective is present, although frequently as an unstated assumption. That is, cultural variation over time and space is considered a natural human condition. All cultures are seen as adaptations to the exigencies of human life and exhibit common as well as distinguishing features.

Criterion VIII. Some of the sociocultural knowledge affecting behavior and communication in any particular setting being studied is implicit or tacit, not known to some participants and known only ambiguously to others. Therefore, a significant task of ethnography is to make what is implicit and tacit to informants explicit to readers. In the modern world, this often means explicit to informants as well. Under controlled conditions, this may cause the ethnographer considerable trouble, for the *implicit* is often implicit to the native because it is unacceptable at the explicit level. We tread a thorny path here.

Criterion IX. Because the informant (any person being interviewed) is one who has the emic, native cultural knowledge, the ethnographic interviewer must not predetermine responses by the kinds of questions asked. The management of the interview must be carried out so as to promote the unfolding of emic cultural knowledge in its most heuristic, "natural" form. This will require the interviewer to "flow" with the informant's style of talk and organization of knowledge without imposing preconceived agendas in the interview interaction.

Criterion X. Any form of technical device that will enable the ethnographer to collect more live data—immediate, natural, detailed behavior—will be used, such as cameras, audio and video tapes, and field-based installments (with the caveats mentioned earlier).

Criterion XI. The presence of the ethnographer should be acknowledged and his or her social, personal, interactional position in the situation described. This may result in a more narrative, personalized style of reporting than has been the case in the past in ethnographic reporting.

References

Devereux, C., 1967. *From Anxiety to Method in the Behavioral Sciences.* Paris and The Hague: Mouton.

Hewett, E., 1904. Anthropology and Education. *American Anthropologist,* 4:574–75.

King, R., 1968. *School at Mopass: A Problem of Identity.* New York: Holt, Rinehart & Winston.

Rosenfeld, G., 1971. *Shut Those Thick Lips: The Ethnography of a Slum School.* New York: Holt, Rinehart & Winston (reprinted by Waveland Press, 1986).

Singleton, J., 1967. *Nichu: A Japanese School.* New York: Holt, Rinehart & Winston.

Spindler, G., ed., 1955a. *Education and Anthropology*. Stanford: Stanford University Press.

_____, 1955b. *Sociocultural and Psychological Processes in Menomini Acculturation* (Vol. 5). University of California Publications in Culture and Society. Berkeley: University of California Press.

_____, ed., 1963. *Education and Culture: Anthropological Approaches*. New York: Holt, Rinehart & Winston.

_____, 1973. *Burgbach: Urbanization and Identity in a German Village*. New York: Holt, Rinehart & Winston.

_____, ed., 1974a. *Education and Cultural Process: Toward an Anthropology of Education*. New York: Holt, Rinehart & Winston.

_____, 1974b. Schooling in Schoenhausen: a Study of Cultural Transmission and Instrumental Adaptation in an Urbanizing German Village. In *Education and Cultural Process: Toward an Anthropology of Education*, G. Spindler, ed., pp. 230–73. New York: Holt, Rinehart & Winston.

_____, 1977. Anthropological Perspectives on American Culture, Core Values, Continuity, and Change. In *We the People: American Cultural and Social Change*, C. D. Renzo, ed. Westport, CT: Greenwood Press.

_____, ed., 1982. *Doing the Ethnography of Schooling: Educational Anthropology in Action*. New York: Holt, Rinehart & Winston (reprinted by Waveland Press, 1988).

_____, ed., 1987. *Education and Cultural Process: Anthropological Approaches*, 2d ed. Prospect Heights, IL: Waveland Press.

Spindler, George, and Louise Spindler, 1965. The instrumental activities inventory. *Southwestern Journal of Anthropology*, 21, 1–23.

_____, 1970. Fieldwork with the Menomini. In *Being an Anthropologist: Fieldwork in Eleven Cultures*, G. Spindler (Ed.), pp. 267–301. New York: Holt, Rinehart & Winston (reprinted by Waveland Press, 1987).

_____, 1982. Roger Harker and Schoenhausen: from the Familiar to the Strange and Back Again. In *Doing the Ethnography of Schooling*, G. Spindler, ed., pp. 21–43. New York: Holt, Rinehart, & Winston.

_____, 1987a. In Prospect for a Controlled Cross-Cultural Comparison of Schooling: Schoenhausen and Roseville. In *Education and Cultural Process: Anthropological Approaches*, G. Spindler, ed., pp. 389–99. Prospect Heights, IL: Waveland Press.

_____, eds., 1987b. *Interpretive Ethnography of Education at Home and Abroad*, pp. 143–70. Hillsdale, NJ: Lawrence Erlbaum.

_____, 1987c. Schoenhausen Revisited and the Discovery of Culture. In *Interpretive Ethnography of Education at Home and Abroad*, G. Spindler and L. Spindler, eds., pp. 143–63. Hillsdale, NJ: Lawrence Erlbaum.

_____, 1989. The Self and the Instrumental Model in the Study of Culture Change and Modernization. *Kroeber Anthropological Society Papers*, 19, 67–70, Berkeley, CA.

_____, 1992. Crosscultural, Comparative, Reflective Interviewing in Schoenhausen and Roseville. In *Qualitative Voices in Educational Research*, M. Schratz, ed., pp.150–75. London, and Bristol, PA: Falmer Press.

Spindler, G., L. Spindler, H. Trueba, and M. Williams, 1980. *The American Cultural Dialogue and its Transmission*. London, and Bristol, PA: Falmer Press.

Spindler, L., 1962. *Menomini Woman and Culture Change*. Memoir of the American Anthropological Association 91, Menasha, WI.

Warren, R., 1971. *Rebhausen: A German Village*. New York: Holt, Rinehart & Winston.

Wolcott, H., 1973. *Man in the Principal's Office*. New York: Holt, Rinehart & Winston (reprinted by Waveland Press, 1984).

5

The Teacher as an Enemy

Harry F. Wolcott
University of Oregon

I don't like Mr. Wolcott
he always make me work
I hate Mr. Wolcott.

A Kwakiutl Indian boy directed these written words to me while he was attending school in his native village on the coast of British Columbia, Canada. At the time I was the teacher at the village school. My purpose in living in the village and teaching at the school was to study the relationship between village life and the formal education of village pupils. An account of my year as teacher and ethnographer at Blackfish Village is contained in *A Kwakiutl Village and School,* which is a case study of the problems of Western education in a contemporary cross-cultural setting (Wolcott 1967).

As the village teacher I had the responsibility for conducting a one-room school for all the resident village children between the ages of six and sixteen. As ethnographer, I wanted to identify and assess the influence of cultural barriers to classroom performance as a way of studying why Native American pupils have so often seemed refractive to the formal educative efforts of the school.

Although I had taught previously in public schools, I was not prepared for the classroom problems which confronted me at the village school. I found there a firmly entrenched pattern of pupil hostility toward the teacher and toward nearly every nonmaterial aspect of the way of life the teacher represented. In the time that has elapsed since the original fieldwork in 1962–1963, I have had the opportunity to reflect upon the experiences of that year and to return for several brief periods of subsequent study. I have been seeking alternative ways of thinking about the role of the teacher in a cross-cultural setting like Blackfish Village.

In a setting in which critical differences between teachers and their pupils are rooted in antagonisms of cultural rather than classroom ori-

Source: Written especially for *Education and Cultural Process.*

gins, I believe that teachers might succeed in coping more effectively with conflict and in capitalizing on instructional efforts if they were to recognize and to analyze their ascribed role as "enemy" rather than to attempt to ignore or to deny it. To those educators who insist that a teacher must always present a facade of cheery optimism in the classroom, the notion of the teacher as an enemy may seem unacceptable, overly negative, perhaps even dangerous. One might question, however, whether cheery optimism and a determination to accomplish "good" inevitably serve the best interests of culturally different pupils, especially pupils from socially and economically depressed or deprived sectors of the population. Any teacher who has faced such pupils in the classroom may have recognized that one alternative is to try to do less harm rather than more good. Even with so modest a goal, any strategy that may minimize psychological harm either to pupils or to their teachers merits consideration. The strategy of regarding the teacher as an enemy is explored here as it relates to formal education in antagonistic cross-cultural settings.

Antagonistic Acculturation

Anthropologists refer to the modification of one culture through continuous contact with another as acculturation. Often one of the contact cultures is dominant, regardless of whether such dominance is intended. Not infrequently the situation of dominance leads to a relationship which breeds antagonism on the part of the dominated group.

Antagonism rises rather expectedly out of feelings that one's own cherished ways are being eroded and lost or that one's ethnic group belongs to a have-not class. Antagonistic feelings may be aggravated by the attempts of members of the dominant society to hasten the process of assimilation. Frequently antagonisms are aggravated by a contradiction between the ideal of assimilation and the reality of prejudicial treatment accorded to minority groups within the dominant society. This was the case at Blackfish Village, not because of any problem unique to the village but because there had been a concerted, although not very successful, effort by both the Canadian and U.S. governments to hasten and even to complete the assimilation of North American Indian groups. Schools run by the federal governments of both countries consciously directed their efforts toward replacing Native American ways with ways more acceptable to and characteristic of the dominant white middle class, although the respective societies have at the same time responded prejudicially to the Native American who attempted to assimilate.

Contemporary social commentary describing the relation of pupils to their schools among the Sioux, along the Mexican-American border, in Harlem and in Puerto Rican East Harlem, in the Deep South, in Boston, in Washington, D.C., or in the inner city everywhere suggests that cultural barriers to classroom performance are not unique to my confrontation with Blackfish pupils. However, I shall relate my discussion to that specific setting. I will describe how the stresses resulting from "antagonistic acculturation" were manifested in microcosm in the behavior of village children in the classroom. First, I shall describe how I perceived the classroom to be organized to thwart my instructional efforts. A rather different picture of the classroom follows as written accounts from some of the older Blackfish pupils suggest how the classroom looked to them.

Classroom Learning Kwakiutl-Style— As Seen by the Teacher

Here are seven important characteristics of the classroom at the Blackfish Indian Day School as I saw it:

1. The pupils set their own pace, not in the ideal sense of an individualized program with each child working independently at an optimum rate, but rather with doing little in lots of time. My inclination, having found them "behind" in their work, was to get them "caught up." Their inclination was, generally, to let the school day slip by without having expended much—or perhaps any—effort in the direction in which I was so anxious to push them. Their whole orientation to school, I believe, was one of patiently enduring. What my pupils wanted most to get out of school was to get out of school. Since maturity provided the only means to achieve that goal, the amount of school work accomplished in a day had no meaning unless one's peers wanted to engage in a self-imposed competition or unless one really valued the praise of the teacher. But neither the rewards this teacher had to give nor the manner in which he gave them were likely to warrant the effort necessary to attain them or the risk of incurring the displeasure of one's fellow pupils for having done so.

2. Classroom assignments were frequently perceived as a group task. My worksheets and practice papers were treated as though my class was a secretarial pool—older or brighter pupils did papers for younger or slower ones, sometimes because the assignments were difficult, sometimes because they were fun. My pupils, as a class, were organized to cope with me collectively, while I was trying to cope with them individually. The nature of this mutual classroom help among pupils had several concomitant aspects described below.

3. Almost invariably, students collaborated as partners in electing to complete or to ignore classroom assignments, in deciding whether

to write long diary entries about their day, in making choices when alternative activities were offered, or in preparing answers to my questions. My "divide and conquer" tactic was constantly subverted. I had great difficulty assessing the progress of any given pupil because pupils so frequently teamed up to write daily entries for each other and to work each other's assignments.

One of the most successful classroom activities of the year was the exchange of a series of letters between the older pupils and a sixth-grade class in a California school. As the exchange of letters progressed, some members of the class began receiving more letters than others. Those who received many letters farmed out the excess and had other pupils write the replies. At another time, I gave eight older pupils a sentence-completion test. I later discovered that instead of eight sets of answers I had received four sets of paired answers in return. Before beginning to complete the sentences each pupil chose a partner with whom he worked out a tentative answer, and then both partners wrote a comparable—or identical—response for each sentence.

4. Teasing and bullying were very disruptive elements in class. Often the teasing was related to inter- or intra-family squabbles which had their origin outside of school. Included in the teasing, however, was a process of pupil socialization in which children learned not to outperform their peers. Particularly, I observed change in the behavior of two children, a fourth-grade girl and a first-grade boy, who came to the village after the school year had begun and who seemed to be particularly capable students. Both underwent continual taunting in class, and both learned to display less overt enthusiasm for school and to restrict their academic prowess to tasks on which they could work alone, while they performed only minimally at those tasks on which greater achievement was apparent to their peers. The boy had come from a provincial school where he was one of few Native American pupils; the girl had been attending a day school in another village, one in which school achievement was more acceptable and school success more frequent. Whether the socialization of these children was due to their ability in school, their being outsiders to the village, or a combination of both, I have never been certain. That the quality and quantity of their academic performance diminished, I am sure. The girl traveled to her parents' village for Christmas and never returned to Blackfish Village; the boy survived the year by learning to perform more like other village boys in school, which meant doing very little on group assignments, although he usually worked well alone. He outperformed all the other pupils in the seclusion of two intelligence tests I administered.

5. At the same time that overperformance was restrained through socialization, there was some tendency to help the slower children of one's age or ability group. Such help differs from the help given to

younger pupils, because that assistance seemed to be used to get the tasks completed (if the teacher was going to insist on them) while the helping to which I now refer served to keep a pupil from appearing too inadequate in the eyes of the teacher. For the teacher, this "equalizing" behavior among the pupils made the task of finding suitable material or diagnosing individual learning difficulties almost impossible.

The most glaring instance was that of a fifteen-year-old boy who was almost a nonreader. In September I assigned to him a fourth-grade basal reader which was being read by several other boys. It was some time before I realized that he was so used to having difficult words whispered to him by his reading mates that during my limited opportunity to hear the children read aloud he did not necessarily look at the pages to appear to be reading from them. Eventually I realized he could read independently only at grade-one level, and as late as May I recorded in my notes, "He gets so much help from other kids that I still doubt that I know his own capabilities."

As a social phenomenon, the cooperative efforts of my pupils may appear both remarkable and praiseworthy. In each case, however, the extent of their cooperation and organization inevitably thwarted my efforts in both assessing and instructing them, according to the expectations which I held for myself as a teacher. Further, to whatever extent I was able to see the positive aspects of pupil cooperation rather than to feel threatened by it, I was still unable to mobilize the cooperative potential of the pupils to accomplish my purposes. I could not make them help each other, be patient toward each other, or socialize each other toward such teacher-approved purposes as keeping the classroom quiet so pupils could read, working quickly enough to allow time for other activities, or letting younger pupils join in the recess play of the older ones.

6.   Antagonistic as they were toward so many aspects of school, my pupils nevertheless held very rigid expectations about the activities they considered appropriate for school work. Insistence on attention to the three R's constituted the only legitimate kind of demand which the pupils both expected and accepted on the part of their teacher. Their notion of an ideal classroom was one in which pupils were busily engaged in highly repetitive but relatively easy assignments for long periods of time, uninterrupted by the teacher. Their notion of an ideal teacher, consistent with this, was a person who meted out assignments but not explanations, a person who had an infinite supply of worksheets and tasks but who never asked a pupil to engage in an exercise he or she could not already perform. The only favors or rewards expected of a teacher were in the distribution of coveted materials (crayons, water colors, compasses, scissors, puzzles, athletic equipment), the allocation of prestige positions (attendance monitor, bell ringer), and the

rationing of school "fun" ("free" time, art periods, extended recesses, classroom parties).

Given their narrow expectations for proper classroom activities, it is not surprising that the pupils responded most favorably to assignments at the specific tasks required in arithmetic and spelling. Occasionally they requested an assignment to repeat a page of arithmetic drill or requested my validation of a self-imposed assignment to write each spelling word three, five, or ten times.

Weeks passed before the older pupils grew accustomed to my daily assignment—making at least a brief entry in a diarylike notebook. Even when they had grown used to this activity as part of our daily program, they were uneasy that I did not "teach" language arts because I did not often use the language arts texts. Although their basal readers and the accompanying workbooks were difficult, dull, and pedantic, the pupils were never satisfied that they were "having reading" unless these readers were before them. They never completely accepted my progressive idea that reading a book of one's own choice was also a legitimate type of classroom reading. Patiently, and sometimes impatiently, they endured my reading aloud to them, because they had been subjected by their teachers to that dubious pleasure for years, but I could seldom induce them to any kind of classroom discussion subsequent to hearing a story. My attempts to relate social studies to their own lives made them uncomfortable both because they perceived this as prying and because I did not depend on textbooks in my approach. They were generally impatient with instruction in concepts that were not included in their texts (for example, notions from the new math). In short, my pupils had very specific expectations for the formal purposes of school, they generally hated school as defined by these expectations, and they refused to have their expectations modified. They disliked school and that is just how they liked it.

7. Let me conclude this description of the classroom as seen by the teacher with one final pattern of pupil behavior, the attempts of the pupils to socialize their teacher. It is misleading to refer to this socialization as "attempts," for my pupils were good teachers and their techniques were effective. The methods they used to socialize me included giving slow, reluctant responses to my directions, ignoring my comments (by not "hearing" them or occasionally by putting their hands to their ears), mimicking my words or actions, constantly requesting to leave the classroom to go to the toilet, and making me the target of spoken or written expletives. To illustrate, the following note was written to me during the daily writing period by a twelve-year-old boy the day after I took a partially eaten apple away from him and inadvertently forgot to return it:

We were packing wood yesterday me and Raymond were packing lots of wood. Oh, you little monkey, little asshole you got my apple why don't you mind your own business you think you smart little asshole. Goodbye, that's all I can say now. Goodbye, no more writing because you throw my apple.

The most direct and telling comments were those that identified me as "White man," the outsider, or drew attention to our different cultural origins: "Just like a White man," "That's the trouble with you White guys," or, twice during the year, an angry stare and the comment, "What's the matter; haven't you ever seen an Indian before?" With such a statement as: "We don't have to tell you anything," I was at a loss to know whether my distinguishing attribute was that I was white, the teacher, a cranky adult, or all of them.

Classroom Learning Kwakiutl Style— As Seen by the Pupils

Although I have referred frequently to the pupils in the class, the classroom picture presented above is entirely a construct of a teacher's perception. Consequently, it is cast primarily in terms of the teacher's instructional goals and how the subculture of the pupils seemed to be organized to thwart them. Written comments of the older pupils provide some insight into how the class and teacher looked to them.

1. This response was written by a fifteen-year-old girl to an assigned topic, "If I Were the Teacher." Note how she relates her concept of the role of a teacher to perpetuating such middle-class values so revered by teachers as cleanliness, quiet, punctuality, and obedience. Note also the emphasis she gives to discipline and punishment. The classroom is an orderly, severe, and punishing place.

If I were the teacher. When I first get here I'd like to meet all the children here. The first day in school I'd tell the pupils what to do. First thing we do is clean the school up then clean the desk and the cupboards. Then straighten the cupboard up for the books. When the school is cleaned up, then I'll give out the books. And ask what grade they're in. Ask how old are they. And give the rules for school. The school starts at 9:00 A.M., recess at 10:30 A.M., dinner at 12:00 P.M., come back in the afternoon at 1:00 P.M., recess at 2:30 P.M. and after school 3:30 P.M. And if anybody's late, they have to write hundred lines.[1] And keep the toilet clean. Their clothes clean and comb hair. First thing they'd do in the morning is Arithmetic, spelling, language, Reading. And the afternoon Science, Social Studies, Health, and free time. And if nobody works they get a strapping. If I had a fourteen year old in my class she or he would take care of grade one and two. And I'd take care of three to eight. If I had a class all in one grade that'll be nice. Then I won't have to bother about other grades except the class I have. And if they get the room dirty they'll sweep the whole classroom. I'd get a monitor for the bath room to be clean and swept. And if anybody talks back. They'd get a strapping. If they get out of their desk they'll have to write lines. If they don't ask permission to sharpen their pencil they'll get strapping. If they wear hats and kerchiefs in class they'll have to stand in the corner for one hour with their hands on their heads. I'd tell the children to draw Indian Design for the room. If they make a noise in class, they all stay in for half an hour. If anybody talks in class they write lines about hundred lines. If anybody's absent they have lots of homework for the next day. And if anybody fights they get a strapping. And I'd have a monitor for the books so nobody touch it except the monitor. Dust the shelves. And on Christmas they'd have to play or sing. And on Halloween they have to dress up for the party.

2. Here is the response of another pupil, a fourteen-year-old girl, to my request for a theme on the same topic, "If I Were the Teacher." Note the contrast she makes between discipline and scholarship. If one of her pupils were to fail to be on time, she would strap him. If he were to fail a comprehensive examination, she would have a talk with him.

If I were the teacher for Blackfish Village, or someplace else, I'd like my class to be very quiet. If not, they would get a straping from me. They would get a straping if they are late.

They would come to school at nine A.M. No sooner nor later. They would have one recess in the morning and one in the afternoon. In the afternoon they would go home at 3:30 P.M.

The subjects I'd give them in the morning are Math, Spelling, Reading. If they do not get it finished they would have it for homework, same in the afternoon. They would have a story, Language, then Library or drawing.

I'd like my class to be very neat, clothes clean, hair neat. In the morning they could sing "God Save the Queen." In the afternoon they would sing "Oh Canada."

I would choose Monitors for toilets, paints and for blackboards, But of course I would do the Attendance myself. I would given them tests before Christmas, Easter, and the final tests at June. After the tests if anyone fails, I would ask them to tell me why. For example if one of my pupils did fail I'd tell that child to write on a paper to tell me why. If that child has a good excuse, I'd tell that child to "smarten up" and pay attention to his or her work more.

I would go to see their parents to see if they have a normal living, like if they go to sleep before nine o'clock, have good meals every day.

Yes sir! If I were the teacher a lot of changes would be made around here at Blackfish Village. The children would have to listen even if I were a girl teacher.

But I didn't plan the future yet. That's for sure I'm not sticking around here in the future.

3. In most cases where the hostility of the children toward the teacher flared up over a specific incident at school the pupils did not record their perceptions of the event in their classroom writing. Typically at such times they refrained from performing any task that might please the teacher, and writing in their notebooks did win teacher approval. The following excerpt reveals one instance where a pupil did record the anger which she shared with several other pupils. I had refused to admit a group of the older pupils into class when they were late in returning from the morning recess, and at least for this fourteen-year-old, trouble at school had precipitated more trouble at home.

Today is a very horrible day for Norma and me. Of course we would be treaten as babies. When we are late in this dump the teacher would [i.e., *did*] tell us to come back in the afternoon. There was Larry, Joseph, Norma, Tommy, Jack, Herman and me. Norma got in trouble too, of course. My brother would tell on me that brat. This is a strict world for some of us. I thought this was a free world. Norma and me can't even go on Larry's boat and for me I'm not aloud to go to their house! My brother said I was in my aunties house. I guess thats why I ain't aloud in their. All the time I was in Sarah's house. The teacher is so lazy to ring the bell I guess he expects us to hear him when he calls us. That's all!!

4. Two final examples suggest the contrast between the pseudo-work and satisfaction of the classroom and the real work and real rewards of adult life. Here is a written comment, in the form of a note to the teacher, from a twelve-year-old boy who recognized that although he was required to attend school, he had a more important contribution to make to his family when he could assist with the work of the men:

I am going to go halibut fishing with my father and Raymond. That's why I asked you is there going to be school tomorrow because I want to go with my father. He always has a tough time when he catches halibut [alone]. We got one halibut yesterday.

In a similar vein, the following was written in November by a fifteen-year-old boy. The note mentions only a week's leave, but it was in fact the boy's last classroom assignment forever, because he has never returned to school:

We are going to Gilford Island tomorrow. I'm going to stay there one week. I'm going to dig clams. There is a big tide this week. I'm not coming to school next week.

The Teacher as an Enemy

In the school at Blackfish Village, or for teachers in any number of comparable settings, I believe there would be real utility in having more than one way of perceiving the reciprocal roles of teacher and pupil. In my own case, experience in both roles prior to my year at Blackfish Village had been within the confines of a middle-class setting of which I am very much part and product. Sometimes, in my twenty years as a student, I had experienced antagonism toward teachers and occasionally I had generated antagonism among my students as a public school and university teacher. Such antagonism, however, was a consequence of immediate psychological or personal incompatibility, never an antagonism rooted in social forces outside the classroom. I had never encountered teachers or pupils with whom I did not share relatively similar expectations regarding behaviors, values, and attitudes.

At Blackfish Village my pupils and I shared few mutual expectations regarding our formal role relationship. Those expectations we did share tended to provide pacts that enabled individual survival in a situation beyond our making rather than opening avenues for trust or understanding. No one, teacher or pupils, ever let his or her guard down very far. If we were not at any one moment actually engaged in a classroom skirmish, it was only because we were recovering from a prior one or preparing for the next. On the last day of school I reflected that I had not won a battle; instead I felt that all year long I had had a tiger by the tail, and we had merely crossed some kind of symbolic finish line together.

I had anticipated that one of my major problems of the year would be to induce my pupils to come regularly to school. Except for the fact that pupils expected to leave school at about age sixteen, however, my pupils and I did not have to do battle regarding school attendance. Economic sanctions could be taken against families who failed to send their children regularly to school, but in fact attendance (other than a perennial problem in getting pupils from certain families to school on time) was not a major concern. Indeed, parents not only sent their children off to school each day but also ritually endorsed the benefits of formal education with such comments as "Education is the only answer."

I had mistakenly assumed that once the pupils were inside the classroom they could be led to a host of new learnings under the guidance of their dedicated teacher. Ever since my year as a teacher at the Blackfish Indian Day School I have been seeking an alternative teaching perspective, one that would have enabled me to present an instructional program without such personal frustration at my lack of success and without nurturing an atmosphere of hostility where I had intended to create an atmosphere of help.

The direction my quest has taken is *not* to ponder how to "out-psych" or outmaneuver my pupils. Training in anthropology had convinced me of the fact that differences exist among groups of human beings and that the differences may touch every facet of human life from household composition to cognition. But I was not assigned to the village to teach villagers their way of life; I was assigned to teach them something about mine.

I think that I might have been a more effective teacher if I had taken the perspective of regarding the *teacher*, me, *as an enemy.* By effective I mean that I would have remained more objective about my lack of success, and I would have been more sensitive to the high cost for each pupil of accepting me or my instructional program. The "enemy" relationship I use here as my analogy does not refer to entering into combat, although on the worst days we may not have been far from it. More appropriate to antagonistic acculturation as manifested in school might be an analogy to a prisoner-of-war camp. Prisoners of war—inmates and captors alike—are faced with the probability that a long period of time may ensue during which their statuses remain unchanged. While great hostility on the part of either group might be present in the relationship, it is not essential to it, because the enmity is not derived from individual or personal antagonism. Nonetheless, the captors, representing one cultural group, are not expected to convert the prisoners to their way of life, and the prisoners are not expected to acculturate the captors.

So far, a teacher in an instructional role has no place in the analogy. Let us extend the analogy one step further. Suppose that along with the usual cadre of overseers the captors have also provided teachers charged with instructing the prisoners in the ways of, and particularly in the merits of, their culture. The purpose of instruction is to recruit new members into their society by encouraging prisoners to defect, and achieving this by giving them the skills so that they can do so effectively. Teachers are expected to provide information about the captors' way of life and about the skills that this way entails. It has been established that prisoners will attend the classes and that they will not be allowed to disrupt classroom proceedings, but beyond these strictures the teachers are not expected to dwell on the negative aspects that have brought their pupils to them. The teachers are not unaware of the probability, however, that since they are perceived as enemies, their pupils may not see them playing a very functional role in the pupils' lives other than as representatives of the enemy culture.

What purposes might be served in cross-cultural education if teachers were to draw an analogy between themselves and enemy captors in trying to understand their relationship with their pupils? There are several potential advantages one might anticipate.

First, teachers who can imagine how pupils might feel toward them as members of a captor society recognize a distinction between having pupils physically present in class and having them psychologically receptive to instruction. Cognizance of the pervasive hostile and suspicious influence of the enemy relationship helps teachers maintain realistic expectations for what they can accomplish in the classroom. Despite the most valiant efforts on the teachers' part to make instruction effective, they are never overcome by feelings of personal inadequacy at a lack of response to lessons. The teachers realize that under certain conditions the energy and resources of their prisoners are utilized in a desperate struggle to survive and to maintain their own identity in the face of overwhelming odds. The teachers recognize that the antagonism of pupils may be addressed to the whole cultural milieu in which they find themselves captive rather than to a teacher as an individual. The teachers understand that any attempt on their part to alter or to ameliorate the basis for antagonism may be met with suspicion. The teachers are not personally disappointed when pupils show tendencies toward recidivism—when they feel themselves being seduced by the constant attention and encouragement of their mentor-enemies. If this is how things seem to the prisoners, the teachers realize that a modification of a lesson plan or an ingenious new teaching technique is not going to make any important difference to them. Taking the point of view of the pupils, teachers can ask themselves, "Just what is it that a prisoner would ever want to learn from an enemy?"

Second, teachers who can entertain perspectives that regard themselves and their pupils as belonging to enemy cultures acknowledge the possibility that there could be important and systematic differences in life styles and in value-orientation characterizing each group. Teachers are not as inclined to share a perception, common among teachers, that if a pupil does not have the same cultural background as the teacher, that pupil does not have any cultural heritage at all. Granted, a teacher can be expected to believe that his or her own life style is right but also recognizes that his or her purposes are not likely to be achieved by insisting that all other life styles are therefore wrong. Anthropologist Ruth Landes has written cogently in this regard, "The educator, or other authority, can advance his inquiries and explanations by taking the position that he represents one culture talking to another. This minimizes personal and emotional involvements by focusing on the grand designs of each tradition. . . ." (Landes 1965:47).

The teachers' instructional objectives are to try to make their own way of life appear sufficiently manageable to the "enemy" pupils that they may choose to explore it further, and, for those pupils who do make this choice, to provide them with a set of survival skills for living in a different culture and having access to its rewards. Children growing up in Blackfish Village, for example, will have to be able to demonstrate the skill aspects of specific middle-class manners and values such as cleanliness, courtesy, responsibility, punctuality, or how to take orders from a white boss in order to survive in the dominant society. They do not, however, need a teacher who insists that such skills are necessary steps on the road to nirvana. They need a teacher who can identify and instruct them in certain specific behaviors which an individual *must* exhibit if he or she is going to move successfully into a society that heretofore has been regarded as an alien one.

We would hardly expect the teacher to engage in much "correction" of pupils except for what was essential to the maintenance of an orderly classroom. The language or dialect used by prisoners need not be singled out for ridicule, correction, or extermination. What the teacher might do, however, is to teach a standard dialect of his or her own language to prisoner-pupils who entertained an intellectual curiosity about it or, especially, to those pupils interested in learning the enemy culture well enough to see if they can survive in it.

Most important, the teacher realizes the meaning that accepting his or her teaching may have for those prisoners who do accept it. It may mean selling out, defecting, turning traitor, ignoring the succorance and values and pressures of one's peers, one's family, one's own people. It can require terrible and anxious decisions for the prisoner, and it may even require severing his or her most deeply-rooted human ties. The teacher needs constantly to review what these costs mean to any human. As a consequence, the teacher interested in "enemy" pupils as humans may be less inclined to act as a cultural brainwasher and more inclined to weigh both the difficulties of cultural transition and the ultimate consequences of change. In the latter regard, a proverb quoted in Robert Ruark's novel *Something of Value* seems particularly appropriate: "If a man does away with his traditional way of living and throws away his good customs, he had better first make certain he has something of value to replace them" (Basuto proverb).

The teacher may feel a greater need to alert pupils to the fact that he or she has *not* been able to provide them with all the prerequisite skills for successfully "passing" in the teacher's own society than to fill them with hopes and promises which few may ever realize. The pupils need to know how much information they actually have, what problems they must anticipate, and which vestiges of their earlier heritage may present almost insurmountable handicaps.

Through the exercise of examining his or her *own* culture as the alien one, the teacher-enemy may be less aggressive about forcing lessons on the prisoner-pupils. The teacher may not accept so unhesitatingly the belief that what he or she is doing is necessarily "good" for them. He or she may be more inclined to think of teaching as an offer of help to members of the dominated group who seek it rather than as an imposition of help from members of the dominant group who insist on giving it. Pausing to consider the possibility of being regarded by pupils as a member of an enemy culture offers the teacher a perspective for understanding why pupils might sometimes appear able but unwilling to accept being taught. This perspective also encourages the teacher to give more help to the potential defectors who seek it, rather than to spend time bemoaning the lack of defection by the prisoner generation of today.

Conclusion

Cultural systems provide us with practical answers to questions of how we should act and what to think about how we act. But no "culture" ever provides its members with a perfect and complete blueprint of how to act in every situation. If cultures accomplished that, they might never change, and we know that change is inherent in human life and human organization. We do not often pause to examine our own behavior, and it can be with a real sense of surprise that in a new role we suddenly discover that we already know exactly how to act; we may even feel we have "known it all the time." Student teachers, as a case in point, provide themselves and observers with remarkable examples of how well they have internalized the teacher behavior associated with the teacher-pupil role relationship even if they have never formally taken the teacher role before.

When circumstances bring us into contact with others who do not share the same cultural orientation, particularly if our "proper" behavior invites inappropriate responses or no response at all, we become more self-consciously aware of our own patterns of behavior. Initially this may result only in our speaking or gesticulating a bit more emphatically, in a manner characteristic of the American tourist abroad. Under conditions of prolonged contact, one might want to do better than simply wave his or her hands more or talk louder. Regardless of how much effort he or she makes at understanding those who are different, however, it is from his or her own repertoire of cultural behaviors that the individual most choose. If there is no perfectly appropriate pattern of behavior, then relevant analogous situations must be found. The choice of analogies is crucial.

The teacher working with culturally different pupils exhibits a natural inclination to draw upon a single analogy, that of the idealized teacher-pupil relationship suitable for the monolithic transmission of culture. I do not imagine that teachers will ever escape from drawing upon this analogy. Their very identity as teachers requires that they have specific notions about teacher behavior. Teachers should not be asked perfunctorily to discard their own "good customs."

I have suggested here that the teacher seek out alternative behavior analogs rather than depend solely on the not-always-appropriate model of the ideal teacher in the ideal setting. Like the role relationship between teacher and pupil, the relationship between enemies is also a culturally based one. The enemy relationship may actually draw more heavily upon universal aspects of behavior than does the teacher-pupil role which has tended to become so crystallized in Western civilization. In spite of the negative implications of an enemy role, and barring extremes of physical cruelty, there are certain ways in which pupils equated with captive prisoners might get better treatment than pupils regarded as allies. For example, in thinking of antagonistic pupils as prisoners of war, one comes to recognize that the classroom is neither the underlying source of intercultural antagonism nor the site of its critical campaigns. Such a realization may also help the reform-oriented teacher to recognize that the proper target for his or her efforts at community reform is the adult community rather than young children in school (Hawthorn et al. 1960:303).

One last dimension of the enemy perspective is that few demands are made of enemy prisoners. Demands are made explicitly; they are not based on assumptions of shared values about fair play, individual rights, ultimate purposes, or the dignity of office. In a sense, the behavior between enemies gives more overt evidence of respecting the other person's cultural ways than does that between friendly groups. Based as it is upon the recognition of vital differences rather than on the recognition of underlying similarities, the perspective of thinking about teachers and their culturally different pupils as enemies invites teachers to examine the kinds of differences cherished by enemies just as they have in the past addressed themselves, at least ritually, to what they and their pupils share in common.

Note

[1] By "write lines" she refers to the practice of repeatedly writing a sentence like "I will not talk out in class" to the satisfaction of a teacher. In my defense I should add that none of the assortment of disciplinary measures she refers to was used in my classroom, although I did have children put their heads down on their desks as a mild disciplinary measure and sent them out of the classroom for a variety of infractions, including that exquisite pupil weapon, sullenness.

References and Further Reading

Goffman, Erving, 1969. The Characteristics of Total Institutions. In *A Sociological Reader on Complex Organizations,* 2d ed., Amitai Etzioni, ed. New York: Holt, Rinehart and Winston. Readers interested in exploring the analogy between pupils and prisoners will find a number of strategies which "inmates" pursue suggested in this essay.

Hawthorn, Harry B., C. S. Belshaw, and S. M. Jamieson, 1960. *The Indians of British Columbia: A Study of Contemporary Social Adjustment.* Berkeley: University of California Press, especially chapter 23, "Schools and Education."

Henry, Jules, 1955. Docility, or Giving Teacher What She Wants. *Journal of Social Issues* 11:33–41.

King, A. Richard, 1967. *The School at Mopass: A Problem of Identity.* CSEC. New York: Holt, Rinehart and Winston.

Landes, Ruth, 1965. *Culture in American Education: Anthropological Approaches to Minority and Dominant Groups in the School.* New York: John Wiley & Sons.

Rohner, Ronald P., 1965. Factors Influencing the Academic Performance of Kwakiutl Indian Children in Canada. *Comparative Education Review* 9:331–40.

_____, 1967. *The People of Gilford, A Contemporary Kwakiutl Village.* National Museum of Canada, Bulletin 225. Ottawa, Ontario: the Queen's Printer.

Rohner, Ronald P., and Evelyn C. Bettauer [Rohner], [1970] 1986. *The Kwakiutl Indians of British Columbia.* Prospect Heights, IL: Waveland Press, especially chapter 4, "Growing Up Kwakiutl."

Ruark, Robert C., 1955. *Something of Value.* New York: Doubleday & Company.

Smith, Alfred G., 1968. Communication and Inter-cultural Conflict. In *Perspectives on Communication*, Carl E. Larson and Frank E. X. Dance, eds. Milwaukee: University of Wisconsin Press.

Wax, Murray L., Rosalie H. Wax, and Robert V. Dumont, Jr., 1964. Formal Education in an American Indian Community. *Social Problems, Monograph #1*, Society for the Study of Social Problems.

Wolcott, Harry F. [1967], 1984. *A Kwakiutl Village and School.* Prospect Heights, IL: Waveland Press.

Part III

EDUCATION AND CULTURAL PROCESS IN THE UNITED STATES

Preview

This part of the book contains eight chapters. In chapter 6, I analyze a broad topic of great importance—the ways in which our schools disadvantage minority students. This is a reversal of the question the public usually asks: "Why do minority students fail in our schools?" Minority students do fail and drop out of our schools in alarming numbers. They drop out not only because they fail in our schools, but also because our schools fail them.

Ray McDermott's chapter has been completely rewritten from the 1987 version. In that version he demonstrated how the incompatibility between minority children and the school system runs deep. He maintains that view in chapter 7, but with a different emphasis. In the 1987 version he saw children so alienated from the school and the mainstream community it represents that failing becomes a measure of self-respect. In the current version he shows us how the entire society is responsible for the failure of minority children. The 1987 paper was designed to show how the *children* failing in school were being fully adaptive to local circumstances. This new chapter is designed to show how much *everyone* in the system is involved in making sense in ways that produce failure. He points out that not only our children are being adaptive in taking up the invitation to fail—so is the rest of the system in organizing so many ways to make their failure possible, apparent, certifiable, and explainable.

In chapter 8, "Racing in Place," Hervé Varenne, Shelley Goldman and Ray McDermott offer a reinterpretation of their 1987 piece. This chapter has an ironic twist to it: We tell each other that education is about the individual and that educational practice is legitimate only to the extent that it fosters individual development. However, when we move from the philosophical level to the level of practice we find that schools continually reproduce situations for the identification of first and second best, and of the failures. Children from "good" homes and families, going to good schools, take tests and fail many of them—but in these schools they get a second chance to take the tests they fail. The chapter is about competition, all-pervasive in the management of the target schools and their classrooms. Perhaps the competitive thrust of the situations described is best conveyed by a question-and-answer game called "screw thy neighbor." The reader will find the interpretive analysis telling.

In chapter 9, John Hostetler demonstrates that minority education can take a different form and succeed. By excluding as much of the mainstream culture and educational input as possible, and by managing their own schools, the Amish and Hutterites maintain their own culture and community successfully.

Maureen Porter demonstrates in chapter 10 how an established, rural, middle-western institution—the county fair—acts as a powerful cultural transmission institution. It provides a context for youth experiences of learning and belonging. The chapter demonstrates that educational institutions are not limited to schools or other formal agencies in U.S. culture.

In chapter 11, "Teaching and Learning through Mien Culture," Lorie Hammond tells a fascinating story of how the expertise and cultural know-how of both Mien adults and their children have been incorporated in a science curriculum project at a Sacramento elementary school. Her work can serve as a model for school-community relationships in regard to other minority groups and to other areas of culture content.

I analyze in chapter 12 the adjustment of Beth Anne, a "well-adjusted" mainstream child who turns out not to be so well adjusted after all. The cost of successful conformity to high-level expectations from teachers and parents and the cultural compulsions that define success are the focus.

In chapter 13, Margaret Gibson describes the severe prejudice with which Punjabi children have to cope as they negotiate the American school system. In this chapter, many of the particular problems of minorities in U.S. schools are demonstrated when the schools are dominated by the mainstream. In schools that have become "minority dominated" the situation is, of course, different.

The Editor

6
Why Have Minority Groups in North America Been Disadvantaged by Their Schools?

George D. Spindler
Stanford University

In Harlem School?

A description of a first-grade class in a black ghetto in New York City follows. It is not a school in the poorest of the districts. It was considered "typical" for the grade.

> The teacher trainee (student teacher) is attempting to teach "rhyming." It is early afternoon. Even before she can get the first "match" (for example, "book" and "look") a whole series of events is drawn out.

> One child plays with the head of a doll, which has broken off from the doll, alternately hitting it and kissing it.

> The student teacher tells a boy who has left his seat that he is staying in after school. He begins to cry. Another child teases that his mother will be worried about him if he stays in after school. The boy cries even harder and screams at the teacher: "You can't keep me in until 15 o'clock."

> A girl tries to answer a question put to the class but raises her hand with her shoe in it. She is told to put her hand down and to put her shoe on.

> Another child keeps switching his pencil from one nostril to another, trying to see if it will remain in his nose if he lets go of it; he is apparently wholly unconcerned with the session in progress.

> One child is lying down across his desk, pretending to sleep while seeing if the teacher sees him. Just next to him another child leads an imaginary band. Still a different child, on his side, stands quietly beside his seat, apparently tired of sitting.

> While this is all going on the regular teacher of the class is out of the room. When she does return, she makes no effort to assist, or criticize,

the student teacher. The student teacher later informed me that the regular teacher was not "just being polite." She rarely directed the student teacher, but simply let her "take over" the class on occasion. The student teacher also remarked that things were no different in the class when the regular teacher held forth.

Fifteen minutes had gone by, but little "rhyming" had been accomplished. A boy begins to shadow box in the back; another talks to himself in acting out a scene he envisions.

Still another child shakes his fist at the student teacher, mimicking her words: "cat-fat, hop-stop."

Two children turn to each other and exchange "burns" on one another's forearms, while another child arranges and rearranges his desk materials and notebook, seemingly dissatisfied with each succeeding arrangement.

A girl in the back has an empty bag of potato chips but is trying to use her fingers as a "blotter" to get at the remnants. She pretends to be paying attention to the lesson.

Another child asks to go to the bathroom, but is denied.

After a half-hour I left. (Rosenfeld 1971:105)

As Gerry Rosenfeld, who taught in a Harlem school and did an anthropological field study there, pointed out, the schooling of these children is already patterned for them at the age of six or seven. "Not much is expected from them," they are from poor families, they are black, and they are "disadvantaged." By high school many of them will be dropouts, or "pushouts," as Rosenfeld terms them. As they get older they become less docile than the children described above, and some teachers in ghetto schools have reason to fear for their own safety. The teachers of this classroom did not have reason to fear their pupils, but they were ignorant about them. Their preparatory work in college or in teacher training had not prepared them for a classroom of children from a poor ghetto area in the city. The student teacher knew nothing about the neighborhood from which the children in her class came. She knew only that she "did not want to work with 'these' children when she became a regular teacher" (Rosenfeld, 1971:105).

As a teacher and observer at Harlem School, Rosenfeld found the teachers held an array of myths about poor children that they used to account for their underachievement and miseducation. At the benign liberal level there are beliefs about the nature of poverty and cultural disadvantage. These conditions become accepted as irrevocable givens: The child comes from such a background; therefore, there is nothing I, as a teacher, can do but try to get minimal results from this misshapen material. Among teachers who are explicitly bigoted in their views of the poor and black, the explanations for failure may be less benign. According to Rosenfeld, and his observations are supported by others, an underlying ethos pervades the slum school which prescribes and accepts failure for the child.

> Assistant principals function not as experts on curriculum and instruction but as stock boys and disciplinarians. Boxes are constantly being unpacked and children are being reprimanded and punished. The principal seems more concerned with maintaining a stable staff, irrespective of its quality at times, than with effecting school-community ties and fashioning relevant learning programs. Education appears as a process where children are merely the by-products, not the core of concern. Guidance counselors and reading specialists are preoccupied with norms and averages, not with the enhancement of learning for all the children. Theirs is a remedial task, and where one would not exist, they create it. School directives and bulletins are concerned with bathroom regulations and procedures along stairways, the worth of the children being assessed in terms of their ability to conform to these peripheral demands (Rosenfeld 1971:110).

The new teacher, however idealistic he or she may be at first, will be affected by the environment and become a part of the social structure of the school. A socialization process occurs so that personal commitment and philosophy become ordered around the system. The clique structure among staff personnel also forces the newcomer to choose models and cultivate relationships. Communication must occur. There must be others with whom one can commiserate.

Teachers who keep their idealism, tempered as it is after a time by reality, turn more and more inward toward their own classrooms. There one sees the results of the years of educational disenchantment. In the middle grades and beyond, the children are already two or more years behind standard achievement norms. The teacher realizes that for the children the school is an oppressive and meaningless place. He or she comes to understand also that children have developed counter-strategies for what they have perceived as their teachers' indifference, confusion, despair, and in some cases, outright aggression. But if the teacher persists in the effort to understand his or her pupils, eventually they become individuals. Most are alert and active. They are potentially high learners and achievers. Some are subdued and permanently detached. Some are irrevocably hostile towards schools, teachers, and white people. Others have surface hostilities but are willing to give trust and confidence when it is justified. Some are fast learners with strong curiosity and an eagerness to learn about the world. Others are apathetic or simply dull. Once the children become individuals, with sharp differences, they can no longer be treated as objects or as a collectivity.

The next step for the teacher who is going to become effective as a cultural transmitter and agent of socialization, as all teachers are, is to learn something of the neighborhood and of the homes from which the children come. But this is a step that is rarely taken. Rosenfeld describes the situation at Harlem School.

> Though Harlem School belonged to the neighborhood, it was not psychologically a part of it. On the contrary, teachers felt unwanted, estranged. Perhaps this was why few ventured off the "beaten paths" to the "hinterland" beyond the school, into the side streets and the homes where the children played out their lives. Some teachers at Harlem School had never been to a single child's household, despite the fact that they had been employed at the school for many years. Nothing was known of community self-descriptions, the activity and social calendar in the neighborhood, the focal points for assembly and dispersal, or the feelings of residents toward the "outside world." Teachers could not imagine that they could foster a genuine coming-together of neighborhood persons and themselves. They hid behind their "professionalism." They failed to realize that the apathy and disparagement they associated with parents were attributed by the latter to them. It is not to be underestimated how "foreign" teachers feel themselves to be at Harlem School, how disliked by the children. Why then do they remain on the job? Part of the answer is in the fact that the rewards of one's work are not always sought on the job itself, but in the private world. Teachers have little stake in the communities in which they work; that is why it may be necessary to link more closely teachers' jobs and children's achievement. It is my guess that all children (except those with proven defects) would achieve if teachers' jobs depended on this. (Rosenfeld 1971:103)

It is clear that there are some parallels between the relationship of the school and teachers to the pupils and community in minority populations in the United States and the like relationship that has developed in many of the modernizing nations. Although there are profound differences in the two situations, the similarity is that the educational institutions in both cases are intrusive. These institutions stem from a conceptual and cultural context that is different from that of the people whose children are in the schools. This tends to be true whether "natives" or aliens are utilized as teachers and administrators for the schools. In the modernizing populations, as among the Sisala, the teacher, even though Sisala himself, is alien by virtue of his having been educated, removed from his community, socialized to norms, values, competencies, and purposes that are not a part of his community's culture (Grindal 1972). He is a member of a different class, for which there is as yet no clear place in the Sisala cultural system. He feels isolated from the community, and this isolation is reinforced by the character of the school in which he teaches. In Harlem School, or its prototypes, the teacher tends to be an alien whether he or she is white or black. Even among black teachers only some can maintain or acquire an identification with the people and community in which the school exists. The same processes of socialization and alienation that have taken place for the Sisala teacher have taken place for the black teacher in the United States. This is particularly true for the black teacher who comes from a middle-class background to begin with, then goes on to the university for advanced training. This teacher may be as far removed from the black community in a slum school as is any white teacher. Of course not all black communities are in slums, but the slum school is the one we have been talking about.

At Rosepoint?

The interactions we are describing between school and culture occur elsewhere than in the urban slum. Martha Ward describes a community in what she calls Rosepoint, near New Orleans (1971). Rosepoint is a very small rural community, a former plantation occupied now by some of the people who once worked on it, plus others. Rosepoint has its own culture—that of the black South, together with a heavy French influence characteristic of the area as a whole, and the unique ecological characteristics of a community built along a levee of the Mississippi River. Martha Ward was particularly concerned with language learning and linguistic features. She found that there were many substantial differences in speech and learning to speak among Rosepoint adults and children and white people. These differences contribute to the separation between community and school, which is the focus of our attention, since the school is taught mostly by whites, although they are by no means the sole cause of this separation.

Rosepoint parents believe that most of the teachers in the schools their children attend—black or white—are authoritarian and punitive. They also see that their children attending white schools for the first time are subjected to discriminatory practices, sometimes subtle, sometimes very obvious. There is little communication between the home and the school, whether primary or high school. Parents have little notion of how the school is run, what their children are taught, or how to cooperate with the school or teachers. And the schools show no understanding of the social problems or cultural characteristics of Rosepoint. The conflicts are profound. The irrelevancy of the school for most Rosepoint children is measured by a high dropout rate and low rates of literacy. From about eleven years of age on, states Martha Ward, staying in school is a touch-and-go proposition, especially for males. She describes certain characteristics of the school environment and expectations that are at odds with those of the Rosepoint children.

> The school creates for the Rosepoint child an environment not as much unpleasant as unnatural. For years he [or she] has been determining his own schedule for eating, sleeping, and playing. The content of his play is unsupervised and depends on the child's imagination. His yard does not

contain sand boxes, swings, clay, paints, nor personnel obliged to supervise his play. At school, however, play is supervised, scheduled, and centers around objects deemed suitable for young minds. There are firm schedules for playing, napping, eating, and "learning and studying" (with the implication that learning will occur only during the time allotted for it). The authority buttressing even minimal schedules is impersonal and inflexible with an origin not in face-to-face social relationships but in an invisible bureaucracy.

Moreover, the Rosepoint home relies on verbal communication rather than on the written word as a medium. Adults do not read to children nor encourage writing. Extraverbal communication such as body movements or verbal communication such as storytelling or gossip are preferred to the printed page. The lack of money to purchase books, magazines, and newspapers partly explains this. . . . [sentence omitted] . . . for children of a culture rich in in-group lore and oral traditions the written word is a pallid substitute.

Another conflict arising out of the home-school discrepancy is language—specifically, "bad" language. Remember, the Rosepoint child is rewarded for linguistic creativity. . . . [three sentences omitted]

In the classroom such language has an entirely different interpretation on it. Some educators discretely refer to it as "the M-F problem."[1] [sentence omitted] A nine-year-old girl was given a two-week suspension from classes for saying a four-letter word. This was her first recorded transgression of the language barrier. The second offense may be punished by expulsion. . . . [two sentences omitted to end of paragraph] (Ward 1971:91–92)

The problems of Rosepoint and the schools that are intended to serve it are probably less overtly intense than those of Harlem School, its staff, and the community, but they are closely related to each other, and in turn to the problems of education among the Sisala, the Kanuri, and in Malitbog. The schools in all of these situations are intrusive and the teachers are aliens. Resentment, conflict, and failures are present in communication from all sides.

We should be very careful here to realize that what we have been describing is not a problem of black minority populations alone. To some extent the disarticulation described between the school and community will be characteristic in any situation where the teachers and school stem from a different culture or subculture than that of the pupils and their parents. There is disarticulation between any formal school and the community, even where the school and community are not culturally divergent. Conflicts ensue when the school and teachers are charged with responsibility for assimilating or acculturating their pupils to a set of norms for behavior and thought that are different from those learned at home and in the community.

Education for minorities in North America is complicated by a variety of hazards. Harlem School operates in a depressing slum environment. No one wants to go there, and the people there would like to get out. The conflicts and disarticulation germane to the school-community situation we have described are made more acute and destructive because of this. Rosepoint and its schools have their special circumstances also. The Rosepoint population has inherited the culture and outlook of a former plantation-slave population. They are close to the bottom of the social structure. The teachers, particularly if they are white, have inherited attitudes toward black people from the South's past. Let us look for a moment at a quite different place and people, the Indians of the Yukon Territory of Canada and the Mopass Residential School.

In the Mopass Residential School?

The children who come to this school represent several different tribes from quite a wide area of northwestern Canada. Many of these tribal societies adapted quickly to the fur trade economy that developed soon after the first white men arrived, and many became heavily acculturated to the other aspects of European culture. One could not say that on the whole the Native Americans[2] of this area resisted the alien culture. In fact, they welcomed many of its technological and material advantages. As the northern territories have been opened for rapid development during the past decade, however, the Native Americans already there have found it increasingly difficult to find a useful and rewarding place in this expanding economy. The reasons for this are altogether the fault of neither the white Canadians nor the Indians, but certainly prejudice has played a role. One of the serious problems of the Native Americans, however, has been that, on the whole, they have had neither the skills that could be used in the expanding economy nor the basic education upon which to build these skills. The task of the school would seem to be that of preparing young Native Americans to take a productive and rewarding role in the economy and society now emerging in the Northwest Territories. This is what it is like at Mopass Residential School, according to Richard King, who taught there for a year and did anthropological observations during that period.

> For the children, the residential school constitutes a social enclave almost totally insulated from the community within which it functions; yet Mopass School reflects in a microcosmic, but dismayingly faithful, manner the social processes of the larger society. Two distinct domains of social interaction exist independently: Whiteman society and Indian society. Where these domains overlap, they do so with common purposes shared at the highest level of abstraction—but with minimal congruence of purposes, values, and perceptions, at the operating levels of interaction. The Whiteman maintains his social order according to his

own perceptions of reality. The Indian bears the burden of adaptation to a social order that he may perceive more realistically—and surely he perceives it with a different ordering of reality—than does the Whiteman. From his perceptions the Indian finds it impossible to accept the social order and, at the same time, impossible to reject it completely. He therefore creates an artificial self to cope with the unique interactive situations.

In the residential school, the Whiteman staff and teachers are the end men of huge bureaucratic organizations (church and national government) that are so organized as to provide no reflection of the local communities. These employees derive their social, economic, and psychological identity from the organizations of which they are members. . . . [Four sentences omitted]

. . . The children of the school are little more than components to be manipulated in the course of the day's work. . . . No job at school is defined in terms of *outcomes*, expected, or observable, in children. (King 1967:89–90)

King goes on to describe the factionalism among the adult faculty and staff in the school. He suggests that many of the people who take teaching jobs in the residential school are deviant or marginal personalities, and that the isolation of the school and its nature as a closed system tend to create a tense interpersonal situation. The children have to adjust to this as well as to the alien character of the institution itself.

The school children become uniquely adept at personality analysis, since their major task is to cope with the demands of shifting adult personalities. But this analysis is limited to their needs as the children perceive them in specific situations. (King 1967:88)

An artificial self is developed by Native American children to cope with the total situation in which they find themselves. King says that the children sustain themselves with the conviction that their "real self" is not this person in the school at all. Through this, and other processes, the barriers between Whiteman and Indian are firmly developed

not so much by a conscious rejection on the part of the Whiteman as by a conscious rejection on the part of the Indian child. The sterile shallowness of the adult model presented by the school Whitemen serves only to enhance—and probably to romanticize—memories of attachments in the child's primary family group, and to affirm a conviction prevalent among the present adult Indian generation that Indians must strive to maintain an identity separate from Whitemen. (King 1967:88)

There is much more we could say about the social and learning environment that this school provided[3] the children who attended it. King's case study should be read in order to understand it more thoroughly, for it is a startling example of miseducation—and with the best of intentions on the part of the sponsoring organizations and the teaching and administrative personnel of the school itself. All the features of disarticulation, isolation and nonrelatedness we have ascribed to the other schools discussed are present, but in a special and distorted form because the school is a closed residential institution even more removed from the community that it is intended to serve than the other schools. It is also a church school, run by the Episcopalian church for the Canadian government. Its curriculum is even less relevant to the Native American children who attend it than the curriculum of the Sisala school was to the Sisala children, for it is the same curriculum that is used in other Canadian schools at the same grade level. It appears that the Mopass Residential School intends to recruit children into the white culture and a religious faith (since religious observances and education are a regular part of the school life). It fails in these purposes and, in fact, creates new barriers to this recruitment and reinforces old ones. More serious by far is the fact that it does not prepare the children who attend it to cope with the new economy and society emerging in the north. The children leave the school without necessary basic skills, alienated from what they see as white culture, alienated from themselves, and nonrelated to their own communities. This kind of schooling creates marginal people.[4]

Is There a Way Out of the Dilemma?

In the discussion so far we have dealt only with minority peoples who have had to operate in what some would describe as an essentially colonial situation. That is, they may have the theoretical rights of self-determination and self-regulation, but in fact do not and could not exercise these rights. There are now strong movements underway towards self-determination. Some are very militant, separatistic, and nationalistic. Others are more accommodative. But all share in striving for self-determination, and regulation of the schools is an important aspect of this determination. These people recognize, perhaps in different terms, what we have said—that education is a process of recruitment and maintenance for the cultural system. For minority people the schools have been experienced as damaging attempts to recruit their children into an alien culture. Their self-images and identities were ignored or actively attacked.

There are some minority communities that have successfully resolved the problem. They have done so by creating and maintaining a closed cultural system that maintains a more-or-less defensive relationship toward the rest of the society. The Old Order Amish and the Hutterites are good examples of this solution. Both are nonaggressive, pacifistic peoples, communal in orientation, and socioreligious in ideology and charter.

Amish communities are distributed principally throughout Pennsylvania, Ohio, and Indiana but are also found in several other states. The total Old Order Amish population is estimated at about 60,000. They are agrarian, use horsepower for agricultural work and transportation, and wear rather somber but distinctive dress. They strive to cultivate humility and simple living. Their basic values include the following: separation from the world; voluntary acceptance of high social obligations symbolized by adult baptism; the maintenance of a disciplined church-community; excommunication and shunning as a means of dealing with erring members and of keeping the church pure; and a life of harmony with the soil and nature—it is believed that nature is a garden and humans were able to be caretakers, not exploiters. The goals of education are to instill the above values in every Amish child and maintain, therefore, the Amish way of life. John Hostetler and Gertrude Huntington describe the concept of a true education from the Amish point of view.

> True education, according to the Amish, is "the cultivation of humility, simple living, and resignation to the will of God." For generations the group has centered its instruction in reading, writing, arithmetic, and the moral teachings of the Bible. They stress training for life participation (here and for eternity) and warn of the perils of "pagan" philosophy and the intellectual enterprises of "fallen man," as did their forefathers. Historically, the Anabaptist avoided all training associated with self-exaltation, pride of position, enjoyment of power, and the arts of war and violence. Memorization, recitation, and personal relationships between teacher and pupil were part of a system of education that was supremely social and communal. (1971:9)

Realizing that state consolidation of schools constituted a severe threat to the continuity of their way of life and basic values, the Amish built the first specifically Amish School in 1925. By 1970 there were over three hundred such schools, with an estimated enrollment of ten thousand pupils. When the population of the United States was predominantly rural and the major occupation was farming, the Amish people had no serious objections to public schooling. In the rural school of fifty years ago in most of the United States a curriculum much like that of the present Amish school was followed, the teacher was a part of the community, and the school was governed locally. Consolidation of schools in order to achieve higher educational standards shifted control away from the local area, and the educational innovations that followed were unacceptable to the Amish. The Amish insist that their children attend schools near their homes so that they can participate in the life of the community and learn to become farmers. They also want qualified teachers committed to Amish values. Teachers who are merely qualified by state standards may be quite incapable of teaching the Amish way of life or providing an example of this way of life by the way they themselves live. The Amish also want to have their children educated in the basic skills of reading, writing, and arithmetic; but training beyond that, they feel, should be related directly to the Amish religion and way of life. They do not agree with what they perceive to be the goals of the public schools, ". . . to impart worldly knowledge, to insure earthly success, and to make good citizens for the state." Ideally, from the Amish point of view, formal schooling should stop at about age fourteen, though learning continues throughout life. They feel that further schooling is not only unnecessary but detrimental to the successful performance of adult Amish work roles. The Amish pay for and manage their own schools in order to attain these goals (Hostetler and Huntington 1971:35–38).

Naturally there have been serious conflicts with state authorities about the schools. Forcible removal of the children from Amish communities has been attempted in some cases, and harassment in legal and interpersonal forms has characterized the relationship of state authority to the Amish in respect to the problem of education. The Amish have doggedly but nonviolently resisted all attempts to make them give up their own schools, for they realize that these schools are essential to the continuance of their cultural system. They have made accommodations where they could, as for instance in providing "vocational" schooling beyond elementary school to meet state educational age requirements concerning duration of schooling.

The Amish story is one about which anyone interested in the processes and consequences of separatism should know. Hostetler and Huntington's study is a good up-to-date overview that presents the case for the community-relevant school clearly and objectively and with a sympathetic understanding of the Amish point of view and lifeway.

The Hutterite culture is similar in many ways to that of the Old Order Amish, as seen from the outside, although the Hutterites are more communal in their economic organization and they use advanced agricultural machinery as well as trucks and occasionally cars. Hutterites are Anabaptists, like the Amish and the Mennonites, originating during the Protestant Reformation in the sixteenth century in the Austrian Tyrol and Moravia. They arrived in South Dakota in 1874 and have prospered since. There are about 18,000 Hutterites living in more than 170 colonies in the western United States and Canada. They are noted for their successful large-scale farming, large families, and effective training of the young.

Hutterites are protected from the outside world by an organized belief system which offers a solution to their every need, although they, like the Amish, have been subjected to persecution and harassment from the outside. The community minimizes aggression and dissension of any kind. Colony members strive to lose their self-identity by surrendering themselves to the communal will and attempt to live each day in preparation for death and, hopefully, heaven. The principle of order is the key concept underlying Hutterite life. Order is synonymous with eternity and godliness; even the orientation of colony buildings conforms to directions measured with the precision of a compass. There is a proper order for every activity, and time is neatly divided into the sacred and the secular. In the divine hierarchy of the community each individual member has a place—male over female, husband over wife, older over younger, and parent over child. The outsider asks, "Why does this order work? How can it be maintained?" The implicit Hutterite answer is that "Hutterite society is a school, and the school is a society." The Hutterites, like the Old Amish, do not value education as a means toward self-improvement but as a means of "planting" in children "the knowledge and fear of God" (Hostetler and Huntington 1967).

We will not go into detail concerning Hutterite schools. Although they differ somewhat from the Amish schools in curriculum and style, particularly in being more strict and "authoritarian," the basic principles are the same. The Hutterites also understand that they must retain control of their schools and teachers if they are to retain their separatistic and particularly their communal and socioreligious way of life. They do this by retaining a "German school" that is in effect superimposed upon the "English school" required by the state or provincial law. The two schools have rather different curricula and teachers, and, of the two, the former is clearly the one that carries the burden of cultural transmission that recruits youngsters into the Hutterite cultural system and helps maintain that system most directly.

The Hutterites serve as another example of how to solve the problem faced by the Sisala, the people of Malitbog, the Kanuri, the children of Harlem School and their parents, the people of Rosepoint, and the children in the Mopass Residential School.

The problem all of these people face is how to relate a culture-transmitting institution that is attempting to recruit their children to a cultural system different from that of the community, class, area, or minority from which the children come. The school and teacher are alien in all of these cases, and they are charged, by governments or the dominant population, with the responsibility of changing the way of life by changing the children. Understandably the consequences are at least disruptive, and at worst tragic.

The Hutterites and Amish have done exactly what is logical according to the anthropologist viewing the relationship between education and culture. Realizing the threat to the continuity of their way of life from the outside world, particularly from schooling and transmission of concepts and views alien to their fundamental principles, they have taken control of their schools to whatever extent they can, given the exigencies of survival in contemporary North America. The schools are so ordered as to recruit and help maintain the traditional cultural system. They are successful. The way of life, beleaguered though it is in both cases, survives—in fact, flourishes.

It is important to understand, however, that, from another point of view, the cost of this success is too great. The result of success is a closed cultural system in a defensive relationship to the rest of society. That there are restrictions on personal behavior, sharp limits on self-expression, and confinement in the very thought processes and world view in both cases, is undeniable. The values of spontaneity, individual creativity, discovery and invention, pursuit of knowledge, and innovation, that are important to men elsewhere, are not values in these or any other closed cultural systems. There is also a kind of self-created disadvantage imposed by the Hutterites and Amish upon themselves. Since they lack higher education, in fact are opposed to it, and control as vigorously as possible the context of primary education, they cannot participate fully in the give and take of our dynamic society. True, they do not want to; but it is a hard choice, and one that could be very disadvantageous to any minority group. Somehow the modernizing peoples of the world emerging from a tribal and then colonial past, and the minority peoples in vast societies like the United States and Canada, must balance the consequences of a closed system and the educational institutions to support it, and an open system and the educational institutions to support it. It is clear, however, that it is necessary for all peoples to exercise and develop the rights of self-determination and self-regulation in education, as well as in other areas of life. It may be that this can be done without creating closed, defensive, and confining cultural systems. It may help for us all to realize that we actually have little control over what happens in our schools, no matter who we are. The educational bureaucracy in a complex urban system functions in some ways like an alien cultural system in relation to the local community, the children in school, and their parents, whether these parents and children are members of minority or majority groups. We all have this problem in common. In this age of cultural pluralism in the United States it is difficult to discern what else we all have in common. Perhaps it is possible to agree that there are some competencies all children should acquire, such as functional literacy, concepts of mathematical processes, and so forth, that are necessary if they are not to be severely handicapped in later life in a complex society. But in the area of specific values, ideologies, and world views we cannot repeat the mistakes of the past, when we assumed that the melting pot would melt all ethnic differences down to the same blendable elements. The cultures of Native Americans, African Americans, Mexican Americans, and Asian Americans did not disappear as our ideology said they would. The challenge is to recognize and accept the differences without creating disadvantageous separatism or segregation, whether self-imposed or imposed from the dominant group. There are many paradoxes in the relationships we are discussing, and they are not easily resolved.

Notes

[1] Refers to the use of obscenities in the school, including "Motherfucker."

[2] The term *Native Americans* is preferred by many American Indians. We use Indian and Native American interchangeably in recognition of this preference.

[3] The school was closed in 1969. The "ethnographic present" is used in this description to be consistent with the other analyses.

[4] Mopass Residential School is neither better nor worse than other residential schools for Native Americans because it is Episcopalian, and certainly not because it is Canadian. Most of the same conditions exist in residential schools in both the United States and Canada, in Protestant, Catholic, and nondenominational schools.

References

Grindal, Bruce T., 1972. *Growing Up in Two Worlds: Education and Transition among the Sisala of Northern Ghana.* CSEC. New York: Holt, Rinehart and Winston.

Hostetler, John A., and Gertrude E. Huntington, 1967. *The Hutterites in North America.* CSCA. New York: Holt, Rinehart and Winston.

_____, 1971. *Children in Amish Society: Socialization and Community Education.* CSEC. New York: Holt, Rinehart and Winston.

King, A. Richard, 1967. *The School at Mopass: A Problem of Identity.* CSEC. New York: Holt, Rinehart and Winston.

Rosenfeld, Gerry [1971], 1983. *"Shut Those Thick Lips!" A Study of Slum School Failure.* Prospect Heights, IL: Waveland Press.

Ward, Martha C. [1971], 1986. *Them Children: A Study in Language Learning.* Prospect Heights, IL: Waveland Press.

7
Achieving School Failure 1972–1997

Raymond P. McDermott
Stanford University

I spent much of 1972 working on what was right about minority students in my class "choosing" to fail in school. The work was based on two years of teaching grade school in New York City and two years as a graduate student reading about children, learning, and social structure. By now, twenty-five years later, the question has been redefined, and new concepts and methods have been applied to analyses and applications. Has there been progress? Yes and no: No, for the country continues to bifurcate into the few who have and the many who have not, and the problem of recorded school failure gets worse; but yes, because we have better concepts to work with, and, if we are diligent and tough, they might prove helpful.

George Spindler kindly included a version of the work in the first edition of *Education and Cultural Process* (1974). Now, for that book's grandchild, he has offered a more terrifying opportunity, namely, to use that paper, *Achieving School Failure* (McDermott 1974), as a benchmark for identifying any subsequent progress in addressing and confronting school failure. In another twenty-five years, I expect him to offer me still another chance to expose the role of school failure in the mystification of social structure in the United States. Barring major social change in the direction of democracy and equality, I suspect I will have to try again.

By current standards, *Achieving* had a great title, a flawed analysis, and a weak conclusion. If we hold onto the title and reframe the analysis, the conclusion takes on a new strength that says more about the world than did the first effort. The new framing also shows how the ethnography of schooling has moved forward in developing concepts that better capture and confront our present circumstances. There have been some surprises over the past twenty-five years, and it is pleasure to identify some of them.

Source: Prepared especially for *Education and Cultural Process*, 3rd Edition.

The Title

The title (and the portions of text consistent with it) have real merit. School failure *is* an achievement of a kind. School success is also an achievement, of a related kind, and they must be understood in terms of each other. School failure is not a simple absence of school success but an actively constructed option for all children, an option taken by about half of them before the end of high school. Together, success and failure are the two perfectly normal ways to go through school. To understand the relationship between success and failure, we must learn to appreciate the sensible efforts of all the participants, of those who achieve success *and* those who achieve failure, of those who orchestrate the designation and interpretation of school failure *and* those who are orchestrated by it.

To consider failure an achievement is more than semantically playful. It harbors three serious claims:

1. School failure takes work on the parts of everyone in the system.
2. School failure makes sense to most participants at most levels of the system.
3. In ways depending on one's place in the system, school failure is in various ways adaptive.

    Each claim deserves a turn.

Work: Who is involved in the production of school failure? A better question would be: Who is not? Every Monday morning through to every year's graduations, it is part of most every U.S. citizen's work to help make school failure a cultural fact that is attended to, worried about, avoided, tested, resisted, paid for, remediated, explained, and condemned. The list of participants, the full *dramatis personae*, is exhaustive, a roster that covers most everyone in the culture:

- the children, of course, although they would seem to be least responsible, even if they are the most highlighted;
- their teachers, only a little more responsible and a little less highlighted, and their administrators—perhaps above all;
- the parents with strong investments in having their children do better than others;
- the testing agencies that document who is doing better than whom;
- the researchers who study school failure;
- the receiving institutions (colleges, entry-level jobs) that keep the sorting system so commonly sensible;
- and finally all those juggling their degrees to negotiating job markets and the inequalities of the wider system.

After all these school-failure workers are seen in place, we can analyze the success and failure of individuals as mere nodes in a wider network of activities that remake the social order of yesterday into the social order of tomorrow, a network of activities that moves yesterday's social structure into today's drama and back again into tomorrow's social structure.

Making sense: The near ceaseless renewal of what for the most part has been *always already there* not only takes work, but it makes sense at most levels of the system. In fact, school success makes so much sense that it can be carried out by almost all the persons caught inside the assumptions of the system. Right after *Achieving* was published, I was asked to speak to school principals about how cultural differences between teachers and children might cause misunderstandings and result in misbehavior on the part of the children. During the presentation before mine, the principals, lined up in rows and being spoken to as students, were chewing, rolling, and spitting wads of paper at each other. More than miscommunication was at play; something more systematic was occurring. The instructions to act inappropriately were in the air: Treat them like kids, and even principals can act up.

A focus on individual motives does not reveal the configurations of which we are all a part. The message to act up does not come from kids alone. It is a symptom of the system, and even the bad performances of principals can be understood as having made sense. After worrying all week about the absurdities of spitball management, it was *their* turn to have someone worry about *their* attention deficits. Making sense as a principal requires many people in the system to lend a hand. Everyone in a school must help construct the environments that allow principals to do a proper job, to interpret and constrain their behavior as principal appropriate. On Monday morning, schools supply strong instructions that principals not get caught playing with spitballs, just as the Saturday morning workshop with lecturing researchers can fill the air with instructions to act like children.

Adaptive failure: In addition to implying that school failure takes work and makes sense, the *Achieving* title suggests that failure is, at various levels of the system, adaptive—so adaptive that sensible people can be found working hard on its daily reproduction. I thought it was my job twenty-five years ago to show failure as a sensible adaptation for children in school. As a teacher, I had watched many teachers, me included, standing in front of children asking them what they were going to do when they grow up and imploring them to understand the importance of education in carving out a good life. There was no shortage of "get-your-education" speeches, and I watched many kids reject such talk. As children, they believed in the words, of course. They could repeat them and did so to those younger than them, but they did not live the words. I had watched many kids reject future talk in favor of the far stronger contingencies of the present. I had adored the children in my classes and thought they were enormously bright, even if they were doing terribly at school. Two years in the library had given me the tools to make a case. Socioinguists and cross-cultural psychologists had taken aim at the myth of the culturally deprived child, and I had only to add a dash of ethnomethodology, ethnoscience, and kinesics to claim that there was complexity and wisdom everywhere available in the lives of the children, at least to observers who knew how to look. Not only were the kids smart, said I, but the perfect measure of their smartness was how much they had embraced school failure: they figured out the odds against their doing well in school, went the opposite direction, and worked at actively achieving school failure.

Certainly there was a price to pay for taking such a route. Teenage toughs may be successful at rejecting school and giving teachers a hard time, but they pay in the long run. Still we can appreciate their effort and the ingenuity they bring to it. There is reason to appreciate how, in their terms, they were doing the best that could be done for their personal identities as kids in a system that was stacked against them. In terms of peer-group prestige, there was no doubt that doing well at school was not going to pay off as well as confronting the system.

In the spring of 1969, while teaching my first sixth-grade class, I heard Labov (1972) present linguistic data from Harlem street gangs. He convinced me, and I remain convinced, that the same children who could be made to look stupid at school and utterly without self-esteem at the counselor's office could defend themselves in ritual insult games in ways as clever and self-possessed as any children ever on record; more importantly, we could see the same competencies at hand if we looked inside their families, where they carried responsibilities that would dwarf those of a middle-class child (Burton, et. al., 1995; Stack 1974). How could we have not seen their strengths? How could we not be aware of the limitations of our own vision as part of the problem, part of the environment to which they had to adapt?

Same Title with a New Cultural Emphasis

There is a theoretical and political edge that separates the above paragraphs from my past effort. The older paper was designed to show how the *children* failing in school were being fully adaptive to local circumstances. The above paragraphs suggest instead how much *everyone* in the system is involved in making sense in ways that produce failure. If the first effort relied on a motivational analysis of the individual, albeit in a social context, the present phrasing emphasizes the world in which individuals are interpreted by others using the concepts available in the wider culture. Not only are children being fully adaptive in taking up the invitation to fail, so is the rest of the system in organizing the means to make failure possible, apparent, certifiable, and explainable.

This is a significant difference. By offering a more inclusive tally of how many people are involved and in what ways, we invite a more cultural account of school failure. In a cultural account, we seek not so much to explain the behavior of individuals as we seek to describe the interpretations to which individual behavior is made subject. For school failure, we seek not so much an account of why this child and not that child fails in school, but an account of how failure is an interpretation to which so much U.S. behavior is assigned. My question in the early effort was: "How could smart kids get fooled into thinking that school failure is going to help them?" My question now is: "How could 240 million people in the United States get fooled into thinking that producing so much failure is going to help them?"

As anyone who has ever filled out a school report card knows, the U.S. school asks how much better one child is doing than another. Culturally and institutionally it is the only question, and it spurs a fierce competition that leaves us with a school system that hands out credentials that mirror the sorting of the political economy: a few experts with access to the rewards of the system and a growing majority who eventually, thoroughly, and for all to see, fail. As a people, what are we thinking when we celebrate success? Do we know we systematically degrade the less successful as failures? A few points on this test or that—as if education were the Olympic Games—are enough to separate a child, regardless of potential, from success. In such a system, it is those who interpret test results so harshly—test-makers, school administrators, competitive parents, college admission officers—who achieve school failure for the rest.

The analytic transition from children and their characteristics to culturally designated characteristics and their children, a *major theme* in all social thought, has developed slowly in the anthropology of education. George Spindler told me then and tells me no less often now that the successful but tortured student, Beth Anne (see chapter 12), and the successful but lethal teacher, Roger Harker (Spindler 1974, 1982), did not simply emerge through their own peculiar adaptations to socialization in the United States in the 1950s. Rather, they emerged with the help of others; they were continually maintained in their successes and failures by all around them. Forty years after Spindler (1959) and Jules Henry (1963, 1973) started exposing school success and failure as a cultural sham, the transition from studying the characteristics of children to studying of the characteristics of culture continues to develop slowly even in the anthropology of education.

Symptoms of the slow transition from a focus on characters and their characteristics to a focus on cultures and their heuristics still dominate the anthropology of education. The original *Achieving* paper is an example. Although the title announces a cultural perspective, the analysis maintains the perspective on only an every-other-line basis. Yes, the paper argues that failure is not just an individual trait and that it takes a world—more than a village—to construct failure as something to be achieved by a kid. Still, *Achieving* harbors assumptions that stiffen the analysis and resist a more fully cultural analysis.

The Analysis

A number of claims made in the original *Achieving* paper need reframing. Essentially, the argument was that:

1. Children raised in different cultural, ethnic, racial, and class groups develop different procedures and expectations for communicating with others.

2. In cross-group school settings, these differences in turn produce miscommunication, which, if not repaired, causes enough discomfort and misunderstanding to make minority children inattentive to learning and the rewards of schooling (there is even the suggestion that the patterns of inattention become physiologically based to such an extent that minority children can appear neurologically disabled).

3. This negative spiral develops to the point that minority children embrace school failure as a way to celebrate themselves.

Each step of the argument is based on a problematic assumption that interferes with the paper delivering on its promise of a cultural analysis. They are:

- Named ethnic/racial groups are easy-to-use units of analysis that successfully gloss the behavior of their members;

- The motivated, thinking individual is the only unit of analysis for the study of learning; and

- Individual failure and success can be documented and explained without an account of the work people do to make failure a category applicable to children who in other circumstances would be kids growing up the way kids have regularly grown up.

Each assumption still has a life in the anthropology of education and must be challenged forcefully if we are to make progress. I knew vaguely about the problems twenty-five years ago, and I tried to say then what I can say a little better now. A group of friends and coworkers has pushed me along, but my stumbling efforts can be used still as a mirror of mistakes.

Achieving ethnicity: The defining characteristic of any group is its borders. In any kin group, ethnic group, or corporation, it is crucial for people inside a group to know not only who is inside, but who is specifically outside, immediately on the other side of the border. Although this has been the main principle of structural anthropology since early Levi-Strauss (1969) and a main tenet of the work I was reading on ethnic groups while writing *Achieving* (Barth 1969; Moerman 1974; Suttles 1974), it is a difficult notion to use carefully and consistently. In the United States, we are invited to ask about the content of cultural (and subcultural) ways of being alive rather than to focus on the surrounding groups that help keep each group seemingly locked inside itself. As U.S. citizens, we are invited to ask what Jews, African Americans, Vietnamese, and Hispanic Americans look like and how they behave. Sometimes we are invited to know how their behavior explains their position inside U.S. social structure, and stereotypes are available to guide our explanations. Only rarely are we invited to understand the conditions for a group being recognized, stereotyped, analyzed, diagnosed, and condemned. Only rarely are we invited to examine the role of mainstream bias in the organization of borders, stereotypes, and the social structural outcomes that maintain the borders.

In *Achieving*, the temporal and emergent dimensions of ethnicity, although stated, were muted by the assumption that once socialized into a group, people were stuck in the habits of that group. This violated not only the theory of how ethnic groups shaped each other at the borders, it violated my own experience. In New York, I grew up in an Irish house in a "changing"—that is to say, increasingly African American—neighborhood and went to a mostly Italian high school before attending a mostly Jewish college (where I spent most of my time studying Chinese). *Ad seriatim*, I have been a honky, mick, goy, *yanggweizeren* (the last is a foreign devil), and the list can now be expanded considerably. For each group I had a different body, a different walk, talk, and agenda. At my best, I was a tribute to the changes people could make in the face of difference, but I was no doubt also a tribute to how much a member of one group, be it specifically Irish or generically white (or my favorite, a New Yorker), could help to redefine once again, and never for the last time, the borders of the other groups. I must now take my identity from being "a not yet dead white male" and, my least favorite, a "Euroamerican." I would not have created these identifications for myself, but few have ever been allowed to weave a recognizable identity from patterns not prescribed by others. Neither "not yet dead white male" nor "Euroamerican" are designations of glory, I understand, but they at least have the power of pointing to my half of the equation that delivers the traditional divisions of U.S. social structure. I may not like them, they may not speak for all of what I am trying to accomplish in life, but they carry well some of the responsibility I owe our shared situation.

In 1973, when I returned to an elementary school to study children learning how to read, I realized immediately that ethnic differences must be studied at the sites of ethnic conflict and in terms of the conditions that turned mere ethnic differences into ethnic borders. I also read a sterling paper that summer by Fred Erickson (1973; see also Erickson and Shultz 1982; Erickson 1997), in which he described people from different groups who put aside their differences to achieve "pan ethnic" amalgams that seemed to be better predicted by local allegiances across class and race lines than by the troubles of talking across the different communicative patterns developed inside ethnic groups. Thus, Polish and Irish students, on the one hand, and African American and Hispanic students, on the other hand, found it easier to communicate with each other than across those combinations.

Once I had videotapes from classrooms, it was immediately apparent that the children were more complex than a simple designation of their ethnicity could begin to cover. The borders separating African American children from white or Hispanic children were both porous and invisible, and my search for the characteristics of children from different groups was transformed into a more interesting effort to document *when* race or ethnicity occurs, under what conditions, by virtue of what work performed by participants, and to what effect[1] (McDermott and Gospodinoff 1979).

In *Achieving*, I had argued that "because behavioral competence is differently defined by different social groups, many children and teachers fail in their attempts to establish rational, trusting and rewarding relationships across ethnic, racial or class boundaries in the classroom" (1974:118). The problem is not that this statement is sometimes untrue; the problem is that it is mostly uninteresting even when it is true. No sooner did I set out to make the case for miscommunication than the very groups I had predecided as my units of analysis disappeared *analytically*. I was still a member of the culture. I could always go into a classroom and separate white kids from black kids, and both of them from Hispanic kids, and any trip through the wider community would certainly show the salience of ethnic and racial borders in the organization of neighborhoods and access to material goods. But that only means that racism was at work, my own included. An analyst can join the rest of the United States with a high interrater reliability in separating African American and white children, but this does not give analytic permission for a claim that any behavior by any African American child is an instance of what African American children do.

In an ethnographic analysis, the identification of a behavior as African American requires that people identify it as such (the analysis of "things" that people, the anthropologist's natives, do not identify, but which are nonetheless crucial in their lives, takes greater attention to detail and more elaborate interpretative schemes). By this criterion, I saw little behavior in classrooms that was anything other than classroom behavior. Ethnic and racial behavior was rarely identified by the participants, and, when it was, because it occurred in interaction, I was forced to ask not how it was an instance of what is essential to one group or another, but how it came about *in situ*, across persons, at exactly that time, and to what end.

The great bulk of work in the anthropology of education continues to identify the characteristics of children from different groups as if such identifications constitute findings. We should stop this practice. Any proposed consistency between a group identity and particular ways of behaving should be the topic of our work and not a resource for analyzing some other problem (Garfinkel 1967). To any statement like:

Asian American children prefer . . .

Children from Hispanic families think . . .

You have to handle African American children by . . . ,

we must raise a suspicion. Stereotypes created by social scientists are still stereotypes, and they are not useful as explanations of the problems people face. Should we really call this stereotyping ethnography? In its stead, we should confront how ethnography can contribute to the ugly politics of creating hostile borders among peoples who could just as easily be understood as being the same.

At the very least, we should wonder how we get organized by those around us to clump people into received categories, to look for and find certain behaviors as markers of the so-called groups, and why it makes sense to others to deliver such descriptions (Gilmore, Smith, and Kairaiuak 1997). As a correction, we can always go to another culture or another era of our own and find different groups being called the same names or the same groups different names (for rich examples of the "genesis of kinds of people," see Frake 1980, 1997; for an update on the Japanese Burakumin, an important example in *Achieving*, see Rohlen 1978, 1983). Any proposed consistency between a group identity and particular ways of behaving should be the very point of fascination that raises questions about how we do identifications. Instead of asking why one group does better than others in school, we should ask how one group—white people, for example—forms environments that define other groups (for instance, African Americans as only, essentially, and irrevocably nothing more than African American) as the kinds of people who can be found failing in school. At the same time, and in complimentary fashion, we must find ways to break through ethnic borders (Goldman, Chaiklin, and McDermott 1994).

Ethnicity is not an explanation of failure. Ethnicity is, like school failure itself, a product of people using U.S. culture to organize each other. It is an achievement.

Achieving learning: Essential to the arguments in *Achieving* is the assumption that the thought processes and decision making of the motivated individual child are the key to understanding school failure. The problem, I thought then, is that many minority children do not learn how to read. This lack of learning is what had to be explained. Instead of taking the mainstream stand that they did not learn to read because they were developmentally impoverished, I argued that they learned how *not* to read. Alienated from school as an institutional setting where they were misunderstood and put upon by the standards of the white middle class, they embraced an alternative life celebrating noncompliance. My effort was to reframe their not learning as an institutionalized, social event rather than as a one-by-one failure in psychological development. I was headed in the right direction, but I left their non-learning analytically intact. I did not challenge, and had few grounds to challenge, the common-sensibly obvious fact that many individual minority children were not learning in school. There is a reality in the test scores that arrived every June—there still is in fact—but not as stated (on the complexity of what tests do deliver, see the extraordinary work of Hill and Parry [1994]). The school system said that this individual failed and that one didn't, and I should not have believed them.[2]

In the mid-1970s, two events greatly complicated my understanding of learning and the difficulties of analyzing it in the real world. First, after a year of fieldwork in a school and a second year analyzing films taken from one first-grade classroom, I could not find anyone learning to read. Certainly children worked on reading tasks occasionally, and certainly some seemed to read much better than others. Mostly they talked with each other and handled classroom procedural demands (Mehan 1979). Chit chat is the site of most learning, even in classrooms, but I did not know that then.[3] Learning, then and now, is hard to see; it develops over time and is embedded in myriad activities that hold a child long enough for something to change enough that the next day's activities look different.

There is a reason why psychologists moved the study of learning into the laboratory: learning is difficult to see. But there is a price to leaving it in the laboratory; clean, experimental results have little to do with the messy lives of people in the world. Ethnography, even the kind that focuses on the organization of individual behavior one film frame (24/second) at a time, does not make learning easily available analytically. Maybe we are all looking for the wrong thing. Maybe—and this is an important shift—learning is less about the individual than it is about the world that others hold together, the world in which individuals learn again and again about the usefulness of the knowledge that they once gained elsewhere (see Rohlen 1992 for the Japanese case). Take away the world, and most of our learning becomes hard to maintain—mere useless memories. Keep the world in the analysis, and the unit of learning becomes many people over time, arranging circumstances for things to be done and for individuals to take their place in relation to these doings. With such a focus, there is no one who is not learning, only people with a well organized and systematic relation to the doings of the wider culture. With such a focus, those made to appear as if they are not learning are *not* not learning, but learning in relation to ongoing arrangements that keep them locked in yesterday's social hierarchies. With such a focus, it is clear that the doings of the wider culture are not seriously arranged to offer equal opportunity for all, but to keep everyone learning how to remain in the same place one generation after another.

The second event that changed my understanding of learning occurred in my next fieldwork, again in a school, but this time as part of a team of psychologists interested in understanding children in their sociohistorical context. We set out directly to find various kinds of thinking—attending, remembering, problem solving—in their natural state in classrooms, the very place where learning is supposed to happen. After a month of fieldwork, we had nothing in our notes, and we instead organized our own environments—cooking clubs, for example—where we hoped to see children thinking their way through recipes and making their learning more analytically available to us. The great excitement of this work was the erasure of individual learning as the necessary focus of any inquiry into how learning was organized (Cole, Hood, and McDermott 1978; McDermott and Hood 1982; for current efforts, see Cole 1996; Hutchins 1995; Lave 1988; Lave and Wenger 1991; Newman, Griffin, and Cole 1989; McDermott 1993; Suchman 1987).

In the clubs, the children and their adults did things together. Analysts could call subsets of their behavior attending, remembering, and problem solving, but it was not easy to know which individual was working on what version of what problem. Contributions came from all sides as the participants performed tasks and then defined, recorded, worried about, and remediated their performances. Life in the world, unlike life as it is assumed to be when whittled down in laboratory settings, does not often require individual learners each poised to make the right move as much as it requires participants creating and solving problems that address the contexts that brought them together and that constrain the conditions for their entrance back into subsequent social events.

For decades before us, philosophers and psychologists tried to enlarge our conception of the many points of contact necessary over time between a person and the world if any sustained learning is to occur. In essays written in the 1930s, Kurt Lewin (1951) asked us to think in terms of "fields" and "topologies," and Lev Vygotsky (1987) pointed to the necessity of postulating a "zone of proximal development" that guides a child's reflexive alignment with the social world. And in the first decade of the century, albeit in a quite different idiom and as part of quite different political circumstances, John Dewey (1899) and George Herbert Mead (1964) were urging us to understand the communicational and communal contexts for all learning. Yes, it is true that learning can be broken down into many little pieces and children can be measured absorbing them at varying speeds. But it is a foolish culture that allows such measures to become the measure of the person. Learning is not ultimately a piecemeal enterprise, but a cumulative process that requires continuities in the organization of persons, continuities that allow participants to make use of their learning in various settings over time. Instead of asking what individuals learn, we should be asking what learning is made possible and necessary by social arrangements. Instead of asking about how individuals acquire a culture, we should be asking about how a culture acquires its individuals.

This shift in perspective is more than rhetoric, for it allows a new approach to school failure. Instead of asking why half the individuals in a culture do less well than the others, we can ask why a culture would acquire so many individuals in failing positions. Instead of asking why so many individuals do not learn what they need to get around in the culture, we can ask why a culture would organize opportunities for individuals to learn to behave in ways that would make them look like failures.

By now I have been to hundreds of schools in United States, and there is something amazingly consistent about them. In varying proportions relative to the socioeconomic status of the people they serve, they all have some who succeed and some who fail; and those who fail look amazingly the same across the system. Albeit with variations across race, class, and regional lines, they have the same culturally well-defined problems across the system. They curse the same adults, listen to the same genres of music, complain about the same injustices, express the same dreams of how to beat the system, and get crushed by the same lack of a future. This is learned behavior. This is a cultural pattern. This is an achievement. Instead of focusing on what individuals do not learn, if we focus on what is collectively learned by various groups, and how what each group learns is related to what the other groups learn, we might begin to understand failure as a systematic product of the collective background we build for it. We might begin to grasp what it means to achieve school failure.

Achieving failure: Ten years after writing *Achieving*, I realized I had been the butt of a joke. I had started an analysis of school failure with a focus on the individual, and I was proud of myself for moving to an account of why whole groups had consistently failed. Self-congratulations were not warranted. There is little progress in moving from individuals to collections of individuals for an explanation of a behavior pattern if in fact the behavior to be explained is not what it appears. I had never questioned the reality of a failure. I really believed that the African American children in my classes were not only failing to learn school skills, they were failing to learn life. They were already and would continue to be failures. It was my job to explain their failure with rigor and respect. I would explain it to those who created the system, the powers that be, and they would fix the problem. The joke was on me. The failure was not what I had thought it was. I never found the powers that be; or worse—they were me. For accepting minority school failure as an established fact, I was the powers that be.

Fortunately, the grounds gave way. Unfortunately, they gave way slowly. First I learned that African Americans, or any other group on the U.S. scene, must be understood in terms of all other groups, all mutually defined and caught up in a battle for access and resources. Then I lost the traditional theory of learning and had to start grappling with an alternative that stressed everyone's learning as part a distributed system for politics and economics as much as education. The final challenge comes with the realization that there is no such thing as school failure with everyone in the culture organizing such a thing. The very thing I was trying to explain, school failure itself, was a fabrication, a mockup—a massively consequential one, of course—but a sham nonetheless. Harumi Befu arranged for me to spend 1980 in Japan, where it is hard to find school failure of the type we organize.[4] At Teachers College, I started working with Hervé Varenne for whom all things American, like all things cultural, stand in a complex, constitutive, and often contradictory relation to the pressing realities of daily life. Baseball and apple pie, racism and democracy, education and failure, they are arbitrary conventions—attractive enough to keep everyone in the game and relentlessly consequential to anyone on the same field of play—but conventions nonetheless and distorting mystifications to any who take them as realities in their own terms (Varenne 1977, 1983, 1992; Varenne and McDermott, in press).

Fifty years ago, it was not possible to be learning disabled, although now it defines the school experience for one of every seven children in the United States; Japan and Denmark, on the other hand, have highly successful school systems with no learning disabilities. Similarly, whole countries get by without too much attention to school failure. In January 1942, there was no school failure problem in the United States (Berg 1969). Some people knew more than others, and some had gone to school more than others, but everyone was needed. The game had changed. Failure was not an option. Everyone had to learn new machinery. Everyone, including women and African Americans, had to up the ante on learning what had been systematically unavailable to them only months before. Everyone was mobilized. Doing a job had become more important than doing it better than others.

My father turned 80 in 1984. "I learned something about myself this week," he told me at the party we gave him. "I am a dropout." He had quit high school sixty-five years before to go to work, and he labored all his life as a handyman. He was not a dropout in 1919. He was a worker, eventually a husband, a father, a grandfather, and for his last twenty years a retired worker. These were all labels he liked. "Work will save us," he always said, often to no one in particular. By the late 1970s, the United States was going through a "dropout crisis." Anyone who did not finish high school for any reason but early death—so says the governmental agency that counts such things—was called a dropout. By the numbers, the United States had too many dropouts, and they were going to cost the country money. Those problem kids had become something to worry about, count, build policy for, and remediate. So it came to be that my father had been reclassified. What had once been a normal and responsible act had become exactly the wrong thing to do. "So Dad," I asked, "how long have you been a problem child?" Never one to answer a question directly, he should have replied with one of the double-edged, mostly true half-jokes with which he kept us organized—something like, "I was so busy taking care of you guys, I never had any time to have any problems of my own." I had missed his mood. He was more serious and said, as he had rarely said before, "Maybe I would do it different if I had to do it all over again." He read six New York papers (all but the *Times*) every day, voted in every election, and hardly missed an opportunity to work hard for sixty-four years, but, on his eightieth birthday, none of that counted. He had been reading about the dropout problem in the newspaper, and, for a moment, he knew himself only and perhaps totally as a dropout.

Whole societies have done without a dropout problem (Spindler and Spindler 1989), and whole societies can go without fabricating a constant concern for failure. In chapter 8 in this book, Varenne and his colleagues document life in a highly successful middle school where everyone has to worry daily about new competitions, new occasions for sorting out—as if once and for all—those who will succeed and those who will fail. Imagine that for twelve-year-olds. Imagine that for six-year-olds. Imagine a country where the latest middle-class fad is to send children to school as late as possible in order to increase their competitive powers. Instead of having their children in the younger half of their first grade class, U.S. parents are increasingly "red-shirting" their children for another year of growth and development relative to their peers. Education in the United States is all strategies. School failure is not a matter of disruptions in growth and development but a matter of strategic planning, some of which can be taught with good effect (Mehan, et. al., 1996). Without everyone in the system being so anxious to show everyone else's failure, without everyone in the system creating the competitive situations around which everyone else must strategize, we would not have a school failure problem in the United States.

There is a reason why it takes so long to move from mainstream to alternative theories of school failure. Common sense is easy to use but hard to escape. *Achieving* was written after four years of my trying to escape commonly sensible ideas about the factual reality of group membership, individual learning, and school failure. It took a full decade before these categories could be reframed and momentarily liberated from helping to create the very realities they would feign only to describe. It is difficult to confront and reframe key categories for problems that had seemed only in need of description and tinkering, for all the categories reinforce each other. I knew early in life that theories of racial inferiority did not describe the world and that their statement made things worse. But as long as I thought individual African American children were really not learning and were really failing in school (as different from merely participating in larger social patterns organized precisely to give different people differential access to the appearance of knowledge and other resources that make their success or failure documentable), then I was immersed in a system that was racist—unconsciously so, but racist nonetheless.

Stages in the Explanation of School Failure, 1960–1997

In this section I offer three theories of school failure that have emerged over the past thirty-seven years. The first, Deprivation theory, developed with the work of Martin Deutsch in 1960 (see his essays collected in 1967). The original *Achieving* paper can be read as an unsuccessful attempt to get beyond Deprivation. By 1980, after fifteen years of critique by linguists and anthropologists, Deprivationist thinking had become so unfashionable that I thought we were rid of it forever. By the late 1980s, it was back stronger than ever. Even anthropologists have been contributing to it. The second theory, Difference theory, was the immediate context for writing *Achieving*, although I was trying to develop, again unsuccessfully, an answer to the more political question of how various groups could have made each other so different. The third theory is a more Political account built around ideas of reproduction (Bowles and Gintis 1975; Bourdieu and Passeron 1977) and resistance (Willis 1977; Apple 1982; Giroux 1983; Gilmore 1984; Scott 1984; see Wexler 1982, for the best single essay in the field). Theoretically obtuse, ethnographically impoverished, practically inarticulate, and institutionally undeveloped, the Political account still represents a major advance in our understanding of schooling. It is necessarily and likely forever under construction. Nothing less than equal education for all would complete its course.

The point is that one cannot move simply from one theory to another without reformulating ideas on a wide range of issues. For each of the three theories, I have listed nine interlocking areas of concern, namely: the diagnosis of the problem, the population under scrutiny, the disciplines used in a description of the problem, the theory of learning that supports both the definition of the problem and the proposed solution, the theory of culture that circumscribes the stated problem, the epistemology that guides an analysis, the implications for policy, the visions of success, and the drawbacks of doing the work. *To move from one theory to the next, it is necessary to change one's mind about all nine* (and the list could be expanded considerably). No wonder there is so much confusion in the field. No wonder most writers slide conceptually between positions.

A full elaboration of the theories would take a volume. The abbreviated treatment I offer here is meant to be a clarifying grid against which papers dealing with school failure can be read. In *Achieving*, I tried to write a Political account in the idiom of a Difference account, and I slid conceptually in and out of a Deprivation account. Most papers in the field fit such a description. As a field, we are angry about how schools work; look for easy and make-nice solutions, such as urging everyone to respect cultural differences; and, to the extent that we work with mainstream categories and audiences, fall once again into wondering what is wrong with minority populations. This is a bad mix and requires constant vigilance against taking our assumptions as realities. After presenting the charts, I use them as a grid for locating the assumption sliding that guided *Achieving*.

Three Theories of School Failure[5]

I. The deprivation stand that will not go away, 1960–

Diagnosis: Children not learning in school have been broken by impoverished experiences; in addition to suffering a restricted environment, they are now restricted kids.

Target Population: Minorities (who need to be explained)

Disciplinary Resources: Cognitive and educational psychology, with an explicit reliance on a theory of individual differences defined against a background of supposedly stable, well defined standardized tasks

Theory of Learning: Knowledge enters heads and makes kids ready for adaptive behavior, just in case they are ever engaged in the real world.

Theory of Culture: A collection of traits and skills developed and nurtured by the members of a society. Some individuals may own more culture than others. Those without a full share can be said to be deprived, disadvantaged, or even deviant.

Method: The categories necessary to an adequate description of social realities are available for the asking; the commonsense categories we use to organize each other can be trusted to make our activities clear.

Policy Implications: Intervene, the earlier the better.

Rewards: Much government research and remediation money

Drawbacks: Unfair to the children labeled and disabled. Descriptively inadequate and ecologically (institutionally and historically) invalid. Remediation does not work well.

II. The difference stand that begs the most important questions, 1970–

Diagnosis: Children not learning in school are not broken, although they can appear that way because of constant miscommunication organized by cultural and linguistic differences.

Target Population: Minorities (who still need to be explained, although now against the background of dominant group powers)

Disciplinary Resources: Cross-cultural psychology, sociolinguistics and social interaction analysis. Each has been good at showing how inarticulateness is rarely a linguistic problem, how stupidity is rarely a psychological problem, and how misbehavior is rarely a moral order problem. Each one has helped to socialize competence.

Theory of Learning: Knowledge enters heads and organizes a specific set of skills that can be used in situationally specific ways.

Theory of Culture: A collection of traits and skills developed and nurtured by the members of a society or its subgroups. Although all members can be understood as fully acculturated to some part of the culture, different subgroups might differentially prepare their members for participation in the dominant cultural strand.

Method: The world is hard to see, and the discovery of appropriate categories for description and analysis requires long-term observation.

Policy Implications: Make better use of the know-how available in local communities and take the pressures off the children and the school system to be so homogeneous.

Rewards: The celebration of cultural differences, moderate research money

Drawbacks: Dominant groups do not give up their powers easily. Minorities resent being explained by outsiders. Results are minor.

III. The political stand that is gradually emerging, 1975–

Diagnosis: Children not learning in school are not so much broken or different as they are made to appear that way. Competition is endemic to our society, and the search for inherent intelligence organizes the school day and its children around the issue of successful and unsuccessful competence displays. School failure is a cultural fabrication and is constantly looked for, noticed, hidden, studied and remediated.

Target Population: Labelers and labeled alike—all of us

Disciplinary Resources: Ethnography and critical theory. Movements to a psychology of situated learning, a linguistics of contextual interpretations, and a sociology of events and sequences in which persons become moments and social realities are collusional.

Theory of Learning: Learning is not an individual possession, but a change in the relations between persons and their situation in a way that allows for the accomplishment of new activities. The focus of school management and research must be on the conditions of the system that make learning possible, and not on specific learners.

Theory of Culture: A collection of practices for idealizing certain traits and skills as goals of individual development and status and for recognizing and making institutionally consequential any occasion in which such traits and skills might be missing.

Method: The categories necessary for an adequate description of the organization of social life are fundamentally well hidden. The only way to learn about the world is to try to change it.

Policy Implications: Stop explaining school failure and confront the social conditions that organize apparent learning differentials.

Rewards: Moral indignation and, with great effort, a sense of direction

Drawbacks: People will resist you with all their strength.

These descriptions circumscribe the clarity and confusions in *Achieving*:

- The *diagnosis* seems confused. Mostly, I tried to understand the children as Politically set up and abused by the system; in other passages, I describe the children as only Different; and in still other passages, particularly where I "wetwire" the differences into a biological account of their attention patterns, I wander into a Deprivationist perspective.[6]

- For a *target group*, I used the Difference stand: both we and they were necessary to an analysis. When I looked at how different groups define their differences, I engaged the more interesting Political perspective.

- For *disciplinary resources*, I relied heavily on cognitive versions of all the social sciences. Sometimes, this had me in the Deprivationist camp, where tasks are tasks, skills are skills, and task-skill combinations are a good way to describe individual capabilities. More often I was trying to get beyond this to an account of how all the individuals described were smart in their Different contexts, but I had little idea of how to do this.

- For a *theory of learning*, I was limited to an understanding of culture as an environment and the individual as a recipient who could absorb more or less of what they were offered. With such a theory of learning, it is hard to imagine a theory of schooling that would not be Deprivationist.

- For a *theory of culture*, I relied on two mistakes that support both the Difference and Deprivationist stands: on the one hand, culture was the surround for individual behavior; on the other hand, culture, once internalized, was a personal characteristic of the individual. A more Political formulation would deliver an account of the many people involved in putting together settings where specific behavioral patterns can be recognized, interpreted, reused, repressed, confronted, and transformed (for a theory of culture complete with a theory of agency, see Varenne and McDermott 1997). In the years between *Achieving* and the Political stand, I mostly avoided the use of the term culture.

- Almost invariably, the biggest barrier to a progressive theory of anything social is *methodology*. *Achieving* offers no relief from this generalization, for it offers no systematic means for developing categories to make the world visible in new ways. Without a sustained method for making the world strange to the observer—or better, without a sustained method for showing the world as stacked against those without access to power—little progress can be made in the analysis of outcomes as highly predictable and institutionally overdetermined as minority school failure. In the years following, for methodological intrigue, I tried exhaustively detailed analyses of behavior (a year of analysis for a minute of behavior), living in other cultures, and trying to change the one in which I live. They all help. There are no guarantees.
- For policy *implications*, *rewards*, and *drawbacks*, *Achieving* is completely in the Difference camp.

A New Conclusion:
Beyond the Explanation of School Failure[7]

There is a preoccupation among "us." Because "we" claim to offer good education to many minority people who seem to reject it, we are plagued with the question of "What's it with 'them' anyway?" or "What's 'their' situation that school goes so badly?" *Their* situation! Should we really try to explain "their" situation as if it were separate from "our" situation? Do we have warrant to talk about "their situation" and "our situation?"

There are more productive questions, for example: How do we in the United States keep making minority groups so visible? Why is it part of the situation of every minority group that it has had to be explained? If minority persons from the bottom of the socioeconomic scale are daily led to discomfort, why do they have to put up as well with people explaining their situation? Perhaps there is something better to do with social science. We must be wary of powers of articulation and explanation that can keep us so systematically dumb about our own behavior and its consequences.

Breakthrough comes when we realize that "their" situation is "ours" as well. Those who are successful in school make possible—and are made possible by—those who fail. This being so, what would an ethnography of minority school failure be, but an account of everyone? Would it have to account for anything more than the self-congratulatory explanations of the successful and the role of other people's apparent failures in the maintenance of the successful and their explanations?

And what would a policy for educational change look like, other than a call for a realignment of all groups in relation to each other and to the marketplace?

The fatal flaw in U.S. schooling will not be found in supposed reasons for individual persons or groups failing. Failure is waiting every morning in every classroom in the United States. Before children or their teachers arrive, failure is there. Somebody is going to fail. It is a cultural rule. As citizens, as teachers, even as reformers, we have been fooled into thinking it is a law of nature, that there is only so much success and so much failure to go around. If we take seriously that failure is an institutional fabrication, a mockup for scapegoating, a mystification, a culturally mandated foolishness that keeps us in our respective places, what would an explanation of failure be? And why would we bother to explain failure when we could be confronting it? By making believe failure is something kids do, as different from something done to them, and then by explaining their failure in terms of other things they do, we likely contribute to the maintenance of school failure.

The fact that school failure is an institutionalized event means that it will be staged, and then noticed, documented, and worried about, without regard for the more obvious intentions, desires, and actions of any participants. What would have to happen for us to stage a schooling event that ruled out failure *a priori*? There are such schools in the United States, but they are often small, experimental, and in desperate need of an alternative credentialing system. As a culturally well-defined part of the U.S. school scene, failure does not need explanation, it needs confrontation. Analytically, it is available only as a background expectation until we do battle with it; explaining it will only keep it at a distance, making us its slaves.

The ethnographer's work is better focused on how we in the United States have become so preoccupied with failure and its ascription to particular (kinds of) children. Grade-school failure in the United States is a fragile flower, no less fragile than school success, and both are perfectly normal ways of growing up. School success and failure rely on little more than an institutionalized willingness to allow small and generally uninteresting differences in test-defined learning to become unduly factual. It is in this sense that every failure belongs to us all. Until we focus on how we all achieve school failure, the ethnography of school failure will remain a failure in its own right.

Doing ethnography inside one's own culture commits a person to the study of phenomena that, upon analysis, seem to disappear. In *Achieving*, I tried to explain that a phenomenon is not what it appeared to be. The sentiments that brought me to that problem remain, but the problem has changed. In the ethnography of schooling, we must resist accepting our culture's own definition of its problem. To do this, we must work against our culture in order to study it, and every study must be directed by a vision of change and renewal. Ethnography is radical activity and, as such, difficult to achieve—but it beats achieving school failure.

Notes

[1] The transformation in social theory from a dependence on "who did what" questions to an inquiry into "when and how" has been most relentlessly called for in ethnomethodology. Harold Garfinkel's first publication (1946), a little known and surprisingly well written short story analyzing a single event, recorded a racial confrontation between a bus driver and an African American couple having to ride in the back of a bus. Only a few years later, he was distinguishing Talcott Parsons and Alfred Schutz in terms of their ability to account for the temporal organization of single events lived out by real people (Garfinkel 1953). A similar emphasis was developed in cognitive anthropology of the type offered by Charles Frake (1980; see also his recent papers on when is time and space? (1994, 1996a,b)). Others have followed their lead to address the issues of this paper, for example: when is an ethnic group? (Moerman 1968); when is a context? (Erickson and Shultz, 1977; McDermott, Gospodinoff and Aron 1978); when is a disability? (McDermott 1993; McDermott and Varenne 1995; Mehan 1993; Mehan, et. al, 1986).

[2] The assumptions from which I was trying to escape are still embraced at the heart of most educational anthropology. John Ogbu (1990), for example, consciously assumes what I then unconsciously assumed and now find embarrassing. He starts out with my old question and, like me twenty-five years ago, he tries to answer it: "Why do some minority groups continue to experience difficulty in acquiring literacy?" And what is literacy, but the "ability to read, write, and compute in the form taught and expected in formal education?" In other words, literacy is "synonymous with academic performance" (1990:520). This is accepting too much from mainstream categories. Literacy is much more than "academic performance," and, if he took into account the many kinds of literacy people use when not in schools—and sometimes precisely *because* they have been rejected from schools—he would have no "difficulty in acquiring literacy" phenomenon to explain (for one among thousands of examples, see Gundaker 1997). The relentlessness with which people in a culture create standardized formulations of problems that others can then explain in ways that can make things worse must be understood and confronted (Smith 1986, 1993).

[3] For an early paper on the learning accomplished in between formally organized classroom events, see Griffin (1977); for a current account showing high school students learning physics while in the course of doing social life with each other, see Goldman (1996).

[4] All rumors that I called George Spindler in the middle of the night from Japan to tell him that I had discovered culture might just as well be true.

[5] The charts are updated and expanded from McDermott and Goldman (1983).

[6] The biology seems to me now as foolish as everyone advised me twenty-five years ago. There was a good instinct behind it. In answer to the question, "what is organized in a social organization?", one good answer is "behavior." In the early 1970s, this was not a dominant position, but I was using it as a nascent claim for a theory of agency. There were people alive in every social organization, and I wanted to know what a minute of it looked like; I wanted to know how people behaved the

social order. For that purpose, I was reading biology, neuropsychology in particular, and, for any theory of how the social world worked, I wanted to know if a body, any body, could act in a way consistent with its claims. Most social science continues to theorize about people without bodies. Staying close to biology now looks like a weak idea, but staying close to the body as a testing ground for social theory still seems essential.

[7]Much of this final section is heavily adapted from McDermott (1987).

References

Apple, M., 1982. *Education and Power*. Boston: Routledge and Kegan Paul.

Barth, F., ed., 1969. *Ethnic Groups and Boundaries*. Boston: Little, Brown.

Berg, I., 1969. *Education and Jobs: The Great Training Robbery*. Boston: Beacon Press.

Bond, G., 1980. Social Economic Status and Educational Achievement. *Anthropology and Education Quarterly* 12:227–57.

Bourdieu, P., and J. Passeron, 1977. *Reproduction*. Beverly Hills: Sage.

Bowles, S., and H. Gintis, 1975. *Schooling in Capitalist America*. New York: Basic.

Burton, L. 1995. Intergenerational Family Structure and the Provision of Care in African American Families with Teenage Childbearers. In *Intergenerational Issues in Aging*, K. W. Schaie, V. Bengston, and L. Burton, eds., pp. 79–96. New York: Springer.

Cole, M., 1996. *Cultural Psychology*. Harvard University Press.

Cole, M. , L. Hood, and R. McDermott, 1978. *Ecological Niche-Picking: Ecological Invalidity as An Axiom of Experimental Cognitive Psychology*. Working Paper no. 14. The Rockefeller University.

Deutsch, M., 1967. *The Disadvantaged Child*. New York: Basic.

Dewey, J., 1899. *School and Society*. Chicago: University of Chicago Press.

Erickson, F., 1973. *Talking to the Man*. Paper presented at the American Educational Research Association Meetings, New Orleans.

_____, 1997. Culture in Society and in Educational Practices. In *Multicultural Education, 3d ed.*, J. Banks and C. Banks, eds., pp. 32–60. Boston: Allyn and Bacon.

Erickson, F., and J. Shultz, 1977 When is a context? *Quarterly Newsletter of Institute of Comparative Child Development* 1(2): 5–10.

_____, 1982. *Counselor as Gatekeeper*. New York: Academic Press.

Frake, C. O., 1980. *Language and Cultural Description*. Stanford: Stanford University Press.

_____, 1994. Dials: A Study in the Physical Representation of Cognitive Systems. In *The Ancient Mind*, C. Renfrew and E. Zubrow, eds., pp. 119–32. Cambridge: Cambridge University Press.

_____. 1996a. A Church Too Far Near a Bridge Oddly Placed: The Cultural Construction of the Norfolk Countryside. In *Redefining Nature*, R. Ellen and K. Fukui, eds., pp. 89–115. Oxford: Berg.

_____, 1996b. Pleasant Places, Past Times, and Sheltered Identity in Rural East Anglia. In *Senses of Place*, S. Feld and K. Basso, eds., pp. 229–57. Santa Fe: School of American Research Press.

Frake, C. O. 1997. Abu Sayyaf: Displays of Violence and the Proliferation of Contested Identities among Philippine Muslims. *American Anthropologist*, in press.

Garfinkel, H. 1946. Color Trouble. In *Primer for White Folks*, B. Moon, ed., pp. 269–86. Garden City: Doubleday, Doran.

_____, 1953. *A Comparison of Decisions Made on Four Pretheoretical Problems by Talcott Parsons and Alferd Schuetz*. Unpublished ms., distributed in 1962.

_____, 1967. *Studies in Ethnomethodology*. Englewood Cliffs: Prentice-Hall.

Gilmore, P., 1985. Silence and Sulking: Emotional Displays in the Classroom. In *Perspectives on Science*, D. Tannen and M. Saville-Troike, eds., pp. 139–62. Norwood: Ablex.

Gilmore, P., D. Smith, and A. L. Kairaiuak, 1997. Resisting Diversity: An Alaskan Case of Institutional Struggle. In *Off-White*, M. Fine, et. al, eds., pp. 90–99. New York: Routledge.

Giroux, H., 1983. *Theory and Resistance in Education*. New York: Bergin and Garvey.

Goldman, S. V., 1996. Mediating Micro Worlds. In *CSCL*, T. Koschmann, ed., pp. 45–81. Mahwah: Lawrence Erlbaum Associates.

Goldman, S. V., S. Chaiklin, and R. McDermott, 1994. Crossing Borders Electronically. In *Pathways to Cultural Awareness*, G. Spindler and L. Spindler, eds., pp. 247–84. Thousand Oaks, CA: Corwin Press.

Griffin, P., 1977. How and When Does Reading Occur in the Classroom? *Theory into Practice* 16:376–83.

Gundaker, G., In press. *Diaspora of Signs/Signs of Diaspora*. London: Oxford University Press.

Henry, J., 1963. *Culture against Man*. New York: Vintage.

_____, 1974. *Sham, Vulnerability, and Other Forms of Self-Destruction*. New York: Vintage.

Hill, C. A., and K. Parry, eds., 1994. *From Testing to Assessment*. London: Longman.

Hutchins, E., 1995. *Cognition in the Wild*. New York: Cambridge University Press.

Labov, W., 1972. *Language in the Innercity*. Philadelphia: University of Pennsylvania Press.

Lave, J. C., 1988. *Cognition in Practice*. New York: Cambridge University Press.

Lave, J. C., , and É. Wenger, 1991. *Situated Learning: Legitimate Peripheral Participation*. New York: Cambridge University Press.

Levi-Strauss, C., [1949] 1969. *Elementary Structures of Kinship*. Boston: Beacon Press.

Lewin, K., 1951. *Dynamic Theories of Personality*. New York: McGraw-Hill.

McDermott, R. P., 1974. Achieving School Failure. In *Education and Cultural Process*, G. D. Spindler, ed., pp. 82–118. New York: Holt, Rinehart and Winston.

_____, 1987. Explaining Minority School Failure, Again. *Anthropology and Education Quarterly* 18:361–64.

McDermott, R. P., 1993. The Acquisition of a Child by a Learning Disability. In *Understanding Practice*, S. Chaiklin and J. Lave, eds., pp. 269–305. New York: Cambridge University Press.

McDermott, R. P., and S. V. Goldman, 1983. Teaching in Multicultural Settings. In *Multicultural Education*, L.V.D. Berg-Eldering, F. de Rijcke, and L. Zuck, eds., pp. 145–63. Dordrecht: Foris Publications.

McDermott, R. P., and K. Gospodinoff, 1979. Social Relations as Contexts for Ethnic Borders and School Failure. In *Nonverbal Behavior*, A. Wolfgang, ed., pp. 75–97. Hillsdale, NJ: Academic Press.

McDermott, R. P., K. Gospodinoff, and J. Aron, 1978. Criteria for an Ethnographically Adequate Description of Activities and their Contexts. *Semiotica* 24:245–76.

McDermott, R. P., and L. Hood, 1982. Institutionalized Psychology and the Ethnography of Schooling. In *Children In and Out of School*, P. Gilmore and A. Glatthorn, eds., pp. 232–49. Center for Applied Linguistics.

McDermott, R. P., and H. Varenne, 1995. Culture as Disability. *Anthropology and Education Quarterly* 26:324–48.

Mead, G. H., 1964. *Selected Writings*, A. Reck, ed. Indianapolis: Bobbs-Merrill.

Mehan, H., 1979. *Learning Lessons*. Harvard University Press.

_____, 1993. Beneath the Skin and Behind the Eyes. In *Understanding Practice*, S. Chaiklin and J. Lave, eds., pp. 241–68. New York: Cambridge University Press.

_____, 1996a. *Contextual Factors Surrounding Hispanic Dropouts*. Paper prepared for the Hispanic Dropout Project. University of California, San Diego.

_____, 1996b. *The Study of Social Interaction in Educational Settings*. Paper delivered to the 95th Annual Meeting of the American Anthropological Association, San Francisco.

Mehan, H., A. Hertweck, and L. Meihls, 1986. *Handicapping the Handicapped*. Stanford: Stanford University Press.

Mehan, H., I. Villanueva, L. Hubbard, and A. Lintz, 1996. *Constructing School Success*. New York: Cambridge University Press.

Moerman, M., [1968] 1974. Accomplishing Ethnicity. In *Ethnomethodology*. R. Turner, ed., pp. 54–68. Baltimore: Penguin.

Newman, D., P. Griffin, and M. Cole, 1989. *The Construction Zone*. New York: Cambridge University Press.

Ogbu, J., 1990. Cultural Mode, Identity, and Literacy. In *Cultural Psychology*, J. Stigler, R. Shweder, G. Herdt, eds., pp. 520–41. New York: Cambridge University Press.

Rohlen, T., 1978. Violence at Yoka High School. *Asian Survey*: 682–99.

_____. 1983. *Japan's High Schools*. Berkeley: University of California Press.

_____, 1992. Learning. In *The Political Economy of Japan. vol. 3. Social and Cultural Dynamics*, S. Kumon and H. Rosovsky, eds., pp. 321–63. Stanford: Stanford University Press.

Scott, J., 1984. *Weapons of the Weak*. New Haven: Yale University Press.

Smith, D. M., 1986. The Anthropology of Literacy. In *Acquisition of Literacy: Ethnographic Approaches*, B. Schieffelin and P. Gilmore, eds., pp. 261–75. Norwood: Ablex Publishers.

_____, 1993. Anthropology of Education and Educational Research. *Anthropology and Education Quarterly* 23:185–98.

Spindler, G. D., 1959. *The Transmission of American Culture*. Cambridge: Harvard University Press.

_____, 1974. Beth Anne—A Case Study of Culturally Defined Adjustment and Teacher Perceptions. In *Education and Cultural Process*, G. Spindler. ed., pp. 230–44. New York: Holt, Rinehart and Winston.

_____, 1982. Roger Harker and Schoenhausen. From Familiar to Strange and Back Again. In *Doing the Ethnography of Schooling*, G. Spindler, ed., pp. 20–47. New York: Holt, Rinehart, and Winston.

Spindler, G. D., ed., 1974. *Education and Cultural Process*. New York: Holt, Rinehart, and Winston.

Spindler, G. D., and L. Spindler, 1989. There Are No Dropouts among the Arunta and Hutterites. In *What Do Anthropologists Know about Dropouts?*, H. Trueba and G. and L. Spindler, eds., pp. 7–16. Philadelphia: Falmer Press.

Stack, C., 1974. *All Our Kin*. New York: Harper and Row.

Suchman, L., 1987. *Plans and Situated Activity*. New York: Cambridge University Press.

Suttles, G., 1974. *The Social Construction of Communities*. Chicago: University of Chicago Press.

Varenne, H., 1977. *Americans Together*. New York: Teachers College Press.

_____, 1983. *American School Language*. New York: Irvington Press.

_____,1992. *Ambiguous Harmony*. Norwood: Ablex.

Varenne, H., and R. McDermott, in press. *Successful Failure*. Boulder: Westview Press.

Vygotsky, L. S., 1987. *The Collected Works of L. S. Vygotsky, vol. 1: Problems in General Psychology: Thinking and Speech and Lectures on Psychology*, R. W. Rieber and A. S. Carton, eds., translated by N. Minick. New York: Plenum Press (Orig., 1934).

Wexler, P., 1982. Structure, Text, and Subject. In *Cultural and Economic Reproduction in Education*, M. Apple, ed., pp. 275–303. New York: Routledge.

Willis, P., 1977. *Learning to Labor*. New York: Columbia University.

Acknowledgment

Bud Mehan and Fred Erickson, close partners in the developments reported in this paper, both offered encouraging comments.

8

Racing in Place
Middle Class Work in Success/Failure

Hervé Varenne
Teachers College, Columbia University
Shelley Goldman
Institute for Research on Learning
Raymond P. McDermott
Stanford University

One of the most powerful and controversial of American meta-phors characterizes education as a race on a level field. As the metaphor is extended in discourse, much effort is spent discussing whether the field is level or how it might be made level. As the metaphor is extended in action, it produces programs designed to improve the chances of the children beginning school "behind." It also leads to a wide range of com-petitive activities, some of which are fun—and some of which have fate-ful consequences.

Many educators as well as parents and politicians assert that edu-cation should *not* be a race. In discussions reaffirming fundamental truths, the people of the United States tell each other that education is about individuals and that educational practice is legitimate only to the extent it fosters individual development. In sacred documents, educa-tion is always about growing, finding one's own way, developing one's own potential. Education is a metaphorical journey, a pilgrim's progress. This discourse of individual growth and development is everywhere evident in the everyday political life of schools as institu-tions. From Horace Mann to John Dewey, prophets have passionately argued that it is proper to develop special institutions to nurture chil-dren as they journey and grow into contributing citizens in a liberal democracy. By the same logic, it is proper to evaluate whether schools are achieving their goals, to investigate why certain schools appear to do better than others, and to help and reform the less successful ones.[1]

Source: Written especially for *Education and Cultural Process*, 3rd Edition.

All this makes perfect sense to citizens interested in education. The sticking point is that the success of a school may only be evaluated in terms of the success of the individual children who journey through the school. The metaphorical journey that started with the child as a seedling takes a detour through a thicket of institutions filled with people, technologies, and conflicting interests. The result is the constant evaluation of schools by the relative ordering of children along a continuum of success and failure.[2]

In this chapter, we focus on the range of test-taking and decision-making situations in which students and teachers engage at Allwin Junior High School. Allwin is part of the commonsensically "excellent" school system of Hamden Heights, a suburban town which can be fairly (and again commonsensically) described as "an upper middle-class community of successful businesspeople and professionals."[3] What do the children of the advantaged do in their schools? They take tests and engage in many competitions, they fail at many of them—and they continue to be identified as successful students. Social science has reported for many years that success for these children is highly probable (although parents and teachers continue to worry). In this process, the participants make a world not only for themselves but for those across the Hudson in New York City who will be seen as never having matched the accomplishments of their peers in Hamden Heights.[4]

When we say that the children of Hamden Heights fail many tests and are still known as "successful," we are not being ironic or merely controversial. We are emphasizing that the processes shaping the educational world in which all Americans live are fundamentally cultural, not psychological. Analytically, success in the United States must be approached as (1) a matter of identification in (2) a complex social scene where (3) agents work hard with what they find around them. Success—or, better, "success/failure"—is a structured cultural category within a system of identification. A category, however, cannot activate itself. Its continued relevance to the life of a population depends on the activity of many people doing particular things at particular times. Success/failure does not simply happen. It is an achievement, a *collective* achievement with major consequences, both for those deemed successful and for the rest. Two major points should be recognized. First, the categories "success" and "failure" are historical constructions (rather than a reflection of attributes of a person). Second, identification is not simply a process of recognizing individual attributes. Taking into account constructed categories and the officials enforcing them is not enough. One must deal with the activities of all persons involved—the officials, parents and children (those identified as successful as well as those identified as failures). One must also deal with the consequences of these activities (remembering always the categories and officials). Everyone must work within the same parameters.

Most importantly, everyone's work[5] impacts everyone else's. The children of the upper-middle classes are not simply fated to occupy the place their parents occupied. They must "work" at it, in both the commonsensical and ethnomethodological sense of the verb. It is not simply that their "hard work" gets properly rewarded but rather that their interactional work within the overall categorical system makes someone else's failure at the same time as it makes their own success. For a child to be "the best," others must be "second best," "the rest," or beyond consideration.

In interactional studies and ethnomethodology, "work" is used to focus attention on social life as a continual process. A greeting between two friends is work, telling a joke is work, and so of course is managing a child's career in school. "Work" can also point to the commonsense understanding that we might find in a phrase like "working" (rather than "leisure") class. The people of Hamden Heights, adults and children, get up in the morning, and then they go to work. Work is not play—even if the people enjoy the work and are highly rewarded for it. It may be tiring or painful but, always, there is work to be done—on the job, at home, in school, at play.

Social reproduction does not happen automatically, and it does not happen through enculturation or socialization. Rather, it happens through the continued work that the "favorites" (and all their social supports) in the race perform as they monitor the "laggards" in the distance. Success/failure is a continued achievement with no fixed ending. From schoolroom to boardroom, the identification of success/failure is always to be made: former valedictorians, now CEOs of large firms, remain forever hanging on the next meeting of their evaluators.

The Performance of Success in Everyday Life

Successful children in good schools have always been the reference point in studies of failure, whether personal or institutional. Success is the ground against which failure stands out as "the problem." In the process, success hides itself, and the mutual dependency of success and failure becomes difficult to discuss. Even in the anthropology of education (for example in the powerful works of Oscar Lewis, William Labov, Shirley Brice Heath, John Ogbu, and many others), the emphasis has been on finding the best *explanations* of failure. Neglected have been investigations into the *constitution* of failure as an object of practical social concern (McDermott, chapter 7). In the search for explanations, bad schools and failing children are separated and singled out as if evaluation was absolute rather than relative. Children who consistently fail when compared with others are analytically isolated, as if their fates were not systematically related to the children consistently identified as having succeeded.

There is another possibility: schools and all their children are part of one differentiated system, one society, the product of a complex cultural construction. Success and failure proceed from the same principles; they are facets of the same historical facts. All individuals in the United States struggle with the same aspects of culture as they race each other across educational fields. From the first day at school to graduation years later, one can follow each child's career as a "smart" kid, a "learning disabled" kid, an "underachiever," a "behavior problem," or any number of labels. In other words, the system of identifications is in place before any individual child enters school. Year in and year out, new children are acquired by this system. They, in turn, can accept or resist but have no choice about the system itself.

In this chapter we will follow kids of prosperous parents, using the same cultural tools given to all children. We see them taking tests; we hear teachers talking about the kids and their tests. We see the students competing, struggling with the consequences of taking competition seriously, and resisting the consequences. We do not do this to identify characteristics that might explain the long-term success of either the students or teachers. Rather, our concern is with the mutualities that exist between the children of the suburbs and the children of the inner city. It is easy to see how the people of Hamden Heights construct a pleasant world at a suburban distance from New York City. It is less easy to see, but always important to remember, that the same people also construct, however much not on purpose, another much less pleasant world for the children of inner-city Manhattan and Brooklyn.

William Labov (1972) showed how "successful" children could be on neighborhood streets—despite attending schools where they were known as "failing." Many others have also traced inconsequential success in the midst of generalized failure. In Allwin, we trace the reverse operation: inconsequential failure in the midst of generalized success. One teacher, for example, having decided that "the majority of the kids in this class shouldn't have failed" on a test she had given, gave them another one on the same material. As per the worst nightmare of the literature on self-fulfilling prophecies, because they "should" not fail, they *could* not fail.[6] Meanwhile, across the river in Manhattan, children in the worst schools were taking classroom tests, and some of them were doing well. But their success would inevitably be erased in a later comparison with Allwin students. At Allwin, the teacher looked for a "reason" for the failure (the test was given the day before a three-day camping trip), and then she planned a new review period and a second test. While the camping scenario was rare, it was not uncommon for a teacher to dismiss a student's failure on a particular test as an insignif-icant indicator of the student's eventual success. The failed test would not be averaged, or the student would be given make-up work, etc. A student who was caught cheating on an exam was given a warning with the understanding that "now she will understand that I am watching her." Given an overall identification of "success," any single instance of failure was reconstructed as an aberration—in the same manner as a single instance of success at an inner-city school can be ignored or treated as an aberration within an overall identification of "failure."

Most of the tests the children of Allwin were continually taking were not used to do what the testing technologies are supposedly designed to do—that is, to sort children ever so painstakingly in the most objective and fair ways. The sorting that did take place proceeded through less formal mechanisms, such as by teacher recommendation and committee reviews. If tests are not directly used for sorting at All-win, what are they used for? How do they fit within the overall life of the school and the school's place relative to all U.S. schools?

The Competitions of Everyday Life
in Allwin Junior High

The first thing to realize is the ubiquity of tests, measurements, and miscellaneous competitions in the everyday life of the students and teachers of Allwin. There may not have been a day when the students were not taking a test, preparing for a forthcoming test, or worrying about the results of an earlier one. On every one of these days, the par-ents participated in one way or another. They helped the children pre-pare. They coached and supported them and worried about the outcomes (even though their confidence in their own identifications as "successful" professionals, managers, entrepreneurs, etc., was assured—at least for the moment). Although parents had moved to Hamden Heights to a large extent because of the reputation of its schools in producing collegebound students, they did not treat success as a state of being with fixed results. Every child's trajectory was con-tinually put on the line in new competitions and tests of ever increasing difficulty.[7]

Everyone paid attention to the tests, but not for the obvious rea-son. Failure was rarely consequential. Most children, on most days, failed most tests in the sense that they did not get top rankings. More consequential was not taking tests or being caught not performing on effort indicators (through cheating, for example, or not preparing). A test performed wrongly (which is different from a failure on a test) might lead to escalating interventions, from the obligation to take the test again, detention, or referral to the school psychologist. It might make sense to think of tests and competitions as a form of what Geertz called "deep play" in his interpretation of the Balinese cockfight:

> "Poetry makes nothing happen," Auden says in his elegy of Yeats, "it survives in the valley of its saying . . . a way of happening, a mouth." The cockfight too, in this colloquial sense, makes nothing happen. Men go on allegorically humiliating one another and being allegorically humiliated by one another, day after day, glorying quietly in the experience if they have triumphed, crushed only slightly more openly by it if they have not. *But no one's status really changes.* You cannot ascend the status ladder by winning cockfights; you cannot, as an individual, really ascend it at all . . . All you can do is enjoy and savor, or suffer and withstand, the concocted sensation of drastic and momentary movements along an aesthetic semblance of that ladder, a kind of behind-the-mirror status jump which has the look of mobility without its actuality. (1973:443)

The people of Allwin would likely find this way of talking about their life rather too effete. In their vocabulary, the competitions of everyday life are "fun" or "motivating." Competition transforms the boring into the interesting. Like spices on bland food, they make school routine palatable.

There are three kinds of tests at Allwin: classroom-level tests, school- or grade-level competitions, and standardized tests. This delineation appears usual for upper-middle class, suburban public schools (Page, 1991). The first two are routine while the last is strongly marked as special and out of the ordinary.

Classroom Tests and Competitions

Classroom tests are designed by individual teachers as part of their lesson plans. They take the form of question-answer sequences, games, quizzes, and pen-and-pencil exams. Quizzes and tests punctuate the beginning and ending of work on most units of academic study. All students are required to participate in class tests and quizzes. No one volunteers. Students are usually competing against their own records or the records of their classmates, and the resulting evaluations usually, but not necessarily, contribute to the student's report card grade. Classroom testing is a frequent activity in almost all classes. A classroom test grade is often averaged in with other test grades. It is not unusual for a student to have two or more classroom tests in a day, especially toward the end of a marking period. When teachers do change their opinion about the relative position of a student, an altogether rare occurrence, they rarely cite a particular test score. They refer rather to patterns in grades over long periods.

Classroom games are usually presented as alternate means of drilling content. They are explained by teachers and students alike as having to do with "learning" (rather than "testing"). As such, they are less constrained by ideological strictures and may take other forms than the classical competitions between individuals. It is permissible in this context to make groups within a class, set them up to work cooperatively as a team, and then pit them against each other. Winners and losers temporarily emerge, possibly confirming a teacher's underlying opinion of individual children. The results of such competitions are rarely applied to consequential sorting.

One eighth-grade class periodically played a question-and-answer game called "Screw Thy Neighbor." The official purpose was to review content materials for a later and officially consequential test. The class was split into two teams. Every student prepared several content questions from their readings and notes on a prior humanities unit. The goal of the game was to stump the students on the opposing team by asking them content questions they could not answer. With questions in hand, the students played the game for the entire class period. The teacher moderated and kept score. The students laughed, raised hands, and even begged to ask or answer questions during the game. They played as if the stakes were high: when they answered correctly, they let out sighs of relief, wiped their brows, and shook each other's hands; and when they answered incorrectly, they pouted, cursed under their breath, and stomped their feet on the floor. When the game was over, the students on the winning team cheered, clapped, whistled, and "gave each other five." Students on the losing teams smiled, clapped, booed, and asked the teacher when they could have a rematch. From the name of the game to the over-stylized displays, the message "this is play" was consistently performed (Bateson 1955). "Real" competitions are not officially called "Screw Thy Neighbor." Still, the structure of this game is not an imaginative happenstance but a symbolic evocation of the times when such performances move out of the play frame. "Screw Thy Neighbor," like the Balinese cockfight, does not do anything. Functionally, it is a non-event. It is "just" deep play, and, culturally, it is the stuff of life.

"Screw Thy Neighbor" was least like a consequential test because it was constructed around teams and not individual students. It was more like the team sports central to the symbolic life of U.S. schools, and it is perhaps more like the experience the children will have, if they are lucky, competing in the private bureaucracies that will later employ them (on the former, see Foley 1990; on the latter, see Jackall 1988).

Classroom tests, like standardized tests, like most evaluations of job performance, are structured around individuals confronting questions that will sort those who can from those who cannot. The fundamental principle is that social rewards should only be granted based on the merit of the performer. Most tests do not have to do with learning but with "evaluation." While, as observers, we can see that most tests at Allwin were not radically consequential, they were still constructed by all participants as something "more serious" than games. Tests were less fun than games, and it was proper for some of the students taking tests to display, and probably to experience, various amounts of anxiety. The parents paid attention to the tests and responded with rewards, punishment, or attempts at remediation.

Voluntary Sorting Activities

Besides classroom-level tests, there were also tests and competitions that involved the whole school. This was true of more than sporting events, where the pattern is most elaborately expanded. Interestingly, these competitions were not directly related to the sorting of individual merit. Students were organized into teams and their individuality subsumed by the team.[8] The "Brain Bowl," for example, was a schoolwide contest modeled after a 1960s television show called "The College Bowl" (the label cross-references an academic activity to sports, particularly football, with its end-of-the-season "bowls"). The Brain Bowl consisted of teams of students competing against each other in tournament fashion on general knowledge and trivia questions. Each year, teachers were asked to construct questions. The questions were made into a test given to any student volunteering to participate in the tournament. Students were placed on teams based on their scores on the trivia tests. Next, the play-offs began. Teams were verbally asked questions, and members would try to answer before any members of the opposing team. Points were given for correct answers and deducted for incorrect ones; at the end of a set time period, the team with the most points advanced to the next round. The testing and tournament play took place over several weeks, culminating in a play-off between the final two teams at a special school assembly.

In such a system, many students do not volunteer, and all but the winning team experience a version of failure. This does not bother most people. The Brain Bowl is mostly a spectator event, an enjoyable activity for all. No record is kept of who loses, at what point or by how much. Once the cathartic final assembly is conducted, the sequence can vanish into a vague memory. Winning and losing are both directly inconsequential and tacitly a confirmation of competitive realities.[9] The identity of the winning team held few surprises, as the team with the "top students" generally won. In the process, the emerging organization of the student body as relatively more or less successful was displayed and justified. The success of students in inconsequential competitions demonstrates the "rightness" of the consequential evaluations. If the students who do well on the "real" tests also do well on the "play" tests, then all must be right. This is what Geertz saw in the Balinese cockfight—an occasion to reaffirm the evolving social organization of the local group.

There were also schoolwide events that were not officially organized as competitions. They were presented as pure displays designed to be enjoyed rather than evaluated, for example: an arts festival, fashion shows, woodworking exhibitions, a gallery of student art projects, and a music festival with performances by the band and chorus. Students again participated by choice, but the competitive frame reemerged in student performances. Among the participants, some worried aloud that their display was not "good enough." Many class periods went into the design and construction of the displays. Some class groups even kept their ideas secret from other classes. An award was given to the "best display."

In every competition, students and their families drove the process. Competing was stimulating. The teachers had no problem giving an analysis of the situation couched in the critical language of much social science writing about tests. Like sociologists or anthropologists, they rhetorically distanced themselves from what was happening. Here are a few quotes from a group discussion about competition:

> **In the classroom:** Give them an activity to get them to practice word skills, and they moan and groan at you. You make it into a contest, and suddenly everyone wants to be an expert at defining vocabulary words.

> **In the community:** Did you ever see the way these kids do sports? . . . Competition drives them, so why shouldn't we capitalize on it?

> **In general:** These kids respond real well to competition. They're geared to it . . . They're used to seeing their fathers respond to it at work. . . .

> They've got to learn how to win and lose. They get chances to do both at some point.

Alfred Kroeber and Clyde Kluckhohn (1953:357) made the famous distinction that there are two ways in which culture impacts the lives of human beings—as a model "of" behavior and as a model "for" behavior. The teachers at Allwin invoke both. First, the culture of competition offers a model "of" behavior: it is an observational fact, there to be seen, that students enjoy competition. Second, in the United States, competition offers a model "for" behavior: the students must get used to winning and losing, and it is the responsibility of teachers to ensure that this happens. From our point of view, what is lacking in adult discourse is an awareness of the processes through which the observation "students like competing" was made. How did competition become a model of and for behavior? How has it become a "fact" of life in Allwin? Who was involved historically? Who is involved now?

The Ritual Organization of Sorting: Standardized Times

Educational games can be fun. Routine tests can be viewed as different levels of deep play peculiarly appropriate to demonstrate the validity of the underlying cultural structure. But fun can give way to anxiety when the time comes to take the extra-ordinary tests that stand at the opposite extreme from games like "Screw Thy Neighbor." These tests can be officially used for decisions to sort one student from another or to confirm earlier sorting decisions, even if the eventual outcome is anything but mechanical. These tests are strongly marked performatively. They are not designed by the school or local school boards. They are state, or more often national, tests designed by educational experts from prestigious universities and corporations. They are presented as based on the most up-to-date understanding of testing—from knowledge of a content area to an expertise at test standardization. The local school has no authority to change anything about them. They are "standardized," "on-demand," tests to be treated with proper behavioral respect.

At Allwin, all students take these tests (no choice allowed) several times during their school careers. When they enter the sixth grade, they are given a battery of diagnostic tests for assessing their reading and math levels. Later in the school year, they take nationally normed achievement tests and statewide competency exams, the most formally scheduled and recognized occasions for evaluating student competencies. When the Iowa Test of Basic Skills was administered, the school schedule was changed so that students would not miss more than one period of each subject. Letters were sent to parents during the week prior to the exams to announce the schedule, to state the importance of the tests for determining student placement, and to ask parents to make sure their children ate good breakfasts. Absences were discouraged. The actual test time was handled formally. The students were seated in rows arranged by the teachers; they used paper and pencil supplied by the test company; and they followed instructions read from the testing manuals. Every attempt was made to ensure every student had exactly the same working conditions. Every attempt was made to break any social network and to force the individual to stand alone against the prescribed task. In all these ways, "fairness" was displayed. The field, that day, was as level as educational science could make it; all that mattered was individual talent and preparation.

By this model, the school and its agents abstract themselves from the performance of the children. The fact that the tests are not designed by the school makes the point. The school may be responsible for preparation of the children, but it withdraws at the moment the race is actually run. Like the coach in a sporting event, the school and the parents can only watch from the sidelines, giving last-minute advice and admonitions, before giving the floor to the appointed official arbiters and, through them, to the institutions that design the fields on which the race is to be run.

The Social Organization of Sorting: Meetings in Uncertainty

When the "race" has been run, the official "time" of the child (the score as reported by the testing agency) is entered into permanent record. It becomes an event in the child's history. One cannot escape the reality that has been constructed, but this reality, like any other cultural fact, works in concert with other constructions. The score is consequential, but the consequences are now open to interpretation by, and negotiation among, all involved. As when political results interact with the media that report them, what now becomes important is the "spin" that is given to the "story" that was the actual score. The score does not *prescribe* what the school, parents, or child must do with them. In fact, test makers send various warnings that scores must not be used "mechanically." They are only items to be used in a process that may eventually lead to a transformation in the career of the child.[10]

This process is a complex of conversations among a large number of people: teachers, counselors, administrators, parents, etc. They meet in corridors and lunchrooms, and eventually in formal meeting rooms. This is a ubiquitous, although somewhat hidden, aspect of life in Allwin. People talk in general about their opinions, or they examine in detail the permanent record of the students. They affirm what they have always known about a student, or they make a call for more information. Sometimes they come to a decision that redirects the life of the child. Occasionally, enough time is spent talking that the problem has become moot. Mostly, the talk produces little change and the children stay where they were previously placed.

Still, there is much of this talk, and it is worth focusing on it. Let us look, for example, at a meeting at the end of the school year. Teachers were sorting students entering from elementary school. In principle, they were engaged in something with the potential of making a major difference in the children's lives. They had never met the students, but "the facts"—that is, scores on standardized tests—were before them. The committee was given the task of grouping children into five different classes without giving the impression the classes were tracked. If this had been the goal, then the solution would seem to be simple: group by using a random table. This did not happen. The teachers' first act was to sort the students according to the five traditional ability groups (gifted, high, average, low-average, remedial). The rationale for this sorting was to ensure that the students from each group would be distributed proportionally. The ability sorting was not itself performed mechanically: some students with the same grades and tests scores were placed in different ability groups. Stories pieced together from their "whole" file were different enough to justify differential placement.[11] Once the ability groupings had been made, the randomization of the students into the five classes could proceed.

It would be easy to criticize the teachers for making a mockery of the requirements for fairness in assigning classroom groupings without tracking. But this was not easy for them. They had had long experiences with ability grouping, and they had lived through many difficult moments with "errors." They reminded each other that moving a student from a lower to a higher group is never a problem, but moving a student down is never simple and involves much work by teachers and parents. The teachers argued that the solution was a soon-to-be-tried curriculum design that would eliminate the need for sorting. We quote the conversation at length, for it illustrates the paradox in which the teachers were caught: the more information they had about the students, the more accurate their decisions, the more legitimate "leveling" (as they called it) there could be. And yet, at the very moment when things would appear settled, complaints were made about the danger of formal grouping.

S: We have to think about how to do the leveling. For the first time they've provided me with each student's name, I.Q. score, local percentile ranks on the I.T.B.S., third marking period grades and teacher comments . . . We want our teachers to use this information to set up the groups.

R: I want to throw it up for suggestions. I was thinking of taking two sixth-grade blocks and have them meet at the same time . . . then we could basically come up with two heterogeneously grouped blocks.

T: What do you mean?

R: I'm asking how we should group the kids, how you think it should be done.

S: We have to think about how to do the leveling. For the first time we actually got good recommendations and information from the teachers so we should try to do it carefully.

W: I thought the whole idea of the block was going to be that we would take care of students' needs without singling them out . . . We should make a commitment to either leveling or total integration . . . just, at least for the sixth grade.

S: Well, then, how would we use Fred [the reading and exceptional children's specialist]?

R: Look, we've been living with leveling. I like what Carol is saying . . . if we don't level on sixth, what are we saying, that we'll level on seventh?

S: I think Joyce would like to eliminate all remedial seventh graders.

[*all laugh*]

J: Low-average classes to me are a waste.

[*They continue discussing how they could arrange ability levels at each grade level and decide they could adjust the organization by adjusting schedules.*]

W: I think we should have no grouping in a formal way . . . and for the seventh and eighth grade we should eliminate all groupings except for the accelerated kids . . .

R: O.K. for next year, and then later if we need a remedial group, we can make one.

B: Then there's no stigma. Personally, I'd like to see us get into no grouping.

S: Will the groups be small enough to handle remedial kids next year?

W: Twenty or under certainly seems workable to me.

B: Well, if we group heterogeneously, the level of ability won't be an issue any more in replying with parents' requests for teacher change.

J: Well, how will the parents react . . . you know they like status.

R: They should like it. The sixth grade becomes transitional and a filtering-down process so we can make true levels . . . and it will certainly take away from the demotion problems with the enrichment kids.

R, the reading teacher and testing coordinator, has summarized the working compromise that is often called on when the problems of tracking or not tracking bump into each other. The school will not completely rank the sixth grade; instead it will play a waiting game and establish more legitimate ranks in the seventh grade.[12]

Much about American education can be found in this discussion. The teachers are dissatisfied with ranking. Lack of knowledge about individual children was momentarily remedied. Although it would have been easy to see the added information as an aid to legitimate ranking, the new information is presented as making it less necessary to rank. There is the problem of parents who may protest "because they like status." In addition, since it is probable that integration would be instituted in the seventh grade, why postpone it? There is also the unanswered question about Fred, the expert on special children. If everybody is treated the same, then he and his expertise in making legitimate distinctions among children and all the institutions behind him become unnecessary. The whole point of the exercise is "to take care of students' needs," but the problem is in taking care of individual students "without singling them out."

This is the major problem American educators have never solved: how is it possible to treat all children the same while treating them all differently? Separation (because children are different) is not compatible with equality. But equality (because all must be treated alike) does not allow proper respect for difference. This is more than a logical or philosophical problem. It is an experiential problem for any good teacher, sensitive student, or concerned parent. When children do not do as well as expected, as often happens, people worry. This presents opportunities for any callous teacher, scheming student, or aggressive parent. If a child "fails" on an objective test, one may be able to call a friend of a friend and explain the "special" conditions that led to the failure and to offer arguments legitimizing an exceptional administrative decision.

Allwin Junior High, like all U.S. schools, had several formal settings for the discussion of special treatment. "Team meetings" were called irregularly (but quite often) when teachers (separately at first, then together in a corridor or teachers' lounge) came to the conclusion that "there was a problem" with a student. A meeting was then formally scheduled as an occasion for "talking about the student" in the light of the facts. Let us look at how this was done in the case of "Brian Jones":

> **S:** He's absent so much, how can you pass him? He read an eighth grade novel and got a 48 on the test . . . and he's content with a D.
>
> **B:** His mother doesn't make him make up the work he misses.
>
> **P:** Do you think it would help to hold him back?
>
> **C:** Can we recommend retention?
>
> **P:** I don't know.
>
> **J:** He's a sweet child; it just might help him.
>
> **R:** He's got schoolitis . . . he's out when the going gets rough.
>
> **P:** Maybe we should talk to [the principal] . . . he may need another year, O.K.? I'll talk to him and let you know.
>
> **R:** Ya know, he told me in confidence that the biggest mistake he ever made in his life was allowing his father to remarry.
>
> **S:** He lives with his mother, and he even pays some of the bills in the house.

[*more discussion about his job, his enjoyment of working with
animals and jokes about his being "like one," how unlikely it is
that he will even be able to become a veterinarian's assistant*]

S: Maybe he should be in the zoo.

P: O.K. Let's do this . . . we'll try to encourage the kid to come to
school and do better in every class. I'll talk to [the principal]
about recommending retention.

In this case, the consequences of the teachers' action could be dire:
retention at Allwin is a strong public statement of "failure." The closing
position in this sequence was only "talking" about "recommending."
The evaluation was still not cast in stone, and there were still many ways
for the evaluation to prove not so radically consequential. The principal
might decide not to "recommend" retention, particularly if the parents
protest and promise remedial action.

The People of Hamden Heights and Their Activities

In everyday activities, the "success" of Allwin reveals itself to be
anything but mechanical. It is made in a complex of small actions that
together—test after test, meeting after meeting—make a portrait of each
child along a trajectory that leads to identified success or failure. Eventually, this activity reproduces the position of the school, and of many
of the participants, in relation to other schools in the United States. The
people of Hamden Heights do not simply inhabit their positions. They
are continually at work rebuilding, (perhaps more accurately, "repairing") what they inhabit to make sure that their children are not displaced.[13] Social reproduction is not guaranteed, however much
cultural or economic capital one may control.

In the long run, as seen in the sociological distance of aggregated
data, parental anxiety looks unnecessary, and yet our evidence suggests
that it is real.[14] Statistically, the children of professionals, managers,
and small entrepreneurs generally attain positions similar to those of
their parents. At stake for parents, teachers, and many students is the
possibility they will find themselves among those—a statistically growing number—who will, in one way or another "not make it." Newman
(1988) has recently documented "downward mobility" in the lives of
middle-class adults. Failure is not an abstraction for the people of Hamden Heights. Potentially consequential failure is an integral part of their
lives. To the extent that they have more to lose, there is a sense in which
school failure is a more feared experience for the middle class than for
the failing children of the inner city.

Paul Willis opened his book about working-class "resistance" to schooling with two rhetorical questions: "The difficult thing to explain about how middle-class kids get middle-class jobs is why others let them. The difficult thing to explain about how working-class kids get working-class jobs is why they let themselves" (1977:1). Willis then gave a version of how social reproduction is actively performed by those involved. In his analytic practice, he seems to have been interested only in the activity of the working-class kids who "let" other kids get the middle-class jobs. This can be misleading unless the related question is also asked: "Given that working-class kids let middle-class kids get middle-class jobs, why is it that middle-class kids work so hard at getting them?"

We understand that this question requires a complex answer. Working-class kids do not simply "let" middle-class kids succeed. They are, eventually, defeated in a generalized, altogether impersonal, and still quite real struggle. Middle-class kids and their parents are not passive combatants. They are intimately engaged in a multipronged struggle they cannot be sure of winning. Only one person can win the race. Everyone else will have to play second, third, or no fiddle at all. Failure to ensure social reproduction is always possible. All prosperous parents know that some of their friends' or peers' children have drifted "down" and will never achieve what their parents had. A 95 on a test is not an 85 is not a 75, and only a few students receive the first grade. All the others know they did not quite measure up, even if some would agree with what one student once told his mother: "B is cool, mom!" Well, a B is not enough to get one into Columbia College, and parents are sensitive to the difference a B makes. Both students and parents are correct. Getting a B from a successful school like Allwin is to do well, but not quite well enough if the goal is admission to an elite university where high school Bs won't earn a student a first-place ranking.

Work, Mutualities and Resistance In and Through the Culture of Success/Failure

We have used the word "work" to refer to the activity of everyone at Allwin, because, as mentioned earlier, the word indexes various traditions of analyses. There are many ironies emphasized by the use of the word, particularly when we place together, as must be done, the people of Hamden Heights and the people of inner-city New York whose children attend West Side High School.[15] The former are all employed, many of the latter are not. The children of the former spend most of their childhoods working at school, both during school time and at home, filling in endless workbook pages. The people of Hamden

Heights often think they occupy their position because of the work they did and continue doing, and that anyone who worked as hard as they did would also succeed. Teachers, professionally, believe that the more school work one does, the better one will be at school work. There is much cognitive psychology that demonstrates that this must be so: musicians and athletes, however talented, must work ever more diligently the more talented they are. But such common sense can be extremely dangerous when two unwarranted generalizations are made: the poor and unemployed "do not work," and "work produces success." For all analytic purposes, the poor work just as much as the nonpoor, but with radically different resources and always in different positions within the social field. They take on another range of work that may not always be recognized as such (Burton 1995).

The point here is that the work people as individuals (or in a small or large group) may perform on their own time and in their own space cannot determine the consequences of the work (rewards and punishments) when it is placed on the overall social field which the person or group shares with others persons or groups. Practice makes perfect, but it does not make "success/failure." Success/failure is a secondary identification dependent on a different kind of work, performed at other times and places with other tools. It is not trivial to point out that one cannot be known as a great pianist without a complex world of agents, reviewers, and concert halls, along with standards of taste. One cannot be known as a great scholar without a similar social apparatus. Homework is important to school success, but only to the extent that it is noticed and evaluated by school personnel.

This leads us to the final, and most fateful, irony. Our last comment cannot be the end, for it implies a simple solution: train school personnel always to recognize talent and work, and the trick will be done. This is not the solution since it does not take into account that people's work is never done. Better training will produce ever more imaginative practices using the tools of the system to gain what some apologists for the success/failure system might consider unfair advantage. The parents of Hamden Heights will resist. More sensitive testing will increase their anxiety, and they will work harder for their children, using ever more of their resources. This work will make something: children who rank high on tests. It will also make something else: children who rank low on tests.

When Jules Henry titled his book on U.S. education *Culture Against Man* (1963), he was talking as a humanist appalled at the way a cultural system could silence an individual's self. This chapter could have been titled "People Against Culture" to emphasize our understanding that people—big and little, rich and poor, privileged and disenfranchised, white and minority, male and female—are never completely defeated in this struggle. They are active, pushing the limits of the conditions they are given. The members of the upper-middle-class community of Hamden Heights do not maintain their position by relying on the cultural predestination that theorists of culture call early socialization. Instead, they must race hard to stay in place. Success is not the inevitable product of a purported fit between family and school environments. Those who win in the United States do not win because they impose "their" culture on people with "different" cultures. We might better say that "America" is imposed on all people in the United States, and all resist it with varying consequences for themselves and for the many, in the social distance, whom they may never notice.

Notes

[1] In this sentence, and in many others, we use the word "success" to index the commonsensical, clichéd, and ultimately dangerous discourse about the fate of people in the United States. We offer no definition of success precisely because we think of it as a cultural category.

[2] For a more detailed account of the historical interplay between high progressivism (as Dewey attempted to inscribe it) and practical progressivism (as inscribed in the institutional evolution of the American school, its curriculum, tests, and attendants), see Cremin (1961, 1988). Lagemann (1989) gives further details about the process that transformed a subtle concern with the shaping of an individual into a citizen into a set of practices intended to measure the extent of the shaping.

[3] A high school in a nearby town was studied by Varenne (1983). Teenage girls in still another nearby town were studied by Joyce Canaan (1986, 1990). To round off an ethnographic overview of a child's progress through the schools of New Jersey in the 1970s and 1980s, see Moffatt's (1989) study of student life at Rutgers, Ortner's emerging work (1993) on remembrances of life in a Newark high school, and Taylor and Dorsey-Gaines (1988) on literacy in inner-city families.

[4] West Side High, an alternative public high school for students who have been failed from other high schools in New York City was studied by Rizzo-Tolk and Varenne (1992). The present paper is best read in tandem with this publication and those listed in note 3.

[5] We emphasize that "work" says something that the social reproduction theories (Bourdieu and Passeron 1977; Giroux 1983) on which we have relied do not say clearly enough. Social reproduction was designed to focus our attention on the practices of agents, but it is threatened by its reliance on theories of enculturation, socialization or internalization. Social facts, we believe, do not have to be internalized to be effective; they only have to be inscribed on the social landscape so they cannot be missed. This is a complex position, which we sketch in detail elsewhere (Varenne and McDermott, in press).

[6] The famous Pygmalion studies (Rosenthal and Jacobson 1968) focused only on the attitudes of individuals in arranging the self-fulfilling prophecies of success and failure. Cultural accounts instead focus on the symbolic order in terms of which certain attitudes are made available to individuals in particular settings (Spindler 1959; McDermott and Aron 1978). The suburbs and the inner city not only draw from the same resources, they make each other possible.

[7] This is not a "new" phenomenon of the 1980s. The same attention to tests was reported by Henry (1963) for the 1950s and by the Lynds ([1929] 1956:218) for the 1920s. Our analysis is an extension of Henry's, although we talk less of the "absurdity" of tests and competitions and more about their fundamental efficacy as reconstructions of, commentaries on, and resistance to a cultural pattern.

[8] Teams may be one of the ways the historical processes in America have transformed the fundamental structures of democratic ideology. In contrast, France gives few occasions for students to organize themselves into teams. The importance of teams perhaps has to do with the strength of the "community" ideology in American culture (Varenne 1977).

[9] Some consider these wins and losses dangerous only to the extent that a winner, or loser, may misinterpret the success. John Updike's famous "Rabbit" series is the story of a man who overinterpreted his success as a high school basketball "star." By definition, being a star is a rare occurrence. More common are the students who interpret their failure as more than what it is culturally constructed to be. For the same problems handled differently in another culture, see Moore (1975) on African marriages and Plath (1980) and Rohlen (1983, 1992) for Japanese schooling and career lines.

[10] As is well known, an interesting aspect of American education is the absence of the national exams that control educational results in an absolute fashion, as in Europe or Asia (Amano 1990; Eckstein and Noah 1993; Miyazaki 1976). In France, as in most other countries, individual results on the baccalauréat are not open to educational negotiation: a failure to pass is an absolute event.

[11] This is a process that has been observed in other studies. See Cicourel and Kitsuse (1963), Erickson and Shultz (1982), and Mehan, Hertwerk and Meihls (1986) for a discussion of the role of guidance counselors and other school personnel in the ranking of students.

[12] A variation on this process is well documented in Lacey (1970). In the English context of an elite school drawing only the very best students from other schools, he traces the reproduction of academic stratification.

[13.] In our forthcoming volume, we use Robert Frost's poem about repairing walls that make good neighbors to illustrate this point: cultural processes construct facts for all to take into account. Some people (hunters in the poem) break down the walls. Others (the neighbor) insist that they be rebuilt. Others (the narrator) question the need for the wall but acquiesce. This is a range of reactions to cultural facts that is well-illustrated in our observations at Allwin.

[14] In the same vein, Ortner (1995) has reported difficulties getting adult middle-class informants to talk about anything other than fear for their own children when she wanted them to talk about their own educational experiences.

[15] In the aforementioned paper on West Side High (Rizzo-Tolk and Varenne 1992), we showed what this can mean in the everyday life of an alternative school and in some of its special programs. One example was the completion of a class project. In a fifteen-minute discussion, a half-dozen students both demonstrated considerable interactional and academic skills related to the project and performed the one thing that allowed some teachers (in a later discussion) to say "they have not learned anything!" The students' discussion was videotaped. For a few seconds, the students laughed at a joke. They were, for all analytic purposes, working at completing a complex collective task which they brought to its appointed closing. Like the students of Allwin playing at "Screw Thy Neighbor" tests, they were also enjoying themselves—laughing and playing with possibilities. They were "at cultural work," making a world for themselves and others. Some of the teachers, when they watched the tape of the students laughing, were also at cultural work when they

identified the laughter as proof that the students had not learned. It is easy for us to show that this identification is wrong. But the identification was made, and this is what must concern us.

References

Amano, Ikuo, 1990. *Education and Examination in Modern Japan*. Tokyo: University of Tokyo Press.

Bateson, Gregory, 1955. The Message "This is Play." In *Group Processes: Transactions of the Second Conference*, B. Schaffner, ed., pp. 145–242. New York: Josiah Macy, Jr. Foundation.

Bourdieu, Pierre, 1977. *Outline of a Theory of Practice*, trans. by R. Nice. Cambridge: Cambridge University Press.

Bourdieu, Pierre, and Jean-Claude Passeron, 1977. *Reproduction in Education, Society and Culture*, trans. by R. Nice. Beverly Hills: Sage.

Burton, Linda, 1995. Intergenerational Family Structure and the Provision of Care in African American Families with Teenage Childbearers. In *Intergenerational Issues in Aging*, K. Schaie, V. Bengston and L. Burton, eds., pp. 79–96. New York: Springer.

Canaan, Joyce, 1990. Passing Notes and Telling Jokes: Gendered Strategies among American Middle School Teenagers. In *Uncertain Terms*, F. Ginsburg and A. Tsing, eds., pp. 215–31. Boston: Beacon Press.

_____, 1986. Why a "Slut" Is a "Slut": Cautionary Tales of Middle-class Teenage Girls' Morality. In *Symbolizing America*, H. Varenne, ed., pp. 184–208. Lincoln: University of Nebraska Press.

Cicourel, Aaron, and John Kitsuse, 1963. *Educational Decision Making*. Indianapolis, IN: Bobbs-Merrill.

Cremin, Lawrence, 1961. *The Transformation of the School: Progressivism in American Education, 1876–1957*. New York: Random House.

———, 1988. *American Education: The Metropolitan Experience, 1876–1980*. New York: Harper & Row.

Eckstein, Max, and Harold Noah. 1993. *Secondary School Examinations: International Perspectives on Policies and Practice*. New Haven: Yale University Press.

Erickson, Frederick, and Jeffrey Shultz, 1982. *The Counselor as Gatekeeper: Social Interaction in Interviews*. New York: Academic Press.

Foley, Douglas, 1990. *Learning Capitalist Culture: Deep in the Heart of Texas*. Philadelphia: University of Pennsylvania Press.

Geertz, Clifford, 1973. Deep Play: Notes on the Balinese Cockfight. In *The Interpretation of Cultures*, C. Geertz, ed., pp. 412–53. New York: Basic Books.

Giroux, Henry, 1983. *Theory and Resistance in Education*. South Hadley, MA: Bergin and Garvey.

Goldman, Shelley, 1982. *Sorting out Sorting: How Stratification Is Managed in a Middle School*. Doctoral Dissertation. New York: Teachers College, Columbia University.

_____, 1996. Mediating Microworlds: Collaborating on High School Science Activities. In *CSCL: Theory and Practice of an Emerging Paradigm*, T. Koschman, ed., pp. 45–81. Mahwah, NJ: Lawrence Erlbaum Associates.

Goldman, Shelley, and Ray McDermott, 1987. The Culture of Competition in American Schools. In *Education and Cultural Process*, 2d ed., G. Spindler, ed., pp. 282–99. Prospect Heights, IL: Waveland Press.

Henry, Jules, 1963. *Culture against Man*. New York: Random House.

Jackall, Robert, 1988. *Moral Mazes*. New York: Oxford University Press.

Kroeber, A. L., and Clyde Kluckhohn, 1953. *Culture: A Critical Review of Concepts and Definitions*. New York: Random House.

Labov, William, 1972. *Language in the Inner City*. Philadelphia: University of Pennsylvania Press.

Lacey, Colin, 1970. *Hightown Grammar: The School as a Social System*. Manchester: Manchester University Press.

Lagemann, Ellen, 1989. The Plural Worlds of Educational Research. *History of Education Quarterly* 29:185–214.

Lynd, Robert, and Helen Lynd, 1956 [1929]. *Middletown: A Study in Modern American Culture*. New York: Harcourt, Brace and World.

McDermott, R. P., and Jeffrey Aron, 1978. Pirandello in the Classroom: On the Possibility of Equal Educational Opportunity in American Culture. In *Futures of Education*, M. Reynolds, ed., pp. 41–64. Reston, VA: Council on Exceptional Children.

Mehan, Hugh, A. Hertwerk and J. Meihls, 1986. *Handicapping the Handicapped*. Stanford: Stanford University Press.

Moffatt, Michael, 1989. *Coming of Age in New Jersey: College and American Culture*. New Brunswick: Rutgers University Press.

Moore, Sally, 1975. Selection for Failure in a Small Social Field. In *Symbol and Politics in Communal Ideology*, S. Moore and B. Myerhoff, eds., pp. 109–43. Ithaca, NY: Cornell University Press.

Miyazaki, Ichisada, 1976. *China's Examination Hell: Civil Service Examinations of Imperial China*, trans. from the Japanese by C. Schirokauer. New Haven: Yale University Press.

Newman, Katherine, 1988. *Falling from Grace: The Experience of Downward Mobility in the American Middle Class*. New York: The Free Press.

Ortner, Sherry, 1993. Ethnography among the Newark: The Class of '58 of Weequakic High School. *Michigan Quarterly Review* 32:411–29.

Page, Reba, 1991. *Lower-track Classrooms: A Curricular and Cultural Perspective*. New York: Teachers College Press.

Plath, David, 1980. *Long Engagements: Maturity in Modern Japan*. Stanford: Stanford University Press.

Rizzo-Tolk, Rosemarie, and Hervé Varenne, 1992. Joint Action on the Wild Side of Manhattan: The Power of the Cultural Center on an Educational Alternative. *Anthropology and Education Quarterly* 23:221–49.

Rohlen, Thomas, 1992. Learning. In *The Political Economy of Japan, Vol. III. Socio and Cultural Dynamics*, S. Kumon and H. Rosovsky, eds., pp. 321–63. Stanford: Stanford University Press.

———, 1983. *Japan's High Schools*. Berkeley: University of California Press.

Rosenthal, Robert, and Lenore Jacobson, 1968. *Pygmalion in the Classroom*. New York: Holt, Rinehart and Winston.

Spindler, George, 1959. *The Transmission of American Culture*. Cambridge: Harvard University Press.

Taylor, Denny, and Catherine Dorsey-Gaines, 1988. *Growing Up Literate:*

Learning from Inner-city Families. Portsmouth, NH: Heinemann.

Varenne, Hervé, and R. P. McDermott, 1986. "Why Sheila Can Read: Structure and Indeterminacy in the Reproduction of Familial Literacy." In *The Acquisition of Literacy*, P. Gilmore and B. Schieffelin, eds., pp. 188–210. Norwood, NJ: Ablex Publishing .

Varenne, Hervé, 1977. *Americans Together: Structured Diversity in a Midwestern Town*. New York: Teachers College Press.

——, 1978. Culture as Rhetoric: The Patterning of the Verbal Interpretation of Interaction in an American High School. *American Ethnologist* 5(3): 635–50.

——, 1982. Jocks and Freaks: The Symbolic Structure of the Expression of Social Interaction among American Senior High School Students. In *Doing the Ethnography of Schooling*, G. Spindler, ed., pp. 210–35. New York: Holt, Rinehart and Winston.

——, 1983. *American School Language: Culturally Patterned Conflicts in a Suburban High School*. New York: Irvington Publishers.

——, 1986. Love and Liberty: La Famille Américaine Contemporaine. In *Histoire de la famille*, A. Burguiere, C. Klapisch-Zuber, M. Segalen and F. Zonabend, eds., pp. 413–35. Paris: Armand Colin.

——, 1987. Talk and Real Talk: The Voices of Silence and the Voices of Power in American Family Life. *Cultural Anthropology* 2:369–94.

——, 1992. *Ambiguous Harmony: Family Talk in America*. Norwood, NJ: Ablex Publishing Corp.

Varenne, Hervé, and Ray McDermott, in press. *Successful Failure: The School America Builds*. Boulder, CO: Westview.

Willis, Paul, 1977. *Learning to Labor: How Working Class Kids Get Working Class Jobs*. New York: Columbia University Press.

This chapter offers a reinterpretation of Goldman (1982) and Goldman and McDermott (1987). It shares a main title and some content with chapter 5 of Varenne and McDermott (in press).

9
Education in Communitarian Societies—The Old Order Amish and the Hutterian Brethren

John A. Hostetler
Temple University

In the United States it is generally assumed that every citizen, regardless of personal values or ethnic membership, must be educated to the limit, that democracy will prevail when education is made available to all, and that the national goals should become the personal goals of everyone. Education is believed to be important not only for national life but also for personal fulfillment and a wide range of social and economic goals. "Ultimately," says *The Report of the President's Commission on National Goals* (1960:81), "education serves all of our purposes—liberty, justice and all our other aims. . . . The vigor of our free institutions depends upon educated men and women at every level of society. And at this moment in history free institutions are on trial." The goals of education in the United States tend to be in the direction of self-development and fulfillment of individual wants, development of rational powers, and the enhancement of personal freedom. Thus we read in a publication of the National Educational Association (Educational Policies Commission 1961:8) that

> A person with developed rational powers has the means to be aware of all facts of his existence. In this sense he can live to the fullest. He can escape captivity to his emotions and irrational states. He can enrich his emotional life and direct it toward even higher standards of taste and enjoyment. He can enjoy the political and economic freedoms of the democratic society. He can free himself from the democratic society. He can free himself from the bondage of ignorance and unawareness. He can make of himself a free man.

Within the United States there are "little" societies which are threatened by the sweeping effort to educate every citizen. They reject the premise that man "can make of himself a free man." The NEA statement

Source: Written especially for *Education and Cultural Process.*

of goals, for example, contrasts sharply with that of the Hutterian Brethren, who say:

> Our children are our noblest, highest, and dearest possession. We teach them from the beginning to know God, to humble and abase oneself before God, to bring the flesh into subjection, and to slay and kill it. We permit them not to go to other schools since they teach only the wisdom, art, and practices of the world and are silent about divine things. (Rideman 1965; 1938 ed.)

In reply to the question: What is a good education? an Amish bishop (Bontreger 1910:77) says:

> A good education does not mean simply book learning, or the acquiring of a great store of information, or a scholarship that has mastered the many branches of learning that are taught in the schools, colleges, and universities of this day. It does mean, however, a store of practical knowledge and skill, a knowledge that can discern between that which is good and useful and ennobling, and that which is a useless accumulation of learning in worldly arts and sciences.

The success of communitarian societies in evading the pervasive educational values of the "great" society, or of integrating some of the insights of public schooling into their indigenous educational system, varies greatly. Many traditional societies have been "swept out by the broom of our industrial and urban civilization," as Everett Hughes (1952:25) has put it. Communitarian societies are faced with the task of not only transmitting their distinctive culture but also maintaining their identity. They engage in what Siegel (1970:11) has aptly called "defensive structuring," defined as "a kind of adaptation that recurs with great regularity among groups that perceive themselves as exposed to environmental stress of long duration with which they cannot cope directly and aggressively."

Over a period of several years the writer has observed differences in the defensive structuring of two communitarian societies, the Amish (Old Order) and the Hutterites (Hutterian Brethren) with respect to education. In this chapter we shall discuss defensive structuring and relate it to community self-realization. At the outset we shall describe the world view and social structure of the two cultures, the areas of tension in relation to education, and then consider the differences in assimilation and disruption patterns. Generalizations dealing with education and the viability of the two cultures will conclude the chapter.

World View and Social Structure

Similarities in World View

Common to both Amish and Hutterites is the dualism of Christianity and of Anabaptism in particular. The doctrine of two kingdoms, the kingdom of God and the kingdom of Satan, light versus darkness, the carnal versus the spiritual, the perishable versus the eternal, and paradise versus wilderness are dominant themes in juxtaposition running through the indoctrination activity and the social structure of the subcultures.

The belief consistently set forth by the Anabaptists (Simons 1956) was that they, like the apostolic community, sought to be the blameless church consisting of those personally awakened and called by God. They believed that those who have been born again, and they alone, are brethren of Christ, because they, like him, have been created in spirit directly by God (Weber 1958:145). Taking the life of the first generations of Christians as a model and "avoiding the world"—in the sense of all unnecessary intercourse with "worldly" people—has been a cardinal principle with the Anabaptists wherever they have lived.

Thus an Amish or Hutterite person must live "unspotted from the world" and separate from the desires, intent, and goals of the outside or outer world. The literalness with which the basic doctrine of separation is practiced is evident in the symbolic systems of dress, in the taboos against forming economic partnerships or alliances with non-members, and in forbidding marriage with outsiders. Both groups view themselves—but in different ways—as "a chosen people," "a remnant people," and "a peculiar people." Because they considered infant baptism invalid and began baptizing only adults on confession of faith, they were called rebaptizers or Anabaptists and were greatly harassed by state churches in the sixteenth and seventeenth centuries. Both groups refuse to bear arms or serve in public office, practices which earned them the title of "radicals" during the Protestant Reformation (Williams 1962). Both have strong ascetic tendencies in Max Weber's sense, and in both persecution has been an important element in perpetuating a sense of distinctiveness. Each has an impressive record of martyrs.

The Old Order Amish today number about 60,000 persons. Their Swiss origin and history from the Rhineland to Pennsylvania and to other midwestern states has been well known (Bachman 1942; Hostetler 1963). The Hutterian Brethren number about 20,000 persons. Like the Amish, they are a Germanic-speaking people but of Tyrol and Moravian origin who have subsequently migrated to Slovakia, Romania, the Ukraine, South Dakota and Montana, and Canada (Peters 1965; Bennett 1967). Hutterite and Amish groups have different dialects, but both use High German in their ceremonial activity. Both societies are communitarian in the sense of having an ideological emphasis on sharing and community, in limiting individual initiative, and in subordinating individual freedom and rationality to community values. The Hutterites are strictly communal, for their basic social unit is a colony, a social entity practicing the community of goods.

The Amish Community

The central integrating institution in Amish society is the ceremonial "preaching service" held every two weeks on Sunday in the home of one of the members. The Amish community consists of a number of farm households in proximity, bonded by a common tradition and faith, articulated in a local church district (congregation), and limited to a few square miles (due to their reliance upon horse-drawn vehicles). Amish and non-Amish farms are interspersed in the same region. The Amish do not own blocks of land as a corporation. Farm machinery, livestock, and individual household units are individually owned. The only property held in common in an Amish church district are the hymn books, and in some districts, the benches used for the church service which are rotated among the households. Sharing and mutual aid in times of fire, sickness, death, or catastrophe are highly characteristic but voluntary.

The authority of the Amish community is vested in the congregation of baptized members, headed by a bishop and several other ordained persons. The basis of all policy is the *Ordnung* (discipline) to which every individual gives assent on his knees when he takes the vow of baptism. The *Ordnung* embodies all that is distinctive of the group and includes common understandings taken for granted. Hence, these rules are unwritten, and most are learned and known only by being a participant member. The *Ordnung* is essentially a list of taboos, reflecting the peculiar problems and encounters of a local congregation. At the basis of any change in the *Ordnung* are the borderline or questionable issues. Any changes are recommended by the ordained and presented orally to the congregation twice each year just prior to the communion service. Each member is asked to approve any changes of the rules. A unanimous expression of unity and "peace" with the *Ordnung* is necessary before the congregation can observe communion. A member can be excommunicated at any time by violating one of the basic rules, but in the case of minor infractions, these must be reconciled before communion. Variations of rules from one congregation to another may be observed, but the most distinguishing rules among all Old Order in the United States are no electricity, telephones, central-heating systems, automobiles, or tractors with pneumatic tires. Required are beards but no moustaches for all married men, long hair (which must be parted in the center if parting is allowed at all), hooks and eyes on dress coats, and the use of horses for farming and transportation in the community. No formal education beyond the elementary grades is a rule of life.

For the Amish farmer who cannot assent to the *Ordnung* there are two means of mobility. Both are difficult and inconvenient. One way is to join a more liberal congregation, but the difficulty is that one may have to be shunned for life by one's kin. The other way is to move the household to a community where there is a more compatible *Ordnung*. The *Ordnung* does not prevent a farmer from moving to another community or another state. This degree of freedom is constantly exercised by families who wish to move either because the *Ordnung* is too strict or not strict enough.

The Hutterite Community

A group of married families (from eight to twelve) and their children who live on a Bruderhof or colony constitute a Hutterite community (Hostetler and Huntington 1967). The family is assigned rooms in a long dormitory according to its size and needs. A colony may vary from 70 to 140 persons. With all its dwellings, communal kitchen, schoolhouse and kindergarten, livestock and poultry buildings, storage and machine buildings, a colony may have up to a total of 70 buildings. A colony integrates not only religious ceremonialism but an economic enterprise, kinship, socialization processes, and property institutions. This basic community structure is very unlike the nucleated households of the Amish. From their beginning in 1528 the Hutterites equated communal living with the primitive and true expression of Christianity. They rejected as pagan the private ownership of property. Thus, land is owned by the colony corporation. Ownership of farm equipment and the purchase of all goods require the consent of the corporation. The colony is the self-sustaining unit within which the needs of all the members are met.

The authority of the colony is centered in the baptized men of the colony and is headed by a council of five to seven members, one of whom is a preacher. He is ordained by an assembly of preachers and is responsible for the moral leadership of a colony. Although a colony may make its own rules, it must also abide by the rules of a confederation of colonies, the *Leut*. All executive functions of the colony are implemented by the council of five to seven men, headed by the preacher. The sale and purchase of goods is the responsibility of the steward, who must give an accounting to the colony. From infancy the individual is socialized to be cheerful, to be submissive and obedient to the colony discipline, and never to display anger or hostility or precipitate quarrels. Individual initiative and self-development are deemphasized. Travel is limited but permitted among colonies, and there are occasional trips to trading centers. Respect for order, for authority, hard work and cooperativeness, and submission of the individual will to that of the colony are dominant in the life style of Hutterite personality. The individual never receives schooling outside of the colony, but attends kindergarten from ages three to five, the colony German school and the English school during the school years, and is baptized at the age of about twenty. Ultimate good is achieved by identification with the colony, its communal work and sharing of goods, and only in this way can God be worshipped and honored properly.

The Areas of Tension and Defensive Structuring

The conflict of the two communitarian groups with the state over educational policy has received widespread publicity. School officials view the problem as one of law enforcement. The Amish and Hutterites view the issue in religious terms and as one of survival. Lawyers interpret the problem in legal categories. Citizens of the community often view the conflict as a "fight" between the old and new sentiments of the community. From the viewpoint of anthropology we are interested in contrasting one culture with another, touching on the significant areas of culture contact, formal and informal, and in defensive structuring as manifested in the socialization process. By concentrating on the areas of greatest tension we may obtain knowledge about the defensive structuring and the consequences for the communities themselves.

Amish Education

Acquiring literacy and skills for their young without subjecting them to a change in world view confronts the Amish community with a fundamental human problem (Hostetler and Huntington 1972). "The Amish as a whole," as one Amish spokesman has pointed out, "are very much interested in teaching their children the three basic parts of learning: reading, writing, and arithmetic" (Kanagy in Stroup 1965:15). The Amish child typically grows up in a large family in a farm environment. The child's first formal schooling begins when he or she is six or seven years old. His or her first major task is to learn the English language. This is not a major problem, with brothers or sisters in the same school. While attending school the child is expected to assist with farm chores and related family responsibilities at home, as do other members of the family. After completing grade eight, the formal schooling period—with some exceptions as noted below—is over.

During the period when the American youngster is in high school, the Amish child is learning to identify with his or her culture. High school comes at a time in the life of the Amish child when isolation is most important for the development of personality within the culture. During this period he or she is learning to understand his or her own individuality within the boundaries of Amish society. As an adolescent the child is learning for the first time to relate to a group of peers beyond immediate family. As with most adolescents, the child is testing his or her powers against parents and the rules of the community. It is important for the Amish community that the child's group of peers include only other Amish persons. If the child should acquire competence in the "English" (non-Amish) culture at this stage, he or she is likely to be lost to the Amish church. While the parents are loosening their direct control and the community has not yet assumed much control, the period is too critical to expose the child to outside influences.

High school would break down this needed period of isolation by taking the youth away from the family farm and by teaching him or her to identify with non-Amish associates. This is what the Amish mean when they say that high school is "a detriment to both farm and religious life." The public high school also teaches ideas that are foreign to the Amish culture and not appreciated by the community. The "way of life" of the high school is feared perhaps even more than the curriculum itself. If the child is removed from the community for most of the working hours of the day there is virtually no chance that he or she will learn to enjoy the Amish way of life. The incentive to comprehend his or her individuality, to master the required attitudes and skills necessary to enjoy life as an Amish person, are achieved during adolescence within the context of family, kinfolk, and church-community.

The Amish family needs the help of its teen-aged children more than the typical American family. The child also feels the family's need. To know that the family needs his or her physical powers and to know that he or she is an economic asset to the welfare of the family is important to the individual. Quitting school after the elementary grades for greater identification with family and for the rewards of participation in adult society is normative. The typical Amish boy or girl who learns to enjoy his or her family and way of life has little regret when leaving school. Rather than relying on authority as a means of controlling the child, parents now exercise control by showing the adolescents clearly how much the family needs them. The young person who works on the farm can understand and feel the contribution he or she is making to his family.

The formal objections to public education are based on religious precepts such as "The wisdom of the world is foolishness with God" (I Cor. 3:19). The world is educated, the Amish would point out, but is plainly corrupt. Education has produced scientists who have invented bombs to destroy the world, and through education the world has been degraded. A "high" education is believed to militate against humility and obedience to Christ.

Given the educational goals of "practical knowledge and skills" and avoidance of "that which is a useless accumulation of learning in worldly arts and sciences," the rural elementary public school has from the viewpoint of the Amish been workable in the past. Parents fear a strong, progressive public school. They recognize that its aim is to make the child self-sufficient outside of the Amish community and perhaps moral, although not necessarily Christian. They fear what teachers they do not know are teaching their children. They resent the school for taking too much time away from the family and from the discipline of farm work. Learning, or reading, for purposes other than the goals of the culture are looked upon with suspicion. But in spite of the adverse influences the small public elementary school has had on the Amish child, it helped to make of the child a good Amish person. It provided enough contact with outsiders to enable the child to participate minimally in two worlds, and just enough indoctrination into the outer culture to make the child feel secure in his or her own family and community.

Until about 1937 the Amish generally accepted most of the legal school requirements. As consolidation became widespread, however, the Amish established private schools as a matter of policy. The intent was not so much to teach religion as to avoid the "way of life" promoted by consolidated school systems. The Amish prevailed upon the school boards to keep the one-room schools open. In the process of consolidation, the public school officials often regarded the strongly populated Amish areas as a "problem" in attaining votes for reorganization (Buchanan 1967). All states with Amish populations have attempted to compel the Amish to meet the minimum standards required by law.

Pennsylvania was the first state to attempt widespread enforcement of the school-attendance law affecting the Amish. The law required children to attend school until their seventeenth birthday, but children engaged in farm work were permitted to apply for a permit which excused them when they reached the age of fifteen. However, many had repeated the eighth grade and were still not old enough to apply for a farm permit. The conflict erupted when schools were no longer willing to tolerate the practice of allowing the Amish children to repeat grade eight. School officials tried withholding the farm permits. When the parents did not send their children to the consolidated high school, the parents were summoned to court and fined. They refused to pay the fines on grounds that this would admit to being guilty and were sent to jail. Anonymous friends and businessmen frequently paid the fines to release the parents from prison. Some were arrested as many as ten times. The Amish fathers and mothers took the position that compulsory attendance beyond the elementary grades interferes with the exercise of their religious liberty, and that the values taught in the public school are contrary to their religion. Attorneys and friends of the Amish who took the case to the courts found no legal solution. After many confrontations and embarrassments, Governor George Leader, in 1955, arranged a reinterpretation of the school code to legitimize a compromise plan, the Amish vocational school (Policy for Operation of Home and Farm Projects in Church-Organized Day Schools 1955). Amish lay leaders took the initiative in developing the vocational schools for those pupils who were not of legal age to obtain a farm permit. Under this plan, known as "The Pennsylvania Plan," the pupils perform farm and household duties under parental guidance, keep a daily journal of their activities, and meet a minimum of three hours per week until they reach their sixteenth birthday. The schools are required to teach certain subjects and to file attendance reports, but teachers are not required to be certified.

The showdown in Iowa between the Amish and the public school officials in 1965–1967 illustrates not only how intense the feelings can become in a rural community but also the social processes when coercion is used (Erickson 1969). In a small Amish settlement centering in Buchanan County, Iowa, school authorities forced their way into an Amish private school to transport the children to a consolidated town school. The press recorded the scene as frightened youngsters ran for cover in nearby corn fields and sobbing mothers and fathers were arrested for noncompliance with an Iowa school law.

A few public school districts have maintained country schools in the more heavily populated Amish areas, thus forestalling the establishment of private schools by the Amish. The boards of these schools seek teachers sympathetic to the Amish way of life and, in keeping with respect for cultural diversity, see that religious values of the pupils and parents are not offended. The few schools that are following such a policy have achieved remarkable results. The arrangement provides for state-certified teachers, more modern curricula and facilities than is possible in the private Amish schools, and for enlightenment that is fitted to the culture. The agreement between the Amish and the Department of Education of the State of Indiana (1967) was an attempt to use means other than the courts to solve differences in educational policy.

In summary, defensive structuring in the case of the Amish takes the following forms: The Amish will vote against school consolidation to protect their group solidarity, and they establish private schools for the same reason. There is a conspicuous absence of formal dialogue between the Amish and the school officials (Buchanan 1967). The Amish are almost wholly dependent on verbal agreements with school officials which the Amish accept at face value. The turnover of school personnel at local and state levels often operates at a great disadvantage to the Amish. Amish parents will refuse to send their children to school even when it appears to school officials that no religious principle is involved. It seems ironic that the Amish are forming private schools not for teaching religion but for obtaining literacy and practical skills under conditions that enable the culture to survive. Pressure from local residents to make the Amish conform to school-attendance laws is often reinforced by longstanding antagonisms. When negotiations break down on the district level, state officials intervene and usually arbitrate either informally or in the courts. School administrators have, in many cases, not learned the difference between those issues on which the Amish will "bend" and those on which they will not compromise.

Amish Controls Over the Socialization Process

The Amish have no control over the philosophy of education presented in the elementary public school and their response is to form private schools. In communities where Amish attend public school, the school experience is accepted as necessary, but with great reservations. The attitude toward public schooling is defensive. Efforts are made to keep methods and ideology from changing. Schooling beyond the elementary grades is not approved and parents will go to prison if necessary to defend this position. An Amish youth who insists on going to high school or college becomes a deviant. The high school is viewed as a system that prepares the individual for living in the "world," not in the Amish community.

The elementary school experience is considered a normal part of life, but if the school is public, then it is regarded as a part of the domain of the outside world. The public school is outside of the central integrating activity of the Amish community. When the school is private, its activity is also carefully guarded so that in many Amish private schools it is not permitted to teach religion, for this would compete with the roles and function of church officials.

In selecting the curriculum, the Amish have no control over the materials selected by the public school. In the private school some of the older texts discarded by the public school are used. They are less objectionable because they have less emphasis on science, modern technology, and physiology. The need for texts appropriate to the private schools is keenly realized. A few have been written by the Amish and others are in preparation.

Typically the one-room school building is located in the country, somewhat central to the Amish farm community. Whether the school is public or private, the distance to school is essentially the same. Many of the Amish live within walking distance, although some hire buses to transport their children to private schools. The school building is midway between the community and the outside world and is least integrated with other Amish institutions.

Hutterite Education

The constitution of the Hutterian Brethren Church (1950) assures every child of an education in skills and in religious training. The initiative for formal training in school belongs to the colony and not to the nuclear family. At all levels in socialization, the family supports the colony. Hutterite society from its beginning has had a highly institutionalized and effective system of formal education for all the age-sets. The major levels of formal education are kindergarten *(Klein-schul)*, German school *(Gross-schul)*, and Sunday school *(Suntag-schul)*, aside from the English or public school taught by an outside certified teacher (Hostetler and Huntington 1996).

When the group settled in the Dakota territories from 1874 to 1879, schools were formed on each of the three founding colonies and were taught by colony members. After 1889 the Hutterite teachers had to qualify for teaching certificates by written examinations. The first outside teacher was hired in 1909 in the Bon Homme colony (Deets 1939:40). By 1931 all the colonies were staffed by non-Hutterite teachers since few members were able to procure teaching certificates. When the Hutterites moved to Alberta in 1918 the establishment of an ungraded rural school in each of the colonies was acceptable to the province. The Alberta Department of Education appointed an official trustee for each school. When school districts were formed, the Hutterites refused to send their children to schools away from the colony grounds. Three private schools were founded as a result. However, in most of the 140 or more Canadian colonies today, the colony school is not a private school. The teacher is appointed and paid by the Department of Education (in consultation with the colony) and the building, heating, and maintenance is provided by the colony.

The agreement between divisional school boards and colonies in Alberta states that "if the colony insist that they shall have their own school apart from the schools for the division, the other rate payers of the division should not be asked to bear any of the cost of the school in the Hutterite Colony" (Knill 1958:86). Three acres, fenced, with an approved building and a residence for the teacher are to be supplied by the colony. The division appoints and supplies the salary of the teacher, supplies school equipment and books, but permits the building to be used by the colony for church activities. The Alberta School Act does not allow divisional boards the right to impose centralization on any school districts opposed to it. The Department of Education has thus far hesitated to enforce transportation of Hutterite pupils to schools outside their colonies. If this were done, Hutterites would exercise the option of establishing private schools. The Hutterites want and need the benefits of an outside teacher, and the Provincial authorities do not want to force the colonies into a situation where they would form private schools. Hutterites have also resisted forming a centralized school for several of the colonies. When the South Dakota colonies moved to Alberta, the several Hutterites who had teacher's certificates were not approved for teaching in Alberta. The colonies permitted four of their young men to attend high school and Calgary Normal School to obtain teacher training. The experiment was considered a failure, for only one boy returned to become a teacher in the colonies. Through such attempts in the past some of their young men in both the Ukraine and in North America deserted the colonies. Although there are presently three college-educated Hutterite men teaching colony English schools, the practice is not favored with unanimity by the leaders. The reason as given by one spokesman is: "It is better to have the worldly school taught by a worldly person so that we can keep the lines straight."

The attitude toward English school is that it is important, especially in the early grades, for all children must know arithmetic and be able to use the language of the country. One leader said: "We expect our children to learn math, reading, and science as required by the Department of Education. We must learn English to understand the people around us." When asked what is most undesirable about the English school, these answers were given: "When the teacher does not cooperate with the German teacher or the preacher; taking pictures and then distributing them to the children or when dancing is held in the school, as it happened once. Learning the worldly ways would lead to their damnation. The old physiology books were all right, but the modern health books contain too much about dating, sex education and anatomy."

Aside from acquiring a good knowledge of arithmetic and reading, the only additional goal for Hutterites is that discipline be maintained in the English school. Teachers are expected and often encouraged to "lay down the law," and if they cannot maintain order, they are considered failures. A German teacher advised a new English teacher to "use the willow, for it's the only language they understand." A common complaint of teachers is that the children lack self-discipline and have less respect for an outside teacher than for the colony's German teacher. Greater respect for colony authority can be maintained if the English school also supports the prevailing authoritarian pattern. The English school on a colony becomes a disruptive force when social distance is not properly maintained. In its place, the school contributes to colony cohesion. Keeping the English school "in its place" is crucial, for here is where the ideology of the world and of the colony compete for the loyalty of the young minds. For the child who has not responded properly to colony indoctrination, the English school can become an important influence leading to possible desertion. In school the child can function as an individual and learn about the world outside the colony from books and from the teacher. Intimacy between teacher and pupil can lead to defection. Friendships can lead to marriages with outsiders, to changes of denominational loyalties. In some instances, teachers have helped young Hutterites find jobs and leave the colony. Young single teachers, male or female, are greater risks than older teachers who are married and have children of their own.

All children of school age attend the English school of the colony. The colony makes a point of not interfering with the living pattern of the teacher, who may have a radio, a television, and even a separate mailbox. The home of the teacher is a potential source of worldly knowledge to colony people and a source of intrusion if not properly controlled.

The teacher is given moral encouragement in ways that aid the colony pattern, mainly as a strong supporter of discipline. The teacher cannot encroach on the child's colony time pattern by asking a child to stay after school, by staying during the lunch hour, or by homework assignments. A child may not be punished by deprivation of food. Discussion of a teacher's shortcomings in the presence of children limits the teacher's influence. Many of the colonies complain about receiving poor teachers. Indeed some are inferior as teachers, but there is evidence that many of the marginally good teachers like to teach in the colonies. Relatively inferior academic teaching is tolerated, and teachers are virtually free from the informal supervision of superiors. There is little pressure from parents for excellence and no parental interference in teaching. Unlike most school teachers, who must participate and relate to the wider activities of the community, the teacher in a colony enjoys a type of privacy and freedom from such demands. The formal relations between colony adults and teacher are cordial. Those with cooperative attitudes, including the poorer teachers, are more readily absorbed into the environment of the colony than teachers who are truly competent by outside standards and demand independent thinking of their pupils. Even then, there is little danger that the teacher will become a model for the children. When the teachers will emulate the colony pattern, in dress or by wearing a beard, disruption patterns are minimized and the children tend to show greater respect for the teacher.

Laws intended to raise the minimum attendance age, requiring children to take formal schooling through the ninth or tenth grades, are now adversely affecting colonies in some states and provinces. A few young Hutterites take correspondence courses from state colleges. Some of the teachers who are assigned to teach in the colony are willing to tutor or to give instruction beyond the elementary grades. Exploratory efforts have been made to establish high schools for Hutterite young people in regions where there are many colonies. All such efforts to take the pupils from the colony grounds have run counter to Hutterite religion. The consequences of having to attend school beyond the time when one is accepted as an adult in Hutterite society (age fifteen) adversely affects the pupil. At this age young people are given adult work privileges. They serve as apprentices to skilled adults under supervised conditions of learning. There is a tendency for the young Hutterite to feel deprived of status as a growing person when forced to attend formal schooling beyond the age required by the Hutterite culture.

The farther the child goes in school, the less that child is said to learn. From the colony's point of view this is correct, for once a child has mastered the basic skills, much of the rest of the subject matter learned has little relevance to their way of life. The colony German school teaches the children how to live, and the English school teaches facts, many of which are of little use to them. German school teaches proper ritual, the English school teaches worldly knowledge. The schools are clearly different, but both are regarded as necessary. In the ideal colony there is little conflict between the two schools, and the normal child receives an integrated learning experience from the viewpoint of Hutterite culture.

Hutterite Control Over the Socialization Process

While Hutterites have no formal control over the educational philosophy of the school, they exercise severe informal controls over the secular educational philosophy. They accept the benefits of the public school system and prefer it to operating their own private school. Leaders want their young to learn enough of the skills of arithmetic, writing, and English to become leaders among themselves in the future. While the "worldly" philosophy is brought into the colony, its influence is carefully guarded in a controlled informal environment.

The Hutterites tolerate the public school experience but reject the elements that are dysfunctional to the colony. Hutterites have a deliberate and well-formalized program of education for all the age-sets. The public school is only one of several "schools" in the life of the pupil, and its effects are diminished. From the ages of two to five the child is in kindergarten daily to recite, sing, write, and think as required by the system. When he or she enters the English school on the colony, the child is already fortified against a foreign culture. During his or her school years the child attends in the morning, and often in the afternoon, the colony's German school. This is the "real" school from the viewpoint of the pupil. The noxious effects of the public school are minimized by the German teacher. Instead of sending their children away to the English school as do the Amish, the Hutterites bring the English school into their environs and attempt to control the learning process.

The curriculum is selected by the divisional school boards, and the Hutterites have no formal and direct control over text materials. Whether the school is private or public, the curriculum is similar to that in the rural schools. The physical proximity of the school to the colony allows for a great deal of informal visits and a strong degree of informal control over the teacher. This indirectly affects what is taught in the school. Teachers who are assigned to a colony for the first time are typically given a "lecture" by the preacher at the start or with the first offense against the colony. He outlines the colony's expectations of the teacher and sets the limits of practices which are "against our religion." The gifts in kind from the colony to the teacher and teacher's family who reside on the colony may obligate the teacher to comply with the wishes of the preacher. Colonies prohibit the use of radio, projected films, and record players in the school rooms. Since the building is used for church in the evening, all art work and visual materials must be removed at the end of the day. Because the role of the teacher in the colonies is a very difficult one for these reasons, some of the most capable teachers by outside standards are not attracted to Hutterite colonies.

The school building is integrated within the colony layout. Its presence in the colony is symbolic of those aspects of schooling that are important to the colony. The colony accepts the English school complex but restrains its influence to serve colony ends. The school and teacherage are on the grounds, but they are oriented to one side of the colony and can function without major interference. The English school remains emotionally outside the colony. The time patterns, schedule, and colony holidays suggest superior loyalties. The first language learned and the first writing skills acquired are in German. German school is held at the start of the day, followed by English school. In effect, the English school is held in the visible presence of the elders, suggested by the council bench in front and the pews in the rear of the school. Thus the English school is encapsulated by the colony pattern, and ideally its influence cannot go beyond the bounds set by the culture.

Assimilation and Disruption Patterns

The type of controls exercised by communitarian societies over the educational offensive of the great society may be a significant variable for explaining why some "little" societies dissolve faster than others. The effectiveness of the controls (and defensive structuring) may be assessed in various ways. We have chosen to examine the extent of assimilation in the two cultures as reflected in the loss of members. A society with the least deserters would be one where we would expect a high degree of solidarity and one whose defensive mechanisms are effective.

Patterns of Mobility in Amish Society

In Amish society there is a constant movement from the orthodox to the more liberal groups of Amish-Mennonites. Individuals, family heads and their children, or entire congregations change their religious affiliation. Thus an Amish farmer who wishes to use a tractor for farming, or drive an automobile instead of horses, will usually affiliate with a Mennonite denomination. In virtually all communities where there are Amish people there are also liberalized Amish or Mennonite groups. These groups form a continuum from conservative to liberal positions with respect to the rules of discipline (figure 9.1). Thus a deviating person may move from a conservative to a more liberal group without losing his identity as an Anabaptist. Although there are many divisions (as is evident from the different forms of dress and material culture), there is a common value orientation. The most orthodox groups lose the smallest number of members while the more liberal groups lose the most. The gains in the more progressive groups are a consequence of the secularization process and not the result of evangelistic activity. Most defectors from the Amish justify their change in affiliation for religious reasons. To turn against the moral training of early life, against kin, and the severe discipline learned in the formative years is not accomplished in the life of some defectors without cultural and religious shock. Religious revivalism, guilt, and conversion are important stages in the experience of the liberalizing Old Order Amish person.

An intensive study of defection in one Amish church in Pennsylvania revealed that 30 percent of the offspring did not join the church of their parents. Of all those who did not join the church of their parents, 70 percent joined a Mennonite group and less than 10 percent joined other Protestant groups.

In a study of religious mobility in the Mennonite Church, it was found that 24 percent of the converts came from Amish churches, while that denomination lost only 3 percent of its members to the Amish (Hostetler 1954:257). The loss of members varies considerably with affiliation, discipline, and church district.

Figure 9.1. Cognitive orientation of Amish-Mennonite groups from "low" to "high" church in Mifflin County, Pennsylvania.

The problem of land room is generally alleviated by the rather sizable number of persons who leave the orthodox groups. They then join the liberalized groups, who are usually engaged in occupations other than farming. The size of ceremonial affiliations is in many instances kept small by the disagreements over the discipline. Among groups who exercise the rigid form of excommunication and shunning, divisions are an alternative to migration. Migration to other rural areas is another alternative where social distance breaks down between the different groups. The assimilation patterns suggest that the Amish, who make the least use of formal education, whether indigenous or nonindigenous, are most vulnerable in terms of losing members.

Patterns of Mobility in Hutterite Society

In Hutterite society the loss of members is low. Some single boys leave the colony during the summer but usually return in the fall. Of those who attempt to leave permanently, many return after they have "tried the world." The transition from the communal to individualistic style of living appears to be unnatural for them. Intensive moral indoctrination from kindergarten through adolescence helps to offset attractions in the world. Only 258 men and 11 women left the colony voluntarily from 1880 to 1951 (Eaton and Weil 1955:146), but over half returned.

Our study of Hutterite defection suggests that the communal socialization patterns are so effective that the small number who do abandon the colonies are those who were deprived of the normal communal training usually given a child (Hostetler 1965). The loss of members varies with "declining" versus "cohesive" colonies. A declining colony has chronic problems of internal leadership or dissension that have not been resolved. The rules of mobility do not permit a member to move from one colony to another colony of choice. Of 38 defectors interviewed in depth, it was found that half had come from five nuclear families and all were located in declining colonies. In a few cases the school teacher was blamed for leading the young astray, teaching anti-Hutterite doctrine, and for finding jobs for them outside the colony. One colony girl eloped with the school teacher.

In Hutterite society there are no legitimate ways to become a non-Hutterite, not even Mennonite. Mobility is essentially blocked. Most male defectors interviewed tended to be indifferent to religion. They showed little interest in making distinctions between the vast number of denominations that are not Hutterite. The absolutist position of the Hutterite religion continues to structure the thinking patterns of those who defect permanently. The religion taught to them in childhood is basically respected by them in such statements as: "If I ever want religion, I know where to find it." One who had abandoned the colony forty years ago said that during the intervening years, "the little faith that you had was right there to sort of guide you. The guardian angel was always with you, it seemed like."

All colony roles are psychologically marked by strong elements of dependency, especially for women. Any woman who cannot accept the definition of the role given to her will have more difficulty than a man in finding alternative avenues of expression. Several groups of sisters who abandoned a colony gave as their reasons that the colony was no longer Christian. An underlying factor is that these sisters who found company in each other's misery rejected the submissive Hutterite role assigned to women. Their conversion to an individualistically oriented fundamentalist denomination permitted a rational way of escape.

Emphasis on individual self-development constitutes a disruptive influence in a communal society. It is rare that an individual will receive sufficient personal attention to develop adequate personal security to leave the protective environment of the colony. Parents who show favoritism to a child or entertain ambitions for a child beyond those sanctioned by the colony introduce dissident elements and increase the probability of defection. This relationship is understood by Hutterites. They say that if one is too good to a single child he or she is more likely to leave. The favored child who obtains attention and privilege above others in the family or in the colony acquires self-confidence above his or her peers. Interests are developed and needs are felt beyond what the colony can provide. A child that does not experience the same rejection as his or her peers will not be frightened by problems that require imagination and individual solution. A father who wanted his son to become an engineer (a goal not attained by others in the colony) entertained noncolony goals for him. A father who wanted his son to become the English school teacher on the colony entertained a vocation for him that led to defection. An able leader who exceeds the limits (usually intellectually) or engages in certain privileges may unwarily pave the way for subsequent deviation by his children. When children are treated as separate personalities in the formative years, individualism tends to develop to such an extent that it constitutes a threat to the colony. The system works best when the preeminence of the collective welfare over individual welfare is cheerfully and unquestioningly accepted by all the members. Although the Hutterites recognize real difficulties in maintaining the loyalty of their young, it will be observed that they have a different pattern of assimilation than do the Amish.

Conclusions

1. In American society it is assumed that the vigor of national life depends upon educated men and women at every level of society. The goals of education are directed toward self-development and

fulfillment of individual wants, the enhancement of rational powers and personal freedom. The two communitarian societies we
have described emphasize submission of the individual to community goals and the subordination of personal freedom and
rationality to community values. Individual fulfillment is realized
primarily within the bounds of the culture rather than outside of
it. Science, technology, and science-oriented education are held
in moderation in order to preserve the social order.

2. While American young people are in high school, Amish and
   Hutterite adolescents are learning to identify with their culture.
   The task of acquiring the necessary attitudes and skills to enjoy
   life in the little society are achieved in the context of family, kinship groups, work, and community. Socially it is an age span
   when greater freedom is permitted. The vows of the church and
   the commitment to the moral values have not yet been assumed,
   and during this period young people are allowed maximal freedom to voluntarily test their beliefs and find their identities.
   These communitarian societies recognize the danger of exposing
   their young people to an alien peer group during adolescence.
   The high school is recognized for what it is: an institution for
   drilling children in "values, preoccupations, and fears found in
   the culture as a whole" (Henry 1963:287). The extent to which
   the communitarian society can control the social patterns of
   interaction and fulfill the basic needs of personality during the
   adolescent period is directly related to its viability.

3. The differences in assimilation patterns between the Amish and
   the Hutterite groups are related to the differences in social structure and defensive structuring. Given the same religious background and values, the communitarian society with the most
   integrated educational experience has the least amount of assimilation. The individual as well as the family in the Amish society
   has greater freedom of mobility, where and when he or she will
   travel and where he or she will live, than does the individual in
   Hutterite society. Amish persons who leave their culture often
   associate with groups similar to their own in religious orientation. Hutterites often show little inclination for religious affiliation after defection. The Navaho and Zuni adaptations to culture
   change (Adair and Vogt 1949) appear to have some similarities
   to these two Anabaptist groups.

4. Hutterites maintain formal education through all ages to maturity. There are "schools" fitted to all ages. The Amish depend
   entirely on informal education except for the elementary school
   period. The effect of introducing one more formal system of education (public) in the Hutterite colony is minimal since there is

already a great amount of formal instruction. The Hutterites rather than the Amish manifest the least apprehension in accepting certain aspects of public education. The Hutterites integrate certain aspects of public education into their system of total socialization in a manner that maximizes their communal life and neutralizes any noxious effects. Formally they accept the inevitability of public education, but informally they "tame" its pagan influences.

5. The management of crises over educational policy in the Amish and Hutterite groups differ significantly. The conflict is felt more directly by the Amish child than by the Hutterite child, who may not even know that a "school problem" exists. Amish children often know they are the objects of controversy. When a legal code is enforced against a Hutterite parent, the government is faced with religious leaders who are also the school officials and the real defendants. Amish parents who may be charged with violations must appraise their own commitment to the church, seek informal support from their church officials, obtain legal counsel at their own expense, or defend their position in court without either legal aid or representation from their church. Social solidarity is thus best maintained in a communitarian society that institutionalizes its contacts with the great society in contrast to one where the individual must represent his or her own position in an alien culture. This analysis has not dealt with the products or the personality types developed in the two communitarian societies. These topics are discussed in greater detail in two case studies (Hostetler and Huntington 1967, 1971). Through internal discipline and community support, often in the face of court action and scant legal protection, the two communitarian societies have transmitted the skills and attitudes required by their cultures. Both have been able to mitigate, at least temporarily, the onslaught of the large consolidated school and its associated values.

References

Adair, John, and Vogt, Evon, 1949. Navaho and Zuni Veterans: A Study of Contrasting Modes of Culture Change. *American Anthropologist* 51 (1947): 547–61.

Bachman, Calvin G., 1942. *The Old Order Amish of Lancaster County, Pennsylvania*. Norristown, PA: Pennsylvania German Society. Reprinted 1961.

Bennett, John W., 1967. *The Hutterian Brethren: Agriculture and Social Organization in a Communal Society*. Stanford: Stanford University Press.

Bontreger, Eli J., c.1910. What Is a Good Education? In *The Challenge of the Child*, J. Stoll, ed. Aylmer, Ontario, Pathway Publishing Company, 1967, p. 77.

Buchanan, Frederick R., 1967. *The Old Paths: A Study of the Amish Response to Public Schooling in Ohio*. Ph.D. dissertation, Ohio State University, Columbus.

Deets, L. E., 1939. *The Hutterites: A Study of Social Cohesion*. Gettysburg, PA: privately printed.

Eaton, J. W., and R. J. Weil, 1955. *Culture and Mental Disorders*. New York: The Free Press.

Educational Policies Commissions, 1961. *The Central Purpose of American Education*. Washington, DC: National Education Association.

Erickson, Donald A., 1969. *Public Controls for Non-Public Schools*. Chicago: University of Chicago Press.

Henry, Jules, 1963. *Culture Against Man*. New York: Random House.

Hostetler, J. A., 1954, *The Sociology of Mennonite Evangelism*. Scottdale, PA: Herald Press.

_____, 1963. *Amish Society*, rev. 1968. Baltimore, MD: The Johns Hopkins Press.

_____, 1965. Education and Marginality in the Communal Society of the Hutterites. University Park, PA (mimeograph).

Hostetler, J. A., and Huntington, G. E., 1992. *Children in Amish Society: Socialization and Community Education*. CSEC. Fort Worth: Harcourt Brace.

_____, 1996. *The Hutterites in North America*. CSCA. Fort Worth: Harcourt Brace.

Hughes, Everett C., 1952. *Where Peoples Meet*. New York: The Free Press.

Hutterian Brethren Church, 1950. *Constitution of the Hutterian Brethren Church and Rules as to Community of Property*. Winnipeg, Manitoba.

Indiana, Department of Public Instruction, 1967. Articles of Agreement Regarding the Indiana Amish Parochial Schools and Department of Public Instruction. Richard D. Wells, Superintendent.

Knill, William, 1958. *Hutterian Education*. M.A. thesis, University of Montana, Missoula.

Peters, Victor, 1965. *All Things Common, The Hutterian Way of Life*. Minneapolis: University of Minnesota Press.

President's Commission on National Goals, 1960. *Goals for Americans*. Englewood Cliffs, NJ: Prentice-Hall.

Redfield, Robert, 1955. *The Little Community*. Chicago, IL: University of Chicago Press.

Rideman, Peter, 1965. *Account of Our Religion*, English ed. 1950. London: Hodder and Stoughton, Ltd.

Siegel, Bernard J., 1970. Defensive Structuring and Environmental Stress. *American Journal of Sociology* 76 (July): 11–32.

Simons, Menno, 1956. *The Complete Writings of Menno Simons*. Scottdale, PA: Mennonite Publishing House.

Stroup, J. Martin, 1965. *The Amish of the Kishacaquillas Valley*. Lewistown, PA: Mifflin County Historical Society.

Weber, Max, 1958. *The Protestant Ethic and the Spirit of Capitalism*. New York: Charles Scribner's Sons.

Williams, George, 1962. *The Radical Reformation*. Philadelphia: Westminster Press.

10

The Bauer County Fair
Community Celebration as Context for Youth Experiences of Learning and Belonging

Maureen K. Porter
University of Pittsburgh

The county fair has long been an important institution for popular education in rural communities across the United States. A precious few endure as community celebrations that give center stage to inter-generational learning. The fair is multidimensional, reaching back to sustain activities that have been central to local lifeways, reaching out to incorporate each succeeding generation, and reaching forward to stretch participants' horizons. Those elements that emerged as critical to young participants' experiences of learning and belonging are summarized in this report of 5 years of participant observation in Bauer County, Wisconsin.

For 140 years, "The Biggest Little Fair in Wisconsin" has played a pivotal role in maintaining and transmitting the rural lifeways that sustain Bauer County[1] as a viable, vital place. While other county fairs have gone the way of the drugstore cafe counter or have been so commercialized and homogenized as to bear little resemblance to the particular locale sponsoring the fair, the Bauer County Fair has endured as a community celebration. The key to its continued attraction lies in the fact that from its inception, the fair's central mission has been public education. It has provided a uniquely effective, nonschool means through which traditional cultural values, skills, and relationships are transmitted from generation to generation. Through the intergenerational events that constitute the fair, young participants are drawn into an engaging community celebration of both learning and belonging.

Like the colorful images created in a kaleidoscope, fairs are never the same from year to year or from person to person. Each time they

Source: Also appeared in the *Journal of Research in Rural Education* (winter 1995), Vol. 11, No. 3, 139–56. Reprinted with permission of the author.

are experienced, the intersecting patterns come alive for the viewer in unique ways. Fairgoers synthesize symbols, roles, and images from overlapping spheres, bringing them together in ways that present coherent pictures of ever-evolving local lifeways. It is not in the regularity of these patterns, but the fascinating number of possible recombinations from a limited number of constituent parts that the fair's enduring appeal may be understood. In this research, I identify the varied and vivid elements critical to young fairgoers' experiences of learning and belonging. How do they make meanings of the resulting patterns, both for themselves and their futures? Further, as in a kaleidoscope backed with a mirror, young participants also see images of themselves reflected, inverted, and exaggerated through the prism of the fair. Delving further into young participants' multilayered experiences, this research then explores the ways in which this county fair also contributes to a critical understanding of themselves and their communities.

The County Fair

Since its founding, the Bauer County Fair has served as a gathering space and time for people from this rural Wisconsin county. It was once the premier annual festival when people from the many little towns and open lands came together. Although it now must compete with cable television, shopping malls, and large outdoor concerts as a provider of entertainment and education, this fair has retained a prominent place in the annual cycle of special events.

The Bauer County fairgrounds are located on the edge of the county seat, tucked between a wooded riverside, new houses on the edge of town, and the edges of sprawling wheat and corn fields. Compared to some of its neighboring festivals, it is a small fair without pretense, made up of buildings that look much like those in the surrounding countryside. The white, wooden grandstand and the cross-shaped exhibition hall built in 1896 stand as reminders of the long history of the fair. The three newer, aluminum-siding barns that fill the far end of the fairgrounds portend continued, if slow, growth. The merchant's hall, the 4-H dairy bar, the fair office, the 4-H exhibition building, and the Farm Bureau and Jaycees' food stands fill in the middle of the fairgrounds. Even though they are, in theory, movable from year to year, machinery row, the beer and entertainment tents, and the midway all have their traditional places.

Although small in size, the Bauer County Fair brings in a big crowd. In the 5 years of my study, the mean fair attendance was 27,089, or the equivalent of 80 percent of the county's population. The total attendance reflects a steady increase over time that has remained commensurate with gains in the county's population. People from many walks of life and generations attend the fair; as many come for several days as come only for the big-name entertainers in the evening. However, the fair is primarily designed to be a family event. Entrance fees reflect this emphasis; in 1995, a family of four could enter the fair for less than $10. Senior citizens make the trip to spend the day playing bingo or listening to old friends in the shade of the beer tent. Couples, perhaps visiting from the nearby suburbs, proudly show off their newest additions to relatives and friends. Young adults who have just completed their first week away at college come back to see high school pals and "fair friends."

Fair week dominates local social calendars, drawing in even those who do not have exhibits to show. The importance of this annual event in a county without a large mall, teen center, or many social events for geographically isolated youth should not be overlooked. When asked why he came, a non-exhibiting teen reflected the relative excitement of the fair: "Where else would I go this weekend? Everybody hangs out here—it's the only place anything is happening."

The history of the growth of the Bauer County Agricultural Association and their annual fair parallels that of many other similarly positioned communities. The Agricultural Association has its roots in the model that Elkanah Watson set down in 1810. Interested in developing an informed consumer base for the wool of his imported Merino sheep, Watson hosted a fair that included exhibit categories for products from both farm and home, from men and women. The opportunity for the average "dirt farmer" to participate in this fair set these celebrations apart from the elite gentlemen's sheep fairs of the colonial past that never enjoyed a popular following.

Encouraged by the response, Watson also founded a "practical society" in order to cultivate support for the nascent county fair movement that he had helped to spark. Such agricultural societies have remained the organizing force for county fairs in this country. Societies organized along his "Berkshire Plan"—those that held public education about agriculture in paramount importance, hosted fairs as their primary activity, and remained locally controlled—were readily adopted, becoming the predominant rural institution in nineteenth-century America (Cremin, 1980, p. 329).

Throughout the Great Plains region that in the mid-nineteenth century formed the western frontier of the expanding United States and Canada, towns were springing up, and with them, local fairs. They were variously advertised as "county fairs," "fat stock shows," or "fall harvest festivals," but all shared the same essential features (Neely, 1935; Waters, 1939). These celebrations served to mark these aspiring communities as "a place" (Coates, 1985; Doyle, 1982), displaying to self and others "the earnestness of our own efforts to build a greater and more wholesome city" (Centennial Pageant Committee, 1948). Such public events provided ready material for politicians to extol the virtues of a nation coming of age. President McKinley, in an oft-quoted speech, declared, "Fairs and exhibition are the timekeepers which mark the progress of nations. They record the country's advancement; they stimulate the energy, enterprise and intellect of the people and quicken human genius" (Jones, 1983, p. 18).

In the dislocating eras of frontier exploration and settlement, ethnic and national identities were being contested, constructed, and conglomerated. At the same time, the county fairs reinforced a sense of group identity, highlighting that which was unique to the hosting region or county. Fairs "absorbed the truly American traditions that went along with barn raisings, corn huskings, and quilting bees" (Augur, 1939, p. 251), building on community solidarity and a sense of uniqueness. A fair provided for local and visitor alike "an image of its setting, providing a glimpse of how fair people view themselves and their region, what they feel they have accomplished and what they see as still needing to be done" (Coates, 1985, p. 211). In its own way, each fair evolved its own particular traditions, remaining "truly native, keeping close to the ground and to the people who earn their living out of the ground" (Augur, 1939, p. 232).

Throughout the rural frontiers, county fairs provided unduplicated educational forums that played a pivotal role in the acceptance and adoption of scientific approaches to agriculture. These "farmer's universities" (Augur, 1939, p. 252) embodied the ideas of progress. Fairgoers learned that wheat was not the only thing that could be grown profitably (Doyle, 1982, p. 5), but that such strange crops as Chinese sugar cane existed (Sellinger, 1952). A wondrous array of products were on display: windmills, artificial teeth, sarsaparilla and birch beer, tropical birds, fine millinery, and more. New inventions like the Universal clothes wringer, sewing machines, threshers, and refrigeration were displayed (Craycroft, 1989; Frost, 1947; Gasch, 1988; Sellinger, 1952). Through exhibition and example, new ideas were presented to fairgoers that they were challenged to try out for themselves. Like most other chroniclers of fairs, Jones (1983) extolled the value of a fairtime education, while recognizing the sometimes reluctant nature of the farmers to change their ways:

> Ideally, the competition was an apprenticeship. Moved by criticism of their exhibits, the also-rans and the ignorant would, in theory, discard their shoddy workmanship and inefficient ways, their inferior crops and defective seeds, their second-rate machinery and scraggly stock. Soon they would become paragons for others to follow. Uplifted by the knowledge that the fairs propagated, they would be equipped to feast on the finest in life and to cope with the worst. (p. 3)

Because they were local, people of average means could load their families into their buckboards or, later, pack a hamper into the rumble seat and spend several days at the fair (Gasch, 1988; Sellinger, 1952). Fairs were a vital link to the wider world that provided information, comparison, and conversation for those who did not or could not attend lectures or subscribe to journals (Nesbit, 1985, p. 25). Especially in isolated rural regions, "the fairs were," as a farm woman said in 1913, "the schools we could afford to attend" (Jones, 1983, p. 136). Such an embodiment of pride and progress were these celebrations to their individual communities, that members of an Edmonton, Canadian town vehemently opposed regional fair consolidation on the charge that "removing the country fair is equivalent to the removal of the public school in rural districts" (Jones, 1983, p. 139).

Once the preeminent place to exchange the latest techniques, innovations, and trends, county fairgrounds still serve as important venues for continuing education. However, there has been a marked shift away from adult vocational education towards an emphasis on youth at county fairs. And in the shift, fairs like the one in Bauer County have taken on renewed importance as forums for cultural transmission and investment in the younger generations. As service club members stated from their food stand, now "everything's for the kids."

Today, youth clubs such as Future Farmers of America (FFA) and Future Homemakers of America (FHA), the Boy and Girl Scouts, and 4-H provide organized means for young people to develop skills and then bring exhibits to the fair. Indeed, as these groups became more widely popular in the rural towns in the Midwest and agriculture and manual training classes more widely offered in the high schools, county fairs came to organize their youth divisions along categories of exhibits that matched the projects and coursework provided through these other groups (Centennial Pageant Committee, 1948; Craycroft, 1989; Doyle, 1982; Neely, 1935; Sellinger, 1952). However, at present, exhibit categories are not just limited to those items that are regularly produced at school. Therefore, the fair offers additional niches for youth to explore. Once an appendage tacked on to the regular fair program, today the youth exhibits and events are the heart of the Bauer County Fair.

The incorporation of younger generations into fair activities has had, and continues to have, a pragmatic base. In the early twentieth century, organizers of the Bauer County Fair recognized that the exodus of talented and ambitious young people from rural areas posed a threat, and they increased efforts to recruit youth to more meaningful participation in the fairs. As exemplified by an ad placed in the 1927 premium book, calf clubs and special youth classes at the fair were instituted in large part to establish ties between youth and agriculture that could last a lifetime. Under the picture of a boy and his calf with the caption "A proud boy," the text reads, "DEVELOP AN INTEREST IN FARMING BY OWNERSHIP. Every Boy Likes to Care for His Calf or Pig IF HE OWNS IT. It ties them to the Farm." The text by the second picture of another boy and his calf reads, "Why should he leave the farm, When He Is a Partner in the Business?"

Celebration

The Bauer County Fair is a celebration on a highly personal scale. Celebrations are multifaceted, highly educational events. As cultural performance, they dramatize the ideals, aims, and aspirations of the participants in a public and playful manner. As collective symbolic representation of who we are, they carry within them the seeds of who we might be. As communally experienced, choreographed events, festivals hold within them the power to evoke, organize, fascinate, and synthesize. As rites of passage, they incorporate younger generations into the heritage that gives modern life context and a sense of continuity. In festival, people of many different groups come together, whereas in other contexts they may be divided because of socially significant differences in occupation, residence, or age. Through celebration participants educate themselves and one another.

A separate space. The fair is time and space reserved to celebrate the common orientations around which communities coalesce. Fairtime is a time set apart to enjoy oneself and one's fellows. It is a quasi-religious space spatially and temporally removed from the spaces where one engages in the serious business of life, whether it be earning a living or earning good grades. "See you at the fair!" declares the sign above the business that has closed its doors and moved itself to the fairgrounds for the weekend. The fairgrounds themselves have become an "elaborated place" (Abrahams, 1982, p. 161), both the setting and symbol of rural folklife (Fitchen, 1991). It is indeed a space located betwixt and between, an event that unites the everyday with the transcendent, the literal with the symbolic.

The annual fair sets aside time, at least temporarily, to suspend the influence of the mass public culture and to concentrate on what makes the people of this county distinctive. Focus turns inward. Especially for groups that feel threatened by accelerating changes to their traditional lifestyles, this time to take stock and reflect is particularly valuable. Burke states that such "exclusive moments—coalescing around class or ethnicity—are associated with a resistance to modernization and a (re)affirmation of an oppositional identity" (1992, pp. 293–94). However, such moments can also lead to greater recognition of strategic—and not necessarily undesirable—interdependence with the outside world.

The fair is a special event that comes only once a year. However, the transitory nature of the fair enhances rather than dilutes its experience, for the fleeting nature of the sensory smorgasbord encourages participants to soak it all in at once. Overabundance, whether of cheese curds, hogs, or tractors, encourages indulgence. Fairgoers find themselves caught up in a boisterous arena of celebration. This condensation of expressive devices in a time when the audience is prepped for leisurely consumption magnifies their power to reinforce one another (Abrahams, 1982, p. 166).

Place within the yearly cycle. As important as these fleeting experiences are, it is the setting of the fair—and fairtime insights—in meaningful relation to the rest of the year that reinforces its significance as an educational event. The extended late summer weekend of the fair is a cyclical renewal. Just as the fair displays the fruits of the summer's labors, it also showcases the maturing of each generation. As a reflection of community vitality, each fair illustrates how ready succeeding generations are to assume valued roles within the community. Conversely, as a reflection of divisions within the community, the fair highlights residents' propensity to detach and distance themselves from their hometowns.

As an event that happens only once a year, the county fair presents itself as an important opportunity to infuse money and energy back into the community. In a celebration of this size, many hands are needed. Service clubs are hired to work at the Bauer County Fair based on the local use that they intend for their fairtime earnings. Whether paying for the annual town Christmas lighting or sponsoring a children's recreation program, groups must reinvest the money. "We don't hire people who don't put the money back in," declared a fair officer. Further, by acting on their commitment to help out their "neighbors," participants affirm valued roles for themselves and their civic groups in the larger community. Connections and alliances are made that can facilitate long-term regional development efforts. Aronoff (1993), in a study of rural Michigan communities, found that "celebrations offer residents a low-risk area in which to develop a region-wide identity, social relationships, and organizational linkages that subsequently become available as resources for direct economic planning" (p. 3).

Creating the public. The fair unites on one festival grounds the creative endeavors and business enterprises of the various constituent communities that make up the county. People come from the scattered townships and villages that in earlier times competed for resources, or today are divided by high school sports rivalries. At the fair they come together as a county, an entity that transcends one sense of place or set of interests. In this way, the fairtime assemblage embodies an imagined community (Anderson, 1983).

The familiar and largely known script of the county fair enables participants to concentrate on its socially creative dimensions. Geertz (1973) emphasizes that such celebratory and evocative cultural performances are, like the Balinese cockfights that he describes, "stories people tell about themselves" (p. 448). Collective representations make the invisible visible (Durkheim, 1915), displaying through art and artifact who we are, e.g., modern pioneers on a nearly-lost frontier. Community fairs, as integrative dramatizations that emphasize things held in common, can offer participants more than the literal truth, presenting—in essence, creating—a unified sense of place even when there inherently is none (Lavenda, 1983).

Incorporation. The gathering aspect of festival integrates the individual, if only for a short time, into a larger collectivity that transcends both the individual and the era. By joining in the annual festival, the young person can be part of something that his or her parents and peers also may have experienced and remember. When the act of taking part in the celebration is infused with a religious or moral dimension, it takes on an added level of meaning to those who subscribe to the celebrated ideology.

Sometimes becoming a communicant member requires formal induction, and if so, rituals of incorporation may be embedded within a highly prominent celebration. Rites of passage exemplify the ritualistic incorporation of youth into adult worlds. Van Gennep (1960) describes these rites as liminal phases, literally crossing of the threshold between one stage and the next. As Bettleheim (1954) noted, initiation ceremonies attempt to quell anxieties about (adult) roles by contextualizing the initiation within a recurring and ritualized celebration of maturity. Such declarations gain added power by their public nature. Therefore, these rites of passage for youth are conducted before the assembled crowds. Through their participation, both participant and spectator are strengthened in their commitment to the lifeways so vividly represented as well as the moral imperatives that underlie these lifeways. After being set apart during the rite, they are reincorporated into the adult or high-status group with enhanced standing.

The Importance of play. People continue to come to the fair year after year, "'cause it's fun!" However frivolous and trivial fairtime activities may appear on the surface, the aspect of play inherent in the fair is a particularly potent form of education. Play is that which is construed to have no serious meaning yet is infused with meaning (Kridel, 1980). Fairs combine many kinds of play: storytelling between exhibitors and spectators, public speeches, competitions of various kinds, races, and contests. Play is integrative; through games we model valued traits (e.g., of stealth and strategy) and partake in a personally engaging kind of moral education (Kridel, 1980). In a setting where the rules are explicit and provide safe bounds of play, the challenge of personal accomplishment comes to the fore. Play is purposeful.

The playful, or ludic, aspect of festival gains its evocative power partly through inversion. That is, festivals invert the prescribed social order; the private becomes the public, abstinence becomes indulgence, the street becomes the home (Marcus, 1986; Raphael, 1976; Turner, 1982). It is a "time out of time" (Falassi, 1987) where normal social relationships are suspended. Those who hold power or social status are participant-observers just like everyone else, although sometimes, for the enjoyment of that same crowd, they may become dunk tank victims or dressed-up caricature figures. Senators converse freely with those represented in the leveling forum of the fair. In a like manner, youth, arguably maintained as marginal members of their home communities, take center stage at the county fair.

Play is also highly creative. Play infuses festival with ironic juxtapositions that call for consideration and knots of images that provoke disentangling. The fair provides a rich forum for creating new understandings and trying out innovative modes of expression. For example, polka bands may revive forms of musical expression from the ethnic heritage while combining old tunes with new lyrics. The risks of failure are few and the public rewards for success are numerous. Explicit encouragement of risk taking can lead to innovation, whether that leads to a breakthrough in using a particular medium or simply in an individual trying something entirely new for the first time.

In the carnival-like freedom of the fair, mirth can become a political tool, used by the oppressed (Marcus, 1986; Scott, 1990) to critique the political order and create themselves anew as powerful agents. In the festive world of carnival, creative ambiguity provides space for the expression of forbidden thoughts and desires. In the relatively low-risk setting of the fair, dissatisfaction with traditional (sex) roles and privileges or social hierarchies can be more openly voiced. Actions that move beyond those deemed gender-appropriate can be taken. Tensions can be expressed and frustrations diffused through the socially sanctioned safety valves of satire and jokes.

But such serious play can also lead to syntheses of disparate elements, the trying on of new and more powerful roles, and the dramatization of new identities. Those same satires and jokes define new kinds of insiderness and a sense of corporate identity. It is this kind of reflective citizenship that Dewey considered essential for a community of life-long learners. Durkheim posited that social formations give rise to symbolic expressions (1915). But in the transient, loosely structured modern world, the opposite may be equally true. Social solidarity may arise through symbols; we are a "fair family" who shares activities, affinities, and interests. Identities enacted in celebrations can provide nodes of identification that then serve as starting points for more finely articulated organizational myths that constitute certain groups in opposition to or contrast with others. Thus, for example, urban street fests such as Juneteenth, by reconstituting the celebrants in relation to the external world, can contribute to a change in political relations between minority and majority groups.

Intensification. Celebrations like the county fair intensify understanding of and commitment to rural lifeways. This is accomplished first by bringing to consciousness those organizing and synthesizing elements of the culture that continue to distinguish country life. One critical way that this is accomplished is by dislocation, the contrasting or setting out of order (Douglas, 1966). At fairtime, the accouterments of personal lifeways are laid out for all to see. Thus, by displaying a cow and a milking stall outside of a barn, by arraying clothes outside of private closets, by presenting a curd curler separate from its operational function as a tool in a cheese factory, they become evocative symbols of activities pursued elsewhere. Objects are seen in new light: A saw blade becomes a thing to be painted upon, abstracted as an art object.

A second kind of intensification is the embodiment of core ideas through displays. The overflowing exhibit halls of the county fair present a cornucopia of symbols of increase (Abrahams, 1982), the harvest of the "fruits of enterprise." One end of the Bauer County fairgrounds is reserved for a larger-than-life exhibition of the grand machinery of progress—the combines, tractors, feeders, and other tools that make impressive harvests possible.

A third way that participants' awareness is enhanced is through exaggeration and explicit statements of standards. Just as the exaggerated features of the Ndembu initiation masks provocatively display relevant personal attributes (Turner, 1967, p. 103), explicit comments by judges in fairtime judging events make clear the rules, standards, and organizing principles that novices are expected to learn.

Methodology

The present study builds on five rounds of research at this site, and draws on more than a decade of participation in county fairs in Wisconsin. The Bauer County Fair was selected for closer investigation because of its apparent success and resiliency in a county that is continuing to undergo significant economic and social shifts. An additional advantage to this site was my familiarity with the region and acquaintance with several fair officers and residents of the county. These personal contacts enabled me to work in a highly diverse array of participant-observer roles. I served in such capacities as a judge's assistant, fair tag distributor, grandstand "handyman," errand runner, cage assembler, hawker, county extension survey distributor, and dunk-tank victim.

Structured and semistructured interviews formed the core of data for this analysis. Given the emphasis on youth learning, the core interviews focused on fair participants aged 7 to 18 and their families. My main sample comprised several dozen young exhibitors of different ages, sexes, and exhibitor categories with whom I met either alone or in groups. I interviewed many of these young people over subsequent years. Whenever possible, I interviewed one or more of their parents.

Additional interviews supplemented these meetings. A series of semistructured interviews was conducted with those with core responsibilities for running the fair: the officers, major event judges, and board members. I also conducted interviews with prominent actors, including the fair royalty ("Fairest of the Fair,") judges, extension agents, and the carnival operator, whose family has come to this fair for years. These interviews were repeated at least twice during the course of the 5 years with the individual in those positions to test for reliability as well as change over time. In addition, I conducted Expressive Autobiographic Interviews (Spindler, 1970) with senior fairgoers who were able to reflect on changes and consistencies in the fair during their lifetimes. Finally, a sample of nonexhibiting fairgoers stratified by age, gender, and family status were polled to ascertain general attitudes toward participation in the fair.

These contacts were complemented by observations of large-group entertainment, religious, and judging events. As the emphasis is on intergenerational teaching and the translation of values and relationships, I paid special attention to the interaction of people from several generations. I particularly looked at key events that formally express standards and expectations for youth, such as judging and the Junior Livestock Auction. The emerging analyses were triangulated with follow-up interviews with key actors and with those working behind the scenes.

Beginning in the second year of the project, I emphasized building photographic and video portfolios of the events, people, and social groupings that comprise the fair. I analyzed patterns of interactions, as well as the assumptions and acknowledgments that participants expressed. Using these portfolios, I gave a multimedia presentation at the annual Fair Appreciation Banquet and received useful critique that shaped the last round of data gathering. The presentation, as well as the permanent photography exhibit that was displayed in the fair office at fair time, also served as the vehicle for fairgoers' personal reflection and informal commentary that frequently spilled over into more formal interviews.

For context, I used fair-related documents from the Smithsonian Museum of American Folklife, the Wisconsin State Historical Society, statewide fair participation and revenue records, the county library, town archives, and Fair Board minutes. Officers and county residents who became interested in my work collected the local newspapers, even digging back into newspaper microfiche to retrieve past documentation. A particularly rich resource was a history of the fair written by a past president (Gasch, 1988). This, coupled with Bauer County Fair premium books dating back to 1921, provided important information about how the fair advertised itself to its prospective constituents. Boxes of pictures, ribbons, and other personal memorabilia that informants drew out of closets and archives also enriched the data.

Finally, in the time between the annual Wisconsin fairs, I visited fairs in large metropolitan, suburban, and rural areas for comparative purposes. I participated in local as well as state-level celebrations in California, Kentucky, Tennessee, Ohio, and Minnesota. Many of these visits included semistructured interviews with fair officials and informal conversations with participants.

An important element in this structuralist research program is the primary emphasis on participant and insider perspectives. Several long-term trends in fair participation underscore this as an appropriate focus. First, the continued popularity of this particular fair is reflected in the high proportion of residents who come. Second, most people attend the fair again and again, setting aside that weekend just to spend time at the fair. For many respondents, it was nearly inconceivable to imagine that the fair might not come again every year, for as one senior fairgoer stated, "It's a part of my life." Third, fairgoers collectively construct the meaning of the fair. Whether exhibitor, grandstand fan, or officer, their paths inevitably cross on the small fairgrounds. Thus, because of their compact distribution, it was possible to draw a diverse subsample from fairgoers, both youth and adult.

Findings

The influence of the fair extends far past the specific weekend when it takes place. The fair is multidimensional, reaching back to sustain activities that have been central to local lifeways, reaching out to incorporate each succeeding generation, and reaching forward to stretch participants' horizons. Two major aspects of the fair emerged from the data, celebrations of learning that intensify understanding of and commitment to rural lifeways and celebrations of belonging that incorporate members of the younger generations into community networks. In the next two major sections of this article I have distilled the two fundamental elements that young fairgoers find most meaningful in their experiences at the Bauer County Fair: learning and belonging.

Learning

The fair provides a unique public forum for celebrating achievement and inspiring excellence. It is a time to focus on the positive. It may be seen as a complement to the schools, strategically providing educational elements that are not highlighted in the standardized curriculum. It also provides a fundamentally different, playful forum in which young people are encouraged to take risks and to explore roles. For many, the fair provides an unduplicated opportunity that they eagerly anticipate. When surveyed, the general consensus among young exhibitors was that "the fair gives you something to work for."

In this section, I present the most salient aspects of young participants' fairtime learning experiences. I draw primarily on numerous examples from face-to-face judging events and showmanship classes—the preeminent venues for youth to display their growing skills and understandings.

The public aspect of the fair. When asked to reflect on how participating in the fair compared to completing work at school, young exhibitors most frequently mentioned the highly visible nature of the fair. A major purpose of the Bauer County Fair is publicly recognizing and collectively celebrating achievement by youth. When awards are bestowed in judging events, the winners' names are announced along with their parents' names. And after the "junior fair" exhibits have been judged, the exhibitors' names are revealed and displayed on tags attached to the project. Large oak cases, crafted in memorial to former fair participants, display what youth have learned through their gun safety projects, model airplanes, computer programs, house plants, and baked goods. "People get to see what you do," stated Ryan, contrasting work done for the fair with schoolwork "that maybe the teacher reads and nobody else." "At the fair, you receive credit for it," added Hannah.

People of all ages can be seen wandering the exhibit halls, looking at the displays, and looking for projects done by their neighbors, students, church members, friends, and rivals. "Maybe somebody will appreciate it," said Darrin hopefully, referring to his photography display. A dedicated few carry notebooks to record who earned what prize, and to note down judges' comments for future reference. A fair officer perhaps put it best:

They make something that's really special and then they have all these people coming through and admiring it and they see the name—so and so made this. And if this youngster who made it is just walking through and hears that, you have to have a needle and thread to sew his button back on! (laughing). He popped his button off his shirt!!

Recognition of their efforts was a recurring theme to young people's stories of why they brought things to the fair. In addition to public recognition, "junior exhibitors" earn cash rewards depending on the ribbon that they are awarded. The symbolic importance of this money far outweighs the actual amount earned. In 1991, youth earned a mean of $12.62 for their several projects, a net income that seldom covers the cost of completing even one item. However, it was the opportunity to "get extra money off it" that they had earned themselves that impressed these young people. Most had grand plans for their fair checks. Respondents planned to put it towards fashionable sports shoes, a bike, clothes, a 14-foot trampoline, or as Stacey said, excitedly realizing how much her check might be, "roller blades—or maybe a pack of gum."

Trying new roles and modes of expression. Exhibits are harvested from the kitchen, field, farm, and basement workshop. They also come directly from the schoolroom, as at the Bauer County Fair most of the elementary schools still each fill a group booth with selected dioramas, posters, and the like. There are numerous categories for exhibits at this fair. Fruit growing, computer, child development, woodworking, and conservation studies projects are, at their best, the culmination of a year-long process of learning from others and about oneself. Conversely, they may also represent a crash course in getting a project done with just a few days to go before the fair. "The fair makes you get it done," admitted Karl.

Young people are encouraged to try out new areas, especially those that are not offered in their rural schools, in their parochial schools, or through home schooling. Eric, who had completed a significant woodworking project, said that through 4-H he was able to seek out teachers to show him the craft because his high school only offered one cabinet-making class, and he would have to wait 2 years yet to take it. The number and diversity of projects that youth bring testify to their diverse interests. In 1991, 891 Bauer County kids prepared 5,473 exhibits, or a mean of 6 apiece. Some really run with the opportunities offered by the fair. Kristin finished 41 exhibits, explaining simply, "I like to do crafts."

At the voluntary, free-wheeling fair, young people can try on new activities and explore parts of themselves that they or their peers may not deem appropriate in other settings. At the fair, they can push back boundaries that they would be more reluctant to test in the more highly circumscribed and regulated social worlds of Bauer County's small rural high schools. Two examples of different kinds of exploration illustrate this point. First, junior class exhibitors are less constrained by notions of gender-appropriate exhibit categories than the adults, who show more rigidly circumscribed patterns of division by gender in the open (adult) classes. A young man who has sewn clothes and a horse blanket stated his reason for wanting to produce a show shirt himself, "'cause in the store it's $40–$50, and I can make it for less." A second kind of stereotype that exhibitors push back was described by Jennifer. She and her sister brought woodworking, goats, sheep, beef, hogs, clothes, moccasins, a leather dog collar, and more. Her interest in these things was allowed free and unabashed expression at the fair. "In school," Jennifer explained, "they'd make fun of you. They don't know me as anything but a sports jock." But at the fair, these interests are validated: "You can show off to everyone your stuff. 4-H is not a bunch of farmers. There are some regular people—city kids."

Judges as encouraging experts. The most influential fairtime teachers are the judges who have been hired to evaluate the youth exhibits. Face-to-face judging of youth exhibits has become the dominant form of interaction at the Bauer County Fair. Five years ago, a major shift was made towards face-to-face meetings between the judge and the exhibitor in response to the overwhelmingly positive response by parents and young people. It now fills the Saturday on the weekend before the fair.

In these specially designated youth classes, the judges make explicit statements about standards, highlighting and exaggerating desired qualities so that they are more apparent to the novice. Aspects of accomplishments are pointed out to the fairtime student. Seventeen-year-old Mike said, "It's more fun at the fair—you learn more. You know you did a good job, the judge congratulated you, told you what you did right. At school it's just 'Good job'." Judges also offer constructive criticism. Rob, also seventeen and an experienced exhibitor, stated, "in face-to-face you learn from your mistakes, how to be judged, how to be criticized versus just look for praise." However, this mentoring relationship only works if the judge is perceived to be unbiased, fair, and if her or his standards are consistent with past expectations. Unfair judging can become the grounds for public outcry. The second year of the study, parents complained about arbitrary standards and criteria because a judge who simply did not like birds ranked exhibits that used or depicted birds lower than others.

As representatives of "expert" communities, judges use the pronoun "we" in ways that indicate to the novices that there is some sort of established body of experts who set the criteria with which they are being judged. "We like to see a straight hem" and "If we can't see the seams [on the finished ceramic piece] that's a very good job." This inclusive pronoun is extended to more accomplished exhibitors, subtly bringing them into the guild of master crafters. The welcome, "We have five pieces here" indicates that, together, the judge and exhibitor are going to assess the item. Congratulating an advanced exhibitor on a thorough job, the judge said, "we sure need to work hard to get it this good," adding that "when we put a second coat (on ceramics), we skilled artists need to be careful about drying times." After a lesson to an older exhibitor on a better way to mat a charcoal drawing, the judge told him, "you be the expert now and go teach your leader."

Just as important as conveying standards, the judges interact to build self-esteem in the exhibitors. Their comments relay that the judges believe that youth have within them the capacity for excellence, and "they want your very best work to come through" at fairtime. Mike added that he was proud of what he had selected to bring to the fair, "It was fun to do and challenging and it took a while. You can pick out your best and bring it to the fair." The element of personal challenge was a repeated theme with exhibitors of all ages. "Just knowing that I can" and "just that I completed it was good" illustrate this point of pride. Carrie added that, "At school you get a grade—you do it for the teacher. At the fair you do it for yourself." Judges encourage personal ownership of both the product and the effort, recognizing both in their decision to award a certain ribbon. One judge frequently asked often amazed exhibitors, "What do you like about it?" to which a plucky young man responded candidly, "I deserve a first 'cause [I] like it and I'm proud of it!" Judges want their students to claim their work, and as one prodded, "sign it—so that when you're rich and famous people will know when you did it."

Although technical skill is clearly emphasized, judges also recognize progress towards a goal as an achievement worthy in and of itself. Comments representative of this kind of approach include, "I'd really like to give you a first [prize], but maybe next year, eh?" Another judge, handing out a red (that denotes second place), said that this is "'cause you're going to know how to do it better next time." Summing up, a judge said to a disheartened recipient of a white (third place) ribbon, "Don't quit, just do it better."

Linking instrumental competencies with underlying values. Face-to-face judging events are the most prominent times for youth to talk explicitly about what they are learning. In often animated interactions, the judges ask pointed questions of exhibitors that bring to consciousness the values underlying fine workmanship and the production of specific objects. They ask questions that probe exhibitors' understandings of, for example, why a certain technique was used, where their pattern or idea came from, what it took to raise a certain vegetable, why the components of their flower arrangement were chosen, and so forth. Through the explanations that youth give about why they made an object or what the intended use is, young people are involved in the vital process of affirming the cultural values that underlie the production of such items and that continue to make them relevant to modern life in the Hinterland (Spindler & Spindler, 1990). They actively link skills learned with recognition of the aesthetic choices, affinities, and inter-personal relationships that endow their exhibits with personal mean-ing. Afterwards in individual interviews with exhibitors after judging, I asked them to further elaborate on their projects.

Since multiple dimensions of the project are equally important, ribbons recognize artistic skill and expression as well as the conditions under which the item was produced. The exhibitor's understanding or intentions when creating an object are also taken into account. Refer-ring to an unorthodox paint job on a model car, a judge stated, "I won't judge an item down if I think that's what he wanted, that's the way he prefers it." Through these educational events, young exhibitors intensify their understandings of and commitments to the lifeways that make their projects meaningful. In the process, they may also come to a reas-sessment of their own future roles (e.g., as crafters or workers).

Building on the work of Douglas (1966), Hall (1977), Toelken (1979), and Seeger (1966), Moore outlines a framework for interpreting the production of cultural items (1989). Moore's model depicts three "Circles of Tradition," umbrella categories under which cultural items can be placed. These categories include the Integrated Tradition, the Perceived Tradition, and the Celebrated Tradition. Like the judges above, these categories take into account form, the mode of production of an object, the relevant aesthetic standards, the creator's intended use, personal relevance, and the diverse meanings that the object evokes and represents. Exploring how these aspects of exhibitors' projects are linked together is key to understanding the multivalent meanings that the projects have for them. This is true not only for the meanings that exhibits take on though their dislocated exhibition at the fair, but also for the meanings that the former exhibits have when they are reintegrated with the personal context from which the objects or animals originated.

Projects that exemplify an Integrated Tradition focus on meaning. To illustrate how a particular project can be classified, it is useful to look at the example of birdhouses. Perennial fairtime favorites, a bird-house could belong in any of the Circles of Tradition. However, an example of a birdhouse that falls in this first category is Jeremy's easily recognizable marten house. Because they are integral parts of their sur-roundings, items in this circle reflect common ideas about aesthetics and form, usually falling within a conservative genre of decoration, shape, size, color, and material. Therefore, Jeremy explained to the judge, it seemed obvious to him to build his white apartment birdhouse in the classic, two-story style and to set it upon a tall pole. In this way, it was clearly recognizable to both Jeremy and the judge, and ultimately to his family, as a marten house. In addition, items in this circle are infused with meaning through the place that the items have in the life and work cycles of an individual or family. Jeremy's home for the mosquito-eating martens is valued because of the importance of encouraging these birds to nest at his parent's rural farmstead. Further, items in this circle express a degree of continuity with the past: Jeremy felt that he should replace the old marten house with a new one, "because we've always had one."

Other projects illustrate additional aspects of this first circle. Traditional symbolic representations are often incorporated into the design of items intended for ritual or holiday use. Micah's Christmas tree skirt and Elizabeth's white, crocheted Christening gown for her new baby brother each have easily recognized designs integrated into them. In this circle, the intended use is significant. Often items are prepared as gifts for a family member or friend (e.g., a wagon for a younger sibling or a bird feeder for an aged neighbor in a nursing home). The gift may be for the family to use as a unit, as in a gunrack for the family room or a dinner-napkin holder for the table. Further, an item's meaning is central to the existence of an object. Items made seem to be obvious choices, necessary provisions for roles and activities that young people see themselves having now and/or in the future. Thus Melissa decided to build a cedar-lined hope chest, where she plans to gather a trousseau of linens in preparation for her own household. Finally, items can express a sense of spiritual community. Luther, who told an engaging story about how he came to make a shelf out of "Grandpa's wood," and Aaron, who exhibited a cutting from "Dad's roses," both derived great pride from the connections that their projects engender.

Projects in the Perceived Tradition focus on function. A birdhouse in this circle need not necessarily conform to highly codified aesthetic standards. Rather, the purposes that it serves are paramount. Rachel's popsicle-stick birdhouse provides her not only with a way of attracting and providing for birds in the backyard, but also reinforces her relationship with the project leader who helped her construct it. Forms are more fluid in this circle. Young artists can meld ideas and themes, making Bart Simpson the subject of an oil painting or a Mighty Morphin Power Ranger the key figure on a leatherworking project.

More important than particular form is the mode of production and the personal relevance of an item. In a similar way, David's large doghouse makes use of aluminum siding salvaged from his Dad's home renovation project. A part of David's pride in telling the story of how it came to be built is derived from knowing that he made good use of scraps that would have been wasted if they had not been recycled in such a clever way. Likewise, in the exquisitely crafted woodworking storage bench that Elise brought, workmanship is dovetailed with enhanced self-sufficiency, the value that the bench embodies. Echoing local values of self-reliance, building for the future, and pragmatism, the judge asks her how her grandchildren will use her storage bench and why her creation is better than one bought in a store. The idea that "sometime in your life you're going to have to grab a hammer and nails and a saw fix something" infuses this project with significance.

Perceived tradition projects can proclaim affiliation, as Mary Katherine's ceramic horse proclaims her love of horses, even though she now lives in the suburbs and cannot have one of her own. Completion of projects enable young people to identify with a community of people they may have seldom interacted with, as Kyle's rocketry exhibit prompted him to say, "I'm going to be an astronaut." The personal relevance of an item may be discovered en route. Teenage Scott said he not only "learned that I had the talent of refinishing," but now sees it as a likely and enjoyable complement to his anticipated career as an engineer. Scott found that working as an artist enriched his life and made him feel like he belonged to a small cadre of accomplished refinishers.

Projects in the Celebrated Tradition focus on form. Two birdhouses were shown at the latest round of the fair that exemplify objects in this circle. They were made out of worn cowboy boots that had holes cut into the fronts. Old Wisconsin license plates formed the bent roofs, and the whole thing was suspended by a loop of barbed wire. These birdhouses are not as functional as they are decorative or provocative. Items in this circle are usually a self-conscious pursuit, one that attempts to use new forms, materials, or modes of production to create an item as well as to create conversation. Forms may be chosen because they are pleasing and the act of creating them is simply fun. Strange and exotic vegetables cultivated to take on wild proportions, new colors, and grotesque shapes fill this bill. The rejection of convention, whether in who makes an item or what it is made out of, provide a commentary on traditional roles and styles.

Especially when condensation symbols become the objects of such artistic play, they gain renewed stature at the same time that they may be caricatured. In this self-proclaimed "Milk Vein of the World," just such a condensation symbol is the Holstein cow. Jason's project illustrates the unconventional use of this common cultural icon. He came up to the judge with a three-foot tall piece of plywood that had been cut out and painted to depict a dancing Holstein cow. It has reflectors in its eyes; when the cutout is staked alongside the entrance to his driveway, it serves to demarcate an entrance that easily disappears among the rolling landscape as twilight approaches. In this way the family can also display to passers-by that they identity with this local icon.

Items in this last circle may be significant for the creator because they proclaim affiliation with a community or heritage that is not necessarily related to the person's own background, ethnic group, or social roles. Projects may hearken back to a different time or be a revival of an art. For example, Sandy made jam, not because it was an essential part of preparing for winter, but because she wanted to try it and enjoy an indulgence of "homemade," rather than the kind she usually found in the store.

Learning to present oneself. Participating in the fair provides a space for young people to develop abilities that could be considerable assets in the future. In addition to concurrently gaining skills in the production of objects and insight into the values that underlie their acquisition, young exhibitors also are encouraged to develop themselves as public actors. Fair events provide a hands-on education in gaining confidence in relating to the public, learning about competing fairly, and practicing presenting themselves in public arenas. These highly transferable abilities will serve young people well in whatever fields they ultimately enter.

First, the fair brings together people from diverse backgrounds who often harbor divergent, if not conflicting, views. Young people, especially those who spend long hours keeping watch over their animals in the barns, frequently become engaged in casual conversations with the fairgoers who wander through these areas. "People ask questions about goats. Some people want to learn," said Stacey, wrestling with several great kids eager for their evening meal.

Other kinds of interactions also are possible in the open forum of the fair. Over the course of this study, there was an increase in tensions from animal rights activists who saw this fair, like others in the region, as a particularly opportune moment to confront young people, carnival operators, and fair officers with their concerns about cruelty to animals and the politics of carnivorism. These activists were usually cast as meddling outsiders who come to agitate and upset the kids unduly. In response, parents and leaders stressed to young exhibitors that they were wrong about meat consumption and encouraged kids to report any "troublemakers." But it most often fell on youth themselves to represent themselves and to defend their activities, stressing that they have been taught about the importance of keeping an animal clean, cool, comfortable and consistently well fed.

Friendly competition, the second transferable skill, is seen as an important means through which talents are honed and skill displayed to one's peers. An important element of competition is instruction in "the Fair way" of relating. An officer stated that at the fair:

> You're participating against your friend—you've got that fight to exceed, to win, but yet when that [exhibiting] class is over you're still all friends. It teaches them good sportsmanship, citizenship, gives them responsibility. I guess that's why it's survived.

Good sportsmanship in particular is an essential skill that is reinforced in subtle and explicit ways. A young man is told that no matter how tense things get in the ring, a good neighbor will sit "as friends" with others in the evening. In addition, competing fairly means deferring to (adult) authority. Later, this young exhibitor's disappointment with his ranking is countered with a statement reinforcing the authority of the judge and the importance of deference to adults' greater experience.

The third transferable skill, showmanship, is cultivated through an entire set of exhibit categories designed specifically for this purpose. The goal of these classes is not to judge the exhibit, but how well the exhibitors conduct themselves and present their dress, sow, or public speech. Showmanship prizes recognize effort, confidence, and poise, things that are not so easy. As Lissa said, "it's hard to look elegant and lead a sheep at the same time."

Parents were more likely than youth to emphasize the value of working for showmanship. A father who had grown, alongside his children, in his fair involvement from uninterested parent to project leader to barn superintendent emphasized the common view that it was important to "just get out there and do it." In addition, he felt that the showmanship categories were a place where those children who came from hobby farms or whose parents did not invest in high-price breeding stock could have an equal footing. This suggests that with the growing shift away from primary incomes from farming, the importance of categories that are attractive to nonfarm families (e.g., pet animals or hobby farming) may grow in importance. A mother of several exhibitors commented that she felt showmanship ribbons were perhaps more telling of the child's effort:

> You can buy an animal or you can raise an animal, I guess, and some people like to buy a good quality animal . . . but my kids work for showmanship. Showmanship is on the kid, how you clean the animal and how you present it and when, ah!, they come home with a showmanship [ribbon], I don't care a what, it makes me feel darn good!
>
> [Q: What does a showmanship ribbon mean to you?]
>
> That they were working on it, and they wanted it hard enough that they wanted to show the people that they knew how to do it and that they were the best there—that's what I like. (Recounts how well her offspring have done.) I know they did their best, even if they might not have come

home with a trophy, I know they did their best, and I'm proud of that fact. (Tells how in their home all of the fair awards are displayed on equal footing with sports trophies.)

Belonging

The Bauer County Fair also provides young people and those who wish to invest in youth opportunities to work together. Teens and even elementary-age kids can take on service and leadership roles at the fair, some of which are seldom otherwise offered to them because of their age or background. But at a small, local fair people need to pull together; there is the potential for each person to find a niche where her or his services are needed. By being a meaningful part of a long established festival, young participants gain a sense of belonging and enhanced perspective about where they might fit in as adults. In this section I present several examples of the ways that youth are brought into community work through the fair and the discourse about volunteerism and service that accompanies such participation. Then, to illustrate how succeeding generations are incorporated into the *communitas* (Turner, 1969), I highlight two annual celebrations of belonging: (a) the Junior Livestock Auction, which incorporates youth into professional networks, and (b) the Sunday church service, which reminds fairgoers that they are inherently part of a larger, moral occupational community.

Learning about the work of building community. Participation is not limited to those who bring exhibits; there are many work roles for people of different generations to fill. Volunteerism has long been the cornerstone of the fair. Today, as in the past, a veritable legion of superintendents, recorders, ticket takers, taggers, breakfast servers, and car parkers keep the fair running smoothly. Often these teams are composed of multi-age groups or families.

Impromptu work groups are a common scene at a small fair; everyone has to pull together to make events happen. Late one night a volunteer crew of officers, their relatives, and other fairgoers disassembled the main stage, a sturdy platform with a backdrop and lighting frame that was built upon three hay wagons. The next morning, these wagons would be moved to the wooded glen along the river that bounds the fairgrounds and the stage rebuilt for a different band's show the next night. A young conscript commented that he felt appreciated because, "Everyone is important, everyone has a contribution to make. Here you're not among strangers—you know people." This aspect of familiarity was important to him, because "you can work better together." Becoming known as someone whom people can call upon is important in a Gemeinschaft—a social system based on personal relationships—whereas it is less crucial in a Gesellschaft—which is more typical in transient, urban settings and where contractual relations are the basis for relationships between people.

Those who volunteer their materials, as well as those who give of their time and energy, reinforce their sense of belonging, feelings that can strengthen and deepen over their lifetimes. Under signs that read "Mueller Memorial Building" or "Dedicated to the Memory of Peter Herman, Fair Officer and 4-H leader for 43 years," young people see their contributions as a continuous line from those made by their foreparents, whether these are literal kin or not.

Metaphors of blood and family underscore these understandings. By helping, "the fair gets in your blood." Many of those who have grown into leadership roles, particularly the fair officers who are responsible for day-to-day operations, "grew up with the fair." Officers felt that they were now full members of the "fair family."

There are many service roles available. Young people become part of teams that staff food booths, keep watch in the barns at night, help in the racetrack pit, or work on the grounds. A teenage boy whose family had not traditionally been involved with the fair but who became a core member of the all-male maintenance squad through a summer groundskeeping job, stated; "I like working up here and knowing that I did something that everyone's going to see. I like helping out." A youth leader stated that working at such a public-supported event provides young workers with a larger sense of belonging. Enthusiastically reflecting on her own positive experiences, she felt that it gives young people

a sense of community work. . . . When these kids come here they come from all areas of the county. They all become friends, working side by side. I think that ability, say, "I'm from Dunwiede" or "I'm from Carver," but we can all work together to make this fair grow, and maybe make our county grow, and make our state be better, you know, just by working like that . . .

By working and playing together, fairgoers collectively construct the meaning of what it means to belong to a community. A fair officer underscored the importance of a celebratory context in which to nurture desired character traits: "If we can teach that to these kids in a fun way with other youngsters at their age, we're just building a character for this child for all the years that he's going to be on this earth." For example, the importance of personal responsibility, the value of working collaboratively, and the importance of service in community life are all skills that young fair participants see modeled by adult leaders and teen leaders. A parent, taking her turn in the 4-H youth dairy bar and grill, stated that when working in multi-age groups in the stand, youth learn more than just how to count change:

They learn the ability to wait on people and be happy and present themselves. That says "Hey, this is a nice county that we can be proud of."

[Q: Why is that important?]

It's important when you go to the 4-H stand and these kids rush up to you and ask, "Can I help you?" And you do see the sense of "I really do want to help you, to do something for you."

These encounters are two-way, as fairtime provides residents of the county with opportunities to see youth in action on a much larger scale than they would otherwise encounter. Negative images of youth are inverted, replaced at least temporarily by positive ones. It is a time set aside to celebrate the accomplishments of young people and to feel optimistic about the group whom event announcers constantly refer to as "our youth." A newspaper reporter there to do the annual opening-day coverage of the fair and several youth leaders concurred with an extension agent's comment that fair provides a singular chance to see youth in positive roles:

Sometimes they say "Ah, gee the youth are going downhill." I think that the county fair is a good example of seeing the youth in action, whether they are showing off, or modeling at the style review, whether they're helping at the food stand or helping as an assistant to a superintendent. But seeing them in different roles—that's important for not only the senior citizens, but also their parents, the adult volunteers they work with, and also their peers.

Another kind of inversion that takes place at the fair is "farm kids" becoming experts and insiders. Bauer County schools bring together students from a wide range of backgrounds, ranging from isolated rural to suburban. Sometimes chided by their nonfarming peers as "hicks," fairtime is a safe space in which farm youth are among those given center stage. Fairgoers who do not live on farms, whether they be visitors from a nearby city or Bauer County residents, have the opportunity to see "real, live farm animals." And they can see young people readily handling boars or cows and fielding fairgoers' often naive questions about animals. The rural young person who is thus cast in the role of expert feels a degree of pride in competently performing a fascinating activity. The pleasure derived from having insider or expert knowledge, especially as compared to the sometimes condescending suburbanites, was reflected in the joke told by a teen leader. Chris recounted the oft-retold tale about the town kids "who'll see a [brown] Guernsey and they say 'Hey, Mom there's a cow that gives chocolate milk!' You have to educate them that all milk is white, the chocolate comes later." The pleasure of the joke comes not from its truth in representing all non-farm visitors, but in the telling of the tale among insiders.

The junior livestock auction and professional networking. The webs of relationship that are woven at the fair also serve to integrate young people into professional networks that can assist them in becoming full-fledged, productive members of the community. The junior livestock auction is the most notable example of how the fair offers young people an unduplicated means to become part of the countywide agribusiness network. Participants are launched on the way toward a life-long set of relationships that will be critical to their abilities to earn a living within the local set of farms, banks, industry, and businesses. In this rural area, business relations are significantly influenced by personal reputation and mutual respect. By participating as "real sellers," young people take the first steps toward becoming serious partners. Even if they do not choose to pursue careers in the region, or choose ones only peripherally related to this core network, the skills and recognition that they gain through the Auction will be assets. This event has no counterpart beyond the fair, so those who do not participate are at a disadvantage.

At the Auction, respected adults invest in youth, publicly supporting these future adult members of the extended community. Bankers, feed dealers, hair stylists, butchers, insurance agents, teachers, and more all eagerly lined up to register to bid. The eager spectators sat on bleachers along the gaily decorated center arena, leafing through programs that list the names of the exhibitors due to appear with their cattle, sheep, and pigs. Prospective bidders marked, at least by sight, the names belonging to the particular family farms they wish to support. "It's about business," a long-time bidder explained. They get ready to bid, fully aware that the prices are inflated to many times the market rate in order to reward youth for a job well done.

Each year, the public spectacle that accompanied the bidding drew a large crowd that grew to spill out of the metal-sided barn building. The names of the highest bidders on each animal were called out, and the runners up in that round of bidding were also acknowledged and thanked for their support. Trying to encourage even higher bids, the auctioneer called to the crowd, "Thanks for bidding! You're giving these kids a real education!" Youth who had earned the grand championship ribbons or who had earned showmanship awards were almost always awarded even higher premiums on their animals. In 1995, the Grand Prize sheep reaped $884 for the young person, the top pig brought in $1,719, and the best beef steer commanded $2,835.

Auction events remained prominent past the Sunday afternoon when it was held. Buyers of the championship animals would later be spotlighted in the local paper, standing with the animal, the exhibitor, and the Fairest of the Fair. After the sale, these buyers not only took the animal, but also kept the championship banner and trophy for dis-

play in their places of business as a public announcement of their support. Almost immediately upon returning to the pens with their animal,
the successful young sellers wrote the name of the buyer up on the entry
sheets that hung above the pens, usually in the form of "Thank you,
Bauer National Bank, for buying my sheep." A few days after the fair,
the young sellers wrote letters of thanks to the buyers as well as to other
case competitors in the auction.

For their part, the exhibiting youth can earn up to several hundred
dollars for top-flight market pigs and sheep, and well over a $1,300 for
a steer. In 1995, $60,231 was invested in young people at the Auction.
Especially for those exhibitors who are too young to find regular
employment, the financial incentives to bring an animal to the fair and
present it at the Auction can be compelling. The clear majority reported
that they take the money and, after paying back their parents a prear-
ranged amount for barn rental and feed, they put the rest in a college
savings account.

The Auction also serves as a public rite of passage. Through the
Auction young farmers must confront the essential dilemma in market
animal production, the sale of the animal for meat. The presence of
many youth selling off animals, the inflated financial rewards given to
every participant, and the involvement of parents, their friends, and
business associates all contribute to the pressures and rewards for
youth to conform to adult expectations at the sale. Individual performance in the Auction show ring is highly ritualized, and there are
numerous adult guides on hand to assist. Young people do not have to
guess how to behave; they simply wait their turn.

In addition to exhibiting the appropriate selling behavior in the
show ring, this liminal stage requires that the young person successfully
resolve the inherent conflict between attachment to and separation
from the animal. They do so by emphasizing profit or "being grown-up"
over emotional attachment to an animal that they may have spent considerable time training and grooming. Often coaching from an older
exhibitor or parent is needed to reinforce the "correct" choice. Corrie,
10-year-old veteran of the lamb scene, said that she was a little worried
about her younger sister who was going to be part of the Auction for the
first time: "It bothered me a little when I was young, but it doesn't any
more."

In another part of the main barn, a farmer cheerfully explained the
purpose of the Auction as her daughter, Amanda, leaned against the
huge pig as she fed him: "Tomorrow is the auction—that's when you are
going to sell him." To Amanda's confused and somewhat anxiety-ridden
gestures, she countered, "Remember, that's why we brought him. Hey,
what are you going to do with your money?" Jason, 18, echoed the
importance of financial incentives, recalling that it may be hard for

young kids to let go of an animal that they've been working with all summer, "but once they see that check, it doesn't affect them too much." Nevertheless, some sellers do have tear-streaked, red faces as they approach the Auction ring, even those who are older and experienced in the Auction ritual.

A moral occupational community and the church services. In addition to learning about the social networks that are important to the smooth functioning of the county as a unit, fairgoers, whether exhibiting or not, are drawn into a public dialogue about the importance of farming, especially family farming, in the life of the county. Although fewer and fewer young people of Bauer County will become full, or even part-time, farmers, the occupation of farming, and in particular, dairying, command the place of honor at the Bauer County Fair.

This celebration explicitly proclaims the organizing myth of independent family dairy farming as the linchpin that secures converging parts of the community while still allowing them considerable individual flexibility. As the large wooden sign over the youth livestock pens reads, "Farming is Everybody's Bread and Butter." In years past, there have been booths glorifying the role that "Victory Farming" played in securing the future of a nation at war. Likewise, today political candidates hand out flyers extolling the importance of residents in the rural "Heartlands" in maintaining a strong national moral commitment to land, ecology, competitive production, and "family values."

Family images pop up again and again at this intergenerational festival. Above the overstuffed tables of vegetables, there is another wooden billboard that reads "Family Living," showing a logo with cupped hands and the slogan, "We've got the future in our hands." The annual fairs emphasize that the "roots" of agriculture are planted in youth, thus the banner in the background of the refrigerated cheese case proclaims hopefully, "Young Farmers Belong." These and other spotlighted displays at the fair reinforce agriculture as the critical juncture in the local concept of self. It is the one thing that all locals can participate in, even if only vicariously once a year at the county fair. For nonfarmers, the idea that there is a highly valued occupational pursuit common to many in the county provides a sense of distinctiveness, cohesion, and importance. The fact that this rural way of life is seen to be infused with a moral dimension and that, together, farmers and their customers comprise a moral occupational community, imbues it with an even greater sense of importance.

Nowhere is the concept of a moral occupational community expressed more clearly than at the ecumenical Christian church service held on Sunday morning in the grandstand or in a revival tent. Those who gather reflect the diversity of ages and roles represented on the fairgrounds, although their numbers may vary from barely a dozen one year to nearly eighty. Many of the worshipers have spent the night keeping watch in the barns or have arrived early to begin another long day at the fair.

The pastor welcomed them, stating, "We come from all corners of the county. We don't all know each other, but here we are called to be one people in God." They gather together to be reminded that the fair exists within a larger scheme of life and that their work is infused with a larger sense of purpose and importance, something larger than any single person (Warner, 1953).

As part of the readings, the officiate recounts to the assembled faithful the story of Genesis. Over the morning lowing of the cows that emanated from the barns next door, he quotes from memory:

> According to our liking let him have dominion over the fish over the sea, and over the birds of the air and over the cattle, and over all the wild animals of the earth, and over every creeping thing that creeps upon the earth.

The rightness of "man's" stewardship over animals and "his" responsibility to care for them properly is equated with fulfilling God's ultimate plan for humans. The fact that genetic engineering can be easily incorporated into the modern understanding of this mission is reflected in the following passage from the sermon:

> I just want you to think of the creativity that's taking place in these [Bauer] County fairgrounds with all the animals and all of the displays of stock. The creation of things isn't done here, and the important thing for us to remember this morning that God involves us in the creation, we are coworkers with God. So the animals that are here being shown are probably quite different from those that started out on the day of creation. We have been capable of doing, God working together with us, for you see, God doesn't do everything for us. Like any parent realizes that to have a child grow up, gradually they have to take on more responsibility. You can't do it all for 'em. But as time passes they have to grow up in order to be the next generation.

It is interesting to note that the pastor draws parallels between the ways that Bauer County parents should provide opportunities for their children to grow, just as God, as The Father, is using the fairgrounds as a training place to show His children how to take on the responsibilities that they are expected to demonstrate as mature beings.

"God wants us to participate," the officiant repeats, exhorting those gathered to a life of service that begins with the most basic relationships with animals and extends to those fellow human beings needing food and shelter. As a nondenominational service, most of the chosen songs are patriotic ones that reflect civil religious values (e.g., *God Bless America* and *America the Beautiful*). Sitting high in the grandstand above real-life "amber waves of grain," worshipers sing of the ways that God has blessed them through the bountiful harvests that "allow us to continue to feed the world." In this way, those gathered are once more reinforced in their sense of being a chosen people with a renewed sense of purpose and importance in the world.

Conclusion

Participating in the Bauer County Fair is important to the young people who come to show their projects, wander through the barns and grandstand, work on the grounds, volunteer in the Dairy Bar, and just watch other people. Young fairgoers actively seek ways to make sense of the patterns that they see in motion around them. Through the kaleidoscope of the fair itself, young people are able to make the pieces fall into place.

While each person finds meaning in her or his own way through the individualized projects and activities that they have voluntarily sought out, several common elements unite their experiences. Opportunities to complete projects and then participate face-to-face in judging provide opportunities for young exhibitors to learn about their craft as well as themselves. In the process of articulating the values and relationships that give their projects personal meaning, such structured interactions with experts intensify participants' understandings of why they should strive to achieve. Further, because of the public nature of youth exhibits and showmanship classes, young people are recognized as they try out new roles and ways of presenting themselves. Youth also encounter settings in which they belong. Their labor, services, and barn supervision are necessary, not trivial, contributions to this small fair. More formalized experiences of belonging also provide transition points for maturing young people. These rituals and rites of passage incorporate young people both into the agribusiness networks vital to community prosperity as well as into the underlying Christian ideologies that inform local lifeways.

The Bauer County Fair should not be seen as a static re-enactment of obsolete cultural patterns, somehow surviving as a relic of a bygone age. Instead, participants of several generations are engaged in a hands-on dialogue, synthesizing symbols, roles, and images from overlapping spheres of culture. The Bauer County Fair provides a week set aside to integrate the often conflicting messages of rural life on a rapidly-expanding urban periphery. It has been this dynamic process of cultural transmission, the ongoing modification of roles, and the creative adaptation of the cultural legacy which have sustained this particular county fair as a meaningful, intergenerational celebration.

Elements Critical to Their Experiences of Learning

Purposeful, playful education infuses the Bauer County Fair with meaning. By providing competitions that bring together judges and youth in face-to-face interactions, fairs provide explicit encounters in which young people learn from teachers drawn from all walks of life. What young artists, gardeners, dog trainers, goat farmers, clothing style review models, and woodworkers produce are given center stage at this small fair.

The fair offers unique judging and competitive forums for youth to learn the skills and values that underlie rural life in Bauer County. The county fair accentuates the positive, highlighting achievements in learning culturally valued pursuits. Young people are rewarded for accomplishments as well as progress toward mastery. Whichever Circle of Tradition their projects falls into, youth are encouraged to feel worthy of the challenge of completing their chosen project. Exhibitors are caught in the public eye, where they see themselves and their abilities reflected and critiqued. They are challenged to redefine who they are and what they are good at doing. It is important to note that for many of the young people whom I interviewed, this fair is the only place where they can safely explore projects otherwise proscribed them because of their age, gender, or "jock" image at school.

The fair provides many opportunities to explore new areas with few risks and, seen through the eyes of youth, relatively large rewards. It is illuminating to contrast how parents sum up what youth learn through the fair with how youth summarize their experiences. Parents felt, on average, that the most important reasons for encouraging their children to participate were enhanced self-esteem and the opportunities to take responsibility, learn how to help others, and meet other kids. Youth, on the other hand, were far and away the most motivated to exhibit by the prize money. This is a fascinating finding, because the average "fair check" barely covers the cost of completing even one project. Despite the fact that county fair premiums have remained nearly the same since the 1970s, young exhibitors reported that the fair check represented to them "money I earned myself." For those who participate in the Junior Livestock Auction, and thus for whom the premiums are substantially inflated, the money may at least partially appease whatever qualms they may have about selling off their animal for slaughter. Other common reasons cited by youth were a sense of accomplishment in meeting a challenge that they had sought out themselves and the opportunity to compete with others and thereby gain ideas about how to improve or what else they could try. These were followed by the opportunity that the fair offered to receive feedback from expert judges "who know something." The fact that most of those interviewed felt that schoolrooms did not provide them with the same kinds of learning experiences or rewards is significant.

At the same time that they reinforce hinterland values, competitions open up significant room for the inversion of roles, critique, recombination, innovation, and humor. Thus, while Jason's dancing Holstein may satirize this oddly shaped creature, at the same time it reinforces the hegemony of the dairy cow as the preeminent condensation symbol of the county. Modes of expression can be used to comment on rather than just glorify life in Bauer County. The fact that more drawings are of decrepit, weather-worn barns than there are of flower-filled active farmsteads, evokes in the person wandering through the exhibition hall a sense of loss, even decay, of a once dominant lifeway based on family farming.

Elements Critical to Their Experiences of Belonging

The Bauer County Fair provides central rather than peripheral roles for young people. Instead of being incidental spectators, young participants come together with members of older generations in events that require their joint efforts in order to be successful. By enlisting in the legion of volunteers needed to run the fair, young workers can gain first-hand knowledge of the amount of work that it takes to make a fair like this happen year after year. Experiencing how they are treated and their contributions acknowledged or not provides insight into what kinds of positions they can anticipate as adults. By participating in the Auction and attending the on-site church services, young fairgoers encounter the norms and assumptions that provide the framework that has linked different elements of the county together for generations.

First, the fair offers young people meaningful ways to belong to a community of workers. Through experiential education working in the grandstand, in the barns, in the 4-H stand, and as traffic controllers in the parking areas, young people are invited to have fun while working. At the same time, they are learning more about what it means to do the work of building community. Those who take on leadership roles experience first-hand the challenges of motivating their peers, not to mention those older than themselves. Participants learn early in life the considerable contributions of time and energy that are the necessary prerequisites for small community celebrations dependent on the local labor supply. Successful fairtime experiences lead youth to see themselves as long-terms participants in this cross-generational activity. They are welcome to return as adults, whether as exhibitors, as officers, or as volunteers. Conversely, perceptions that judging has been unfair, their efforts were not rewarded, or that their participation was discounted may lead to an early decision to disassociate with the fair as a time-consuming and irrelevant activity.

Through this animated celebration, fairgoers collectively construct what it means to be part of the *communitas,* both now and in the future. Participants gain a critical perspective on what it means for them as young men and women to live in an urbanizing, yet still rural county, that depends to a large extent on external markets and resources. Young participants are continually encouraged to reinterpret and reinforce their commitment to their hometown region and the underlying values that make belonging meaningful. Looking up to the young lady chosen as "Fairest of the Fair," they are asked to emulate someone who embodies the ideal characteristics valued by the local committee: scholarship, leadership, service, understanding of the regional economy, plans for higher education, etc. For many youth interviewed, the rural lifestyle that they envisioned in their future was not an "either-or" choice. Several indicated that they are searching for ways to combine the instrumental competencies that they enjoyed displaying at the fair (e.g., refinishing furniture or designing sustainable agriculture plans) with careers in engineering, ecology, nursing, or teaching. While most young people do have the real option of moving away from their hometowns, being part of this rural fair gives them a more complex understanding of what it would take to create a satisfying lifestyle locally.

Second, through the Junior Livestock Auction, the most prominent rite of passage at the fair, future farmers, homemakers, teachers, and business people are dramatically brought into the circle of agribusiness professionals. Sellers in the auction need to be able to internalize the assumptions of the value system that makes the raising—and then selling—of market animals acceptable. Most notably, young sellers need to believe that the sale should not arouse feelings of loss or sadness, at least not in "mature" exhibitors. If the young person is not able to do this, the Junior Livestock Auction may serve as a pivotal point in his or her decision not to engage in livestock farming in the future.

Third, at the Bauer County Fair there are numerous opportunities for those who agree with the dominant paradigms of "traditional" or "family values" to display their messages. The fairgrounds are the field upon which the average person sees inscribed the relationships and ideologies that knit together regional endeavors. By highlighting the production and display of objects and skills, fairtime competitions underscore the values and relationships necessary for their creation and continued use. At the fair people gather with others who share similar views about a moral occupational community that draws inspiration from the values expressed through family farming. Above these clusters of fairgoers, on billboards such as "Farming is Everybody's Bread and Butter," participants are presented with explicit statements about the condensation symbols, understandings, and organizing myths around which their communities coalesce.

Those who disagree—for example, with images of God as "Father" or an embryo's "Right to Life"—are not encouraged to debate the issue. Instead, no one follows up if, for example, they decide not to have their own booth in the Merchant's Hall. The idea that "this is our time," and "if you don't like it here you can go somewhere else" parallels the message given to young people who face the very real option of leaving the county if they do not comfortably fit in.

Areas for Further Research

There is need for additional research on this and other community celebrations as forums for youth experiences of learning and belonging. As opportunities for intergenerational co-education, they offer opportunities for both intensification of understanding as well as incorporation of diverse groups. However, the extent to which such fairs do not adequately reach out to all members of their host communities needs to be more fully explored. Those disaffected teens who are detached from local social networks are one group that needs to be better integrated; whether the county fair and its associated clubs are the most appropriate means for doing so remains to be seen.

Nonparticipants' experiences and perspectives should be analyzed and then taken into account by those who wish to further expand the constituent base drawn to the fair. Those who feel that the exhibit categories do not match their own interests should be interviewed to see how the fair can become more inclusive of the actual activities and interests of those who live in this rapidly changing region. While the fair offers opportunities for explicit recognition of a certain array of values and ideologies, organizers need to become more alert and responsive to those who do not feel that they would be heard at this forum. How county residents engage in self-silencing is as important a topic for further study as is an investigation of how people express their mainstream beliefs. If the fair is not to become narrow or stagnant, leaders need to assess the extent to which this celebration is able to accommodate dynamic exchange.

By investigating the fair as celebration, an expanded history of the fair could be written that is not limited to a listing of which buildings were constructed when. Seeing the fair as a reflection of the county leaders' desires to present, to themselves and to others, Bauer County's potential, further research could document histories that illustrate the emerging sense of self as a leading agricultural center. A historical study of how the fair has changed over time, including the significant shift away from adult vocational education to the current emphasis on youth, would be another important contribution. Looking at ways that roles,

especially gender roles, have been reified by the structure of exhibit categories (e.g., the "Women's Department") would be valuable. Lastly, a
comparison of the changing relationship between school-based learning and fairtime learning could shed light on the differences between a
context of celebration and one of academic competition.

This prominent community celebration can play a critical role in
drawing out valued elements of the county's heritages and in shaping
new conceptions of the county's future. Investing in young people is a
critical place to begin. However, future research by the fair's officers as
well as researchers interested in the potential of community celebrations should be concerned with understanding how—and if—young
participants make the transition to adult participants. Participating in
the Bauer County Fair remains a voluntary activity. This optional, personally sought-out nature of participation underscores many of the
most valued aspects of young participants' experiences. It also means
that fair leaders will have to continue to maintain an emphasis on reaching out to younger generations in ways that they find meaningful and
engaging.

Note

[1] Pseudonyms are used throughout.

References

Abrahams, R., 1982. The Language of Festivals: Celebrating the Economy. In
    Celebration. Studies in Festivity and Ritual, V. Turner ed., pp. 161–77.
    Washington, DC: Smithsonian Institution Press.
Anderson, B., 1983. *Imagined Communities: Reflections on the Origin and
    Spread of Nationalism*. London: Verso.
Aronoff, M., 1993. Collective Celebration as a Vehicle for Local Economic Devel-
    opment: A Michigan Case. *Human Organization*, Winter.
Augur, H., 1939. *The Hook Affairs*. New York: Harcourt, Brace and Company.
Bettleheim, B., 1954. *Symbolic Wounds*. Glencoe: Free Press.
Burke, P., 1992. *History and Social Theory*. Cambridge: Polity Press.
Centennial Pageant Committee, 1948. *"Harvest of a Century" Dodge County
    1836–1948*. No. Dodge County Board of Supervisors, Centennial Commit-
    tee.
Coates, K., 1985. *Pride of the Land. An Affectionate History of Brandon's Agri-
    cultural Exhibitions*. Winnipeg, Canada: Peguis Publishers.
Craycroft, R., 1989. *The Neshoba County Fair: Place and Paradox in Missis-
    sippi*. Jackson, MS: Center for Small Town Research and Design, Missis-
    sippi State University.
Cremin, L., 1980. *American Education: The National Experience 1783–1876*.
    New York: Harper and Row.
Douglas, M., 1966. *Purity and Danger*. London: Routledge and Kegan Paul.
Doyle, M., ed., 1982. *A Commemorative History of the Buffalo County Fair*

1872–1982. Alma, WI: The Buffalo County Historical Society.

Durkheim, E., 1915. *Elementary Form of the Religious Life.* London: G. Allen and Unwin.

Falassi, A., ed., 1987. *Time out of Time: Essays on the Festival.* Albuquerque, NM: University of New Mexico Press.

Fitchen, J., 1991. *Endangered Spaces, Enduring Places: Change, Identity and Survival in Rural America.* Boulder, CO: Westview Press.

Frost, F., 1947. *Windy Foot at the County Fair.* New York: Whittlesey House McGraw-Hill Book Company.

Gasch, R., 1988. *The Bauer County Fair: 1856–1988.* The Bauer County Agricultural Association.

Geertz, C., 1973. *The Interpretation of Cultures.* New York: Basic Books.

Hall, E. T., 1977. *Beyond Culture.* Garden City, NY: Doubleday.

Jones, D., 1983. *Midways, Judges, and Smooth-Tongued Fakirs. The Illustrated Story of Country Fairs in the Prairie West.* Saskatoon, Saskatchewan: Western Producer Prairie Books.

Kridel, C., 1980. The Play Element in Culture and the Use of Festivals in the General Education Curriculum. *The Journal of General Education* 32(3), 229–38.

Lavenda, R. H., 1983. Family and Corporation: Celebration in Central Minnesota. In *The Celebration of Society: Perspectives on Contemporary Cultural Performance,* F. E. Manning, ed., pp. 51–64. Bowling Green, OH: Bowling Green University Popular Press.

Marcus, L., 1986. *The Politics of Mirth.* Chicago, IL: The University of Chicago Press.

Moore, W., 1989. Circles of Tradition: Toward an Interpretation of Minnesota Folk Art. In *Circles of Tradition. Folk Arts in Minnesota,* pp. 1–23. St. Paul: Minnesota Historical Society Press.

Neely, W. C., 1935. *The Agricultural Fair.* Morningside Heights, NY: Columbia University Press.

Nesbit, R., 1985. *The History of Wisconsin.* Stevens Point, WI: Worzella Publishing Company.

Raphael, R., 1976. *Edges: Backcountry Lives in America Today on the Borderlands between the Old Ways and the New.* New York: Alfred A. Knopf.

Scott, J., 1990. *Domination and the Arts of Resistance: Hidden Transcripts.* New Haven: Yale University Press.

Seeger, C., 1966. The Folkness of the Non-folk vs. the Non-folkness of the Folk. In *Folklore and Society: Essays in Honor of Benjamin Botkin,* B. Jackson, ed., pp. 1–9. Hatboro, PA: Folklore Associates.

Sellinger, P., 1952. A *Guide to the Sheboygan County and the Fair: Past and Present.* Sheboygan Falls, WI: The R. E. Lindner Company.

Spindler, G., 1970. Fieldwork among the Menomini. In *Being an Anthropologist: Fieldwork in 11 Cultures,* G. Spindler, ed., pp. 267–301. New York: Holt, Rinehart and Winston.

Spindler, G., and L. Spindler, 1987. *Education and Cultural Process: Anthropological Approaches,* 2nd ed. Prospect Heights, IL: Waveland Press.

Toelken, B., 1979. *The Dynamics of Folklore.* Boston: Houghton Mifllin.

Turner, V., 1967. *The Forest of Symbols: Aspects of Ndembu Ritual.* Ithaca, NY: Cornell University Press.

Turner, V., 1969. Liminality and communitas. In *Ritual Process*, V. Turner, ed., pp. 94–131. Chicago, IL: Aldine Pub. Co.

_____, 1982. Introduction. In *Celebration: Studies in Festivity and Ritual*, V. Turner, ed. Washington, DC: Smithsonian Institution Press.

Van Gennep, A., 1960. *The Rites of Passage.* Chicago, IL: University of Chicago Press.

Warner, W. L., 1953. An American Sacred Ceremony. In *American Life*, W. L. Warner, ed., pp. 1–26. Chicago, IL: The University of Chicago Press.

Waters, H. W., 1939. *History of Fairs and Expositions: Their Classifications, Functions and Values.* London, Ontario: Reid Bros. and Co.

11

Teaching and Learning through Mien Culture

A Case Study in Community-School Relations

Lorie Hammond
University of California at Davis

Openings

Mesmerized by the smell of cilantro and garlic, the chop, chop, chop of hand-forged knives against large wooden blocks; by the haziness of incense wafting from the makeshift altar, where a just-bled chicken awaits ritual cooking among glasses of wine, burning incense, and Chinese scrolls; captured by the chanting of Chiem Chow, the Shaman, its rhythm broken only by sharp claps of bamboo dice, by singsong annotations by Chiem Chow's wife, and by the occasional cry of an infant—one can almost imagine the mountains of Laos in the background, the jungle birds and warm moist air. It is hard to believe that the backdrop is really a subsidized housing complex in West Sacramento, on the opening day of the Southeast Asian (SEA) Family English Literacy Project. How can the ways of these people—so recently uprooted by war from a carefully preserved oral culture, a five-thousand-year tradition of farming and hunting—be validated in California in the 1990s? How can the Mien people make meaning of their crowded apartments beside the freeway, the tall buildings of the state capitol visible on the horizon, or the ninety-eight-cent store just around the corner? Yet in an act of bravery and desperation they are here, ready to leave the apartments where they have been huddled for years, depressed and nonparticipant in the world around them, watching their children board yellow school buses while they are left behind. This project is for them—and because the project's coordinator, Cyndi Thompson, is willing to accommodate their ways, and since it is not on a school site, it can open in proper fashion, with a blessing ceremony.

Source: Written especially for *Education and Cultural Process*, 3rd Edition.

"What is the Shaman saying?" I ask Joe Liow, our Mien interpreter, as the chanting continues.

"He is negotiating with the spirits of our ancestors. The Shaman is afraid that the ancestors will be concerned about the program, because we are working with American people. When they did not respond to his requests, he knew that they could not find Cyndi's Portuguese ancestors, and so he substituted some of mine to be responsible for the project. Now the negotiations are going better." After two hours of chanting and throwing down bamboo dice, the ancestors are appeased. An agreement, inked in ancient Chinese, is completed and hung on the wall, and the program is granted good fortune for one year, at which point a pig is promised in payment for the favor. To seal the agreement, a large pile of hand-embossed spirit money is burned so that its smoke will reach the heavens.

As soon as the transaction with the spirits is complete, efficiency takes over. The chicken is removed from its place of state and dropped into an already boiling pot of water. With little discussion, thirty women and a few men hunker on the floor, where they chop vegetables from their gardens for stir fry and egg rolls, produce both steamed and sticky rice made at home, and prepare a feast for over fifty people within an hour. Toddlers and babies abound, watching and playing. When they cry, they are placed on their mothers' backs in elaborately embroidered cloth carriers and fall asleep. The food is traditional except for the Mien salad, which is a compromise. Iceberg lettuce and tomatoes have replaced the green papaya available in Laos, enabling a strange but delicious mix of rice noodles, American salad ingredients, and bottled ranch dressing enhanced with peanut butter, cilantro, garlic, lemon grass and lime juice. How many new ingredients can be incorporated before the spirit of the old is lost?

The next day these tribal people, babies on backs, will be seated at desks and even at computers, learning English and recording their own life stories. They will be learning to tutor their children in school, to make playdough in the Mien preschool in the next apartment, to become citizens of the United States. What can we, in turn, learn from the wisdom they bring?

A mile away, at the elementary school the Mien children attend, an opening staff meeting is held, with two hours devoted to discussing the proposed school-community garden project. Barbara Githens, the principal, begins this meeting by bestowing her own "blessing" on the project, saying, "I didn't just want to open up the garden and put a fence up and say, 'Let's go'; I wanted to have a *conscious plan*, some participation guidelines for parents, and some classroom plot guidelines. . . ." Along with her teachers, Barbara wants to see the garden project work for two reasons: to involve children in garden science, and to bring the community into the school. She continues:

> I feel that this is a great opportunity to bring in not only our Mien parents but some of our other parents, to kind-of open the door for them to feel comfortable coming to school, to be part of the campus. It's not only an educational opportunity for our students to learn parents' expertise about gardening, but it also gives us an opportunity to interact with parents on a positive basis.

She then turns the meeting over to me, to serve as a "technical expert" sharing the experiences of other schools, helping the teachers to plan integrated curricula related to the garden, and to plan the garden itself. Many issues arise. Will teachers be given curriculum resources? Will the garden be fenced against vandals, and will parents be given keys? Will teachers be liable if kids get hurt working with tools? We discuss strategies that have worked at other schools. I distribute a survey, in which teachers respond whether they would like to have a garden plot, to serve on a steering committee, or to help plan curriculum. Many ideas are shared about crops that can be planted and ways they might fit into the existing curriculum.

While both the Mien parents and the school staff are eager to find ways to work together, the contrast between their two cultures needs to be understood, lest it affect their ability to do so. As is illustrated by their opening gathering, the Mien culture is oral, collective, and spiritually based. The Shaman speaks as the voice of his people in assuring an environment in which they can thrive. The community focuses on maintaining continuity with the past through the ancestors and on accomplishing concrete tasks in the present. Little attention is paid to time, rules, or other quantitative measures. Knowledge is practical and empirical, connected to farming and to learned skills, such as sewing and metalsmithing. Literacy is possessed by the Shaman, passed on to his sons, and reserved for sacred documents in which ancient wisdom is preserved. Its purpose is to maintain a harmonious relationship between this generation and the spirits of the ancestors nine generations back.

School culture, on the other hand, is literate, individualistic and secular. Each teacher has a voice, and it is often difficult to get people to agree. The focus is on planning for the future. Children are seen as future adults who must be taught certain skills to succeed, and the planning of lessons and activities is a constant practice. Time is important and is carefully regulated by a bell schedule. Knowledge is generally seen to come from books, and teachers tend to have abstract rather than experiential knowledge. The purpose of school is to create literate and academically skilled children who can function in the technological society and global economy of the twenty-first century.

Despite the contrasts between the Mien blessing and the meeting at school, there are some similarities. Both groups operate in complex and assumed patterns of which they are not aware, and which, like members of any culture, they consider "normal." Both opening meetings help their members to prepare for the potentially stressful experience of working with the other group. The Mien recognize that it is a potential hazard to their ancestors—that is, to their traditions—to learn school ways and to venture into the mainstream community. School staff members, on the other hand, recognize that while they want to become more involved with the community, they would like to keep some control. That is why discussions about who will have keys, about garden rules, fencing, and liability are so important. There is a natural fear on both sides that something unpredictable could happen.

This chapter is an account of the ongoing experience of building a collaborative relationship between the two communities described above: the Mien families and the public elementary school their children attend. The role I play is that of coordinator of a curriculum project that focuses on making science and other subject matter accessible to language minority students. Although I work with several schools, this discussion focuses on a garden science program which joins three agencies: a community-based Family English Literacy Project (FELP), Evergreen Elementary School, and the Bilingual Integrated Curriculum Project (BICOMP), all of which are based in Washington Unified School District (WUSD), West Sacramento, California. My purpose, however, is not simply to describe the evolution of the Evergreen school-community garden. Rather, it is to illustrate how this particular experience is *a case of a mainstream school learning to collaborate with a nonliterate language-minority community, using a constructivist model which builds on community knowledge.*

Background

My participation in this project began about ten years ago, when, as a classroom teacher and MA student, I started working as a research assistant for Dr. Barbara Merino, Professor of Linguistics and Teacher Education at U. C. Davis (UCD). Dr. Merino was involved in the development of science curriculum for Spanish bilingual students in WUSD. This project had grown out of concern on the part of Merino and of WUSD bilingual staff members that their students were learning English and Spanish but were not being exposed to rich content area curriculum, especially in science and technology. Several reasons were given for this situation. There were no textbooks available that limited-English-speaking students could read. The material in textbooks was not relevant to the children's lives. Teachers had limited experience with science themselves and did not know how to build science curriculum related to their students' lived experience.

A collaboration developed among bilingual teachers and coordinators in WUSD and Dr. Merino and her colleagues in the division of education at UCD. The result of this collaboration was the Bilingual Integrated Curriculum Project (BICOMP), an approach to science-centered, integrated curriculum adapted to Spanish bilingual students' needs. Materials were developed in English and Spanish; units covered themes, such as weather and agriculture, about which the predominantly farm-worker parents were expert; and teachers were encouraged to collaborate on "spin-off" activities that followed children's interests and experiences. In addition, the curriculum developed advanced thinking skills and was designed to enable bilingual students to work at or above grade level. Over a five-year period, Merino was able to document in 1989 that participation in the BICOMP integrated curriculum enabled students to make significant gains in English, reading, and math as measured on standardized tests. BICOMP applied for and received both California Exemplary Status in 1989 and a federal Title VII Academic Excellence dissemination grant in 1990. At that point, I ceased being a classroom teacher-participant and became coordinator of the dissemination project, the purpose of which was to establish the program in other bilingual schools in WUSD and throughout the United States. In 1993, I also entered the doctoral program in education at UCD.

During the late 1980s, WUSD enrolled large numbers of refugee students from both the Soviet Union and Southeast Asia. By 1990, students from immigrant and refugee families totaled 30 percent or more of the elementary school population. These students generally came to school from families where no one spoke English. Whereas WUSD had an established Spanish bilingual program with Spanish-speaking teachers at every grade level K–6, few Russian teachers and no teachers speaking Southeast Asian dialects could be located. Like many California cities, West Sacramento was faced with the question of how to integrate families with vastly different life experiences and no common language into the school system.

The district responded creatively to this challenge. Because research showed that students will be more successful academically if they are reinforced in their primary languages as much as possible (Peal and Lambert, 1962; Snow, 1990), WUSD schools were reorganized by language. Although every school enrolled English speakers from its neighborhood, language-minority students were clustered into schools by language group so that language assistants could be hired to work with each group. Two Spanish bilingual schools and a Russian, Mien, and mixed-language school were organized. The BICOMP research team began to develop strategies to teach the new school populations effectively. This chapter traces one BICOMP project, the Evergreen School-Community Garden, a half-acre of land where parents farm their own plots of land, and where K–5 classrooms conduct a school science project. This garden has become an intercultural space where two very different subcultures, the elementary school and the Mien community, can learn to create common ground.

Methodology

Two methodological questions which had to be resolved in writing this chapter require clarification. The first is the question of group versus individual identity. This chapter rests on the assumption that cultural groups, including the immigrant families and American teachers discussed herein, operate within specific, shared "cultural dialogues" (Spindler, 1987; Spindler and Spindler, 1987) that can be described. Understanding these dialogues is essential to cross-cultural comparisons, yet I am fully aware of the pitfalls involved in stereotyping people within group identities, without noting either the variations in how individuals experience their own group or the hybrid and protean nature of group identity among people in diverse communities. For example, it is a given that Mien children attending school in the United States experience and come to identify with at least the two cultures of home and school as well as the variety of peer cultures to which they are exposed. This chapter was written for practical purposes: (1) to illustrate how the gap that exists between teachers and immigrant families is cultural as well as individual in nature; and (2) to suggest a practical process that school staffs can use to incorporate community cultural knowledge into the school curriculum. A more complete study, which is in process, would include the story of how individuals from each group construct, expand, and transform their identities through contact with each other and with the complex communities in which they live.

A second question is that of voice. I have used real names in this chapter, so that people can be credited with what they say. I have also chosen to write in the first person singular and plural. One might wonder why I do both, and who the "we" voice is. I attempted to use the first person singular when stating an idea of my own, but also to acknowledge in general that this is not my project alone. It is accomplished only through daily dialogue with the many players involved and, hence, has developed a kind of "we" identity as a project. I am fully aware, however, that while key players have been shown this work and approved its publication, the ultimate responsibility for what is stated rests with me.

Working with Mien People

Each refugee group provides unique challenges to a school community. The Mien are a little-known minority group from Laos who, along with the Hmong and some smaller tribal groups, were forced to flee their country on foot, under fire, only to find themselves imprisoned in Thai refugee camps for up to ten years before immigrating to the United States. The following passages exemplify their stories:

Soldiers and their families that have worked for the CIA were being sought and killed. Little villages were being burned down and bombed. . . . My dad was a rebel soldier fighting alongside other Mien people in Laos.

The moon was like the crescent shape shining dimly over our farm near the Mekong River. I laid on my hard wooden bed. I could see the moon through a tiny hole in our roof, listen to the splashing of the river's currents on the shore, and listen to nature and its creatures calling to each other. I couldn't really sleep that night because we would finally depart from our homeland.

My father quietly whispered to us, "Wake up. We need to go." The next thing I noticed, we are out the door with our belongings and headed toward the river. I was walking quietly alongside my family on the damp and slippery grass and branches. It was so quiet that I could hear "squeeze squeeze" as we walked down the poorly built steps toward the river. There waiting for us I saw three Thai men with whom my dad had made a deal so they could take us across to the Thailand side of the border. I could see and hear in their voices that they were just as frightened as we were. Sitting in the middle of the river in the single-engine boat which sounded so loud, I wondered if it would give us away and cost us our lives. Little drops of the cold river water landed on me, making me shiver to my spine.

Finally . . . we unloaded our belongings on the banks. I was about to relax and say to myself that it was over and we were safe, when five men jumped out from behind the thick bushes and shrubs. Two of the men were carrying M-16 rifles. Three masked men began to search our bodies for valuables. . . . Even my shoes were taken off and checked. . . . After about thirty horrifying minutes, we were left alone without any money or valuables.

The memory of this terrible place is vividly stored within my memory. When I go out into the woods, I feel I am being watched. . . . But I guess any ordeal can be overcome if we somehow can find the right tools to help us overcome it.

—Joe Liow, FELP interpreter

We came to Bannamyaw Refugee Camp. It doesn't have a hospital. I had been shot. . . . . I am lucky not to die. . . . In camp I didn't have money to buy something to eat. I escaped to the city of Nan. I worked in the rice fields. . . . Some soldiers saw me. They put me in jail and beat me. They put me in jail 80 days. . . . In 1990 I was moved to Panutnicomp camp. I was learning English for six months. . . . I and my family flew to San

Francisco. . . . I saw my brother-in-law and my brother. I felt happy. I went to my brother's house. I felt sick. I saw many different things, not the same as my country. I can't speak English. . . .

—San Chow Saetern

I think back to my country. I often felt homesick. I saw many people in America. But not my mother, brother or sister. When I felt depressed I cried sometimes for a long time. I went to school to learn English. I feel better. But America is freedom. Everybody has a telephone, a car, lights, and hot water in a house. This country has many hospitals, schools, and libraries. This country is better than my country. But I want to go back to my country, because I want to see my mother.

—Liew Fow Saetern

In addition to bearing the traumas and losses they experienced during the war and in the camps, Mien people face the daily culture shock of transition from a subsistence, slash-and-burn agricultural society to modern life. They still function as a tribe; share animist beliefs; and are highly skilled at gardening, hunting, fishing, embroidery, and metalsmithing. Not surprisingly, they have had trouble applying these skills to life in the United States. Most Mien do not speak English, have never attended formal schools, and are illiterate. There is no traditional written Mien language, although some people are in the process of writing down their language in Roman letters. Most Mien live together in subsidized housing projects, such as the apartment complex where the FELP is located, and are supported by public assistance. As skilled farmers and craftsworkers, they find this situation intolerable. Ricky Saelee, a Mien language assistant at Evergreen School, describes how people feel.

Down by Sandalwood apartments and Pine Street apartments there live many, many refugees from Southeast Asia struggling in their little apartments. I have seen many families of six or seven people in the one- or two-bedroom apartments. These people get funded from the government just enough for their rent. They really want to work, but there is one thing: They can't read, write, and speak enough English to get a job. Many people say they can do anything with their hands, but there is no job just using hands.

Many families say they miss their homeland. They didn't have to know how to read or write there, and they could get a job. These people were mostly farmers. They worked very hard—if they didn't they would starve. They planted their own food and many kinds of vegetables. Right now these people miss a lot. That is why you see many refugee families having their little garden around their apartment because this is the only hobby they have. Many of them don't have a garden, but they are willing to clean up their neighbor's backyard for them so that they can have a little garden for themselves.

Around the refugee community people are still talking about their homeland. They want to know what happens over there. Many people try to
leave everything behind them and start a new life, but it's very hard for
them. They say: "It's not easy to start a new life, if you don't have land or
property."

Until the FELP project began in January, 1995, the Mien adults
in Sandalwood apartments spent their days in their apartments, unable
to learn English or to participate in meaningful work. Their one outlet
was a community garden that offered small plots. They are always looking for more land to farm. They are expert farmers, and their biggest
frustration is lack of access to land.

Now forty families attend FELP English classes each day. The
project offers English as a Second Language (ESL), citizenship classes,
parenting skills, and a preschool program conducted in Mien. Its purpose is to help the Mien and other Southeast Asian people to learn
English so that they can integrate into the job market and into American
life. FELP Coordinator Cyndi Thompson, who works with several language groups, is committed to building on each community's strengths
as a foundation for its integration into American society. For example,
she has purchased sewing machines so that Mien women can create
garments for sale, incorporating their embroidery skills. Similarly, it is
her hope that the garden project might help some families to develop
commercial gardens.

A second FELP project goal corresponds with BICOMP's purpose:
to integrate Mien families with their children's schooling. Mien people
are avid horticulturists. By centering the school science curriculum
around gardening, a subject which Lifelab[1] has shown can be used as
the basis for a complete elementary science curriculum, we enable Mien
parents to enter the school through a medium in which they already
have expertise. *Our goal has been to find effective ways to bring Mien
community knowledge about garden science into the school curriculum, as well as to engage Mien family members as expert contributors to the school community.* The obvious challenge is that Mien
parents have limited proficiency in English and in school practices, and
teachers have limited experience both in communicating with people
from another cultural group and in using the community as a source
of knowledge.

My role has been to serve as a mediator. I have interviewed Mien
parents, have worked with a teacher mentor to write and pilot a curriculum unit which uses students as ethnographers, and have given
teacher workshops in which I share what I have learned. My purpose
is not simply to trace the interaction between one school and one community, but to develop a model of how to build school science and lit-

eracy from community knowledge. The following four processes have emerged as useful.

Step 1: Find natural bridges. Determine a body of knowledge about which the target community is expert and which has intrinsic meaning to this community. Choose subject areas that lend themselves to curriculum development. If possible, create a real project based upon the chosen body of knowledge.

Step 2: Gather community knowledge about the chosen subject area. This can be done through a variety of informants, but the most available translators between home and school are the students themselves. Home-based homework assignments enable students to serve as mini-ethnographers while validating their own language and culture.

Step 3: Devise a curriculum based on community knowledge. Parents and children together create family books which record community knowledge and, in the process, develop family literacy skills.

Step 4: Incorporate parents as expert participants in the school teaching team. Involve language-minority parents as teachers in their primary languages and as expert participants in the community of learners.

These four steps repeat and recycle. For example, as teachers work with parents and student-ethnographers, new community "funds of knowledge"[2] become unearthed as future sources of curriculum. Unplanned projects emerge from the process itself. The interaction between Evergreen School and the Mien community is by no means complete and will continue to evolve. The following descriptions are meant to illustrate some ways in which each step in the process has worked in this one situation. While each community is different in its strengths and therefore in its curriculum themes, it has been our experience that the same general process works with a variety of communities.[3]

Step 1: Find natural bridges. Determine an issue in which the community is already involved.

> Long, long ago there were a young man and a young woman who were sister and brother. A great flood came, and they climbed up to the highest lands. After the flood, they could find no one else alive. In a panic, they asked the bamboo, the oldest and wisest plant, where they could look for the other people. The bamboo said that they were the only survivors, and that they must procreate. They did not believe the bamboo, and in their anger and frustration, they chopped him up into little pieces.

They began walking, searching for other people. Eventually they met a turtle. They asked him what to do, but his answer was the same as the bamboo's. Again in anger, they chopped him to pieces and went on.

The pair walked on, but eventually realized that there was no one else. They felt bad that they had not listened to the wise bamboo and turtle, so they put them back together. That is why, to this day, the bamboo has sections and the turtle's shell is like a puzzle.

Finally, they decided they would procreate. When the woman had a baby, it was not a human, but a large squash with many seeds. The woman sent the man out to plant the seeds all over the earth, especially in the lowlands, where they would grow well, but he tripped and became confused, and most of the seeds fell in the highlands. That is why there is only a small tribe of Mien up in the highlands, and other tribes of people inhabit the rest of the earth.

—Mien creation story, told by Joe Liow

It is hard to overestimate the spiritual and practical importance of gardening and farming to Mien people. At blessing ceremonies, the Shaman asks advice of the spirits by throwing down bamboo dice, because the bamboo is old and wise and was present at the time of the ancestors. As illustrated by their creation story, Mien people view themselves as having grown from squash seeds, which came up in the highlands where they were scattered. Bamboo and other plants are seen as more powerful than people, because they can grow by themselves from the earth, from seeds, whereas people can only survive through dependency on plants.

On a day-to-day level, gardening is one of the few things that reminds refugees of their old activities and makes them feel good again. The plants they grow today are descendants of the seeds and the cuttings of their medicinal herbs they first brought from Laos five to ten years ago. They almost never buy seed and feel very strongly about propagating the same strains of vegetables and herbs which they knew in Asia. Three Mien men recently told me: "When we see a well-grown garden, it reminds us of a particular season in our country, and it is a good feeling. To have a garden is a new beginning for us. Our bodies do not feel right if we do not farm, and we are afraid that our children will not know how."

When we started our first science garden at another Southeast Asian school, we asked parents to help dig up the classroom garden at a Saturday work party. Although they had not shown up at the planning meetings, most of the Hmong and Mien who had children in the school arrived early that morning. It soon became clear that there had been a misunderstanding. We thought that they were coming to help with classroom gardens, but they thought they would be a given a piece of land to garden for their own use. We began to realize the importance of land to them. Luckily, the principal was creative and came up with a compromise solution: they would be given family plots if they would help children and teachers to tend the classroom plots, and would weed and water during school breaks. The parents were very pleased, and this arrangement has become the system at all of our Southeast Asian schools. What we have now learned, however, is that the school garden needs to be as large as possible, because the parents want large enough plots to grow all their vegetables. At one school, we found that small plots were being exchanged on the black market, because people were so eager to get more land!

Our most recent Southeast Asian school gardens, including the one at Evergreen, are about one-half acre, with about one-third of the land going to classroom plots and two-thirds to family plots. The family plots are always beautifully tended and become teaching environments in themselves, where children can observe plant growth, do scientific illustration, catch insects, and watch traditional farmers at work. The challenge is to create a workable relationship between parents and teachers. Initially, we thought that parents would tend their plots and "help" teachers to tend theirs. We now think that asking parents to act as a secondary agent for teachers—the traditional "parent assistant" role—is not workable in this setting. From a practical perspective, parents are more expert than teachers about gardening and have their own non-Western ways of doing it. The situation soon becomes comic. Teachers, reading the Lifelab manual or some other reference, attempt to tell parents what to do. Parents feel unempowered, because they have never done things in the way they are being asked to do them. The situation is exacerbated by the fact that teachers generally do not really know how to garden, as well as by the language barrier between the two groups. When teachers attempt to use parents as an extension of themselves, both parties feel that the other one is "doing it wrong" and become frustrated.

What role should parents play? After working with parents and teachers in a variety of gardens over the past year, I have come to support the notion of parents as master gardeners who teach children directly how to do garden procedures, using an apprenticeship model. The master-apprentice relationship is based on modeling and seems to be the home teaching method of most traditional families. Mien parents generally report that they teach their children by "showing" them what to do. By contrast, teachers are encouraged to teach science to students through an inquiry model, in which they ask questions, explore hypotheses, etc. Such a model is central to the "constructivist" science reform currently encouraged by state and federal guidelines and by the BICOMP project. The goal of constructivist teaching is not to feed information to students, but to encourage them to dialogue with their own assumptions through experimentation.

Given the contrast between apprenticeship and exploratory teaching models, there is a gap between the discourse styles in which parents and teachers naturally engage. When teachers tell parents what to do, parents report feeling inadequate at doing things the teachers' way. More importantly, teachers never find out what the parents really know how to do, because they never give them a chance to do it. Parents pass on their cultural knowledge not only by planting a garden or sewing a scarf, but also by operating in their traditional language and discourse style.

What we propose is simple: Create an arena at school, such as the garden, in which parents can operate relatively freely, carrying out and sharing activities they know how to do. Children can participate with them as apprentices. Unless the teacher specifically wants to garden, let the parents manage the school plots as well as their own. Simultaneously, use parent-initiated activity as a laboratory in which inquiry science, as well as cultural and literacy study, can occur. This is where teachers and students alike can don the hat of inquirers. Chronicle what the parents do in the garden at various times of the year. Ask them questions about why they do it. Observe the garden itself: its growth, its problems, its insects. Ask parents to cook foods from the garden and chronicle how they do it. Write cultural cookbooks. Perhaps most importantly, ask parents to tell their stories about what they do. Make bilingual books (discussed later as a topic in itself).

If we want to learn about minority communities as whole cultures that create their own webs of meaning, we must give them arenas in which they can share what they know and do through their own discourse styles and in their own languages. If the job of school is to create literacy—that referential process in which we read, write, discuss and measure reality—what richer laboratory could we invent in which to be literate than an active piece of community life?

An obvious question would be whether, by focusing school curriculum on a traditional community pursuit like gardening, we create a provincial education which limits students' experiences in the broader world. This question has particular significance for low-income, minority students who already lack opportunities to interact outside of their community. This is where the ingenuity of the teacher comes in. While essential science concepts, such as the idea that ecosystems are made up of living and nonliving things, may occur in the garden, it is the teacher's job to point out how this principle is played out in other environments as well. While we might begin with Mien creation stories, we can move to other creation stories as well, which can be compared and contrasted. Obviously, we must expose students to as many opportunities to read, write, use computers, and quantify the world as possible. The point is not that we are limited to or by community knowledge, but that we show students how to tie what they already know into that great body of knowledge that human beings can and do amass, which will be available to them as educated people. If students are to maintain essential ties to their parents as their first and most important teachers, then schools must show that the language and knowledge students learn at home are part of and essential to the broader body of knowledge they access at school.

A mediating factor that softens the contrast between home and school knowledge and discourse styles is the fact that parents and teachers are learners too and will learn from each other *if* they are exposed to each other's ways. Although the Mien community has traditional gardening practices to which they are loyal, I have found them extremely open to new ideas. For example, when we opened the Evergreen School garden, the Mien discovered that the soil was not good. Their plants grew slowly and yellowed, and the soil did not hold water. Their first reaction was that we should garden somewhere else, as had been their tradition as slash-and-burn agriculturalists. When the soil became depleted, they moved on. I explained to them that in the United States, we can't move on. We had already invested in a fence and irrigation system for their garden, as well as negotiated to use the land. I hired a soil-testing agent to analyze the soil and to report the results to them. He explained that the soil was sandy and lacking in nutrients, and that we would have to amend it with fertilizer and compost. The Mien were very interested in the process and added the necessary amendments, even though this had not been their practice before. Mien parents have also shown openness to growing crops new to them, which teachers indicated they would like in the garden plots. The Mien have an intense curiosity about new ideas related to farming, since this subject is so important to them, and they are willing to learn new techniques. While the Mien people would describe themselves as traditional, they are keenly open to experimentation. They realize that their life in the United States is an experiment in which they will have to adapt to survive.

The point of this discussion is not that gardens *per se* are the answer for all communities, although the growing and eating of food provides a universal theme for science study. Our point is that each community has strengths that it could share at school, but that many immigrants are so disenfranchised that they (1) have stopped valuing the skills they had in the "old country," or (2) do not realize that their skills would have any application in the classroom. Similarly, teachers usually have no way of assessing community strengths and have never thought about how their curriculum could be expanded to include parents' knowledge.

Finding the natural bridge, the fund of knowledge which is already important to a particular community, is the first step in collaborating with a community. Having been a classroom teacher, I am anticipating the question which I would have at this point: How can teachers know what issues are important to the communities they teach? Teachers are busy people, with endless activities to accomplish within the classroom. Unless they are paired with university researchers, how can they have time to collect and analyze community knowledge? Many times teachers do not even speak the same language as parents. However, regardless of how limited school staffing is, there are people present who can find the natural bridges between home and school. Those people are the students themselves.

Step 2: Gather community knowledge—use students as ethnographers. If a teacher is not from the same community as his or her students, it is important to find a "cultural informant" who can serve as a liaison between teacher and community. In our schools, primary-language assistants are usually available. They are invaluable as a bridge, not only to translate at meetings and parent conferences, but to help teachers to assess what issues are important to the community.

Community-relevant curriculum can be designed in several ways. As a start, a teacher can take the standard curriculum and figure out ways that it can be connected to home issues. One example of this is the traditional study of family holidays that led Diana Charmbury, the Language Development Specialist at Evergreen School, to study Mien New Year and, in the process, to learn about the contrast between using "official" and community knowledge. Diana knew that her Mien students celebrated their New Year according to the Chinese calendar, so she went to the library to gather stories about Asian New Year celebrations, most of which featured a dragon parade. Her students read these stories and made elaborate and beautiful cardboard dragon costumes to wear in the school parade. The day before the parade was to occur, she decided to ask her Mien aide to see if parents would be willing to play their traditional instruments. The parents responded that they would be willing to help, but that the school should know that dragon parades are not a part of the Mien New Year celebration. Rather, the Mien make dyed eggs in woven cases as symbols of fertility and good luck. It is the Chinese who hold dragon parades.

Luckily Diana was able to create a joint event, in which the dragon parade was followed by egg dying demonstrated by Mien parents, who honored the school by wearing their elaborate ceremonial costumes. They were very pleased to be asked to demonstrate their actual New

Year rituals, which they had never before been asked to share. The next week, we did a "language experience" story (a description of which follows) with these Mien parents so that we could make a book about Mien New Year that we could reproduce for teachers and parents. The information they shared was not in the library. It was in the community.

The production of bilingual/bicultural children is a joint effort that must be shared between school and home. However, it is too simple to assume that it will occur naturally. The pursuit of English and the acquisition of American culture are so pervasive in both school and popular culture that children quickly devalue the offerings of their homes unless schools reinforce these offerings as a part of the important, "official" knowledge that they must learn. I believe that a curriculum based on home knowledge, acquired through the home language, creates a significant change in the power relationship between home and school.

The mechanism we use to gather home knowledge is simple, yet rich with possibilities. It is illustrated through a curriculum called *Project Food*, which I wrote and piloted jointly with Diana Charmbury in her ESL classes at Evergreen School. This curriculum was written as a preliminary to the garden project, as a way to assess what foods should be grown in a traditional garden representing the cultures in the classroom. The students who participated were predominantly Mien, although several Hmong, Khmer, Russian, and Afghani students participated, and the same curriculum could be used with native English-speaking students as well.

Our goal in writing this curriculum was to use home curriculum content to teach challenging school-processing skills, and to promote the oral and written use of both the students' primary languages and English. The processing skills emphasized in BICOMP are the discourse acts that children must have in order to succeed at science, such as the ability to describe a phenomenon, to narrate a set of events, and to explain what has been experienced. Using these discourse acts, students must be able to follow the scientific method: create a question, make a hypothesis, test results, and draw conclusions. Both science and social science can fit this constructivist framework. The content to be studied can be gathered in the community, through observation of either the social or the natural world. It can be based on information derived from children's experiences. However, it is important that this information is used analytically once it is brought to school, so that students are cognitively challenged and develop higher-order thinking skills.

In addition to taking an experimental approach, students gathering social science data need to learn simple field-study techniques. In other words, they must be trained to be mini-ethnographers studying their own cultural experiences. Like adult ethnographers, they are

trained to interview, to make observations, and to document and analyze data. In lesson 1 of *Project Food*, we introduced the idea of interviewing. The first interview question was simple: Students were asked
to collect data on what they had for dinner that night. Their job was to
observe their dinner, record what they ate, then ask their parents for
information about the ingredients that went into the dinner. To prepare
students for this project, we modeled interviewing each other in English
and in Mien, using our Mien interpreters. Children were told that if they
could not write everything they heard, they could draw pictures. They
were given special journals to take home and to return to the classroom
with field notes each day.

Before beginning this interviewing activity, we asked students as
a group to reflect on what they already knew about food and what they
wanted to learn. This information was recorded on large charts posted
in the classroom. Students were encouraged to compare what they
knew to what they had learned as the unit progressed. The Mien stu-

Figure 11.1: One Mien student's illustration of the family dinner

dents' perspective on food revealed that they shared the connection to agriculture previously attributed to their parents. The comments of third-grade newcomers to English began as follows:

What do you know about food?
Rice is a food.
We grow food.
Food makes us grow.
We water the food.
We put slug medicine on the food. . . .

When asked about food, most of the commentary was on gardening. It is clear that these children view food and agriculture as closely linked. They also appear to see themselves in the same kind of growth cycle as the food. In contrast, when a classroom of English-speaking children in a BICOMP school went on a field trip to the supermarket and were asked which of the foods they had seen could have been grown in a garden or on a farm, they could not think of any examples. When questioned about their dinners the night before, more than one-third said that they went out for fast food.

When the ESL students returned with information about their dinners, they were asked to construct these dinners out of felt, styrofoam, and paper on a paper plate and in a cup, mounted on a construction-paper placemat. They then had to label the foods they ate, along with the ingredients that went into them, in English and in their primary language when possible. Mien has not traditionally been a written language, but members of the Mien community are currently attempting to write it down using the Roman alphabet. Some of the children attempt to sound out the words they know. This is a difficult process, however, since the last letter of Mien words is not a sound but rather an indicator of tone, and because there is not one agreed-upon version of sound-symbol relationships.

When everyone's dinners were displayed, students were asked to make a chart of how many people ate which food. This chart was then translated into a graph, from which generalizations (such as "More people ate rice than any other food" and "Almost nobody ate bananas") were suggested by the students. Their home stories were treated as data that could be analyzed using charting, graphing, and analyzing techniques. Hence, science and social science literacy skills were taught using information gathered at home.

In the next assignment, students were asked to think about the data from their dinners and predict what their parents would consider the most important foods. The idea of prediction was illustrated through guessing how many candies were in a glass jar. Students could see that a prediction is a guess that is based on evidence. They were asked to base their predictions on the components of not only their own dinners, but all the dinners from their ethnic group reported by the class. Students filled out a chart predicting the five most important foods in their homes, writing the words for these foods in their home languages and in English, and predicting where these foods came from. One chart follows.

What are our most important family foods ?

food (picture)	name (English)	name (home language)	Where do we get it ?
1)	rice	maang x	store
2)	mustard green	Iai Jaqix	Store
3)	fish	mdiaux	river
4)	milk		store
5)	mushroom	Chio	store

Figure 11.2: Lo Kuong Saelee's predictions of important family foods

Students left their predictions at school, then went home with a clean chart to fill out with their parents at home. When they returned, they compared the two results to see how accurate their predictions had been, recorded the sources of food reported by their parents, and commented on what they had learned. Since some students are very new to English, all of these discussions were facilitated by a Mien language assistant.

The ESL teacher and I were fascinated by the students' responses. Many sources of food were reported. In addition to the supermarket foods, almost every parent listed some items which came from the garden, from the Asian store or farmers' market, from the river (fish), or from the fields (herbs or mushrooms). Mien people, accustomed to growing or finding in the jungle everything they need, have obviously carried their resourcefulness to their new environment. While some practices are worrisome, such as gathering herbs and mushrooms near the freeway or fishing in the river using illegal nets, they reflect ingenuity. In addition, we saw that people cooperate within the Mien tribe. Some people go fishing and sell fish to each other. Others go to the farmers' market and get food for several families. Since both cars and money are at a premium, these efficiency tactics are important. In addition, they show how, while the Mien have limited English skills, they have figured out how to use the broader community to find what they need for daily life.

Students' comments on what they had learned surprised us in that several students in each class reported that they enjoyed learning to write their home language. One Hmong girl came to school eager to use the Hmong-English dictionary because her father had not known the word for one of her favorite foods, "apple," in Hmong, since they did not have that fruit in Laos. Although we thought that students would eventually appreciate the practice in their primary language provided by these homework assignments, we were astonished by the importance the students immediately attributed to this facet of the project. We decided that in addition to gathering community knowledge, home-interview homework served several purposes: (1) enabling and requiring parents to help with homework, (2) affording students practice in their home languages, and (3) forcing students to practice English through translation of their answers for the class the next day. Given that students had previously thrown away homework on their way out the door, stating that their parents could not read it, interactive homework involving families created a major change. Perhaps most significantly, the ESL teacher reported that students were more eager to share the results in their home interviews than they had been to speak in class about school-based assignments.

Step 3: Devise a curriculum based on community knowledge—language-experience stories and family books. A question which interested me in approaching this project is: What is the body of knowledge that Mien people know about gardening? How is it the same as or different from Western scientific knowledge about botany and/or agriculture? I thought about school science, which generally comes from books, and about UC-Davis, the major agricultural research university with which our project is connected. How is knowledge gathered, stored, and transmitted at the university? How is this the same as, or different from, the knowledge taught in an elementary science classroom? How does all this relate to the way the Mien keep and pass on their knowledge about agriculture?

The questions particularly interest me because Mien children attending American schools will have two sources of knowledge—one at home and another at school. I was curious about the similarities and differences between these two bodies of knowledge, and about how children integrate them. Osborne and Freyberg (1985) describe how even children from Western backgrounds hold developmentally immature concepts of science long after they are presented with other information at school. Unless they have direct experiences that change their perspectives, children can memorize factual knowledge without changing their own conceptions of the world. If this is the case, how much of the scientific information that we teach at school is absorbed by Mien children? How do they resolve the conflicts, if any exist, between the body of knowledge they receive at home and that which they receive at school?

I decided that the first step in designing community-relevant curriculum was to find out how the Mien parents construct their own knowledge of plants. I began to interview the Mien parents in the ESL classes, initially by asking questions in English that were translated by Joe Liow, the FELP language assistant. Their answers were tape recorded and transcribed later by Joe. The whole process was cumbersome and took up a lot of Joe's time. Moreover, I had little notion of what was going on and could not interact with the discussion.

Later I found that *language-experience stories*, an ESL technique I had used in teach elementary English learners, could double as an information-gathering tool for me and as English instruction for the Mien parents. This technique consists of asking questions in English that generate discussion in Mien, which is then translated back into English to create a narrative. I write down what parents say on a big chart. Every so often, the parents read their "story" back to me as an English literacy lesson. Although they cannot read an English text they have not seen before, they understand what they are reading because they have supplied the information. (This same technique works for ESL students and with young children learning to read in the elementary school.) We go over difficult words or anything they do not understand. Once they all understand the text, they correct what is written. A very informal interview process emerges from this technique. Often one description leads to another.

After we finish a session, I type a report of the results and hand it to the parents at the beginning of the next meeting. More recently, Mien parents have begun to type their own stories, thus practicing both literacy and computer skills. We read the story together again, and parents suggest corrections. It is important to all of us that the information be correct, because we will use the text to make a book for use in the school and in their homes. When the text is corrected, we type it in large print, a few lines per page, to create a children's book, and parents take pages home to illustrate them. Sometimes they use photos from Laos; sometimes they draw pictures of what life was like. When everyone turns in their illustrated pages on a certain subject, we xerox them and bind them into a book, which is given to Mien families and to teachers at the school.

The parents are very excited about these books because they have few written records of their lives. They recognize that the mechanisms for handing down their oral culture are not being continued in this country and that they must record things in writing if they are to be remembered. The FELP Coordinator, Cyndi Thompson, has encouraged her students to write personal books on the school computers. They are very interested in recording their own life stories. In the process, they are learning English.

The first book we wrote was a description of the Mien New Year. Now we are working on a book about rice, which goes with a curriculum unit Diana has been developing. Diana decided to do this unit on rice because when her ESL classes were asked, during *Project Food*, about what they eat, all of the Asian children began with rice. Phoeun Khon, our Cambodian interpreter, expresses many immigrants' feelings:

> I lived on a farm with my parents. . . . They worked on a rice field every day. I used to help my parents with the farm work when I was only five years old. Rice fields are very important to our lives. We can't live without rice because it is our daily meals.

Following the students' lead, Diana decided she would grow rice in large tubs in the classroom, as well as taste and study foods that come from rice. Simultaneously, we began to create a language experience book on the subject of rice. It began with a technical account about how to grow rice, of which a short excerpt follows:

> We build a special rack called a *biow hang* to dry the rice. It is made of bamboo and wood, with a rice stalk roof to keep off the rain. The rice is hung in rows. . . . Each family has two racks, one for sweet rice (sticky rice: *biow butte*) and one for steamed rice (*biow tze*).

The fathers telling this story got excited about the possibility of demonstrating at school how to harvest and process rice. We began to discuss the garden huts they built in Laos for this purpose and the tools they used for the harvesting process. We then discussed the possibility of building a traditional bamboo hut at the school garden to demonstrate traditional techniques. The fathers are willing to do this, and we plan to do it in the fall. This discussion illustrated to me how parents' reflections can lead naturally into new projects.

After we wrote a long account about how to grow and process rice, I became concerned about whether children would enjoy such a technical document. I suggested that we write it as a story, from the point of view of a child helping with the harvest. While this idea might work, it overlooked an obvious point: traditional stories about growing rice already exist. When I asked the Mien parents about their stories, they produced the story of Mm Gou Tzum. "Mm" is a respectful term for old woman, whereas "Gou Tzum" means "one who can make things grow again." Hence Mm Gou Tzum is an important figure, the old woman who can make things grow again, the Earth Mother. I believe that this short excerpt captures the richness of the story:

The Mien people did not know how to grow enough rice to feed their families, so the spirit of the sky took pity on them. The spirit sent down a lady called Mm Gou Tzum. No one knew about her. She did her magic at night. During the harvest, they cut down the rice and left the stalks. The next day they came back and the rice grew again. She did this for them three times.

On the third night, a Mien woman got tired of harvesting her crops because she had to do it so many times. She got lazy, so she sent her dog to chase Mm Gou Tzum away. Mm Gou Tzum ran for her life and climbed up a tree. She blew her nose and put her mucus and feces on the tree stump below her.

Mm Gou Tzum cursed the Mien people, saying: "If you are lucky, you will find my mucus to eat. If you're not lucky, you won't even find my feces to eat." Her mucus turned into a Mien potato called *doi mien*. It is sweet and tastes good, but it grows deep and is hard to find. Her feces turned into another potato called *doi chu* (chu=dog), which is unpleasant, bitter, and smelly. Doi chu is easy to find because it grows as a vine on the trees. If Mien can't grow enough rice, they have to eat these things. . . .

> —story told by members of the Saetern, Saejao, and Saechao families

In the course of the story, reminiscent of the Bible since it traces a gradual fall from Eden into our present condition due to various human acts of frailty, each aspect of Mien rice growing is explained. Mien and other children can use the stories we produce as part of their school literacy program. In the process of creating them, Mien parents are learning English literacy, as well as computer and bookmaking skills. The Mien interpreter at Evergreen School, Ricky Saelee, is one of the few people who has learned to write the emergent Mien script. While making a book with San Chow Saetern, he taught him this script. San learned to write Mien in two days because he was so excited about the possibility. Now, between San and Ricky, we will be able to produce books in both English and Mien.

Step 4: Incorporate parents as expert participants in the school teaching team. Our goal is to involve language-minority parents in school in ways that empower them as (1) linguistic experts, teaching in their own languages; (2) technical experts, teaching specific skills; and 3) decision makers. During *Project Food*, Diana invited Mien parents to school to cook a traditional meal and later to demonstrate dying eggs for Mien New Year. Both activities were very popular with students and staff alike, but we realized that we were still not involving parents as part of the teaching staff. They were demonstrating while students watched.

In June of 1996, BICOMP, FELP, and EVENSTART, another family literacy project that works with Latino and Central Asian families, staged an eight-day summer science institute on the theme, "literacy and parent involvement through the garden." The summer science institute had been held for several years as a teacher training project, with language assistants occasionally incorporated. The institute works on a peer-coaching model. After receiving inservice training on the summer's theme and working together on curriculum to address that theme, teachers are placed in teams of four to six people who team-teach a summer school class in the morning and are given time for planning and debriefing in the afternoon. Themes are science-based but involve all subject areas.

The 1996 institute was unique in that language-minority parents were placed on each team. For example, in a classroom serving Mien and American students, the teaching team consisted of two or three teachers, a bilingual language assistant, and two or three Mien parents. It was the job of this group to plan and carry out a week's curriculum together with a group of students. All parties involved would be considered teachers.

The institute provided an opportunity to test some new roles for teachers and parents. Teachers were seen as facilitators whose job was to organize the curriculum so that it met students' academic needs, integrating both community knowledge and existent curriculum requirements. Parents were expected to take master-apprentice roles in teaching groups of students. Over the course of the institute, each group was expected to accomplish certain tasks, such as planting something or doing some kind of project in the new school garden at the summer school site. Another task was organizing teachers and students to prepare a traditional ethnic lunch for students in the class, as well as for the fifty institute participants. Parents organized the menu and ordered ingredients, which the BICOMP secretary purchased. They then organized students and teachers to help them prepare the food. Yet another task was to produce at least one traditional language-experience book per classroom.

Before the teaching days began, parents and teachers had three days to get to know each other and to become familiar with the model. Teachers began by interviewing parents in their groups about what they do in their gardens at different times of the year and about major events which highlight their calendars. Teachers then met in grade-level teams to plan how to incorporate their new community knowledge into the standard curriculum they need to teach. Parents had their own training, in which they learned about the ecology of the garden; practiced various illustration techniques; learned to use the bookbinder, laminator, and computers, and so on. The second week, both parents and teachers taught what they had planned together. Generally, parents worked with small groups of students, usually in their own language, to accomplish specific tasks. Teachers, on the other hand, focused on building literacy and numeracy through the activities.

Most popular were the ethnic lunches. Each group began to outdo the last. In the course of a week, everyone experienced Mien, Mexican, Cambodian, Hmong/Lao, and Pakistani lunches.

How well did this activity meet our original goals for parent involvement? Parents definitely served as both linguistic and technical experts. As members of the planning team, they also participated in decision making. However, one of the things we learned was that parents' idea of empowerment is not always the same as what we had imagined.

Teachers often define parent power as holding positions on school committees, such as the school site council. Although it is important for minority parents eventually to learn how to participate in these decision-making bodies, these bodies are in themselves a part of the school's cultural structure, which may be very foreign to minority families. In some cases, *the most empowering way to deal with parents is to allow them to create arenas in which they determine the course of action according to their own cultural norms.* A creative staff can create meaningful activity from situations that emerge from the community. If teachers are willing to be flexible enough to abandon plans when they become unworkable in order to follow new directions initiated by students or parents, then new experiences and cultural possibilities begin to emerge. As teachers, we are taught to equate responsibility with being in control. If we redefine our role and view ourselves as mediators and coordinators rather than controllers, power is automatically redistributed to the other members of the teaching/learning team.

On the last day of the institute, we asked parents from each language group to discuss and share their ideas about what the school could do to encourage immigrant parents to be more involved in school. The Mien response was as follows:

> *What things do you want to do to help in the classroom?*
> Use our own language in the classroom.
> Preview lessons in our own language so that students can
>   understand.
> Help keep students at work.
> Tell traditional stories.
>
> *What is the most difficult or challenging thing?*
> Speaking or reading English.
>
> *What can teachers do to make it easier or harder?*
> Be flexible.
> Allow younger children to come to school.
> Communicate and plan with us.

Give parents a space where we can work on books or art with students, on our own. . . . Create a parent work center.

What would you like to do as a parent garden expert?
Show students the process of gardening.
Show proper use of tools.
Show why we plant different plants in different ways.
Teach students to distinguish plants and know their uses.

What/how do you teach your children?
By modeling/showing.
We want them to learn our cultural heritage.
Responsibility.
To use polite language and respect the teacher.

The parent groups from various countries reflected similar sentiments. They felt that teachers need to be flexible, allowing them to bring younger children to school if necessary, and allowing ongoing projects on which they can work with students independently, in the garden or at parent work centers. This input surprised some teachers, who have been told that the parents in this community do not take initiative and need to be "trained" and directed. For example, it is common to hold parent workshops to train parents to read American books to their children. An alternative pursued during our institute was to encourage parents to tell their own stories in the classroom, either to students who speak their language or with the help of translators, and then to create their own books. Parents are much more enthusiastic about the latter project.

We hope to institutionalize our parent-teacher team model during the school year by making it a part of both our family literacy projects and our elementary science program. Perhaps teachers and parents can work together on teams at each school one morning per week. We also hope to enable parent leaders from each school community to work as garden managers.

In the model of parent involvement we are proposing, minority parents gain power not so much by playing "important" roles in our structures but by being granted community space and time within schools where they can initiate activities in their own cultural style. Parents become teachers in a master-apprentice model, modeling and accomplishing tasks agreed upon by the school community. Teachers validate parents' activities by encouraging them, and by using them as a source of curriculum. In the process, each group inevitably begins to learn the others' ways.

Reflections

Like a camera zooming in to view one niche in a larger environment, we have been examining one example of a larger theoretical framework. The Evergreen school-community garden project rests on research traditions that should be acknowledged, and it suggests its own dialogue with these traditions.

Fundamentally, I have drawn from the tradition of cultural anthropology as it sheds light on the educational process. The work of George and Louise Spindler has enabled me to understand that schools operate as cultural institutions representing the dominant society. If schools are to build on rather than assist in the destruction of immigrant communities, then they must redefine their boundaries to include immigrant cultures. This inclusion cannot be piecemeal, through the addition of a folktale here and a language class there. It must be holistic, because cultures are organic structures that include language, content, discourse style, and that invisible web which makes them whole.

The Spindlers suggest that people have both "enduring selves," defined as that sense of continuity one has with one's own past—"a personal continuity of experience, meaning, and social identity" (1994:13)—and "situated selves," which enable them to function in the instrumental, daily tasks of existence. In a continuous, traditional community, situated skills are built on the foundation of a cultural and spiritual value system. Immigrant children and other disenfranchised children in our diverse and sometimes fractured modern society do not experience such continuity. This puts them fundamentally at risk. To develop as whole people, children need to reconcile their deep identity, their "enduring selves," with the roles they need to play in society. For many immigrant students, the connection is not made at school. Most often, children confronted with discontinuity will feel that they have to choose between worlds. They can succeed at the expense of their identity, or they can fail in the interest of maintaining this identity. Ethnographers (among them Boggs et al., 1985; Heath, 1983; Philips, 1983) have chronicled the ways in which discontinuity between home and school expectations lead to school failure for many minority students.

How can schools incorporate minority cultures? The approach we have taken is eclectic, combining several research traditions. The Spindlers suggest that teachers need to become conscious of their own cultural impact and judgments, so they can encourage rather than reject the identities of minority children who enter their classrooms. They call this process "cultural therapy." A major thrust of the Evergreen project has been and continues to be informing teachers about ways the Mien community can enhance their curriculum and school community, as well as dialoguing about cultural misunderstandings.

Our attempts to find "natural bridges" between community and curriculum draw heavily on the work of Luis Moll and his colleagues (1994), who suggest that all communities possess "funds of knowledge" which can be used as a basis for curriculum. The methodology we use to research these "funds of knowledge" derives from teaching children and teachers ethnographic field techniques such as interviewing, observing, and compiling data. The language-experience stories and family books draw heavily on Sudia Paloma-McCaleb's (1994) concept of "building communities of learners." The idea of social constructivism, of building curriculum around community-relevant projects and issues, derives from both the progressive education tradition in American education dating back to John Dewey (1916, 1938) and the work of Paolo Friere (1983).

Important to our own evolution within the BICOMP project is the dialogue among the researchers, teachers, interpreters—and, increasingly, parents—that helps us determine our direction. Barbara Merino has created our initial and ongoing vision of a research-based educational approach that draws eclectically from what we know about language acquisition, constructivist reform, and cultural empowerment for minority students. Rosalinda Quintanar, our colleague at San Jose State University, brings the perspective she gained from working with Friere on community-based education in Mexico. John McFadden at California State University, Sacramento, adds a continuous spirit of dialogue and questioning to our project. Most important, however, are the dialogues that occur within each school community among teachers, interpreters, and parents. It is there that all theories are validated or made irrelevant.

What have we learned from the case of the Mien school community garden? Most fundamentally, we have reinforced our premise that *community knowledge and experience can become the content through which academic constructs are taught.* However, we have done more than prove what we believed in the first place. We have experienced, and continue to experience, a broader educational process than we had imagined. My original goal was to teach English and meaningful curriculum to a group of immigrant students. The goal of the Family English Literacy Project was to teach English and school skills to parents. By combining our efforts, we have created a model of family education that is more powerful than we expected. Mien parents who were not literate at the beginning of the school year are now initiating the writing of books both in English and in the emergent Mien written language. In order to do this, they have made a leap into Western culture, accepting the idea that they must record their oral history if it is to be preserved. I believe they have become willing to make this leap because we, and especially the staff at the family literacy project, have so constantly reinforced the value of their knowledge and traditions. We also have given them places—in the garden, the sewing room, and the kitchen—where they can act out some small part of the way of life they know.

Our situation is not a bed of roses. The Mien people are still on welfare and currently face imminent welfare cuts that might make their struggle with life on a day-to-day basis even more difficult than it has been. The larger community in and around Evergreen School is heavily at risk, and both immigrant and native-born children must learn not only to negotiate school culture but also to survive a peer culture which can be dangerous and destructive. Teachers must still juggle the many requirements and traditions of school culture against their emergent desire to work more closely with a community that is still quite challenging and foreign to them.

Yet in our project there is a sense of emergence and expectancy. I think this is because we are all learning so much. It is not that we are teaching and the Mien community is learning; it is that we are teaching each other. Each of the two cultures represented by the Mien community at Sandalwood apartments and the staff at Evergreen School reflects a wealth of human possibilities that can only be expanded by exposure to each other. From the school community we gain literacy in English, skills in mathematics and computers that access the world, a science tradition that enables us to fix the soil, and much more. We bring scientific knowledge about photosynthesis and plant categorization, and efficient—if sometimes environmentally questionable—modern agricultural practices. When they are not intimidated, the Mien community is thirsty for this new knowledge. Parents and their children now attend school each day, eager to learn.

If we left the story at this point, we would lose at least half of its value. The Mien community has many things to teach to us. This community brings to us a deep sense of connection to the earth, acted out through a horticultural tradition that is continuous and sustainable. It brings a knowledge of how to work together for the good of the group. It brings a rich tradition of cooking and growing food; of embroidering and telling stories. If we believe we are incorporating Mien culture into our schools simply to enable Mien children to succeed in American society, it will seem like a troublesome accommodation of which we will tire. But when we as teachers see that by incorporating another cultural perspective into our learning community we too can become learners, we become as motivated as our students.

What can two cultures learn from each other? In simple terms, we can learn that there is another way to view the world. This is a kind of knowledge once confined to anthropologists and foreign travelers. I do not mean simply that we can learn a new recipe for soup or a new song, although these are important aspects of life and culture. Every time I "teach" science *with*, rather than *to*, an immigrant parent group, I learn new things, as I did one day when we were sorting seeds. Americans generally sort seeds into categories such as color, shape, and size—by their properties as objects. The Mien did something different. They sorted seeds by whether they would germinate easily or with difficulty, whether they would need trellises, whether they grow in spring or summer, etc. Perhaps American farmers would do the same, but I realized that Mien people see seeds not as objects but as part of a life cycle. I found this startling and interesting. As teachers, we often rate children by whether or not they can fit reality into certain categories. Kindergartners are tested to see if they know color, shape, and size. Did we ever think to ask them how a seed fits into the life cycle? Did we ever consider that seeds could be viewed in more than one way? I felt a chink developing in my window of perception, through which another reality came faintly into focus.

Another day, I put a large piece of butcher paper on the wall, carefully measured to match the dimensions of a school garden plot. I imagined that I would teach the Mien parents how to plan a garden on paper, while gathering information from them about what we should plant in the school plot. They looked quizzically at the paper, then shook their heads. I asked Joe to translate that this was like looking at the garden from on top, as if from an airplane. I thought they did not "get" what we were doing, but their problem was of a different nature. Finally they explained it to me: A garden can't be planned on a piece of paper. It is necessary to go out and feel the soil. Where it is soft, the little seeds like cilantro will grow. Where it is wet, put the mint.

For just a moment, as I abandoned my lesson plan, I was able to glimpse an approach that works with nature as it is, rather than bulldozing it to make reality as we would have it—a qualitative worldview, which experiences more and measures less.

When I think of our troubled urban kids, who walk through the garden smashing pumpkins, I realize how much we have to learn from a people who save the largest pumpkin each year so that there will be seeds for the years to come. With the Mien people, I am learning to save seed.

Notes

[1] Lifelab is an elementary curriculum project centered at UC–Santa Cruz and supported by the National Science Foundation. Its purpose is to provide curriculum and training for schools that would like to teach their complete science curriculum through the medium of the garden, a "living laboratory." BICOMP teachers receive Lifelab training and materials.

[2] Luis Moll and his colleagues (1994) use the term "funds of knowledge" to refer to bodies of knowledge possessed by any community. Our approach draws heavily on his rationale, that valuable community knowledge exists in language-minority com-

munities and can be used as the basis for meaningful and empowering curriculum. [3]BICOMP currently conducts parallel projects in Mexican, Russian, and multilingual schools.

Bibliography

American Association for the Advancement of Science (1990). *Science for all Americans: Project 2061*. New York: Oxford University Press.

Boggs, S. T., assisted by K. Watson-Gegeo and G. McMillen, 1985. *Speaking, Relating and Listening: A study of Hawaiian Children at Home and School*. Norwood, NJ: Ablex.

Delgado-Gaitan, C., 1990. *Literacy for Empowerment: The Role of Parents in Children's Education*. Bristol, PA: the Falmer Press.

Delgado-Gaitan, C., and H. Trueba, 1991. *Crossing Cultural Borders: Education for Immigrant Families in America*. Bristol, PA: the Falmer Press.

Dewey, John, 1916. *Democracy and Education*. New York: the Free Press.

_____, 1938. *Experience and Education*. New York: Collier Books.

Friere, Paolo, 1983. *Pedagogy of the Oppressed* (Ramos, M. B., trans). New York: The Continuum Publishing Company.

Heath, S. B., 1983. *Ways with Words: Language, Life and Work in Communities and Classrooms*. Cambridge: Cambridge University Press.

Moll, L. C., C. Amanti, D. Neff, and N. Gonzalez, 1994. Funds of Knowledge for Teaching: Using a Qualitative Approach to Connect Homes and Classrooms. *Theory into Practice*, xxxi (2), 132–41.

Osborne, Roger, and Peter Freyberg, 1985. *Learning in Science: The Implications of Children's Science*. Auckland: Heinemann Education.

Paloma-McCaleb, S., 1994. *Building Communities of Learners*. New York: St. Martin's Press.

Peal, E., and W. E. Lambert, 1962. The Relation of Bilingualism to Intelligence. *Psychological Monographs*, 76.

Philips, S. U., 1983. *The Invisible Culture: Communication in Classroom and Community on the Warm Springs Indian Reservation*. New York: Longman.

Snow, C. E., 1990. Rationales for Native Language Instruction: Evidence from Research. In *Bilingual Education: Issues and Strategies*, A. M. Pedilla, H. H. Fairchild and M. Valdez, eds., pp. 60–74. Newbury Park, CA: Sage.

Spindler, G. D., ed., 1987. *Education and the Cultural Process: Anthropological Approaches*, 2d ed. Prospect Heights, IL: Waveland Press.

Spindler, G. D., and L. Spindler, eds., 1987. *Interpretive Ethnography of Education at Home and Abroad*. Hillsdale, NJ: Lawrence Erlbaum Associates, Publishers.

_____, 1994. *Paths to Cultural Awareness: Cultural Therapy with Teachers and Students*.

Trueba, H., L. Jacobs, and E. Kirton, 1990. *Cultural Conflict and Adaptation: The Case of Hmong Children in American Society*. Bristol, PA: the Falmer Press.

Vasquez, O. A., L. Pease-Alvarez, and S. M. Shannon, 1994. *Pushing Boundaries: Language and Culture in a Mexicano Community*. Cambridge: Cambridge University Press.

12

Beth Anne—A Case Study of Culturally Defined Adjustment and Teacher Perceptions

George D. Spindler
Stanford University

This case study of Beth Anne will demonstrate how culturally unsophisticated perceptions of children by teachers may damage the "successful" middle-class child as well as the academically "unsuccessful" minority child in the school. The situation is in many respects the reverse of those portrayed in chapters 6 and 7 by Raymond McDermott and myself, but in both chapters the basic theme is the influence of the teacher's culture and the school upon perceptions and interpretations of children's behavior. For this purpose I am using a case study carried out when I was one of three people working in a school system under the aegis of the Stanford Consultation Service, directed by Dr. Robert N. Bush.[1]

Our purpose as a service team was to perform various studies of whole classrooms, teachers, individual children, other groups in the school, and even of whole school systems, as well as top supervisory personnel. Unlike the practice in a usual field study, we shared the data we collected and the analyses of those data with our informants. By so doing we hoped to share any benefits that might result from our research and direct them toward the improvement of the schools and the professional competence of teachers and related staff.

In this particular school, which we will call Washington Elementary School, we had entered to work with the whole staff of twelve teachers and the principal. First, we asked the assembled staff what it was they would like to study. They proposed a study of the "adjusted"—rather than the maladjusted—child in the classroom and in interaction with teachers and peers. We accepted this novel idea enthusiastically and proceeded to set up a mechanism whereby "ad-

Source: Written especially for *Education and Cultural Process*.

justed" children could be selected for study. After some discussion the teachers helped out by deciding upon several specific children. These children's classes were approached as a whole for volunteers for the study. Among the volunteers were the children picked out by the staff.

The studies were cleared with their parents, and we proceeded over a period of about three months to collect data and periodically to discuss these data and our interpretations with the assembled staff of the school. Beth Anne, a fifth-grade pupil, is one of the children studied.

The Classroom and Beth Anne's Place in It

The fifth-grade class consisted of 35 children ranging in age from 9 years, 8 months to 11 years, 8 months. The I.Q. range as measured by the California Mental Maturity Test appropriate to this age level was 70–140 with a mean of 106. There were three reading groups in the room, highly correlated with I.Q. scores as well as with reading achievement scores.

The classroom consisted of 20 children who could be described as Anglos whose socioeconomic status ranged from upper lower to upper middle (using the scales drawn from the studies of H. Lloyd Warner and his associates). The other 15 children were from the minority groups represented in the community surrounding the school and included 3 blacks, 2 Filipinos, 3 Japanese-Americans, and 7 Mexican-Americans (the term "Chicanos" was not current at that time).

Beth Anne was 10 years and 3 months old, just 3 months below the average for the whole class. She was in the top reading group and at the 95th percentile with her I.Q. test score of 132.

Excepting for occasional minor illnesses Beth Anne was apparently in good health, according to her parents and to records from the school office. She was dark haired, clear skinned, well developed for her age, had regular features and almond-shaped brown eyes, and wore braces on her front teeth. She always came to school extremely well dressed and was polite and considerate in her relations with her teachers; she appeared to be slightly reserved but equally considerate with her peers. The members of the team as well as the teachers in the school were impressed with her appearance and manners and regarded her as an exceptionally nice-looking child of good background.

Beth Anne was described by the teachers as an "excellent student," one of "the best students in the school," one who is "extremely conscientious," "cooperates well," "never has caused trouble in any of her classes," and who is "well liked by the other children." Further comments from the faculty were elicited in discussions of Beth Anne and the other children selected for study before the studies began.

Her former first-grade teacher said, "She was a very bright little child, perhaps not too friendly. At first she didn't respond too readily to me, but gradually began to work well and by the end of the year appeared to have made an excellent adjustment." Her present fifth-grade teacher said that "Beth Anne has attended very regularly this year. She is very interested in her class work and activities and performs at top level in everything. She even does excellent work in arithmetic, and she plays very well with the other members of the class and in general with children of her own age." The principal said, "Her home would certainly be classified in the upper-middle bracket. The parents are middle-aged, having married late. They have a very nice home and provide every cultural experience for the children." She went on to say that "one of the things that has concerned me a little, however, is a kind of worried look that Beth Anne has sometimes. It seems that if she doesn't understand the very first explanation in class, she is all concerned about it. She hasn't seemed so much that way this year but I have noticed it a lot in the past." Another teacher said, "Well, the mother has always been very interested in her children and has worked to give them many advantages. Beth Anne and her brothers and her parents go to many things and places together." Another teacher agreed, "Yes, they go to symphonies, I know. And they all went to the football game at Orthodox U."

Several times, and in different ways, we asked the teachers whether they regarded Beth Anne as a "well-adjusted" child. There were no explicit reservations expressed except for the comment by the principal about her "worried look" and the comment by her first-grade teacher that at first "she didn't respond too readily." The teachers all expressed verbal agreement that she was indeed very well adjusted, both academically and socially. Several teachers went out of their way to say that she was not only accepted by her peers but was considered a leader by them.

The Evidence

The study consisted of weekly classroom observations, watching playground activities, interviewing teachers, and administering psychological and sociometric tests. After having established the conditions of our study, our first step was to explain to Beth Anne what we would be doing and why. With her apparent enthusiastic consent, we proceeded then to a first interview followed by administration of the Rorschach projective technique and the Thematic Apperception Test (TAT). Within the following two weeks we also administered a sociometric technique to the classroom group. This technique included the questions, "Whom would you like best to sit next to?" "Whom do you like to pal around with after school?" and "Whom would you invite to a birthday party if you had one?" The sociometric maps of the choices expressed by the children were made up from the results elicited by these questions. They were quite consistent with each other. The sociometric map (sociogram) resulting from the responses to the first question is shown in figure 12.1. We also administered a status-reputation technique that included thirty-two statements such as, "Here is someone who fights a lot," "Here is someone who never has a good time," "Here is someone who does not play fair," "Here is someone who is good looking," "Here is someone who likes school," "Here is someone who plays fair," and so forth. The children were to list three names in rank order following every statement.[2] Following are summaries of these categories of data.

Observations

The reports by our three-man team of observers of Beth Anne's behaviors in the classroom and around the playground were monotonously similar. Beth Anne did not cause trouble. She was obedient, pleasant, and hard-working. She responded to questions in a clear voice and was noticeably disturbed when she was unable to provide the answer to a question in the arithmetic section. She read well and easily.

However, she interacted only infrequently with the other children in the classroom, either in the room or on the playground. She seemed quite reserved, almost aloof. Apparently she had a fairly strong relationship with one girl who looked and acted much as she did and who seems to have come from the same general social and cultural background.

Sometimes she chose to stay in the classroom when recess was called and would go out only at the urging of the teacher. She played organized games but not enthusiastically and seemed to find aggressive handling of a ball or other play equipment difficult.

Psychological Test Results

The Rorschach and the TAT were administered the day after the preliminary interview with Beth Anne and before any other observations or other methods of data collection had been implemented. Without becoming involved with the many problematic aspects of their interpretation, I will summarize the results of these psychological techniques. In general we found these projective techniques to be of considerable use in our studies of individuals, though we regarded them with a certain flexibility.

Thematic Apperception Test Analysis

Most of the pictures in the TAT are of people engaged in social interaction, and the subject is asked to tell a story about each picture. This story should state what the people are doing and thinking, what probably happened before the situation pictured, and what probably will happen. Beth Anne did not like to tell stories of this kind. Picking up the TAT pictures, she stated perfunctorily who the people were and what they were doing and then laid them down with what appeared to be an impatient air of finality. She was not able to say more upon probing, though she appeared to be at least superficially eager to comply. The TAT record is consequently rather sparse, though it is revealing.

The resistance to letting her imagination guide her to a creative solution to problems of human relationships as suggested by the pictures seems to be the most important feature of her protocol. She does not seem to like to be in a situation where she has to turn to her own creativity and utilize her emotions for interpretation. She does not seem to be able to empathize freely with the people in the pictures, even when she sees them as children. When asked what they might be feeling or thinking. she answered "I don't know," and if pressed by the interviewer, "How should I know?"

It is hard to pick out the most revealing instance of this aspect of her personality from the large amount of evidence in the TAT protocol. Upon seeing a picture of a little boy sitting in front of a log cabin she said, "It looks like he lives in a log cabin." ("What is he doing there?") "He's probably sitting there thinking about something." ("What is going to happen?") "Probably he is going to do what he is thinking about after a while." ("What is he thinking about?") "I don't know what he's thinking about. He's just thinking about all the things there are to think about!" In my experience with the administration of this technique with children her age, this is an unusual response. Most children as intelligent as Beth Anne seemed to embrace the task of telling the story about each picture with considerable spontaneity and creativity. Not so Beth Anne, who did not seem to be able to let herself go.

In another instance, when she was presented with a blank card and told to put a picture there by telling a story, she said, "There's nothing to make up that I can think of." That appeared to be literally true. She did not seem to be able to dip into any reservoir of imagination.

Beyond this prevailing feature in her TAT protocol, we can say that she shows some overt hostility toward authority. She also shows a certain amount of depression that is fairly rare for children her age, and she is made quite uneasy by symbols of open aggression.

There is no direct evidence of what could be called a pathological character development. What seems to be apparent is a lack of spontaneity and a refusal or inability to use her imagination to interpret the behavior of others.

Rorschach

Beth Anne gives evidence in her Rorschach protocol of possessing superior intelligence. She produced forty-eight appropriate responses, a result which is not only well above the average for her age group but higher than most adults achieve. She exhibits a high regard for detail and specification but does not embark upon any flights of fantasy, nor does she often put the details together to form an integrated whole perception.

Both qualitatively and quantitatively her protocol suggests that she is more constricted emotionally and intellectually than her superior productivity would lead one to expect. She has a well-developed perception of the concrete world about her, but these perceptions seem to stop at the level of concrete detail.

There is some evidence that she feels herself to be at times overwhelmed by forces beyond her control. There is also evidence that she has strong feelings that are not channeled into manageable interpersonal relationships or self-development.

It may be misleading to say that she lacks "creativity," but there is little imaginative spontaneity and little use of emotions for interpretive purposes. Beth Anne is what is sometimes known as a "tightrope" walker who sees what it is safe to see. She seems to avoid aspects of the inkblots that may have strong emotional implications for her and does not go deeply within herself for responses that would be emotionally meaningful. She avoids entanglements in emotionally laden material.

Furthermore, she seems to be fairly restricted in her ability to empathize with human motives or feelings. She does not seem to be able to put herself into another person's shoes, possibly because she has suppressed many of her own drives and feelings. At times, this may affect her intellectual performance, since she appears to be led off into inconsequential details and fails to see the larger whole.

Beth Anne is not likely to be a troublemaker. She conforms even at her own personal cost. She says "Thank you" every time a Rorschach card is handed to her and "Oh, pardon me!" when she drops a card an inch onto the desk and it makes a little noise. She seems very concerned about performing adequately and asks continually if she has given enough responses.

There is evidence that there are some definite problems in the handling of emotions. Generally speaking, the emotions seem to be suppressed or avoided, but when they are confronted they seem overwhelming. Given this evidence within the context of a personality adjustment that can be described as constricted and at the same time achievement-oriented, one would predict the probability of some form of hysterical behavior, probably in the form of conversion to somatic disturbances or to chronic invalidism. We shall see later that this prediction was supported.

The Rorschach psychogram is reproduced here (fig. 12.1). For those familiar with Rorschach interpretation, one can note the heavy

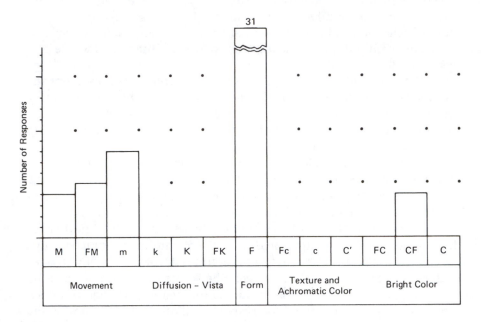

Figure 12.1. Beth Anne's Rorschach profile.

emphasis upon the "m" response and upon the "F" category, the absence of textural or shading responses, the absence of controlled color responses, and the presence of several relatively uncontrolled color responses. This psychogram is accompanied by 6 percent whole responses, 51 percent large usual-detail responses, 20 percent small usual-detail responses, and 23 percent unusual-detail or white-space responses. Beth Anne's average reaction time for all responses was 11.5 seconds. As everyone who has worked with the Rorschach knows, not too much faith should be placed upon the formal psychogram. It happens in this particular case that the psychogram relates closely to interpretations that flow from the qualitative nature of the responses. This tends to support the interpretation but does not validate it.

Sociometric Results

The sociogram (fig. 12.2) maps the results of class responses to the question, "Whom would you like to sit next to?" Without attempting an analysis of the classroom as a whole, I will only say that it is not unusual at this age level, there is a definite separation between boys and girls. While the boys tend to cluster around certain leaders or "stars of attraction," the girls usually relate to each other in smaller cliques or even dyads.

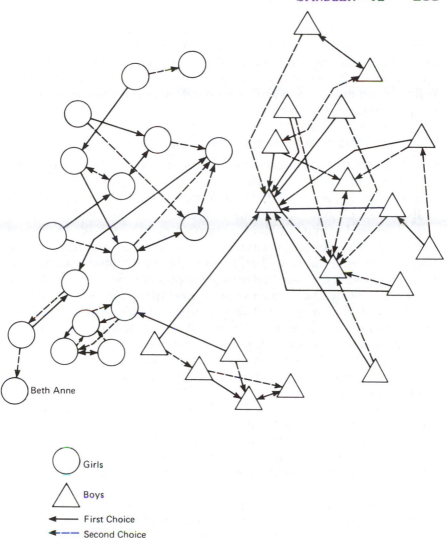

Beth Anne

◯ Girls

△ Boys

◀—— First Choice

◀--- Second Choice

Figure 12.2. Sociogram for Beth Anne's fifth-grade class.

Beth Anne's position in the classroom group insofar as these data show is extremely marginal. She is the second choice of a girl whom she considers (inferred from other data) to be her best friend. She made no choices herself. Her social situation is not significantly altered according to the social mapping of the results of the responses to the other two questions, "Whom would you like to pal around with after school?" and "Whom would you like to invite to a birthday party?"

Responses on the status-reputation test from the classroom group are impressively consistent with the results of the sociometric technique. Beth Anne is rated minimally: once for "Never having a good time" and once each for "Liking school" and "Being good looking."

The results from both techniques indicate that Beth Anne is marginal in the classroom group. She is given very little attention—either favorable or unfavorable. It is almost as though she were not there at all. These results are consistent with direct observations made of her behavior and interactions with other children in the classroom and on the playground during recess.

Home Visit and Parent Interview

Her parents were informed that the study of Beth Anne was under way. They had given their enthusiastic permission for the study when they were told, as was true, that Beth Anne was selected as a particularly well-adjusted child for special study. After the data collected above had been discussed within our team, an appointment was made to discuss the material with the parents and I was elected as the team representative. By that time the study had become primarily mine, although all three members of the team had engaged in observations and we had discussed the data as they came in during weekly seminar sessions.

Beth Anne's home was decidedly upper-middle class in furnishings and exterior appearance. The interior appointments were luxurious, and a two-car garage with a beautifully landscaped lawn completed the picture. Her father's occupation as the manager of a large building materials manufacturing company was appropriate to the socioeconomic status assignment.

When I entered the house Beth Anne's mother was waiting for me and said that her husband would come soon because he was very interested also. We discussed their recent trip to Alaska until Mr. Johnson arrived. Mrs. Johnson's attitude seemed very cooperative, and in fact she appeared pleased that the school had arranged to have a home visit and interview.

As soon as Mr. Johnson arrived we began a cordial discussion over coffee. I wished to make it clear at the very beginning that we were not dealing with Beth Anne as a "problem" case, so I reviewed the circumstances of the selection. We were working with the faculties of several schools in the community in an attempt to improve understanding of the adjustments of children at different grade levels—academically, socially, and emotionally. Having set the stage in this positive manner, I asked what aspects of our results they were particularly interested in. The father, a dynamic doer who wasted no time getting to the point, asked three questions as one, "What did you do, what did you find out, and what are you going to do about it?"

Rather than answer all these questions, I explained the techniques used in our study in some detail, including observations, sociometric materials, and projective tests. I explained why we used these techniques and what each contributed to a rounded picture of the child's adjustment. The parents seemed interested but obviously had some other concerns on their minds.

Mrs. Johnson queried, "Did you find that Beth Anne was temperamental or nervous at all?" I asked her to explain what she meant by that. She went on to explain that Beth Anne was "always complaining about her health. If any little thing is wrong with her, she wants to go to bed—and she is always thinking that she is getting sick." She elaborated upon this at some length and then went on further to say, "She used to have a tic. . . . I guess that's what you would call it. When she was reading, and she reads a lot, she would draw her stomach up into a tight little knot and then let it go and the abdominal muscles would jerk back and forth." She continued, "I took her to the doctor, of course, and he said that she was tense and nervous but not to worry about it, that it was just an abdominal tic. He said that she would get over it eventually, and as a matter of fact she is better now." This condition had apparently become obvious about a year ago.

Using this as leverage, I asked the parents if she were not rather a perfectionist—if she didn't seem to feel that everything she did, particularly at school, had to be done perfectly. Both parents agreed quickly and rather enthusiastically that this was the case. They appeared to regard my question as somewhat of a compliment. Possibly they could regard the pattern I described as evidence of a high achievement drive. They confirmed the observation implicit in the question with several examples concerning her behavior at home, in her room, her dress, and maintenance of personal possessions. After some minutes of this, I asked them if they thought this perfectionism might not cost her too much in tension and loss of spontaneity. While both parents nodded assent to this, they did not agree as wholeheartedly as they did when I asked them if she were not a perfectionist. They apparently could accept the definition of Beth Anne as an achievement-oriented youngster, but they could not bring themselves to accept the possibility that the standards of achievement could be so high as to make the cost so great. I did not press the point. When a silence in the conversation developed, I did nothing to fill it.

At this point Mr. Johnson said, "There's something else. . . . I'm not so concerned about it but Mary [the mother] is. . . ." And then the mother took up the cue, saying, "There are several junior high schools here [and she named them], now you have had a lot of experience in schools, could you tell us which one is the best?" I replied by asking her what she particularly wanted of the school selected. She said, "Well, we've been wondering whether or not we should move to a different neighborhood when Beth Anne is ready for junior high school. Washington School has been fine and we both appreciate all the things the teachers have done for Beth Anne, but you know there are all kinds of children over there—Mexicans, Italians, Chinese, Japanese, and even Negroes. Now, I believe in being democratic, but I feel that Beth Anne should associate with children that are, well . . . more her *equals!* [emphasis hers]. When she gets into junior high school this will be more important than it is now, but she feels it even now. She came home just the other day and said, 'Oh Mother, do I *have* to dance with them?' I think she should go to a school that doesn't have such a mixed group, where the children are all more her kind . . . don't you think so?"

In response I pointed out that the choice of a school was a decision that should be made by the parents in consultation with the child, and that what was important to one might not be important to another. Furthermore, it seemed to me that two points of equal importance in respect to a child's associates are, first, that the child be given a sense of belonging to a particular group and, second, that he or she should have broad experience with a wide variety of people from different backgrounds. This should enable the child to adjust well in any situation and to respect differences in others. When the parents pointed out that the two seemed contradictory I agreed, stating, however, that both could be accomplished if the parents' attitudes were supportive. To probe their attitudes a bit, I then suggested that they send their daughter to a private boarding school. Mrs. Johnson said that she wanted Beth Anne to be under her supervision, which would not be possible if she went away. However, she said, she wanted Beth Anne to be able to choose her own friends, with no attempt at reconciliation of the contradiction this posed with her other statements. I ended this phase of the discussion by saying that whatever the situation, Beth Anne's attitudes toward her classmates would reflect in significant degree what the parents thought.

I asked if there was any other specific topic they would like to discuss. The father asked how well Beth Anne was liked by her classmates. I replied, "She was not rejected more than a very few times by any other child; apparently they do not dislike her." While this did not tell the whole truth, it was at least in the direction of the truth, and I thought it was about as much as the parents could accept. I then asked if any of Beth Anne's friends were in her class, and Mrs. Johnson named three. My next statement was that Beth Anne was not chosen often either, and that in my opinion some of her classmates may have felt that she was critical of them. However, I told them also that the only negative trait on our status-reputation test was that she was rated as never having a good time. I could not explain the exact meaning of this, but assumed that it represented the children's feeling that she was serious about her school work. Before leaving I reassured them that "Beth Anne is a very excellent student and the teachers all like her a great deal." With reference to the points they had brought up, I told them that it might be important to see that she is encouraged to relax a little more and enjoy life as it comes. I said I thought her school work would keep up since she is very intelligent, even though her parents make this appear less important. I left thanking them for their cooperation and saying that it was a pleasure to talk with parents who were as cooperative as they were. They both uttered the usual pleasantries and said that they very much appreciated my coming to talk with them.

Teachers' Responses to the Evidence

By the end of our study period all of the evidence described above, plus many more details, had been shared with the staff. The teachers' responses could be described as ranging from surface compliance and agreement to deep covert resistance and resentment. I will draw a few representative comments from the tape taken during the final session with the faculty.

"I have her in art for 80 minutes a week where we try to bring out creative ideas, but actually she never offers any ideas. She usually looks at me as if to say, 'Well, what do I do next?'"

"I know Beth Anne and her family quite well and she knows this, but she is aloof with me. Does she impress the rest of you that way?"

"She reads so much. I should think this would aid her imagination. She reads stories about girls, camping, fairy stories, everything that children her age and even older read."

"She belongs to a group that went to camp last summer, but I don't think she went. She does have that little frown or worried look. I remember it bothered you, Mrs. Smith."

"I suppose that when a teacher has thirty-five children she tends to think of normal and adjusted in terms of how well they conform."

"Well they do have a very nice home. The parents just returned from a month's trip to Alaska and they hired a trained nurse to stay with the children. They have always been very thoughtful about their welfare."

"Well she has certainly done outstanding work academically, all the way through since kindergarten right up to the present in this school."

"She was always absent a lot in third grade and she never was particularly friendly. I always felt that she looked down her nose at the other children in the class who weren't quite up to her . . . I don't know whether she just didn't want to enter into things or whether she was fearful of making a mistake or what. Though she did good work, I always had a queer little feeling about her. I don't know just what it was."

"I don't think you have to worry about Beth Anne. She is going to arrive. Her family and their standing will see to that and she represents them very well."

"I agree. She'll be successful! She'll belong to a sorority."

"Well, anyway, she's a great reader!"

Interpretation

This case study virtually tells its own story and in that sense little interpretation is needed. Not all cases are as neat. This one was selected out of a much larger group—not for its representativeness but rather for its ideal-typical characteristics. It pulls together in one configuration dynamic processes that are present in some form in many other cases. It seems to be in part a reversal of the relationship between the teacher and the fifth-grade class and the counselor and his class that I have discussed elsewhere (1959). It is actually only a variation in this relationship. In all of these cases and in many others that we studied during our several years of field research and consultation, it became apparent that teachers, usually quite contrary to their expressed intentions and ideals, were selecting children for the fruits of success in our social system or for the ignominy of defeat and alienation on the basis of undeclared, and probably unknown, cultural biases.

Beth Anne was selected by the teachers by consensus as exceptionally well adjusted. It is difficult to know exactly what "adjusted" means to anyone, though it was a term used very widely in the fifties and sixties in American public schools. These particular teachers said during our preliminary consultations that adjustment meant "conformity to the rules and regulations of the classroom," "success at school work," "the ability to achieve according to the expectations of parents and teachers," "an ability to get along well with one's peers," "a person who is not too conflict-ridden when he or she attempts to get along with their work and play," and "a child who works and plays well with others." The teachers were clearly not all of a single mind concerning what adjustment meant, but their definitions tended toward an adaptation to the situation as defined by teachers, by rules, and, by the culture which the school represented. This is not unreasonable. In every cultural system those who accept the rules and achieve the goals laid down within the system are "adjusted" and those who do not are deviant, maladjusted, or criminal. The teachers' definitions do not pay much attention to what is inside Beth Anne's mind and, in fact, do not have much to do with Beth Anne at all. They have more to do with the school than with the child. This is understandable too.

However, we are faced with the fact that the teachers, even given their own criteria of adjustment, inaccurately perceived Beth Anne's situation. It is true that she achieved well according to the formal standards of academic performance. This achievement, however, was apparently at considerable psychic cost which was almost completely overlooked. Even more startling is the fact that the teachers misread the degree of her social adjustment. She did not "work and play well with others." In fact, she interacted with other children very little and was definitely marginal, really isolated within the classroom group.

Beth Anne's social marginality and isolation within the school was accompanied by severe internal distress in her own psychic system. She was compliant, a high achiever, but fearful of not achieving. She was unable to express her own emotions and had begun to evolve into a very constricted personality—all the more sad because she was such an intelligent girl. These processes had gone so far that a form of hysteric conversion had occurred. The prediction made on the basis of Rorschach evidence that the conversion would take the form of a somatic disturbance or possibly chronic invalidism was strongly supported. She wanted to stay in bed "on the slightest pretext" and suffered an "abdominal tic."

It would be easy to conclude that the teachers misperceived Beth Anne simply because she was academically successful—a high achiever in those areas where the teachers are directly responsible. This is, indeed, part of the cause for the misreading, but it is not a sufficient cause.

As I interpret the whole pattern of Beth Anne's adaptation and the perceptions of others of this adaptation, I see the teachers' perceptions as a self-sustaining cultural belief system. Beth Anne was selected not only because she was a high achiever but because in every other way she represented the image of what is desirable in American middle-class culture as it existed at the time of the study in the fifties and still exists today in slightly modified form. Beth Anne and her family represented success and achievement, the value of hard work, the validity of gratification delayed for future satisfaction, the validity of respectability and cleanliness, of good manners and of good dress as criteria for behavior. Beth Anne fit the criteria by means of which the teachers were selecting behaviors and children for the single channel of success and adaptation for which the school was designed as an institution representing the dominant mainstream culture.

I have characterized the belief in these values and selective criteria as self-sustaining because negative evidence was rationalized out of the system. Despite behaviors and attributes that any alert observer could have picked up in Beth Anne's case without the aid of outside experts or foreign instruments, Beth Anne was seen as one of the best-adjusted children in the school because she fit the belief system about the relationship between certain symbols, certain behaviors, and success as culturally defined.

This belief system, like most, can and does work. When belief systems stop working entirely they cease to exist, but they can continue to work partially for a very long time at great cost. In this case the cost to Beth Anne was profound. The culturally induced blindness of her teachers was in a certain real sense killing her and in ways no less painful than those in which minority children were and are being "killed" in many American schools.

Conclusion

I am not blaming teachers personally for what I have described in this case analysis. The teachers, the children, the administrator, and all of the other actors on the stage are acting out a cultural drama. What I am striving for as an anthropologist of education is an understanding of this drama as a cultural process. As an anthropologist teaching teachers I want to promote *awareness* of this cultural process. None of the teachers that I have described here or elsewhere in my writings in this book are people of bad intent. Most teachers are idealistic, many are quite liberal in their political and social beliefs, but they *are products of their culture* and live within the framework of values and symbols that are a part of that culture. By being made aware of what they are and do, they can be freed from the tyranny of their cultures; in turn, they will be able to free children from the damaging effects of premature, inaccurate, or prejudiced estimates and interpretations of their behavior that are culturally induced.

This awareness is not easily gained. Though the teachers were exposed to intimate details of Beth Anne's case as these details developed, and though we exercised responsible skill and sensitivity in the dissemination of this evidence in open and closed discussions, the resistance of the teachers to the implications of the evidence was profound. The educative process had some effect, probably, but I doubt that it was very significant as far as the future behaviors of the teachers is concerned. Nor is a course or two in anthropology the answer. A year's fieldwork in a foreign community where one's assumptions, values, and perceptions are profoundly shocked by raw experience would make a significant difference, but not always in a direction that would be useful in the classroom. Matters have improved since the study of Beth Anne, but they have not improved enough. In my opinion a substantial part of the energy and time devoted to training teachers should be devoted to learning how to cope with the kinds of problems that I have been discussing in this and other case studies.

We were somewhat more successful with Beth Anne and her family as individuals than we were with the teachers. We explicitly recommended that the standards of excellence be lowered somewhat for Beth Anne and that she be given to understand that such achievements were not all that was important. Beth Anne seemed considerably improved according to a short follow-up observation the next year. But we cannot be sure of what happened. It may be that doing the study had a positive effect. Beth Anne at least knew that someone else had found out what it was like to be Beth Anne, and her parents discovered that it was possible to face a problem that they intuitively felt to be there because an outside agency had detected the same problem.

Notes

[1] Details of time and place are left ambiguous, certain minor details of fact are altered, and all personal references are disguised in order to protect all parties involved with the case study.

[2] With the wisdom of hindsight, I would not administer this technique again. It is potentially destructive to children's self-feelings and stimulates corrosive interpersonal evaluation.

Reference

Spindler, George D. 1959. *The Transmission of American Culture*, Third Burton Lecture, Harvard University. Cambridge: Harvard University Press.

13

Playing by the Rules

Margaret A. Gibson
University of California at Santa Cruz

Immigrant minorities have been found to do well in school in many parts of the world. Examples of Asian immigrant success are well known in the United States, but perhaps less well known are studies of successful immigrant groups in Australia, Canada, and Britain. I will review briefly some of the studies in these countries and then turn to my own study of the Punjabis in California.

In Australia, the children of non-English-speaking immigrants, notably Greeks, Yugoslavs, and Italians, have been found to stay in school longer and to like school more than Anglo-Australian youths of similar class background. Australian research suggests that the educational aspirations of immigrant parents are more important to school persistence than students' IQ or socioeconomic status (Marjoribanks 1980; Martin and Meade 1979; Taft and Cahill 1981). Immigrant parents place greater importance on respect for school rules and hard work than on a child's ability.

Canadian studies show language minority immigrants of low socioeconomic background to perform better in school than either the French-Canadian minority or the English-Canadian majority (Anisef 1975; Masemann 1975; Wolfgang 1975). Canadian-born children of non-English-speaking immigrants tend to be overrepresented in college-preparatory classes compared to students whose first language is English (Cummins 1984). Like the Australian studies, the Canadian work indicates that immigrant youth are "more committed to education as the route to a better life" than are indigenous students (Anisef 1975:127). Immigrants also are less likely than indigenous students to relinquish their goals of a university education when their performance in school is poor (ibid., p. 128).

In Britain, where students of working-class backgrounds have been found to have far less opportunity to enter universities than is the case in America, again we find a group of immigrants outperforming

Source: Written especially for *Education and Cultural Process*.

indigenous students of comparable class background. A higher percentage of Indian-born males entered British universities in 1979 than UK-born males. In addition, significantly more of the Indians were sons of manual workers than were the UK-born (Ballard and Vellins 1985). So striking is the general pattern of success among students of South Asian origin that a government-appointed committee in Britain has recently asked the question: What is it that enables South Asian young people to surmount, to the degree that they do, both the influence of prejudice and discrimination and that of low socioeconomic status? (Swann Committee 1985:86).

All of these studies—British, Canadian, and Australian—reveal considerable success on the part of immigrant youth of non-English-speaking and working-class backgrounds to use formal education as an avenue to middle-class occupational status.

Not all immigrant groups perform well in school, however. In Britain, for example, students of West Indian origin do very poorly (Swann Committee 1985; Taylor 1981; Tomlinson 1983), as do the children of Turkish workers in West Germany (Castles 1984; Skutnabb-Kangas 1981) and Finnish students in Sweden (Paulston 1982:40; Skutnabb-Kangas 1979). Yet my own research in the American Virgin Islands showed West Indian immigrants to be doing quite well academically, and far better, in the case of boys, than the native Crucian West Indian population (Gibson 1982, 1983a). There also are studies indicating that children of Turkish and Finnish origin in Australia appear to be doing better in school than their counterparts in Germany and Sweden (Inglis and Manderson n.d.; Troike 1984:50).

What does all this mean? It means to me that in addition to the social structure of the host society and the cultural background of the minority group, we must attend very carefully to the specific nature of the minority group's relationship to the dominant group.

Most minority students face substantial barriers in school. Those most frequently cited as having an impact on educational performance are low socioeconomic status, a home language other than that used in school, unequal employment opportunities, the tracking system of many schools, home-school cultural discontinuities, and the prejudiced attitudes of the dominant group toward the minority. The question I would like to focus on is not *how* these different barriers impede classroom learning, but *why* some groups more readily transcend these barriers than others.

The Punjabi Case

Let us turn now to my study of Punjabi Sikh immigrants in a rural California school district (Gibson 1983b, 1987).[1] Those who settle in

"Valleyside" (my name for the research site) differ in a number of essential respects from the urbanized and highly educated Asian Indians, including many Sikh professionals, who have settled since 1965 in metropolitan areas throughout the United States (Gardner, Robey, and Smith 1985; Leonhard-Spark and Saran 1980; Minocha 1984). Most Valleyside Sikhs have few saleable skills, speak little English, if any at all, and, in the case of women in particular, have had little formal education. Most must work, at least initially, in back-breaking and low-paid jobs as farm laborers in Valleyside's fruit orchards. The median family income in 1980 for Valleyside Punjabis was $15,000, just half that of the average white Valleyside family.[2]

The study revealed sharp differences in the performance patterns of Punjabi students who receive *all* their education in America, or English-medium schools, and those who enter the American system after fourth grade. Almost 90 percent of those who arrive in grades five, six, seven, or eight are still limited in English during high school.[3] These later arrivals are an extremely high-risk group, with little prospect of achieving their educational and occupational aspirations.

Punjabis who enter the American school system no later than second grade have a distinctly different pattern of school performance. In high school Punjabi girls educated from childhood in this country do as well academically as their white majority-group classmates, and Punjabi boys do even better. Not only do these boys receive higher marks, but more significantly they take more of the tough college-preparatory classes in science and math. More Punjabis, proportionately, than white Valleysiders graduate from high school. Although Punjabi immigrants encounter many problems along the way, still they persist with their education.

In school, Punjabi children have to cope with severe prejudice and sharp conflicts between home values and those promoted by the school. Punjabi students are told they stink, directly by white peers and indirectly by their teachers. They are told to go back to India. They are accused of being illegals. They are physically abused by majority-group students, who spit at them, refuse to sit by them in class or on buses, crowd ahead of them in line, stick them with pins, throw food at them, and worse. They are labelled troublemakers if they defend themselves. In one way or another they are told constantly that India and Indian culture are inferior to Western and American ways. They are criticized for their diet, their dress, and their hair style. They are faulted because they place family ahead of individual interests, defer to the authority of elders, accept arranged marriages, and believe in group decision making. They are condemned most especially for not joining in majority-dominated school activities and for resisting as best they can the forces for Anglo conformity.

While teachers commend Punjabi students for their diligence in the classroom, they are perplexed by their refusal to participate in team sports, clubs, and other non-academic school activities. They don't "fit in socially," which, for many teachers, is the chief criterion for school success.

The more the schools pressure Punjabi children to conform, the more tightly their parents supervise their behavior and advise against contact with non-Punjabi peers. Punjabi parents define "becoming Americanized" as forgetting one's roots and adopting the most disparaged traits of the majority group, such as young people making decisions on their own without parental counsel, leaving their families at age eighteen to live independently, dancing, dating, and arranging their own marriages. Punjabi adolescents are warned repeatedly that they will dishonor themselves, their families, and their community if they adopt the values and behaviors of white peers. Such warnings are coupled with community gossip about those whose behavior deviates from Indian village norms. If inappropriate behavior persists the family will likely decide to withdraw the offender from school, first for a period of time and then permanently. A boy is put to work in the peach fields and a girl is kept at home until her marriage can be arranged. The individual who insists on having his or her own way risks being cut off from family and community.

Punjabi teenagers themselves criticize those who socialize at school with non-Punjabis. They say, "He's Anglo, or he thinks he's white. He's not one of us." Punjabi students stick with their own because, as one student put it, "you don't want to be an outcast from your own people." Punjabi young people, in effect, are forced to choose sides. Few find it possible to mix socially in both worlds.

No similar pressure is brought to bear on Punjabi students for accepting the authority of white teachers or doing well in school. Adapting oneself to teachers' expectations, even when their expectations conflict with traditional Indian or Punjabi values, is not viewed as "acting white." Quite the reverse. Students are encouraged to excel academically and teased when grades or behavior are poor. Parents remind their offspring that they have made great sacrifices for them and that the parents' lives will have been wasted if their children are not successful. Young people are also told that those who do well in school can expect to find better marriage partners, that their accomplishments bring credit to their family, and that they set an example for other younger Punjabis to follow. These are powerful messages.

Punjabi parents have high expectations for their children's achievement. If a child does poorly, however, only rarely do they blame the system, or the teachers. "If the child does not wish to study, then what can the teacher do?" parents remark. "Those who wish to learn, will learn," is the general attitude.

Punjabi adolescents, for their part, know firsthand the drudgery of manual labor and the precarious nature of orchard farming. They want a better, more secure future. Almost all Punjabi children have direct contact with adults who have overcome substantial obstacles and, in the words of one young Sikh informant, "have been able to beat the system and the whites at their own games" (Gibson and Bhachu, 1986). Academic achievements, in the Punjabi view, represent what can be done even without parental wealth and education. Parents urge their children to become proficient in the ways of the majority culture. They take pride in the fact their children can speak English well and can help them deal with the host society, *providing* they also are maintaining strong roots within the Punjabi community.

Punjabi students conform to their teachers' expectations to the degree possible, but they are nevertheless no bunch of goody-goodies or pushovers. Punjabi Sikhs have a tradition of toughness in the face of abuse. Boys are instructed, for example, that they must protect the honor of family and community. "Turn the other cheek once, twice," Sikhs say, "but the third time defend yourself." The current activist Sikh radicalism in India and abroad, and the Ghadr Party Marxism of Sikh immigrants earlier in the century (Juergensmeyer 1981; Singh 1966), show Sikhs' readiness to resist their oppressors when they feel no other alternative exists.

Punjabi parents are not unmindful of the difficulties their children face in school. They are especially disturbed by the prejudiced attitudes and actions of white youths, but they choose to downplay the problems. They urge their children to ignore racist remarks and to avoid fights. The parents recognize that they are operating from a position of weakness and that they have little power to turn things around. Their response to prejudice stems from this reality. But it is also a deliberate and conscious strategy of putting education first. The parents I surveyed stated specifically that a situation of response and counterresponse would only promote greater ill will between groups and would distract their children from their studies.

Sikh parents advocate a strategy of *accommodation and acculturation without assimilation.* Adapt to the formal demands of the classroom—do what you must to get a high school education—but resist the forces for total cultural assimilation. "Dress to please the people," Punjabis frequently say, "but eat to please yourself."

My study of Punjabi Sikhs, coupled with the general literature on immigrant adaptation patterns, make it quite clear that immigrants perceive their situation very differently and respond to it very differently from many indigenous minority groups. Immigrants bring a comparative perspective: schooling, jobs, and overall chances for getting ahead are far better here than back where they came from. They measure their success not in terms of the white majority, but in terms of other Punjabis settled in this country and back in Punjab. To understand school response patterns we must, as John Ogbu has long argued, attend very carefully to folk theories of success and failure (Ogbu 1974, 1978; Ogbu and Matute-Bianchi 1986). Punjabis, like many immigrants, view formal education as the avenue to a better life. They put up with all kinds of difficulties in school because they believe so strongly that there will be a payoff later. This is true even though many immigrant groups did not pursue education with the same vigor back in their homeland. The context has changed. Their situation has changed. And so too, do their strategies change.

Why do some minority groups have an easier time than others playing the classroom game by the rules? The explanation involves, I believe, a complex and dynamic interaction among three sets of variables, namely: the cultural preferences of the group, the historical context of settlement in the host society, and the group's response to its current situation.[4]

Conclusion

Comparative research worldwide suggests that school performance is directly and strongly affected by, first, minority attitudes about the probable payoff for playing the school game, and, second, minority attitudes about the dominant group and dominant culture. When parents and students do not believe there will be a sufficient return for investing their time and energy in schooling, they turn their energies elsewhere. Likewise, if they feel hostility and suspicion toward the school system and those in authority, it is more difficult for students to accept this authority and to seek to become skilled in the ways of the dominant group.

"Why study immigrants?" I have been asked. There are many reasons, but let me suggest three that are especially pertinent to the field of minority education. First, research on immigrant minorities provides fresh insight into the role of family and community in promoting successful school adaptation patterns. Second, immigrants provide a rich and useful perspective on both the strengths and weaknesses of the American system of schooling. Third, immigrant studies bring into sharp relief the barriers to equal educational opportunity for minority students.

The Valleyside study and others suggest that non-English-speaking immigrants who enter American schools after fourth grade are an extremely high-risk group (cf. Masemann 1975:111, 119). They, especially, need a supportive learning environment and good ESL, or bilingual, instruction. With respect to bilingual education, we need to attend carefully to the views of the target population. Many immigrants are strongly opposed to any instruction whatsoever in their mother tongue, and this certainly was the case for the Punjabis whom I studied. They wanted an all-English curriculum. Bilingual education may not be an appropriate instructional strategy for all groups of language minority students, and this is something we need to learn more about.

What the Punjabis do want is a far more rigorous English-as-a-second-language program taught in such a way that immigrant students are not segregated from the mainstream, nor handed cheap credits and shuffled along through the system with only the pretense of a decent education. Punjabis also want an end to the racial prejudice in school and to the pervasive and intense pressure to conform to the dominant culture. However hard they may work in class, outside of class they are labeled un-American because their behavior deviates from majority norms.

This is what educational programs need to address—this oppression of those who demand the right to be different. Immigrants, too, if beaten down long enough will fight back and will come to view the dominant group with suspicion and hostility. And when they do, they likely will reject the authority of teachers and administrators and resist playing the classroom game by the rules.

References

Anisef, Paul, 1975. Consequences of Ethnicity for Educational Plans among Grade 12 Students. In *Education of Immigrant Students*, A. Wolfgang, ed. Toronto: Ontario Institute for Studies in Education.

Ballard, Roger, and Selma Vellins, 1985. South Asian Entrants to British Universities: A Comparative Note. *New Community* 12(2): 260–65.

Castles, Stephen, 1984. *Here for Good.* London: Pluto Press.

Cummins, Jim, 1984. *Bilingualism and Special Education.* Clevedon, Avon: Multilingual Matters.

Gardner, Robert W., Bryant Robey, and Peter C. Smith, 1985. Asian Americans: Growth, Change, and Diversity. *Population Bulletin* 40(4).

Gibson, Margaret A., 1982. Reputation and Respectability: How Competing Cultural Systems Affect Students' Performance in School. *Anthropology and Education Quarterly* 13(1): 3–27.

_____. 1983a. Ethnicity and Schooling: West Indian Immigrants in the United States Virgin Islands. *Ethnic Groups* 5(3): 173–98.

_____, 1983b. Home-School-Community Linkages: A Study of Educational Opportunity for Punjabi Youth. Final Report to the National Institute of Education, Washington, D.C.

_____, 1987. Punjabi Immigrants in an American High School. In *Interpretive Ethnography of Education at Home and Abroad*, George D. and Louise S. Spindler, eds. Hillsdale, NJ: Lawrence Erlbaum.

Gibson, Margaret A., 1988. *Accommodation without Assimilation: Sikh Immigrants in an American High School.* Ithaca, NY: Cornell University Press.

Gibson, Margaret A., and Parminder Bhachu, 1986. Community Forces and School Performance: Punjabi Sikhs in Rural California and Urban Britain. *New Community* 13 (Spring/Summer).

Inglis, Christine, and Lenore Manderson, n.d. Education and Reproduction among Turkish Families in Sydney. Department of Education, The University of Sydney (unpublished manuscript).

Juergensmeyer, Mark, 1981. The Gadar Syndrome: Ethnic Anger and Nationalist Pride. *Population Review* 25 (1/2): 48–58.

Leonhard-Spark, Philip J., and Parmatma Saran, 1980. The Indian Immigrant in America: A Demographic Profile. In *The New Ethnics: Asian Indians in the United States,* P. Saran and E. Eames, eds. New York: Praeger.

Marjoribanks, Kevin, 1980. *Ethnic Families and Children's Achievements.* Sydney: George Allen and Unwin.

Martin, Jean I., and P. Meade, 1979. *The Educational Experience of Sydney High School Students* (Report No. 1). Canberra: AGPS.

Masemann, Vandra, 1975. Immigrant Students' Perceptions of Occupational Programs. In *Education of Immigrant Students,* A. Wolfgang, ed. Toronto: Ontario Institute for Studies in Education.

Minocha, Urmil, 1984. Indian Immigrants in the United States: Demographic Trends, Economic Assimilation in the Host Society, and Impact on the Sending Society. Honolulu: East-West Population Institute (unpublished manuscript).

Ogbu, John U., 1974. *The Next Generation.* New York: Academic Press.

_____, 1978. *Minority Education and Caste: The American System in Cross-Cultural Perspective.* New York: Academic Press.

Ogbu, John U., and Maria Eugina Matute-Bianchi, 1986. Understanding Sociocultural Factors: Knowledge, Identity, and School Adjustment. In *Beyond Language: Social and Cultural Factors in Schooling Language Minority Students.* Sacramento: California State Department of Education.

Paulston, Christina Bratt, 1982. Swedish Research and Debate About Bilingualism. A Report to the National Swedish Board of Education, Stockholm.

Singh, Khushwant, 1966. *A History of the Sikhs: Volume 2, 1839–1964.* Princeton: Princeton University Press.

Skutnabb-Kangas, Tove, 1979. Language in the Process of Cultural Assimilation and Structural Incorporation of Linguistic Minorities. Rosslyn, VA: National Clearinghouse for Bilingual Education.

_____, 1981. Guest Worker or Immigrant—Different Ways of Reproducing an Underclass. *Journal of Multilingual and Multicultural Development* 2(2): 89–115.

Swann Committee Report, 1985. *Education for All.* The Report of the Committee of Inquiry into the Education of Children from Ethnic Minority Groups. Cmnd. 9453. London: HMSO.

Taft, Ronald and Desmond Cahill, 1981. Education of Immigrants in Australia. In *Educating Immigrants,* Joti Bhatnagar, ed. New York: St. Martin's Press.

Taylor, Monica J., 1981. *Caught Between.* Windsor: NFER-Nelson.

Tomlinson, Sally, 1983. *Ethnic Minorities in British Schools.* London: Heinemann.

Troike, Rudolph C., 1984. SCALP: Social and Cultural Aspects of Language Proficiency. In *Language Proficiency and Academic Achievement,* Charlene Rivera, ed. Clevedon, Avon: Multilingual Matters.

Wolfgang, Aaron, ed., 1975. *Education of Immigrant Students.* Toronto: Ontario Institute for Studies in Education.

Notes

[1] The fieldwork on which the findings reported here are based was funded by the National Institute of Education (Grant Number 80-0123). I gratefully acknowledge the support of the Institute and the contribution of fellow research team members· Amarjit S. Bal, Gurdip K. Dhillon, and Elizabeth McIntosh.

[2] These income statistics are based on family background information gathered from 45 Punjabi seniors and their parents, and a comparable number of white Valleyside seniors and their parents.

[3] This figure is based on an analysis of school records for all 231 Punjabi students attending Valleyside High, grades 9–12, in 1980–81.

[4] I discuss the interaction of these three sets of variables more fully in *Accommodation without Assimilation: Sikh Immigrants in an American High School* (Ithaca, NY: Cornell University Press, 1988).

Part IV

CULTURAL PROCESS IN EDUCATION VIEWED TRANSCULTURALLY

Preview

A transcultural perspective on education is essential, for education is a cultural process and occurs in a social context. Without attention to cultural differences and the way education serves those differences, we have no way of achieving perspective on our own culture and the way our educational system serves it or of building a comprehensive picture of education as affected by culture.

My purpose as one of the founders of the field has been to give the anthropology of education a focus by defining the field's special area to be cultural transmission. Recently this position has been challenged, and I welcome the challenge. Harry Wolcott, in particular, has raised issues about cultural uniformity and diversity and has pointed out that a cultural acquisition model accounts for the diversity found in all cultures more adequately than a cultural transmission model. If, however, we take the position that *intentional intervention* in the learning process is displayed in the way adults manage the education of their children, we can find adequate reason for diversity. These interventions—from weaning and toilet training to kindergarten, to instruction in high school, occupational training, and the rituals of death—never teach what they are intended to teach—for human beings never learn only one thing at a time. Concomitant learning always takes place. In the internally consistent cultural systems the concomitant and intended learning will be at least congruent. In inconsistent or disintegrating cultural systems the intended and concomitant will often be at odds. In chapter 14 I sample selected aspects of cultural transmission in fifteen situations emphasizing nonliterate, traditional cultures. This chapter serves as an introduction to the treatment of single cases, and, along with Wolcott's chapter 15, explores the complex relationship between cultural transmission and the learning of culture. Wolcott's chapter serves to alert us to a need for a diversified approach to the study of the complex processes we subsume under headings such as "transmission" and "acquisition."

Nevertheless, our area of greatest strength as anthropologists is our understanding and experience with culture. No one else understands culture as we do or as well as we do. The enactment of culture, culture as a uniquely human adaptation to the problems posed by life on this planet, culture as a "smorgasbord" of possibilities in the form of instrumental behaviors and goals from which individuals can draw (and increasingly from cultures that are not of their own heritage), culture as a continuity of meaning linking generation to generation and providing identities, culture as the stuff from which enduring and situated selves are created—all of these, and many more aspects of culture and cultural process are too important to allow our attention to wander.

In both Dorothy Eggan's chapter 16 on the Hopi and Steve (as he is known to friends) Hart's on the Tiwi (chapter 17) there is a dominant theme—the transition from childhood to adolescence and later to maturity through initiation rituals. This theme appears in many ethnographies of traditional communities and has been the subject of discussion and the focus of theory for much anthropological writing. In both Hopi and Tiwi cultures the initiates experience sharp discontinuity in role relationships. Formerly friendly or aloof adults suddenly become threatening and punitive. The initiate is coerced, cowed, treated as a know-nothing neophyte and is taught esoteric content that must be kept secret. Dissonance is aroused. The childish neophytes are anxious about what is happening to them and experience pain and deprivation. Doubts about one's ability to survive the initiation are raised. Finally, all doubts and fears are resolved by the successful conclusion of the initiation and the transformation of the former child to beginning adulthood. The initiate becomes committed to the very cultural patterns and their symbols that were threatening him (or, less frequently, her). Resolution of dissonance appears in most educational contexts cross-culturally, not solely in the initiation setting. In fact, it may be one of several fundamental education processes that we tend to blur and ignore, with our cultural focus on individual development and social and personal "adjustment." Resolution of dissonance in the course of education as cultural transmission may be an essential mechanism in the maintenance of cultural systems if it engenders, as we hypothesize it does, commitment to one's culture.

Sindell's report in chapter 18 on the educational experience of Mistassini Cree children points to a related process. Discontinuity of culturally patterned experience and social roles is created for the Mistassini children—not by a dissonance-resolving initiation ceremony, but by removal from the native community to a residential school run by aliens. The children never learn fully the culture of their parents; they only partially, and with ambivalence that is rarely resolved, learn the alien culture. There are parallels in the experience of children from any culturally differentiated ethnic group in the United States as they adapt, or fail to adapt, to mainstream schools.

Vera Michalchik's chapter 19 on the display of cultural knowledge in cultural transmission on the Pacific Island of Kosrae is of quite a different order than any of the previous chapters in this section. Displays of cultural knowledge occur in any interactional context on Kosrae. Michalchik focuses on the family, the church, and the school. In these contexts children are called upon to display cultural knowledge and must display it correctly or be censured. They must not only know the content to be displayed but when and how it is appropriate to display it. The nuances of the conditions of display remove this aspect of cultural transmission from the formal, ritual context of formal institutions and place it within the framework of everyday social intercourse. Michalchik's chapter thus gives this section a balance that would otherwise be lacking and moves the analysis of cultural transmission and cultural acquisition to a better resolution of opposing interpretations.

The Editor

$$14$$

The Transmission of Culture

George D. Spindler
Stanford University

This chapter is about how neonates become talking, thinking, feeling, moral, believing, valuing human beings—members of groups, participants in cultural systems. It is not, as a chapter on child psychology might be, about the growth and development of individuals, but on how young humans come to want to act as they must act if the cultural system is to be maintained. A wide variety of cultures are examined to illustrate both the diversity and unity of ways in which children are educated. The educational functions that are carried out by initiation rites in many cultures are emphasized, and the concepts of cultural compression, continuity, and discontinuity are stressed in this context. Various other techniques of education are demonstrated with selected cases, including reward, modeling and imitation, play, dramatization, verbal admonition, reinforcement, and storytelling. Recruitment and cultural maintenance are analyzed as basic educative functions. The chapter is not about the whole process of education but about certain parts of that process seen in a number of different situations.

What Are Some of the Ways That Culture Is Transmitted?

Psychologists and pediatricians do not agree upon the proper and most effective ways to raise children. Neither do the Dusun of Borneo, the Tewa or Hopi of the Southwest, the Japanese, the Ulithians or the Palauans of Micronesia, the Turkish villagers, the Tiwi of North Australia, the people of Gopalpur, or those of Guadalcanal. Each way of life is distinctive in its outlook, content, the kind of adult personalities favored, and the way children are raised. There are also many respects

Source: Reprinted with minor revisions from *Culture in Process*, 2nd Edition, by Alan R. Beals, George D. Spindler, and Louise Spindler. Copyright © 1967, 1973, by Holt, Rinehart and Winston. Reprinted by permission of Holt, Rinehart and Winston.

in which human communities are similar that override cultural differences. All major human cultural systems include magic, religion, moral values, recreation, regulation of mating, education, and so forth. But the *content* of these different categories, and the ways the content and the categories are put together, differ enormously. These differences are reflected in the ways people raise their children. If the object of cultural transmission is to teach young people how to think, act, and feel appropriately this must be the case. To understand this process we must get a sense of this variety.

This Is How It Is in Palau

Five-year-old Azu trails after his mother as she walks along the village path, whimpering and tugging at her skirt. He wants to be carried, and he tells her so, loudly and demandingly, "Stop! Stop! Hold me!" His mother shows no sign of attention. She continues her steady barefooted stride, her arms swinging freely at her sides, her heavy hips rolling to smooth the jog of her walk and steady the basket of wet clothes she carries on her head. She has been to the washing pool and her burden keeps her neck stiff, but this is not why she looks impassively ahead and pretends not to notice her son. Often before she has carried him on her back and an even heavier load on her head. But today she has resolved not to submit to his plea, for it is time for him to begin to grow up.

Azu is not aware that the decision has been made. Understandably, he supposes that his mother is just cross, as she often has been in the past, and that his cries will soon take effect. He persists in his demand but falls behind as his mother firmly marches on. He runs to catch up and angrily yanks at her hand. She shakes him off without speaking to him or looking at him. Enraged, he drops solidly on the ground and begins to scream. He gives a startled look when this produces no response, then rolls over on his stomach and begins to writhe, sob, and yell. He beats the earth with his fists and kicks it with his toes. This hurts and makes him furious, the more so since it has not caused his mother to notice him. He scrambles to his feet and scampers after her, his nose running, tears coursing through the dirt on his cheeks. When almost on her heel he yells and, getting no response, drops to the ground.

By this time his frustration is complete. In a rage he grovels in the red dirt, digging his toes into it, throwing it around him and on himself. He smears it on his face, grinding it in with his clenched fists. He squirms on his side, his feet turning his body through an arc on the pivot of one shoulder.

A man and his wife are approaching, the husband in the lead, he with a shorthandled adz resting on his left shoulder, she with a basket of husked coconuts on her head. As they come abreast of Azu's mother the man greets her with "You have been to the washing pool?" It is the Palauan equivalent of the American "How are you?"—a question that is not an inquiry but a token of recognition. The two women scarcely glance up as they pass. They have recognized each other from a distance and it is not necessary to repeat the greeting. As the couple pass, even less notice is taken of Azu, sprawled on the path a few yards behind his mother. They have to step around his frenzied body, but no other recognition is taken of him, no word is spoken to him or to each other. There is no need to comment. His tantrum is not an unusual sight, especially among boys of his age or a little older. There is nothing to say to him or about him.

In the yard of a house just off the path, two girls, a little older than Azu, stop their play to investigate. Cautiously and silently they venture in Azu's direction. His mother is still in sight, but she disappears suddenly as she turns off the path into her yard without looking back. The girls stand some distance away, observing Azu's gyrations with solemn eyes. Then they turn and go back to their doorway, where they stand, still watching him but saying nothing. Azu is left alone, but it takes several minutes for him to realize that this is the way it is to be. Gradually his fit subsides and he lies sprawled and whimpering on the path.

Finally, he pushes himself to his feet and starts home, still sobbing and wiping his eyes with his fists. As he trudges into the yard he can hear his mother shouting at his sister, telling her not to step over the baby. Another sister is sweeping the earth beneath the floor of the house with a coconut-leaf broom. Glancing up, she calls shrilly to Azu, asking him where he has been. He does not reply, but climbs the two steps to the threshold of the doorway and makes his way to a mat in the corner of the house. There he lies quietly until he falls asleep.

This has been Azu's first painful lesson in growing up. There will be many more unless he soon understands and accepts the Palauan attitude that emotional attachments are cruel and treacherous entanglements, and that it is better not to cultivate them in the first place than to have them disrupted and disclaimed. Usually the lesson has to be repeated in many connections before its general truth sinks in. There will be refusals of pleas to be held, to be carried, to be fed, to be cuddled, and to be amused; and for a time at least there will follow the same violent struggle to maintain control that failed to help Azu. For whatever the means, and regardless of the lapses from the stern code, children must grow away from their parents, not cleave to them. Sooner or later the child must learn not to expect the solicitude, the warm attachment of earlier years and must accept the fact that he is to live in an emotional vacuum, trading friendship for concrete rewards, neither accepting nor giving lasting affection. (Barnett 1960:4–6)

Is culture being transmitted here? Azu is learning that people are not to be trusted, that any emotional commitment is shaky business. He is acquiring an emotional attitude. From Professor Barnett's further description of life in Palau (Barnett 1960) we know that this emotional attitude underlies economic, social, political, even religious behavior among adult Palauans. If this happened only to Azu we would probably regard it as a traumatic event. He might then grow up to be a singularly distrustful adult in a trusting world. He would be a deviant. But virtually all Palauan boys experience this sudden rejection (it happens more gradually for girls)—not always in just this particular way—but in somewhat the same way and at about the same time. This is a culturally patterned way of getting a lesson across to the child. This culturally patterned way of treating the child has a more or less consistent result—an emotional attitude—and this emotional attitude is in turn patterned, and fits into various parts of the Palauan cultural system. What is learned by Azu and transmitted by his mother is at once a pattern of child training (the mother had it and applied it), a dimension of Palauan *worldview* (Palauans see the world as a place where people do not become emotionally involved with each other), a modal personality trait (most normal adult Palauans distrust others), and a pattern for behavior in the context of the many subsystems (economic, political, religious, and so forth) governing adult life.

Azu's mother did not simply tell him to stop depending upon her and to refrain from lasting emotional involvements with others. She demonstrated to him in a very dramatic way that this is the way it is in this life (in Palau at least). She probably didn't even completely rationalize what she did. She did not say to herself, "Now it is time for Azu to acquire the characteristic Palauan attitude that emotional attachments are not lasting and the best way to teach him this is for me to refuse to carry him." Barnett says that she "resolved not to submit to his plea." We cannot be sure that she even did this, for not even Homer Barnett, as well as he knows the Palauans, can get into Azu's mother's head. We know that she did not, in fact, submit to his plea. She may well have thought that it was about time for Azu to grow up. Growing up in Palau means in part to stop depending on people, even your very own loving mother. But maybe she was just plain tired, feeling a little extra crabby, so she acted in a characteristically Palauan way *without thinking about it* toward her five-year-old. People can transmit culture without knowing they do so. Probably more culture is transmitted this way than with conscious intent.

Discontinuity between early and later childhood is apparent in the Palauan case. Most cultures are patterned in such a way as to provide discontinuities of experience, but the points of time in the life cycle where these occur, and their intensity, differ widely. Azu experienced few restraints before this time. He did pretty much as he pleased, and lolled about on the laps of parents, kin, and friends. He was seldom if ever punished. There was always someone around to serve as protector, provider, and companion, and someone to carry him, usually mother, wherever he might go. Much of this changed for him after this day at the age of five. To be sure, he is not abandoned, and he is still shielded, guided, and provided for in every physical sense, but he finds himself being told more often than asked what he wants, and his confidence in himself and in his parents has been shaken. He no longer knows how to get what he wants. The discontinuity, the break with the ways things were in his fifth year of life, is in itself a technique of cultural transmission. We will observe discontinuities in the treatment of children and their effects in other cultures.

How Is It Done in Ulithi?

The Ulithians, like the Palauans, are Micronesians, but inhabit a much smaller island, in fact a tiny atoll in the vast Pacific, quite out of the way and fairly unchanged when first studied by William Lessa in the late forties (Lessa 1966). The Ulithians educate their children in many of the same ways the Palauans do, but differently enough to merit some special attention.

Like the Palauans, the Ulithians are solicitous and supportive of infants and young children.

> Infants are given the breast whenever they cry to be fed or whenever it is considered time to feed them, but sometimes only as a pacifier. They suckle often, especially during the first three to six months of life, when they may average around eighteen times during the day and night. The great stress placed by Ulithians on food is once more given eloquent expression in nursing practices. Thus, if both the mother and child should happen to be asleep at any time and it seems to someone who is awake that the baby should be fed, both are aroused in order to nurse the baby. . . .
>
> The care of the baby is marked by much solicitude on the part of everyone. One of the ways in which this is manifested is through great attention to cleanliness. The infant is bathed three times a day, and after each bath the baby is rubbed all over with coconut oil and powdered with tumeric. Ordinarily, bathing is done by the mother, who, as she holds the child, rocks him from side to side in the water and sings:
>
> > Float on the water
> > In my arms, my arms
> > On the little sea,
> > The big sea,
> > The rough sea,
> > The calm sea,
> > On this sea.
>
> [three sentences omitted]
> An infant is never left alone. He seems constantly in someone's arms, being passed from person to person in order to allow everyone a chance to fondle him. There is not much danger that if neglected for a moment he will harm himself. (Lessa 1966:94–96)

Unlike the Palauans, the Ulithians do not create any special discontinuities for the young child. Even weaning is handled with as little disturbance as possible.

> Weaning begins at varying ages. It is never attempted before the child is a year old, and usually he is much older than that. Some children are suckled until they are five, or even as much as seven or eight. Weaning takes about four days, one technique being to put the juice of hot pepper around the mother's nipples. Physical punishment is never employed, though scolding may be deemed necessary. Ridicule, a common recourse in training Ulithian children, is also resorted to. The child's reaction to being deprived of the breast often manifests itself in temper tantrums. The mother tries to mollify the child in a comforting embrace and tries to console him by playing with him and offering him such distraction as a tiny coconut or a flower. (Lessa 1966:95)

Apparently this technique, and the emotional atmosphere that surrounds it, is not threatening to Ulithian children. We see nothing of the feelings of deprivation and rejection suffered by Azu.

> The reactions to weaning are not extreme, children weather the crisis well. In fact, a playful element may be observed. A child may quickly push his face into his mother's breast and then run away to play. When the mother's attention is elsewhere, the child may make a sudden impish lunge at the breast and try to suckle from it. After the mother has scolded the weanling, he may coyly take the breast and fondle it, toy with the nipple, and rub the breast over his face. A man told me that when he was being weaned at the age of about seven, he would alternate sleeping with his father and mother, who occupied separate beds. On those occasions when he would sleep with his father, the latter would tell him to say goodnight to his mother. The boy would go over to where she was lying and playfully run his nose over her breasts. She would take this gesture good-naturedly and encourage him by telling him he was virtuous, strong, and like other boys. Then he would go back to his father, satisfied with his goodness. (Lessa 1966:95)

We also see in the above account of Ulithian behavior that transmission of sexual attitudes and the permissiveness concerning eroticization are markedly different than in our own society. This difference, of course, is not confined to relations between young boys and their mothers but extends through all heterosexual relationships, and throughout the patterning of adult life.

Given the relaxed and supportive character of child rearing in Ulithi, it is small wonder that children behave in a relaxed, playful manner and apparently grow into adults that value relaxation. This is in sharp contrast with the Palauans, whom Barnett describes as characterized by a residue of latent hostility in social situations, and as subject to chronic anxiety (Barnett 1960:11–15).

Indeed, play is so haphazard and relaxed that it quickly melts from one thing to another, and from one place to another, with little inhibition. There is much laughter and chatter, and often some vigorous singing. One gains the impression that relaxation, for which the natives have a word they use almost constantly, is one of the major values of Ulithian culture. (Lessa 1966:101)

Particularly striking in the transmission of Ulithian culture is the disapproval of unusually independent behavior.

The attitude of society toward unwarranted independence is generally one of disapproval. Normal independence is admired because it leads to later self-reliance in the growing individual, dependence being scorned if it is so strong that it will unfit him for future responsibilities. Ulithians talk a lot about homesickness and do not view this as improper, unless the longing is really for a spouse or sweetheart, the suspicion here being that it is really sexual outlet that a person wants. Longing of this sort is said to make a person inefficient and perhaps even ill. Homesickness is expected of all children and not deprecated. I was greatly touched once when I asked a friend to tell me what a man was muttering about during a visit to my house. He said he felt sad that I was away from my home and friends and wondered how I could endure it. Ulithians do not like people to feel lonely; sociability is a great virtue for them. (Lessa 1966:101)

The degree and kinds of dependence and independence that are inculcated in children are significant variables in any transcultural comparison of cultural transmission. Palauan children are taught not to trust others and grow to adulthood in a society where social relationships tend to be exploitative and, behind a facade of pleasantness, hostile. Palauans are not, however, independent and tend to be quite dependent for direction upon external authority (Barnett 1960:13, 15–16). The picture is confused in Palau by the greater degree of acculturation (than at Ulithi) and the threatening situations that the Palauans have experienced under first German, then Japanese, and now American domination. In American society, middle-class culture calls for independence, particularly in males, and independence training is stressed from virtually the beginning of childhood. But adolescent and adult Americans are among the most sociable, "joiningest" people in the world. Ulithian children are not taught to be independent, and the individual who is too independent is the object of criticism. Palauan children are taught a kind of independence—to be independent of dependency upon other people's affection—by a sudden withdrawal of support at about five years of age. But which is really the more "independent" adult? Palauans are independent of each other in the sense that they can be cruel and callous to each other and exploitive in social relationships, but they are fearful of independent action and responsibility, are never originators or innovators, and are dependent upon authority for direction. Ulithians are dependent upon each other for social and emotional support but do not exhibit the fearful dependency upon authority that Palauans do.

This does not mean that there is no predictable relationship between the training of children in dependency or independence and the consequences in adulthood. It does mean that the relationship is not simple and must be culturally contextualized if it is to make sense.

Every society creates some discontinuities in the experience of the individual as he or she grows up. It seems impossible to move from the roles appropriate to childhood to the roles appropriate for adulthood without some discontinuity. Societies differ greatly in the timing of discontinuity, and its abruptness. The first major break for Azu, the Palauan boy, was at five years of age. In Ulithi the major break occurs at the beginning of young adulthood.

> The mild concerns of ordinary life begin to catch up with the individual in the early years of adulthood and he can never again revert to the joyful indifference of his childhood.
>
> Attaining adulthood is marked by a ritual for boys and another for girls, neither of which is featured by genital operations. The same term, *kufar,* is used for each of the initiations. . . .
>
> The boy's *kufar* is much less elaborate and important. It comes about when he begins to show secondary sex characteristics and is marked by three elements: a change to adult clothing, the performance of magic, and the giving of a feast. All this occurs on the same day. . . .
>
> The outstanding consequence of the boy's ritual is that he must now sleep in the men's house and scrupulously avoid his postpubertal sisters. Not only must he not sleep in the same house with them, but he and they may not walk together, share the same food, touch one another's personal baskets, wear one another's leis or other ornaments, make or listen to ribald jokes in one another's presence, watch one another doing a solo dance, or listen to one another sing a love song. (Lessa 1966:101–2)

Brother-sister avoidances of this kind are very common in human societies. There is a whole body of literature about them and their implications and consequences. The most important thing for us to note is that this is one of the most obvious ways in which restrictions appropriate to the young adult role in Ulithian society are placed on the individual immediately after the kufar. Transitional rites, or "rites of passage," as they are frequently termed, usually involve new restrictions of this sort. So, for that matter, do the events marking important transitions occurring at other times in the life experience. Azu lost the privilege of being carried and treated like an infant, and he immediately became subject to being told what to do more often than demanding and getting what he wanted. One way of looking at Azu's experience and the

Ulithian kufar is to regard them as periods of sharp discontinuity in the management of cultural transmission. Expressed most simply—what cultural transmitters do to and for an individual after the event is quite different in some ways from what they did before. Another way of looking at these events is to regard them as the beginning of periods of cultural compression. Expressed most simply—cultural compression occurs when the individual's behavior is restricted by the application of new cultural norms. After the kufar, the Ulithian boy and girl cannot interact with their mature opposite-sex siblings except under very special rules. Azu cannot demand to be carried and is told to do many other things he did not have to do before.

In Ulithi the girl's kufar is much more elaborate. When she notices the first flow of blood she knows she must go immediately to the women's house. As she goes, and upon her arrival, there is a great hullabaloo in the village, with the women shouting again and again, "The menstruating one, Ho-o-o!" After her arrival she takes a bath, changes her skirt, has magic spells recited over her to help her find a mate and enjoy a happy married life, and is instructed about the many *etap* (taboos) she must observe—some for days, others for weeks, and yet others for years. Soon she goes to live in a private hut of her own, built near her parents' house, but still she must go to the menstrual house whenever her discharge begins (Lessa 1966:102–4).

The discontinuity and compression that Ulithian young people experience after the kufar are not limited to a few taboos.

> Adolescence and adulthood obviously come rushing together at young Ulithians, and the attitude of the community toward them undergoes a rapid change. The boy and the girl are admitted to a higher status, to be sure, and they are given certain rights and listened to with more respect when they speak. But a good deal is expected of them in return. Young men bear the brunt of the heaviest tasks assigned by the men's council. For their own parents they must help build and repair houses, carry burdens, climb trees for coconuts, fish, make rope, and perform all the other tasks commonly expected of an able-bodied man. Young women are similarly called upon to do much of the harder work of the village and the household. Older people tend to treat these very young adults with a sudden sternness and formality lacking when they were in their childhood. The missteps of young people are carefully watched and readily criticized. so that new adults are constantly aware of the critical gaze of their elders. They may not voice strong objections or opinions and have no political rights whatsoever, accepting the decisions of the men's and women's councils without murmur. Altogether, they are suddenly cut off from childhood and must undergo a severe transition in their comportment towards others about them. Only in the amatory sphere can they find release from the petty tyranny of their elders. (Lessa 1966:104)

What Is It Like To Be Initiated in Hano?

Like the Hopi, with whom they are very close neighbors on the same mesa in Arizona, the Hano Tewa hold an initiation ceremony into the Kachina[1] cult at about nine years of age. In fact, the Tewa and Hopi share the same ceremony. Further examination of this occasion will be instructive. Up until that time Tewa children are treated about the way the Hopi children are. They are kept on a cradleboard at first; weaned late, by middle-class American standards; and on the whole treated very permissively and supportively by mothers, mothers' sisters, grandparents, fathers, older siblings, and other people in and about the extended family household; admonished and corrected by the mother's brother; and half scared to death from time to time when they are bad by the Kachinas, or the threat of Kachinas. Of course nowadays the continuity of this early period is somewhat upset because children must start in the government day school at Polacca when they are about seven, and the teachers' ideas of proper behavior are frequently at variance with those maintained by Tewa parents. Excepting for school, though, Tewa children can be said to experience a consistent, continuous educational environment through the early years.

Things change when the initiation takes place at about age nine. A ceremonial father is selected for the boy, and a ceremonial mother for the girl. These ceremonial parents, as well as the real parents and for that matter everyone in the pueblo, build up the coming event for the child so that he or she is in a tremendous state of excitement. Then the day comes. Edward Dozier reports the initiation experience of one of his informants.

> We were told that the Kachina were beings from another world. There were some boys who said that they were not, but we could never be sure, and most of us believed what we were told. Our own parents and elders tried to make us believe that the Kachina were powerful beings, some good and some bad, and that they knew our innermost thoughts and actions. If they did not know about us through their own great power, then probably our own relatives told the Kachina about us. At any rate every time they visited us they seemed to know what we had thought and how we had acted.

> As the time for our initiation came closer we became more and more frightened. The ogre Kachina, the Soyoku, came every year and threatened to carry us away; now we were told that we were going to face these awful creatures and many others. Though we were told not to be afraid, we could not help ourselves. If the Kachina are really supernaturals and powerful beings, we might have offended them by some thought or act and they might punish us. They might even take us with them as the Soyoku threatened to do every year.

Four days before Powamu our ceremonial fathers and our ceremonial mothers took us to Court Kiva. The girls were accompanied by their ceremonial mothers, and we boys by our ceremonial fathers. We stood outside the kiva, and then two whipper Kachina, looking very mean, came out of the kiva. Only a blanket covered the nakedness of the boys; as the Kachina drew near our ceremonial fathers removed the blankets. The girls were permitted to keep on their dresses, however. Our ceremonial parents urged us to offer sacred corn meal to the Kachina; as soon as we did they whipped us with their yucca whips. I was hit so hard that I defecated and urinated and I could feel the welts forming on my back and I knew that I was bleeding too. He whipped me four times, but the last time he hit me on the leg instead, and as the whipper started to strike again, my ceremonial father pulled me back and he took the blow himself. "This is a good boy, my old man," he said to the Kachina. "You have hit him enough."

For many days my back hurt and I had to sleep on my side until the wounds healed.

After the whipping a small sacred feather was tied to our hair and we were told not to eat meat or salt. Four days later we went to see the Powamu ceremony in the kiva. As babies, our mother had taken us to see this event; but as soon as we began to talk, they stopped taking us. I could not remember what had happened on Powamu night and I was afraid that another frightening ordeal awaited us. Those of us who were whipped went with our ceremonial parents. In this dance we saw that the Kachina were really our own fathers, uncles, and brothers. This made me feel strange. I felt somehow that all my relatives were responsible for the whipping we had received. My ceremonial father was kind and gentle during this time and I felt very warm toward him, but I also wondered if he was to blame for our treatment. I felt deceived and ill-treated. (Dozier 1967:59–60)

The Hano Tewa children are shocked, angry, chagrined when they find that the supernatural Kachinas they have been scared and disciplined by all their lives up until then, and who during the initiation have whipped them hard, are really men they have known very well in their own community, their clans, their families. To be treated supportively and permissively all of one's life, and then to be whipped publicly (or see others get whipped) would seem quite upsetting by itself. To find out that the awesome Kachinas are men impersonating gods would seem almost too much. But somehow the experience seems to help make good adult Hano Tewa out of little ones.

If the initiate does not accept the spiritual reality of the Kachina and will not accept his relatives' "cruel" behavior as necessary and good for him (or her), he can stop being a Tewa. But is this a real choice? Not for anyone who is human enough to need friends and family who speak the same language, both literally and figuratively, and whose identity as a Tewa Indian stretches back through all of time. Having then (usually without debate) made the choice of being a Tewa, one is a *good* Tewa. No doubts can be allowed.

There is another factor operating as well. Children who pass through the initiation are no longer outside looking in, they are inside looking out. They are not grown up, and neither they nor anyone else think they are, but they are a lot more grown up than they were before the initiation. Girls take on a more active part in household duties, and boys acquire more responsibilities in farming and ranching activities. And it will not be long before the males can take on the role of impersonating the Kachinas and initiating children as they were initiated. The ceremonial whipping, in the context of all the dramatic ceremonies, dancing, and general community uproar, is the symbol of a dramatic shift in status-role. The shift starts with just being "in the know" about what really goes on in the kiva and who the Kachinas are, and continues toward more and more full participation in the secular and sacred life of the community.

Dorothy Eggan sums it up well for the Hopi when she writes:

Another reorganizing factor . . . was feeling "big." They had shared pain with adults, had learned secrets which forever separated them from the world of children, and now they were included in situations from which they had previously been excluded, as their elders continued to teach intensely what they believed intensely: that for them there was only one alternative—Hopi as against Kahopi.

Consistent repetition is a powerful conditioning agent, and as the youngsters watched each initiation, they relived their own, and by again sharing the experience gradually worked out much of the bitter residue from their own memories of it, while also rationalizing and weaving group emotions ever stronger into their own emotional core—"It takes a while to see how wise the old people really are." An initiated boy, in participating in the kachina dances, learned to identify again with the kachinas whom he now impersonated. To put on a mask is to "become a kachina," and to cooperate actively in bringing about the major goals of Hopi life. And a girl came to know more fully the importance of her clan in its supportive role. These experiences were even more sharply conditioned and directed toward adult life in the adult initiation ceremonies, of which we have as yet only fragmentary knowledge. Of this one man said to me: "I will not discuss this thing with you only to say that no one can forget it. It is the most wonderful thing any man can have to remember. You know then that you are Hopi. It is the one thing Whites cannot have, cannot take away from us. It is our way of life given to us when the world began." (Eggan 1956:364–65)

In many ways the preadolescent and adolescent period that we have been discussing, using the Ulithian kufar and the Hano Tewa initiation ceremonies as representative cases, is the most important of all in cultural transmission. There is a considerable literature on this period, including most notably the classic treatment given by Van Gennep (1960, first published in 1909) and the recent studies by Frank Young (1965), Yehudi Cohen (1964); Gary Schwartz and Don Merten (1968); and Whiting, Kluckhohn, and Albert (1958). Judith Brown provides a cross-cultural study of initiation rights for females (Brown 1963). But these studies do not emphasize the educational aspects of the initiation rites or rites of passage that they analyze.

One of the few studies that does is the remarkable essay by C. W. M. Hart (see chapter 17), based upon a single case, the Tiwi of North Australia, but with implications for many other cases. Hart contrasts the attitude of cultural transmitters toward young children among the Tiwi to the rigorous demands of the initiation period.

> The arrival of the strangers to drag the yelling boy out of his mother's arms is just the spectacular beginning of a long period during which the separation of the boy from everything that has gone before is emphasized in every possible way at every minute of the day and night. So far his life has been easy; now it is hard. Up to now he has never necessarily experienced any great pain, but in the initiation period in many tribes pain, sometimes horrible, intense pain, is an obligatory feature. The boy of twelve or thirteen, used to noisy, boisterous, irresponsible play, is expected and required to sit still for hours and days at a time saying nothing whatever but concentrating upon and endeavoring to understand long intricate instructions and "lectures" given him by his hostile and forbidding preceptors. [sentence omitted] Life has suddenly become real and earnest and the initiate is required literally to "put away the things of a child," even the demeanor. The number of tabus and unnatural behaviors enjoined upon the initiate is endless. He mustn't speak unless he is spoken to; he must eat only certain foods, and often only in certain ways, at fixed times, and in certain fixed positions. All contact with females, even speech with them, is rigidly forbidden, and this includes mother and sisters. (1963:415)

Hart goes on to state that the novices are taught origin myths, the meaning of the sacred ceremonials, in short, theology, ". . . which in primitive society is inextricably mixed up with astronomy, geology, geography, biology (the mysteries of birth and death), philosophy, art, and music—in short the whole cultural heritage of the tribe"; and that the purpose of this teaching is not to make better economic men of the novices, but rather ". . . better citizens, better carriers of the culture through the generations . . ." (Hart 1963:415). In this view Hart agrees (as he points out himself) with George Pettit, who did a thorough study of educational practices among North American Indians and who writes that the initiation proceedings were ". . . a constant challenge to the elders to review, analyze, dramatize, and defend their cultural heritage" (Pettit 1946:182).

Pettit's words also bring into focus another feature of the initiation rituals implicit in the description of these events for the Ulithians, Hano Tewa, and the Tiwi, which seems very significant. In all these cases dramatization is used as an educational technique. In fact a ceremony of any kind is a dramatization, sometimes indirect and metaphoric, sometimes very direct, of the interplay of crucial forces and events in the life of the community. In the initiation ceremonies dramatization forces the seriousness of growing up into the youngster's mind and mobilizes his emotions around the lessons to be learned and the change in identity to be secured. The role of dramatization in cultural transmission may be difficult for American readers to appreciate, because the pragmatization of American schools and American life in general has gone so far.

These points emphasize the view of initiation proceedings taken in this chapter—that they are dramatic signals for new beginnings and, at various times before and throughout adolescence in many societies, the intensification of discontinuity and compression in cultural transmission. Discontinuity in the management of the youngsters' learning—from supportive and easy to rigorous and harsh; compression in the closing in of culturally patterned demand and restriction as the new status-roles attained by successfully passing through the initiation period are activated. Of course this compression of cultural demand around the individual also opens new channels of development and experience. As humans mature they give up the freedom of childhood for the rewards to be gained by observing the rules of the cultural game. The initiation ceremonies are dramatic signals to everyone that the game has begun in earnest.

What Happens in Gopalpur?

In the village of Gopalpur, in South India, described by Alan Beals, social, not physical, mastery is stressed.

> Long before it has begun to walk, the child in Gopalpur has begun to develop a concern about relationships with others. The period of infantile dependency is extended. The child is not encouraged to develop muscular skills, but is carried from place to place on the hip of mother or sister. The child is rarely alone. It is constantly exposed to other people, and learning to talk, to communicate with others, is given priority over anything else that might be learned. When the child does learn to walk, adults begin to treat it differently. Shooed out of the house, its training is largely taken over by the play group. In the streets there are few toys, few things to be manipulated. The play of the child must be social play and the manipulation of others must be accomplished through language and through such nonphysical techniques as crying and withdrawal. In the play group, the child creates a family and the family engages in the production of imaginary food or in the exchange of real food carried in shirt pockets. (1962:19)

Children in Gopalpur imitate adults, both in the activities of play and in the attempts to control each other.

> Sidda, four years old, is playing in the front of his house with his cousin, Bugga, aged five. Sidda is sitting on the ground holding a stone and pounding. Bugga is piling the sand up like rice for the pounding. Bugga says, "Sidda, give me the stone, I want to pound." Sidda puts the stone on the ground, "Come and get it." Bugga says, "Don't come with me, I am going to the godhouse to play." Sidda offers, "I will give you the stone." He gives the stone to Bugga, who orders him, "Go into the house and bring some water." Sidda goes and brings water in a brass bowl. Bugga takes it and pours it on the heap of sand. He mixes the water with the sand, using both hands. Then, "Sidda, take the bowl inside." Sidda takes the bowl and returns with his mouth full of peanuts. He puts his hand into his shirt pocket, finds more peanuts and puts them in his mouth. Bugga sees the peanuts and asks, "Where did you get those?" "I got them inside the house." "Where are they?" "In the winnowing basket." Bugga gets up and goes inside the house returning with a bulging shirt pocket. Both sit down near the pile of sand. Bugga says to Sidda, "Don't tell mother." "No, I won't." Sidda eats all of his peanuts and moves toward Bugga holding his hands out. Bugga wants to know, "Did you finish yours?" "I just brought a little, you brought a lot." Bugga refuses to give up any peanuts and Sidda begins to cry. Bugga pats him on the back saying, "I will give you peanuts later on." They get up and go into the house. Because they are considered to be brothers, Sidda and Bugga do not fight. When he is wronged, the older Bugga threatens to desert Sidda. When the situation is reversed, the younger Sidda breaks into tears. (Beals 1962:16)

In their play, Bugga and Sidda are faithful to the patterns of adult control over children, as they have both observed them and experienced them. Beals describes children going to their houses when their shirt pockets are empty of the "currency of interaction" (grain, bits of bread, peanuts).

> This is the moment of entrapment, the only time during the day when the mother is able to exercise control over her child. This is the time for bargaining, for threatening. The mother scowls at her child, "You must have worked hard to be so hungry." The mother serves food and says, "Eat this. After you have eaten it, you must sit here and rock your little sister." The child eats and says, "I am going outside to play, I will not rock my sister." The child finishes its food and runs out of the house. Later, the child's aunt sees it and asks it to run to the store and buy some cooking oil. When it returns, the aunt says, "If you continue to obey me like this, I will give you something good to eat." When the mother catches the child again, she asks, "Where have you been?" Learning what occurred, she says, "If you bought cooking oil, that is fine; now come play with your sister." The child says, "First give me something to eat, and I will play with my sister." The mother scolds, "You will die of eating, sometimes you are willing to work, sometimes you are not

willing to work; may you eat dirt." She gives it food and the child plays with its sister. (1962:19)

This is the way the child in Gopalpur learns to control the unreliable world of other people. Children soon learn that they are dependent upon others for the major securities and satisfactions of life. The one with a large number of friends and supporters is secure, and they can be won and controlled, the individual comes to feel, through the use of food, but also by crying, begging, and working.

And among the Eskimo?

Eskimo children are treated supportively and permissively. When a baby cries it is picked up, played with, or nursed. There are a variety of baby tenders about, and after the first two or three months of life older siblings and the mother's unmarried sisters and cousins take a hand in caring for it. There is no set sleeping or eating schedule, and weaning is a gradual process that may not be completed until the third or fourth year.

How is it then that, as white visitors to Eskimo villages often remark, the Eskimo have managed to raise their children so well? Observers speak warmly of their good humor, liveliness, resourcefulness, and well-behaved manner. They appear to exemplify qualities that Western parents would like to see in their own children (Chance 1966:22). American folk belief would lead one to surmise that children who are treated so permissively would be "spoiled." Norman Chance describes the situation for the Alaskan Eskimo.

Certainly, the warmth and affection given infants by parents, siblings, and other relatives provide them with a deep feeling of well-being and security. Young children also feel important because they learn early that they are expected to be useful, working members of the family. This attitude is not instilled by imposing tedious chores, but rather by including children in the round of daily activities, which enhances the feeling of family participation and cohesion. To put it another way, parents rarely deny children their company or exclude them from the adult world.

This pattern reflects the parents' views of child rearing. Adults feel that they have more experience in living and it is their responsibility to share this experience with the children, "to tell them how to live." Children have to be told repeatedly because they tend to forget. Misbehavior is due to a child's forgetfulness, or to improper teaching in the first place. There is rarely any thought that the child is basically nasty, willful, or sinful. Where Anglo-Americans applaud a child for his good behavior, the Eskimo praise him for remembering. . . .

Regardless of the degree of Westernization, more emphasis is placed on equality than on superordination-subordination in parent-child relations. A five year old obeys, not because he fears punishment or loss of love, but because he identifies with his parents and respects their judgment. Thus he finds little to resist or rebel against in his dealing with adults. We will find rebellion more common in adolescents, but it is not necessarily a revolt against parental control.

By the time a child reaches the age of four or five, his parents' initial demonstrativeness has become tempered with an increased interest in his activities and accomplishments. They watch his play with obvious pleasure and respond warmly to his conversation, make jokes with him and discipline him.

Though a child is given considerable autonomy and his whims and wishes treated with respect, he is nonetheless taught to obey all adults. To an outsider unfamiliar with parent-child relations, the tone of Eskimo commands and admonitions sometimes sounds harsh and angry, yet in few instances does a child respond as if he had been addressed hostilely. . . .

After the age of five a child is less restricted in his activities in and around the village, although theoretically he is not allowed on the beach or ice without an adult. During the dark winter season, he remains indoors or stays close to the house to prevent him from getting lost and to protect him from polar bears which might come into the village. In summer, though, children play at all hours of the day or "night" or as long as their parents are up. . . .

Although not burdened with responsibility, both boys and girls are expected to take an active role in family chores. In the early years responsibilities are shared, depending on who is available. Regardless of sex, it is important for a child to know how to perform a wide variety of tasks and give help when needed. Both sexes collect and chop wood, get water, help carry meat and other supplies, oversee younger siblings, run errands for adults, feed the dogs, and burn trash.

As a child becomes older, more specific responsibilities are allocated to him, according to his sex. Boys as young as seven may be given an opportunity to shoot a .22 rifle, and at least a few boys in every village have killed their first caribou by the time they are ten. A youngster learns techniques of butchering while on hunting trips with older siblings and adults, although he is seldom proficient until he is in his mid-teens. In the past girls learned butchering at an early age, since this knowledge was essential to attracting a good husband. Today, with the availability of large quantities of Western foods, this skill may not be acquired until a girl is married, and not always then.

Although there is a recognized division of labor by sex, it is far from rigid at any age level. Boys, and even men, occasionally sweep the house and cook. Girls and their mothers go on fishing or bird-hunting trips. Members of each sex can usually assume the responsibilities of the other when the need arises, albeit in an auxiliary capacity. (1966:22–26)

Apparently the combination that works so well with Eskimo children is support—participation—admonition—support. These children learn to see adults as rewarding and nonthreatening. Children are also not excluded, as they so often are in America, from the affairs of adult life. They do not understand everything they see, but virtually nothing is hidden from them. They are encouraged to assume responsibility appropriate to their age quite early in life. Children are participants in the flow of life. They learn by observing and doing. But Eskimo adults do not leave desired learning up to chance. They admonish, direct, remonstrate, but without hostility.

The Eskimo live with a desperately intemperate climate in what many white men have described as the part of the world that is the most inimical to human life. Perhaps Eskimo children are raised the way they are because a secure, good-humored, resourceful person is the only kind that can survive for long in this environment.

In Sensuron?

The people of Sensuron live in a very different physical and cultural environment than do the Eskimo. The atmosphere of this Dusun village in Borneo (now the Malysian state of Sabah) is communicated in these passages from Thomas Williams' case study.

> Sensuron is astir an hour before the dawn of most mornings. It is usually too damp and cold to sleep. Fires are built up and the morning meal cooked while members of the household cluster about the house fire-pit seeking warmth. After eating, containers and utensils are rinsed off with water to "keep the worms off" and replaced in racks on the side of the house porch. Older children are sent to the river to carry water home in bamboo containers, while their mother spends her time gathering together equipment for the day's work, including some cold rice wrapped in leaves for a midday snack. The men and adolescent males go into the yard to sit in the first warmth of the sun and talk with male neighbors. The early morning exchange of plans, news, and recounting of the events of yesterday is considered a "proper way" to begin the day. While the men cluster in the yard center, with old shirts or cloths draped about bare shoulders to ward off the chill, women gather in front of one house or another, also trading news, gossip, and work plans. Many women comb each other's hair, after carefully picking out the lice. It is not unusual to see four or more women sitting in a row down the steps of a house ladder talking, while combing and delousing hair. Babies are nursed while mothers talk and small children run about the clusters of adults, generally being ignored until screams of pain or anger cause a sharp retort of *kAdA!* (do not!) from a parent. Women drape spare skirts about their bare shoulders to ward off the morning chill. About two hours after dawn these groups break up as the members go off to the work of the day. The work tasks of each day are those to be done under the annual cycle of subsistence labor described in the previous chapter. . . .

Vocal music is a common feature of village life; mothers and grandmothers sing a great variety of lullabies and "growth songs" to babies, children sing a wide range of traditional and nonsense songs, while adults sing at work in the fields and gardens during leisure and social occasions and at times of ritual. Drinking songs and wedding songs take elaborate forms, often in the nature of song "debates" with sides chosen and a winner declared by a host or guest of honor on the basis of "beauty" of tone, humor, and general "one-upmanship" in invention of new verse forms. Most group singing is done in harmony. Adolescents, especially girls, spend much of their solitary leisure time singing traditional songs of love and loneliness. Traditional verse forms in ritual, and extensive everyday use of riddles, folktales, and proverbs comprise a substantial body of oral literature. Many persons know much ritual verse, and most can recite dozens of stylized folktales, riddles, and proverbs.

Village headmen, certain older males, and ritual specialists of both sexes are practiced speechmakers. A skill of "speaking beautifully" is much admired and imitated. The style used involves narration, with exhortation, and is emphasized through voice tone and many hand and body gestures and postures. Political debates, court hearings, and personal arguments often become episodes of dramatic representation for onlookers, with a speaker's phrase listened to for its emotional expressive content and undertones of ridicule, tragedy, comedy, and farce at the expense of others involved. The verse forms of major rituals take on dimensions of drama as the specialist delivers the lines with skillful impersonations of voices and mannerisms of disease givers, souls of the dead, and creator beings.

By late afternoon of a leisure day people in the houses begin to drift to the yards, where they again sit and talk. Fires are built to ward off the chill of winds rising off the mountains, and men and women circle the blaze, throwing bits of wood and bamboo into the fire as they talk. This time is termed *mEg-Amut,* after the designation for exchange of small talk between household members. As many as 20 fires can be seen burning in yards through Sensuron at evening on most leisure days and on many evenings after work periods. Men sit and talk until after dark, when they go into houses to take their evening meal. Women leave about an hour before dark to prepare the meal. Smaller children usually eat before the adults. After the evening meal, for an hour or more, the family clusters about the house firepit, talking, with adults often engaged in small tasks of tool repair or manufacture. By 8 or 9 P.M. most families are asleep; the time of retiring is earlier when the work days are longer, later on rest days. (1965:78–79).

Children in Sensuron are, like Eskimo children, always present, always observers. How different this way of life is from that experienced by American children! Gossip, speech-making, folktale telling, grooming, working, and playing are all there, all a part of the stream of life flowing around one and with which each member of the community moves. Under these circumstances much of the culture is transmitted by a kind of osmosis. It would be difficult for a child *not to* learn his culture.

The children of Sensuron do not necessarily grow up into good-humored, secure, trusting, "happy" adults. There are several factors that apparently interact in their growing up to make this unlikely. In the most simple sense, these children do not grow up to be like Eskimo adults because their parents (and other cultural transmitters) are not Eskimo, Dusun cultural transmitters (anybody in the community that the child hears and sees) act like Dusun. But cultural transmitters display certain attitudes and do certain things to children as well as provide them with models. In Sensuron, children are judged to be nonpersons. They are not even provided with personal names until their fifth year. They are also considered to be ". . . naturally noisy, inclined to illness, capable of theft, incurable wanderers, violent, quarrelsome, temperamental, destructive of property, wasteful, easily offended, quick to forget" (Williams 1965:87). They are threatened by parents with being eaten alive, carried off, damaged by disease-givers. Here are two lullabies sung to babies in Sensuron (and heard constantly by older children):

> Sleep, Sleep, baby,
> There comes the *rAgEn* (soul of the dead)
> He carries a big stick,
> He carries a big knife,
> Sleep, Sleep, baby, He comes to beat you!

or, as in this verse,

> Bounce, Bounce, baby,
> There is a hawk,
> Flying, looking for prey!
> There is the hawk, looking for his prey!
> He searches for something to snatch up in his claws,
> Come here, hawk, and snatch up this baby!
> (Williams 1965:88)

None of the things that the adults of Sensuron do to, with, or around their children is to be judged "bad." Their culture is different from Eskimo culture, and a different kind of individual functions effectively in it. We may for some reason need to make value judgments about a culture, the character of the people who live by it, or the way they raise children—but not for the purpose of understanding it better. It is particularly hard to refrain from making value judgments when the behavior in question occurs in an area of life in our own culture about which there are contradictory rules and considerable anxiety. Take, for instance, the transmission of sexual behavior in the village of Sensuron.

In Sensuron people usually deal with their sex drives through ideally denying their existence, while often behaving in ways designed to side-step social and cultural barriers to personal satisfaction. At the ideal level of belief the view is expressed that "men are not like dogs, chasing any bitch in heat," or "sex relations are unclean." Some of the sexuality of Dusun life has been noted earlier. There is a high content of lewd and bawdy behavior in the play of children and adolescents, and in the behavior of adults. For example, the eight-year-old girl in the house across from ours was angrily ordered by her mother to come into the house to help in rice husking. The girl turned to her mother and gave her a slow, undulating thrust of her hips in a sexual sign. More than 12 salacious gestures are known and used regularly by children and adults of both sexes, and there are some 20 equivalents of "four-letter" English terms specifically denoting the sexual anatomy and its possible uses. Late one afternoon 4 girls between 8 and 15 years, and 2 young boys of 4 and 5 years were chasing about our house steps for a half hour, grab-bing at each other's genitals, and screaming, *uarE tAle!* which roughly translated means, "there is your mother's vulva!" Adult onlookers were greatly amused at the group and became convulsed with laughter when the four-year-old boy improvised the answer, "my mother has no vulva!" Thus, sexual behavior is supposed to be unclean and disgusting, while in reality it is a source of amusement and constant attention. . . .

Children learn details of sexual behavior early, and sex play is a part of the behavior of four-to six-year-olds, usually in houses or rice stores while parents are away at work. Older children engage in sexual activi-ties in groups and pairs, often at a location outside the village, often in an abandoned field storehouse, or in a temporary shelter in a remote garden. (Williams 1965:82–83)

We can, however, make the tentative generalization that in cul-tures where there is a marked discrepancy between ideal and real, between the "theory" of culture and actual behavior, this conflict will be transmitted and that conflicts of this kind are probably not conducive to trust, confidence in self and in others, or even something we might call "happiness." We are like the people of Sensuron, though probably the conflicts between real and ideal run much deeper and are more damaging in our culture. In any event, the transmission of culture is complicated by discrepancies and conflicts, for both the pattern of ide-alizations and the patterns of actual behavior must be transmitted, as well as the ways for rationalizing the discrepancy between them.

How Goes It in Guadalcanal?

Many of the comments that have been made about child rearing and the transmission of culture in other communities can be applied to the situation in Guadalcanal, one of the Solomon Islands near New Guinea. Babies are held, fondled, fed, never isolated, and generally given very supportive treatment. Weaning and toilet training both take place without much fuss, and fairly late by American standards. Walking is regarded as a natural accomplishment that will be mastered in time, swimming seems to come as easily. Education is also different in some ways in Guadalcanal. There is no sharp discontinuity at the beginning of middle childhood as in Palau, nor is there any sharp break at puberty as in Ulithi, or at prepuberty as among the Hano Tewa or Hopi. The special character of cultural transmission in Guadalcanal is given by Ian Hogbin:

> Two virtues, generosity and respect for property, are inculcated from the eighteenth month onward—that is to say, from the age when the child can walk about and eat bananas and other things regarded as delicacies. At this stage no explanations are given, and the parents merely insist that food must be shared with any playmate who happens to be present and that goods belonging to other villagers must be left undisturbed. A toddler presented with a piece of fruit is told to give half to "So-and-so," and should the order be resisted, the adult ignores all protests and breaks a piece off to hand to the child's companion. Similarly, although sometimes callers are cautioned to put their baskets on a shelf out of reach, any meddling brings forth the rebuke, "That belongs to your uncle. Put it down." Disobedience is followed by snatching away the item in question from the child and returning it to the owner.
>
> In time, when the child has passed into its fourth or fifth year, it is acknowledged to have at last attained the understanding to be able to take in what the adults say. Therefore, adults now accompany demands with reasoned instruction. One day when I was paying a call on a neighbor, Mwane-Anuta, I heard him warn his second son Mbule, who probably had not reached the age of five, to stop being so greedy. "I saw your mother give you those nuts," Mwane-Anuta reiterated. "Don't pretend she didn't. Running behind the house so that Penggoa wouldn't know! That is bad, very bad. Now then, show me, how many? Five left. Very well, offer three to Penggoa immediately." He then went on to tell me how important it was for children to learn to think of others so that in later life they would win the respect of their fellows.
>
> On another occasion during a meal I found Mwane-Anuta and his wife teaching their three sons how to eat properly. "Now Mbule," said his mother, "you face the rest of us so that we can all see you aren't taking too much. And you, Konana, run outside and ask Misika from next door to join you. His mother's not home yet, and I expect he's hungry. Your belly's not the only one, my boy." "Yes," Mwane-Anuta added. "Give a thought to those you run about with, and they'll give a thought to you." At this point the mother called over the eldest lad, Kure, and placed the basket of yams for me in his hands. "There, you carry that over to our guest and say that it is good to have him with us this evening," she whispered to him. The gesture was characteristic. I noted that always when meals were served to visitors the children acted as waiters. Why was this, I wanted to know. "Teaching, teaching," Mwane-Anuta replied. "This is how we train our young to behave." (1964:33)

It appears that in Guadalcanal direct verbal instruction is stressed as a technique of cultural transmission. Hogbin goes on to describe the constant stream of verbal admonition that is directed at the child by responsible adults in almost every situation. And again and again the prime values, generosity and respect for property, are reinforced by these admonitions.

The amount of direct verbal reinforcement of basic values, and even the amount of direct verbal instruction in less crucial matters, varies greatly from culture to culture. The people of Guadalcanal, like the Hopi, keep telling their children and young people how to behave and when they are behaving badly. In American middle-class culture there is also great emphasis on telling children what they should do, explaining how to do it, and the reasons for doing it, though we are probably less consistent in what we tell them than are the parents of Guadalcanal. Perhaps also in our culture we tend to substitute words for experience more than do the people of Guadalcanal, for the total range of experience relevant to growing up appropriately is more directly observable and available to their children than it is to ours.

> Girls go to the gardens regularly with their mother from about the age of eight. They cannot yet wield the heavy digging stick or bush knife, but they assist in collecting the rubbish before planting begins, in piling up the earth, and weeding. Boys start accompanying their father some two or three years later, when they help with the clearing, fetch lianas to tie up the saplings that form the fence, and cut up the seed yams. The men may also allocate plots to their sons and speak of the growing yams as their own harvest. The services of a youngster are of economic value from the time that he is pubescent, but he is not expected to take gardening really seriously until after he returns from the plantation and is thinking of marriage. By then he is conscious of his rights and privileges as a member of his clan and knows where the clan blocks of land are located. As a rule, he can also explain a little about the varieties of yams and taro and the types of soil best suited to earth.

> At about eight a boy begins to go along with his father or uncles when the men set out in the evening with their lines to catch fish from the shore or on the reef. They make a small rod for him, show him how to bait his hook, and tell him about the different species of fish—where they are to be found, which are good to eat, which are poisonous. At the age of ten the boy makes an occasional fishing excursion in a canoe. To start with, he sits in the center of the canoe and watches, perhaps baiting the hooks and removing the catch; but soon he takes part with the rest. In less than a year he is a useful crew member and expert in steering and generally handling the craft. At the same time, I have never seen youths under the age of sixteen out at sea by themselves. Often they are eager to go before this, but the elders are unwilling to give permission lest they endanger themselves or the canoe. (Hogbin 1964:39)

The children of Guadalcanal learn by doing as well as learn by hearing. They also learn by imitating adult models, as children do in every human group around the world.

> Children also play at housekeeping. Sometimes they take along their juniors, who, however, do not remain interested for long. They put up a framework of saplings and tie on coconut-leaf mats, which they plait themselves in a rough-and-ready sort of way. Occasionally, they beg some raw food and prepare it; or they catch birds, bats, and rats with bows and arrows. Many times, too, I have seen them hold weddings, including all the formality of the handing-over of bride price. Various items serve instead of the valuables that the grownups use—tiny pebbles instead of dog's and porpoise teeth, the long flowers of a nut tree for strings of shell discs, and rats or lizards for pigs. When first the young-sters pretend to keep house they make no sexual distinction in the allo-cation of the tasks. Boys and girls together erect the shelters, plait the mats, cook the food, and fetch the water. But within a year or so, although they continue to play in company, the members of each group restrict themselves to the work appropriate to their sex. The boys leave the cooking and water carrying to the girls, who, in turn, refuse to help with the building. (Hogbin 1964:37–38)

Children seem to acquire the culture of their community best when there is consistent reinforcement of the same norms of action and thinking through many different channels of activity and interaction. If a child is told, sees demonstrated, casually observes, imitates, experi-ments and is corrected, acts appropriately and is rewarded, corrected, and (as in the Tewa-Hopi initiation) is given an extra boost in learning by dramatized announcements of status-role change, all within a con-sistent framework of belief and value, he or she cannot help but learn, and learn what adult cultural transmitters want him or her to learn.

How Do They Listen in Demirciler?

In Demirciler, an Anatolian village in the arid central plateau of Turkey, a young boy, Mahmud, learns by being allowed in the room when the adult men meet at the Muhtar's (the village headman) home evenings to discuss current affairs.

> Each day, after having finished the evening meal, the old Muhtar's wife would put some small earthenware dishes or copper trays filled with nuts or chick-peas about the room, sometimes on small stands or some-times on the floor, and the old man would build a warm fire in the fire-place. Soon after dark the men would begin to arrive by ones or twos and take their accustomed places in the men's room. This was the larg-est single room in the village and doubled as a guest house for visitors who came at nightfall and needed some place to sleep before going on their way the next day. It had been a long time since the room had been used for this purpose, however, because the nearby growing city had

hotels, and most of the modern travelers stayed there. However, the room still served as a clearing house for all village business, as well as a place for the men to pass the cold winter evenings in warm comfort.

The room was perhaps 30 by 15 feet in size, and along one side a shelf nearly 15 inches above the floor extended about 2 feet from the wall and covered the full 30 feet of the room's length. The old Muhtar sat near the center of the shelf, waiting for his guests to arrive. As the men came in, the oldest in the village would seat themselves in order of age on this raised projection, while the younger ones would sit cross-legged on the floor. No women were ever allowed to come into this room when the men were there. The Muhtar's wife had prepared everything ahead of time, and when additional things were occasionally needed during the evening, one of the boys would be sent out to fetch it. Opposite the long bench was a fireplace, slightly larger than those in the kitchen of the other village homes, in which a fire burned brightly spreading heat throughout the room. The single electric bulb lighted the space dimly and so the shadows caused by the firelight were not prevented from dancing about the walls.

Mahmud would have been happier if the electric bulb had not been there at all, the way it used to be when he had been a very small boy. Electricity had been introduced to the village only a year ago, and he remembered the days when only the glow of the fire lighted these meetings.

As the gatherings grew in size, Mahmud heard many small groups of men talking idly about all sorts of personal problems, but when nearly all of the villagers had arrived, they began to quiet down.

The Hoca posed the first question, "Muhtar Bey, when will next year's money for the mosque be taken up?"

"Hocam, the amount has not been set yet," was the Muhtar's reply.

"All right, let's do it now," the Hoca persisted.

'Let's do it now," the Muhtar agreed.

And Mahmud listened as the Hoca told about the things the mosque would need during the coming year. Then several of the older men told how they had given so much the year before that it had been hard on their families, and finally, the Muhtar talked interminably about the duty of each Moslem to support the Faith and ended by asking the head of each family for just a little more than he knew they could pay.

Following this request there were a series of discussions between the Muhtar and each family head, haggling over what the members of his family could afford to give. Finally, however, agreement was reached with each man, and the Hoca knew how much he could count on for the coming year. The Muhtar would see that the money was collected and turned over to the Hoca.

The business of the evening being out of the way, Mahmud became more interested, as he knew that what he liked most was to come now. He had learned that he was too young to speak at the meetings, because he had been taken out several times the year before by one of the older boys and told that he could not stay with the men unless he could be quiet, so he waited in silence for what would happen next. After a slight pause one of the braver of the teen-aged boys called to an old man.

"*Dedem,* tell us some stories about the olden times."

"Shall I tell about the wars?" the old man nearest the Muhtar asked.

"Yes, about the great war with the Russians," the youth answered.

"Well, I was but a boy then, but my father went with the army of the Sultan that summer, and he told me this story." (Pierce 1964:20–21)

Is there any situation in the culture of the United States where a similar situation exists? When America was more rural than it is now, and commercial entertainments were not readily available for most people, young people learned about adult roles and problems, learned to think like adults and anticipated their own adulthood in somewhat the same way that Mahmud did. Now it is an open question whether young people would want to listen to their elders even if there was nothing else to do. Possibly this is partly because much of what one's elders "know" in our society is not true. The verities change with each generation.

At the end of the "business" session at the Muhtar's home an old man tells a story. The story is offered as entertainment, even though it has been heard countless times before. Young listeners learn from stories as well as from the deliberations of the older men as they decide what to do about somebody's adolescent son who is eyeing the girls too much, or what to do about building a new road. Storytelling has been and still is a way of transmitting information to young people in many cultures without their knowing they are being taught. Any story has either a metaphoric application to real life, provides models for behavior, or has both features. The metaphor or the model may or may not be translated into a moral. The elders in Demirciler do not, it appears, make the moral of the story explicit. In contrast, the Menomini Indians of Wisconsin always required a youngster to extract the moral in a story for himself. "You should never ask for anything to happen unless you mean it." "He who brags bites his own tail." A grandparent would tell the same story every night until the children could state the moral to the elder's satisfaction (Spindler 1971). People in different cultures vary greatly in how much they make of the moral, but stories and myth-tellings are used in virtually all cultures to transmit information, values, and attitudes.

What Does Cultural Transmission Do for the System?

So far we have considered cultural transmission in cases where no major interventions from the outside have occurred, or, if they have occurred, we have chosen to ignore them for purposes of description and analysis. There are, however, virtually no cultural systems left in the world that have not experienced massive input from the outside, particularly from the West. This is the age of transformation. Nearly all tribal societies and peasant villages are being affected profoundly by modernization. One of the most important aspects of modernization is the development of schools that will, hopefully, prepare young people to take their places in a very different kind of world than the one their parents grew up in. This implies a kind of discontinuity that is of a different order than the kind we have been discussing.

Discontinuity in cultural transmission among the Dusun, Hopi, Tewa, and Tiwi is a process that produces cultural continuity in the system as a whole. The abrupt and dramatized changes in roles during adolescence, the sudden compression of cultural requirements, and all the techniques used by preceptors, who are nearly always adults from within the cultural system, educate an individual to be committed to the system. The initiation itself encapsulates and dramatizes symbols and meanings that are at the core of the cultural system so that the important things the initiate has learned up to that point, by observation, participation, or instruction, are reinforced. The discontinuity is in the way the initiate is treated during the initiation and the different behaviors expected of him (or her) afterward. The culture is maintained, its credibility validated. As the Hopi man said to Dorothy Eggan, "I will not discuss this thing with you only to say that no one can forget it. It is the most wonderful thing any man can have to remember. You know then that you are Hopi [after the initiation]. It is the one thing Whites cannot have, cannot take from us. It is our way of life given to us when the world began." (See chapter 17.) This Hopi individual has been *recruited* as a Hopi.

In all established cultural systems where radical interventions from outside have not occurred, the major functions of education are *recruitment* and *maintenance.* The educational processes we have described for all of the cultures in this chapter have functioned in this manner. Recruitment occurs in two senses: recruitment to membership in the cultural system in general, so that one becomes a Hopi or a Tiwi; and recruitment to specific roles and statuses, to specific castes, or to certain classes. We may even, by stretching the point a little, say that young humans are recruited to being male or female, on the terms with which a given society defines being male or female. This becomes clear in cultures such as our own, where sex roles are becoming blurred so much that many young people grow up without a clear orientation toward either role. The educational system, whether we are talking about societies where there are no schools in the formal sense but where a great deal of education takes place, or about societies where there are many specialized formal schools, is organized to effect recruitment. The educational system is also organized so that the structure of the cultural system will be maintained. This is done by inculcating the specific values, attitudes, and beliefs that make this structure credible and the skills and competencies that make it work. People must believe in their system. If there is a caste or class structure they must believe that such a structure is good, or if not good, at least inevitable. They must also have the skills—vocational and social—that make it possible for goods and services to be exchanged that are necessary for community life to go on. Recruitment and maintenance intergrade, as you can see from the above discussion. The former refers to the process of getting people into the system and into specific roles; the latter refers to the process of keeping the system and roles functioning.

Modernizing Cultures: What Is the Purpose of Education?

In this transforming world, however, educational systems are often charged with responsibility for bringing about change in the culture. They become, or are intended to become, agents of modernization. They become intentional agents of cultural discontinuity, a kind of discontinuity that does not reinforce the traditional values or recruit youngsters into the existing system. The new schools, with their curricula and the concepts behind them, are future oriented. They recruit students into a system that does not yet exist, or is just emerging. They inevitably create conflicts between generations.

Among the Sisala of Northern Ghana, a modernizing African society, for example, there have been profound changes in the principles underlying the father-son relationship. As one man put it:

> This strict obedience, this is mostly on the part of illiterates. With educated people, if you tell your son something, he will have to speak his mind. If you find that the boy is right, you change your mind. With an illiterate, he just tells his son to do something. . . . In the old days, civilization was not so much. We obeyed our fathers whether right or wrong. If you didn't, they would beat you. We respected our fathers with fear. Now we have to talk with our sons when they challenge us. (Grindal 1972:80)

Not all of the Sisala have as tolerant and favorable a view of the changes wrought by education, however:

> When my children were young, I used to tell them stories about my village and about our family traditions. But in Tumu there are not so many people from my village and my children never went to visit the family. Now my children are educated and they have no time to sit with the fam-

ily. A Sisala father usually farms with his son. But with educated people, they don't farm. They run around town with other boys: Soon we will forget our history. The educated man has a different character from his father. So fathers die and never tell their sons about the important traditions. My children don't sit and listen to me anymore. They don't want to know the real things my father told me. They have gone to school, and they are now book men. Boys who are educated run around with other boys rather than sitting and listening to their fathers. (Grindal:83).

That these conflicts should flare up into open expressions of hostility toward education, schools, and teachers is not surprising. A headmaster of a primary school among the Sisala related to Bruce Grindal what happened when a man made a trip to a village outside Tumu.

> He parked his car on the road and was away for some time. When he returned, he saw that somebody had defaced his car, beaten it with sticks or something. Now I knew that my school children knew something about this. So I gathered them together and told them that if they were good citizens, they should report to me who did it and God would reward them. So I found out that this was done by some people in the village. When the village people found out their children told me such things, they were very angry. They said that the teachers were teaching their children to disrespect their elders. It is because of things like that that the fathers are taking their children out of school. (Grindal: 97–98)

The above implies that the new schools, created for the purposes of aiding and abetting modernization, are quite effective. Without question they do create conflicts between generations and disrupt the transmission of the traditional culture. These effects in themselves are a prelude to change, perhaps a necessary condition. They are not, however, the result of the effectiveness of the schools as educational institutions. Because the curricular content is alien to the existing culture there is little or no reinforcement in the home and family, or in the community as a whole, for what happens in the school. The school is isolated from the cultural system it is intended to serve. As F. Landa Jocano relates concerning the primary school in Malitbog, a barrio in Panay, in the middle Philippines:

> Most of what children learn in school is purely verbal imitation and academic memorization, which do not relate with the activities of the children at home. By the time a child reaches the fourth grade he is expected to be competent in reading, writing, arithmetic, and language study. Except for gardening, no other vocational training is taught. The plants that are required to be cultivated, however, are cabbages, lettuce, okra, and other vegetables which are not normally grown and eaten in the barrio. [sentence omitted]
>
> Sanitation is taught in the school, but insofar as my observation went, this is not carried beyond the child's wearing clean clothes. Children may be required to buy toothbrushes, combs, handkerchiefs, and other

personal items, and bring these to school for inspection. Because only a few can afford to buy these items, only a few come to school with them. Often these school requirements are the source of troubles at home, a night's crying among the children. . . . [sentence omitted] In the final analysis, such regular school injunctions as "brush your teeth every morning" or "drink milk and eat leafy vegetables" mean nothing to the children. First, none of the families brush their teeth. The toothbrushes the children bring to school are for inspection only. Their parents cannot afford to buy milk. They do not like goats' milk because it is *malangsa* (foul smelling). (Jocano 1969:53)

Nor is it solely a matter of the nonrelatedness of what is taught in the school to what is learned in the home and community. Because the curricular content is alien to the culture as a whole, what is taught tends to become formalized and unrealistic and is taught in a rigid, ritualistic manner. Again, among the Sisala of Northern Ghana, Bruce Grindal describes the classroom environment.

The classroom environment into which the Sisala child enters is characterized by a mood of rigidity and an almost total absence of spontaneity. A typical school day begins with a fifteen-minute period during which the students talk and play, often running and screaming, while the teacher, who is usually outside talking with his fellow teachers, pays no attention. At 8:30 one of the students rings a bell, and the children immediately take their seats and remove from their desks the materials needed for the first lesson. When the teacher enters the room, everyone falls silent. If the first lesson is English, the teacher begins by reading a passage in the students' readers. He then asks the students to read the section aloud, and if a child makes a mistake, he is told to sit down, after being corrected. Variations of the English lesson consist of having the students write down dictated sentences or spell selected words from a passage on the blackboard. Each lesson lasts exactly forty minutes, at the end of which a bell rings and the students immediately prepare for the next lesson.

Little emphasis is placed upon the content of what is taught; rather, the book is strictly adhered to, and the students are drilled by being asked the questions which appear at the end of each assignment. The absence of discussion is due partially to the poor training of the teachers, yet even in the middle schools where the educational standards for teachers are better, an unwillingness exists to discuss or explain the content of the lessons. All subjects except mathematics are lessons in literacy which teach the student to spell, read, and write.

Interaction between the teacher and his students is characterized by an authoritarian rigidity. When the teacher enters the classroom, the students are expected to rise as a sign of respect. If the teacher needs anything done in the classroom, one of the students performs the task. During lessons the student is not expected to ask questions, but instead is supposed to give the "correct" answers to questions posed to him by the teacher. The students are less intent upon what the teacher is saying than they are upon the reading materials before them. When the teacher asks a question, most of the students hurriedly examine their books to find the correct answer and then raise their hands. The teacher calls on one of them, who rises, responds (with his eyes lowered), and then sits down. If the answer is wrong or does not make sense, the teacher corrects him and occasionally derides him for his stupidity. In the latter case the child remains standing with his eyes lowered until the teacher finishes and then sits down without making a response. (Grindal 1972:85)

The nonrelatedness of the school to the community in both the content being transmitted and the methods used to transmit it is logically carried into the aspirations of students concerning their own futures. These aspirations are often quite unrealistic. As one of the Sisala school boys said:

I have in mind this day being a professor so that I will be able to help my country. . . . As a professor I will visit so many countries such as America, Britain, and Holland. In fact, it will be interesting for me and my wife. . . . When I return, my father will be proud seeing his child like this. Just imagine me having a wife and children in my car moving down the street of my village. And when the people are in need of anything, I will help them. (Grindal: 89)

Or as another reported in an essay:

By the time I have attained my graduation certificate from the university, the government will be so happy that they may like to make me president of my beloved country. When I receive my salary, I will divide the money and give part to my father and my wife and children. . . . People say the U.S.A. is a beautiful country. But when they see my village, they will say it is more beautiful. Through my hard studies, my name will rise forever for people to remember. (Grindal: 89)

As we have said, the new schools, like the traditional tribal methods of education and schools everywhere, recruit new members of the community into a cultural system and into specific roles and statuses. And they attempt to maintain this system by transmitting the necessary competencies to individuals who are recruited into it via these roles and statuses. The problem with the new schools is that the cultural system for which they are recruiting does not exist in its full form. The education the school boys and girls receive is regarded by many as more or less useless, though most people, like the Sisala, agree that at least literacy is necessary if one is to get along in the modern world. However, the experience of the school child goes far beyond training for literacy. The child is removed from the everyday routine of community life and from observation of the work rules of adults. He or she is placed in an artificial, isolated, unrealistic, ritualized environment. Unrealistic aspirations and self-images develop. Harsh reality intrudes abruptly upon graduation. The schoolboy discovers that, except for teaching in the primary schools, few opportunities are open to him. There are some clerical positions in government offices, but they are few. Many graduates migrate in search of jobs concomitant with their expectations, but they usually find that living conditions are more severe than those in the tribal area and end up accepting an occupation and life style similar to that of the illiterate tribesmen who have also migrated to the city. Those who become village teachers are not much better off. One Sisala teacher in his mid-twenties said:

> I am just a small man. I teach and I have a small farm. . . . Maybe someday if I am fortunate, I will buy a tractor and farm for money because there is no future in teaching. When I went to school, I was told that if I got good marks and studied hard, I would be somebody, somebody important. I even thought I would go to America or England. I would still like to go, but I don't think of these things very often because it hurts too much. You see me here drinking and perhaps you think I don't have any sense. I don't know. I don't know why I drink. But I know in two days' time, I must go back and teach school. In X (his home village where he teaches) I am alone; I am nobody. (Grindal: 93)

The pessimist will conclude that the new schools, as agents of modernization, are a rank failure. This would be a false conclusion. They are neither failures nor successes. The new schools, like all institutions transforming cultural systems, are not articulated with the other parts of the changing system. The future is not known or knowable. Much of the content taught in the school, as well as the very concept of the school as a place with four walls within which teacher and students are confined for a number of hours each day and regulated by a rigid schedule of "learning" activities, is Western. In many ways the new schools among the Sisala, in Malitbog, and in many other changing cultures are inadequate copies of schools in Europe and in the United States. There is no doubt, however, that formal schooling in all of the developing nations of the world, as disarticulated with the existing cultural context as it is, nevertheless is helping to bring into being a new population of literates, whose aspirations and worldview are very different than that of their parents. And of course a whole class of educated elites has been created by colleges and universities in many of the countries. It seems inevitable that eventually the developing cultures will build their own models for schools and education. These new models will not be caricatures of Western schools, although in places, as in the case of the Sisala or the Kanuri of Nigeria described by Alan Peshkin (Peshkin 1972), where the Western influence has been strong for a long time, surely those models will show this influence.

Perhaps one significant part of the problem and the general shape of the solution is implied in the following exchange between two new young teachers in charge of a village school among the Ngoni of Malawi and a senior chief:

> The teachers bent one knee as they gave him the customary greeting, waiting in silence until he spoke. "How is your school?" "The classes are full and the children are learning well, Inkosi." "How do they behave?"
>
> "Like Ngoni children, Inkosi."
>
> "What do they learn?"
>
> "They learn reading, writing, arithmetic, scripture, geography and drill, Inkosi."
>
> "Is that education?"
>
> "It is education, Inkosi."
>
> "No! No! No! Education is *very* broad, *very* deep. It is not only in books, it is learning how to live. I am an old man now. When I was a boy I went with the Ngoni army against the Bemba. Then the mission came and I went to school. I became a teacher. Then I was chief. Then the government came. I have seen our country change, and now there are many schools and many young men go away to work to find money. I tell you that Ngoni children must learn how to live and how to build up our land, not only to work and earn money. Do you hear?"
>
> "Yebo, Inkosi" (Yes, O Chief). (Read 1968:2–3)

The model of education that will eventually emerge in the modernizing nations will be one that puts the school, in its usual formal sense, in perspective, and emphasizes education in its broadest sense, as a part of life and of the dynamic changing community. It must emerge if these cultures are to avoid the tragic errors of miseducation, as the Western nations have experienced them, particularly in the relationships between the schools and minority groups.

Conclusion

In this chapter we started with the question, What are some of the ways culture is transmitted? We answered this question by examining cultural systems where a wide variety of teaching and learning techniques are utilized. One of the most important processes, we found, was the management of discontinuity. Discontinuity occurs at any point in the life cycle when there is an abrupt transition from one mode of being and behaving to another, for example as at weaning and at adolescence. Many cultural systems manage the latter period of discontinuity with dramatic staging and initiation ceremonies, some of which are painful or emotionally disturbing to the initiates. They are public announcements of changes in status. They are also periods of intense cultural compression during which teaching and learning are accelerated. This managed cultural compression and discontinuity function to enlist new members in the community and maintain the cultural system. Education, whether characterized by sharp discontinuities and culturally compressive periods, or by a relatively smooth progression of accumulating experience and status change, functions in established cultural systems to recruit new members and maintain the existing system. We then turned to a discussion of situations where alien or future-oriented cultural systems are introduced through formal schooling. Schools among the Sisala of Ghana, a modernizing African nation, and a Philippine barrio were used as examples of this relationship and its consequences. The disarticulation of school and community was emphasized. The point was made that children in these situations are intentionally recruited to a cultural system other than the one from which they originated, and that the school does not maintain the existing social order, but, in effect, destroys it. This is a kind of discontinuity very different than the one we discussed previously, and produces severe dislocations in life patterns and interpersonal relations as well as potentially positive change.

Note

[1] This word is sometimes spelled Katcina, sometimes Kachina. Voth, used as the source for the description of the Hopi ceremony, spells it Katcina. Dozier, used as the source for the Hano Tewa, spells it Kachina. Either is correct.

References and Further Reading

Barnett, Homer G., 1960. *Being a Paluan.* CSCA. New York: Holt, Rinehart and Winston.

Beals, Alan R., 1962. *Gopalpur: A South Indian Village.* CSCA. New York: Holt, Rinehart and Winston.

Brown, Judith K., 1963. A Cross-cultural Study of Female Initiation Rites. *American Anthropologist* 65:837–53.

Chance, Norman A., 1966. *The Eskimo of North Alaska.* CSCA. New York: Holt, Rinehart and Winston.

Cohen, Yehudi, 1964. *The Transition from Childhood to Adolescence.* Chicago: Aldine Publishing Company.

Deng, Francis Mading [1972], 1984. *The Dinka of the Sudan.* Prospect Heights, IL: Waveland Press.

Dozier, Edward P., 1967. *Hano: A Tewa Indian Community in Arizona.* CSCA. New York: Holt, Rinehart and Winston.

Eggan, Dorothy, 1956. Instruction and Affect in Hopi Cultural Continuity. *Southwestern Journal of Anthropology* 12:347–70.

Grindal, Bruce T., 1972. *Growing Up in Two Worlds: Education and Transition among the Sisala of Northern Ghana.* CSCA. New York: Holt, Rinehart and Winston.

Hart, C. W. M., 1963. Contrasts Between Prepubertal and Postpubertal Education. In *Education and Culture,* G. Spindler, ed. Holt, Rinehart and Winston.

Henry, Jules, 1960. A Cross-cultural Outline of Education. *Current Anthropology* 1, 267–305.

———, 1963. *Culture Against Man.* New York: Random House.

Hogbin, Ian, 1964. *A Guadalcanal Society: The Kaoka Speakers.* CSCA. New York: Holt, Rinehart and Winston.

Jocano, F. Landa, 1969. *Growing Up in a Philippine Barrio.* CSEC. New York: Holt, Rinehart and Winston.

Lessa, William A. [1966], 1986. *Ulithi: A Micronesian Design for Living.* Prospect Heights, IL: Waveland Press.

Mead, Margaret [1928], 1949. *Coming of Age in Samoa.* New York: Mentor Books.

——— [1930], 1953. *Growing Up in New Guinea.* New York: Mentor Books.

———, 1964. *Continuities in Cultural Evolution.* New Haven: Yale University Press.

Peshkin, Alan, 1972. *Kanuri Schoolchildren: Education and Social Mobilization in Nigeria.* CSEC. New York: Holt, Rinehart and Winston.

Pettit, George A., 1946. *Primitive Education in North America.* Publications in American Archeology and Ethnology, vol. 43.

Pierce, Joe E., 1964. *Life in a Turkish Village.* CSCA. New York: Holt, Rinehart and Winston.

Read, Margaret [1968], 1987. *Children of Their Fathers: Growing Up among the Ngoni of Malawi.* Prospect Heights, IL: Waveland Press.

Schwartz, Gary, and Don Merten, 1968. Social Identity and Expressive Symbols: The Meaning of an Initiation Ritual. *American Anthropologist* 70:1117–31.

Spindler, George D., and Louise S. Spindler, 1971. *Dreamers without Power: The Menomini Indians of Wisconsin.* CSCA. New York: Holt, Rinehart and Winston. Reissued (1984), *Dreamers With Power.* Prospect Heights, IL: Waveland Press.

Spiro, Melford, 1958. *Children of the Kibbutz.* Cambridge, MA: Harvard University Press.

Van Gennep, Arnold, 1960. *The Rites of Passage.* Chicago: University of Chicago Press.

Whiting, Beatrice B., ed., 1963. *Child Rearing in Six Cultures.* New York: John Wiley & Sons.

Whiting, John F., R. Kluckhohn, and E. Albert, 1958. The Function of Male Initiation Ceremonies at Puberty. In *Readings in Social Psychology*, E. Maccoby, T. Newcomb, and E. Hartley, eds. New York: Holt, Rinehart and Winston.

Williams, Thomas R., 1965. *The Dusun: A North Borneo Society.* CSCA. New York: Holt, Rinehart and Winston.

Young, Frank, 1965. *Initiation Ceremonies.* Indianapolis: The Bobbs-Merrill Company.

15

The Anthropology of Learning

Harry F. Wolcott
University of Oregon

For a number of years I have been wondering how "the anthropology of learning" might look if we were to make it a subject for systematic inquiry. How might anthropological research inform current thinking about learning, and how might reawakened interest in the topic of learning inform anthropological research? Might an infusion of anthropological concern help human learning recapture the level of interest it deserves and once had?

I have always been skeptical of social scientists or educators who regard teaching and learning as one and the same. I have also been uncomfortable with anthropological nonchalance in seeming to equate the *transmitting* of culture—particularly with self-conscious efforts within a society to do so—with the *learning* of culture. Societies are often portrayed as both overbearing in their domination over the individuals who comprise them and overly successful in their efforts to produce, or *reproduce,* the very type of individual the society wants. If I once had to accept on faith that such complete and exquisite conformity existed in societies that I could only know through reading, I recognized that such uniformity was not present in societies I could observe firsthand.

That anthropologists have shown more interest in reporting what transmitters try to transmit than what learners are actually learning seems understandable. Self-conscious efforts to transmit culture capture our attention and give the fieldworker explicit behavior to observe and to describe. Before we can call this "enculturation," however, we need at least to include someone (in addition to the fieldworker) willing to heed the messages being transmitted. As to what is being made of the messages, the immediate results are hard to assess, but the long-term results are apparent: enculturation works!

Source: Reproduced by permission of the American Anthropological Association from *Anthropology and Education Quarterly*, Vol. 13, No. 2 (summer 1982), pp. 83–108. Not for further reproduction.

My years of teaching "anthropology and education" have provided excellent opportunity for drawing upon anthropological materials as resources for examining teaching and learning in noninstitutional settings. But only recently did I feel ready to pull together some ideas about the "anthropology of learning" as an area of collective academic interest and to invite colleagues to share their views on the topic. We first formalized our thoughts in a symposium on the Anthropology of Learning presented at the American Anthropological Association meetings in December 1980.

Although that event marked the beginning of a dialogue, our effort should be regarded as a renewed interest rather than a new one. A first task that faced each of us was to reflect upon the ways that earlier contributors in anthropology and related social sciences have brought us to where we are today.

In anthropological fashion, our papers show a tendency to link ideas rather closely to the elders with whom we associate them. But, also in anthropological fashion, there are numerous ideas, concepts and hypotheses floating about that have not been subjected to rigorous review. A curious characteristic of anthropology, comforting to those within its sphere and confounding to outsiders, is that hypotheses are conceived rather promiscuously and then abandoned to make it quite on their own. Our effort to talk about an anthropology of learning, no matter how loosely defined, provides an occasion to sift carefully through myriad possible explanations suggested by others. Perhaps academic ideas, like academicians themselves, should be subject periodically to "up or out" scrutiny. Literally and figuratively, which among a storehouse of anthropological ideas related to learning should we be promoting?

Looking Back

I would not dream of drawing attention to the anthropology of learning without acknowledging Margaret Mead's longtime interest in both teaching and learning. Although she was careful to distinguish between them (cf. 1964), I think that, like most anthropologists, her attention was drawn more to processes of teaching than to learning per se. That interest is stated succinctly in *Culture and Commitment*:

> Man's most human characteristic is not his ability to learn, which he shares with many other species, but his ability to teach and store what others have developed and taught him. Learning, which is based on human dependency, is relatively simple. (1970:72)

Mead once proposed a contrast between "learning cultures" and "teaching cultures" (Mead 1942, as noted in Gearing 1973). A "learning culture" refers to a small, homogenous group that shows little concern for transmitting culture because there is virtually no danger of anyone going astray. "Teaching culture" refers to societies that regard it as imperative that those who know inform and direct those who do not know. Mead's view of the contrast between learning and teaching is apparent in her observation in *Culture and Commitment* that "Learning, which is based on human dependency, is relatively simple. But human capacities for creating elaborate teachable systems . . . are very complex" (1970:72).

Mead was usually in the mainstream of ideas. Her cavalier dismissal of learning as "simple" is reflected in the writings of other anthropologists. Ethnographers have not customarily paid much attention to children other than to place them conveniently about so that they could "soak up" their culture, play at it, or help with appropriate tasks. Powdermaker's description of culture transmission in Lesu aptly characterizes how anthropologists have tended to portray children as ever present but minimally engaged, patiently waiting for the onset of puberty before suddenly blossoming into adult roles: "We find the children always observers or minor participants of the adult society" (1971:100).

The work of Bateson, on the other hand, serves as reminder that some anthropologists have extended their interests to include a consideration of learning or have felt free to explore beyond customary anthropological bounds, although Bateson himself did ponder whether anthropologists had anything to offer on the topic of learning other than their questions:

> As is usual in anthropology, the data are not sufficiently precise to give us any clue as to the nature of the learning processes involved. Anthropology, at best, is only able to *raise* problems of this order. The next step must be left for laboratory experimentation. (1972:115)

"Raising problems" was something that Bateson did extremely well, however, and he frequently turned his attention to raising problems about the nature of the learning process. At one time he wrote that "All species of behavioral scientists are concerned with 'learning' in one sense or another of that word" (1972:279). His legacy includes the contract first introduced in 1942 between what he called *proto-learning* (rote learning, or the "simple learning curve") and *deutero learning*: progressive change in the rate of proto-learning, or "learning how to learn." (At one time he even extended the concept to "trito learning," but eventually he settled for deutero learning as adequate to account for meta-learning.) He also proposed a hierarchical classification of learning "levels" based upon the assumption that "all learning is in some degree stochastic (i.e., contains components of 'trial and error')" and thus that the *types of errors to be corrected* provide the basis for a classification of learning levels (1972:287ff).

Zero learning: learning not subject to correction by trial and error.

Learning I: revision of choice within an unchanged set of alternatives.

Learning II: revision of the set within which choice is made, thus the learning of contexts.

Learning III: learning of the contexts of contexts—a corrective change in the system of sets.

I could cite numerous scholars in addition to Bateson, Mead, and Powdermaker to illustrate how anthropologists have variously concerned themselves with, or ignored, the teaching and learning of culture. The topic of education has always received some anthropological attention; occasionally it has provided a major focus and major contribution (e.g., Benedict 1938; Fortes 1938; Gladwin 1970; Pettitt 1946). Recent and noteworthy high points in a modest but persistent interest in learning (as contrasted with the formal transmission of culture) include a symposium held in 1972 at the annual meeting of the American Ethnological Society and the set of papers from that symposium later published in a monograph edited by Kimball and Burnett, *Learning and Culture* (1973). The publication of Hansen's book, *Sociocultural Perspectives on Human Learning* (1979), which includes a twenty-eight-page bibliography, suggests that "anthropological contributions to the study of knowledge transmission" are not withering away.

Why an "Anthropology of Learning" Just Now?

These seem propitious times for expanding the dialogue between anthropologists and educators that has been gaining momentum for a quarter century. In the 1970s, "things ethnographic" definitely caught the educator's eye (cf. Wolcott 1982). Wide interest in ethnography provides us with an unusual opportunity to demonstrate that anthropology has more to offer to the field of education than simply a "fieldwork" approach to research. Perhaps anthropology can serve as a reminder to educational researchers that their preoccupation with method borders on making method an end in itself. Anthropological concern has never been with method per se. Its focus is in making sense of the lived-in world. As usual, Geertz has said it eloquently:

> Like all scientific propositions, anthropological interpretations must be tested against the material they are designed to interpret; it is not their origins that recommend them (1968:vii). . . .

The validity of both my empirical conclusions and my theoretical premises rests, in the end, on how effective they are in so making sense of
data from which they were neither derived nor for which they were originally designed. (p. viii)

Now that "ethnographic method" has caught educator attention,
there is opportunity to get beyond ethnographic *technique* into the
realm of the stuff with which ethnographic research deals, a realm that
Geertz describes as cultural interpretation (1973).

To date, our ethnographic opportunities, both in schools and out,
have focused largely on teachers and teaching. What can we now bring
to the understanding of learners and learning? And, recognizing that
psychologists and educational psychologists have attended to—one
might even say usurped—the question of *learning in school*, what can
we say about learning that is *not* school related?

To begin, we might ask how learning itself has become so uninteresting a topic. Edward Hall refers in *Beyond Culture* to the "miracle of
learning" (1976:173), but one gets little sense of awe or excitement in
psychological treatises on the topic. For most students, "learning" is as
dull and pedestrian a topic of study today as it was for me as an undergraduate years ago; I still hear college students insist that all they need
to know and all they want to know about learning is contained in the
sterile definition, "a change in behavior." Learning has become synonymous with classroom performance for pupils, sophomoric performance for sophomores, and maze performance for mice. What
undergraduate would ever think of comparing the learning drive to the
sexual drive the way Hall does (although I must leave to him the methodological issues involved in this comparison):

> The sexual drive and the learning drive are, if one can measure the rela-
> tive strength of such disparate urges, very close to each other in the
> power they exert over men's lives. (1976:207)

For my part, I have pondered the salutary effect it might have on
the teaching profession if teachers were to take "learning" as their central professional and intellectual concern, committed to knowing what
is known about learning, conversant with and critical of competing theories, thoroughly up-to-date on current research, and intrigued with
understanding how learning occurs not only among their students but
among themselves as well. What a remarkable contribution anthropology could make to teaching if it could help teachers develop a propri-
etary interest in the natural (and very social) process of human learning
and help educators shape a learning-centered rather than a teach-
ing-centered profession.

The Anthropology of Learning: An Inventory

I have begun to identify a corpus of anthropological terms, labels, ideas, and questions related to the topic of learning. A bit of stock-taking seems in order as a starting place. What new light can we bring to these issues? Which concepts and ideas nest with others? Which of the multifarious terms and ideas introduced in recent years continue to warrant attention?

Since I will later take issue with the idea of "gradualness" in learning, let me note that, although I have been accumulating this corpus for years, I think I can trace back to the very moment when the idea of the anthropology of learning first flashed through my mind. The occasion was an informal session at the American Anthropological Association meetings in Washington, D.C., in November 1976, when Solon Kimball and George Spindler were invited to reminisce about the "evolution" of anthropology and education as an area of inquiry. Even as the two men spoke, I found myself reflecting on the different perspective and contribution each had made to the development of anthropology and education, including rather different emphases on teaching and learning.

George Spindler, my esteemed mentor, has always been keenly interested in the processes of cultural transmission and in identifying "cultural antecedents" of behavior. That interest is evident in much of his own writing. It is epitomized in his Burton Lecture on "The Transmission of American Culture" (Spindler 1959) and in his chapter, "The Transmission of Culture" (Spindler 1973:207–45; 1974:279–310 [see chapter 14]). Spindler's concern for processes of cultural transmission has itself been transmitted to his students and provides a theme in much of their work. He has interpreted cultural transmission very literally, focusing almost exclusively on what humans do, consciously and explicitly, to transmit culture. Spindler has pondered aloud—although I think not in public—whether anthropologists rightfully have any professional interest in learning processes at all. Many share what Goodenough describes as this "tempting" view that, since anthropologists are concerned with the patterns characterizing *groups*, they should confine themselves to phenomena at the group level of abstraction (Goodenough 1981:52).

Solon Kimball has also addressed the topic "The Transmission of Culture" in a paper that first appeared in 1965 and has been frequently reprinted, but his interests have often found him writing about the learning of culture as well. He has described his baptism to fieldwork as a process of "learning a culture" (1972). In organizing his own papers for publication in a single volume, he placed six of them, including his chapter on cultural transmission, in a section entitled "Culture and Learning" (1974).

It is hardly surprising that Spindler's comments during that session reflected his interest in processes related to the transmission of culture and that Kimball's comments touched as well upon aspects of learning. At some point during the dialogue, Kimball mentioned that, in his opinion, the literature of anthropology offers a rich resource for the study of human learning. That thought "struck home" as I realized what a fresh perspective anthropology might bring in rekindling interest in learning as a natural process rather than as an activity restricted to laboratories and schools. I believe Kimball stated rather boldly that anthropology has "even better materials on learning than psychology has." Ever since that day, I have been trying to get Kimball to elaborate on that sentence, and he has been trying to recall whether he actually said it. For me, the idea of the anthropology of learning was conceived at that moment. The event of the Kimball-Spindler dialogue provides a starting point for my review.

Point 1: Anthropology as a Resource on "Learning"

If anthropology is a rich resource on learning, it is a largely untapped one and its utility has not yet been demonstrated. To the best of both Kimball's and my knowledge, no one has prepared a bibliography dealing exclusively with anthropological contributions to the study of the learning process and anthropological sources rich with descriptions about learning, although many such references are cited in bibliographies in anthropology and education dealing with closely related topics (cf. Burnett 1974a; Hansen 1979; Harrington 1979).

A first step was to begin compiling such a bibliography. In a project initiated with the help of Barbara Harrison while she was a doctoral student in anthropology and education, I have begun to identify and annotate those references. Our starting point was with studies in language and culture acquisition in natural settings. It is hoped that our "working bibliography" will provide a test of the assertion that the materials are both valuable and interesting.

Point 2: Why Everyone Doesn't Learn Everything

In an open discussion immediately following the Kimball-Spindler dialogue, Fred Gearing posed two related questions that have since proved as provocative for my students as they did at that moment for me. "It's somewhat of a wonder," Gearing began, either in those words or in words to that effect, "that anyone ever learns anything. But, given that they do, then we can also ask why everybody doesn't learn everything!"

Gearing has a special talent for phrasing questions that invite involvement. His questions typically point as well to his own current interests, and so it is with these questions. Stated in what he describes as its more exact form. Gearing and his colleagues have been investigating the issue of "what constraints, necessarily noncognitive and non-motor in nature, reduce the expectable randomness" that keeps almost everyone from learning almost everything (cf. Gearing and Sangree 1979:1).

Point 3: Things Learned versus the Learning Itself

As my previous point suggests, Fred Gearing is among the minority of anthropologists who have expressed long-term interest in the "receiving" as well as the transmitting of culture. In an earlier discussion dealing with the development of "anthropology and education," Gearing once posited a hypothetical juncture in the evolution of cultural anthropology, a juncture at which *processes* involved with the *transmission* of culture, rather than a preoccupation with the *content* of it, might have become the core of anthropological inquiry:

> If learned behavior is the subject matter, then things learned and the learning itself are opposite sides of the same coin. In the historical flip of that coin . . . culture fell up and cultural transmission down. (1973:1225)

Had learning won out at the moment of Gearing's hypothetical coin toss, there would have been no need to develop a special subfield of anthropology and education. But with culture *content* serving as the core of the discipline, the question of how content is transmitted tends to be overshadowed by the endless task of description. The "road not taken" would have led to a more overriding concern for cultural process instead of a preoccupation with cultural content.

Point 4: Through Whose Efforts Does Culture Get Transmitted?

Given their preoccupation with cultural inventory, it is noteworthy that anthropologists have given at least passing attention to educational processes, particularly to child-training practices. Mead's characterization of some societies as "learning cultures," in which there seems so little likelihood of anyone failing to "catch" the cultural heritage that no self-conscious effort is made to transmit it, reminds us how easy it is to regard culture as virtually self-transmitting. Spindler has made the assertion in this regard that "It would be difficult for a child *not* to learn his culture" (Spindler 1973:225). In the broadest sense, of course, that statement is not only true but need not be made with any tentativeness. A comparable statement holds for learning the language(s) heard about us. We neither invent language and culture on our own nor have any options about learning them.

Those anthropologists interested in enculturation have attended almost exclusively to aspects of *transmission.* They follow a normal human propensity to be attracted by novelty and movement and a professional concern for *content* and the manner in which it is presented. Whether or not the children fall asleep while hearing a story or watching a dance, the culture content embedded in the words and actions of the transmitters is there to be recorded. More than that, the very process of transmitting culture is a time for defining it as well, as Pettitt aptly observed in *Primitive Education in North America* (1946):

> Primitive education was a community project in which all reputable elders participated at the instigation of individual families. The result was not merely to focus community attention on the child, but also to make the child's education a constant challenge to the elders to review, analyze, dramatize, and defend their cultural heritage.

Pettitt's oft-quoted words appear in discussions about the process of cultural transmission. I think they help explain why even those anthropologists not particularly intrigued with enculturation per se have nonetheless been attentive to the transmitters. What better source of data for the ethnographer than the self-conscious efforts of elders bent upon reviewing, analyzing, dramatizing, and defending their culture?

Our efforts on behalf of an anthropology of learning now invite careful attention to what it is that learners learn of their culture and to how and why learners attend to some things rather than others. Our starting point is to recognize that we all have to acquire some cultural knowledge in at least one major cultural system and no one, not even the anthropologist, is going to acquire all of it.

What I think we might now attend to, more than we have in the past, is the critical role that learners themselves play in the process of cultural transmission. If it is obvious that there must be a learner in order for cultural transmission to take place, we have not been as attentive to the fact that the learner holds the ultimate answer to the question of what has been transmitted. This idea is hardly a new one, but it has made remarkably little headway. Over 60 years ago Sapir warned against the "convenient but dangerous metaphor that culture is a "neatly packed-up assemblage of forms of behavior handed over piece-meal . . . to the passively inquiring child." Culture is not something "given," Sapir wrote, but something to be "gradually and gropingly discovered" (1934:414).

More recently, Wallace has used the term "rediscover" to convey the magnitude of the task of transmitting culture and the impossibility for the transmitters to accomplish the process solely through their own efforts:

In a radical sense, then, it would appear that much of every culture must
be literally rediscovered in every generation because of the impossibility
of describing, and therefore communicating. (Wallace 1970:109)

Keesing takes a bolder step by suggesting that perhaps cultural
learning "takes place not so much through the child-rearing practices
of a society as *in spite of them*" (1976:203). If Keesing's statement
seems too extreme, how can we better convey our understanding of the
nexus between culture as portrayed and culture as discovered, between
culture as "taught" and culture as "caught"?

Our inquires will no doubt bring us back to fields once figuratively
plowed by anthropologists of the old "Culture and Personality" school.
This time, however, our attention will be, in Wallace's well-posed contrast, to the "organization of diversity" rather than to the "replication of
uniformity" (1970:22ff.). If each of us must literally "rediscover" culture, then an anthropology of learning must attend not only to what
societies insist that their neophytes know, but also to what those neophytes actually learn. We have to account for the inevitable diversity of
each individual's experience, as well as for an incredible human capacity for discerning the patterned regularity that makes culture possible.
For some insight into how the individual learner approaches this task,
we can turn to colleagues who have been doing exciting things in a
related area of natural learning: language acquisition.

Point 5: Language Acquisition as a Model for Cultural Acquisition

Studies in language acquisition seem to offer a promising direction for an anthropology of learning. Language acquisition is hardly a
new field of inquiry, but I share with others a sense of its growing importance for understanding the processes of cultural acquisition (cf. Brukman 1973; Goodenough 1981; Schwartz 1981).

I recognize the long debate regarding the suitability of language
acquisition processes as analog for cultural acquisition, including the
problem that language must then double both as an aspect of cultural
learning and as a model for it. I also recognize the problem of referring
to a language acquisition "model" that implies that linguists are themselves in agreement about how the process occurs. Yet I am intrigued
with the similarities of issues related to the biological basis for language
and cultural learning, the utility of talking about each of them as the
learning of a set of unwritten rules that guides the operation of appropriate (linguistic or cultural) behaviors, and the contrast linguists have
made between *performance* (what one actually does) and *competence*
(the totality of what one understands).

Surely one of the most exciting contributions from linguistics for
the study of cultural acquisition is the conceptualization shared by

many child language learning scholars of the language learner as an *active participant in the learning process,* an incipient but persistent "theory builder" constantly (though not often consciously) sifting and sorting and seeking regularity from a continuous, almost random bombardment of linguistic and cultural elements swirling about.[1] In essence, all human beings are confronted anew with rediscovering—figuring out for themselves—how their social environment "works." Until we figure out how those about us go about getting what they need and want, we cannot get the system to work, or to work predictably, on our own behalf. Each of us must "gropingly discover" the unexplicated rules of our language through deriving a grammar for at least one of the languages spoken around us. As well, each of us must work out a comparable "grammar" of what Geertz calls the "informal logic of actual life" (1973:17).

Psychometricians to the contrary, the tasks of discerning underlying pattern and regularity in that "blooming, buzzing confusion" are not behaviors in which half a population falls below some statistical midpoint. Every normally endowed, normally functioning human is engaged life-long in a constructive and effortful process to figure things out sufficiently well to develop a personal life-style and live out a unique life within some linguistically and culturally bounded system(s). Our ecological environment presents a certain range of possibilities, and biological needs create some urgencies and predispose us toward others. But we learn to cope with these exigencies, and to cope with our fellow "copers" as well, through figuring out underlying "grammars" and recognizing significant variation in the styles those about us use in behaving and in communicating. We are all figuring things out (and only more or less successfully) all the time. In our awe at the magnitude of this task as it confronts the newborn, we lose sight of the fact that for each of us the task of figuring things out continues to the moment we draw our last breath.

Point 6: The Question of Innate Capacity

Do we need to declare a moratorium while we await the answer to the debate on whether or to what extent we are "programmed to learn" (cf. Pulliam and Dunford 1980)? Chomsky's early hypothesis about the innateness of linguistic capacity, that humans are born preprogrammed with a Language Acquisition Device, might seem to offer a convenient wayside resting point for those who insist upon a final resolution of basic heredity-versus-environment issues. Does our analogy to language acquisition require some anthropologist to propose a comparable "Cultural Acquisition Device" to explain how humans are so adept at acquiring culture?

Once again, Bateson points a way out of the seeming morass of the heredity-environment issue. He urges us to attend to the extensive overlap where resolution is not the critical issue:

> The problem in regard to any behavior is clearly not "Is it learned or is it innate" but "Up to what logical level is learning effective and down to what level does genetics play a determinative or partly effective role"? (Bateson 1972:307)

Point 7: Learning "About" versus Learning "To"

Thirty years ago analytical philosophers like Gilbert Ryle, the source of Geertz's notion of "thick description," were making what I find to be a useful distinction between *learning about* (or *learning that*) *versus learning to* (or *learning how*) (cf. Carroll 1968). If such simple and direct language is adequate for our purposes, I suggest we adopt it.

If we wish to build our taxonomies upon anthropological sources, Anthony Wallace (1961) has proposed a classification of learning according to the kinds of "matter" to be learned. He identifies three: *technic* ("how to" learning), *morality* (consideration for the welfare of the group), and *intellect* (a tradition and way of thinking). Technic, as Wallace points out, is the most "conspicuous" matter of learning and has been subject to the most intensive analysis by psychologists and educators. That is hardly surprising in an era when a concern for measurements has been so central in scientific thinking.

Anthropologists, too, have been interested in "how to" learning, but I think their commitment to context finds them particularly suited to inquire into the learning of morality and intellect. I find Wallace's ideas about the learning of morality especially provocative, for he is describing the learning of human qualities that find their expression in placing the welfare of the group above one's own needs or interests. Morality, as Wallace uses the term, is "sharply distinguished from mere propriety, conformity, and respectablitity"; it is the sort of behavior most *conspicuously* exhibited in heroic action but most *commonly* practiced in the "humble endurance of discomfort, protracted over decades, by inconspicuous people in positions of authority" (p. 32). Such learning cannot be explained apart from a cultural context.

Point 8: Intentionality in Learning

How can we best describe and distinguish among the various ways that humans acquire their cultural knowledge? Two frequently heard terms are "observational learning" and "imitation." Neither term seems sufficiently precise. Can we find better words to convey our sense of the processes that are involved?

Personally, I recommend against using the term *imitation*. Although its broad definition includes the ideas of "modeling," I think modeling should be the preferred term when that describes how we believe learning to be occurring, if only because modeling is "less imprecise." I suspect that when my students use the term imitation they are really thinking "mimicking." To say, for example, that we learn any substantial part of language by mimicking (imitating) words and sentences—and I always find some students who insist that's how we do it—is quite absurd. We do not learn to speak by mimicking. If we did, we would be doomed to speak only those words or phrases we have heard before! That our speech resembles the speech of somebody rather than a generalized "everybody" implicates a process of modeling. Modeling seems critical for learning language and for learning culture as well.

The phrase "observational learning" seems to make "learning" synonymous with "watching" or even "seeing." Inadvertently, the phrase cloaks rather than reveals the very processes we are trying to understand. If we "learn" everything we observe, we are back to Gearing's question: Why then don't we all learn almost everything? When my students in Western Oregon insist that we learn what we see around us, I ask them why we do not all become Douglas fir trees, since that is what we see everywhere. And as they explain why we do *not* become Douglas firs, they recognize how observation must be joined to other mental processes before we can associate it with learning.

Both "imitation" and "observational learning" seem more helpful than Spindler's depiction of learning one's culture by a process of "osmosis" (Spindler 1973:225). Yet one can see how Spindler wanted to convey the pervasiveness of cultural influences. Other terms have also been suggested to account for cultural influence. Although they seem preferable to "osmosis," they fail to provide a distinction, if a careful examination of learning requires it, between what one invites into one's mind and what else either tags along or sneaks in uninvited. I am not sure of the origins or use among anthropologists of such related terms as *concomitant learning, incidental learning, unintended learning,* and *latent learning.*

Lawrence Frank may have been responsible for introducing the term "concomitant learning" to anthropologists. I first heard the term used by Spindler. When I subsequently organized a paper of my own around the concept of concomitant learning (Wolcott 1969), I linked that concept to "incidental" and to "unintended" learning and called attention to earlier use that both Jules Henry and George Spindler had made of contrasts between intended and unintended learning in the school setting (cf. Henry 1960; Spindler 1959).

"Latent learning" proves even more elusive, but joins company with such terms as "no-trial" learning and "vicarious" learning suggested by educational psychologists like Gage and Berliner (1975) and social learning theorists like Bandura (1977). Educational psychologist Wittrock reminds us that "People learn . . . sometimes without practice, without reinforcement, and without overt action" (1979:5). Ralph Peterson once recounted how his belated and sudden mastery of a skill required in building a log cabin in Idaho over a period of summers was identified by a neighbor as an example of "winter learning." Have we been sufficiently attentive to folk taxonomies in our examination of learning phenomena?

Such an array of terms provides tempting labels when we want to explain how a member of a society is suddenly able to perform a skill or enact a role that has not previously been mastered and may never have been practiced. Especially when we speak of learning "about," as, for example, in learning about how things were in the "good old days" or learning about experiences like drowning or starving to death, it is obvious that thought processes themselves, rather than practice or firsthand experience, may satisfy the condition that the learner be actively involved. Which of these terms best convey our present level of understanding?

I do not deny that something goes on in human cognition that can be called "observational learning" or even "learning by osmosis." But I hope we can find more precise ways to describe that learning. More importantly, can we find ways to distinguish circumstances when we have every reason to believe learning is taking place from other moments when we believe it might be taking place? Should we make a distinction between intentional learning—dare I introduce such a term?—and incidental learning, "second-order" stuff that *may* or *may not* be retrieved in some future intentional learning effort. Incidental learning, it seems to me, might include everything from minuscule details one may be asked to recall ("Do you remember seeing where I left my car keys?") to those "whole integrated patterns of behavior" we are said to acquire almost subconsciously. (As grandson, was I also learning the complementary social role of how to act as a grandfather?) And if even so vague a notion as incidental learning does not include all the experiences to which a learner is exposed, if learning is something different from the complete osmosis of everything within the range of one's senses, then what are the outer limits beyond which learning does not occur? In a practical, everyday sense, what are the boundaries for what any particular human should learn, might learn, and does learn (cf. Wallace 1961:38)?

Traditionally, anthropologists have attended to the venerable old storytellers, dancers, and singers who go on hour after hour. But what happens if the children are distracted, inattentive, daydreaming, or—worst of all—asleep? When children focus attention on other children, instead of on the formally appointed transmitters, and children are remarkably attentive to other children, then what is *actually* being learned? It is time at least for us to ask.

Point 9: The Polyphasic Nature of Learning

I might have included Henry's idea of *polyphasic learning* among the terms just reviewed, since it, too, deals with peripheral learning. I treat it separately here, consistent with what I take to be Henry's intent in noting not simply that humans can learn more than one thing at a time, but that they are *incapable* of learning *only* one thing at a time (Henry 1955:196ff). Although this seems the kind of pronouncement one must take on faith, I have always felt that Henry's idea of polyphasic learning warrants more attention than it has received. Here is an opportunity to reexamine it.

Point 10: The Importance of the Setting

When anthropologists turn their attention to learning, they do not perforce think of schooling; they have customarily been careful to distinguish "learning done in schools" from learning in other settings. Wallace has proposed what he calls a "scale of generality" for describing human learning:

> It is convenient to arrange the circumstances of human learning in the form of a scale of generality, each category of which is contained in, and implied by, its succeeding category. If we take *schooling* as the initial category, it is followed by *education*, then *enculturation*, then *learning* itself. (Wallace 1961:29)

In a somewhat similar vein, learning modes have been contrasted according to the formality of the setting, distinguishing *formal learning* done in schools, *nonformal* (i.e., noninstitutionalized) *learning* through sources like the media, and *informal learning*, the learning in which individuals engage throughout their lives (cf. Wilbert 1976).

There are other ways to classify learning settings in addition to their formality. Whiting and Child, for example, have noted how the tasks expected of young males in some societies (e.g., the daily herding of livestock) place them in learning environments dominated by male peers, while in the same society young girls might be expected to help with household chores in learning environments dominated by older females (1953). Poirier has noted a similar contrast among nonhuman primates (1973:29). Some years ago Barker and his associates were attempting to examine learning in terms of the "behavior settings" in which it occurred, another way to examine learning environments (cf. Barker 1968).

These various ways of looking at "learning settings" present some problems. For example, a preoccupation with settings themselves rather than with their content invites confusion between quantity and quality. It may be that father's few words of praise or reprimand in the evening are of more consequence than the entire day's opportunities for diversion with other herders. An underlying question is: When, and in what ways, do learning settings make a difference? How, in turn, do elements within the different settings in which we interact (in space and time) serve subsequently as mnemonics to help us recall previously learned behaviors appropriate to them (cf. Harwood 1976)?

Point 11: The Importance of Intimacy or Social Distance

Closely allied with the consideration of settings are questions of who we learn from, the latter characteristically viewed by anthropologists in terms of generation, kinship, or social distance. For even if we adopt Keesing's proposition that cultural learning occurs *in spite of* rather than *because of* child-rearing practices, culture is learned nonetheless, and it is learned from those with whom one is in rather close proximity. Anthropological pronouncements on the influence of "significant others" in this process fare better when examined separately than when viewed collectively.

Little systematic attention has been given to considerations of "generation" in human learning. Anthropologists have raised some interesting questions, however. I can recall when it was vogue to quote (or at least be conversant with) Bruner's "early learning hypothesis": that which is learned earliest (and thus from persons with whom one is close) is the most resistant to change; that which is learned later is most readily discarded, in conditions of culture contact (Bruner 1956a, 1956b). Yet Bruner informs me (personal communication, 1980) that although a literature "grew up around it" and influenced a great deal of his subsequent work, he does not believe that anyone has made a systematic attempt to test the hypothesis. Our stock-taking provides an opportunity to review this concept.

Similarly, Tax once suggested that we glean most of our cultural knowledge from those only slightly older and in turn convey to those only slightly younger most of what they will learn. Tax emphasized the point that "a chief way—not an incidental way, but a chief way—the traditional adult culture is transmitted in all or most societies is through the peer group" in the passage of information "from slightly older to slightly younger people" (1973:50).

Tax observes that it is probably "an illusion of our culture and other cultures that parents, teachers, learners and others teach anything to people 20 or 25 years their junior" (pp. 50–51). As a middle-aged adult, I continue to influence, and to be influenced by, those closest to me in age. On reflection, I am sure this has always been the case for me, and I assume it is largely true for others. Yet I think it erroneous to suggest that we are not influenced by those much older or that we exert no influence on those much younger. The question properly posed directs us to ask how and what we learn from people of various kinship designations and generations.

At the same time that I draw attention to this learn-then-teach cycle that Tax describes as the "short-jump percolation" of information, I must note that anthropologists have rightly called attention to the enculturative influence of every family member. They have made a particular effort to show how certain functions that mainstream American families assume to be the "normal" child-rearing responsibilities of (two) parents are often performed by others (e.g., older siblings, mother's brother, "equivalent" members of extended families) in different societies. But we need not cite exotic circumstances to bring attention to the influence of people in roles other than parents and peers. In our own society, for example, we have given rather slight attention to the role of grandparents in cultural acquisition. Margaret Mead often alluded to the educative influence of grandparents and wrote personally of her experience of grandmothering (Mead 1972:273–94). Ethnographic accounts sometimes mention grandparent-grandchild relationships, especially if they are characterized by special behavior such as the "joking relationship" and reciprocal forms of address noted among some American Indian tribes. Perhaps the anthropology of learning can draw attention to the influence that grandparents exert in our efforts to discover our culture and locate ourselves in it.

I wonder how parents and grandparents play different and complementary roles as models in our learning. Our parents attend to our everyday needs and daily deportment. Do grandparents convey a bigger sense of family and cultural heritage? Did I perchance learn *how* to behave from my parents and *why* I would want to behave that way from my grandparents? Is there any doubt that a grandfather who died years before I was born (hardly a coincidence that I bear his name) nevertheless exerted a benign grandfatherly influence over me whenever I was lauded for seeming to exhibit one of his fondly recalled traits?

Also unsorted is the cross-cultural examination of the circumstances by which persons charged with formal responsibilities as educators are to be regarded as strangers or friends. When the social distance between learner and teacher is great, Tax's hypothesis might suggest that efforts would be made to narrow the gap (e.g., assign teachers only slightly older than the students, or address teachers by kin terms). We often see "beginning" teachers try to effect this closeness, but my sense of the anthropological evidence is that teachers have traditionally been cast in the role of stranger. In the absence of real strangers to perform some formal ceremony or initiation, it has been pointed out that a group can *create* strangers with the use of masks (cf. Hart 1955, including the discussants' comments following his presentation). In our society (and certainly among professional educators), we virtually insist that didactic instruction be given by strangers. We do not want to be "lectured to" by friends. At the same time, we expect public school teachers to be friends, or at least friendly, particularly in the early years of schooling. What cross-cultural and comparative questions could sharpen our perspective?

Point 12: The Essential Continuity of Cultural Acquisition

Previous points dealt with settings and personnel. A related issue, raised but not resolved, is that of continuity in cultural acquisition. Years ago Benedict wrote a remarkable essay, "Continuities and Discontinuities in Cultural Conditioning," in which she noted that "from a comparative point of view, our culture goes to great extremes in emphasizing contrasts between the child and the adult" (Benedict 1938). Ethnographic attention has often been drawn to such contrasts, particularly if the ethnographer perceived a romantic period of carefree youth terminated abruptly at a formal transition into adult status. Hart's provocative paper, "Contrasts between Prepubertal and Postpubertal Education," first published in 1955, makes splendid use of contrasts among preliterate societies that have formal "pre-initiation" education and post-initiation education (see chapter 17). I do not believe we have addressed the issue of whether or not contrasts or inconsistencies in the process of cultural conditioning can reach such proportion as to constitute true "discontinuities."

From the point of view of a society intent on dramatizing the transition from a previous status to a new one, it seems appropriate to speak of efforts to *create* discontinuity. And to an outside observer like the anthropologist, such abrupt transitions might appear as discontinuities. From the point of view of the learner, however, the idea of discontinuity seems suspect. The drama of being inducted into "initiation school" or into the army, or being married to a stranger through prior family arrangement, may be intended to create discontinuity and may seem a discontinuity to the observer. To participants reared with the expectation that someday this would happen, no matter how traumatic and disorienting the event, it seems to me that it is entirely consistent with those expectations. It does not really matter if you cry yourself to sleep as long as you get up when the bugle blows; you knew this was how it would be.

The Anthropology of Learning: Some Next Steps and Some Cautions

There are already anthropologists whose careers are marked with notable contributions to understanding the enculturation process. If we can induce them to include more attention to the learning of culture as well as to the teaching of it, our efforts at "revitalizing" learning will be well rewarded. In addition, perhaps we can spark new interest and enlist a broader commitment to describing learning-related aspects of behavior among those whose major research interests lie elsewhere. To that end, some next steps and some cautions are outlined here.

One way to stimulate broader participation might be to call for more systematic anthropological attention to the learning of *particular* aspects of culture, such as Philips' examination of how lawyers acquire legal jargon (Philips 1982). In a study that must have seemed daring when reported over four decades ago, sociologist Becker provides another model in "Becoming a Marihuana User" (Becker 1953). An opportunity to study urban African beer gardens prompted me to look at "Becoming a Drinker" (Wolcott 1974:205–15). I imagine that careful anthropological attention to the ways particular groups of people acquire particular skills and understandings related to social (and anti-social) behaviors, comparable to contemporary studies of drinking or drug use, could provide a valuable resource for administrators and policy makers who assume responsibility when any pattern of behavior becomes identified as a social issue or social problem. My hunch is that the teaching and learning involved in the acquisition of "antisocial" behaviors are often rapid, secluded, and highly personal circumstances difficult to research but not beyond the ethnographic imagination. In fact, ethnographers are probably at those very scenes right now but are looking at cultural practice rather than cultural acquisition.

We might also invite more systematic attention to discerning the moment in individual life cycles when people learn particular facets of their culture. I remember reading an article in which Margaret Mead reported being questioned (was it during her doctoral oral?) about the point in its life when an infant actually *became* Kwakiutl or Hopi or a member of whatever society. The question proves provocative for turning attention to the continuous process of *becoming*, rather than focusing on a state of *being*. Mead's answer was, in effect, that a Kwakiutl infant of age one month is just that much of a Kwakiutl, a 10-year-old Hopi is just that much a Hopi, and so on.

It is understandable that anthropologists inquiring into a culture are drawn toward older informants who are, in one sense, the best source of cultural knowledge. But in our ethnographic determination to "get right to the source," we inadvertently gloss over the age-grading of knowledge. We lost track of the fact that even our oldest informants continue to learn. I recall a conversation with an old Kwakiutl man who was explaining something of the contemporary form of traditional Kwakiutl social organization. Having been struck by how uninformed my Kwakiutl pupils were about the ways of their people (and having thereby forfeited a golden opportunity to observe cultural acquisition in process), I was wondering about the circumstances under which my elderly informant had become so knowledgeable. I asked him when he had learned what he was now explaining to me, fully expecting him to say that his grandfather had passed this knowledge on to him while he was a young boy. Instead, to my disappointment, he confessed that only recently had he learned much of what he was telling me. I had become so intent on learning how it was to be Kwakiutl that I had failed to realize that my most informed informants were still "becoming" Kwakiutl as they assumed new roles as elders and guardians of their heritage (cf. Wolcott 1967).

The anthropological tenet that the informant is the teacher and the fieldworker is the learner has also kept us from systematic attention to what members of a society do *not* know, do not *yet* know, or may *never* be expected (or even allowed) to know because of their particular circumstances. As Robert Tonkinson has reminded me, informants have a tendency to behave as if they know everything; they feel an obligation to be fully informed. The difficulty of inquiring into what individuals do *not* know is thus complicated by creating the informant role in which an individual is supposed to be all-knowing. But informants do make errors, and the systematic analysis of those errors can lead to a clearer understanding of what informants themselves know or have yet to know (cf. Cancian 1963).

In our call for more anthropological attention to learning, I think attention should be focused on learning that occurs in natural settings rather than on learning done in schools. This is not to say that school learning is unimportant or that anthropologists have nothing to offer; rather, I think, school learning already receives adequate attention and anthropologists are contributing to that work. Of late, "anthropology and education" seems to have focused unduly on schools and given too little attention to education in broader cultural context. Schools should not dominate either our research or our perspective when schooling itself deals with such a narrow spectrum of the cultural repertoire. We should be bringing our anthropology to bear on classroom observations, not drawing our perspectives from them. Perhaps this is why Lave's work on the apprenticing of tailors in Liberia, viewed as an alternative *to* formal schooling rather than an alternative form *of* it, has struck such a note of interest in anthropology and education (cf. Lave 1977, n.d.; see also Lancy 1980).

To whatever extent learning one's language or culture of "orientation" differs from learning alternative forms of it (dialects, microcultures) or alternatives to it (second language, another "macro" or "national" culture), then the frequent and satisfying claim that the anthropologist in the field is "just like a child" also warrants critical review. Perhaps the very opposite of that assertion is true: nothing is more unnatural and unchildlike than the ethnographer learning a culture, since the ethnographer is trying quite self-consciously to learn "another" culture and to make that learning explicit. By contrast, "natural" learners ease into their first culture casually, effortlessly, and essentially unaware of the process. A closer examination of the analog between culture acquisition and ethnographic research could add to our understanding of both processes (cf. insightful comments in this regard in Burnett 1974b).

Some scholars interested in second-language learning make a distinction between language *acquisition* and language *learning.* They use the former, more inclusive term to refer to processes of interaction through which one acquires a feeling for a whole language system. Language "learning," on the other hand, refers to self-conscious processes involving error correction and the presentation of explicit rules (cf. Krashen 1981:2; see also Corder 1967; Lawler and Selinker 1971).

In this chapter I have used the terms acquisition and learning interchangeably. Until scholars interested in second-language learning began making a distinction between the terms, I think they were used interchangeably by most linguists and anthropologists.[2] I wonder now if a more self-conscious anthropology of learning might make better use of this distinction. Of course, "acquisition" may prove in the long run to be no more than a fancy synonym for "osmosis," acknowledging the presence of a complex process without in the least helping us to understand it. Nonetheless, our concern with identifying appropriate terms serves notice of our effort to distinguish broad, pervasive learning "contexts" from attempts to induce learning through purposeful engagement, error correction, and the explicit teaching of rules. Extending the distinction between acquisition and learning into the cultural sphere provides a perspective for understanding why anthropologists, for all their success at "learning" other cultures, seldom achieve the "good intuitions" or "deep understandings" to the degree that the natives have, even though the anthropologist may easily outperform the native in "explaining" a particular society.

What if we were to incorporate the *acquisition* versus *learning* contrast into our dialogues on cultural learning, henceforth restricting our use of the term "learning" to those circumstances where we can muster evidence not only that something has been learned but that there was also a self-conscious effort to accomplish that learning? Linguists already make splendid use of children's "rule-governed errors" in speech (e.g., "He goed") to infer processes in child language acquisition (cf. Corder 1967). We could be making better use of errors to infer processes in children's cultural acquisition as well (cf. Heider 1976 for an example of using errors to posit the sequence in which children come to understand a kinship system). Unless learner errors are subject to intentional efforts at correction and rule explication, however, they provide evidence of the broad and largely subconscious activity of acquiring language or culture rather than evidence of the self-conscious and focused activity of learning.

The distinguishing feature between acquisition and learning seems to be *intentionality*. The term learning, then, could be restricted to those things in the vast repertoire of stuff we carry about in our heads that we have consciously tried to make sense of, or that someone has either succeeded in teaching us or has tried unsuccessfully to teach (thus accounting for things "not learned"). Presumably, we will continue to use "learning" in both its broad "acquisition" sense and in the more restricted sense suggested here. Even a clearer recognition of differing levels of consciousness and degrees of intentionality, however, might help lend precision to our efforts to understand the complex process of cultural acquisition.

The tendency to view learning as "problem solving" seems to me to present another potential problem, that of taking too restricted a view of how learning works. Unquestionably, problem solving creates opportunities for learning, but the idea that learning occurs *only* during problem solving is too restrictive. Years ago Lee pondered the topic in an essay on "Autonomous Motivation" (Lee 1961) in which she asked why humans engage in behavior for no apparent social reason, the kind of behavior reflected in Leigh-Mallory's alleged response about why one climbs mountains: because they are there. In fact, explanations of a social world founded entirely on the concept of "need reduction" seem strained if one looks at humans *as problem finders* as well as *problem seekers*. As Jacob Getzels notes,

> there seem to be as yet ill-defined neurogenic needs that are gratified by stimulation, needs for excitement, novelty, sensory variation, and perhaps above all for the challenge of the problematic . . . The learner is not only a problem-solving and stimulus reducing organism but also a problem-finding and stimulus seeking organism. (Getzels 1974:536)

My hunch is that in attending to the "imponderabilia of actual life" anthropologists have probably observed far more "problem finding and stimulus seeking" behavior than they have reported. They have not made much of such behavior because they have tended to view it as idiosyncratic and individual. If we were to aggregate such behaviors, we might see patterns that reflect cultural influences in terms of the ordinary range of behaviors from which one may select alternatives or "do one's own thing." Do some societies foster problem finding more than others? Stated another way, in what ways do different societies accommodate problem-finding and stimulus-seeking behavior?

Just as we might reexamine whether we are viewing problem solving or problem seeking in our investigations into cultural acquisition, I think we should see what an anthropological perspective brings to the issue of *gradualness* versus *gestalts* (or "spurts") in learning. Gradualness is a compelling notion; clearly the life-long accumulation of knowledge is a gradual process. Neither languages nor cultures are acquired quickly. But the appropriateness of talking about the accumulation of knowledge as a long-term process may mask that, except on the most abstract of levels, learning seems to proceed in spurts, bursts, and flashes. Piaget has posited a number of learning stages for the young. Research on brain growth indicates that the developing brain, too, alternates between periods of rapid growth and periods of rest. (It is also characteristic of our level of understanding that there are arguments over whether growth spurts precede, accompany, or follow learning spurts.) What ethnographic evidence can we provide to illustrate what Beals refers to as "dramatic intuitive leaps" that humans are capable of making (Beals 1973:129)? What kind of evidence from ethnographic observation can we bring to support or refute Hall's observation in *Beyond Culture* that "People learn in gestalts—complete units—which are contexted in situations and can be recalled as wholes" (Hall 1976:130–31)?

Growing out of a reexamination of such comfortable but nonetheless questionable assumptions as learning being *only* problem solving or *always* gradual and continuous, it is probably wise to conclude this assessment of possible next steps by urging that we continue to work from our traditional "worm's eye view" in providing an anthropological dimension to the study of cultural acquisition. Anthropology's most vital contribution to the understanding of learning, for now at least, would seem to be its traditional ethnographic concern for specificness, for details in context. Our task is not to provide a treatise on learning per se but to provide an accumulation of richly contextualized, culturally oriented, easily accessed accounts of learning to be or become *something* or *someone* in a *particular* place, time, and setting. For the anthropologist, the model must be more like Whiting's *Becoming a Kwoma* (1941) than Allport's *Becoming* (1955).

At the same time, and with the advantage of over 50 years of hindsight, Whiting's monograph stands as reminder of the perils of laying out one's data on the Procrustean bed of currently popular theory or of using field research to prove rather than to probe. Whiting describes *Becoming a Kwoma* as a "pioneering attempt to apply learning theory to anthropological data" (1941:xix). He invested heavily in reinforcement ("the most basic of learning principles," p. 172), in a set of four "essential conditions for habit formation" comprised of *drive, response, cues,* and *reward* (p. 173), and in the concept of *imitation* ("one of the most important mechanisms by which culture is transmitted," p. 196). He tells us that

> A Kwoma child learns but a small part of his cultural habits by free trial and error, that is, without some member of his society guiding and directing him . . . He is forced [and, later, "compelled"; cf. p. 200] to learn, not the habits which might be most rewarding to him alone, but the habits which are specified in the culture as being best. (p. 177)

Whiting also dismisses "free trial and error," referring to "learning which takes place without the guidance or interference of any other person" (p. 177n), as an important avenue for learning.

Whiting's confidence that all learning could be explained by the theories he was applying kept him from probing into some theory-shaking subtleties in what he himself observed and reported:

> The circumstances which determine when one should ask for food and when one may take it without asking were too subtly shaded for me to appreciate. I can simply record that Kwoma culture contains both these customs and that children learn to distinguish between them. (p. 42)

The Whitings and their students have, of course, continued to examine these topics throughout a lifetime of study on socialization practices. By 1975, their explanations had moved away from John Whiting's earlier emphasis on reward and deliberate instruction:

> It is in the assignment of tasks and the punishment of disobedience rather than in deliberate instruction or rewarding and punishing specific behaviors that [parents] have the greatest effect . . . Having been assigned a task, children are motivated to imitate the behavior of those who are competent. Their skills are more likely to come from observations than from instruction. (Whiting and Whiting 1975:180)

The softening evident in this latter statement of the primacy Whiting once assigned to deliberate instruction is, I think, indicative of the growing interest being directed to what learners themselves are up to. The irony is that Whiting was at the brink of discovery years ago. With the benefit of hindsight, one wonders what would have happened had he set his "pioneering effort" in a different direction, to use anthropological data to ask what it is of human behavior for which learning theory must account. That same opportunity—and peril—exist today, for we are no less subject to the influence of current theory than was Whiting at the time of his Kwoma research. But the lesson is clear: Our explanations must work in the natural settings in which ethnographic research is conducted. And that stands to be the major contribution from the anthropological study of learning.

Summary

I view rather critically the tendency to equate what cultural transmitters are attempting to transmit with what cultural acquirers are necessarily acquiring. The call proposed here for an anthropology of learning is a call for increased attention to the processes through which individuals continue throughout their lives to "gropingly discover" what they need to know. An anthropology of learning can also serve as a reminder that learning remains an individual matter; culture is, at best, only imperfectly "shared." As Goodenough states, "People learn as individuals. Therefore, if culture is learned, its ultimate locus must be in individuals rather than in groups" (1981:54).

I have examined a number of learning-related terms and concepts that anthropologists have used or introduced. It is time for sifting and sorting. To the end of providing some structure for the anthropology of learning, I have attempted to identify central issues and have raised cautions, primarily with the intent of keeping our attention focused on what we have actually observed, rather than borrowing too heavily from psychological theory or working from popular anthropological assumptions that have not themselves been subjected to scrutiny.

I am quite taken with the generally accepted view among linguists that sees learning as a constructive and effortful process. In that view, learners are seen as active hypothesis makers or theory builders, constantly discovering and refining a set of underlying principles that corresponds closely enough with the behavior of other humans around them to guide the conduct of their everyday lives. A distinction between *cultural acquisition* and *cultural learning,* comparable to the distinction second-language learning scholars are making between language acquisition and language learning, could prove helpful in accounting for the fact that learners accumulate a storehouse of data that far exceeds what they are actively attending to at any given moment.

To be able better to distinguish the learned from the learnable in all that stuff we carry about in our heads would help us with the dilemma of seeming to explain at once so much and so little when we observe that it would be "difficult" for children not to learn their culture. The signal contribution from a rekindled anthropological interest in learning may come not from the recognition of the inevitability of acquiring one's culture but from the reminder that human social learning is essentially a process of active rediscovery. For even as we display new facets of our own linguistic or cultural competence, we only succeed in proving that we have rediscovered, and now claim as our own, what our elders knew all the time.

Notes

[1] Psychologists may insist that they have long touted this view. The importance they have assigned to the learner has varied considerably over the years, however. In a 1974 paper, educational psychologist Wittrock commended "the current welcomed shift" in cognitive psychology "toward reinstating the learner . . . as a primary determiner of learning with understanding and long-term memory" (1974:87).

[2] Cazden notes that, although the terms have not been used contrastively by scholars in the first-language field, the term that individual scholars choose usually reflects their theoretical perspective, the psycholinguists of Chomsky persuasion addressing themselves to the process of language acquisition, and behaviorists consistently employing "learning" as their preferred term (Cazden 1980, personal communication). Anthropologists seem not to have used the terms contrastively: compare Keesing's "Learning a Culture" (1976:201–3) and Schwartz's "Acquisition of Culture" (1981:4–17).

References

Allport, Gordon W., 1955. *Becoming: Basic Considerations for a Psychology of Personality.* New Haven: Yale University Press.

Bandura, Albert, 1977. *Social Learning Theory.* Englewood Cliffs, NJ: Prentice-Hall.

Barker, Roger G., 1968. *Ecological Psychology: Concepts and Methods for Studying the Environment of Human Behavior.* Stanford: Stanford University Press.

Bateson, Gregory, 1942. Social Planning and the Concept of Deutero-Learning. In *Science, Philosophy and Religion, Second Symposium* by the Conference on Science, Philosophy and Religion. New York: Harper & Row.

_____, 1972. *Steps to an Ecology of Mind.* San Francisco: Chandler.

Beals, Alan, 1973. *Culture in Process,* 2d ed. New York: Holt, Rinehart and Winston.

Becker, Howard S., 1953. Becoming a Marihuana User. *American Journal of Sociology* 59:235–42.

Benedict, Ruth, 1938. Continuities and Discontinuities in Cultural Conditioning. *Psychiatry* 1:161–67.

Brukman, Jan, 1973. Language and Socialization: Child Culture and the Ethnographer's Task. In *Learning and Culture,* Solon T. Kimball and Jacquetta Burnett, eds., pp. 43–58. Seattle: University of Washington Press.

Bruner, Edward M., 1956a. Cultural Transmission and Culture Change. *Southwestern Journal of Anthropology* 12:191–99.

_____, 1956b. Primary Group Experience and the Processes of Acculturation. *American Anthropologist* 58:605–23.

Burnett, Jacquetta Hill, 1974a. *Anthropology and Education: An Annotated Bibliographic Guide.* New Haven, CT: Human Relations Area Files Press.

_____, 1974b. On the Analog between Culture Acquisition and Ethnographic Method. [Council on] *Anthropology and Education Quarterly* 5(1): 25–29.

Cancian, Frank, 1963. Informant Error and Native Prestige Ranking in Zinacantan. *American Anthropologist* 65:1068–75.

Carroll, John B., 1968. On Learning from Being Told. *Educational Psychologist* 5(2): 1–10.

Corder, S. P., 1967. The Significance of Learner's Errors. *International Review of Applied Linguistics in Language Teaching* 5:161–70.

Fortes, Meyer, 1938. Social and Psychological Aspects of Education in Taleland. *Africa* 11, No. 4 (Supplement).

Gage, N. L., and David Berliner, 1975. *Educational Psychology*. Chicago: Rand McNally.

Gearing, Frederick O., 1973. Anthropology and Education. In *Handbook of Social and Cultural Anthropology*, John J. Honigmann, ed. Chicago: Rand McNally.

Gearing, Frederick O., and Lucinda Sangree, eds., 1979. *Toward a Cultural Theory of Education and Schooling*. The Hague: Mouton Publishers.

Geertz, Clifford, 1968. *Islam Observed*. Chicago: University of Chicago Press.

_____, 1973. Thick Description. In *The Interpretation of Cultures*. New York: Basic Books.

Getzels, Jacob W., 1974. Images of the Classroom and Visions of the Learner. *School Review* 82(4): 527–40.

Gladwin, Thomas, 1970. *East is a Big Bird*. Cambridge: Harvard University Press.

Goodenough, Ward H., 1981. *Culture, Language and Society*, 2d ed. Menlo Park, CA: Benjamin/Cummings Publishing Co.

Hall, E. T., 1976. *Beyond Culture*. Garden City, NY: Doubleday.

Hansen, Judith Friedman, 1979. *Sociocultural Perspectives on Human Learning: An Introduction to Educational Anthropology*. Englewood Cliffs, NJ: Prentice-Hall.

Harrington, Charles, 1979. *Psychological Anthropology and Education: A Delineation of a Field of Inquiry*. New York: AMS Press.

Hart, C. W. M., 1955. Contrasts between Prepubertal and Postpubertal Education. In *Education and Anthropology*, George D. Spindler, ed. Stanford: Stanford University Press.

Harwood, Frances, 1976. Myth, Memory, and the Oral Tradition: Cicero in the Trobriands. *American Anthropologist* 78:783–96.

Heider, Karl G., 1976. Dani Children's Development of Competency in Social Structural Concepts. *Ethnology* 15(3): 47–62.

Henry, Jules, 1955. Culture, Education, and Communication Theory. In *Education and Anthropology*, George D. Spindler, ed. Stanford: Stanford University Press.

_____, 1960. A Cross-Cultural Outline of Education. *Current Anthropology* 1:267–305.

Keesing, Roger M., 1976. *Cultural Anthropology: A Contemporary Perspective*. New York: Holt, Rinehart and Winston.

Kimball, Solon T., 1965. The Transmission of Culture. *Educational Horizons* 43(4): 161–65.

_____, 1972. Learning a New Culture. In *Crossing Cultural Boundaries*, Solon T. Kimball and James B. Watson, eds. San Francisco: Chandler.

_____, 1974. *Culture and the Educative Process*. New York: Teachers College Press.

Kimball, Solon T., and Jacquetta Hill-Burnett, eds., 1973. *Learning and Culture*. Seattle: University of Washington Press (for the American Ethnological Society).

Krashen, Stephen, 1981. *Second Language Acquisition and Second Language Learning*. Elmsford, NY: Pergamon Press.

Lancy, David F., 1980. Becoming a Blacksmith in Gbarngasuakwelle. *Anthropology and Education Quarterly* 11:266–74.

Lave, Jean, 1977. Cognitive Consequences of Traditional Apprenticeship Training in West Africa. *Anthropology and Education Quarterly* 8:177–80.

_____, n.d. *Tailored Learning: Education and Cognitive Skills among Tribal Craftsmen in West Africa*. University of California, Irvine. Unpublished manuscript (1980).

Lawler, J., and L. Selinker, 1971. On Paradox, Rules, and Research in Second Language Learning. *Language Learning* 21:27–43.

Lee, Dorothy, 1961. Autonomous Motivation. In *Anthropology and Education*, Frederick C. Gruber, ed. Philadelphia: University of Pennsylvania Press.

Mead, Margaret, 1942. Educational Effects of Social Environment as Disclosed by Studies of Primitive Societies. In *Symposium on Environment and Education*, E. W. Burgess et al., eds. Chicago: University of Chicago Press.

_____, 1964. *Continuities and Discontinuities in Cultural Evolution*. New Haven: Yale University Press.

_____, 1970. *Culture and Commitment*. Garden City, NY: Doubleday.

_____, 1972. On Being a Grandmother. In *Blackberry Winter*. New York: Morrow.

Pettitt, George, 1946. Primitive Education in North America. *American Archaeology and Ethnology* 43(1), University of California Publications.

Philips, Susan U., 1982. The Language of Socialization of Lawyers: Acquiring the "Cant." In *Doing the Ethnography of Schooling*, George D. Spindler, ed. New York: Holt, Rinehart and Winston.

Poirier, Frank E., 1973. Socialization and Learning among Nonhuman Primates. In *Learning and Culture*, Solon T. Kimball and Jacquetta Hill-Burnett, eds. Seattle: University of Washington Press (for the American Ethnological Society).

Powdermaker, Hortense [1933], 1971. *Life in Lesu*. New York: W.W. Norton.

Pulliam, H. Ronald, and Christopher Dunford, 1980. *Programmed to Learn: An Essay on the Evolution of Culture*. New York: Columbia University Press.

Sapir, Edward, 1934. Emergence of a Concept of Personality in a Study of Cultures. *Journal of Social Psychology* 5:408–15.

Schwartz, Theodore, 1981. The Acquisition of Culture. *Ethos* 9(1): 4–17.

Spindler, George D., 1959. *The Transmission of American Culture*. Cambridge: Harvard University Press.

_____, 1973. Cultural Transmission. In *Culture in Process*, 2d ed., Alan R. Beals, with George D. Spindler and Louise Spindler. New York: Holt, Rinehart and Winston.

_____, ed., 1978. *The Making of Psychological Anthropology*. Berkeley: University of California Press.

_____, ed., 1987. The Transmission of Culture. In *Education and Cultural Process*, 2d ed. Prospect Heights, IL: Waveland Press.

Tax, Sol, 1973. Self and Society. In *Reading in Education*, Malcolm P. Douglass, ed. Columbus, OH: Chas. E. Merrill.

Wallace, Anthony F. D., 1961. Schools in Revolutionary and Conservative Societies. In *Anthropology and Education*, Frederick C. Gruber, ed. Philadelphia: University of Pennsylvania Press.

_____, 1970. *Culture and Personality*, 2d ed. New York: Random House.

Whiting, Beatrice B., and John W. M. Whiting, 1975. *Children of Six Cultures: A Psycho-Cultural Analysis*. Cambridge: Harvard University Press.

Whiting, John W. M., 1941. *Becoming a Kwoma: Teaching and Learning in a New Guinea Tribe*. New Haven: Yale University Press.

Whiting, John W. M., and Irving Child, 1953. *Child Training and Personality*. New Haven: Yale University Press.

Wilbert, Johannes, ed., 1976. *Enculturation in Latin America: An Anthology*. UCLA Latin American Center Publications, University of California, Los Angeles.

Wittrock, M. C., 1974. Learning as a Generative Process. *Educational Psychologist* 11(2): 87–95.

_____, 1979. The Cognitive Movement in Instruction. *Educational Researcher* 8(2): 5–11.

Wolcott, Harry F. [1967], 1984. *A Kwakiutl Village and School*. Prospect Heights, IL: Waveland Press.

_____, 1969. Concomitant Learning: An Anthropological Perspective on the Utilization of Media. In *Educational Media: Theory into Practice*, Raymond V. Wiman and Wesley C. Meierhenry, eds. Columbus, OH: Chas. E. Merrill.

_____, 1974. *The African Beer Gardens of Bulawayo: Integrated Drinking in a Segregated Society*. Rutgers Center of Alcohol Studies, Monograph No. 10.

_____, 1982. Mirrors, Models, and Monitors: Educator Adaptations of the Ethnographic Innovation. In *Doing the Ethnography of Schooling*, George D. Spindler, ed. New York: Holt, Rinehart and Winston.

16

Instruction and Affect in Hopi Cultural Continuity [1]

Dorothy Eggan

    Education and anthropology have proved in recent years that each has much of interest to say to the other[2] for both are concerned with the transmission of cultural heritage from one generation to another—and with the means by which that transmission is accomplished. And although anthropology has tended to be preoccupied with the processes of cultural *change*, and the conditions under which it takes place, rather than with cultural continuity, it would seem, as Herskovits has said, that cultural change can be best understood when considered in relation to cultural stability (Herskovits 1950:20).

    Both education and anthropology are concerned with learned behavior, and the opinion that early learning is of vital significance for the later development of personality; and that emotional factors are important in the learning process, while sometimes implicit rather than explicit, is often found in anthropological literature, particularly in that dealing with "socialization," "ethos" (Redfield 1953), and "values." From Mead's consistent work, for instance, has come a clearer picture of the socialization process in a wide variety of cultures, including our own, and she examines early "identification" as one of the problems central to all of them (Mead 1953). Hallowell, too, speaking of the learning situation in which an individual must acquire a personality pattern, points out that "there are important affective components involved" (Hallowell 1953:610), and elsewhere he emphasizes a "need for further investigation of relations between learning process and affective experience" (Hallowell 1955:251). Kluckhohn, writing on values and value orientation, says that "one of the severest limitations of the classical theory of learning is its neglect of attachments and attitudes in favor of reward and punishment (Kluckhohn 1951:430). And DuBois states explicitly that, "Institutions which may be invested with high emotional

Source: Reprinted by permission of the *Southwestern Journal of Anthropology*, Vol. 12, No. 4 (1956), pp. 347–70.

value because of patterns in child training are not ones which can be lightly legislated out of existence" (DuBois 1941:281).

In fact, increasing interaction between anthropology and psychiatry (which has long held as established the connection between emotion, learning, and resistance to change in individuals) has in the last decade introduced a theme into anthropology which reminds one of Sapir's statement that "the more fully one tries to understand a culture, the more it takes on the characteristics of a personality organization" (Sapir 1949:594).

Psychologists, while perhaps more cautious in their approach to these problems, since human emotional commitments—particularly as regards permanency—are difficult if not impossible to examine in the laboratory, emphasize their importance in the learning situation, and frequently express dissatisfaction with many existing methods and formulations in the psychology of personality. The shaping factors of emotion—learned as well as innate—are stressed by Asch (1952:29) in his *Social Psychology*, and focus particularly on man's "need to belong." He feels that the "psychology of man needs basic research and a fresh theoretical approach." Allport speaks of past "addiction to machines, rats, or infants" in experimental psychology, and hopes for a "design for personality and social psychology" which will become "better tempered to our subject matter" as we "cease borrowing false notes—whether squeaks, squeals, or squalls . . ." and "read the score of human personality more accurately" (Allport 1951:168–96). And Murphy, starting with the biological foundations of human learning, particularly the individual form this "energy system" immediately assumes, examines man as psychologically structured by early canalizations in which personality is rooted, to which are added an organized symbol system and deeply ingrained habits of perception, and suggests that the structure thus built is highly resistant to change. He says that, "The task of the psychology of personality today is to apply ruthlessly, and to the limit, every promising suggestion of today, but always with the spice of healthy skepticism," while recognizing "the fundamental limitations of the whole present system of conceptions . . ." as a preparation for "rebirth of knowledge" (1947:926–27).

Anthropologists as well as psychologists are aware that any hypotheses in an area so complex must be regarded as tenuous, but since the situations cannot be taken into the laboratory, there is some value in taking the laboratory to the situation. Progress in these amorphous areas can only come about, as Redfield has said, by the mental instrument which he has called a "controlled conversation" (Redfield 1955:148)—this discussion, then, must be considered a conversation between the writer and others who have brought varied interests and techniques to the problem of resistance to cultural changes (DuBois

1955). It begins logically with a recent paper on "Cultural Transmission and Cultural Change" in which Bruner discusses two surveys (SSRC, 1954:973–1002; Keesing 1953; also Spiro 1955:1240–51) of the literature on acculturation and adds to the hypotheses presented in them another which he finds relevant to the situation among the Mandan-Hidatsa Indians. As stated in his summary paragraph we find the proposition: "That which is learned and internalized in infancy and early childhood is most resistant to contact situations. The hypothesis directs our attention to the age in the individual life career at which each aspect of culture is transmitted, as well as to the full context of the learning situation and the position of the agents of socialization in the larger social system" (Bruner 1956a:197).

This proposition will be further extended by a consideration of the *emotional* commitment involved in the socialization process among the Hopi Indians; here the "conversation" will be directed to emotion in both teaching and learning and will center around resistance to cultural change which has been remarkably consistent in Hopi society throughout recorded history, *until the Second World War brought enforced and drastic changes.*[4] At that time the young men, although legitimately conscientious objectors, were drafted into the army. Leaving the isolation of the reservation where physical violence between adults was rare, they were rapidly introduced to the stark brutality of modern warfare. In army camps alcoholic intoxication, an experience which was the antithesis of the quiet, controlled behavior normally demanded of adult Hopi on the reservation, frequently brought relief from tension and a sense of comradeship with fellow soldiers. Deprived of the young men's work in the fields, many older people and young women were in turn forced to earn a living in railroad and munition centers off the reservation. Thus the gaps in the Hopi "communal walls" were, for the first time, large enough in numbers and long enough in time—and the experiences to which individuals had to adapt were revolutionary enough in character—so that the sturdy structure was damaged. It is emphasized, therefore, that in this discussion *Hopi* refers to those members of the tribe who had reached *adulthood* and were thoroughly committed to their own world view before 1941. Much of it would not apply as forcefully to the children of these people, and would be even less applicable to their grandchildren.

The major hypotheses suggested here, then, are:

1. That the Hopi, as contrasted with ourselves, were experts in the use of *affect* in their educational system, and that this element continued to operate throughout the entire life span of each individual as a *reconditioning* factor (Herskovits 1950:325–26, 491, 627); and

2. That this exercise of emotion in teaching and learning was an

efficient means of social control which functioned in the absence of other forms of policing and restraint, and also in the maintenance of stability both in the personality structure of the individual and the structure of the society.

These hypotheses may be explored through a consideration of (a) the early and continued conditioning of the individual in the Hopi maternal extended family, which was on every level, an inculcation of *interdependence* as contrasted with our training for *independence*; and (b) an early and continuing emphasis on religious observances and beliefs (also emphasizing interdependence), the most important facet of which—for the purposes of this paper—was the central concept of the Hopi "good heart."[5]

If we examine the educational system by which a Hopi acquired the personal entity which made him so consistently and determinedly Hopi, we find that it was deliberate and systematic (Pettit 1946; Hough 1915:218). Students of Hopi are unanimous on this point but perhaps it can best be illustrated by quoting one of my informants who had spent much time away from the reservation, including many years in a boarding school, and who was considered by herself and other Hopi to be an extremely "acculturated" individual. In 1938 when she made this statement she was about thirty years old and had brought her children back to the reservation to be "educated." Said she:

> It is very hard to know what to do. In the old days I might have had more babies for I should have married early. Probably some of them would have died. But my comfort would have been both in numbers and in knowing that all women lost babies. Now when I let my little son live on top [a conservative village on top of the mesa] with my mothers, I worry all the time. If he dies with dysentery I will feel like I killed him. Yet he *must* stay on top so the old people can teach him the *important* things. It is his only chance of becoming Hopi, for he would never be a *bahana* (white).

The education which she considered so vital included careful, deliberate instruction in kinship and community obligations, and in Hopi history as it is seen in mythology and as remembered by the old people during their own lifetimes. The Hopi taught youngsters fear as a means of personal and social control and for the purposes of personal and group protection; and they were taught techniques for the displacement of anxiety, as well as procedures which the adults believed would prolong life. Children were instructed in religious lore, in how to work and play, in sexual matters, even in how to deal with a *bahana*. Good manners were emphasized, for they were a part of the controlled, orderly conduct necessary to a Hopi good heart.

Constantly one heard during work or play, running through all activity like a connecting thread: "Listen to the old people—they are wise"; or, "Our old uncles taught us that way—it is the *right* way." Around the communal bowl, in the kiva, everywhere this instruction went on; stories, dream adventures, and actual experiences such as journeys away from the reservation were told and retold. And children, in the warmth and security of this intimate extended family and clan group, with no intruding outside experiences to modify the impact until they were forced to go to an alien school, learned what it meant to be a good Hopi from a wide variety of determined teachers who had very definite—and *mutually consistent*—ideas of what a good Hopi is. And they learned all of this in the Hopi language, which, as Whorf has made so clear, has no words with which to express many of our concepts, but which, working together with "a different set of cultural and environmental influences . . . interacted with Hopi linguistic patterns to mould them, to be moulded again by them, and so little by little to shape the world outlook" (Whorf 1941:92).

Eventually these children disappeared into government schools for a time, and in the youth of most of these older Hopi it was a boarding school off the reservation where Native American children from various reservations were sent, often against their own and their parents' wishes.[6] Here white teachers were given the task of "civilizing" and "Christianizing" these wards of the government, but by that time a Hopi child's view of the world and his or her place in it was very strong. Moreover, trying to transpose our concepts into their language was often very nearly impossible for them, since only Hopi had been spoken at home. Examining Hopi memory of such a method of education, we quote a male informant who said:

> I went to school about four years. . . . We worked like slaves for our meals and keep. . . . We didn't learn much. . . . I didn't understand and it was hard to learn. . . . At that time you do what you are told or you get punished. . . . You just wait till you can go home.

And a woman said:

> Policemen gathered us up like sheep. I was scared to death. My mother tried to hide me. I tried to stay away but the police always won. . . . Then we were sent up to Sherman [in California]. . . . It was far away; we were afraid on the train. . . . I didn't like it when I couldn't learn and neither did the teachers. . . . They never punished me, I always got 100 in Deportment. . . . I was there three years. . . . I was so glad to get home that I cried and cried . . ., glad to have Hopi food again, and fun again.

As children, the Hopi usually solved this dilemma of enforced education by means of a surface accommodation to the situation until such time as they were able to return to their own meaningful world. For, as Park has said, man can "make his manners a cloak and his face a mask, behind which he is able to preserve . . . inner freedom . . . and independence of thought, even when unable to maintain independence of action."[7] In other words, because the inner core of Hopi identification was already so strong, these children were able to *stay* in a white world, while still *living* in the Hopi world within themselves.[8] And while for some there was a measure of temptation in many of the things learned in white schools so that they "became friendly with whites and accepted their gifts,"[9] the majority of these older Hopi acquired a white education simply as a "necessary accessory";[10] they incorporated parts of our material culture, and learned to deal with whites astutely, but their values were largely unaffected.

If we now examine more closely the pattern of integration through which the Hopi erected a communal wall[11] around their children we find in their kinship system the framework of the wall, but interwoven through it and contributing greatly to its strength was a never-ending composition which gave color and form, their religious ceremonies and beliefs.

Let us first contrast briefly the affect implicit in the way a Hopi born into this kinship system experienced relationships and the way in which Western children experience them. In the old days it was rare for a growing primary family to live outside the maternal residence. Normally each lived within it until the birth of several children crowded them out. And in this household each child was eagerly welcomed, for infant mortality was high and the clan was always in need of reinforcement. Thus, in spite of the physical burden on the biological mother, which she sometimes resented, the first strong *clan* sanction which we see in contrast to our own, was the absolute need for and desire for many children. From birth the young of the household were attended, pampered, and disciplined, although very mildly for the first several years, by a wide variety of relatives in addition to the mother. These attentions came both from the household members and from visitors in it. In no way was a baby ever as dependent upon his or her physical mother as are children in our culture. The child was even given the breast of a mother's mother or sister if he or she cried for food in mother's absence. True, a Hopi saying states that a baby is made "sad" if another baby steals his or her milk, but it has been my experience that these women may risk making their own babies sad temporarily if another child needs food.

Weaning, of course, when discussed in personality contexts means more than a transition from milk to solid food. It is also a gradual process of achieving independence from the comfort of the mother's body and care, of transferring affection to other persons, and of finding satisfactions within oneself and in the outside world. Most people learn to eat solid food; many of us are never weaned, which has unfortunate consequences in a society where *individual* effort and independence are stressed. The Hopi child, on the other hand, from the day of his or her birth was being weaned from his or her biological mother. Many arms gave Hopi children comfort, many faces smiled at them, and from a very early age they were given bits of food which were chewed by various members of the family and placed in their mouths. So, for a Hopi, the outside world in which one needed to find satisfaction was never far away. The child was not put in a room alone and told to go to sleep; every room was crowded by sleepers of all ages. The child was in no way *forced to find satisfactions within the self;* rather these were provided for the child, if possible, by the household and clan group. Weaning, then, was from the breast only, and as he or she was being weaned from the biological mother, the child was at the same time in a situation which *increased* emotional orientation toward the intimate in-group of the extended family—which was consistent with the interests of Hopi social structure. Thus, considering weaning in its wider implications, a Hopi was never "weaned"; it was not intended that he or she should be. For these numerous caretakers contributed greatly to a small Hopi's faith in his or her intimate world—and conversely without question to a feeling of strangeness and *emotional insecurity* as adults in any world outside of this emotional sphere. The Hopi were often successful outside of the reservation, but they have shown a strong tendency to return frequently to the maternal household. Few ever left it permanently.

In addition to the extended family, while a Hopi belonged to one clan only, the clan into which he was born, the Hopi was a "child" of his father's clan, and this group took a lively interest in the child. There were also numerous ceremonial and adoptive relationships which were close and warm, so that most of the persons in his familiar world had definite reciprocal relations with the child (Eggan 1950:Chap. II; Simmons 1942:Chaps. 3, 4). Since all of these "relatives" lived in the child's small village, or in villages nearby, his emotional and physical "boundaries" coincided, were quite definitely delimited, and were explored and perceived at the same time. It cannot be too strongly emphasized that the kinship terms which a Hopi child learned in this intimate atmosphere were not mere verbalizations—as, for instance, where the term "cousin" among ourselves is sometimes applied to someone we have never seen and never will see. On the contrary, each term carried with it definite mutual responsibilities and patterns of behavior, and, through these, definite emotional interaction as well. These affects were taught as proper responses, together with the terms which applied to each individual, as he entered the child's life. This process was deliberately and patiently, but unceasingly, worked at by every older individual in the child's surroundings, so by the time a Hopi was grown kinship reaction patterns were so deeply ingrained in thinking and feeling, and in workaday life, that they were as much a part of the Hopi as sleeping and eating. One was not merely told that Hopi rules of behavior were right or wise; one lived them as he grew and *in his total environment* (Henry 1955) (as contrasted to our separation of teaching at home, in school, and in Sunday school) until one was simply not conscious that there was any other way to react. Note that I say *conscious!* The unconscious level of feeling, as seen in dreams and life-history materials, and in indirect behavior manifestations (jealousy and gossip), often presents quite a different picture. But while ambivalence toward specific persons among the Hopi—as with humankind everywhere—is a personal burden, the long reinforced conditioned reaction of *interdependence* on both the emotional and overt behavior level was highly uniform and persistent (See Whorf 1941:87, Aberle 1951:93–94, 119–23). Perhaps the strength of kinship conditioning toward interdependence which was conveyed in a large but intimate group, living in close physical contact, can be best illustrated by quoting from an informant:

My younger sister _____ was born when I was about four or five, I guess. I used to watch my father's and mother's relatives fuss over her. She didn't look like much to me. I couldn't see why people wanted to go to so much trouble over a wrinkled little thing like that baby. I guess I didn't like babies as well as most girls did. . . . But I had to care for her pretty soon anyway. She got fat and was hard to carry around on my back, for I was pretty little myself. First I had to watch her and joggle the cradle board when she cried. She got too big and wiggled too much and then my mother said to me, "She is *your sister*—take her out in the plaza in your shawl."

She made my back ache. Once I left her and ran off to play with the others for a while. I intended to go right back, but I didn't go so soon, I guess. Someone found her. I got punished for this. My mother's brother said: "You should not have a sister to help you out when you get older. What can a woman do without her sisters?'[12] You are not one of us to leave your sister alone to die. If harm had come to her you would never have a clan, no relatives at all. No one would ever help you out or take care of you. Now you have another chance. You owe her more from now on. This is the worst thing that any of my sister's children has ever done. You are going to eat by yourself until you are fit to be one of us." That is what he said. That is the way he talked on and on and on. When meal time came they put a plate of food beside me and said, "Here is your food; eat your food." It was a long time they did this way. It seemed a long time before they looked at me. They were all sad and quiet. They put a pan beside me at meal time and said nothing—nothing at all, not even to scold me. My older sister carried _____ now, I didn't try to go near her. But I looked at my sisters and thought, "I need you—I will help you if you will help me." I would rather have been beaten or smoked. I was so ashamed all the time. Wherever I went people got sad [i.e., quiet]. After a while [in about ten days as her mother remembered it] they seemed to forget it and I ate with people again. During those awful days Tuvaye [a mother's sister] sometimes touched my head sadly, while I was being punished, I mean. Once or twice she gave me something to eat. But she didn't say much to me. Even she and my grandfather were ashamed and in sorrow over this awful thing I had done.

Sometimes now I dream I leave my children alone in the fields and I wake up in a cold sweat. Sometimes I dream I am alone in a desert place with no water and no one to help me. Then I think of this punishment when I dream this way. It was the worst thing I ever did. It was the worst thing that ever happened to me. No one ever mentioned it to me afterward but _____ [older male sibling], the mean one. I would hang my head with shame. Finally my father told him sharply that he would be punished if he ever mentioned this to me again. I was about six when this happened, I think.

This informant was about forty when she related this incident, but she cried, even then, as she talked.

Nor was withdrawal of support the only means of punishment. There were bogey Kachinas who "might kidnap" bad children, and who visited the mesas sometimes when children were uncooperative; thus the "stranger" *joined effectively* with the clan in inducing the "ideal" Hopi behavior. But children *shared* this fear, as they also frequently shared other punishments. Dennis has called attention to the fact that a whole group of children often shared the punishment for the wrong-doing of one (Dennis 1941:263). This method may not endear an individual to one's age-mates, but it does reinforce the central theme of Hopi belief that each person in the group is responsible for what happens to all, however angry or jealous one may feel toward siblings.

Before we examine the religious composition of the Hopi "communal walls," we might contrast more explicitly the emotional implications of early Hopi conditioning to those experienced in our society. From the day of *our* birth the training toward *independence*—as contrasted to *interdependence*—starts. We sleep alone; we are immediately and increasingly in a world of comparative strangers. A variety of nurses, doctors, relatives, sitters, and teachers march through our lives in a never-ending procession. A few become friends, but *compared with a Hopi child's experiences,* the impersonality and lack of emotional relatedness to so many kinds of people with such widely different backgrounds is startling. Indeed the disparity of the relationships as such is so great that continuity of emotional response is impossible, and so we learn to look for emotional satisfaction in change, which in itself becomes a value (Kluckhohn and Kluckhohn 1947:109). In addition, we grow up aware that there are many ways of life within the American class system; we know that there are many choices which we must make as to profession, behavior, moral code, even religion; and we know that the values of our parents' generation are not necessarily ours. If the permissive intimacy in the primary family in our society—from which both nature and circumstance demand a break in adulthood—is too strong, the individual cannot mature so that he or she can function efficiently in response to the always-changing personalities in his or her life, and the always changing demands of the society (Riesman 1955; Mead 1948: 518). The person becomes a dependent neurotic "tentative between extreme polarities (Erikson 1948:198; Murphy 1947:714–733). But precisely because the permissive intimacy, as well as the punishing agencies, in a Hopi child's life were so far and so effectively extended in the formative years, he or she became *interdependent* with a larger but still definitely delimited group and tended always to be more comfortable and effective within it. The Hopi child's self-value quickly identified itself with the larger Hopi value (Hallowell 1955: Chap. 4; Erikson 1948: 198n), and to the extent that the Hopi could continue throughout life to identify with his or her group and function within it, he or she was secure in his or her place in the universe.

We have now sketched the situation which surrounded the young Hopi child in his or her first learning situations, and contrasted these with our own. For descriptive convenience this has been separated from religious instruction, but in the reality experience of the children—with the exception of formal initiation rites—no one facet of learning to be Hopi was separated from others. To understand the meaning religion had for a Hopi one must first understand the harsh physical environment into which he or she was born. While it is agreed that it would not be possible to predict the character or the social structure of the Hopi from the circumstances of this physical environment,[13] it is self-evident that their organized social and ritual activities are largely a response to it. And such activities are at once a reflection of the human need to *be*, and the need to justify existence to oneself and others. If those who doubt that the forces of nature are powerful in shaping personality and culture were confined for one year on the Hopi reservation—even though their own economic dependence on "nature" would be negligible—they would still know by personal experience more convincing than scientific experiments the relentless pressure of the environment on their own reaction patterns. They would, for instance, stand, as all Hopis have forever stood, with aching eyes fastened on a blazing sky where thunderheads piled high in promise and were snatched away by "evil winds," and thus return to their homes knowing the tension, the acute bodily need for the "feel" of moisture. When rains do fall, there is the likelihood of a cloudburst which will ruin the fields. And there is a possibility of early frost which will destroy their crops, as well as the absolute certainty of sandstorms, rodents, and worms which will ruin many plants. These things on a less abstract level than "feeling" resolved themselves into a positive threat of famine and thirst which every Hopi knew had repeatedly ravaged the tribe. Is it possible that the effects of this silent battle between humans and the elements left no mark on successive generations of individuals? It certainly was the reinforced concrete of Hopi social structure, since strongly conditioned interdependence was the only hope of survival.

Thus, the paramount problem for the Hopi was uncertain rain, and the outward expression of their deep need for divine aid was arranged in a cycle of ceremonies, the most impressive of which, at least among the esoteric rituals, were Kachina (Earle and Kennard 1938) dances. These were, for the observer, colorful pageants in which meticulously trained dancers performed from sunrise until sunset, with short intermissions for food and rest. Their bodies were ceremonially painted; brilliant costumes were worn, along with beautifully carved and painted masks which represented the particular gods who were taking part in the ceremony. The color, the singing and the drums which accompanied the dance, the graceful rhythm and intense concentration of the dancers, all combine into superb artistry which is an hypnotic and impressive form of prayer. Ideally, the Hopi preceded every important act with prayer, and with these older Hopi the ideal was apt to be fact. A bag of sacred cornmeal was part of their daily equipment.

In the religious context also, we must remember the intimate atmosphere which surrounded a Hopi child in the learning situation. Here children were taught that if *all* Hopi behaved properly—that is, if they kept good hearts— the Kachinas would send rain. It was easy for the children to believe this because from earliest babyhood these beautiful creatures had danced before them as they lolled comfortably in convenient laps. There was a happy, holiday atmosphere throughout a village on dance days, but while each dance was being performed, the quiet of profound reverence. Lying in the mother's lap, a baby's hands were often struck together in the rhythm of the dance; as soon as he would walk his feet were likewise directed in such rhythm, and everybody praised a child and laughed affectionately and encouragingly as it tried to dance. As the children grew older, carved likenesses of these gods, as well as other presents, were given to them by the gods themselves. And as the child grew in understanding, he or she could not fail to realize that these dancers were part of a religious ceremony which was of utmost importance in his or her world—that the dancers were rain-bringing and thus life-giving gods.

When first initiation revealed that the gods were in reality men who danced in their stead, a *reorganization* of these emotions which had been directed toward them began, and there is much evidence in autobiographical materials of resentment, if not actual trauma, at this point. For some of them the initiation was a physical ordeal, but for those who entered this phase of their education by way of Powamu there was no whipping, although all initiates witnessed the whipping of those who were initiated into the Kachina cult (F. Eggan 1950:47–50; Steward 1931:59ff.).[14] However, the physical ordeal seems to be less fixed in adult memories than disillusion.

In Don Talyesva's account of initiation into Kachina we find:

> I had a great surprise. They were not spirits, but human beings. I recognized nearly every one of them and felt very unhappy because I had been told all my life that the Kachinas were Gods. I was especially shocked and angry when I saw my uncles, fathers, and own clanbrothers dancing as Kachinas. . . . [But] my fathers and uncles showed me ancestral masks and explained that long ago the Kachinas had come regularly to Oraibi and danced in the plaza. They explained that since the people had become so wicked . . . the Kachinas had stopped coming and sent their spirits to enter the masks on dance days. . . . I thought of the flogging and the initiation as a turning point in my life, and I felt ready at last to listen to my elders and live right. (Simmons 1942:84–87)

One of our informants said in part:

> I cried and cried into my sheepskin that night, feeling I had been made a fool of. How could I ever watch the Kachinas dance again? I hated my parents and thought I could never believe the old folks again, wondering if gods had ever danced for the Hopi as they now said and if people really lived after death. I hated to see the other children fooled and felt mad when they said I was a big girl now and should act like one. But I was afraid to tell the others the truth for they might whip me to death. I know now it was best and the *only way to teach* children, but it took me a long time to know that. I hope my children won't feel like that.

This informant was initiated into Powamu and not whipped. She was about thirty when she made this statement to the writer.

Another woman, from a different mesa, speaking of her initiation into the Kachina society, said to me:

> The Kachinas brought us children presents. I was very little when I remember getting my first Kachina doll. I sat in my mother's lap and was "ashamed" [these people often use ashamed for shy or somewhat fearful], but she held out my hand for the doll. I grabbed it and hid in her lap for a long time because the Kachina looked too big to me and I was partly scared. But my mother told me to say "asqualie" [thank you] and I did. The music put me to sleep. I would wake up. The Kachinas would still be there. . . . I dreamed sometimes that the Kachinas were dancing and brought me lots of presents. . . .

> When I was initiated into Kachina society I was scared. I heard people whisper about it. . . . Children shook their heads and said it was hard to keep from crying. . . . My mother always put her shawl over my head when the Kachinas left the plaza. When she took it off they would be gone. So I knew they were gods and had gone back to the San Francisco

mountains. . . . My ceremonial mother came for me when it was time to go to the kiva [for initiation] and she looked sad [i.e., serious]. She took most of the whipping on her own legs [a custom widely practiced among the Hopi]. But then I saw my father and my relatives were Kachinas. When they took their masks off this is what I saw. I was all mixed up. I was mad. I began to cry. I wondered how my father became a Kachina and if they [these men, including her father] would all go away when the Kachinas went back to the San Francisco mountains where the dead people live. Then when my father came home I cried again. I was mad at my parents and my ceremonial mother. "These people have made me silly," I said to myself, "and I thought they were supposed to like me so good." I said that to myself. But I was still crying, and the old people told me that only babies cry. They kept saying I would understand better when I got bigger. They said again that the Kachinas had to go away because the Hopi got bad hearts, and they [the Kachinas] couldn't stand quarreling, but they left their heads behind for the Hopis. I said why didn't they rot then like those skulls we found under that house? They said I was being bad and that I should have been whipped more. . . .

When children asked me what happened in the kiva I was afraid to tell them because something would happen to me. Anyway I felt smart because I knew more than those *little* children. It took me a long time to get over this sadness, though. Later I saw that the Kachinas were the most *important thing in life* and that children can't understand these things. . . . It takes a while to see how wise the old people really are. You learn they are always right in the end.

Before we try to find our way with the Hopi to an "understanding of these things" we must examine their concept of the good heart which functions both in their kinship system and religion to maintain the effectiveness of the "wall of Hopiness." Of greatest significance in all activities among these people, and particularly in their religious ceremonies, is the fact that everything of importance is done communally. Thus each individual who has reached maturity is responsible *to* and *for* the whole community. The Hopi speak of this process as "uniting our hearts," which in itself is a form of prayer. A slight mistake in a ceremony can ruin it and thus defeat the community's prayer for rain; so too can a trace of "badness" in one's heart, although it may not be visible to the observer. Thus their religion teaches that *all* distress —from illness to crop failure—is the result of bad hearts, or possibly of witchcraft (here the simple "bad heart" must not be confused with a "Twoheart," *powaka*, witch), an extreme form of personal wickedness in which an individual sacrifices others, particularly one's own relatives, to save oneself (Titiev 1942; Aberle 1951:94).

This concept of a good heart in *conscious contradistinction* to a bad heart is of greatest importance not only in understanding Hopi philosophy but also in understanding their deep sense of cultural continuity and their resistance to fundamental change. A good heart is a positive thing, something which is never out of a Hopi's mind. It means a heart at peace with itself and one's fellows. There is no worry, unhappiness, envy, malice, nor any other disturbing emotion in a good heart. In this state, cooperation, whether in the extended household or in the fields and ceremonies, was selfless and easy. Unfortunately, such a conception of a good heart is also impossible of attainment. Yet if a Hopi did not keep a good heart he or she might fall ill and die, or the ceremonies—and thus the vital crops—might fail, for, as has been said, only those with good hearts were effective in prayer. Thus we see that the Hopi concept of a good heart included conformity to all rules of Hopi good conduct, both external and internal. To the extent that it was internalized—and all Hopi biographical material known to the writer suggests strongly that it was effectively internalized—it might reasonably be called a quite universal culturally patterned and culturally consistent Hopi "super-ego."[15]

There was, therefore, a constant probing of one's own heart, well illustrated by the anguished cry of a Hopi friend, "Dorothy, *did* my son die as the old folks said because my heart was not right? Do *you* believe this way, that if parents do not keep good hearts children will die?" And there was a constant examination of one's neighbors' hearts: "Movensie, it is those _____ clan people who ruined this ceremony! They have bad hearts and they quarrel too much. That bad wind came up and now we will get no rain." Conversation among the Hopi is rarely censored, and the children heard both of these women's remarks, *feeling*, you may be sure, the *absolute belief* which these "teachers" had in the *danger* which a bad heart carries for everyone in the group.

In such situations, since human beings can bear only a certain amount of guilt,[16] there is a great game of blame-shifting among the Hopi, and this in turn adds a further burden of unconscious guilt, for it is difficult to love properly a neighbor or even a sister who has a bad heart. However, in the absence of political organization, civil and criminal laws, and a formal method of punishment for adults, this consistent "tribal super-ego" has maintained, throughout known history, a record almost devoid of crime and violence within the group,[17] and it has conditioned and ever *reconditioned* a Hopi to feel secure only in being a Hopi.

For through the great strength of the emotional orientation conveyed within the kinship framework and the interwoven religious beliefs, young Hopi learned their world from dedicated teachers whose emotions were involved in teaching what they believed intensely, and this in turn engaged the children's emotions in learning. These experiences early and increasingly made explicit in a very personal way the values implicit in the distinction between a good heart and a bad heart. For public opinion, if intensely felt and openly expressed in a closely knit and mutually dependent group—as in the case of the child who left her baby sister alone—can be more effective potential punishment than the electric chair. It is perhaps easier to die quickly than to live in loneliness in a small community in the face of contempt from one's fellows, and particularly from one's clan from whence, as we have seen, comes most of one's physical and emotional security. Small wonder that the children who experience this constant pressure to conform to clan dictates and needs, and at the same time this constant reinforcement of clan solidarity against outsiders, are reluctant as adults to stray too far from the clan's protective familiarity or to defy its wishes.

There was much bickering and tension within the clan and village, of course, and it was a source of constant uneasiness and ambivalence among the Hopi.[18] But tension and bickering, as I have indicated elsewhere, "are not exclusively Hopi"; the Hopi see it constantly among the whites on and off the reservation. What they do *not* find elsewhere is the *emotional satisfaction* of belonging intensely, to which they have been conditioned and reconditioned. For, as Murphy says, "It is not only the 'desire to be accepted' . . . that presses the ego into line. The basic psychology of perception is involved; the individual has learned to see himself as a member of the group, and the self has true 'membership character,' structurally integrated with the perception of group life" (Murphy 1947:855); Asch 1952:334–35, 605). Actually the Hopi clan, even with its in-group tensions and strife, but with all of the advantages emotional and physical it affords the individual, is one of the most successful and meaningful "boarding schools" ever devised for citizenship training.

In this situation, where belonging was so important, and a good heart so vital to the feeling of belonging, gossip is the potential and actual "social cancer" of the Hopi tribe. It is devastating to individual security and is often senselessly false and cruel, but in a country where cooperation was the only hope of survival, it was the *servant* as well as the policeman of the tribe. Not lightly would any Hopi voluntarily acquire the title Kahopi,[19] "*not* Hopi," and therefore not good. Throughout the Hopi life span the word *kahopi* was heard, until it penetrated to the very core of one's mind. It was said softly and gently at first to tiny offenders, through "Kahopi tiyo" or "Kahopi mana" to older children, still quietly but with stern intent, until the word sometimes assumed a crescendo of feeling as a whole clan or even a whole community might condemn an individual as *Kahopi.*

It is true that we, too, are told we should keep good hearts and love our neighbors as ourselves. But we are not told that, if we do not, our babies will die, *now, this year*! Some children are told that if they do not obey the various "commandments" they learn in different churches they will eventually burn in a lake of hell fire, but they usually know that many of their world doubt this. In contrast, Hopi children constantly *saw* babies die because a parent's heart was not right; they saw evil winds come up and crops fail for the same reason; they saw adults sicken and die because of bad thoughts or witchcraft (to which bad thoughts rendered a person more vulnerable). Thus they learned to *fear* the results of a bad heart whether it belonged to themselves or to others. There were witches, bogey Kachinas, and in objective reality famine and thirst to fear. Along with these fears were taught mechanisms for the displacement of anxiety, including the services of medicine men, confession and exorcism to get rid of bad thoughts, and cooperative nonaggression with one's fellows, even those who were known to be witches. But the best technique was that which included all the values in the positive process of keeping a good heart, and of "uniting our hearts" in family, clan, and fraternal society—in short, the best protection was to be *Hopi* rather than *Kahopi*.

It is clear throughout the literature on the Hopi, as well as from the quotations given in this discussion, that in finding their way toward the goal of "belonging," Hopi children at first initiation had to deal with religious disenchantment, resentment, and with ever-increasing demands made by their elders for more mature behavior. These factors were undoubtedly important catalyzing agents in Hopi personality formation and should be examined from the standpoint of Benedict's formulations on discontinuity (Benedict 1948:423–24). Here we must remember that shock can operate either to destroy or to mobilize an organism's dormant potentialities. And if a child has been consistently conditioned to feel a part of his or her intimate world, and providing that person still lives on in this same world; it seems reasonable to suppose that shock (unless it were so great as to completely disorganize personality, in which case the custom could not have persisted) would reinforce the individual's need to belong and thus would tend to reassemble many of his or her personality resources around this need.

If the world surrounding the Hopi child had changed from warmth to coldness, from all pleasure to all hardship, the discontinuity would have indeed been insupportable. But the new demands made on him or her, while more insistent, were not unfamiliar in *kind;* all adults, as well as the Hopi's newly initiated age-mates, faced the same ones. He or she had shared the shock as he or she had long since learned to share all else; and the Hopi now shared the rewards of "feeling big." The Hopi had the satisfaction of increased status along with the burden of increasing responsibility, as the adults continued to teach the child "the important things," and conformity gradually became a value in itself—even as we value nonconformity and change. It was both the means *and* the goal. Conformity surrounded the Hopi—child or adult—with everything he or she could hope to have or to be; outside if there was only the feeling tone of rejection. Since there were no bewildering choices presented (as is the case in our socialization process), the "maturation drive"[20] could only function to produce an ego-ideal in accord with the cultural ideal,[21] however wide the discrepancy between ideal and reality on both levels.

And since the Kachinas played such a vital role in Hopi society throughout, we must consider specifically the way in which the altered faith expressed by informants gradually came about after the first initiation (Aberle 1951:38–41). First, of course, was the need to find it, since in any environment one must have faith and hope. They also wanted to continue to believe in and to enjoy that which from earliest memory had induced a feeling of pleasure, excitement, and of solidarity within the group. A beginning was undoubtedly made in modifying resentment when the Kachinas whipped each other after first initiation; first, it was again sharing punishment, but this time not only with children but *with adults.* They had long known that suffering came from bad hearts implied by disobedience to the rules of Hopi good conduct and then whipped each other for the same reason; thus there was logic in an initiation which was actually an extension of an already established conception of masked gods who rewarded good behavior with presents but withheld rain if hearts were not right, and who sometimes threatened bad children (Goldfrank 1945:516–39).

Another reorganizing factor explicitly stated in the quotations was "feeling big." They had shared pain with adults, had learned secrets which forever separated them from the world of children, and they were now included in situations from which they had previously been excluded, as their elders continued to teach intensely what they believed intensely: that for them there was only one alternative—Hopi as against Kahopi.

Consistent repetition is a powerful conditioning agent and, as the youngsters watched each initiation, they relived their own, and by again sharing the experience gradually worked out much of the bitter residue from their own memories of it, while also rationalizing and weaving the group emotions ever stronger into their own emotional core—"It takes a while to see how wise the old people really are." An initiated boy, in participating in the Kachina dances, learned to identify again with the Kachinas whom he now impersonated. To put on a mask is to "become a Kachina," and to cooperate actively in bringing about the major goals of Hopi life. And a girl came to know more fully the importance of her clan in its supportive role. These experiences were even more sharply conditioned and directed toward adult life in the tribal initiation ceremonies, of which we have as yet only fragmentary knowledge. Of this one man said to me: "I will not discuss this thing with you only to say that no one can forget it. It is the most wonderful thing any man can have to remember. You know then that you are Hopi. It is one thing whites cannot have, cannot take from us. It is our way of life given to us when the world began."

And since children are, for all mankind, a restatement of one's hopes to be, when these Hopi in turn become teachers (and in a sense they had always been teachers of the younger children in the household from an early age), they continued the process of reliving and rationalizing, or "working out" their experiences with an intensity which is rarely known in our society except, perhaps, on the psychoanalytic couch. But the Hopi had no psychiatrists to guide them—no books which, as Riesman says, "like an invisible monitor, helps liberate the reader from his group and its emotions, and allows the contemplation of alternative responses and the trying on of new emotions" (Riesman 1955:13). They had only the internalized "feeling measure" and "group measure" explicit in the concepts of Hopi versus Kahopi.

On the material level, the obvious advantages of, for instance, wagons versus backs were a temptation. And to the extent to which white influences at first penetrated to these older Hopi it was through this form of temptation. But outside experiences usually included some variation of hostility, scorn, or aggression, as well as a radically different moral code, and these were all viewed and reinterpreted through the Hopi-eye view of the world and in the Hopi language, so that a return to the familiarity of the Hopi world with its solidarity of world view and behavior patterns *was experienced as relief*, and increased the need to feel Hopi, *however great a burden "being Hopi"* implied.

In summary, the hypothesis here developed, that strong emotional conditioning during the learning process was an instrument in cultural continuity among the Hopi, is suggested as supplementary to that of early learning as being resistant to change. It further suggests that this conditioning was *constantly* as well as *consistently* instilled during the entire lifetime of an individual by a circular pattern of integration. For an individual was surrounded by a series of invisible, but none the less solid, barriers between oneself and the outside world. To change oneself, influences had to breach the concentric walls of social process—as conveyed through the human entities which surrounded one and which were strengthened by obligation to teach others—and then to recondition one's early and ever-increasing emotional involvement in Hopi religion, morals, and mutually dependent lineage and clan groups, as well as those attitudes toward white aggression which were shared with all Indians.

In 1938 one old Hopi, who in his youth had been taken away from his wife and children and kept in a boarding school for several years, said to me:

I am full of curiosity; a great *bahana* [white] education would tell me many things I've wondered about like the stars and how a man's insides work. But I am afraid of it because I've seen what it does to folks. . . . If I raise a family, clothe and feed them well, do my ceremonial duties faithfully, I have succeeded—what do you call success? . . . [And again, while discussing fear in connection with a dream, his comment was] Well, yes, we are afraid of *powakas* [witches] but our medicine men can handle them. Neither your doctors nor your gods can control your governments so you have more to fear. Now you are dragging us into your quarrels. I pity you and I don't envy you. You have more goods than we have, but you don't have peace ever; *it is better to die in famine than in war.*

As the old man anticipated, enforced participation in modern warfare soon replaced instruction for Hopi citizenship, and the concentric walls were finally seriously breached. But for these older Hopi the walls still enclose "our way of life given to us when the world began."

Notes

[1] The substance of this paper was originally presented to the Society for Social Research of the University of Chicago in 1943, and subsequently enlarged in 1954 at the request of Edward Bruner for his class in Anthropology and Education. Discussion with him has greatly clarified my thinking on the problems examined here. Some elimination and revision has been made in order to include references to recently published work and suggestions from Fred Eggan, David Aberle, Clyde Kluckhohn, David Riesman, and Milton Singer. But intimate association with the Hopi over a period of seventeen years has given me this perception of the Hopi world.

[2] See, for example, Mead 1931:669–87; Mead 1943:663–39; Whiting and Child 1953; Spindler (ed.) 1955.

[3] Of particular interest in this problem is this paper of DuBois' and the discussion following it. See also Dozier's (1954) analysis of the interaction between the Hopi-Tewa and Hopi; compare Dozier 1955.

[4] An evaluation of these changes has not been reported for the Hopi, although John Connelly is working on the problem; see Adair and Vogt 1949, and Vogt 1951, for discussions of Navajo and Zuni reactions to the war and postwar situation.

[5] The concept of the Hopi "good heart" as contrasted to a "bad heart," which is *Kahopi*, has been documented by every student of Hopi known to the writer, in references too numerous to mention, beginning with Stephen (written in the 1890s but published in 1940) and Hough in 1915. But the clearest understanding of this and other Hopi concepts may be had in Whorf 1941, especially pp. 30–32.

[6] See Simmons, 1942, pp. 88–89, for an excellent description of Don Talayesva of the government's use of force in the educational policy of this period; and pp. 134, 178, 199, and 225 for some of the results of this policy. Cf. Aberle 1951 for an analysis of Talayesva's school years and his later reidentification with his people.

[7] Park 1950:361. Cf. Kluckhohn 1951:388–433, who points out that values continue to influence even when they do not function realistically as providers of immediate goal reactions.

[8] Cf. D. Eggan 1955, on the use of the Hopi myth in dreams as a means of "identification."

[9] Simmons 1942:88, and compare pp. 178, 180.

[10] Bruner 1956b:612, indicates that his Mandan-Hidatsa informants were quite conscious of this "lizard-like" quality of protective coloration in white contacts.

[11] Stephen, 1940a:18 says that the Hopi "describe their fundamental organization as a people" by "designating their principal religious ceremonies as the concentric walls of a house." The concept is extended here to include the entire wall of "Hopiness" which they have built around their children.

[12] In a matrilineal household and clan, cooperation with one's "sisters" is a necessity for the maintenance of both the social structure and the communal unit.

[13] Redfield 1955:31–32; cf. Titiev 1944:177–78; Whorf 1941:91; D. Eggan 1948 (first published in the *American Anthropologist* 1943, vol. 45); Thompson and Joseph 1944:133.

[14] The Powamu society is coordinate with the Kachina society and furnishes the "fathers" to the Kachinas on dance occasions. At first initiation parents may choose either of these societies for their children. It is reported that on First Mesa Powamu initiates were whipped, but my Powamu informants from both Second and Third Mesas were not whipped.

[15] See Piers and Singer 1953:6, where Dr. Piers defines "Super-Ego" as stemming from the internalization of the punishing, restrictive aspects of parental images, real or projected.

[16] See Dr. Piers' definition of guilt and shame (Piers and Singer 1953:5, 16). Hopi reactions are not classified here either in terms of guilt or of shame, since, as Singer points out (p. 52), an attempt to do so can confuse rather than clarify. In my opinion, both shame and guilt are operative in the Hopi "good heart," but it is suggested that the reader compare the material discussed here with the hypotheses in *Shame and Guilt,* particularly with Singer's conclusions in Chap. 5.

[17] Cf. Hallowell 1955, Chap. 4, on the positive role anxiety may play in a society.

[18] In a short paper it is impossible to discuss both sides of this question adequately, but these tensions, and a Hopi's final acceptance of them, are discussed in D. Eggan 1948, particularly pp. 232–34. Cf. Thompson and Joseph 1944: Chap. 16, where Joseph speaks of fear born of the internally overdisciplined self in Hopi children, and its role both in adult discord and social integration. See also Thompson 1945, for hypotheses regarding the integration of ideal Hopi culture. Aberle (1951) discusses various tensions in Hopi society; see especially p. 94. All authors, however, call attention to the compensations as well as the burdens in Hopi society.

[19] See Brandt 1954. In his study of Hopi ethical concepts, *Kahopi* is discussed on p. 92.

[20] See Piers (in Piers and Singer 1953;15) for a discussion of the maturation drive.

[21] Erikson 1948:198, fn.: "The child derives a vitalizing sense of reality from the awareness that his individual way of mastering experience (his ego-synthesis) is a successful variant of a group identity and is in accord with its space-time and life plan."

References

Aberle, David F., 1951. The Psychosocial Analysis of a Hopi Life-History. *Comparative Psychology Monographs* 21:1–133. Berkeley and Los Angeles: University of California Press.

Adair, John, and Evon Z. Vogt, 1949. Navaho and Zuni Veterans: A Study of Contrasting Modes of Culture Change. *American Anthropologist* 51:547–61.

Allport, Gordon W., 1951. The Personality Trait. In *Psychological Theory: Contemporary Readings*, Melvin H. Marx, ed. New York: The Macmillan Company, pp. 503–7.

Asch, Solomon E., 1952. *Social Psychology.* Englewood Cliffs, NJ: Prentice-Hall.

Benedict, Ruth, 1948. Continuities and Discontinuities in Cultural Conditioning. In *Personality in Nature, Society, and Culture*, Clyde Kluckhohn and Henry A. Murray, eds. New York: Alfred A. Knopf, pp. 414–23.

Brandt, Richard B., 1954. *Hopi Ethics: A Theoretical Analysis.* Chicago: The University of Chicago Press.

Bruner, Edward M., 1956a. Cultural Transmission and Cultural Change. *Southwestern Journal of Anthropology* 12:191–99.

____, 1956b. Primary Group Experience and the Process of Acculturation. *American Anthropologist* 58:605–23.

Dennis, Wayne, 1941. The Socialization of the Hopi Child. In *Language, Culture, and Personality: Essays in Memory of Edward Sapir*, Leslie Spier, A. Irving Hallowell, and Stanley S. Newman, eds. Menasha, WI: Sapir Memorial Publication Fund, pp. 259–71.

Dozier, Edward P., 1954. The Hopi-Tewa of Arizona. *University of California Publications in American Archaeology and Ethnology* 44:259–376. Berkeley and Los Angeles: University of California Press.

____, 1955. Forced and Permissive Acculturation. *American Anthropologist* 56:973–1002.

DuBois, Cora, 1941. Attitudes toward Food and Hunger in Alor. In *Language, Culture, and Personality: Essays in Memory of Edward Sapir*, Leslie Spier, A. Irving Hallowell, and Stanley S. Newman, eds. Menasha, WI: Sapir Memorial Publication Fund, pp. 272–81.

____, 1955. Some Notions on Learning Intercultural Understanding. In *Education and Anthropology*, George D. Spindler, ed. Stanford: Stanford University Press, pp. 89–126.

Earle, Edwin, and Edward A. Kennard, 1938. *Hopi Kachinas.* New York: J. J. Augustin, Publisher.

Eggan, Dorothy, 1948. The General Problem of Hopi Adjustment. In *Personality in Nature, Society, and Culture*, Clyde Kluckhohn and Henry A. Murray, eds. New York: Alfred A. Knopf, pp. 220–35.

____, 1955. The Personal Use of Myth in Dreams. In "Myth: A Symposium," *Journal of American Folklore* 68:445–53.

Eggan, Fred, 1950. *Social Organization of the Western Pueblos.* Chicago: The University of Chicago Press.

Erikson, Erik Homburger, 1948. Childhood and Tradition in Two American Indian Tribes, with Some Reflections on the Contemporary American Scene." In *Personality in Nature, Society, and Culture*, Clyde Kluckhohn and Henry A. Murray, eds. New York: Alfred A. Knopf, pp. 176–203.

Goldfrank, Esther, 1945. Socialization, Personality, and the Structure of Pueblo Society. *American Anthropologist* 47:516–39.

Hallowell, A. Irving, 1953. Culture, Personality, and Society. In *Anthropology*

Today: An Encyclopedic Inventory, A. Kroeber, et al., eds. Chicago: The University of Chicago Press, pp. 597–620.

———, 1955. *Culture and Experience.* Philadelphia: University of Pennsylvania Press.

Henry, Jules, 1955. Culture, Education, and Communications Theory. In *Education and Anthropology*, George D. Spindler, ed. Stanford: Stanford University Press, pp. 188–215.

Herskovits, Melville J., 1950. *Man and His Works: The Science of Cultural Anthropology.* New York: Alfred A. Knopf.

Hough, Walter, 1915. *The Hopi Indians.* Cedar Rapids, IA: The Torch Press.

Keesing, Felix M., 1953. *Culture Change: An Analysis and Bibliography of Anthropological Sources to 1952.* Stanford: Stanford University Press.

Kluckhohn, Clyde, 1951. Values and Value-Orientations in the Theory of Action: An Exploration in Definition and Classification. In *Toward a General Theory of Action*, Talcott Parsons and Edward A. Shils, eds. Cambridge: Harvard University Press, pp. 388–433.

Kluckhohn, Clyde, and Florence R. Kluckhohn, 1947 American Culture: Generalized Orientations and Class Patterns. In *Conflicts of Power in Modern Culture*, 1947 Symposium of Conference in Science, Philosophy, and Religion, Chap. 9.

Mead, Margaret, 1931. The Primitive Child. In *A Handbook of Child Psychology.* Worcester, MA: Clark University Press, pp. 669–87.

———, 1943. Our Education Emphases in Primitive Perspective. *American Journal of Sociology* 48:633–39.

———, 1948. Social Change and Cultural Surrogates. In *Personality in Nature, Society, and Culture*, Clyde Kluckhohn and Henry A. Murray, eds. New York: Alfred A. Knopf, pp. 511–22.

———, 1953. *Growing Up in New Guinea.* New York: The New American Library. A Mentor Book (First published in 1930, by William Morrow & Company.)

Murphy, Gardner, 1947. *Personality: A Biosocial Approach to Origins and Structure.* New York: Harper & Row.

Park, Robert Ezra, 1950. *Race and Culture.* New York: The Free Press.

Pettit, George A., 1946. Primitive Education in North America. *University of California Publications in American Archaeology and Ethnology* 43:1–182. Berkeley and Los Angeles: University of California Press.

Piers, Gerhart, and Milton B. Singer, 1953. *Shame and Guilt: A Psychoanalytic and a Cultural Study.* Springfield, IL: Charles C Thomas, Publishers.

Redfield, Robert, 1953. *The Primitive World and Its Transformations.* Ithaca, NY: Cornell University Press.

———, 1955. *The Little Community: Viewpoints for the Study of a Human Whole.* Chicago: The University of Chicago Press.

Riesman, David, 1955. The Oral Tradition, The Written Word, and the Screen Image. Founders Day Lecture, no. 1, Antioch College, October 5, 1955.

Riesman, David, in collaboration with Reuel Denney and Nathan Glazer, 1950. *The Lonely Crowd: A Study of the Changing American Character.* New Haven: Yale University Press.

Sapir, Edward, 1949. The Emergence of the Concept of Personality in a Study of Cultures. In *Selected Writings of Edward Sapir in Language, Culture, and Personality*, David G. Mandelbaum, ed. Berkeley and Los Angeles:

University of California Press, pp. 590–97.

Simmons, Leo W., 1942. *Sun Chief: The Autobiography of a Hopi Indian.* Published for The Institute of Human Relations by Yale University Press, New Haven, CT.

Social Science Research Council Summer Seminar on Acculturation [SSRC], 1954. Acculturation: an Exploratory Formulation, *American Anthropologist* 56:973–1002.

Spindler, George D., ed., 1955. *Education and Anthropology.* Stanford: Stanford University Press.

Spiro, Melford E., 1955. The Acculturation of American Ethnic Groups. *American Anthropologist* 57:1240–52.

Stephen, Alexander MacGregor, 1940. *Hopi Indians of Arizona.* Southwest Museum Leaflets, no. 14. Highland Park, Los Angeles: Southwest Museum.

Steward, Julian H., 1931. Notes on Hopi Ceremonies in Their Initiatory Form in 1927–1928. *American Anthropologist* 33:56–79.

Thompson, Laura, 1945. Logico-Aesthetic Integration in Hopi Culture. *American Anthropologist* 47:540–53.

Thompson, Laura, and Alice Joseph, 1944. *The Hopi Way.* Indian Education Research Series, no. 1. Lawrence, KS: Haskell Institute.

Titiev, Mischa, 1942. Notes on Hopi Witchcraft. *Papers of the Michigan Academy of Science, Arts, and Letters* 28:549–57.

____, 1944. *Old Oraibi: A Study of the Hopi Indians of Third Mesa.* Papers of the Peabody Museum of American Archaeology and Ethnology, Harvard University, vol. 22, no. 1.

Vogt, Evon Z., 1951. *Navaho Veterans: A Study of Changing Values.* Papers of the Peabody Museum of American Archaeology and Ethnology, Harvard University, vol. 41, no. 1.

Whiting, John W. M., and Irvin L. Child, 1953. *Child Training and Personality: A Cross-Cultural Study.* New Haven: Yale University Press.

Whorf, B. L., 1941. The Relation of Habitual Thought and Behavior to Language. In *Language, Culture, and Personality: Essays in Memory of Edward Sapir*, Leslie Spier, A. Irving Hallowell, and Stanley S. Newman, eds. Menasha, WI: Sapir Memorial Publication Fund, pp. 75–93.

17

Contrasts between Prepubertal and Postpubertal Education

C.W.M. Hart

This chapter represents an attempt to use the body of generally accepted anthropological information as a baseline for considering the educational process. It might be paraphrased as "the educative process, anthropologically considered." I assume that "anthropologically considered" is equivalent to "cross-culturally considered," and I assume that education refers to any process at any stage of life in which new knowledge is acquired or new habits or new attitudes formed. That is, I have taken the question which forms the core problem of this volume and tried to develop a few generalizations about that problem from the general anthropological literature. But it follows that since they are anthropological generalizations their usefulness to education is a matter of opinion. All I claim for them is the old basis upon which anthropology has always justified its preoccupation with the simpler societies, namely that by studying the simpler societies we gain perspective and proportion in really seeing our own society and from that better perspective comes better understanding of common human social processes. I hope that the material contained in this chapter will at least enable the readers interested in education to see our own educative process in better perspective and help them separate what is distinctively American in it from what is general-social and general-human.

My starting point is a distinction that is made by Herskovits. In his chapter on education in the book called *Man and His Works* (1948) he finds it necessary to stress that the training of the young in the simpler societies of the world is carried on through two different vehicles. The child learns a lot of things knocking around underfoot in the home,

Source: Reprinted with minor revision by permission of Stanford University Press from George D. Spindler, Editor, *Education and Anthropology*, © 1955 by the Board of Trustees of the Leland Stanford Junior University.

in the village street, with his or her brothers and sisters, and in similar environments, and he or she learns a lot of other things in the rather formidable apparatus of what is usually called in the anthropological literature the initiation ceremonies or the initiation schools.

Herskovits stresses that initiation education takes place outside the home and is worthy to be called schooling, contrasts it with the education the child receives knocking around the household and the village long before the initiation period begins, and decides that the main feature of the latter is that it is within the home, and that it should therefore be called education as contrasted with schooling. There he, and many other writers on the subject, tend to leave the matter.

This tendency, to leave the problem at that point, is rather a pity. Further exploration of these two contrasting vehicles for training of the young will pay rich dividends, and it is to such further exploration that the bulk of this chapter is devoted. But before going on, certain unsatisfactory features of Herskovits' treatment must be mentioned. To suggest, as he does, that preinitiation education is "within the home" is misleading to people unacquainted with the character of primitive society. While initiation education is very definitely outside the home and—as we shall see later—this remoteness from home is a very essential feature of it, it does not follow that the other has to be, or even is likely to be, "within the home." The home in most primitive societies is very different indeed from the connotation of "home" in America, and the type of education to which Herskovits is referring takes place in every conceivable type of primary group. The young child in primitive society may be subjected to the learning process in his or her early years in the household (Eskimo), or in a medley of dozens of households (Samoa); the parents may ignore the child and leave him or her to drag him- or herself up as best he or she can (Mundugumor); the child may be corrected or scolded by any passer-by (Zuni); a boy's male mentor may not be his father at all but his mother's brother (many Melanesian cultures); and so on.

I do not intend to explore the social-psychological results of this variety of primary-group situations; the reason I mention them here is to demonstrate how misleading it is to lump them all together as comprising "education within the home." About the only things they have in common is that they all take place in the earlier years of life and that they don't take place within the formal framework of initiation ceremonies. I propose therefore to call all this type of education by the title "preinitiation" or "prepuberty" education (since most initiation ceremonial begins at puberty or later), and the problem I am mainly concerned with is the set of contrasts that exists between what societies do with their children in the preinitiation period and what is done with them in the postinitiation period. In other words, Herskovits' distinction between education and schooling becomes clearer and more useful if they are simply called prepuberty education and postpuberty education.

One further explanatory comment is necessary. Not all primitive societies possess initiation ceremonies of the formal standardized type with which anthropology has become familiar in many parts of the world. How "schooling" or post-puberty education is handled in those primitive societies which lack initiation ceremonies, and the results of such lack for the adult culture, are interesting questions; but they are outside the scope of the present chapter. What we are concerned with here is the set of contrasts between prepubertal and postpubertal education in those numerous and widespread societies which include formal initiation ceremonies in their set of official institutions.

Prepubertal and Postpubertal Education— How Do They Differ?

If attention is directed to the ways education is carried on in the prepuberty and postpuberty periods in a large number of simple societies—those "with initiation ceremonies"—some very impressive contrasts begin to appear. They can be dealt with under four heads: (1) Regulation, (2) Personnel, (3) Atmosphere, (4) Curriculum; but the nature of the data will require us to jump back and forth between these four divisions, since they are all interwoven.

1. Regulation

Postpuberty education, in such societies, does not begin until at least the age of twelve or thirteen, and in many cases several years later than that. By that age of course, the child has already acquired a great deal of what we call his or her culture. How has the child acquired the things he or she knows at the age of twelve or thirteen? The traditional anthropological monographs are said to tell us little or nothing about "early education." I suggest that the reason the older literature tells us so little that is definite about the early prepubertal training of the children is basically for the same reason that we know so little about preschool education in our own culture, or did know so little before Gesell. Until the appearance of *The Child from Five to Ten* (Gesell and Ilg 1946), the information on the preschool "enculturation" of the American child was just as barren as the anthropological literature. Whether Gesell has really answered the question for the American child and whether a Gesell-like job has been done or can be done for a primitive society are questions which need not concern us here except to point up the real question: Why is it so rare to find clear information as to what goes on in the learning process during the preschool years, in any culture?

One possible answer is that preschool education is rarely if ever standardized, rarely if ever regulated around known and visible social norms.[1] It is an area of cultural laissez faire, within very wide limits of tolerance, and society at large does not lay down any firm blueprint which all personnel engaged in "raising the young" must follow. If, instead of asking for a "pattern" or "norm," we ask the simpler question, "What happens?" it seems to me that the literature is not nearly so barren of information as has been argued. It tends to suggest that anything and everything happens in the same society. For instance Schapera's account of childhood among the Bakgatla is pretty clear: "The Bakgatla say that thrashing makes a child wise. But they also say a growing child is like a little dog and though it may annoy grownups, it must be taught proper conduct with patience and forbearance" (Schapera 1940). As Herskovits has pointed out, this mixture of strict and permissive techniques is also reported for Lesu in Melanesia by Powdermaker, for the Apache by Opler, and for the Kwoma by Whiting (Herskovits 1948). This list can readily be added to.

There is no point in counting how many cultures use severe punishment and how many do not. The explicit statements of the fieldworkers just cited are at least implicit in dozens of others. Do the natives beat their children? Yes. Do they fondle and make a fuss over their children? Yes. Do they correct them? Yes. Do they let them get away with murder? Also yes. All this in the same culture. I repeat that it is pretty clear what happens in the prepuberty years in the simpler societies. Anything and everything from extreme punishment to extreme permissiveness may occur and does occur in the same culture.

The fieldworkers do not tell us what the pattern of early education is because there is rarely any one clear-cut pattern. What each individual child learns or is taught or is not taught is determined pretty much by a number of individual variables. A few such variables are: interest or lack of interest of individual parents in teaching their children, size of family and each sibling's position in it, whether the next house or camp is close by or far away, whether the neighbors have children of the same age, the amount of interaction and type of interaction of the particular "peer-groups" of any given child. The number of variables of this type is almost infinite; the child is simply dumped in the midst of them to sink or swim, and as a result no two children in the same culture learn the same things in the same way. One, for example, may learn about sex by spying upon his or her parents, a second by spying upon a couple of comparative strangers, a third by getting some explicit instruction from his or her father or mother (or elder brother or mother's brother), a fourth by listening to sniggering gossip in the play group, and a fifth by observing a pair of dogs in the sexual act. Which of these ways of learning is the norm? Obviously none of them is, at least not in the same sense as that in which we say that it is the norm for one to inherit the property of one's mother's brother, or to use an intermediary in courtship, or to learn certain important myths at Stage 6B of the initiation ceremonies.

In asking for a uniform cultural pattern in such a laissez faire, anything-goes area, we are asking for the inherently impossible, or at least the nonexistent. There are, of course, some cultural limits set in each society to this near-anarchy: there will, for example, be general outrage and widespread social disapproval if one family shamefully neglects its children or some child goes to what is by general consensus regarded as "too far," but such limits of toleration are very wide indeed in every society. The household is almost sovereign in its rights to do as much or as little as it likes—that is, to do what it likes about its offspring in the *preschool* years. The rest of society is extraordinarily reluctant everywhere to interfere with a household's sovereign right to bring up its preschool children as it wishes. And most primitive parents, being busy with other matters and having numerous children anyway, leave the kids to bring each other up or to just grow like Topsy.

There are other strong lines of evidence supporting this judgment that prepuberty education in the simpler societies is relatively so variable as to be virtually normless. One is the self-evident fact, which anybody can verify by reading the monographs, that no fieldworker, not even among those who have specifically investigated the matter of child practices, has ever found a tribe where several reliable informants could give him or her a rounded and unified account of the preschool educational practices of their tribe comparable to the rounded and generalized picture they can give, readily and easily, of the local religion, or the folklore, or the moral code for the adults, or the local way of getting married, or the right way to build a canoe or plant a garden. This difference can best be conveyed to an anthropologist audience, perhaps, by contrasting the sort of answer fieldworkers get to such questions as "Tell me some of your myths," or "How do you make silver ornaments?" or "How do you treat your mother-in-law?" with the answer they get to a question like "How do you bring up children?" To the former type of question (not asked as crudely as that, of course) the answers will come (usually) in the form of norms—stereotyped and generalized statements that do not differ a great deal from one informant to the next, or, if they do so differ, will always be referred to a "right" way or a "proper" way: the "right" way to build a canoe, the "proper" way to treat one's mother-in-law, the "correct" form of a myth or a ceremony, and so on. Even in the type of sentence structure the answers come in, they will have this official character—"We do it this way" or "It is our custom here to do thus and so"—and often in case of conflicting versions an argument will develop, not over what the informant does but over whether what he or she says is "right" or socially sanctioned as "the right way."

But given the opportunity to perform a similar generalized descriptive job upon "how children are or should be brought up," informants fail dismally to produce anything of this kind. They either look blank and say little or nothing, or come up with a set of empty platitudes—"All boys should be brought up good boys," "They should all respect their elders," etc.—which clearly have no relation to the facts of life going on all around the speaker; or (most common of all) they fall back onto their own life history and do a Sun Chief or Crashing Thunder sort of job. That is, they give in endless and boring detail an account of how they individually were brought up, or how they bring up their own children, but they clearly have no idea of whether their case is typical or atypical of the tribe at large. And the anthropologist equally has no idea of how representative or unrepresentative this case is. This happens so constantly that we are left with only one conclusion, namely, that if there is a cultural tradition for preschool education (comparable with the cultural tradition for religion or for tabu observance or for technology), then the average native in a simple society is completely unaware of what it is.

This same conclusion is also supported by another line of evidence, namely, the complete change that comes over the picture when we move from prepuberty education to postpuberty education. Postpuberty education is marked in the simpler societies by the utmost degree of standardization and correctness. At puberty the initiation rituals begin, and perhaps the most universal thing about these is their meticulously patterned character. Every line painted on a child's body, every movement of a performer, every word or phrase uttered, the right person to make every move, is rigidly prescribed as having to be done in one way only—the right way. A wrongly drawn line, a misplaced phrase, an unsanctioned movement, or the right movement made by the wrong person or at the wrong time, and the whole ritual is ruined. They belong to the same general type of social phenomena as the English Coronation ceremony or the Catholic sacrifice of the Mass; there is only one way of doing them, regardless of the individuals involved, namely the "right" way. By contrast that meticulously patterned feature throws into sharp relief the haphazard, permissive, and unstandardized character of the education that *precedes* the time of puberty.

2. Personnel

So far, then, our stress has been on the unregulated character of primitive preschool education. Certain further things become clearer if at this point we switch our attention from the focus of regulation to the focus of personnel—i.e., from the question of whether the education is controlled and standardized to the question of who imparts the education. Anthropologists are coming more and more to realize the importance of the "Who does what?" type of question in fieldwork, and perhaps nowhere is it so important to know who does what than in the area we are discussing. From whom does the child learn in the simpler societies? As far as the preinitiation years are concerned the answer is obvious: The child learns from his or her intimates, whether they be intimates of a senior generation like parents or intimates of his or her own generation like siblings, cousins, playmates, etc. In the preinitiation years the child learns nothing or next to nothing from strangers or near-strangers. Strangers and near-strangers are people who the child rarely sees and even more rarely converses with; and, since learning necessarily involves interaction, it is from the people with whom he or she interacts most that the child learns most, and from the people with whom he or she interacts least that the child learns least.

This is so obvious that it needs little comment. But one important point about intimates must be made. In all cultures it appears as if this "learning from intimates" takes two forms. The child learns from parents or other senior members of the family and also learns from play groups. And the interaction processes in these two situations are different in several important respects. The parents are intimates and so are the members of the play group, but there is the important difference that parents, to some extent at least, represent the official culture (are the surrogates of society, in Dollard's phrase), while the play groups do not. All the work upon play groups in Western society has tended to stress what autonomous little subcultures they are, each with its own social organization, its own rules, its own values. The family is a primary group, but one which is tied into the total formal structure of the society and therefore subject to at least some overall social control. The play group is an autonomous little world of its own, whose rules may be, and often are, directly at variance with the rules of the home or of the wider society.

If, then, as suggested above, it is true that in most societies—simple or modern—each household is allowed a great deal of freedom to bring up its children pretty much as it chooses, and if this wide degree of tolerance leads in turn to a wide variation in the ways in which the culture is presented to different children, then obviously such variation is enormously increased by the role of the play group. Even if we were told of a culture in which all households standardized their child-training practices, it would still fall far short of being convincing evidence of a standardized child-training situation because of the great amount of knowledge which children in all cultures acquire without the household or at least the parents being involved in the transmission process, namely the knowledge which the child "picks up somewhere."

Once we recognize the influence of this second group of intimates on how the child acquires certain aspects of his or her culture, the case for wide variation in early child training is greatly strengthened. There seems to be no evidence that would suggest that the play group in simple societies functions in any notably different way from the way it functions in modern societies, but unfortunately we have few studies of the "subcultures" of the playworld in other than Western cultures. Among child psychologists dealing with Western cultures, Piaget in particular has some findings that are relevant to the present discussion (Piaget 1929, 1932). These findings tend to show that at least by the age of ten or eleven the child has become empirical and secular in attitude toward rules and norms of play behavior, partly because he or she has learned by that time that each primary group has its own rules, so that there is no "right" way, no overall norm—at least for children's games such as marbles—to which all play groups conform. Piaget, of course, is describing European children, but primitive children spend at least as much time in unsupervised play groups as European or American children; and since their preschool period is certainly many years more prolonged, there is no apparent reason why this conclusion of Piaget should not have cross-cultural validity.

However, I am not trying to develop a theory but merely to follow through some of the difficulties that are hidden in the simple statement above that preschool learning is between intimates. There are different sorts of intimacy because of the child's dual relation to the home and to playmates, and some of his or her culture is mediated by each. We don't know nearly enough about degrees of intimacy, and we may be forced by further research to start making classifications and subdivisions between the different sorts of intimate relationships (different "levels" of primary groups?) to which the child in any culture is exposed in the preschool years. Even if we do, however, the fact still remains that in the preinitiation years the child in primitive society learns nothing from strangers or near-strangers. And this leads to the second comment under the head of Personnel, which is that in the child's *postpuberty* education in contrast to that of *prepuberty* he or she *has to* learn from strangers or near-strangers and cannot possibly learn from anybody else. When puberty arrives and the boy is therefore ready for initiation (or the girl for marriage), that child's family, siblings, gangs, village, all the intimates to whom training or learning has been left up to now, are roughly pushed aside and a whole new personnel take over his or her training. Who these new teachers are varies from culture to culture, but a very common feature is that they be nonintimates of the child, semistrangers drawn from other sections of the tribe (opposite moieties, different districts or villages, hostile or semihostile clans, different age groups, and so on), people with whom he or she is not at all intimate. Who they are and what they represent is made painfully clear in the ritual. An actual case will help to make clear the nature of the transition.

Among the Tiwi of North Australia, one can see the traumatic nature of the initiation period in very clear form, and part of trauma lies in the sudden switch of personnel with whom the youth has to associate. A boy reaches thirteen or fourteen or so, and the physiological signs of puberty begin to appear. Nothing happens, possibly for many months. Then suddenly one day, toward evening when the people are gathering around their campfires for the main meal of the day after coming in from their day's hunting and food gathering, a group of three or four heavily armed and taciturn strangers appear in camp. In full war regalia they walk in silence to the camp of the boy and say curtly to the household: "We have come for So-and-So." Immediately pandemonium breaks loose. The mother and the rest of the older women begin to howl and wail. The father rushes for his spears. The boy himself, panic-stricken, tries to hide, the younger children begin to cry, and the household dogs begin to bark. It is all terribly similar to the reaction which is provoked by the arrival of the police at an American home to pick up a juvenile delinquent. This similarity extends to the behavior of the neighbors. These carefully abstain from identifying with either the strangers or the stricken household. They watch curiously the goings-on but make no move that can be identified as supporting either side. This is particularly notable in view of the fact that the strangers are strangers to all of them, too; that is, they are men from outside the encampment or outside the band, who, under any circumstances, would be greeted by a shower of spears. But not under these circumstances (see also Hart and Pilling 1960).

In fact, when we know our way around the culture we realize that the arrival of the strangers is not as unexpected as it appears. The father of the boy and the other adult men of the camp not only knew they were coming but have even agreed with them on a suitable day for them to come. The father's rush for his spears to protect his son and to preserve the sanctity of his household is make-believe. If he puts on too good an act, the older men will intervene and restrain him from interfering with the purposes of the strangers. With the father immobilized the child clings to his mother, but the inexorable strangers soon tear him (literally) from his mother's arms and from the bosom of his bereaved family and, still as grimly as they came, bear him off into the night. No society could symbolize more dramatically that initiation necessitates the forcible taking away of the boy from the bosom of his family, his village, his neighbors, his intimates, his friends. And who are these strangers who forcibly drag the terrified boy off to he knows not what? In Tiwi they are a selected group of his senior male cross-cousins. To people who understand primitive social organization that should convey most of what I want to convey. They are "from the other side of the tribe," men with whom the boy has had little to do and whom he may have never seen before. They belong to the group of men who have married or will marry his sisters, and marriage, it is well to remember, in a primitive society is a semihostile act. As cross-cousins, these men cannot possibly belong to the same clan as the boy or to the same territorial group; and since only senior and already fully initiated men are eligible for the job they will be men in their thirties or forties, twenty or more years older than he.

By selecting senior cross-cousins to conduct the forcible separation of the boy from the home and thus project him into the postpuberty proceedings, the Tiwi have selected men who are as remote from the boy as possible. The only thing they and he have in common is that they are all members of the same tribe—nothing else. If, then, we have stressed that all training of the child in the prepuberty period is carried on by intimates, we have to stress equally the fact that the postpuberty training has to be in the hands of nonintimates. Anybody who is in any way close to the boy—by blood, by residence, by age, or by any other form of affiliation or association—is *ipso facto* ineligible to have a hand in his postpuberty training.

I selected the Tiwi as my example because the case happens to be rather spectacular in the clarity of its symbolism, but if one examines the literature one finds everywhere or almost everywhere the same emphasis. Those who prefer Freudian symbolism I refer to the initiation ceremonies of the Kiwai Papuans (Landtmann 1927), where during initiation the boy is required to actually step on his mother's stomach; when Landtmann asked the significance of this he was told that it meant the boy was now "finished with the place where he came from" (i.e., his mother's womb). Van Gennep has collected all the older cases in his classic *Rites de passage* (Van Gennep 1909), and no new ones which invalidate his generalizations have been reported since his time.

I therefore suggest two reasonably safe generalizations about initiation rituals: (a) The rituals themselves are designed to emphasize in very clear terms that initiation ceremonies represent a clear break with all home, household, home-town, and friendship-group ties; and (b) as a very basic part of such emphasis the complete handling of all initiation proceedings, and initiation instruction, from their inception at puberty to their final conclusion often more than a decade later, is made the responsibility of men who are comparative strangers to the boy and who are thus as different as possible in their social relationships to him from the teachers, guiders, instructors, and associates he has had up to that time.

3. Atmosphere

It should now be clear what is meant by the third head, Atmosphere. The arrival of the strangers to drag the yelling boy out of his mother's arms is just the spectacular beginning of a long period during which the separation of the boy from everything that has gone before is emphasized in every possible way at every minute of the day and night. So far his life has been easy; now it is hard. Up to now he has never necessarily experienced any great pain, but in the initiation period in many tribes pain, sometimes horrible, intense pain, is an obligatory feature. The boy of twelve or thirteen, used to noisy, boisterous, irresponsible play, is expected and required to sit still for hours and days at a time saying nothing whatever but concentrating upon and endeavoring to understand long intricate instructions and "lectures" given him by his hostile and forbidding preceptors (who are, of course, the men who carried him off to initiation, the "strangers" of the previous section). Life has suddenly become real and earnest, and the initiate is required literally to "put away the things of a child," even the demeanor. The number of tabus and unnatural behaviors enjoined upon the initiate is endless. He mustn't speak unless he is spoken to; he must eat only certain foods, and often only in certain ways, at fixed times, and in certain fixed positions. All contact with females, even speech with them, is rigidly forbidden, and this includes mother and sisters. He cannot even scratch his head with his own hand, but must do it with a special stick and so on, through a long catalogue of special, unnatural, but obligatory behaviors covering practically every daily activity and every hour of the day and night. And during this time he doesn't go home at night or for the weekend or on a forty-eight-hour pass, but remains secluded in the bush, almost literally the prisoner of his preceptors, for months and even years at a time. If he is allowed home at rare intervals, he has to carry all his tabus with him, and nothing is more astonishing in Australia than to see some youth who the year before was a noisy, brash, boisterous thirteen-year-old, sitting the following year, after his initiation is begun, in the midst of his family, with downcast head and subdued air, not daring even to smile, still less to speak. He is "home on leave," but he might just as well have stayed in camp for all the freedom from discipline his spell at home is giving him.

The preoccupations of anthropologists with other interests (that of the earlier fieldworkers with the pain-inflicting aspects of the initiations, and the recent preoccupation with early physiological experiences) have directed attention away from what may well be the most important aspect of education in the simpler societies, namely, the possibly traumatic aspect of the initiation ceremonies. From whatever aspect we view them their whole tenor is to produce shock, disruption, a sharp break with the past, a violent projection out of the known into the unknown. Perhaps the boys are old enough to take it in their stride and the experience is not really traumatic. If so, it would seem that primitive society goes to an awful lot of trouble and wastes an awful lot of time needlessly. Actually we don't know what the psychological effects of initiation upon the initiates are. All that can be said safely is that judged by the elaboration and the minuteness of detail in the shocking and disruptive features of initiation rituals, they certainly appear to be designed to produce the maximum amount of shock possible for the society to achieve.

This may suggest that our own exaggerated concern with protecting our own adolescents from disturbing experiences is quite unnecessary. If the grueling ordeal of subincision, with all its accompanying disruptive devices, leaves the young Australian psychologically unscathed, we needn't worry that Universal Military Training, for instance, will seriously upset the young American. But perhaps something in the prepuberty training prepares the young Australian and makes him capable of standing the trauma of the initiation period.

4. Curriculum

What is the purpose of all this elaboration of shock ritual? Ask the natives themselves and they will answer vaguely, "to make a child into a man." Occasionally a more specific verb is used and the answer becomes, "to teach a boy to become a man." What is supposed to be learned and what do the preceptors teach in the initiation schools? Perhaps the most surprising thing is what is *not* taught. It is hard to find in the literature any case where the initiation curriculum contains what might be called "practical subjects," or how to make a basic living. (There appear to be certain exceptions to this generalization, but they are more apparent than real.) The basic food-getting skills of the simpler peoples are never imparted in the initiation schools. Where practical subjects are included (as in Polynesia or in the Poro schools of Liberia and Sierra Leone), they are specialized crafts, not basic food-getting skills. Hunting, gardening, cattle-tending, fishing, are not taught the boy at initiation; he has already learned the rudiments of these at home in his intimate groups before his initiation starts. This is a surprising finding because of the well-known fact that many of these people live pretty close to the starvation point, and none of them manage to extract much more than subsistence from their environment. But despite this, the cultures in question are blissfully oblivious of economic determinism and blandly leave instruction in basic food production to the laissez-faire, casual, hit-or-miss teaching of parents, friends, play groups, etc. When society itself forcibly takes over the boy in order to make him into a man and teach him the things a man should know, it is not concerned with teaching him to be a better hunter or gardener

or tender of cattle or fisherman, even though the economic survival of
the tribe clearly depends on all of the adult men being good at one or
another of these occupations. The initiation curricula cover instead
quite a different series of subjects, which I am tempted to call "cultural
subjects"—in either sense of the world "culture."

Of course, there is much variation here from tribe to tribe and
region to region, but the imparting of religious knowledge always occu-
pies a prominent place. This (in different cultures) includes such things
as the learning of the myths, the tribal accounts of the tribe's own origin
and history, and the performance, the meaning, and the sacred connections and connotations of the ceremonials. In brief, novices are taught
theology, which in primitive society is inextricably mixed up with
astronomy, geology, geography, biology (the mysteries of birth and sex),
philosophy, art, and music—in short, the whole cultural heritage of the
tribe. As Pettit has pointed out (dealing with North America, but his
statement has universal anthropological validity), the instruction in the
initiation schools is "a constant challenge to the elders to review, analyze, dramatize, and defend their cultural heritage" (Pettit 1946). That
sentence "review, analyze, dramatize, and defend their cultural heritage" is very striking, because you can apply it equally aptly to a group
of naked old men in Central Australia sitting and talking to a novice in
the middle of a treeless desert, and to most lectures in a college of liberal arts in the United States. It serves to draw attention to the fact that,
in the simpler societies, the schools run and manned and controlled
and financed by the society at large are designed not to make better economic men of the novices, or better food producers, but to produce better citizens, better carriers of the culture through the generations,
people better informed about the world in which they live and the tribe
to which they belong. It is here finally, through this sort of curriculum,
that each adolescent becomes "enculturated," no matter how haphazard and individualized his or her learning and growth may have been
up to now. It is through the rigidly disciplined instruction of a common
and rigidly prescribed curriculum that the youth assumes, with all his
fellow tribe members, a common culture. This is where standardization
occurs in the educational process of the simpler societies. Everybody
who goes through the initiation schools, generation after generation, is
presented with the same material, organized and taught in the same
way, with no allowances made for individual taste or choice or procliv-
ity, and no substitutions or electives allowed. When we realize how standardized and rigid and uniform this curriculum is, it should help us to
realize how variable, how un-uniform, how dictated by chance, acci-
dent, and the personal whims of individual parents, individual adult
relatives, and the variation in peer and play groups is the "curriculum"

on or in which the individual child is trained during the long impressionable period that precedes puberty.

Conclusion

The above discussion has, I hope, provided the basis for some helpful generalizations about education in primitive societies, or at least has opened up some new avenues for further exploration. The main points of this discussion may be summed up as follows:

1. There are typically (though not universally) in primitive societies two sharply contrasting educational vehicles, the preschool process, lasting from birth to puberty, and the initiation procedures, beginning around puberty or a little later and lasting from six months to fifteen years. These two educational vehicles show some highly significant contrasts.

2. From the point of view of regulation, the preschool period is characterized by its loose, vague, unsystematic character. Few primitive societies follow any set standards or rules on how children shall be brought up. It is true that there are frequently, perhaps usually, pretty clear rules (which are actually followed) telling mothers how to hold a baby, correct methods for suckling or weaning, and standardized techniques of toilet training (though I suspect some of these are nothing but copybook maxims), but outside the "physiological areas of child-training" (which therefore have to bear all the weight the Freudians put upon them), it is rare indeed to find in primitive cultures any conformity from family to family or from case to case with regard to anything else in the child's early career. This is not, of course, to deny that there are differences from culture to culture in the degree to which children are loved and fussed over or treated as nuisances or joys. I am not questioning the fact, for example, that the Arapesh love children, whereas the Mundugumor resent them. What I am reiterating is that there is still a wide variation not only possible but inevitable in conditioning and learning between one Mundugumor child and the next.

3. If this view is correct, it raises certain interesting possibilities for theory. Because of the heavy Freudian emphasis in the literature on child training in recent years, there exists a strong and unfortunate tendency to talk of child training as if it were coterminous with swaddling, suckling, weaning and toilet-training practices. But these "physiological" areas or "bodily functions" areas are only a small part of the preschool education of the primitive child. Even if in primitive cultures the physiological areas of

child training are relatively standardized (and this is by no means certain), there is no evidence that the nonphysiological areas are. On the contrary, the evidence points in the other direction. Among adult members of the same society there may be, for example, great variation in apparent strength of the sex drive, or in the overt expression of aggressive or passive personality traits (Hart 1954). Where does such "personality variation" come from? From childhood experiences, say the Freudians. I agree. But in order to demonstrate that personality variation in adult life has its roots in early childhood experiences, it is necessary to show not that childhood experiences are highly standardized in early life and that child training is uniform, but that they are highly variable. How can we account for the self-evident fact of adult personality variation by stressing the uniformity of standardization of childhood training? Surely the more valid hypothesis or the more likely lead is to be found in those aspects of child training which are not uniform and not standardized.

4. So much for the preschool training. But there is also the other vehicle of education and youth training in primitive society, the initiation rituals. The initiation period demonstrates to us what standardization and uniformity of training really mean. When we grasp the meaning of this demonstration we can only conclude that compared with the rigidities of the initiation period, the prepuberty period is a loose, lax period. Social scientists who find it necessary for their theories to stress uniformity and pressures toward conformity in simple societies are badly advised to take the prepuberty period for their examples. The natives themselves know better than this. When they are adults, it is to the happy, unregulated, care-free days of prepuberty that they look back. "Then my initiation began," says the informant, and immediately a grim, guarded "old-man" expression comes over his face, "and I was taken off by the old men." The same old men (and women) who sit around and indulgently watch the vagaries and idiosyncrasies of the children without correction become the grim, vigilant, reproving watchers of the initiates, and any departure or attempted departure from tradition is immediately reprimanded.

5. Who are the agents of this discipline? Primitive societies answer in loud and unmistakable tones that discipline cannot be imposed by members of the primary group, that it has to be imposed by "outsiders." The widespread nature of this feature of initiation is, to my mind, very impressive. Making a boy into a man is rarely, anywhere, left to the family, the household, the village, to which he belongs and where he is on intimate terms with people.[2]

The initiation schools are directed at imparting instruction that cannot be given in the home, under conditions as unlike home conditions as possible, by teachers who are the antithesis of the home teachers the boy has hitherto had. The symbolisms involved in the forcible removal from the home atmosphere; the long list of tabus upon homelike acts, homelike speech, home-like demeanor, homelike habits; the selection of the initiators (i.e., the teachers or preceptors) from the semihostile sections of the tribe—all tell the same story, that the turning of boys into men can only be achieved by making everything about the pro-ceedings as different from the home and the prepuberty situa-tion as possible. Everything that happens to the initiate during initiation has to be as different as it can be made by human inge-nuity from the things that happened to him before initiation.

6. This becomes pointed up still more when we remember that what is actually being taught in the initiation schools is the whole value system of the culture, its myths, its religion, its philoso-phy, its justification of its own entity as a culture. Primitive soci-ety clearly values these things, values them so much that it cannot leave them to individual families to pass on to the young. It is willing to trust the haphazard, individually varied teaching methods of families and households and peer groups and gossip to teach children to walk and talk, about sex, how to get along with people, or how to be good; it is even willing to leave to the individual families the teaching of how to hunt or to garden or to fish or to tend cattle; but the tribal philosophy, the religion, the citizenship knowledge, too important to leave to such haphazard methods, must be taught by society at large through its appointed and responsible representatives.

In doing this, society is asserting and underlining its right in the child. The fact that, for example, in Australia it is a group of senior cross-cousins, and elsewhere it is men of the opposite moiety or some other specified group of semihostile relatives, who knock on the door and demand the child from his mourn-ing and wailing family, should not be allowed to disguise the fact that these men are the representatives of society at large, the native equivalents of the truant officer, the police, and the draft board, asserting the priority of society's rights over the family's rights in the child. Clearly in every society there is always a fam-ily and there is always a state, and equally clearly both have rights in every child born into the society. And no society yet—Western or non-Western—has found any perfect way or equal way of adjudicating or harmonizing public rights and pri-vate rights. The state's rights must have priority when matters of citizenship are involved, but the assertion of the state's rights is always greeted with wails of anguish from the family. "I didn't raise my boy to go off and get subincised," wails the Australian mother, but he is carried off and subincised just the same. "I didn't raise my boy for the draft board or the school board," says the American mother, but her protests are of no avail either. It is an inevitable conflict, because it arises from the very structure of society, as long as society is an organization of family units, which it is universally. The only solution is to abolish the family or abolish the state, and no human group has been able to do either.

7. The boy is not ruined for life or a mental cripple as a result of the harrowing initiation experience, but is a social being *in a way he never was before.* He has been made aware of his wider social responsibilities and his wider membership in the total society, but more important in the present context, he has been exposed to a series of social situations in which friendship counts for naught, crying or whining gets one no place, whimsy or charm or boyish attractiveness pays no dividends, and friends, pull, and influence are without effect. The tribal tradition, the culture, treats all individuals alike, and skills and wiles that were so valuable during childhood in gaining preferential treatment or in winning approval or avoiding disapproval are all to no avail. He goes into the initiation period a child, which is a social animal of one sort, but he comes out a responsible enculturated citizen, which is a social animal of a different sort.

8. Primitive societies, then, devote a great deal of time and care to training for citizenship. They make no attempt to even start such training until the boy has reached puberty. But once they start, they do it thoroughly. Citizenship training in these societies means a great deal more than knowing the words of "The Star-Spangled Banner" and memorizing the Bill of Rights. It means exposing the boy under particularly stirring and impressive conditions to the continuity of the cultural tradition, to the awe and majesty of the society itself, emphasizing the subordination of the individual to the group at large and hence the mysteriousness, wonder, and sacredness of the whole individual-society relationship. In Australia, the most sacred part of the whole initiation ritual is when the boys are shown the *churinga*, which are at the same time their own souls and the souls of the tribe which came into existence at the creation of the world. Citizenship, being an awesome and mysterious business in any culture, cannot be imparted or taught or instilled in a secular atmosphere; it must be imparted in an atmosphere replete with symbolism and

mystery. Whether it can be taught at all without heavy emphasis on its otherworldliness, without heavy sacred emphasis, whether the teaching of citizenship can ever be a warm, friendly, loving, cozy, and undisturbing process, is a question I leave to the educators. Primitive societies obviously do not believe it can be taught that way, as is proved by the fact that they never try.

9. One last point, implied in much of the above but worth special mention, is the rather surprising fact that technological training, training in "getting a living," is absent from the initiation curricula, despite its obvious vital importance to the survival of the individual, of the household, and of the tribe or society. Mastery of the food-obtaining techniques by the children is left to the hit-or-miss, highly individualistic teaching processes of the home, to the peer groups, and to the whimsies of relatives or friends. The reason for this omission from the socially regulated curricula of the initiation schools is, I think, pretty clear. In the simpler societies there is nothing particularly mysterious, nothing spiritual or otherwordly about getting a living, or hunting or gardening or cattle-herding. It is true that there is apt to be a lot of magical practice mixed up with these things, but even this heavy magical element is conceived in very secular and individualistic terms. That is, it either works or doesn't work in particular cases, and each man or each household or clan has its own garden magic or cattle magic or hunting magic which differs from the next man's or household's or clan's magic. Dobu, for instance, is a culture riddled with garden magic; so is that of the Trobriands, but each group's magic is individually owned and comparisons of magic are even made between group and group. For this reason, garden skills or hunting skills, even though they include magical elements, can still safely be left by society to the private level of transmission and teaching. Public control, public supervision is minimal.

This leads to two further conclusions, or at least suggestions. (1) On this line of analysis, we can conclude the primitive societies, despite their marginal subsistence and the fact that they are frequently close to the starvation point, devote more care and attention, *as societies*, to the production of good citizens than to the production of good technicians, and therefore they can be said to value good citizenship more highly than they value the production of good food producers. Can this be said for modern societies, including our own? (2) This relative lack of interest in standardizing subsistence-training, while insisting at the same time on standardizing training in the ideological aspects of culture, may go a long way toward enabling us to explain the old sociological problem called cultural lag. Everybody who has taken an introductory course in social science is acquainted with the fact that change in technology is easier to achieve and takes place with less resistance than change in nontechnological or ideological fields. I do not suggest that what we have been talking about above offers a complete explanation of the culture lag differential, but it may at least be helpful. I would phrase the relation between culture lag and education like this: that because prepuberty education in the simpler societies is loose, unstructured, and left pretty much to individual household choice, and because such laissez-faire prepuberty education typically includes food-getting techniques and the use of food-getting tools (spears, harpoons, hoes, etc.), the attitude toward these techniques and tools that the child develops is a secular one and he carries that secular attitude toward them into his adult life. Hence variations from or alternatives to such tools and techniques are not resisted with anything like the intensity of feeling with which variations from or alternatives to ideological elements will be resisted. From his childhood, the boy believes that in trying to get food anything is a good technique or a good tool, provided only that it works, and he is familiar too with the fact that techniques and tools differ at least slightly from household to household or hunter to hunter. Therefore, as an adult he is, in relation to food-getting techniques and tools, both a secularist and an empiricist, and will adopt the white man's gun or the white man's spade when they are offered without any feeling that he is flouting the tribal gods or the society's conscience. The white man's ideology, or foreign importations in ideology, are treated in quite a different way. They are involved with areas of behavior which have been learned not in the secular, empirical atmosphere of the home and the play groups, but in the awesome, sacred atmosphere of the initiation schools, wherein no individual variation is allowed and the very notion of alternatives is anathema.

To avoid misunderstanding, a brief comment must be made about societies like that of Polynesia and the "schools" of Africa such as the Poro, where specialized technical knowledge is imparted to the adolescent males in special training institutions. The significant point is that in such societies ordinary food-gathering techniques (fishing in Polynesia, gardening in West Africa, cattle-tending in East Africa) are still left to the haphazard teaching methods of the individual household, whereas the craft skills (woodcarving in Polynesia, metalworking in the Poro) are entrusted to vehicles of instruction in which apprenticeship, passing of exams, standardized curricula, unfamiliar or nonintimate teachers, heavy emphasis on ritual and the sacred character of the esoteric knowledge which is being imparted, and the dangers of the slightest variation from the traditional techniques of the craft are all prominent. In such societies, despite the inclusion of some technology in the "schools," basic food-getting techniques remain in the common domain of the culture and are picked up by children haphazardly—only the special craft knowledge is sacredly imparted. (Even as late as Henry VIII's England the crafts were called the "mysteries," the two words being apparently interchangeable.)

To conclude, then, we may pull most of the previous discussion together into one final summary. In primitive society there are two vehicles of education, the prepuberty process and the postpuberty process. No Western writer has ever succeeded in contrasting them as much as they need to be contrasted, because they are in every possible respect the Alpha and Omega of each other. In time of onset, atmosphere, personnel, techniques of instruction, location, curriculum, the two vehicles represent opposite poles. Everything that is done in or through one vehicle is the antithesis of what is done in the other. Standardization of experience and uniformity of training is markedly present in the postinitiation experience: it is markedly absent in the prepuberty experience of the growing child. If this is accepted as a base line, it has very important implications for the whole field of personality studies, especially for those studies which seem to claim that personality is very homogeneous in the simpler societies and for those allied studies which allege that child training and growing up in primitive society are very different from their equivalents in modern Western cultures. It is suggestive also as a base for attempting to answer a question that nobody has yet attempted to answer: Why do individuals in simple cultures differ from each other so markedly in personality traits, despite their common cultural conditioning? And it furnishes us finally with another link in the complicated chain of phenomena which exists between the problem of personality formation and the problem of culture change.

All these things are brought together, and indeed the whole of this chapter is held together by one single thread—namely, that childhood experience is part of the secular world, postpuberty experience part of the sacred world. What is learned in the secular world is learned haphazardly and varies greatly from individual to individual. Therefore no society can standardize that part of the child's learning which is acquired under secular circumstances. My only claim for this chapter is that the use of this starting point for a discussion of primitive education enables us to obtain some insights into educational and cultural processes which are not provided by any alternative starting point.

Notes

[1]*Editor's note:* Nonanthropologist readers should be aware of the fact that Prof. Hart's statements concerning lack of uniformity in prepubertal child training would be contested by many anthropologists, though the same ones might accept his basic position that in comparison to pubertal and postpubertal training the earlier years of experience are *relatively* less structured and less subject to the pressure of public opinion.

[2]In the original draft of this paper I mentioned the Arapesh as one of the few exceptions. At the Stanford conference, however, Dr. Mead pointed out that while it is true that initiation in Arapesh is carried out by intimates, they wear masks. To me this correction of my original remark dramatically emphasizes the main point. The Arapesh social structure is such that there are no "strangers" to use for initiation; therefore they invent them by masking some intimates.

References

Gesell, Arnold, and Frances L. Ilg, 1946. *The Child from Five to Ten.* New York: Harper & Row.

Hart, C. W. M., 1954. The Sons of Turimpi. *American Anthropologist* 56:242–61.

Hart, C. W. M., and Arnold R. Pilling, 1960. *The Tiwi of North Australia.* CSCA. New York: Holt, Rinehart and Winston.

Herskovits, Melville J., 1948. *Man and His Works.* New York: Alfred A. Knopf.

Landtmann, Gunnar, 1927. *The Kiwai Papuans of British New Guinea.* London: The Macmillan Company.

Pettit, George A., 1946. Primitive Education in North America. *University of California Publications in American Archaeology and Ethnology* 43:182.

Piaget, Jean, 1929. *The Child's Conception of the World.* New York: Harcourt, Brace Jovanovich.

_____, 1932. *The Moral Judgment of the Child.* London: Routledge & Kegan Paul.

Schapera, I., 1940. *Married Life in an African Tribe.* London: Sheridan House.

Van Gennep, Arnold, 1909. *Les rites de passage.* Paris: E. Nourry. Translated paperback edition, 1960, Chicago: University of Chicago Press.

18

Some Discontinuities in the Enculturation of Mistassini Cree Children

Peter S. Sindell

> The establishment of Western schools, especially boarding schools, and curricula in non-Western societies is likely to constitute an extreme type of culture discontinuity and may do much to force "either-or" choices on their learners. (DuBois 1955:102)

Some of the discontinuities which five- or six-year-old Mistassini children experience when they first attend the residential school at La Tuque will be described in this chapter. The world in which these children live before starting school is almost wholly Cree in character. The language spoken at home is Cree, and preschool children have little direct interaction with Euro-Canadians, or "whites." For the small Cree child the most striking figure in the white world is probably the *wabinkiyu*, a form of bogeyman who is thought of as white. When children misbehave parents frequently tell their children that wabinkiyu is going to take them away.

In the preschool period the children have clear-cut traditional models for identification: parents, grandparents, elder siblings, and other close kin. Most of these kin display behavior and attitudes which conform to traditional Cree values and role expectations.[1] In addition, these kinfolk reward their children, implicitly and explicitly, for conformity to traditional norms.

When the children enter school they must act according to norms which contradict a great deal of what they have learned before, master a body of knowledge completely foreign to them, and communicate in an incomprehensible language in a strange environment.

Source: Printed with permission of the Director of the Canadian Research Center for Anthropology.

In this chapter I shall discuss self-reliance and dependence, the character of interpersonal relations, cooperation and competition, the expression and inhibition of aggression, and role expectations for children. For each topic the traditional milieu and the first year in the school environment will be compared and contrasted.[2]

As the children attend school, they form ties with their teachers and counselors and learn more about Euro-Canadian culture. Eventually, older students face situations different from those they faced as small children. Upon reaching adolescence, most students experience a conflict in identity which reflects the cultural discontinuities they experience in school, and in alternating between the urban residential school in winter and the trading post during the summer.

The data on which the following discussion is based were gathered during fieldwork at Mistassini Post and at the La Tuque Indian Residential School from July 1966, to September 1967.[3] The school is operated by the Anglican Church of Canada for the Indian Affairs Branch. It is located in La Tuque, Province of Quebec, which is 180 miles northeast of Montreal and 300 miles south of Mistassini Post by road. Most Mistassini Cree children between the ages of six and sixteen attend the residential school for ten months of each year while their parents go into the bush to hunt and trap. Other children from Mistassini attend the day school at the post or attend high school in Sault Ste. Marie, Ontario, while living with white families. Only since 1963, when the La Tuque school opened, have the majority of Mistassini children attended school on a regular basis.

In studying the children, interviews were conducted with the children, their parents, teacher, and counselors before, during, and after school. In addition, a series of behavior-rating forms was utilized with the counselors and teacher, and hypotheses about the role of imitation and modeling in acculturation were tested in an experiment. Finally, observational protocols were collected on the children's behavior at the post and in school. The theoretical framework utilized in the study is that of social learning theory as developed by Bandura and Walters (1963). This theory stresses the importance of such concepts as modeling, imitation, and social reinforcement in the analysis of behavioral and attitudinal change.

The study of the thirteen children who entered school for the first time in September 1966 is that of the first generation of people who will receive extensive formal education. Many of the cultural conflicts discussed below adumbrate those which the children will face as adolescents and adults when they attempt to adapt changing economic and social conditions in the Waswanipi-Mistassini region.

Self-Reliance and Dependence

Before Cree children enter school they experience few limits on their behavior. As infants they are fed on demand. When they grow older they eat when they feel hungry and are free to choose from whatever food is available. Usually something—bannock, dried fish, or dried meat—is readily available. Sleeping too is not rigidly scheduled; and the children simply go to sleep when they are tired.

Further, children are free to explore their natural surroundings, either alone or with siblings or playmates. There are no demarcated territorial boundaries which limit their wanderings at the post. The number of children in any particular hunting group varies, and therefore, a child may spend much or all of the winter without playmates from his or her own age group. As a result, children learn to depend upon themselves for amusement. They learn to utilize whatever is available—an old tin stove, a few soft drink bottles, a dead bird, sticks, or stones. Anything the child can reach is a legitimate object for play. If the object is dangerous, parents divert the child's attention or take the object away, but do not reprimand the child. For instance, two- or three-year-old children often handle or play with axes. In general, the only limits placed on a child's behavior relate to specific environmental dangers, for example, children are not allowed to go out in boats alone.

Whereas at home the children have experienced a few limits on their freedom of action, at school there are many. In order to cope with the large number of children (277 at the time the study was made), the school requires them to conform to many routines. They must eat three times a day at specified hours, must wake up and go to sleep at set times, and must learn to obey many other seemingly arbitrary rules. For example, children are not allowed in the front foyer of the dormitory and are not allowed to use the front stairway. Their environment is circumscribed also by the boundary of the school yard. Occasionally the children leave the school property, but only in the company of an adult.

The child is dependent upon others to satisfy almost all of his needs. He must depend on the counselor in his living group ("wing") for clean clothes, soap, toothpaste, and even toilet paper when it runs out. Furthermore, he or she must line up to receive these supplies at the counselor's convenience. Practically the first English phrase which every child learns is "line up!"

The school, then, reinforces the children into submissive, nonexploratory behavioral patterns. These contravene their previous experiences, which led to self-reliant and exploratory behaviors highly adaptive for life in the bush.

Interpersonal Relations

After a child is weaned, he or she is cared for not only by his or her mother but increasingly by a wide range of other kin, such as older siblings, young uncles and aunts, and grandparents. Consequently, each child forms close ties with several kinfolk. Fairly frequent shifts in residence and in hunting group composition, early death, and the Cree patterns of adoption mitigate against the development of extreme dependency on only one or two members of the nuclear family. In fact, it seems likely that some frustration of dependency needs results from the disruption of social relationships noted above. Parents and children interact primarily within networks of close kin. Thus, before they go to school, children gain little experience in interacting with people with whom they do not have close affective ties.

As children enter the school at La Tuque, they interact primarily in the context of large groups: the school class, the wings, and the age groups—Junior Girls (age six to eight) and Junior Boys (age six to ten). The children sleep in rooms with siblings of the same sex, but due to differing schedules on most days they see them only at meals and early in the morning. Since practically all activities are segregated by sex, brothers and sisters have few opportunities to talk to each other. Thus, children's social ties begin to shift from warm affective relations with a small, multigenerational kin group comprised of both sexes to shallow contacts with a large peer group of the same sex. Preston notes the implications of this shift for the internalization of social controls (1966:6).

While their peer group expands, the number of adults with whom the children interact shrinks. Each beginning pupil is cared for by only two or three adults: teacher, wing counselor, and junior counselor. Since each wing counselor is also responsible for an age group, one of the wing counselors is the junior counselor.

With a large number of children competing for a single adult's attention in any given situation, the children learn to beg for nurturance which they could take for granted at home. Dependent behavior, such as crying and yelling, is reinforced as the children discover its effectiveness in eliciting a response from the adult. At home self-reliance and independence are valued and, therefore, crying is ignored from an early age and children learn not to cry. Children learn in school that the smallest scratch will elicit a great deal of concern because the counselors fear that impetigo will develop. Thus, their early training in silently enduring pain is also contradicted.

In summary, the children openly express far more dependence in school than at home, and this dependence is focused on two or three adults rather than upon a multigenerational kin group. At home the children have supportive relationships, but these do not involve a high level of overt expression of dependence (see Spindler 1963:384). Furthermore, the children interact with others far more than they did at home and come to need a high degree of social stimulation.

Cooperation and Competition

Most of the tasks which a child performs at home are done cooperatively and contribute to the welfare of the whole group, usually a nuclear or extended family. Children perform these tasks with siblings, parents, or other kin. Cooperation in hunting and in household chores is extremely adaptive, since it makes the most efficient use of the group's limited labor resources. Sharing food as well as labor is of major importance in traditional Cree culture. Religious values reinforce this since "*mistapeo*," the soul spirit, "is pleased with generosity, kindness and help to others" (Speck 1935:44).

Children observe this extensive sharing and cooperation within the kin group and participate directly in it. For example, during the summer, young children often are used to carry gifts of fish, bannock, fowl, and so on, between kin. Observations indicate that the children themselves usually share food and toys readily.

Competition rather than cooperation is the keynote of school life. In class the students are encouraged to compete with each other in answering questions, and those who answer most promptly and correctly gain the teacher's attention and win his or her approval. Both in school and in the dormitory the children must constantly compete for places in line. Those who are first in line get their food or clothing first or get outside to play soonest. Also, because the dormitory is understaffed, each child must compete with many others to ensure that the counselor attends to his or her individual needs.

Although the teacher finds it difficult to stimulate many children to respond competitively in class, many older children learn to compete aggressively for food and refuse to share their belongings.

Expression and Inhibition of Aggression

Inhibiting the overt expression of aggression is highly valued in Cree culture and serves to maintain positive affective ties among kin, particularly within the hunting-trapping group. Aggression is defined broadly by the Cree and includes not only fighting but also directly contradicting someone else, refusing a direct request, and raising one's voice inappropriately. (These statements apply particularly to relations between kin.) These forms of behavior are unacceptable except if one is drunk and, thus, considered not responsible for one's actions. Fighting when drunk is common and appears to arouse anxiety in children observing this. Laughing at people's mistakes or foibles is not usually defined as aggressive behavior. Gossip, teasing, and the threat of witchcraft are covert means of expressing aggression which are prevalent among the Cree. During enculturation fighting and quarreling are punished.

Punishment seems to be infrequent and usually consists of teasing, ridicule, threats of corporal punishment or reprisals by wabinkiyu, and, occasionally, yelling. But corporal punishment is rare and most often is limited to a light slap with an open hand on top of the head or just above the ear.

In contrast to what they have been taught at home, in school the children learn to express aggression openly. Counselors and teachers disapprove greatly of the children's constant "tattletaling," which serves to express aggression covertly. On the other hand, overtired and frustrated with the demands of controlling large numbers of children, the adults in the school often yell at the children, speak to them sternly, and occasionally swat them. Television and observation of white children are other sources of models for openly aggressive behavior. It is apparent from observing the children that these television models, such as Batman and Tarzan, are very important. Mistassini children also learn to express aggression openly because they are forced to defend themselves against some of the more aggressive children from Dore Lake.

Role Expectations for Children

Cree children learn very early in life the basic components of adult roles through observing their parents and elder siblings. As soon as a child is able to walk, he or she is given small tasks to perform, such as carrying a little water or a few pieces of wood. If he or she does not perform these tasks, the child is not punished, because Cree parents think he or she is not old enough to "understand" yet. When the child walks out of the tent for the first time on his or her own, the "Infants' Rite" is held.

> The essence of the baby's rite is the symbolization of the child's future role as an adult. A boy "kills," brings the kill to camp, and distributes the meat; a girl carries in firewood and boughs. (Rogers and Rogers 1963:20)

All but one of the thirteen children in the sample participated in this rite.

At about five or six years of age children begin to perform chores regularly and are punished if they do not obey. Among their new chores are caring for smaller siblings and washing dishes; in addition, they begin to carry significant quantities of wood, water and boughs. Children also begin to contribute food to the family at this age. They pick berries, snare rabbits, hunt birds, and sometimes accompany their parents into the bush to check traps or to get wood, water, or boughs. At approximately the same time as the child begins playing a more responsible role in performing tasks, the parents believe that his or her ability to conceptualize develops.

Parents conceive of their children as developing gradually into responsible adults. Much of the children's play imitates the activities of their parents and, thus, rehearses adult roles. For example, little girls make bannock out of mud, make hammocks and baby sacks for their dolls, and pretend to cook. Little boys hunt birds and butterflies, play with toy boats, and pull cardboard boxes and other objects as if they were pulling toboggans. Little boys and girls sometimes play together in small "play" tents which their parents make for them.

On the other hand, when they go to school, counselors and teachers expect children to live in a world of play unrelated to their future participation in adult society. There are few chores to do, and these are peripheral to satisfaction of the basic needs—food, heat, and water—which concerned them at home. Keeping one's room clean and tidy and making one's bed are the principal chores which smaller children are expected to do. Young children are expected to spend most of their time playing and going to school. In school and in the dormitory most play involves large groups of thirty to forty children and consists mainly of organized games such as "Cat and Mouse," "Simon Says," "London Bridge," and relay races. When play is nondirective, children frequently resort to imitative play as they did before coming to school, but sometimes with a new content, for example, playing "Batman," "Spaceghost," or "Counselors."

In discussing the child-rearing practices of some societies like the Cree, Benedict says: "The essential point of such child training is that the child is from infancy continuously conditioned to responsible social participation, while at the same time the tasks that are expected of it are adapted to its capacities" (1954:23–24).

Attending school radically disrupts this development. After only one year of school parents report that their children "only want to play" and are not interested in performing their chores. Thus, children have already begun to reject their parents' definitions of proper behavior. This kind of intergenerational conflict increases dramatically with each year of school experience. It is exacerbated because the children are in school all winter and thus fail to learn the technical skills related to hunting and trapping as they mature. This has serious implications for identity conflicts in adolescence, since the children are unable to fulfill their parents' expectations. Children who do not attend school are able to assume adult economic roles at about the onset of puberty. For example, boys begin to trap seriously and girls can contribute significantly to the cleaning and preparation of pelts.

Conclusions

Traditional Cree enculturation takes place primarily in the context of multigenerational kin groups and stresses food sharing and cooperative labor, indirect rather than open expression of aggression, and self-reliance. Interpersonal relations within the kin group are supportive, but verbal expression of dependence is discouraged. Children are viewed as "little adults" and contribute labor and food to the kin group commensurate with their level of maturity. Children's self-reliance is placed in the service of the kin group.

During their first year of residential school the beginners experience radical discontinuities in their enculturation. The values, attitudes, and behavioral expectations which motivate the dormitory counselors and teacher in their interaction with the children differ sharply from those of Mistassini Cree parents. In school, children have few tasks, and these rarely relate to the welfare of the whole group. Competition and direct expression of aggression are reinforced rather than punished. The children interact primarily in large groups—school class, age group, and wing—and come to need a high rate of social stimulation. Dependence becomes focused on two or three adults, and overt expression of dependence increases since it is effective in eliciting nurturant behavior.

As the data presented in the body of the chapter make clear, during their first year of formal education Mistassini beginners are exposed to great cultural discontinuity. They learn new ways of behaving and thinking and are rewarded for conformity to norms which contradict those which they learned before coming to school. Consequently, after only one year of school they have already begun to change significantly toward acting in ways which are appropriate in Euro-Canadian culture but inappropriate in their own. As they continue their education, this process accelerates. After alternating for five or six years between the traditional milieu in the summer and the urban residential school in the winter, severe conflicts in identity arise.

In the six years before starting school the children learn behavioral patterns and values which are highly functional for participating as adults in the traditional hunting-trapping life of their parents. Because they must go to school, their development into trappers or wives of trappers is arrested. Prolonged residential school experience makes it difficult if not impossible for children to participate effectively in the hunting-trapping life of their parents. Not only do they fail to learn the requisite technical skills, but they acquire new needs and aspirations which cannot be satisfied on the trapline. Yet most Mistassini parents want their children to return to the bush. It remains to be seen how the students will resolve their dilemma.

Notes

[1] This is changing now to a certain extent since some of the older children, who have been to school for many years, act in ways which are not traditional. Therefore, they provide their younger siblings with other models for emulation and identification.

[2] This chapter was written while the author was in the field; therefore, many aspects of the shift from the traditional context to the school environment are not dealt with here. Furthermore, many of the ideas expressed must be considered preliminary until further analysis of the data is completed. The usual biographical apparatus is also attenuated for this reason.

[3] I would like to state that my understanding of Cree culture and enculturation has been greatly enriched by reading the works of A. Irving Hallowell on the Ojibwa, George and Louise Spindler on the Menomini, and Edward and Jean Rogers on the Mistassini. The works of Albert Bandura in the field of social learning theory have also influenced my thinking considerably.

References

Bandura, Albert, and Richard H. Walters, 1963. *Social Learning and Personality Development.* New York: Holt, Rinehart, and Winston.

Benedict, Ruth, 1954. Continuities and Discontinuities in Cultural Conditioning. In *Childhood in Contemporary Cultures,* Margaret Mead and Martha Wolfenstein, eds. Chicago: University of Chicago Press.

DuBois, Cora, 1955. Some Notions on Learning Intercultural Understanding. In *Education and Anthropology,* G. D. Spindler, ed., pp. 89–105. Stanford: Stanford University Press.

Preston, Richard J., 1966. Peer Group versus Trapline: Shifting Directions in Cree Socialization. Paper presented at the Annual Meeting of the Pennsylvania Sociological Society, Haverford, PA, October 15 (mimeographed).

Rogers, Edward S., and Jean H. Rogers, 1963. The Individual in Mistassini Society from Birth to Death. In *Contributions to Anthropology, 1960.* Part II, pp. 14–36 (Bulletin 190, National Museum of Canada, Ottawa: Roger Duhamel).

Speck, Frank, 1935. *The Savage Hunters of the Labrador Peninsula.* Norman: University of Oklahoma Press.

Spindler, George D., 1963. Personality, Sociocultural System, and Education among the Menomini. In *Education and Culture,* G. D. Spindler, ed., pp. 351–99. New York: Holt, Rinehart and Winston.

Acknowledgments

The research reported on this paper has been supported by the U.S. National Institute of Mental Health grant number MH 13076-01, which is attached to the author's NIMH Pre-Doctoral Fellowship, number 5-F1-MH-24,080-04. This support and the assistance provided by the staff of the McGill-Cree Project are gratefully acknowledged. The author would also like to express his deep appreciation to the Rev. J. E. DeWolf and Mrs. Cynthia Clinton, respectively principal and senior teacher of the LaTuque Indian Residential School.

19

The Display of Cultural Knowledge in Cultural Transmission
Models of Participation from the Pacific Island of Kosrae

Vera S. Michalchik
Stanford University

"Puhlakfohn!" (A Stupid Child)

"Ahset! Ahset!" the small child cried brightly at me as I walked by. Lore has it that the term, referring to white-skinned foreigners, derives from the locals overhearing the nineteenth-century American sailors yell, "Ah, shit!" as they went about their days of shore leave on the Micronesian island of Kosrae in the western Pacific.

I turned and replied with a cheery *lotu wo* ("good morning" in Kosraean, the local language) to both the petite four-and-a-half-year-old and her mother. The little girl watched my approach with interest while her mother warmly returned my greeting. But as I asked the child, as clearly as I could, her name—*"Suc inem an?"*—the young girl looked down and melted into the folds of her mother's skirt. When I repeated my question, in a rather clumsy attempt to fill the silence, the little child seemed to disappear even more. Her mother intervened. *"Fahk! Fahk!"* (Say it! Say it!) she insisted, tapping and shaking the child's arm as she instructed her to speak. This did nothing to make the girl talk. I was starting to protest that it didn't matter when the child's mother brought the brief episode to a close. *"Puhlakfohn!"* (Stupid!) she said, giving her daughter a light swat. After another moment, the mother and I exchanged good-byes and I continued on my way.

Little Sepe, as I later came to know her, of course knew her own name quite well. She knew it in the ordinary conversations of her everyday life: when gathering fallen breadfruit from the yard with her grandmother, when splashing about on the reef flat with other children, when climbing into the back of an old pickup with aunts and cousins to go to

Source: Written especially for *Education and Cultural Process*, 3rd Edition.

393

a relative's funeral in another village. In all these circumstances, both she and those around her knew and used her name as it helped them in their daily lives. Today, in her meeting with the *ahset*, little Sepe was asked to know her name in a new and strange way. She was asked to *display* her knowledge of it, to respond to an unfamiliar type of question that, while extremely common in American culture, has limited use on Kosrae outside of contexts that are shaped by American culture.

This accidental encounter—with my question, Sepe's nonresponse, and her mother's negative evaluation of her performance—as an isolated event was not terribly important in any of our lives. When taken together, however, events like this, which I call *knowledge displays*,[1] have tremendous import in the way the social world is constructed and the way individuals experience it on Kosrae. As it turns out, the story of Sepe is quite useful in helping us understand the cultural dynamics of knowledge display within Kosraean society. As we will see in this chapter, knowledge displays as a type of event are in fact quite important on Kosrae, having a significant role in determining one's place, relative to others, in Kosrae's social order. Understanding how this is so on one small Micronesian island gives us insight as to how it may be the case elsewhere in the world.

Places to Show What You Know: Church, Family, and School

These special performative moments, moments that make it possible for someone like Sepe to be called smart or dumb, able or unable, wise or foolish, are not of only one sort on Kosrae. That is, there are lots of different ways in which Kosraeans are held accountable for just how knowledgeable they show themselves to be. In proving their knowledgeability,[2] Kosraeans do not follow one simple set of rules of when to act smart. They live in a complex world that brings together in one small space a variety of cultural and institutional factors deriving from Kosrae's own traditions and from its Western influences. All Kosraeans learn to live and act appropriately in their families, to participate in the array of events organized within their church, and to make sense of the processes of formal schooling. Church, family, and school are three institutions which touch the lives of all Kosraeans and shape their experiences from an early age. Within each of these institutional complexes, displaying one's knowledgeability matters a great deal in how one *participates* in social life and what types of *status* one achieves.[3]

Following are a short overview of the recent history of Kosrae and an introduction to some of the basic ways in which knowledge displays on Kosrae fit within patterns of participation in the three institutions discussed.

Kosrae and Its Settings

A lush tropical island of 42 square miles, Kosrae lies just north of the equator roughly halfway between Hawaii and the Philippines in the western Pacific. Its volcanic peaks promote heavy rainfall, its fertile lowlands support cultivation of a variety of crops, and its fringing reef protects the coastline and makes for easy access to the sea's harvest. For sailors aboard nineteenth-century American whaleships looking for fresh food, water, and recreational diversions, Kosrae's sheltered harbors were the perfect place to anchor for refreshment while cruising equatorial waters in the winter. Within a few short decades after first contact with explorers from the West in 1824, Kosrae was regularly host to vessels loaded with ocean-weary whalers anxious for respite from the misery of their days at sea. The effect this had on the island was disastrous. In addition to bringing Western goods and an increasing awareness of the world beyond the local region's islands, the whalers inadvertently brought disease and infertility on such a scale that the population of the island decreased from several thousand to only seven hundred by the end of the whaling period in the 1860s. Over the next two decades, the population continued to dwindle until it was just two or three hundred.[4]

The Church

The rapid loss of life on the island left Kosrae's highly hierarchical political system in utter confusion. The island's leaders traditionally were drawn from the lineages of noble subclans, but many of these subclans had disappeared altogether with depopulation, leaving no one to assume many of the island's key political titles. In the last decade of the whaling period, another powerful influence began to take hold of the island. The American Board of the Commissioners of Foreign Missions, which had achieved great success in the Hawaiian islands, set its sights for missionary expansion westward, and Kosrae was the first of the Micronesian islands to receive a Christian mission. Established in 1852, the mission was abandoned ten years later because its leader, the Reverend Benjamin Snow, believed that the Kosraean population would soon be extinct and the missionization efforts for naught.[5] In spite of his dire predictions, however, the Kosraean population recovered. Furthermore, Snow's efforts to convert the islanders from their traditional religion to Christian belief and practice proved in time to be tremendously successful. By the late nineteenth century, under the guidance of the local pastors and deacons whom Snow had trained, the Kosraean Congregational Church not only commanded complete sacred authority but held tremendous civil authority on the island as well.[6]

The end of the regime of hereditary chiefly authority on Kosrae and the beginning of the new, church-related system meant a dramatic shift in the way Kosraeans accounted for and achieved sociopolitical status. Leadership no longer depended on kinship, but rather, as Kosraeans came to see it, on stewardship—the proven ability to explicate the Bible and guide others in matters related to the church. The pastor, in his ability to clarify for others, embodied this ideal. In time, the Kosraean church developed an elaborate organizational structure that served to channel individuals who demonstrated their worth up the ranks to the highest of church statuses. Along with this organizational structure came a set of practices that encouraged active participation based on daily reading of the Bible and regular presentation of scripture or commentary before the assembled congregation. The hereditarily ascribed authority of a few decades before gave way to an order founded on the public display of one's knowledgeability in preaching the word of God and leading others squarely into the Christian fold. Authority now belonged to those most able to make a new kind of sense for Kosraeans of what life and death were about.

The Family

Although the church gave new order and meaning to much of Kosraean social life, Kosraean practice still remained similar to that of pre-contact times in the daily subsistence activities associated with family life: farming, fishing, cooking, cleaning, and child rearing. The family and church—two distinct spheres of activity representing vastly different historical origins—thus were co-existing side by side in daily life on the island. Even today, family life is much as it was two hundred years ago, before the first Western ships set anchor in Kosrae's harbors and long before the Congregationalist mission took its hold. Together the practices within these two institutional domains came to comprise neo-traditional Kosraean culture, what Kosraeans call *facsin kosrae* (the Kosraean "fashion" of doing things). Family and church, for the best part of one hundred years, organized the activities in which Kosraean children learned most everything they learned about their world.

Today, as it was long ago, from an early age Kosraean children participate in the work done in their families. As they begin to understand and use language, toddlers are given simple tasks, like fetching and carrying, that involve them in what their elders are doing. Three- and four-year-old boys gather leaves and vines from a patch of land being cleared by their fathers. Five-year-old girls tote their little brothers, more than half their own size, back up the road to their homes after a rowdy period of play with neighbors. At any age, Kosraean children learn within their families by watching, imitating, and also by obediently doing what they are instructed to do.

Knowledge displays within the family are tightly woven into the very activities with which they are concerned. For example, within the family setting, a female child's knowledge is displayed in her everyday practical accomplishments. These practical accomplishments themselves prove her ability, and this is the basis of her assuming more responsibility and authority in the daily activities of her family over the years. As a young girl helps care for even younger children, she is all at once learning about child care, contributing to a vital family activity, and demonstrating her own increasing ability to do so.

The School

Forms of Western-style schooling have existed on Kosrae since the days of the nineteenth-century missionaries. The early mission schools, training a small handful of Kosraeans in religious matters, fit squarely into the church and into a model of Kosraean society, in which family and church serve as the primary settings for cultural transmission. Gradually other forms of schooling, along with new economic and political structures, came to be established on the island. A succession of colonial powers in the region—Spanish, German, Japanese and American—brought with them successively more formal and comprehensive school systems. Starting in the 1960s, based on policy decisions within the Kennedy administration, all Kosraean children were required to attend American-style schools up through the eighth grade, with many students continuing on to high school.[7] This new mandate established an enduring, bureaucratic educational system in the American mold.

Modern bureaucratic schooling on Kosrae has served in supporting the development of Kosrae's bureaucracy. Successful high school and college graduates have preferentially been chosen for the government jobs that have been created with political change over the past few decades. Like elsewhere in the world, the knowledge displays characteristic of school—for example, answering questions in class discussions and on tests—result in kinds of certification that are taken seriously in the job market. The increasing scarcity of available government jobs on Kosrae has led to an intensification of competition among young persons having recently completed their education.

Levels of school achievement also affect the lives of Kosraeans in domains far removed from the job market. Schooling, because it is so widespread and its measures are so tidy and seemingly absolute, tends to serve as a kind of universal yardstick by which individuals can be easily compared one against the other. "A" students can readily be compared to "C" students; a fifty-seven-year-old who forty years ago finished only fourth grade can be compared to her niece who is about to complete high school. This kind of status signification has become prevalent on Kosrae and again points to the way in which knowledge displays come to shape individual lives according to the logic of particular institutions.

Knowledge Displays in Teaching and Learning Culture

As the historical overview indicates, with the establishment of widescale compulsory schooling a third institution came to lay broad claim to the life experiences of Kosraean children. Like family and church, schooling carries with it certain practical requirements for individual display of knowledgeability. In each of these three institutional domains, persons are held accountable for knowing certain things at certain times and places. The ways in which this happens varies a great deal, however: family, church and school have their own versions of what being a knowledgeable person is. To understand what it means for a Kosraean to know something and how this "meaning of knowing" plays itself out socially, we must look at the different types of knowledgeability created in each of the major enculturating institutions on the island.

What does an approach focused on knowledge displays really gain us? For those of us concerned with how culture—broadly defined as the knowledge needed to appropriately live in one's world—is transmitted to a new generation, this focus on the display of knowledge leads to a better understanding of the transmission process. There are three parts to this understanding. First, we can see that a significant part of cultural knowledge is *knowledge of when to display* one's knowledge. Although little Sepe knew her name, she knew nothing about the conditions I had created for her to "show" this knowledge. Her mother, by contrast, was familiar with the general patterns of questioning in school, and also with the particular importance of questions like "What is your name?" within American-based school culture. Confronted with this school-like situation, and also with an American woman in age and manner not unlike the teachers from the mainland she had known in her youth, Sepe's mother construed my question in a way that helped create the knowledge-display event previously described.

This raises a second point regarding knowledge displays in cultural transmission. Knowledge displays are closely tied to cultural notions about learning. They serve to identify both *what valued knowledge is* and *who should know it*. A clear example of this comes from school, where students are regularly asked to display knowledge (for example, on tests) of particular curricula (the valued knowledge) according to a schedule that specifies who should know the material and when they should know it (e.g., what a second grader should know after a week of instruction on a topic). For little Sepe, this type of situation quickly developed, with her mother enforcing a test-like accountability for Sepe's proper recital of her name once I had asked my question. Sepe's practical knowledge of the appropriate social behavior immediately became valued in this situation.[8]

Finally, knowledge displays deepen our understanding of the cultural transmission process by helping us focus on the *consequences* of the display. This point is crucial. For each display event there are necessarily outcomes, consequences that come directly from the positive or negative evaluation of the display. "*Puhlakfohn!*" and a painless swat are probably all that Sepe suffered after her failure to speak that day; but within the family, church and school settings I have described, the consequentiality of knowledge displays is far more complex and far reaching. Cumulatively, these consequences have major effects in individual lives as persons are judged and socially situated in relation to one another.

In sum, the displays of knowledgeability required of individuals in family, church and school on Kosrae are in themselves important pieces of cultural know-how. They also act as markers or pointers of sorts, making more identifiable key components of learning situations: what should be known and who should know it. This know-how of the cultural rules for displaying knowledge varies from setting to setting, making for differences in the processes of cultural transmission and differences in personal learning experiences within these settings. The cultural rules for displaying knowledge generally correspond to institutional domains. However, they also spill over from one domain—one set of circumstances—to another, as the distinctions between what constitutes a knowledgeable person in the classroom and in the living room sometimes are not all that neat. Ultimately, to be knowing, able, smart and wise in one domain is distinct from being so in the others, not so much because of the practical differences in the ways that persons display their knowledge, but because of the differences in consequences that knowledge displays engender in the varied domains. The meaning of knowing depends primarily, then, on the ways in which displays of knowledgeability affect the lives of the people involved.

Some Knowledgeable Kosraens

In the following sections we will look at examples of Kosraeans displaying (or not displaying) their knowledge in the cultural transmission processes associated with church, school, and family. In doing so, we will learn more about teaching and learning on Kosrae and also more about the way that institutions shape our understanding of these processes.

Issues of Participation

Emily reached out with the bundle of dried coconut leaf spines, the local-style broom, and gave a good swat to the newly laid linoleum floor near where she was sitting. "*Suhmaht!*" (from the English "smart") Emily exclaimed with a chuckle. She was referring to the housefly she'd been trying to get, noting its successful evasion of her potentially fatal blow. With her left arm she held the youngest of her grandchildren, eleven-month-old Castro, who had been fiddling with Emily's shiny gold earring but was now beginning to fuss. Castro's mother was busy combing and styling his sister Mariannie's long black hair. At ten years of age the oldest child in the family, Mariannie always dressed neatly and tidily for church, but today was a special Sunday and her mother was helping her look just right. Mariannie and her eight-year-old brother Arnie were both to be presenters in the *kalwen*, a quarterly review of the Sunday School lessons from the previous three months.

Arnie bounced back into the one-room house from taking his shower and rummaged around in the modest collection of toiletries on a small shelf near the front door. When his mother asked him what he wanted, he held up a tube of his father's hair gel and showed it to her with a glint in his eye. As soon as he had filled his hands with the stuff (and a bit too much of it), his grandmother told him to fetch her the baby's biscuit, his bottle and a clean cloth diaper from across the room. A whimper and a quick wipe of his hands through his hair later, Arnie was across the room, considering how he was going to manage the task of carrying the baby's things with his still-gooey hands. "Wait a second" (*kolyac*), his sister insisted as her mother secured the last barrette through the braid she had twisted atop her daughter's head. Mariannie stood up and, brushing past her brother, delivered the things unsullied to her grandmother.

The children's father walked in from behind the partition where he had been sleeping. "There's soup" (*oasr sup*), his wife said, gesturing with her head towards the cookhouse as she took the baby from her mother-in-law. Cousins of Mariannie and Arnie's, who lived in houses around the same courtyard, poked their heads in the door. "*Kom wi alu?*" (Are you going to church?) Emily asked as each one appeared. "Hurry up and get dressed if you're going!" (*Ssuhlahklahk som ahkolah*), she ordered. Mariannie and Arnie's father, still sleepy, had stretched out again on the cool, cleanly swept linoleum near where his wife nursed their baby. "*Kom wi alu?*" she asked him as the others were preparing to leave. "I'm tired. I'll go in the afternoon" (*Nnga ullac, nga wi tahfuhn lwen tok*), he replied.

Around the family courtyard, as Emily, Mariannie and Arnie waited for their ride, the phrase *Kom wi?*—which literally translates as "You with?"—rang out as the extended family of elderly brothers and sisters, with their children, grandchildren and other relatives, organized the trip to church. Pickups and sedans filled with people set out at different intervals for the mile-long bounce down the dirt road to the Lelu village church. Along the way, the stream of friends and neighbors making their way to the morning service on foot were invited to squeeze in with those already getting rides. The standard invitation *Kom wi?* would be yelled out, the appreciative pedestrians either running to climb into the slowing pick-up or waving the vehicle on. Amidst the busy comings and goings of Kosraean life, the little, ever-present phrase, *Kom wi?* helps people keep track of one another's activities and also helps them in their efforts to help each other.

On any Sunday, Kosraeans pay a lot of attention to who is (or isn't) participating in church events. The following four sections discuss church participation more fully, particularly as it relates to concepts of knowledge display and status. Meanwhile, it is worth noting here that participation is similarly important in small-scale, informal events as well. In the story just recounted, Arnie's participation in the care of his baby brother, although limited to something as minimal as fetching a baby's bottle, nevertheless indicates that he has responsibilities in this arena of activity and is acting obediently to fulfill them. However, as this example shows, participation in itself is not the only thing that is important. Just *how well* one participates sometimes matters, too. With his hands all full of hair goo, Arnie could be judged to be less competent than his sister.[9] Participation, knowledge displays, and status can often be tightly intertwined.

At Church

Presenting the kalwen. Standing before the assembled congregation, Arnie's wiry little eight-year-old body was as tall and poised as he could make it. Between him and the distant doors of the simple whitewashed building, hundreds of tightly packed people looked up at him: the men of Lelu village from the pews on his left, the women from the pews on his right, and the children from the woven pandanus mats in the large area directly before him. They were gathered for the quarterly *kalwen*, a review of the Sunday School lessons of the previous thirteen weeks. Arnie was well prepared, along with other children representing each of the Junior Sunday School classes, to give his short summary of part of one week's lesson. He held the microphone steadily in his hand and spoke clearly about Jesus' miracle with loaves and fishes. When he finished, he hesitated for a moment and then turned just a bit the wrong way before correcting himself and heading off to his right. Arnie's earnestness succumbed to a wide smile, and he trucked to his sideline position to the accompaniment of the congregation's light chuckles.

The next boy in line had already started to speak. Midway through his recitation, he halted, eyes searching the wide spaces around him for words that didn't come. He began again from the beginning, this time finishing smoothly. When the next presenter, a small eight-year-old, took the microphone, he delivered his carefully memorized lines in a big, bellowing voice tinged with an accent affected just for the performance. Laughter rang out from the church into the quiet of the cloudy and peaceful Sabbath day. Up until this point, today's *kalwen* had been especially sober, with child after child—even if stumbling over words or forgetting a line—giving a serious performance. This deliberate bit of humor made today's event more like the adult *kalwen*, where occasional clownish elements—funny voices, exaggerated enunciation, dramatic postures—are uniquely what produce audience responses.

Kosraeans laugh and comment when a presenter is notably funny. But, generally, the audience for the *kalwen* gives no other indication of the quality of individual performances. This is not to say that Kosraeans do not recognize the characteristics of a good *kalwen*. At the first adult *kalwen* I attended, a friend seated next to me whispered to me, after one woman had just finished, "*Aenpat!*" The word *aenpat* is from the English "iron pot," an implement introduced to Kosrae by Westerners in the last century. Along with "fry," these words for new and popular cooking styles came to refer to something especially good or likable— something that is in its own way delicious.[10] My friend at the *kalwen* that day was informally acting as my guide, helping me as a newcomer understand what Kosraeans already know about *kalwen* presentations. She elaborated on what she had meant by referring to the presentation as *aenpat*: the woman spoke in loud voice, her speech itself was "nice" (*kahto*), and overall it was *suhmaht*.

Except in unusual circumstances, very little gets said about the quality of church performance. My friend did not afterwards congratulate the presenter she had admired on a job well done. No one offered any praise to Arnie or to Mariannie, who had both given fine *kalwen* presentations, as the children sauntered home from church that day. Instead, the Sunday after the *kalwen*, all the two dozen or so children who had presented, including Arnie and Mariannie, received the small prize of $1.00 each for their participation in the event. Before passing out the money, the adult leader of the Sunday School joked with the children that their prizes were nothing more than an ordinary banana, worth little other than as a token of their involvement. On the same day, Arnie and Mariannie also received certificates of recognition for their perfect attendance in the previous quarter's Sunday School classes. For both the *kalwen* and Sunday School more generally, importance is placed almost exclusively on the fact of participation itself, not on a relative quality—for example, good versus bad—attributed to the participation.

Knowledge displays in Sunday school. Mariannie and Arnie's church participation began early. In infancy, Kosraean children are carried by their mothers and grandmothers into the main Sunday morning service, where they are held and nursed during hymns, homilies and offerings.[11] Past toddlerhood, children take part in "little church" (*alu srihsrihk*) services that parallel the adult services and are held in an adjacent building. Siblings hold on to squirmy younger participants, who anticipate the jubilant singing that sometimes drowns out the adult services in the building nearby. Like the adults, Kosraean children are encouraged to stay for Sunday School after the service. Mariannie and Arnie are in the junior section of the children's Sunday School, which is almost identical in format to the adult version. After songs, prayer, and an introduction to the lessons, the children break up into small, same-sex groups.

Mariannie is seated with her small group on the large expanse of hand-woven mats in the "little church" building on this Sunday. The Sunday School teacher has just finished taking roll; twelve of the twenty girls assigned to this group are present today. One of their two teachers, who also teaches sixth grade at the local elementary school, has just delivered a baby and will not be back for a few weeks. Lucinia, the teacher there today, does not read English and has not prepared the lesson, which comes from a booklet distributed by an American association for Bible study. So, after taking roll, instead of giving an explanation of the day's lesson, Lucinia sits quietly, saying nothing to the twelve ten-year-old girls who smack gum, occasionally whisper, and sometimes get up and talk to a friend in another group. It is not too unusual for a teacher to sit quietly with her group like Lucinia does today; no one comments or seems to mind.

Around the large room, the teachers for the other groups are very softly and monotonously delivering the week's lesson. Today it is from Genesis, about Joseph in Egypt during the great famine.[12] Many of the students in these groups seem to be no more involved than those in Mariannie's group. Yet, in spite of this apparent inattention, the teachers never comment, never tell the students to look up, to be quiet, to stay put, to remove their gum. They continue their lesson and at the end of their explanations ask their students some review questions. Almost always, at least one or two of the students offer answers; if they don't, the teacher simply provides the answer herself and then moves on to another question.

Once the small-group lessons are over, the whole Junior Sunday School reconvenes. Mariannie squeezes in between two of her friends on the girls' side of the room, a sea of colorful polyester dresses and large, lacy hair bows that contrasts with the plain shirts and slacks worn by the boys. The leader has taken the microphone at the front of the church and quiets the room. Before posing his own questions about the day's lesson, he urges the children to be bold in offering answers, arranges a little competition between the girls and boys, and emphasizes the importance of wisdom (*lalmwetmwet*) in living a good life. His first question goes to the boys. After a sixth grader stands up and gives the answer, the leader teases by repeating what the boy has just said in a comical, almost mocking voice. The children all laugh.

It's the girls' turn. "Who was Joseph's wife?" (*Kuh suc muhtwacn kiacl Joseph?*), the leader asks. Mariannie whispers the answer, and says it again louder as her neighbor, Shirline, turns to her for a confirmation. When the other girls around them tacitly agree, Shirline stands up and answers, "Asenath." The questions continue to go back and forth, to the boys and to the girls, for a few more turns until it is time for songs before announcements and the final prayer.

The collaborative nature of answering questions—of displaying knowledge—that we have seen with Mariannie, Shirline, and their friends is characteristic of Sunday School life and of church life more generally. However, it is more than the collaboration itself—Mariannie helping Shirline—that makes this example interesting. In it, as in other knowledge display events within the institutional domain of the church, knowledge displays are not used to hold *individuals* accountable for demonstrating what they know. The students who answer questions are not part of a system that, in the short run, is trying to determine individual levels of learning and to distinguish one person from another, as would be characteristic in school. Although the cultural transmission events themselves are very school-like—lectures, memorization, question and answer, and even overt competition—the accountability is not. As long as *someone* answers the question, filling the slot for this behavior, then everyone has acted appropriately within the structure of church activities. The agenda has been carried forward. In a sense, one person's knowledge display is as good as everyone's.

Processes of cultural transmission within the church embody the notion that there will always be many opportunities to learn church-related material. A Kosraean ideally spends a lifetime participating in religious activities in which Biblical passages and stories will be revisited again and again. Mariannie will hear of Joseph's prophesying and his marriage to the Egyptian high priest's daughter in other lessons in the years to come. Mariannie's familiarity with the person of Asenath on this Sunday comes from having read the pertinent scripture earlier in the week with her family.[13] In the face of *kung fu* videos and other contemporary distractions, Mariannie's family still practices the Kosraean tradition of reading together most mornings and evenings from the Bible. Her great-grandfather, who died around the time she was born, was a well-beloved, longtime pastor on the island; many of her older relatives who live in her family compound act to uphold the standards set by the pastor for Christian devotion and service to the church.

Knowledge displays in a lifetime of church participation. Mariannie and Arnie's early church experiences lay the foundation for patterns of knowledge display that span a lifetime on Kosrae. While still children, they will have had practice with types of display, such as the *kalwen*, that are both in form and in meaning almost identical to those in which adults regularly participate. Even at their young age, Mariannie and Arnie understand that knowledge displays within the church are intrinsic to participation in the church, signifying an individual's commitment to what Kosraeans consider to be the Christian way of life. By attending services and Sunday School, and by participating fully in the range of activities which are part of these regular church events, they affirm both their own commitment and the general importance of the church within Kosraean society.

For Kosraeans of any age, participation in church activities is synonymous with learning; as is said with regard to these activities, one learns by doing, and by doing one learns. Kosraeans have the opportunity to return to these learning activities again and again during their lives, with no one being considered too old or inexperienced to join in the process. Furthermore, within the institutional structure of the church there is no judgment or relative value placed on the efforts of those who do participate. In discussing the requirement that lay persons conduct services in the process of becoming full members of the church, one pastor said to me that the only thing he could think of that would count as doing a "bad job" under such circumstances would be saying or doing something directly against the teachings of the church.

Even though learning and participation, as part of a closely intertwined bundle, are emphasized within the church, there is also great flexibility and tolerance for those who for whatever reason do not participate fully in church activities. An adult who feels inadequate to the task of preparing a commentary or leading a service will be given a great deal of encouragement and time. Those who have left the church outright and spent years or even decades in oppositional behavior[14] are always given opportunities to return to the congregation. The ultimate purpose of the Kosraean Church is always emphasized: to provide for all Kosraeans the means to attain salvation and everlasting life (*moul ma paht paht*). Kosraeans do not see salvation, however, as strictly an individual matter. Although everyone must individually choose his or her own path (*inkacnek*), it is up to everyone else to encourage choice of the right path.

Thus, knowledge displays serve a very particular purpose in the Kosraean Church. They are the means by which Kosraeans, both young and old, gain experience in performing what is considered to be a basic and essential social function. To be able to skillfully and successfully explicate scriptures for others, to be able to guide them to understanding religious truths and prescriptions for living, are responsibilities that ideally all Kosraeans share. Knowledge displays seen as such fit within a scheme of *service*, to particular others and to the community at large. Even at the ages of three and four, young Kosraean children learn to speak publicly, to take seriously the scriptural admonition that all take up the responsibility of preaching God's word.

Within such a framework, Mariannie and Arnie are free from being characterized as especially "good" or especially "bad" at being part of their church. Regardless of their performance in the *kalwen* and similar events, they are received as legitimate participants in church activities. Their acceptance and inclusion is not predicated on particular types of performance, and they are not differentially situated in the church based on their presentations. While display of her knowledge could lead someone like Mariannie to a more prominent role in the church later in life, there are no letter grades, no higher or lower sections, and no serious consequences to those who fail to offer, for example, answers to the questions asked by the leader during a Sunday School lesson. The same is true for adults. Questions posed by Sunday School leaders have the rhetorical quality of not requiring an answer and leave all attendees free from obligation to display declarative knowledge of the Biblical text. Knowledge displays within the church are more about service than about stratifying people based on their demonstrated competence.

Knowledge displays and status in the church. While the display of knowledge in the church functions to serve as an ideal of Christian responsibility, there is also within the Kosraean church an elaborate organizational structure that specifies a large number of leadership positions. Election or appointment to these positions depends on many factors; one of these is a person's proven ability to speak publicly and explain well to others. Status within the church, then, does depend *in part* on knowledge displays. Mariannie and Arnie's Great Uncle Peter, active in the church today, studied scripture carefully during his youth with his father, the pastor. Throughout the many and varied events which call on congregation members to present on scriptural matters, Peter has always shown a depth and clarity of understanding. His appointment as a lay minister reflects this.

Knowledgeability, as demonstrated within the knowledge display events organized within the church, is only a part of what makes for status ascent within the church. Kosraeans view a person's knowledgeability in terms of how this knowledge is *used*. When asked about how they choose their leaders, Kosraeans speak of looking for persons who have lived lives of service to their church and community. They look for persons who actively serve others and who serve as examples of upright Christian living.[15] Any church leader, including a pastor, who does not maintain these standards is removed from his or her position.

There are other important ways in which the consequence of knowledge displays in status ascent within the church is reduced or attenuated. For one, there is no single or deciding display event, no one *kalwen* or worship service, which determines how one's ability is judged. Kosraeans come to know each other over the course of a lifetime. These lifetimes are characterized by countless changes in levels of involvement with and commitment to the church. Very little meaning is attributed to isolated events, and judgments of character as well as knowledgeability accrue very slowly and also very tentatively. Many high-status persons within the church today spent years as sinners, completely "outside" church guidelines and practice (*muhtuhn alu*). Devoted churchgoers of one year might become quite uninvolved the next. Church participation on Kosrae is characterized by extreme flexibility, and this affects the way in which behavior in church activities at any given time is judged.

Another important reason that knowledge displays take on less significance in determining church status is that there is an assumption that *everyone* can and will, in time, learn. Throughout the many events and activities sponsored by the church, none, even those intended specifically as training or instruction, has something analogous to a school examination. Without deadlines and schedules for when learning should take place, there is little reason to evaluate individuals to see if they have grasped the material. Without this kind of systematic and regular means of holding persons accountable for displaying what they have individually learned, there is no standard by which to compare persons to one another. What this means is that no one ever fails at church because of inadequate knowledge displays. Those who seem to be doing well at any moment are, in the long view, not necessarily considered to be doing much better than their peers.[16]

Finally, although knowledge of the Bible and Christian theology matters in the selection of pastors and other church leaders, humility in one's demeanor and attitude toward others matters perhaps more. No one who "makes like a big shot" (*orek big shot*) gains status within the church; campaigning, even for the most administrative and temporary of elected church offices, always backfires. It has become standard on Kosrae for pastors to be chosen from among those who have received special training at divinity schools or special institutes elsewhere in the Pacific or the United States. In a way, these persons' "knowledge displays" become embodied in the certificates they hold. Although these credentials are influential in the process of selecting pastors, everyone realizes that they are only one part of this process. Among the few who have been able to get theological training off-island, far fewer—perhaps three or four within each generation—are accorded the status of pastor in the Kosraean church. Knowledge displays figure crucially but in a highly circumscribed way into the judgments that affect this kind of status achievement.

At School

Little things (knowledge displays) making big differences. "These are the smartest kids of all," jokes a young teacher recently returned from college in Hilo, Hawaii. He has just finished teaching a period of English composition, forty minutes of drilling on grammatical rules with the lowest ability-grouped section of the third grade at the elementary school barely a hundred yards from Mariannie and Arnie's house. Arnie is one of the pupils in this class. Another teacher comes into the classroom, and the two continue, above the drumming of rain on the school building's tin roof, to make humorous comments to me about the abilities of these children. At this school of 650 students, serving the largest municipality on the island, tracking begins in the third grade. Based on their grade-point averages at the end of the first quarter, the children are regrouped into equivalent-sized class sections, and everyone at the school is acutely aware of who is considered to be smart and who is not. The teachers talking to me during my visit to Arnie's class, rather than merely poking fun, were doing a very culturally appropriate thing: they were making light of something they saw as inescapably true and regrettable and thereby lightening the burden of this fact.

However, the burden of this "fact"—that while some children are smart, others unavoidably are not—seems to be relative to the setting.[17] The Arnie and Mariannie that we have seen in church, for example, are very different from the Arnie and Mariannie of school. In church, they participate in activities where they read, recite, present, answer questions, and display their knowledgeability overall in ways that are very similar to those in the school—but their participation does not result in their relegation to distinct categories such as good or bad, smart or dumb, "A" level or "C" level. The quality of their participation is not scrutinized for such purposes. Rather, their participation itself, according to Kosraean cultural assumptions about their church, brings its own rewards: knowledge, wisdom, goodness, service, salvation.[18] In church, Arnie and Mariannie are essentially equals. Both children participate and, without question, benefit from their participation, as do other church-goers on the island.

In school, however, their lives diverge. Mariannie is in the "A" section, the best student among the best; Arnie is assigned to section "C," reserved for the lowest achievers. When visiting his third-grade class, I see the same energetic, inquisitive Arnie I know from other settings. On certain days he looks out the window a bit more frequently, talks to his friends a little longer, or blurts out an answer with less worry as to whether it is right or wrong than do some of his peers. When it comes time to take tests, he may be a few facts—or a few increments of savvy, or maybe just a few seconds of attention—away from the leading edge of the third grade. Still, he reads and writes, subtracts and adds, and multiplies. For Arnie, and for other children like him, the problem is not that they are not participating or not learning, but that their knowledge displays are used to document their comparative inadequacy. Simply put, others in the third grade display their knowledge better. This means that even though Arnie's behavior is substantially just like that of other children his age, Arnie belongs to a group of students identified as C-level, as slow, or—like little Sepe, who didn't say her name—as *puhlakfohn*. By contrast, Mariannie, who sits in the front row of her fifth-grade class, away from friends, earns the label *suhmaht* (smart). The worst and the best students at the school are indistinguishable except for a few occasional and usually unremarkable behaviors.

These small distinctions can easily get turned into very large differences in children's lives. As Kosrae makes a transition from its traditional subsistence economy to a cash-based economy, schooling has come to matter more and more on the job market. A high income is viewed as the key to a high-quality life, all the more so as the island becomes more populous and as Kosraeans come to depend more on Western technology and goods. Like elsewhere in the world, school grades and academic reputation are used in job placement. Changes in the demography and economy on Kosrae are making jobs more scarce just as more and more young people are finishing school, untrained in traditional ways, hoping against the odds to land a job to earn the wages that increasingly provide the primary means for what is considered to be an attractive life. The high rates of alcoholism and suicide among the young on Kosrae and elsewhere in Micronesia are often attributed to this process of the loss of the old combined with the elusiveness of the new.[19]

Such concerns may be far from young Arnie's mind, but they nonetheless affect his life. When I first meet Arnie and his family and mention that I am interested in the lives of Kosraean children, I am told that Mariannie is very smart, but Arnie is very stupid. "He likes to play too much at school," the adults in his family say. His father, mindful of the information distributed by Kosrae's Public Health Service, suggests that maybe he was not breastfed long enough; this could account for his slowness. Mariannie, on the other hand, offers more hope. Her family would like to see her spend some of her school years in the United States, perfecting her English skills and getting situated even more solidly at the top of her academic echelon. This would improve her chances for high-level employment and gaining the means to contribute financially to her family.[20]

Both in school and out of school, Arnie's classification as a poor student follows him around. This is not the case all of the time. As a playmate or brother or Sunday School speaker or apprentice gardener—during many of the activities of his everyday life—Arnie is free from the burden of his reputation, from being talked about and treated as though he were stupid. But this classification, borne of the evaluative moments characterizing school knowledge displays, is always available for others to use in accounting for Arnie's inadequacies. In this way, school spills over into other domains of the little boy's life. Its ready, standardized categories—such as grade point averages or number of years completed—make it easy to compare brother to sister, elder to child, even local to outsider. Its foreign origins simultaneously make it almost impossible not to make such comparisons; the material and technological superiority of the industrialized world testifies to the intrinsic worth of its institutional ways. Schooling, seen uncritically as the primary vehicle for economic and social advancement, sets an unassailable standard for ways of measuring, categorizing, and treating individual persons.

When Arnie is held up to the universal yardstick of schooling, he is found wanting. In church, he is not. Without institutionalized forms of comparisons among children, which stigmatize some on the basis of their knowledge displays, church invites Arnie to participate at his own pace. The results of this are evident. Even among the children who are quietest in church, none is identified as a failure; none is said to fail to learn to read the Bible, to fail to learn to sing hymns, to fail to be a knowledgeable member of the church community. The pervasiveness on Kosrae of the ability to read the Bible—a particularly impressive form of literacy—stands as a tribute to the success, for all participants, of the system of learning embedded in church life.[21] Yet little Arnie, away from the church and closer to settings governed by the logic of schooling, is reminded in numerous ways on most days that he is less than others when it comes to just how *suhmaht* he is. Just as participation in church life amounts to learning, participation in school life, for half the children, amounts to indications of their inadequacies in learning and knowing. Arnie experiences this daily.

A story about stars. One of Mariannie and Arnie's cousins, Kimberly, a fourth grader who lives in the house adjacent to theirs, also received an award for perfect attendance in Sunday School this quarter. I come to know her from the play areas around her house, from her neighborhood children's choir, and from her presentations in church. Her parents and older sisters are my friends. During one of my visits to the municipal elementary school, the fourth-grade English reading teacher, Melinda, welcomes me to spend time observing in her classroom. Like Arnie's teachers, Melinda laments the differences in abilities among her students. After my first hour there, spent quietly taking notes in the corner, Melinda tells me that I had just observed Section A; the students she will be teaching after the short break are the Section C students, and they really have problems. Several of the Section C students, in Melinda's view, belong in an even lower category: in "special," as Kosraeans refer to special education classes. Melinda identifies Kimberly as one of these students.

Melinda offers an explanation of her Section C students. "These aren't the ones whose parents work in the government, or have those good jobs, like the students in Section A." Melinda never elaborates on any reasons why this would be so, although she repeats her theory many times. As we go through her class lists over the next few days, it becomes clear to me that children with parents in the government's employ, generally earning the highest wages on the island, are distributed fairly equally among the three fourth-grade sections. Two of the four children, including Kimberly, who are named as needing "special" have fathers with exceptionally high-status and high-paying jobs. In spite of its inaccuracy, I am struck by how sensible Melinda's theory seems. It fits squarely with common-sense views in the United States and elsewhere that students categorized as lower achievers are intrinsically disadvantaged because of their social or genetic backgrounds. Even in a place like Kosrae, where terms like race, class, and socioeconomic status are relatively meaningless, people struggle to account for low-ranked students as belonging to a social category that makes them inherently deficient.

Melinda has what seems to be proof of the lower achievers' deficiencies posted on her wall. For each of the fourth-grade sections, there is a large sheet of construction paper with the names of the students listed down the left side. Each time a child raises his or her hand and answers one of the teacher's questions correctly, that child earns a shiny metallic star that goes alongside his or her name on the chart. Some of the children have long rows of stars beside their name; a few of the children have none. At a glance anyone can see who does the best in each section, and how the sections compare. Students in Section C have far fewer stars than those in other sections, and, of course, Section

A students accumulate the most of these symbolic indications of their successful knowledge displays.

I watch closely for a week, counting raised hands, right answers, posted stars. In Section A, four children—Nolte, Jennie A., Jennie H., and Selpalik—lead the pack, accumulating several stars each. It is late May, near finals time, and there are lots of questions being posed by the teacher during review of the semester's material. Section C looks quite similar to Section A in many respects. Hands shoot up, nearly yanking children out of their seats whenever it seems the teacher is about to ask a question. The children on whom she calls give good answers, but there are some differences between the two sections. Although in section C she includes the same material in her review, Melinda lectures more, *asking fewer questions*. More importantly, *fewer children ask for or are offered stars* after giving the right answer.

Conrad has the most number of stars in Section C. Conrad seems to understand better than some others the stakes in the classroom each day. He attends acutely to his classmates' moves in the knowledge-display race. Today Conrad has gotten off to a bad start, having gotten caught not knowing his place in the textbook. Other students jump in when he hesitates, lost, after the teacher asks him to read the selection. The lesson continues. Two other children successfully define vocabulary words, and Conrad finally gets his chance to do the same. Rather than giving a memorized English definition, Conrad negotiates with the teacher to let him describe the meaning of the word, free-form, in Kosraean. Even he knows that although he gave a reasonable rendition of the meaning of the word, this marginal performance doesn't deserve a star. As the lesson proceeds, twice more his hand shoots up first, and both times his answer is wrong. The teacher then asks for the meaning of the word "busy." As soon as Nadine, a slight girl who sits next to Kimberly, is called on, Conrad complains, "Hey, I had my hand up before you!" (*nga pihsrpihsr liki kom*). Nadine recites, "Busy: full of activity." The teacher offers her a star. As she slips by Conrad's seat to add this star, her third for the entire school year, to the chart after her name, Conrad mutters, "I'm going to kill you!"[22]

Rema, the quietest girl in the class, has no stars on the chart on the wall. Melinda is continuing the review of the story in the students' reader. "Name three of the characters," Melinda directs. "Rema, *fahk sie*" (say one of them), she tells the quietest girl in the room. Rema asks, very much to the point, "*Mwet?*" (people?). Once the teacher affirms her interpretation of the term "characters," Rema says "Mother," giving a fine answer to a question regarding a story about a young boy's love for his parents. Melinda says, "Very good," and Rema says nothing. She finishes the fourth grade without ever getting a star by her name.

Rema, Kimberly, and other children like them will continue to learn to do many varied and interesting things in their lives. They will most likely remain active participants in the church, and will use their abilities to read and write, to present and analyze, in a lifetime of service to that institution. They will also continue to help in the cleaning, cooking, gardening and sewing, the planning and administrating that are part of family life, becoming gradually more competent in these skills as the years go by. But they will probably leave school as soon as possible, having already learned by the age of nine that they are inevitably losers in a contest where the success of some is defined by the mandated failure of others. Moments of knowledge display, and the fallout from these moments, are at the core of this stratification process.

At Home

Caring: Doing it, learning it, knowing it, showing it. The arrival of Mariannie's baby brother Castro closely followed the birth of three other babies in the cluster of houses where Mariannie and her extended family live. When Arnie, her younger brother, was born, Mariannie at the age of two was too young to help much with child care. Two other younger siblings, both girls, were reluctantly given to friends and family—adopted out, as is customary on Kosrae in certain situations.[23] For Mariannie, then, Castro is the first baby for whom she can assume significant responsibility. As the oldest daughter in the family, she takes such responsibilities very seriously.

Like other Kosraean children, Mariannie has been in training for these responsibilities for a long time. Even as a two-year-old, she helped care for babies in rudimentary ways, fetching things, noticing the babies' needs, following whatever simple instructions she could. Although mothers are typically the primary caregivers, infant care is shared among closely residing relatives on Kosrae, and nearly every household has a baby about, at least some of the time. Mariannie has been at the periphery of baby care for years, and now she is ready to move to a more central position, taking more charge in this activity of seeing to an infant's well-being. Adding to her responsibilities, Mariannie's mother works at one of the island's largest retail stores until seven o'clock or later most evenings. While her mother is working, Mariannie's grandmother, Emily, has charge of the new infant. But after school, on weekends, and during holidays, Mariannie gets very involved.

On this particular evening, Castro is just three months old. Emily is across the courtyard bathing, and Mariannie is providing for all of Castro's needs during this time: giving him his bottle, arranging his bedding, changing his soiled clothes, carrying him and comforting him with swaying and songs. When Emily returns from bathing, Mariannie moves to other activities. Emily, as an adult, is presumed to be more able in caregiving and automatically steps into this role.

In family life, as in church, participation leads to learning; no one worries that over time children will fail to become increasingly more competent at producing goods, providing services, orchestrating events, and doing what else is required of adults in daily domestic life. Doing and learning go hand in hand. Mariannie both cares for Castro and learns about caring for Castro in the moments when she is involved in doing so. As Mariannie participates in Castro's care, not only is she doing and learning, she is also showing to others that she is competent in this activity; she is displaying her knowledge. Over time, on the basis of these steady and implicit demonstrations, her responsibilities become greater and greater. This is the fundamental mode of cultural transmission, of participation and learning, in family life. It is also a mode of status ascent, of moving from being less like a child to being more like an adult.

However, there can be complications in this process. There are times when the move from a more peripheral to a more central place in an activity will not take place without a bit of a push on the part of the person making the move. These "pushes" include forms of knowledge displays. Once Emily has returned to care for Castro, Mariannie's further involvement is dependent on Emily's authority in this matter. If Emily asks Mariannie to help, and if Mariannie does so according to her instructions, then all goes smoothly. If Mariannie tries to do more than this, however—to assume responsibility that her grandmother has not given her—then she has a burden of proof; she must bid for this additional responsibility and do so by indicating its advantages. We see this type of event as we set about to play a game of cards later this evening.

A game of cards: participation, knowledge displays and status. Mariannie is playing solitaire while Emily holds Castro, trying to put him to sleep at the other side of the room. Arnie moves about, watching what each of them are doing, dabbling in this and that for a moment or two at a time. As is typical of Kosraean homes, there is little, if any, furniture in this room. Most activities are conducted on the floor, with mats, blankets, or pillows used when needed. Over the past few nights, the family has been enjoying card games together here, and tonight I suggest to Mariannie that we play the one game I recognize, Crazy 8's.

As we begin to get organized to play, it becomes clear that there are three preliminaries that need to be attended to: Emily must decide what to do about Castro, the playing space needs to be prepared, and the game participants need to be determined. Emily voices all three issues, giving instructions about the first two and asking Mariannie about the third. In matters of childcare and housekeeping, Emily has clear authority: she tells us to gather around where she is sitting with Castro so that she can keep holding him while we all play, and she tells Mariannie to sweep the floor in this area so that our playing surface is clean. Mariannie protests. Her main concern is about Castro, and several times she suggests that instead of in Emily's arms the baby would be better off on his pillow and mat. When she brings his bedding to where we are sitting, Emily orders her to push it away. Mariannie ultimately does what she is told, but meanwhile she has made several bids, all unsuccessful, to assume more responsibility in caring for Castro this evening. Tonight she remains peripheral in the baby's care, under the authority of someone older and generally more able. Nonetheless, Mariannie's accumulating experience in caring for Castro is also the impetus for a change in her status—and a change in her status depends on a display of her knowledgeability in this regard.

Although Mariannie must defer to Emily on matters of childcare, she is readily given control of organizing the game. On Kosrae, as elsewhere, being regarded as less knowledgeable in some areas does not necessarily mean being regarded as less knowledgeable in others. In playing cards, Mariannie is a skilled scorekeeper, clear on all the rules of the game and attentive during the play. Even though Emily expresses skepticism about Arnie joining in the game, several times questioning whether or not he knows how to play, she defers to Mariannie's judgment to include him.

When Arnie sees that Mariannie has drawn up the score sheet to include him, he repeats with anticipation, "Let's see who the winner will be. Let's see who the winner will be" (*akuhtuhn mwet se itto*). Arnie is in search of favorable comparisons to others, looking to tonight's game as a validation of his skill or knowledge, or even his luck. He has assumed a dual burden: first, he must maintain his legitimacy as a participant in the game by displaying his knowledge of how to play; second, he must try to win. As soon as the game begins, Arnie begins to suffer. He hesitates to lay a card down when it is his turn, and both his sister and grandmother find fault with this. When he plays an eight, he is reminded to change the suit. Changing it to spades, he hears his grandmother joke, "Spades! He probably doesn't even have any!" in a reference to what would be Arnie's least strategic move. Arnie does his best to keep up, avoiding playing out of turn by asking "Me?" (*nga?*) prior to each of his plays. He stays in the game, coached by his sister a bit, but he is still vulnerable both to loss and to expulsion.

Hand after hand, Arnie does, in fact, lose. Once, after a particularly disappointing round, he tries to change the game to another simpler game he has played more often and is more likely to win. His sister ignores his request. By now, Emily has temporarily left the game, moving to another part of the room to lay Castro down to sleep. After yet another loss, Arnie checks the score sheet and tries to change the "game" again, this time by kicking his sister and curling up on the floor. His efforts to change the activity prove effective. Mariannie calls their grandmother's attention to what has happened, and Arnie becomes the main topic of discussion and the focus of activity, even while he is quietly collapsed on the floor.

Arnie's behavior is interpreted as evidence of his insufficient knowledge of the game, and also his insufficient knowledge of how to behave well. He has demonstrated a *lack* of the knowledge needed to improve his status either as a card player or as a competent social actor. His grandmother scolds him, repeatedly emphasizing that if he did not know how to play he should not have joined in the game. He has violated a basic rule of family life: a person should not try to do more than he or she can do. The long period of apprenticeship that is necessary for learning the duties and responsibilities of daily life on Kosrae is predicated on the assumption that learning will ultimately take place. But learning comes with time, and individuals must establish their knowledgeability before taking on responsibility. For Arnie tonight, this logic has created a tension. He has not struck an acceptable balance between doing and learning, knowing and showing.

Tonight's card game presents an especially tricky situation for Arnie. Unlike most family activities, the card game is discrete; one is either playing or one is not. Such games are generally not structured for incrementally increasing participation. Furthermore, games are intrinsically competitive, designed to highlight differences in skill among participants. Games are activities both bracketed apart from much of the rest of ordinary activity and structured to identify winners and losers. They are, in many ways, like school exams. In participating in the card game tonight, Arnie again found himself at the lowest end of a hierarchy, clearly identified as a loser based on his knowledge displays.

Most of the time in family life Arnie does not get marked in this way. He participates in a range of activities, both playful and serious, that allow him a safe place in which to act and to learn. Around the house, if his grandmother or parents complain about him, it is usually because he has been lazy or disobedient, not because he has demonstrated a lack of knowledge. Tonight, the situation was special, not just because it was a card game but because there was a foreigner, an American guest, present. My interest in playing the game made it especially important that Arnie not detract from it, that he play only if he knew how to behave like a fully competent player. Arnie's participation hinged on his knowledge displays especially because of this. When, after some time of the sulking and scolding, I ask Arnie if he would like to rejoin the game, my interest in his participation is clear to the others and readily accommodated. Arnie's grandmother tells him to rejoin the game, to sit closely in the circle between her and me. Instead of invoking a context where Arnie, like the aforementioned little Sepe, was to be judged on the basis of his knowledgeability, those present created something different. From this point forward, as the game went on, Arnie was treated like the little boy he was, on a path to learning more in all the areas of his life. Arnie's immediate world, within a moment, had changed: stupidity, failure, incompetence, and exclusion no longer loomed over him as threats.

The Story of Roger

For Mariannie and Arnie, as for starless Rema and the other children on Kosrae that we have seen, knowledge displays matter in a variety of settings in their lives. For the most part, however, it is only in school where knowledge displays are used in an immediately consequential way to label, sort, and categorize children. The influence of school does not always stay contained unto itself, however. It easily spills over into other domains of life, not only because its measures are so neat and clear but also because its rationale is so powerful. Schooling is seen as paving the road to modernity, as providing the means for sophistication, advancement, and the array of benefits associated with the industrialized world.

What will later become of Arnie, Rema, and the other students relegated to the lowest strata or margins of school life? By looking at a man named Roger, we see that the school's definition of knowledgeability is not omnipotent; those who are failures at school can be respected, useful and competent in other places in their lives. However, as Kosrae falls into step with the rest of the world, individuals increasingly experience the effects of being judged according to the standards of modernity and schooling. In Roger's case, this has been particularly harsh.

"Puhlakfohn!" (a stupid adult). "Hey, I saw your friend today," jokes Katsuo Isaac, Administrative Officer for Kosrae's Department of Education. We're a comical combination, Roger and me, and Katsuo chuckles about it every time he sees me. Roger is the janitor in the department. A man in his mid-forties, Roger's main job is to cut back the thick tropical vegetation that continually threatens to overtake the concrete and tin buildings on the departmental grounds. He is also called on to do a variety of jobs that others don't want. A hundred teachers and administrators boss him around all day, keeping him busier than almost anyone else. Roger is a warm and kindly person whom I have been happy to have as a friend. The library for which I worked during my time on Kosrae is near the main administrative offices and high school campus where Roger is kept busy.

I'm around a lot and I get to see a lot. Some of it isn't nice, in particular the many jokes at Roger's expense. One day, a few of the men in the building and maintenance division were throwing stones at Roger. He finds a way to laugh at many such abuses, but, even for someone with a disposition like Roger's, sometimes it's too much. During the construction of a new library facility, I often investigated the source of some group hilarity and found Roger to be the only one not laughing. It was never hard to figure out who the object of ridicule was.

Roger is the butt of almost all public jokes at the department. When a baseball team was being formed, the posting that listed the members included "Roger Abraham, Department of Education Executive Chief" as the captain, although Roger was not invited to be on the team. This was typical. When I asked, as I occasionally did, why Roger was disliked, I was told that he smelled bad because he never bathed. There were a few other things about Roger that were not mentioned: his slow, deliberate pattern of speech; a lazy eye that gave him a quizzical, cocked-head demeanor; his reputation for being dull.

People who see me talking with him say, "Hey, can he talk with you?" He is presumed not to speak English. While there are several department staff members who do not speak English, Roger speaks it fairly well, usually sticking with English even though I often speak to him in Kosraean. One day, he was not remembering the English word for "egg" and, instead of using the Kosraean *ahtro*, said to me: "You know, those white balls that come out of chickens, those little white balls." He laughed as he explained this, and when I said, "Oh, you mean eggs!" Roger laughed and laughed some more. Over the next few years, he several times recounted that incident to me with glee.

Tulpe and Mayleen are the other two custodians who work for the central office of the Department of Education. They sweep the floors of the main building, they clean the women's room, and they do some light work on the grounds, mostly cultivating flowers. They often say unflattering things about Roger. Although they share the same place in the organizational chart of the department with Roger, they dissociate themselves from him and his work.

As the new library was under construction, Roger asked if he could work inside the facility with our staff after it opened. He came into the still-incomplete building most workdays to sweep and clean. Sweeping is distinctly women's work on Kosrae. One day when we were alone in the office, Roger said that he would really like to work with the books. He told me that he never finished high school, only eighth grade, and even then, at 12:00 each day he would leave the campus and go back home. "I was bad; I didn't want to go. Now I want," he says.

He asks me if I can teach him "one word every day," saying, "If it's not fast, if it's one word at a time, I can do it." I pick up *Little Danny*

Dinosaur from my desk and he says, "Little," looking at the title page. He repeats the sounds of "Danny." Lee Roy, a co-worker, comes into the room, and Roger stops. When Lee Roy leaves Roger says, "Don't say about this to anyone." He takes the book home for the night. The next day he asks me to say his new word again, since he forgot. I suggest simple books in Kosraean written for first and second graders, and we continue the process of me repeating the words, at his request, over and over so that he can remember them. I emphasize the sounds and point at the consonants as I do. A lot of time when he is trying to "read," instead of looking at the book he is looking at me—my face, my eyes—for cues. After taking the book home for the night, Roger usually says that he has forgotten his new word the next day.

At some point he and I are talking about the kids he has seen in school, and he says, in reference to their academic work, "Those kids, they know how! No one taught them; they see it and they do it. They just know how!" It is one of many conversations of which I am a part wherein a Kosraean talks about who knows how to do what and how they might have come to learn it. Roger talks about these things as well. He comes from an accomplished family. One of his brothers was a municipal mayor for years; another is the twelfth-grade biology teacher who, for a time, was in medical school in Hawaii.

Roger often asks if I mind helping him. He also wonders if it's all right to be learning school things at his age. During one of these discussions he asks, in Kosraean, if it's true about the country-western musician Johnny Cash that "he knows how to sing but doesn't write or read" (*el etuh on; tiyac na sihm, rit*). He adds that he wonders "if it's TV lies." I say that I don't know, either, about Johnny Cash, but that it's quite possible; there are people in America who don't read. Roger's eyes get big and he breaks into a smile. "*Puhlakfohn!*" he exclaims.

As eagerly as Roger sought out duties in the library, the women custodians opposed an expansion of their duties to include the new library. They refused to help with library maintenance unless they were given overtime pay, something rarely available and not a possibility in this case. But even though others were not willing to do it, neither the departmental administration nor the library staff thought Roger was the right choice to clean the library. Because he was a man, he was unsuited for a job that is considered to be women's work; because he was Roger, he was unsuited to operate in a library. The woman who was organizing the circulation desk had worked in libraries for ten years. When Roger's name came up, she would say, "*El nihkihn*" (he doesn't know how to do these things).

Another side of Roger. One day, in the midst of these discussions, I walked past the foyer of the main department building and noticed something that surprised me. Roger was sitting on a locally fashioned bench holding the thigh of Mayleen, one of the two women custodians. Tulpe, the other woman custodian, sat nearby. People working in the department walked in and out. Everyone behaved as though the scene were normal. I came back for a second look. It was the first time I had seen physical contact between any man and woman, married or not, on Kosrae. This was a particularly surprising pair for such a public display. I walked up to them and asked Mayleen how she was. She said, "*Arlac ngal niyuhk*" (my leg really hurts). Roger added, "I make massage."

As I came to find out, Roger's talents as a healer were in high demand all over the island. There were many times, after that day, when Roger described to me his past evening or weekend by mentioning that there was an old man in one village or a sick person in another who needed to be massaged. Many days he came to work tired because he had been performing his healing massage late the night before. He sometimes mentioned that relatives of a sick person had come to his house in the deep of night seeking his help.

Modern Western medicine is practiced and very important on Kosrae. The hospital dispenses large volumes of antibiotics and pain killers every day. People often ask to be admitted into its wards if they are troubled by a stomach ache or other vague malady. Most babies are born in the hospital. But the predominance of Western medical techniques has not entirely displaced the indigenous healing tradition. The few who know and practice traditional medicine are still respected and sought out for their skills. Above and beyond the technical knowledge needed for traditional forms of healing, the personal characteristics of the healer—his or her wisdom, sensitivity, and willingness to help—matter a great deal. Reputations are based on both technical skills and character. People know who is good and who is not, and Roger is considered one of the best.

Roger kept busy in other ways as well. On occasion, when passing through the village where Roger lived, I would notice him working with a group of young teenage boys on some community-oriented project or another. I initially assumed that he was participating as a supervisor for some youth service group, but I was wrong. I came to learn that these projects were of Roger's own creation. He would have an idea of something that would be good to do and would organize a group to do it. Roger was the organization, and the young men would simply choose to give up an evening or a Saturday to work with him on his project.

One such project involved the dedication of the new library, which was being named in honor of Rose Mackwelung, the woman considered to be the mother of education in Kosrae.[24] The current generation of Kosrae's leaders were all her students. Since the library is part of the Education Department complex, Roger had the duty of getting the grounds in shape after the construction. It was part of his job, and he did it in the solitary fashion that was typical for him at work. Outside of work, though, he had the idea that Rose Mackwelung's grave site should be cleared and tended as well. Graves in Kosrae, particularly of those of respected elders, are carefully designed and elaborate, but they can easily get overgrown and obscured by the tropical vegetation. On the eve of the dedication of the library in her name, after his other work was done, Roger led a group of young men to beautify Rose Mackwelung's grave.

Making Rogers. The Roger we have seen clearing debris from the government construction site and the Roger cutting back vines from the grave of an honored friend are two different Rogers. The differences are not in the earnestness of his efforts, the capabilities he brings to the job, or the smile he has for passers-by. The differences do not really come from Roger. What we find, when we take a close look, is that Roger is made into different kinds of persons according to different sets of socially arranged criteria. These criteria are not natural; they are not given in the order of the world. Instead, the criteria used to classify and locate Roger—as someone to like, to avoid, to trust, or to humiliate—come from ways of talking and acting. These ways are part of culture, shaped by particular social institutions and brought to life in the day-to-day actions of ordinary people working together within these institutional frameworks.

Like Roger, all people are subject to being smart or dumb or simultaneously both, depending on what their culture makes possible. Different cultures allow for different kinds of persons and use a variety of criteria for making its people into what they are. On Kosrae, the kind of person most typically called *puhlakfohn* is a person who is made out to do badly at school. The rest of the time, Kosraeans use words like *puhlakfohn* and its opposite, *suhmaht*, not to label people but to describe particular actions. Under these circumstances, *puhlakfohn* and *suhmaht* don't stick; they are temporary and generally are important only as indicators of levels of progress rather than levels of personhood. Roger, when working as a healer or working as a part of his community, when away from schools and bureaucracies and other imported institutions with a particular sort of stigmatizing power, is not made into a fool.

Conclusion

Arnie and Mariannie, Sepe, Rema and Roger, along with the others we have seen on Kosrae, all share this same experience of being made into what they are by their culture. This process is not uniform throughout the many times and places of their lives. Different settings, operating by the varying logics of different institutions, shape the actions—the ways of talking, the ways of behaving—of the people in these settings. The actions of the people around them are what give particular shape to the lives of the individuals we have discussed here. At school, at home, and at church, Arnie is subject to different social processes for determining where he fits in relation to others. He can be ordinary, extraordinary, or not ranked at all, depending on the possibilities that are available within each of the pivotal institutions in his life. By comparing the workings of these institutions—school, family, church—this chapter has focused on presenting some of the culturally determined ways in which displays of knowledge situate persons within the culturally given range of possibilities.

Knowledge displays and the status they bring are a function of participation in activities within social institutions. In family and church on Kosrae, participation is seen as in itself leading to more competence. Everyone who participates learns. Knowledge displays serve, within the ordinary workings of family and church life, as indices of participation and learning. They are used primarily to include persons in more central positions of participation; they are used to allow persons to assume progressively higher levels of responsibility during the course of their lifetime. In the family, knowledge displays contribute to the means for survival; in church, they contribute to the goal of salvation (see figure 1).

Figure 1 Participation and Different Levels of Knowledge Display

Family Participation—>everyone:	doing —> survival learning knowing DISPLAYING never leads to nonparticipation
Church Participation—>everyone:	doing —> salvation earning knowing DISPLAYING rarely leads to nonparticipation
School Participation—>some:	learning knowing DISPLAYING —> stratification
—>some:	not learning not knowing (NOT) DISPLAYING often leads to nonparticipation

School works somewhat differently. Participation leads to the identification of some students as successes and the identification of others, if not as outright failures, as only marginally better. There are set limits to the time in which any individual can display that he or she has learned. Without the open-ended provisions characteristic of family and church, school participants risk becoming nonparticipants. Their time can run out. Although the aim of schooling ideally is education, when viewed from a perspective that includes both successes and failures the more practical outcome is economic and social stratification. Not making the grade amounts to forms of nonparticipation, in relation to both school and other domains of activity that make use of school certification.

Within any society, cultural knowledge necessarily includes as one of its subsets awareness of, and understanding about displaying, this knowledge. To evaluate what any person knows, those around that person must rely on displays. (No one anywhere has yet figured out how to get this information by looking inside someone else's head.) Kosrae is by no means exceptional as a place in the world where moments for the evaluation of people's knowledgeability are socially arranged. A day or two of watching will reveal multiple knowledge-display events in the lives of most North Americans, and this may be true throughout the world.

If we consider the varieties, at one end of the spectrum knowledge displays blend seamlessly into ordinary activity, emerging only when useful in determining where people best fit in the accomplishment of practical tasks. This is the type of activity in which Mariannie helps clean house, her cousins carry away weeds from a patch of farmland their father is clearing, or her mother rehearses the soprano part of a hymn for an upcoming church performance. In each case, knowledge displays help organize the activity by situating persons within it. At the other end of the spectrum, knowledge displays can operate as institutionally sanctioned schemes to categorize persons within rigid structures based on arbitrary criteria.[25]

Knowledge displays, as we have seen them on Kosrae and portrayed them in this chapter, generate evaluations. They give others the opportunity to call little Sepe *puhlakfohn* or to ordain her uncle a pastor. Evaluations are not ends in themselves, however. They are part of systems of consequences, resulting from knowledge displays, that typically cycle back into the processes that are responsible for the transmission of cultural knowledge. Rema's knowledge displays in school during one day are likely to affect what happens to her there the next day. In serving to situate and resituate persons in the activities of everyday life, knowledge displays shape the wide variety of forms of teaching and of learning culture by shaping the very structure of participation in human activity.

Notes

[1] The three basic elements of *knowledge display*, as I use the term here, are illustrated by what happened with Sepe. First, a situation is socially defined or organized so that someone is required to show to others some particular of what they know. Second, the person responds to this requirement. Third, there is an implicit or explicit evaluation of the person's response. Cf. Mehan (1978) on Initiation-Response-Evaluation schemes in American classroom lessons.

[2] In the type of socially focused analysis presented here, my use of the term *knowledgeability* is intended to refer only to what is evident and attended to by other social actors, not to refer to a "real" measure of the knowledge or ability someone has acquired and stored within their person.

[3] This approach derives from the work of a number of psychologists concerned with development (e.g., Rogoff, 1995) and cognition (e.g., Greeno, 1994), as well as the work of several cultural anthropologists (Lave and Wegner, 1991; McDermott, 1993; Spindler and Spindler, 1989).

[4] The population of Kosrae is now approaching 8,000.

[5] As cited in Ritter (1978).

[6] Operating according the democratic model of New England Congregationalism, the Kosraean church continued to directly or indirectly influence the selection of leaders and policies on the island, even as colonial governments—German, Japanese, and American—came and went.

[7] Kosrae was then part of the U.S. Trust Territory of the Pacific Islands, an entity established through a United Nations Trusteeship that gave Japan's former colonies in the Pacific to the United States. The Kennedy administration established a policy aimed, in part, at generating an identification on the part of Micronesians with the United States so that in a general plebescite islanders would chose to retain political affiliation with them. The right tool with which to effect this attitudinal change, to officials in the Department of Interior, was education (Peacock, 1990). Schools, staffed by American teachers or Peace Corps Volunteers, were built in most of the municipalities of the region.

[8] Ironically, for little Sepe this was premature. Within a year or so she would become like her cousins Conan and Minnie and the other half-dozen slightly older children of her neighborhood who have come to recognize a set of generic conditions for boldly pronouncing their own names. The first few days of kindergarten, with its drill on response to rudimentary questions like "What is your name?" would make this difference.

[9] Arnie, then, ended up in a situation very similar to Little Sepe's: he was given a task, others observed his performance, and his lack of success made him subject to a negative evaluation. For Arnie any negative consequences resulting from this event were implicit; no one yelled "*puhlakfohn*," gave him a swat, or gave him a failing letter grade. But a difference in status with his sister that centers on issues of competence could have been reinforced as a consequence of this interaction.

[10] A pretty new dress, for example, might bring the reaction "*fuhraei*" ("fry") from others seeing it for the first time.

[11] Frequently a baby is passed down the pew to another woman who has made some indication that she would like to hold it. If the baby cries, the caretaker quickly leaves the building and visits with other women holding babies just outside the main church doors.

[12] Many of the teachers have read at least part of the week's selection from the booklet in English and are translating loosely from it. For those who have difficulty reading

the English text, the booklet serves as an index to the Biblical chapter and verse being emphasized.

[11] The Kosraean church distributes a booklet called "Guiding Words" (*kahs in kol*), which lists the readings that relate to the topic to be covered in Sunday School each week.

[14] This could take the form of sinning, such as drinking or smoking, or it could take the form of joining one of the relatively new "other" churches on the island. Most notable among these is the Mormon Church, which has established a significant mission on Kosrae.

[15] Kosraeans speak of this in terms of abiding by the commandments and also living within the guidelines of the church. It is generally understood that smoking, drinking and fornication are outside the parameters of these guidelines.

[16] The assumption that learning, per se, is not a problem extends to Kosraean views about literacy. Kosraeans equate literacy with participation in normal community and church events. It is not regarded as a function of schooling, since many older Kosraeans have attended little or no school (see also footnote 20).

[17] On the social construction and use of such facts, see McDermott and Varenne, 1995.

[18] Beyond this, only a lifetime of devoted service, as others see it, would qualify them for the rare kind of status held by deacons or pastors, and for most Kosraeans most of the time, such status considerations are irrelevant.

[19] See, e.g., Rubinstein, 1994. Cf. Marshall, 1979.

[20] When they talk about this, her family members laugh that her grandmother Emily, widowed and worried about money, only finished the third grade. The only jobs she can ever hope for are cleaning hotel rooms or the few houses occupied by expatriates on the island. A constant source of comment and amusement is my interest in spending time with her and learning things Kosraean from her. "But she left school in third grade!" people laugh, indicating that she would have nothing to offer someone well-schooled like me.

[21] It is almost humorous to a Kosraean, even to someone who grew up in an era without schools, to try to conceive of not being able to read. The assumption that persons living in the world will come to know how to read ties into the assumption that everyone on the island can read. No one on Kosrae worries about literacy rates, as conventionally conceived. Senior officials in the Department of Education, whose job it is to identify such things, find that the only persons unable to read are those with severe organic impairments that make reading at a functional level physically impossible for them. There are only a few such Kosraeans.

[22] It is physically easy for Nadine and others in Section C to add stars after their name. Their chart is down low, directly beneath the Section B chart. Section A students have to stand on a chair or table to reach their chart. During Section A classes, there is an animated up-and-down motion, with students climbing on furniture, one after another, to place their newest star on the chart.

[23] Adoption has been important in sharing resources, maintaining descent groups, and achieving social solidarity in Micronesia for a very long time. Even though it is a well established practice, parental attachments can conflict very strongly, as was the case in Mariannie's family, with social obligations to honor requests for adoption of one's baby. Rather than a sign of lack of care, adoption transactions in Micronesia indicate the intense devotion to and value of children there, with adopted children sometimes having the highest status among a family's children (Oneisom, 1994; Wilson, 1976).

[24] At the end of the Japanese occupation in 1945, she recognized the importance of

English in the island's future and organized classes to teach it. When an island-wide council was formed in the early 1950s, "Mother Rose," as she is often remembered, was appointed the first superintendent of education. She established Kosrae's first school system.

[25] In his discussion of the evolution of legal systems, Weber calls this "formal irrationality." This same kind of thing is rendered in caricature in a scene from *Monty Python and the Holy Grail*. In it, a troll grants permission to pass his bridge based on the would-be passers' ability to answer irrelevant and obscure questions. Those who give wrong answers are immediately hurled to their death.

Further Reading

Greeno, J., 1994. Understanding Concepts in Activity. In *Discourse Comprehension: Essays in Honor of Walter Kintsch*, C. A. Weaver, III, S. Mannes, and C. R. Fletcher, eds. Hillsdale, NJ: Lawrence Erlbaum.

Lave, J., and E. Wegner, 1991. *Situated Learning: Legitimate Peripheral Participation*. Cambridge, UK: Cambridge University Press.

Marshall, M., 1979. *Weekend Warriors: Alcohol in a Micronesian Culture*. Palo Alto, CA: Mayfield.

McDermott, R., 1993. Acquisition by a Child of a Learning Disability. In *Understanding Practice*, S. Chaiklin and J. Lave, eds., pp. 269–305. Cambridge: Cambridge University Press.

McDermott, R. and H. Varenne, 1995. Culture as Disability. *Anthropology and Education Quarterly*, 26, 324–48.

Mehan, H., 1978. Structuring School Structure. *Harvard Educational Review*, 45, 311–38.

Oneisom, I., 1994. The Changing Family in Chuuk: 1950–1990. *The Micronesian Counselor*, 6. Pohnpei, FM: Micronesian Seminar.

Peacock, K., 1990. The Maze of Schools: Education in Micronesia, 1951–1964: "The Gibson Years." Unpublished doctoral dissertation, University of Hawaii, Manoa, HI.

Ritter, P., 1978. The Repopulation of Kosrae: Population and Social Organization on a Micronesian High Island. Unpublished doctoral dissertation, Stanford University, Stanford, CA.

Rogoff, B., 1995. Observing Sociocultural Activity on Three Planes: Participatory Appropriation, Guided Participation, Apprenticeship. In *Perspectives on Sociocultural Research*, A. Alvarez, P. Del Rio, and J. V. Wertsch, eds. Cambridge, UK: Cambridge University Press.

Rubinstein, D., 1994. Changes in the Micronesian Family Structure Leading to Alcoholism, Suicide, and Child Abuse and Neglect. *The Micronesian Counselor*, 15. Pohnpei, FM: Micronesian Seminar.

Spindler, G., and L. Spindler, 1989. Instrumental Competence, Self-efficacy, Linguistic Minorities, and Cultural Therapy: A Preliminary Attempt at Integration. *Anthropology and Education Quarterly*, 20, 36–50.

Wilson, W. S., 1976. Household, Land and Adoption on Kusaie. In *Transactions in Kinship*, I. Brady, ed. Honolulu: University of Hawaii.

Part V

TRANSCULTURAL COMPARISONS

Preview

In chapter 20 of this section, Mariko Fujita and Toshiyuki Sano interpret the philosophies of U.S. and Japanese daycare centers using more-or-less standard ethnographic techniques and a procedure called reflective cross-cultural interviewing. This technique of interviewing was first developed by myself and Louise Spindler in our comparative study of Schoenhausen and Roseville Elementary Schools.

The technique is based on the showing of videos taken of each school to the teachers (and, in the Schoenhausen/Roseville case, the children and administrators as well) and using these videos of their own classrooms to stimulate reflective discussion. However, the technique goes beyond this in that the videos of the "other" school, in this case Japanese, German, or American, are shown to these same teachers and others to further enhance culturally reflective discussions. This engages the principals involved in an interpretation of their own situation that is complex and satisfying. Chapter 22 also provides some insights into the effect of position (administrator, child, or teacher) on perception of culture as well as the common cultural elements perceived by all three.

The problem of "comparison" appears significantly in the discussions by the respective authors. Fujita and Sano conclude that true comparison is not possible between Japanese and American daycare centers because dependence and independence—the characterizations that they selected for focus—do not have the same meaning in both the Japanese and American cultures. From our point of view the comparative method truly worked in order to produce this conclusion, so that the meaning of "comparison" *is* different in American and Japanese culture. Some critics would use this kind of difficulty as a reason for not doing comparative ethnography. To us the implication is quite the opposite: doing ethnography in this fashion sharpens the nature of comparison and provides illuminating results.

Chapter 21, by Victoria Baker, is quite different in its emphasis and provides an expansion of this section to larger dimensions of relationships. On the basis of visits to schools in more than sixteen developing countries where Baker did case studies, she posits that the formalism so characteristic of these schools is not something to be disparaged and attacked by progressive Western educators. After considerable rumination about formalism, schooling, and Western views, Baker has assumed an incrementalist position rather than attacking formalistic pedagogy and striving to replace it by Western-based practices. A better approach may be one that does not critically question the teaching abilities of legions of educators—many of them remarkably dedicated—working under extremely difficult conditions. Improving the quality of education means improving it in terms of the recipients' own values and within their own cultural context, within which formalistic approaches may fit better, for the time being, than progressive, Western-based procedures. Again, a comparative approach seems to have produced useful results.

The Editor

20

Day Care Teachers and Children in the United States and Japan

Ethnography, Reflexive Interviewing and Cultural Dialogue

Mariko Fujita
Hiroshima University
Toshiyuki Sano
Nara Women's University

Introduction

In this chapter we explicate two different philosophies underlying early childhood education in Japan and the United States. Early childhood is a period when core cultural values are taught (Caudill and Weinstein 1969; LeVine 1984; Masuda 1969). Studying educational processes in day care centers in different countries, therefore, may reveal different cultural transmission processes of core values, such as "independence" in American culture (Fujita 1984; Hsu 1973, 1981; Rapson et al. 1967; Varenne 1977) and "dependence" in Japanese culture (Doi 1973; Fujita 1977; Kiefer 1970). However, a cross-cultural study of cultural transmission will immediately put us face to face with complex problems. It is not difficult merely to find two comparable, socioeconomic groups in two different countries. The comparative study involves a more profound and perhaps more important problem—that of finding a concept such as "independence" that is applicable to different cultures. If the meanings of concepts are culturally constructed (e.g., Shweder and LeVine 1984; Marcus and Fisher 1986), how can we compare the educational processes of two different countries, simultaneously being sensitive to the cultural construction of the differing meanings underlying these two systems?

Source: Adapted by the authors especially for *Education and Cultural Process*, 3rd Edition, from *School and Society*, Henry T. Trueba and Concha Delgado-Gaitan, eds. New York: Praeger Publishing Co., pp. 73–97.

This chapter attempts to answer this question by examining daily activities at an American day care center, Maple Day Care in Central Wisconsin, and a Japanese day care center, Kawa Day Care in suburban Tokyo.[1]

In the first section, we will describe similarities and differences in the American and Japanese day care centers using participant observation and interviews. Our purpose, however, is not a straightforward comparison of the two cultures. We are trying to show that the American and Japanese teachers do not interpret such key concepts as "independence" in the same way. Our contention is that it is inadequate to determine which system produces more independence-oriented children. For such a purpose it is vitally important to understand the difference in meanings of the key concepts in each cultural context. Judging two cultures using a single criterion blinds us to an understanding of the two different philosophies of education operating in these two centers (e.g., Frake 1980).

In the second section, to discern different educational assumptions operating under the two systems we describe a research procedure, "reflexive cross-cultural interviewing,"[2] following a procedure which George and Louise Spindler (1987a; 1993) created. Activities at both centers were recorded on videotape.[3] Both American and Japanese videotapes were shown to the teachers in these two centers. While watching these videotapes with the teachers, we interviewed them concerning their explanation of their own activities. Then we asked them to compare the American and Japanese day care centers shown on the tapes. We used these tapes as evocative stimuli to let the teachers talk about their cultural assumptions.

We will then discuss the multiplicity of meanings of "independence" and "dependence." We will point out that the Japanese and American teachers interpret the same behavior patterns differently and therefore hold two different systems of symbols and meanings (Geertz 1973a; Schneider 1972).

Finally we will analyze the difference in the underlying cultural assumptions and conceptions of two sets of "cultural dialogues" (Spindler and Spindler 1987b; 1990) that the reflexive cross-cultural interviewing reveals. Both American and Japanese teachers interpret the others' system within their own cultural framework. They are not really comparing American culture with Japanese culture and vice versa. Instead they are engaged in cultural dialogues by talking about their "pivotal concerns" while contrasting them with what is disturbing within their own educational system. We also analyze teachers' interpretations, especially their discrepancies, as clues in understanding the two sets of cultural dialogues. We will clarify differences in underlying educational philosophy between the American and Japanese day care centers,[4] using as examples the concepts of "time," "space," "teachers" and "children."

Ethnographic Observation and Interview

Description of the Day Care Centers

Place, term and class. Maple Day Care is located in Riverfront City (population 22,000), Wisconsin. The center is at the east end of the city on the border of the residential area and is adjacent to the commercial area. Parents bring children by car from all over the county.

Kawa Day Care is located in the northeastern suburb of Tokyo, in Tama City (population 121,000). The center is in the middle of high-rise apartment buildings. It is conveniently located within only a ten-minute walking distance from a railroad station which connects Tama city to the central part of Tokyo in 30 minutes. Parents who live relatively close to the center bring children mostly by bicycle, on foot, or rarely by car.

The Maple Day Care center is open five days a week, Monday through Friday. It has seven classes, including two classes of three-year-olds. They are formed in September and are organized by age group. Once a child reaches a specific age (between two and five), he or she can move to the next class, depending on the teachers' evaluation of the child's growth and development as well as the availability of a vacancy. The parents can choose which days of the week to send children to the center. A certain number of children use the center only two or three days a week. The parents pay an hourly fee that is competitive with those of several day care centers in this city. There is one handicapped child at the center.

Japanese parents bring children every day to the Kawa Day Care center because there is no part-time system like the one at Maple. The center is open Monday through Saturday (Saturday is a half day). Parents pay a monthly fee directly to the municipal office, although Kawa Day Care is operated by a private, nonprofit organization. The fee is determined by the official schedule according to both parents' (if single parent, his or her) income tax of the previous year. The center accepts a few handicapped children (currently two). The classes are organized by age group. They are formed once a year in April according to the children's ages as of April 1. If the child's age is between one and two, he or she belongs to the class called *sumire-gumi* (violet class) or *issai-ji gumi* (one-year-old class). There are four other classes for two-, three-, four-and five-year-olds. Unlike the Maple children, the Kawa children can move to the next class only once a year in April.

The child/teacher ratio which the Maple and Kawa centers employ is set by local authorities (that is, the State of Wisconsin and the Tokyo Prefecture, respectively). In comparison, the ratio is the same in both centers for younger children (4:1 for age one, 6:1 for age two, 8:1 for age two-and-a-half in Maple Center only, 10:1 for age three). However, the Kawa teachers take care of twice as many older children (25:1 for age four and five) as the Maple teachers (13:1 for age four and 16:1 for age five).

Floor plan and playground. Maple Day Care is a two-story building with the entrances at the mezzanine level. At an entrance, there are two sets of stairs; one leads to the lower level where classrooms for younger children (ages one to three) are found. Classrooms for older children are upstairs. Entering or leaving the building is not especially easy, for only two doors lead to the outside. Classrooms are connected with small halls, and each room is divided into areas for specific activities. The floor is carpeted. People enter the building without taking off their shoes. Bare feet are not allowed by state regulations. There is no staff lounge. However, Maple Day Care has a dining room, unlike Japanese day care centers. The playground is divided into three parts: the largest part is cement, the next largest one is sand, and there is a grassy area in front of the building. The playground is fenced. There is a shed for the toys in the sandy area.

Kawa Day Care is a one-story building. All the classrooms face the playground, with sliding doors that enable children to have easy access through the porch to the playground. The porch of the classroom for the youngest children (age one) is fenced to prevent them from running out to the playground. Immediately outside of each classroom are water faucets where children wash their hands and brush their teeth. At Kawa Day Care, there is a long straight hallway (*roka*) in the building. The floor is hardwood. People take off their shoes and put on "inside shoes" when they enter the building at the main entrance. Going barefoot is permitted. There is a staff room for relaxation and changing clothes. Teachers change clothes for working. The playground is covered with compressed sand. In the playground along the fence are slide, swings, jungle gym, and sandbox.

Daily schedule. The Maple and Kawa Day Care centers have similar daily schedules of general activities. Most activities are performed according to the age group, except in the very early morning and very late afternoon when only a small number of children attend the center. In those cases, activities are performed in a mixed group. The daily schedule at both centers is: (a) group activity such as singing, painting and story telling; (b) snack; (c) group activity such as reading a story and dancing; (d) lunch; (e) nap; (f) snack and (g) free play. One difference between these two centers is that a morning snack is provided only to the children of one- and two-year-old age groups at Kawa Day Care, while everyone receives a morning snack at Maple. The Maple center is open at 6:30 A.M. while the Kawa center is open at 7:20 A.M. Both are closed at 6:00 P.M.

Teachers. The staff of the Maple center is all female except for one male teacher, who is the assistant director and also works with the four-year-old group. The staff of the Kawa center is all female. The personnel of the Maple center include one director, one bookkeeper, seven teachers, three teacher aides and two cooks. That of the Kawa center includes one director, one head teacher, eleven teachers, one janitor and two cooks. The American teachers are graduates of a four-year college and the teacher aides are usually graduates of a two-year junior college or a two-year technical school. The Japanese teachers are mostly graduates of a two-year junior college or a two-year special training school. Each Maple teacher's aide works with a teacher. Hereafter, we use the term "teachers" to cover both teachers and teacher aides unless otherwise noted.

Activities and "Independence" versus "Dependence"

In this section we will compare some of the activities at the Japanese and American day care centers through participant observation. One temptation here is to try to determine which system produces more independent-oriented (or dependent-oriented) behavior among children. However, can we really decide on this issue? We will consider several cases to illustrate the difficulty involved. Our contention is that we cannot settle this issue if the meanings of key concepts held by American and Japanese teachers (such as "independence") are different.[5]

In the classroom. Maple teachers connect the concept of "independence" with that of "choice"—they often stress the importance of children's "choosing" an activity. The American children at Maple are constantly asked to choose from two or three activities. The Maple teachers believe that giving choices to the children will make them sort out their wishes and express their desires to engage in an activity without being forced to do so. Therefore, letting children choose is a step toward independence and freedom. In contrast, the Kawa teachers do not stress the importance of giving choices to the children. They do not make a point of asking their children to "choose" an activity.

The Maple teachers expose their children to a variety of activities by dividing each class of older children (from age three) into three groups, especially during the morning classroom activities. The teacher takes care of a group of seven or eight children who are involved in one project, while another teacher (teacher aide) attends to a second group with a different project. The rest of the children in this class are assigned to play on their own with toys in the classroom. After about fifteen minutes, the children rotate and engage in a different activity. At the end of the rotation process, all the children have experienced each of the three activities provided in this classroom. At Kawa Day Care, however, usually there is only a single activity for all children in an age group, even when there are two teachers per group.

By setting up a variety of activities in the classroom, American teachers seem to encourage children to be more independent than Japanese teachers do. However, if we look at the ways of controlling children's behavior in the activities set by teachers, we gain a different view of the meaning of "choice" that children experience.

In our observation, the Maple teachers use disciplinary measures more frequently than the Kawa teachers do. Whenever a teacher finds a child not engaging in the activity in which he or she is supposed to be involved, the teacher tells the child to join the group activity. "Time-out" is frequently used as such a measure at Maple Day Care—when the child disturbs other children, or when the child's side activity attracts other children's attention away from the teacher, the teacher pulls this child out of the group and lets him or her sit alone and reflect on his or her conduct. After five to ten minutes, the teacher allows that child to rejoin the group activity. However, if the misbehavior is excessive, the teacher asks the child why he or she was disciplined. If the child acknowledges his or her fault, then he or she is allowed to rejoin the group and to resume the activity. This disciplinary measure is observed several times in each activity session for all the children except for the very youngest.

At Kawa Day Care, although the teachers claim that they sometimes withdraw distracting children from group activities, this "time-out" is not recognized as a disciplinary measure and is rarely used. In observing the classroom activities in any age group, we find some children not participating in the group activity. An example from a class of four-year-olds illustrates the content of a Japanese class. The group activity was to walk on a balance beam designed for children and engage in a game called *jan-ken-pon*.[6] Meanwhile, at one corner of the classroom two girls were talking together, and at a different corner three boys and a girl were playing with toys. Three other children were running around the room. The children who were engaged in these side activities were not disciplined by the teacher, as they would be at Maple. The teacher takes it as a matter of course that some children do not want to participate in the group activity and that they choose to play on their own. "After all, they are only children. This is not a school, but a day care center. It is a place to play. They should have happy times."

When a child distracts other children, Kawa teachers use a technique called *kibun-tenkan* instead of trying to discipline the child (Sano 1989a). They try to divert the child's focus from his or her preoccupation in other activity. For example, one day two children were teasing each other by the little pool during their swimming time. Their teacher came, lifted one of the children and jokingly said, "You are so mischievous. I'm going to throw you into the pool!" She pretended that she was actually going to throw this child into the swimming pool. In this situation everyone knew that she was joking. No one took it as an emotionally abusing threat to the child, as some Americans might interpret the situation. The child also took it as a joke and started giggling. The point here, according to the Kawa teachers, is to change the child's mood rather than trying to teach him or her what is right and wrong.

Although the Maple teachers emphasize the importance of having choices for their children's activities as a key to independence, they do not talk about the fact that the range of activities from which the American children can choose is always set by the teachers. If the children engage in activities other than those set by the teachers, the teachers are likely to interpret these side activities as distracting to other children and to utilize some disciplinary measures such as the "time-out." On the other hand, the Japanese children are allowed not to participate in group activities and can engage in almost any activity of their choice in the classroom without penalty as long as they do not disturb or injure other children. Even though the Japanese teachers do not verbally emphasize the importance of having choices, as do the American teachers, do the Japanese children not have a wider range of choices and find themselves in a less restricting environment than the American children?

Mealtime and nap time. At both the Maple and Kawa Day Care centers, hot lunch is served. The Maple center has a separate uncarpeted dining room. The meals are served in two shifts, one for younger children (ages one to two-and-a-half) who eat first and one for older children (ages three to five). At the Kawa center, lunch is served in each classroom, and children eat by age group.

In Maple's dinning room, there are seven large rectangular tables, where ten people can be seated. The children usually sit with their classmates. The teachers also sit with their own children and eat with them. At the beginning of the meal, they recite a short prayer in thanksgiving for the food. Meals are served family style. Quantities of each item on the menu are put on large plates or in bowls that the teachers ask the children to pass among themselves. The teachers tell children to take a small amount of every item on the menu—if they want to have more, they may ask for seconds. If they do not like a certain food, the teachers ask them to "at least try it." The Maple teachers regard lunch as a social time. They encourage the children to talk. At the same time, the teachers supervise the children's table manners.

One way that American teachers emphasize "independence" is during the meal, by encouraging children to eat on their own. At Kawa the teachers sometimes feed even three-year-olds, who are slow eaters.

However no one, even the youngest child (age one), is fed at Maple. The Maple teachers think it important that each child is able to eat with his or her own utensils. They regard it as a step toward independence. Feeding children, even if they are slow eaters, is not thought to be a good idea, because it is believed that they would soon stop making an effort to eat unassisted and would expect teachers to feed them constantly. It is felt that other children would compete for the extra attention, causing a chaotic situation (Fujita 1986).

The Kawa teachers consider it important to do things for younger children. Each teacher brings food for his or her children on several trays from the kitchen to the classroom. For younger children (ages one to four), teachers set the table for the children. Each item on the menu is served on a separate plate or bowl for each child instead of on communal plates and bowls.

However, among the oldest children, one boy and one girl are assigned duty each day. These children, called *toban*, serve the individual, already-filled plates and bowls from the trays to each child. Meanwhile the other children are supposed to wait quietly. When the children on duty finish serving, they stand in front of everyone and say *itadaki-masu* ("I will gratefully receive this food"), and the others follow. The teacher puts the children on a rotation schedule so that every child has an equal opportunity to be a *toban*. Each child knows from the schedule when his or her turn comes. A Kawa child does not consider this duty system as an imposition; instead, he or she takes pride in being responsible and also in being able to do the task as well as other children do. It is a sign of being a "big child." The Kawa teachers believe that this *toban* system makes children responsible.

Although the Maple teachers encourage children to help the teachers, no duty system such as the *toban* is used at the Maple center. At snack time, teachers solicit help, but, they think it important that the children volunteer rather than assigning a task to them. Hence, when a teacher asks, "Who wants to wipe the table?", two or three children usually raise their hands. A Maple child likes to be chosen as a helper; it means that he or she chooses to help the teacher without being forced to do so and that the teacher recognizes his or her willingness. Because children regard helping as a reward of recognition, the teachers say that they see to it that everyone has a chance to help the teachers over a period of time. However, to maintain an appearance of voluntariness, the rotation is implicit and the children do not know when their turn will come. For the children, helping is a competition among themselves.

The concept of duty can be observed in preparing for naps in Kawa Day Care. Both centers have a daily nap time for all children. At Maple Day Care, the teachers set up portable cots for napping in each classroom. Setting up these cots is considered to be the teachers' duty and no child helps the teachers.

At the Kawa Day Care center, both teachers and the older children prepare their classrooms for napping. For the oldest group (age five), for example, the teacher first vacuums the floor. Then, the children bring *futon* (cotton mattresses) from the closet and set them on the floor. Although not all the children always help, preparing the room for napping is seen as a shared duty between teachers and children.

From the observation of lunchtime and preparation for napping, what can we say about "independence" and "dependence?" The American teachers train children to eat on their own by not feeding them from the very earliest stage of development. In view of the fact that some Japanese three-year-olds require occasional assistance and the attending teachers are willing to give that help, the American system seems to produce more independence-oriented children. To the Maple teachers, The Japanese teachers seem to be overprotective of their children. However, the Japanese teachers encourage the children to assume duties through the *toban*, or by sharing some tasks with the teachers, such as putting down mattresses for napping or cleaning the classrooms. In this sense, they are neither overprotective nor indulgent. The Japanese system does not necessarily seem to encourage dependent behaviors.

During transition. Perhaps one of the most remarkable differences between Kawa and Maple Day Care is the way in which the teachers move children from one activity to the next. The Kawa teachers, in comparison with the Maple teachers, use very little verbal instruction, instead relying on nonverbal measures to signal the transition. An example from the class of three-year-olds at Kawa Day Care will illustrate this point. One of the two teachers was reading a book to the children. When it was time for swimming, the teacher said, "Let's go swimming. Let's do *basha-basha*" (children's talk for swimming.) Some children who know the routine better than others spontaneously go to the bathroom, and others follow. The children seem to imitate what the other children are doing rather than following the teachers' verbal instruction. They come back to their classroom and start changing into their swimming suits. Then, the children pull out dry towels and the clothes which they will wear after swimming from their individual lockers and give these items to the teacher. When the teacher plays a record, the children gather in a circle to exercise before swimming.

The Kawa teachers can expect the children to complete this series of actions without giving step-by-step instruction. Indeed, when the teachers give instructions, they say only a few words in passing, addressing two or three children nearby. However, the Kawa teachers frequently use music to signal the transition. When one of the teachers announces snack time, the other teacher starts playing piano. There are specific songs for the beginning and end of snack time, for washing hands, for brushing teeth and so forth, as cues for the children to begin a new activity.

At Maple Day Care, on the other hand, teachers find it important to explain procedures to the children before each activity, relying exclusively on verbal instruction. At the beginning of each school day, the teacher tells the children what they are going to do that morning. At the beginning of each activity the teacher repeats what she expects from the children. When the teacher gives an instruction, all the children are supposed to gather and sit down. For example, before they go outside to play in wintertime, the teacher gives a series of instructions to the entire group of children in the three-year-old class. "Now, we are going outside to play. Before you go out, I want you to go to the bathroom. Then, come back here and put on your coats and boots. Don't go outside yet. You must line up in front of the classroom and be quiet. If you are noisy, we are not going outside. Then, we go out together. O.K.? Now, go to bathroom." The teacher waits for all the children to come back to the classroom. "Put on your coats and boots, " says the teacher. She helps some children put on their coats. "Now, I want you to line up in front of the classroom." Those children who have put on their coats start lining up and wait for the others. After everyone lines up, the teacher gives another set of instructions. "Now, we are going outside. When we finish, I want you to come back right away and line up in front of the building, O.K.?" Then the teacher leads her children quietly outside. Although the children may or may not know these actions as a routine, they seem to wait for the teacher's instructions.[7]

The teachers place different emphasis and importance on verbal instruction in these two centers. The Kawa teachers believe that for the children at this age it is not sufficient just to tell them what to do. It is more important to show them by action, either demonstrating examples for them, or letting them follow some children who can perform the task. The Kawa teachers regard demonstration and example as a better way of teaching children. They also believe that young children respond better to music than to words. The Maple teachers, on the other hand, believe it important that the children understand why they are doing what they are doing. To avoid blind obedience, it is important for them to verbally explain to the children the reasons for what they are going to do before the action takes place.

The difference in the teachers' attitudes regarding the verbal instructions can be seen in the ways that they deal with fights among the children. At the beginning of the school year, the Maple teachers set up several lessons to talk about "fights" with the children—for example, why fighting is bad, how it feels to be hit, and what they should do instead of fighting—and establish some rules. The Maple teachers believe that they can minimize the chances of fighting among the children in this way.

The Kawa teachers, on the other hand, wait for an actual fight to occur before saying anything to the children. They think it important to teach children what is right and wrong in a particular incident. According to them, rules are dependent on individual cases, so there is no point in teaching children rules in the abstract. One teacher even said that she did not teach children not to fight, because she believed fighting (within certain limits) was a form of communication or expression of individual emotions.

In observing activities at Kawa Day Care we can see that, although the Japanese teachers give fewer verbal instructions than do their American counterparts and do not employ a disciplinary measure such as the "time-out," there is certainly an orderly flow of activities. Even if at any given moment the Japanese children are noisier than the American children, programs in the Japanese day care center are carried out very smoothly.

As the above examples indicate, it is impossible to determine which system produces more independence-oriented behavior among children without clarifying exactly what we mean by "independence." Here we face a fundamental problem—that is, do the American and Japanese teachers share the same meaning of "independence?" For instance, to an American teacher, a three-year-old being fed by a teacher is typical of dependent behavior. However, do Japanese teachers consider feeding oneself an essential key to independence, as do American teachers? As we shall see below, the Japanese teachers do not interpret independence in the same way as the American teachers do. When they do not share the same interpretations of these key concepts, it is fruitless to try to determine which system is more independence-oriented by using a single criterion. Rather, the underlying assumptions and patterns of meanings that shape the teachers' conceptions of "independence" and "dependence" must be determined. Before we proceed, informants must examine concrete behaviors and must be encouraged to make statements that are culturally meaningful. For this purpose, reflexive cross-cultural interviewing is useful.

Reflexive Interviewing and Cultural Dialogue

Notes on Procedures

In order to conduct reflexive cross-cultural interviewing, we have taken the following steps:

Videotaping. We took videotapes of several activities at both the Maple and Kawa Day Care Centers on which we came to focus while we conducted participant observations—for instance, group activity, lunchtime, and free play. To do this, one of us was videotaping while another was taking notes. For interview use, we chose scenes on videotape which captured similar activities at both the Japanese and American day care centers.

Interviewing with videotape of themselves. We first interviewed the American teachers individually or in pairs while they watched the videotapes of the Maple Day Care center. The first interview with the Japanese (Kawa Day Care) teachers was conducted in a group of six while they watched videotapes of Kawa Day Care.

Interviewing with videotape of the "other" culture. We then interviewed the American teachers a second time, individually or in pairs, while showing the videotapes of the Japanese day care center. The second interviews with the Japanese teachers were conducted with six teachers at a time while they watched the videotapes of Maple Day Care.

Directors of both centers graciously allocated the time for interviewing during the nap time for one-and-a-half hours. We conducted individual interviews with Maple teachers, allowing each teacher choose the most convenient day for him or her. At Kawa Day Care, we conducted two group interview sessions, one with the teachers of younger children and the other with those of older children. We invited the director and the head teacher to join in.

Here we should clarify the differences between the first and second type of interviews. In the first set of interviews, we showed the teachers the videotapes of their own day care center while the interview was in progress. Viewing the videotapes of the teachers' interaction with the children made our interview questions more concrete. As the teachers are usually interested in seeing themselves and their own children on the TV monitor, the videotapes also helped the teachers relax and get involved in our interviews (Erickson and Wilson 1982; McDermott 1976). More importantly, viewing the videotapes enabled both the teachers and us to engage in open-ended conversation. In the second type of interview, a *reflexive cross-cultural interview*, we showed Japanese videotapes to American teachers and American videotapes to Japanese teachers. In this second set of interviews, we encouraged the teachers to talk about their impressions, feelings and interpretations of similarities and differences between an American and a Japanese day care center as well as between the two cultures.

The roles that we as anthropologists play in the two types of interviews are different. In the first type, we are "interviewers" of our informants, asking questions in the way anthropologists usually conduct ethnographic research. In the case of the day care center interviews, we asked the teachers about whatever we did not understand in their inter-action and activity scenes. As the teachers answered our questions, we paid special attention to how they talked about the children's charac-teristics, attitudes, feelings, achievements, and sometimes about the children's family members. The first type of interview included some open-ended conversation among the teachers and ourselves, not only about the specific scenes of the videotapes but also about the broader, more general issue of ways of caring for the children.

In the second, reflexive type of interview, our role is quite different from that in the first type—we act as active moderators of cultural dis-cussions. In the day care interview sessions, we attempted to facilitate a "conversation" between the American and Japanese teachers. Viewing the videotapes of another culture enabled the American and Japanese teachers to have a "virtual" discussion—as if the teachers from both cul-tures were engaging in an actual conversation—through us, as active cultural moderators. First, teachers from one culture asked us ques-tions about the scenes in the videotapes from the other culture. We explained the content of the scenes. We also gave them some basic infor-mation about the other culture's day care center. For example, we men-tioned the number of children and staff, the number of days a week the center is open, the child/teacher ratio, location and operating organiza-tion. In this sense, we acted as cultural consultants.

The teachers made professional comments on the performances of the other culture's teachers as if they were observing and talking to them. When that happened, we encouraged the teachers to elaborate on their comments. They also sought explanations for "the other's" way of doing things. We tried to answer the questions in a way we believed the teachers of the other culture would answer. For instance, a Japanese teacher remarked on the fact that American children wear shoes while taking a nap, which she thought quite odd and even dirty. We explained to her that, unlike the Japanese, Americans generally do not take off their shoes inside the house, that going barefoot is not allowed at Maple Day Care by state regulation, and that children sleep on vinyl cots instead of on *futon* (cotton mattresses) placed directly on the floor.

We sometimes relayed observations and interpretations from the teachers of one culture to the teachers of the other culture. For instance, we said to the Kawa teachers, "American teachers often say, 'We are teachers, and not baby-sitters.' Do you view yourselves in the same way?" In this way, we opened up the "discussion" between the Maple and Kawa teachers and solicited their views. In this type of interview, we played a far more active role with informants than anthropologists normally would, by encouraging them to reflect on the meanings of their day-to-day activities.

Teachers' Views of American and Japanese Cultures

Following is a summary of comments the Maple and Kawa teachers made about themselves and the others, obtained through our reflexive cross-cultural interviewing. We will first examine the views that the Maple teachers had of the Japanese teachers and day care as seen on the videotapes. After each comment, we will discuss the Kawa teachers' "reply" on the same issue, obtained through our role as cultural translators and discussion leaders in reflexive cross-cultural interviewing. After examining the Maple teachers' views, we will turn to the Kawa teachers' views.

The strongest impression that the Maple teachers have is that the Japanese center is too noisy and even looks chaotic. The Japanese children are talking out loud all the time. Some children are walking and even running around, while others are listening to the teacher. The Maple teachers think the reason for this disorderly behavior must be the high child/teacher ratio. With that high ratio, the Maple teachers feel that there is no way the teachers can adequately control the children. Their concern about control often centers around maintaining a safe environment for children.

When we interviewed the Kawa teachers, we raised this issue of the high ratio between teachers and children expressed by the Maple teachers. We also told them that at Maple, one class was often divided into smaller groups. We asked their opinion of having several teachers lead a class. The Kawa teachers think that two or three teachers would not necessarily make things easier. They believe one teacher can often lead children better, because she can run the whole class in the way she wants and can see the progress of the children better, and the teacher can respond to the individual child's pace of development better. The Kawa teachers do not regard their work load as heavy. Incidentally, the Kawa teachers were quite surprised when we told them that the Maple teachers thought the Japanese children were too noisy. It was only after they viewed our videotapes on Maple Day Care that they noticed their high noise level.

The American teachers see their Japanese counterparts as working not *with* but *around* children by preparing things for them. The Maple teachers think that most of the time the Japanese teachers prepare things for the children rather than teach them. For example, during lunchtime, the Japanese teachers set up tables and wipe them, whereas American teachers would let other people such as cooks wipe tables. During play time, especially outdoors, the Japanese teachers do not supervise the children. There is no one watching what they are doing. The American teachers question the safety of the children.

The Kawa teachers think the American teachers do not play with children; they seem to just sit by them and watch them. To Kawa teachers, the American teachers who do not play with children appear lazy, not doing a proper job. A good teacher, according to the Kawa teachers, is one who can join the children's world, can communicate with the children in a way they understand, and can play with them at their level.

Another impression that the Kawa teachers have is that American children are treated as if they are adults instead of children. They dress like adults—for example, they wear leather shoes and jeans made with tough materials which the Kawa teachers think inappropriate for children. Commenting especially on younger children (ages one and two), a Kawa teacher said, "The material for pants seems so tough. Jeans fit them so tightly. Isn't it awkward, when they (teachers) take children to the toilet? Do they have enough time?" The Kawa teachers think that children should wear something soft and loose for their comfort. They also think that the plastic glasses that the American children use during lunch are not the children's size, but the size that adults would use.

We pointed out to the Kawa teachers that the American teachers encourage the children to be self-sufficient as soon as possible. For example, even one-year-old children are expected to eat on their own without any help from the teachers at the Maple Day Care center. The Kawa teachers view the attitude of the American teachers as strict, rigid and Spartan, reminding the Japanese director (the oldest member of the staff) of the educational method in pre-war Japan, under which she grew up. They think it acceptable to help younger children to eat, especially slow eaters. They said that at one time they used to encourage self-help at an earlier stage. In recent years, however, they changed their policy because they discovered that too much pressure on self-help would make children less motivated in later years, when they reach age four or five. Even though these children can take care of themselves, they refuse to do so. Until the children reach three years of age, it is necessary to provide lots of attention and care and sometimes to indulge them. "When they are satisfied, they start doing things on their own. But, if they are deprived of care at a very young stage and given pressure to do things on their own, they just lose interest later on." The Kawa director, even though she is running a day care center, thinks that ideally every mother should stay at home and raise her child until the child reaches three years of age, instead of taking the child to day care, because no one can provide as much love as a mother can.

The Maple teachers have a very different opinion on self-sufficiency, especially in eating, from that of the Kawa teachers. When the Maple teachers saw the videotape of the Japanese day care center, they took special note of the feeding of children, especially the three-year-olds. They asked us whether these children were sick on that day or were handicapped. They think it is not a good idea to feed a child, even a one-year-old, if he or she is healthy and normal. The Maple teachers comment on feeding as follows: "If you start feeding one child, other children also want to have extra attention and to be fed. Then, there is no way you can control the children." By feeding them, teachers felt that they would spoil the children's self-effort. The children will soon take advantage of the teacher's attitude and stop eating without assistance. The Maple teachers believe that being able to eat on one's own is a first step toward independence that should be encouraged as soon as possible.

How do the Maple and Kawa teachers summarize American and Japanese cultures? How do they account for the differences between these two centers? The Maple Day Care teachers believe that American culture stresses individualism and individual development. To paraphrase their summarization,

> Americans are so individualistic. It is important to teach children to think on their own. For this purpose, children should be given ample opportunities to exercise their choice. However, children at this age need to be closely supervised and be under constant control. As a society, the Japanese are far less individualistic, more structured, paternalistic, and traditional. In the videotapes, teachers do not seem to interfere with children. But, because the society itself is so structured, traditional values can control the children and keep order in the day care center.

The Kawa Day Care teachers believe that things occur in stages. They summarize the cultural difference as follows:

> Americans seem to have a consistent rule applicable to any age and place—the same rule at school, at home, or in public, and for adults as well as for children. These rules are very strictly enforced. For Japanese, rules are relative and not absolute. We tend to be inconsistent in applying rules. Maybe we are indulging children, but we also need to consider the particular time, place, and occasion in applying rules. Childhood is a separate stage from the rest of the life cycle. Children are different from adults; they have their own world apart from adults. They have their own ways of thinking and acting, and we should respect that. We cannot impose adult values on them. It is better to leave things to their natural pace of development.

Note here the difference in central concerns on which the Maple and Kawa teachers focus. The Maple teachers' cultural comparison focuses on individualism and the issue of power and control over the children, whereas that of the Kawa teachers focuses on time—for example, the time for disciplining, and the time of childhood in the life cycle.

An Analysis of Two Sets of Cultural Dialogues

We have seen the different ways in which the Maple and Kawa teachers characterize some aspects of American and Japanese cultures. We must next proceed to analyze the significance of these differences. Are they really comparing the two cultures, or are they telling us something else? To answer this question, we need to examine more closely how they describe these two cultures and analyze their descriptions as texts (Geertz 1973b, Fujita 1989). What are these teachers telling us when they describe things as the "Japanese way" or the "American way?"

First, we should note a peculiar feature of their descriptions. Both the Maple and Kawa teachers underplay the similarities between these two day care centers. They simply omit some similarities—for example, when the Maple teachers talk about the high ratio between teachers and children at the Japanese day care center, they ignore the fact that the ratio for younger children is the same for both centers. Similarly, when the Kawa teachers describe the American teachers as being strict, rigid and even Spartan, they do not comment on the affection that the Maple teachers physically demonstrate—for instance, hugging and kissing the children. Both groups of teachers highlight the differences, not the similarities, between these two centers.

Contrast the differences between the Kawa teachers' view of the "American way" and the view held by the Maple teachers, and note the discrepancy between them. The Kawa teachers describe the American teachers as being strict and rigid, imposing absolute rules on the children regardless of their stages of development. However, the way the Maple teachers characterize the "American teachers" or "American way" is different from the one described by the Kawa teachers. The "American teachers," according to the Maple teachers, are the teachers who are sensitive to the individual needs of the children and, thus, give choices to the children—but because of the children's age, the teachers must exercise control.

Similarly, there is a discrepancy between the way the Maple teachers described the "Japanese way" and the self-image held by the Kawa teachers. The Maple teachers describe Japanese society as structured, paternalistic, and traditional, and they view both teachers and children as being governed by traditional values that are beyond individual power. The Kawa teachers, however, do not consider themselves as slaves to traditional values. On the contrary, they view themselves as sensitive to the nature of a particular situation, judging accordingly, and responding to the children's pace of development.

Clearly, both the Maple and Kawa teachers misinterpreted each other. It is a misinterpretation in the sense that there is an acute discrepancy between the outsider's interpretation and that of the insider. Our point here is not to criticize either the Maple or Kawa teachers for misunderstanding Japanese or American culture. After all, no one among the Maple nor Kawa teachers spent any time in the other's country or were especially familiar with that country. Our argument here is that both the Maple and Kawa teachers' descriptions are not a comparison of two cultures, but a self-dialogue about one's own cultural system.

The Kawa teachers contrast their system with the pre-war Japanese education, which employed tougher disciplinary measures starting at a very early stage of the development. The fact that the Kawa director compared the "strict, rigid and Spartan" system of American teachers to her own pre-war educational system is significant. When these teachers describe the other culture, they are telling us what is disturbing to them. They are establishing their own self-identity by reconstructing something that occurred within their own culture that is different from the way they currently see themselves and labeling it as "American." They are making a sharp contrast within their own cultural framework. They describe the other culture as negating the values of their own culture, and by doing so they are indirectly affirming their own system.

The Maple teachers' contrasts are less explicit. When they emphasize the individualism in their own system and compare it to the more structured Japanese society, they are contrasting their system with a more totalitarian system. When they emphasize the importance of the teacher's control over children and view Japanese teachers as relatively noninterfering by comparison, they also contrast their philosophy with a more laissez-faire type of education, characteristic of their concept of "progressive" education. In Middle America, the educational philosophy found at Maple Day Care is certainly a mainstream type—a sort of middle ground between two more extreme philosophies, as the Maple teachers' analysis of their system shows.

If the Maple and Kawa teachers' descriptions are not cultural comparisons between American and Japanese cultures but rather ways of talking about their own systems, how do we proceed from this point to an analysis of the meanings of the underlying concepts which shape their systems? The best way seems to be to treat their descriptions as two sets of distinct "cultural dialogues." Here we adopt George and Louise Spindler's definition of a cultural dialogue as "the exchange of patterned meanings and significations among actors in social contexts." The following quotation defining American culture clarifies what is meant by the "cultural dialogue":

> We claim that there is an American culture because since prerevolutionary times we have been dialoging about freedom and constraint, equality and difference, cooperation and competition, independence and conformity, sociability and individuality, puritanism and free love, materialism and altruism, hard work and getting by, and achievement and failure. . . . It is not because we are all the same (we are not), or that we agree on most important matters (we do not), that there is an American culture. It is that somehow we agreed to worry, argue, fight, emulate and

agree or disagree about the same pivotal concerns. (Spindler and Spindler 1987b:2)

When both the Maple and Kawa teachers describe their own and the other's day care centers and educational orientations, they are undoubtedly talking about their "pivotal concerns." In this sense, their descriptions are cultural dialogues. We should point out here that their cultural dialogues are not the same but rather two distinct dialogues. The Maple teachers' description uses the idioms of control and power, whereas that of the Kawa teachers employs the idiom of time. Their central, "pivotal concerns" are different. Because of the difference in the central themes of the cultural dialogues, they are most likely to misinterpret each other when they compare the two systems—as they actually did.

Given that the Maple and Kawa teachers describe educational philosophy in the idioms of power and control and of time respectively, what are the meanings of the key concepts (such as "teachers," "children," "time" and "space") that shape their educational orientations? How do these concepts influence their actions?

The most fundamental contrast between the Maple teachers' educational philosophy and that of the Kawa teachers is the concept of "children." The Kawa teachers emphasize the separation of the distinct stage of childhood from the rest of the life cycle. They believe that "children" have their own world, their own ways of communicating, and their own rules apart from the world of adults. Although the Maple teachers do recognize childhood as a stage in the life cycle, they believe that children should not stay in this stage too long and should learn the rules which are applicable to adults and children alike as soon as they can. Thus, the Maple teachers encourage their children to be self-sufficient, especially in the area of self-care, whereas the Kawa teachers are more willing to offer assistance to their children in the same area.

The concept of "teachers" that the Maple and Kawa teachers have also differs. The Maple teachers conceptualize a "teacher" as someone who supervises and controls children's behavior. The Kawa teachers, on the other hand, believe a "teacher" at a day care is someone who facilitates and maintains a flow of activities. Rather than that of a supervisor, their image of a "teacher" is closer to that of a navigator or a guide.

Both the Maple and Kawa teachers use the word "natural" to describe children's behavior, yet the nuances that they convey are very different. When the Kawa teachers use the Japanese word for nature (*shizen*), they mean something positive. "The children should be left as natural as possible (*shizen no mama ni*)." What they mean by this phrase is that the children are innocent and should be left uninterfered with and unrestrained—left as they are. When the Maple teachers talk about "natural" behavior of the children, they convey the impression that children are unpredictable and disorderly if "left as they are"—that their behavior must be supervised and controlled.

The Maple and Kawa teachers' perceptions of "time" and "space" in the context of the day care centers are also different. The Kawa teachers' focus is the flow of activities over an entire day, whereas that of the Maple teachers is activities in each moment. Thus, the Kawa teachers are bothered less by the children who do not participate in a particular group activity, so long as they join other activities some other time and the series of activities flows smoothly. The Maple teachers focus on each activity. They often give verbal instructions at the beginning of each activity; they supervise the children and strongly encourage them to join in each activity. If a child misbehaves during an activity, the teacher exercises a disciplinary measure such as "time-out," regardless of the child's conduct in other activities.

The spatial orientations of the Maple and Kawa teachers are different as far as the area of the children's activities are concerned. Although the Kawa teachers prefer that the children stay in their classroom, they do not stop children from going to other classrooms, to the hall, or sometimes even to the playground, as long as they stay within the perimeter of the day care center. The Maple teachers expect their children to stay in their own classroom, and those who wander around in the building are likely to be taken back to their own rooms. The difference in the spatial orientations of the teachers are reflected in the floor plan of the buildings. Each room at Kawa Day Care has several sliding doors, which are usually open during the classroom activities, and the children have easy access to other rooms through the hallway and also through the porch. At Maple Day Care, each room is enclosed and has only one door. The children do not have access to other rooms without going through several doors, which are usually closed during the classroom activities.

Conclusion

To answer our initial question—how can we understand cultural differences in educational processes, being sensitive to the underlying cultural meanings?—we have employed reflexive cross-cultural interviewing, using videotapes as well as conventional ethnographic methods, participant observation, and interviews. Our analysis has made explicit the cultural assumptions and conceptual frameworks underlying the American and Japanese educational processes.

This analysis also demonstrates the following implications of our method of research. The use of audiovisual and reflexive cross-cultural interviewing in addition to participant observation exposes us to fundamental differences in the cultural assumptions and meanings of the key concepts in cross-cultural, comparative research. Thus, employing this method can prevent researchers from applying unconsciously only a single framework to compare two cultures.

Moreover, the use of audiovisuals, especially those showing comparable scenes from different cultures, greatly encourages informants to make explicit, culturally meaningful statements. The role of an anthropologist who employs this method is no longer that of a simple participant observer but that of a cultural moderator, who encourages the informants to engage in reflexive activities and cultural dialogue.

Finally, this interviewing process often helps informants to establish their own identity in juxtaposition to something different from them—something by which they are disturbed. In this way, this research procedure brings to the surface not only the cultural assumptions of the informants, but also the tension in a wider social context surrounding the informants. Through informants' characterization of their own identity, we as anthropologists begin to appreciate the tension within a society.

Notes

[1] This chapter is a revised version of our earlier paper (Fujita and Sano 1988). The material is based on three field studies. The American data are part of broader fieldwork jointly conducted in Riverfront City, Wisconsin, from fall 1984 to spring 1986 (Sano 1989b). The Japanese material was collected through observations and interviews during the summer of 1986 at a Japanese day care center (Kawa Day Care) in a suburb of Tokyo. Sano also conducted research on young children's behavior patterns at a different day care center (Hato Day Care) in 1978–79 in a different suburb of Tokyo (Sano 1983, 1988). During this research, he recorded extensively on videotape the interactions between teachers and children. The Japanese videotapes shown to the American teachers were the ones that Sano recorded at Hato Day Care.

[2] Though the Spindlers use the term "reflective," we prefer to use the term "reflexive" in order to convey the nuance of deeper consideration, meaning-seeking, and evocation.

[3] See also Tobin et al. (1989) for the use of video in comparative studies.

[4] The reflexive cross-cultural interviews at the American day care center were conducted in March 1986, before we did our fieldwork at the Kawa Day Care center. When we went to Japan for research in the summer of 1986, we tried to conduct more intensive fieldwork at Hato Day Care because of the familiarity with this center from the previous research. However, because of many changes in staff and some miscommunication, it was practically impossible for us to resume our research at Hato Day Care. Instead, we chose Kawa Day Care in a different suburb. The Hato and Kawa Day Care centers share many similarities. The differences between these centers are limited to the fact that the Kawa center is a one-story building operated by a private organization, while the Hato center is a two-story building operated by the city. In fact, both centers have very similar educational philosophies and daily activities, the same child/teacher ratio, identical floor and playground arrangements, similar backgrounds of the children's parents and almost the same age distribution of staff. Most importantly, the types of activities

about which the American teachers commented while viewing the videotapes of the Hato center (such as the noise level, help in eating, or the duty system, which we will subsequently describe) are also commonly observed at Kawa Day Care. Therefore, we have judged that both sets of videotapes from the Hato and Kawa Day Care centers are adequate for the present study.

[5] See Shinohara and Sakai (1995) for comparative studies of American and Japanese teachers at elementary schools.

[6] In this game, the children are divided into two groups. Two children from each group face each other and walk on the balance beam from the opposite ends. When they meet, each child extends his or her hand showing one of the following three forms: *gu* (stone, by making a fist), *choki* (scissors, a fist with the index finger and the middle finger extended) or *pa* (paper, by opening a hand). The stone is stronger than the scissors but weaker than the paper. The scissors defeat the paper but lose to the stone. So, if a child extends his other hand showing paper, and the opponent shows stone, the first child wins, but if the opponent shows scissors, then the first child loses. The child who loses goes to the end of the line, and the next child in the group walks on the balance beam to compete with the winner.

[7] The difference in the amount of instruction the teachers give in these two centers may be due to the difference in the attendance patterns of the children. The Kawa teachers can expect to see the same group of children every day in their classes for an entire year; whereas some of the children at Maple are part-time, do not come every day, and can move up a class on their birthdays even in the middle of the school year. Hence, the group of children a Maple teacher has for her class changes quite frequently. Repeating instructions for the changing group may be necessary.

References

Caudill, William, and Helen Weinstein, 1969. Maternal Care and Infant Behavior in Japan and America. *Psychiatry* 32:12–43.

Doi, Takeo, 1973. *The Anatomy of Dependence*. Tokyo: Kodansha International Ltd.

Erickson, F., and Jan Wilson, 1982. *Sights and Sounds of Life in Schools: Research Guide to Film and Videotape for Research and Education*. Research Series No. 125. East Lansing: Institute for Research on Teaching, Michigan State University.

Frager, Robert and Thomas P. Rohlen, 1976. The Future of a Tradition: Japanese Spirit in the 1980s. In *Japan: The Paradox of Progress*, Lewis Austin, ed. New Haven: Yale University Press, pp. 255–78.

Frake, Charles O., 1980. Plying Frames can be Dangerous: Some Reflections on Methodology in Cognitive Anthropology. In C. O. Frake, *Language and Cultural Description*. Stanford: Stanford University Press, pp. 45–60.

Fujita, Mariko, 1977. The Concept of *Amae* in Western Social Science. Unpublished Master's thesis (Spring Paper), Stanford University.

_____, 1984. The Cultural Dilemmas of Aging in America. Ph.D. dissertation, Anthropology, Stanford University.

_____, 1986. Independence and Sharing: A Symbolic Analysis of Meal Programs for the Elderly and Pre-school Children. In *Essays by the Second Year Spencer Fellows*. Cambridge: National Academy of Education.

_____, 1989. "It's All Mother's Fault": Child Care and Socialization of Working Mothers. *Journal of Japanese Studies* 15:67–91.

Fujita, Mariko, and Toshiyuki Sano, 1988. Children in Japanese and American

Day Care Centers: Ethnography and Reflective Cross-Cultural Interviewing. In *School and Society: Learning Content through Culture*, Henry T. Trueba and Concha Delgado-Gaitan, eds. New York: Praeger Publishing Co., pp. 73–97.

Geertz, Clifford, 1973a. Religion as a Cultural System. In C. Geertz, *Interpretation of Cultures*. New York: Basic Books, pp. 87–125.

_____, 1973b. Deep Play: Notes on the Balinese Cockfight. In C. Geertz, *Interpretation of Cultures*. New York: Basic Books, pp. 412–54.

Hsu, F., 1973. Rugged Individualism Reconsidered. *Colorado Quarterly* 9:145–62.

_____, 1981. *Americans and Chinese: Passage to Differences*. Honolulu: University of Hawaii Press.

Kiefer, Christie W., 1970. The Psychological Interdependence of Family, School, and Bureaucracy in Japan. *American Anthropologist* 72: 66–75.

LeVine, Robert A., 1984. Properties of Culture: An Ethnographic View. In *Culture Theory: Essays on Mind, Self, and Emotion*, R. A. Shweder and R. A. LeVine, eds. Cambridge: Cambridge University Press, pp. 67–88.

McDermott, R. P., 1976. *Kids Make Sense: An Ethnographic Account of the Interactional Management of Success and Failure in One First Grade Classroom*. Ph.D. dissertation, Anthropology, Stanford University.

Marcus, G. E., and M. Fisher, 1986. *Anthropology as Cultural Critique: An Experimental Movement in the Human Sciences*. Chicago: University of Chicago Press.

Masuda, Kokichi, 1969. *Amerika no Kazoku—Nippon no Kazoku* (American families and Japanese families). Tokyo: Nippon Hoso Shuppan Kyokai.

Rapson, Richard L., et al., 1967. *Individualism and Conformity in the American Character*. Boston: Heath.

Sano, Toshiyuki, 1983. Behavior Patterns of Mother and Child in Separation and Greeting at a Japanese Day Nursery. *Journal of Anthropological Society of Nippon*, 91(4): 435–54.

_____, 1988. Children's Access Behavior to an Observer: Age Group Differences at a Day Care Center in Japan and Their Cultural Implications. *Journal of Ethology*, 6:9–20.

_____, 1989a. Methods of Social Control and Socialization in Japanese Day-Care Centers. *Journal of Japanese Studies*, 15:125–38.

_____, 1989b. *Caring Americans: An Ethnography of Riverfront, a Middle-Sized Town in the Midwest*. Ph.D. Dissertation, Stanford University.

Schneider, David M., 1972. What is Kinship all About? In *Kinship Studies in the Morgan Centennial Year*, Priscilla Reining, ed. Washington DC: The Anthropological Society of Washington, pp. 32–63.

Shimahara, Nobuo, and Akira Sakai, 1995. *Learning to Teach in Two Cultures: Japan and the United States*. New York: Garland Publishing.

Shweder, Richard A., and Robert A. LeVine, eds., 1984. *Culture Theory: Essays on Mind, Self, and Emotion*. Cambridge: Cambridge University Press.

Spindler, George, and Louise Spindler, 1987a. Prospect for a Controlled Cross-Cultural Comparison of Schooling Schoenhausen and Roseville. In *Education and Cultural Process: Anthropological Approaches,* 2d ed., George Spindler, ed. Prospect Heights, IL: Waveland Press.

Spindler, George, and Louise Spindler, eds., 1987b. Editorial Introduction to Part I, Ethnography: An Anthropological view. In *Interpretive Ethnography of Education at Home and Abroad*. Hillsdale, NJ: Lawrence Erlbaum Associates.

_____, 1990. *The American Cultural Dialogue and its Transmission*, with Henry Trueba and Melvin D. Williams. London; New York: Falmer Press.

_____, 1993. Crosscultural, Comparative, Reflective Interviewing in Schoenhausen and Roseville. In *Qualitative Voices in Educational Research*, Michael Schratz, ed. London; Washington, DC: Falmer Press.

Tobin, Joseph J., David Y. H. Wu, and Dana H. Davidson, 1989. *Preschool in Three Cultures: Japan, China, and the United States*. New Haven; London: Yale University Press.

Varenne, H., 1977. *Americans Together: Structured Diversity in a Midwestern Town*. New York: Teacher's College Press.

Acknowledgments

This study is supported in part by the Spencer Fellowship, National Academy of Education, which was awarded to Mariko Fujita (1984–87). The authors would like to express our gratitude toward George and Louise Spindler, who have always been helpful to us not only as university professors, but also as colleagues and friends, ever since we took their courses at Stanford University. We are grateful to the people of Maple and Kawa Day Care who gave us their valuable time. We also thank Susan Zack for her editorial comments, and Sharon Traweek for the discussions we had.

21

Does Formalism Spell Failure?
Values and Pedagogies in
Cross-Cultural Perspective

Victoria J. Baker
Eckerd College

Your teaching methods are fun and entertaining for the children. They
love to be in your class, and it's a good opportunity for them. As for us,
however, the inspectors and the parents expect us to follow the school
syllabus; and we also don't have the resources to buy special materials
for projects like you do. In the end, the children need to respect authority, and your methods would not work for us.

—-from an interview by the author with a Sri Lankan teacher, 1984

Over the past twelve years I have visited schools in more than sixteen developing countries and have done case studies in many of them.
In Sri Lanka I taught English for a year in a remote rural school where
I did my dissertation research; and in Ethiopia I watched a former student of mine, Andrew Haines, cope with many problems as he took on
a teaching job in a privileged girls' school. Through the years I have mel-
lowed and softened my culture-bound judgments of the formalism so
apparent in the majority of the schools I have visited: rote recitation,
copying exercises, "chalk and talk," and passive seatwork. Both Andy
and I learned that it is difficult to successfully export Western pedagogical methods that involve participatory learning or exercises to promote
creative or critical thinking. Formalistic teaching seems to be right in
settings where the cultural values are congruent with formalism: where
national identities may conflict with modern or Western-oriented pedagogies, and where there is a colonial history of formalism or ideologies
linked with strict religious or political principles.

While looking at formalism in a new perspective, I have also
become more aware of the issues of appropriate learning, cultural con-

Source: Written especially for *Education and Cultural Process*. 3rd Edition.

textualization and pedagogical innovation. Formalism may be the best approach for many cultures because it is congruent with their cultural values and context. At the same time, it may be inappropriate for other cultures which operate with different value systems. This often can be seen in contexts where minority children are struggling in mainstream school situations.

For this chapter I have poured over my field notes and historical notes from seven countries around the world, looking at the degree to which formalism is employed by the teachers and how it fits with the cultural values of the pupils, parents and educators. I have come to the conclusion that formalism is not necessarily an anachronism which merits far-reaching programs for change; rather, it is compatible with numerous traditional values. Formalistic models can be effective and can be improved through incremental change. All pedagogies, whether formalistic, participatory/inquiring, or somewhere in between, should be consistent with the values of the teachers and learners in question.

Notes from Fieldwork Observations

In most of the following cases I was an observer rather than a participant observer in the strict sense of the term. It is likely that my presence altered the behavior of the teachers and learners to some extent. On the other hand, most of the teachers tried to do their task a little better than usual—with their best foot forward, according to the ideals and expectations of their system—when being observed by an outsider, as I have always done when my teaching was observed. For this reason, if I saw formalistic approaches and behavior, it is probably because this is considered to be the expected and best way. Having gained long-term, firsthand experience in a remote rural school in Sri Lanka, that is a good place to begin.

Sri Lanka

A nation with a proud educational heritage, Sri Lanka has an excellent reputation among developing countries in the field of education. Its list of glowing statistics had even improved and grown lengthier in the decade between my two field research periods, despite the ethnic violence there. Public education is free from year 1 (age 5) through university level. The total number of schools has risen along with the growing population, and primary pupils rarely have to walk farther than 4 km to school. The overall teacher:pupil ratio is an admirable 23.5. The literacy figures are reported to have improved from an 86.5 percent overall literacy ten years ago to an estimated 90.2 percent today. The country is on the threshold of achieving universal primary education

(99 percent intake); and its education flow statistics are enviable among developing countries: 97 percent of grade-one entrants complete primary school, and of these 92 percent go on to secondary school.

I went to Sri Lanka in 1983 to study education in rural areas and spent sixteen months (1984–1985) in the village of Suduwatura Ara. There I occupied an excellent vantage point as participant observer, for I taught English in the thatch-roofed school and lived in a small wattle-and-daub house that the villagers built for me on the school premises. In that period I also visited thirty randomly selected village schools in the underdeveloped Moneragala District, interviewing the principals and observing classes. I was investigating what made some schools function more effectively than others within the framework of the Sri Lankan Ministry of Education's goals. Returning to the village for a sabbatical year of leave in 1994–95, I was again able to follow the workings of their new and bigger school from the same vantage point.

Despite Sri Lanka's overall good record, there were many grumblings about quality decline, and the composite picture of the typical rural school is far from rosy: high teacher absenteeism; alienation between the school and community, with teachers and parents both complaining that the other does not take education seriously; low attendance rates, with pupils performing poorly and classes that are far behind on the curriculum calendar; and dissatisfied teachers and principals, with a minimum of supervision, who feel they are on punishment assignments in places with primitive living conditions.

Lamentably, the village school where I lived and worked fell into this "failing" category, particularly in the second fieldwork period. The schools which could be placed (according to a given set of criteria, such as performance of students on state examinations) in the category of "promising" schools were those in which there were dedicated principals and teachers who took pride in their work (Baker 1988:270). In these schools order and discipline are strict, the curriculum is closely followed, and the teaching methods are traditional. Approaching these schools during lesson time, it is likely that choral recitation will be heard, or that students are seated neatly in rows, copying exercises from the board or from a book that would be labeled "dull and colorless" by Western standards. Such formalism permeates all aspects of the school's practices; and it is a rare class that allows for deviation from the day's prescribed lesson, letting children use what they have learned, ask questions, or be independently creative.

Into such an atmosphere I brought my Western teaching experience, complete with various antics, skits, and games; using puppets made by the class, giving cut-and-paste projects, and teaching all the children's songs I could recall from my repertoire. The children responded to these lessons and delighted in them, partly of course because it was a curiosity to have a white woman "entertain" them in ways to which they were unaccustomed. The parents, too, were appreciative to have anyone—especially an outsider—take an interest in their children and their school.

I was depressed in the beginning that the children had been conditioned not to think and not to use what they had learned, but rather to parrot English phrases in a Pavlovian style. When they heard me say an English phrase, they repeated it without knowing the meaning—for example, "come with me" or "very good." Though I was able to make some progress with them, teaching them the meaning of common directions I gave in class and having them do substitution exercises, it was clear that much of their "learning" in all their classes was learning without thinking.

My innovative (for Sri Lanka) teaching methods made the other teachers at the school uncomfortable, especially during the second fieldwork. I was not oblivious to some of their disapproving glances as I played "Simon Says" or danced the "Hokey-Pokey" with the children. For teachers, persons in positions of authority and alleged respect, this was considered undignified behavior, with the danger of undermining the required discipline and inviting the children to take too many liberties. The attitude of those teachers is expressed in the opening quotation of this chapter. They probably were right when they said that my pedagogical approaches would not work for them. Their values and those of the villagers were more consistent with traditional formalistic methods; and they also saw poverty as a constraint to doing many "creative" activities that necessitated buying materials. At the same time, both teachers and pupils know it is very possible to have good quality formalistic instruction, achieving the goals of the Ministry of Education, with the children performing well on the state examinations—when the teachers go about their jobs with dedication, taking special interest in the children they teach, albeit with strict discipline; and when the community and the school have active reciprocal support. Such were the effectively functioning schools in the district.

Vietnam

Among the countries where I have done comparative fieldwork in rural schools, Vietnam is an interesting example for consideration of values and national identity. I was allowed to observe and interview at several rural Vietnamese schools in 1992 and 1995. Here there has been a long tradition of respect for education, as Vietnam is the home to one of the oldest universities in the East, founded in 1070 to educate the sons of Mandarins. More recently, Vietnam has raised its literacy rate from a mere 10 percent in 1945, when it freed itself from the French after sixty-two years of oppression, to almost 94 percent today.

This accomplishment is even more remarkable when one considers its decades of warfare, the expensive involvement in Cambodia, and the long U.S. economic embargo. Although Vietnam is one of the poorest countries in the world, 86 percent of all children aged 6–10 attend primary school.

The schools I was allowed to visit epitomized formalism. The school day started with formal exercises to the beat of a drum. The classrooms were bare and austere, with wooden tables and benches lined in rows and only a blackboard and a picture of Ho Chi Minh adorning the walls. The teacher wrote lessons on the board; the 50–55 pupils recited lessons in unison on command. The teacher asked questions; the children raised their hands in stiff, salute form and stood when called on to give their answers. Occasionally a child would be asked to write a phrase or do a sum on the board. In the arithmetic classes the pupils did their work on small slates with chalk. Periodically the teacher asked them to hold up their slates so she could check their sums. Reading lessons consisted of children standing in turn to read a passage aloud from their reading book, often with a socialist message in the text, as I was to find out after showing one of my Vietnamese college students the videos I made. Factual questions were asked about the text, but there was no discussion of the meaning. At all times the children were well behaved, usually with their arms folded on the tables.

One of the schools I visited was considered the best in the rural area around Hanoi. When I asked the accompanying Ministry of Education official what made it a good school, he replied that they followed most closely the rules set by the Ministry. In their very centralized communist system, no room is left for innovative or flexible teaching, even if a teacher were so inclined. This is reflected in the present educational reform in Vietnam, which aims "to turn out citizens equipped with socialist spirit, national character and professional abilities" (Vietnam Ministry of Education 1991:15).

Vietnam is also interesting for consideration of its cultural contextualization, because its values are couched in Confucianism and Buddhism: filial piety, discipline, obedience, respect for parents, elders and teachers. Added to these are the rigid socialist values imparted by the political system and its ideology, in which production and study are linked, education and indoctrination are on an equal par, and instruction is aimed at increasing the pupils' usefulness to society. Watching the earnest faces of the children at their benches, the best of whom were wearing the red bandannas of the "Young Pioneers," they seemed to personify the values of socialism—both in appearance and in behavior. Going to school is serious business and best accomplished if all are following rigid rules.

Formalism is thus an educational model compatible with the Vietnamese traditional values and those of its political regime. The Ministry acknowledges that educational quality must be improved; it even includes terms such as "individual development" and "capacity of imagination" in its discussion of aims (1990:19). For the moment, however, a formalistic approach is the only one feasible. Considering the (recent) historical, social, and financial constraints, the story of Vietnam's educational development can be seen as a success story—one where the teaching/learning strategies are appropriate for the prevailing cultural values.

Morocco

Another good example for consideration of values and cultural contextualization in a tightly controlled Islamic monarchy is Morocco. It is a country with a tradition of literacy brought by Arab conquerors in the eighth and ninth centuries; its Kairouine University, founded in 862 as a center for higher Islamic studies, is one of the oldest universities in the world. Recent history has seen substantial school enrollment increases since independence from France in 1957; the ratio of the six- to eleven-year-old cohort enrolled in primary school was 63 percent in 1995, up from 55 percent in 1991; but the literacy rate was still under 44 percent, with great male/female disparities.

The village primary school of Maraahdar, housed in three separate small buildings and located in a remote and little-developed area, serves five hamlets. There are no latrines and no water at the school. The day starts with the head teacher clapping his hands sharply, a sign for the pupils to line up at their individual buildings. In the bare rooms are only tables, chairs, and a blackboard with King Hassan II's picture above it. The school abundantly exemplified the characteristics of formalism when I was there in 1992. The 103 pupils (78 boys, 25 girls) were taught by six male teachers who dominated the classes with strict authority. Typically the teacher stood at the blackboard with a pointer and pointed to words which had to be read or recited. Memorization in a tightly controlled classroom was the norm. The use of the pointer and the sharp commands lent a tension and sense of threat to the classroom, which gave way to boredom when the teacher was not present or in his controlling mode. School was clearly not a place to go for fun. As in the schools described by Boubekri (1990:136–38), I observed the same pattern time and again: teacher giving a command, pupils responding. The teacher always took the initiative and directed the operations; the pupils waited for assignments and remained in a dependent situation, lacking spontaneity. Repetition, rote memorization, rigidity and austerity marked the activities and atmosphere. I got the feeling that as a woman my prying eyes were not welcome. Even the most pleasant and compassionate of the six teachers took a defensive stance, saying that it was hard to get the rural children interested in education.

I noticed in the schools I observed that the linguistic situation also made it difficult to do or expect more than memorization. The children speak Moroccan Arabic at home, and they memorize classical, Koranic Arabic at the local Koranic preschool. They go to the first two grades learning standard Arabic. In the last three grades they are confronted with two language streams: they study history, geography and religious morality in Arabic; and they start learning the French language, which is also the language of instruction for science and math. It is little wonder that this is a formidable program for poor rural children of illiterate parents, in a school with the bare minimum of educational equipment and supplies.

State education is preceded by two years of Koran school—a tradition which pre-dates the public school system by a millennium and probably contributes to the formalistic mind-set. Although these Koranic schools are not part of the public school system, it is strongly recommended that preschoolers attend. The main goal of traditional Koranic education was, and remains, memorization of the Koran. In the Koran school the Moroccan/Islamic values of respect for authority and good behavior are impressed on the children. Parents express their approval of such schools as an important religious opportunity, where their children learn the rudiments of attention behaviors, literacy skills, and obedience. However, any tendency toward critical or creative thinking is squelched at an early stage.

In many ways Morocco is on the right track in achieving its goals, such as higher enrollments and better trained—or at least longer trained—teachers; but it is far from smoothing out urban-rural and gender inequities or achieving classroom dynamics with active pupil participation. There are fundamental values (for example, strict discipline and respect for authority; memorization of sacred texts; family responsibility and loyalty above individual achievement; cooperation and community; protection and seclusion of females) which clash with the Western values that create the models for economic and educational development (such as cultivation of the individual, self-reliance, a questioning attitude, democratic and participatory input, and success-orientation). Moroccan values are entrenched in Islam, enculturated in the home and preschool, held equally dear by the public school teachers, and unlikely to be changed in the foreseeable future.

Tanzania

As in Vietnam, education in Tanzania is supposed to play an integral role in molding the socialist society. The Tanzanian plan was proposed by President Julius Nyerere in 1967, and similar objectives to those of Nyerere are outlined in a recent booklet published by the Tanzanian Bureau of Statistics:

Primary education which is both compulsory and universal aims at giving pupils a permanent ability in literacy and numeracy with emphasis on reading, writing and arithmetic. It also intends to give pupils education which is complete in itself, inculcating a sense of commitment to the total community and to help the pupils accept the values appropriate to Tanzania's future as well as preparing learners for further education. (1992:22).

Like the declining literacy figures since 1987, however, the quality of rural schools leaves much to be desired.

A good example of this can be found in the town of Missungui in northwestern Tanzania, where I did fieldwork in 1993. Missungui has three schools; the smallest and newest of these had three teachers and 180 children in grades 1–5 at the time of my fieldwork. The school was housed in three rooms of the municipal administrative building, in addition to an incomplete, separate, two-room building originally designed as a storage unit. All the rooms were bare except for desks and a blackboard. In the small building with dirt floor, a portable blackboard was propped against the wall. Although the books were free and supplied by the government, they were very old: the Swahili book dates from 1969, the geography book from 1977, and the science book from 1986. There were no posters or teaching materials, and the only sports equipment consisted of two old tennis balls. The children's school supplies were equally scarce. Most of them had put newspaper covers on their exercise books; and many had their pencils tied to a string and attached to a book or article of clothing to prevent losing these precious items. The pupils wore ragged, torn uniforms and no shoes.

The teaching style and classroom dynamics were equally sober. The students sat in rows of desk-bench units, three seated at a unit built for two. Most of their activities consisted of copying from the board or doing exercises from their textbooks, which were then taken to the teacher for brief correction. All movements appeared to be strictly formal. The male teacher even drew lines on the painted blackboard before writing the lesson.

In the supervised classes, teachers were quick to reprimand any talking. The unattended classes were chaotic, and children often spent that time on the playground. The supervised behavior was very rigid, from the repeated drills in unison to the standing position each child assumed when answering a question or reading aloud. Female students made a small curtsy when approaching the teacher for any reason, as is the custom in the Sukuma tribe, the dominant tribe of this village. Corporal punishment was common. The end of the school day was marked by calisthenics done in formal lines. Even during these exercises a child could be called forward and given a blow on the hand or rear.

Although the drab austerity and seeming unfriendliness of the school may make it a target of criticism by Western observers, the values reflected in the educational goals and the teaching strategies are congruent with those of the Tanzanian culture and national identity: respect for authority, a sense of commitment to the total community, and learning literacy and numeracy, not critical thinking. Although I got the distinct impression that more compassion from the teachers would be welcomed by the pupils, it is doubtful that innovative teaching methods would meet with success in this setting of subsistence farmers. The latter harbor the dream that their child may be one of the few who passes the state examination, goes on to secondary school and gets a salaried job. Any changes in the traditional path toward achieving that idealistic goal would be eyed with the greatest suspicion.

Cuba

When it comes to using education to inculcate the values of national identity, few better examples can be found than in Cuba. I had wondered how the island's educational system—long hailed as a model—would be faring now that the country had lost 70 percent of its trade after the demise of the former Soviet Union, and now that the continued U.S. economic embargo was squeezing the country dry. After visiting both urban and rural schools in 1994, it was evident that this nation was holding on tenaciously and proudly to its educational reputation and the accompanying values of respect for authority, community and nation.

I asked permission to visit more than the acclaimed Ciudad Escolar Libertad, a square-mile complex of eight schools in Havana, converted from a military base of the Batista period and dedicated to excellence in scholastic achievement as well as physical education. I wanted to see some "average" urban schools and some rural schools in remote areas, making unannounced visits.

Transportation was a bigger problem than permission. I found that Cuba was indeed "running on empty" with regard to food and fuel—but not when it came to human educational resources. Wherever I stopped to visit, the schools were functioning in good form, and a formal curriculum was followed down to the last detail. In every Cuban school there is a bust of Jose Marti, revered as their greatest writer and patriot, near the flag which is raised at 8:00 A.M. with a short ceremony. Every class had a teacher and a teacher's assistant, and no class had more than 33 pupils. The curriculum included a course in "practical work" that dealt with things like gardening so the children would learn to help solve food problems in the "Special Period," carpentry, cooking and sewing, as well as a course in "civil defense." The children were all dressed in clean uniforms, shoes and socks—blue uniforms and ties for the Pioneras Moncadistas (grades 1–3), and red ones for the Pioneras Jose Marti (grades 4–6). The government provides cloth coupons for only one uniform per child every two years, "but the families pass them down and share," confided a teacher.

I was determined to visit a remote rural school, but getting out into the countryside was no small task: buses are sporadic, overcrowded and undependable. I had to pay an exorbitant price to the taxi driver of a rickety old Lada to take me 185 km to the remote village of Macurije, where I was able to visit two tiny village schools. The visits remained unannounced, as Macurije and surrounding hamlets have no telephones—nor electricity and running water, for that matter.

The tiny Guillermo Montagut School had fifteen pupils in grades one through six, and two teachers. It was housed in a two-room wooden structure that the parents helped build. The young male teacher in charge of grades five and six was also a lawyer who defends the rights of workers in the area. The same immaculate white bust of Jose Marti stood in front of the school, graced with a bouquet of fresh flowers. At 8:00 sharp the handful of rural children, dressed in the same uniforms found across the island, lined up for the flag-raising ceremony. Every child, when called on, recited lines or verses by Marti. Inside the classroom the children worked on their lessons quietly and in a disciplined fashion. The teacher gave instruction at the board, but the small number of pupils allowed for individual control.

Even this small school had the traditional "mural" with cutouts of Cuba's revolutionary heroes. It also had a cabinet of books designated as the mini-library; a latrine; and a well-tended garden with fruits, vegetables and medicinal herbs. The teachers assured me that enrollment of all school-aged children was necessary and normal and that attendance was excellent. "There is enough social control from the Federation of Women and the Youth Organization to prevent anyone from keeping their children at home," one said. The other remarked that all parents agree that the fundamental task of a child is to go to school and study.

The children were learning the rigid values of the nation's socialist system: selflessness, community and sharing, and submission to authority. It was not a system where the Western values of individualism or critical questioning would be given a chance, but it worked for Cuba.

Ethiopia

Among the sub-Saharan African nations, Ethiopia has perhaps the richest cultural history and the oldest educational tradition. Not only has it shared in the Islamic past with Koranic schools in the large Muslim community; it also has been served by widespread church schools of the Ethiopian Orthodox Church since Ethiopia adopted Christianity in the fourth century A.D. It is ironic, therefore, that this nation is one of the poorest and most educationally deprived in the world today. Despite some brief success in literacy campaigns after the socialist revolution of 1974, continuing ethnic tension, political upheaval, civil war with Eritrea, drought and famine shifted the focus from educational development to survival. Recent figures place the literacy rate for those 15 years and older at 35.5 percent (45.5 percent male; 25.3 percent female). There continue to be glaring educational inequities, not only between the sexes, but also between urban and rural areas.

In the summer of 1993 I visited schools of different types in Ethiopia, running the full continuum from urban private schools in Addis Ababa to the most humble village schools. Most interesting for the comparative examples presented here is the case study of the Yehiwot Berhan School in Addis Ababa, a privileged protestant girls' school where my former American student, Andy Haines, taught English for two years. His experiences shed additional light on the dilemmas encountered when trying to employ Western teaching methods in a setting with very different values.

The school was founded in 1924 by American missionaries, who brought foreign expertise and resources, and it gained the reputation of being the best school in the country. After the Ethiopian revolution in 1974 it was turned over to the Evangelical Lutheran Church of Ethiopia. The school remains church affiliated today, but it receives relatively little funding from the United States; it is now at the lower end of the privileged and prestigious educational institutions in Addis Ababa. The director tells with pride that there is a maximum enrollment of 60 students per class in grades 1–8 in this school of 820 girls. Given the common situation of 90–120 pupils per class in Ethiopian public schools, both urban and rural, 60 is a small number.

The classes are conducted in a very formalistic manner. The desks are arranged in four rows of two desks side by side. The students rise to greet the teacher and also rise every time they speak to give an answer; they then wait to be given permission to sit down. The fourth-grade English class is a typical example. The girls are enthusiastic in giving answers to prelearned lessons, although many of the lessons are learned by heart. They raise their hands, waving and whispering loudly, "Teacher!" Despite the "small" size of these private-school classes, many of the teachers consider order and discipline among the girls to be a problem; they often resort to corporal punishment, hitting the girls on the hand or shoulders with a length of rubber hose. Haines says he could not bring himself to hit the girls. At the same time, he feels his classes were more rowdy than the others because of that.

Although the teachers and administrators at this school think that a "Western" approach to education is desirable, there is a decided clash of traditional values with Western pedagogies that include the inquiry method, critical thinking, and participatory interaction. Consequently, the approaches espoused by Haines—inspired by his TESL (Teaching English as a Second Language) training at the University of Florida, and given a noble and determined try by him in the beginning—ran into barriers. For example, his request to use textbooks other than the government's *English for New Ethiopia* was denied. While the government text is culturally relevant, the topics often relate to communism and revolution, which Andy considered inappropriate for children. Also, the emphasis is on written rather than spoken language, and the testing assesses grammatical knowledge as opposed to communicative ability. It was feared that the use of another textbook might be perceived as acting against the government's wishes, and using another text or his own material might jeopardize the students' success on the standardized national examinations.

The non-Western, dependence-training values of respect for rigidly enforced discipline, as well as a cooperative, collective (as opposed to individualist) attitude, could additionally be found in Haines' aborted attempts at using new teaching strategies and Western ideals. He reports that his main goal in teaching was to promote greater independent thinking with increased interaction between the students and teacher. On one occasion he asked his fourth-grade students with three prior years of English simply to write one sentence in English. Of the 63 students in the class, 12 wrote an original sentence, 20 wrote a sentence that recently appeared in their textbook examples, and the rest could not write one.

Further, the act of learning was shown to be a communal effort rather than an individual one. Giving a fellow student an answer was the norm. Cheating on tests and homework was not considered to be wrong, as cheating was perceived as a way of helping someone to succeed. Most of the Ethiopian teachers deducted 5–10 percent from the grade if a student was caught cheating on an exam. Haines' policy, considered to be the most stringent in the school, was to fail the student on the particular test. Despite the comparative severity, the frequency with which his students cheated was no less than in other teachers' classes. Andy's idealism and innovative ideas gradually gave way to conformity and acceptance that outside approaches and values are not easily introduced in a traditional Ethiopian setting—even one that pays lip service to the desirability of Western strategies.

Haines' experiences further corroborated my own in Sri Lanka. New teaching strategies by an enthusiastic teacher can have some limited, temporary success; but they will probably succumb to the more powerful pressures of traditional enculturated values held by the administrators, teachers, parents and pupils.

Aboriginal Australia

The schools in Australian Aboriginal communities are government schools operating with the dominant Western-oriented values of a modern industrial society. In the summer of 1991 I did case studies in two remote Aboriginal communities in Queensland together with a student of mine, a Ford Foundation Apprentice Scholar, Angela Matusik. These studies showed a problem of contextualization in which the values of the mainstream Australian education system are inconsistent with Aboriginal values.

Australian Aboriginal communities are plagued by innumerable problems. Many of these are interrelated with broader, more general troubles that permeate diverse levels of Aboriginal life and perpetuate a vicious cycle: high unemployment due to lack of skills and training; unacceptance, racism and prejudiced attitudes encountered among white Australians; and alcoholism and violence in Aboriginal communities. Such dilemmas are reflected in the problems facing educators and learners—for example, the difficulty in getting trained Aboriginal teachers and/or dedicated white teachers and principals; high dropout rates and poor attendance among students; and a low percentage of students who go on to secondary or higher education. An all-pervasive tension exists in the Aboriginal communities and is seen in the volatility of student behavior and the lower attainment of goals. The schools are pulled between two general models. One stresses preservation of cultural identity and traditions, reinforcing pride in ethnic origins and adopting educational strategies appropriate to Aboriginal lifestyles. The other stresses uniformity of education and the aim of preparing Aboriginal children to fill a place in the modern industrial system of the dominant Australian society. This means inculcating (or trying to inculcate) the values of individualism, competition, efficiency, success-orientation and even materialism—values which are incongruent with those of the Aboriginal society.

One of the schools I visited was Palm Island State School, located on a lush green, coral reef island about 45 miles north of Townsville and 30 miles off the mainland coast: a seemingly idyllic tropical paradise. A closer look, however, shows that the quality of life is far from ideal. The island served as a penal colony early in the century, to which

Aboriginals from many different tribes were deported for various offenses. The population on the island has grown to over 3,000, making it the largest Aboriginal community in Australia. It was not until 1984 that Aboriginal Councils were elected to take the job of Local Government Authority, but the Palm Islanders were in no way prepared to take over the responsibility of running their local government. A tense situation has prevailed, and Palm Island continues to be ridden with a shocking record of violent crime, a high incidence of alcoholism and family abuse, a lack of income-generating activities, and 90 percent unemployment. The community "cantine" (bar) is the biggest profit-making enterprise through the sale of alcoholic beverages, and there are few other recreational facilities, not even a movie theater. Living "off the dole" has become a way of life for most inhabitants.

The Palm Island State School is housed in an attractive set of buildings, centrally located, with up-to-date supplies and equipment. The Australian government has spared no cost in the school's physical attributes. There is a comfortable teacher's lounge, bright classrooms with modern desks and cabinets, a separate manual arts building full of woodworking and other shop equipment, a computer center with a terminal for each class member, a fully equipped home economics room, an arts center, and a library. It was clear that if there are educational problems, they are not due to material shortages.

At the time of the case study the school had an enrollment of 288 pupils, of which 280 were Aboriginal (the rest being children of temporary white residents). There were nine teachers in addition to the principal; all were white except for one Maori. The teachers said they dreaded coming to Palm Island and experienced culture shock and a sense of isolation when they arrived. They had no special training to deal with Aboriginal culture and had difficulty understanding the pidgin English. They found it hard to bridge the gap with the community, given the suspicion with which they were viewed and their temporary status. Most disturbing of all, according to the teachers, were the high suicide and murder rates and the high incidence of physical abuse on the island.

The teachers pointed out that the Palm Island children are about two years behind those in mainstream schools and that truancy is a big problem. Typical problems that were difficult to address in class included the verbal abuse, aggression and volatility of the children. The teachers had given up on trying to enforce punctuality, for the children stay up very late in the overcrowded, noisy households and are extremely tired in the morning; they come to school any time they please and stay away with equal ease. A common behavior of Aboriginal children is that of "teasing," taunting their peers who may try to conform to the rules or who try to excel in the class. In the school, as well as in the community, ambition and competition are not values prized by the Aboriginal tradition. The leveling mechanism of teasing serves to frustrate the white teachers, who are trained to encourage, reward and teach children through competitive activities.

On Palm Island there is a second school, different from the State School—St. Michael's, a smaller private Catholic school, where three of the seven teachers were black and each class also had an Aboriginal teacher aide to serve as a liaison between the teacher and the community. The teachers were there because they wanted to be. They had followed the AITEP program at James Cook University (Aboriginal and Islander Teacher Education Program) and served as role models and carriers of indigenous values. The program's research makes clear that there is a "fundamental weakness in any curriculum where non-Aboriginal educators are taking responsibility for teaching Aboriginal knowledge to Aboriginal students through non-Aboriginal learning processes in non-Aboriginal institutions" (Miller 1989:127).

Observations of the first grade taught by an Aboriginal teacher showed a very relaxed atmosphere in a relatively unstructured setting. The teacher was often literally down on the rug with a group of children in the reading corner, while other children were carrying out creative projects with a black teacher's aide. Using teaching strategies with non-competitive, cooperative values—compatible with the indigenous culture—helped eliminate the teasing and taunting so prevalent in the Palm Island State School.

I could not help but draw an analogy in my mind between these Australian situations and those of some Native Americans in the United States. The Australian case studies illustrate the difficulty of imposing Western values on a non-Western culture through schooling, and the usefulness of considering the core values of the receiving culture when judging the effectiveness and success of educational strategies. In many ex-colonial cultures the present-day Western strategies are not formalistic enough to suit the values and expectations of the receivers. It is an ironic twist, however, that many Western educational values (such as punctuality, regular attendance, abiding by the rules, and participating in organized, competition-based activities) tend to be too formal for these Aboriginal children. They respond better in a culturally appropriate context, underscoring the idea that pedagogical strategies must be carefully considered.

Reflections

The observations and experiences over the years have changed me—from an idealistic and optimistic "true believer" in the primacy of participatory approaches to teaching, reinforced by innovative teacher training programs—to a cautious skeptic who realistically acknowledges the enormous obstacles faced by developing countries as they strive for universal primary education and quality improvement. In addition to the practical problems is the question of enculturated values, powerful elements of any culture. Reduced to some basic common denominators, fundamental differences can be signaled between the values of non-Western developing countries in mostly rural settings and those of Western industrialized nations. Generalizing further, the set of values in developing countries—especially those with colonial histories and conservative religious schooling—are usually found in tandem with formalistic pedagogies. Trying to transfer "innovative" teaching programs or programs with competitive underpinnings from the West to schools in developing nations where other values prevail may well turn out to be an exercise in futility.

Several questions remain. Are these schools in developing countries—the majority of all schools in the world—simply "lost causes"? Must more effective ways be found to transfer innovative, participatory, pupil-centered, inquiry-based teaching methods and learning programs to developing countries, so that the students can be better prepared for living in the modern world? To answer yes to a culture-bound assumption such as this—and there will be many who do—will mean that more Western-oriented and idealistic experiments are in store, some destined for unavoidable failure. As Guthrie states in an article defending traditional teaching, "Formalistic teaching is not an aberration distorting the goals of education systems. It is frequently part of, and highly compatible with, a symbiotic whole" (1990:231). It is possible to see, with a glance at Japan, South Korea, and other rapidly industrializing Asian nations, that formalistic pedagogies can be found in countries where enviable modernization has taken place. Inquiry methods and active student participation are not a *sine qua non* for promoting technological change, if that is the goal.

More important is the employment of pedagogical practices that are consistent with the norms and values of a given culture. I felt a kindred spirit in Musgrove when he stated, "Even the most relativist of modern educationists assume that non-directive, discovery methods have a universal validity and should be imposed impartially on all cultures whatever their past traditions and current problems." He went on to say that what other cultures want from the West is strenuous and disciplined pursuit of knowledge: "And we persistently refuse to give it. The arguments are educational, the imperialism pedagogic" (Musgrove 1982:179–80).

Rather than experimenting with Western-styled innovations, there is boundless room for quality improvement within the formalistic pedagogies already in place. In many cases it is a matter of finding solutions to practical problems and constraints. For example, some of the "promising avenues" suggested by Lockheed and Verspoor include providing good textbooks and teacher guides, setting and maintaining standards for instructional time, and introducing snacks or simple meal programs (1991:115–16). These kinds of changes do not run counter to the sets of values that are brought to school by teachers and that are reinforced in their cultural settings. Improving educational elements related to the administration, the school, the principal and the teachers can be done with incremental reforms. As was evident during my own sixteen-month study of education in a remote district of Sri Lanka, some schools are functioning much better than others within the framework of the Ministry of Education's goals (Baker 1988:275–85). Such studies can provide insights into feasible improvements which are consonant with formalistic pedagogies. At the same time, qualitative case studies can show how Western-based methods may be inappropriate for certain cultural groups, often minorities. In these cases, values such as individualism and competition imbedded in the Western pedagogies can be counterproductive, turning children away from schooling. Here, employing the ideas and experiences of native teachers would be a more useful strategy.

As an anthropologist and comparative educationist, I adhere to an incrementalist position taken after the Sri Lankan study (Baker 1988:27–28) and supported by my observations in rural schools around the world. Rather than attacking formalistic pedagogy and striving to replace it by Western-based practices, a better approach may be an incremental one that does not critically question the teaching abilities of legions of educators—many of them remarkably dedicated—working under extremely difficult conditions. In this context I must agree with Guthrie: "The tendency is to look for complex solutions to complex problems, but on occasion simple solutions may suffice" (1990:232). Improving the quality of education means improving it in terms of the recipients' own values and within their own cultural contexts.

References

Baker, Victoria J., 1988. *The Blackboard in the Jungle: Formal Education in Disadvantaged Rural Areas—A Sri Lankan Case*. Delft: Eburon Publishers.

Boubekri, M., 1990. *The International Financial Crisis of the 1980s and its Impact on Educational Reform in Morocco, with a History of Moroccan Education and Policy Recommendations*. Ph.D. dissertation. University of Michigan.

Britannica, 1996. *Britannica Book of the Year, 1996*. Chicago: Encyclopaedia Britannica.

Guthrie, Gerard, 1990. In Defense of Traditional Teaching. In *Teachers and*

Teaching in the Developing World, V. D. Rust and P. Dalin, eds. New York: Garland Publishing.

Lockheed, Marlain E., and Adriaan M. Verspoor, 1991. *Improving Primary Education in Developing Countries*. Oxford: Oxford University Press.

Miller, Greg, 1989. A Reflective Analysis of Cross-Cultural Curriculum Planning: The Development of the Diploma of Teaching (Early Childhood Education). In *Succeeding Against the Odds: The Townsville Aboriginal and Islander Teacher Education Program*, Noel Loos and Greg Miller, eds. Sydney: Allen & Unwin.

Ministry of Education of the Socialists Republic of Vietnam, 1990. *45 Years of Educational Development in Vietnam*. Hanoi: Education Publishing House.

Musgrove, Frank, 1982. *Education and Anthropology: Other Cultures and the Teacher*. Chichester: John Wiley & Sons.

Rust, Val D., and Per Dalin, eds., 1990. *Teachers and Teaching in the Developing World*. New York: Garland Publishing.

Tanzanian Bureau of Statistics, 1992. *Women and Men in Tanzania*. Dar es Salaam: United Republic of Tanzania, Bureau of Statistics.

22
Crosscultural, Comparative, Reflective Interviewing in Schoenhausen and Roseville

George and Louise Spindler
Stanford University

Voices

"Voices," for us, means the voices of our "native" informants in the Schoenhausen and Roseville elementary schools, the sites of our comparative research. The voices include those of the administrator, the children, and, most importantly in this exercise, the voices of two teachers teaching in comparable schools, one in Germany, the other in the United States. The voices in our study are elicited by using evocative stimuli in the form of films taken by us in the Schoenhausen and Roseville schools. We have arranged for textual space so that informants have their own voices, and made the dialogue between ethnographer and informants explicit, as appropriate to a study in modernist format. Our analysis is directed at culturally phrased assumptions apparent in the voiced discourse of the informants. The voices of the ethnographers, ourselves, are heard in the quest for assumptions in the discourse phrased by the natives, but our voices are muted, since we try to elicit the discourse in such a manner that it is self/other reflective. Our method is therefore called the "crosscultural, comparative, reflective interview."

The Research Sites

Schoenhausen is a village of about 2000 in a semi-rural but urbanizing area in *Land* Baden Württemberg, southern Germany. Schoenhausen was known, and still is to some extent, as an *ausgesprochener Weinort* (emphatically a wine-making place). The native-born are *swaebisch* and protestant. Most of the "newcomers" originally migrated from

Source: Reprinted with permission of Falmer Press from *Qualitative Voices in Educational Research*, M. Schratz, ed. (1993), pp. 150–75.

the former east zone, Sudetenland, or other areas from which Germans were expelled or from which they fled after World War II. They are somewhat more urbanized as a rule, and more often than not Catholic (Spindler 1974). The *Grundschule* (elementary school) is charged with the responsibility for educating all of the children and preparing them for a changing Germany and world. Its 127 children are distributed in four grades staffed by six teachers and a *Rektor* (principal), and various other special services personnel. The Schoenhausen Grundschule has enjoyed a good relationship with the community and with the parents whose children attend it. Partly, at least, this relationship is due to the benign influence of the *Rektor*, who has been in that position since the beginning of our study in 1968.

The Roseville elementary school, located in central Wisconsin, includes kindergarten through eighth grade and is somewhat larger than the Schoenhausen school, but is comparable in every other respect. The school district is rural but has many commuters that work in nearby towns, some of them as much as forty or fifty miles distant. The majority of children attending the school come from small dairy farms. This school also enjoys good relationships with its community and with the parents, who eagerly attend school functions whenever possible. The principal is himself a farmer as well as an educator and is well-liked. The predominant ethnicity of the Roseville School District is German (Spindler, 1987a, 1987b and 1990).

Purpose

Our purpose in this chapter is to demonstrate one particular kind of research technique and the text that it produces—the crosscultural, comparative, reflective interview (CCCRI). The technique has been discussed only briefly in our own publications and demonstrated somewhat more extensively in a study in which a Japanese and an American pre-school furnished the cultural "brackets" in the form of films (or video) from each location, for interviews with teachers (Fujita and Sano, 1988 [see chapter 20 for an updated version of their paper]). Our research in Schoenhausen began in 1968, and continued in 1977, 1981 and 1985. In each of the field visits we had specific research objectives that are discussed in "Schoenhausen Revisited and the Discovery of Culture" (Spindler, 1987a). Our overall objective was to explore the role of the school in culture change in comparable areas in Germany and the United States.

As with all instruments or special techniques used in our research, the CCCRI developed out of field experience *in situ*. It was fully applied for the first time in 1985 though we had used films as evocative stimuli (Collier and Collier, 1986) in interviews before that, though not in an explicitly comparative and reflective framework.

The interviews conducted with teachers, children and administrators were directed at cultural differences and similarities, both between Schoenhausen and Roseville and among the named "audiences." The diagram below expresses the overall relationship in both sites.

The diagram shows us that all three kinds of natives in the Schoenhausen and Roseville elementary schools shared some perceptions and assumptions and diverged in others. The divergence appears to represent positional differences. Both the "shared" and "divergent" sectors may be considered cultural phenomena. The anthropologist is not a native, but participates in the situation, perceives, and assumes. His and her (G. and L. Spindler) perceptions and assumptions are no less influenced by position as well as by shared experience and participation in the dialogue of the two research sites.

The CCCRI are designed to stimulate dialogue about pivotal concerns on the part of natives in comparable cultural systems. Some form of audiovisual material (in this instance films of classrooms) representing two cultures (conceivably more) is used to "bracket" the interview. That is, the interview is conducted as an inquiry into the perceptions, by the native, of his/her own situation and that of the "other," and the assumptions revealed in reflections about those perceptions. We regard both the perceptions and assumptions as cultural phenomena.

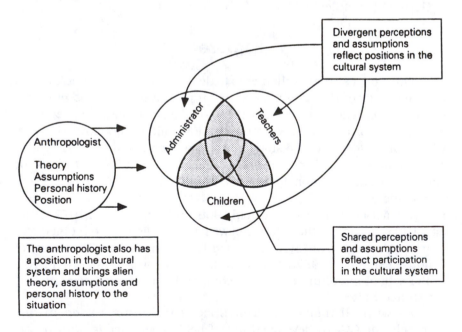

Figure 22.1: The crosscultural comparative reflective interview (CCCRI)

We believe that a "complete" ethnography should include explicit recognition of this complex dialogue in both its shared and divergent aspects.

The Crosscultural Comparative, Reflective Interview (CCCRI)

The basic procedure for the CCCRI is simple—we filmed in Schoenhausen and we filmed in Roseville; and we showed the teachers, the children, and the administrators in both sites the films from both places.[1] We conducted interviews about what they saw in their own classrooms and in those of the "other" and how they interpreted what they saw. These interviews are of a different quality than anything that we had collected previously. They are *reflective* in depth and with a subtlety that had heretofore been lacking, and they are cultural translations by *natives*. The observed differences in the action in the two settings, Schoenhausen and Roseville, caused teachers and children to reflect back on their own behavior at the same time that they were pronouncing perceptions of the behavior of the other. In a sense they were experiencing what we have experienced as ethnographers. After working in the Schoenhausen school in 1968, 1977 and 1981, our visits to the Roseville school beginning in 1983 caused us to reexamine what we were observing in Schoenhausen. This reorientation was fully implemented in our 1985 visit. We had come to accept the Schoenhausen school and community as "normal," as familiar, and it had become increasingly difficult to "see" what it was we were observing. The Roseville experience sharpened our perceptions and caused us to think about them in a different way. In order to observe anything, anywhere, it seems necessary to make it a little "strange" (Spindler, 1988).[2]

The rest of this chapter will be devoted to an examination of some texts produced by the crosscultural, comparative, reflective interviews. Though we have extensive interview material from all of the teachers, the administrator, and from the children in both school settings, we will present only two interviews from teachers, one in Schoenhausen and the other in Roseville; provide some excerpts from the perceptions of the children when they saw the films of their counterparts; and provide a brief excerpt from a longer monologue by a high official in the school district of which Schoenhausen is a part, when he saw the Roseville films. The reactions of the children follow, excerpted from group interviews conducted in the Schoenhausen and Roseville schools. The children's responses will be followed by those of the administrator, and finally the two teachers, Mrs. Schiller (Roseville) and Frau Wanzer (Schoenhausen).[3]

Diverse Reflections

Children's Reactions to Films

Schoenhausen

We showed the films of Roseville classrooms to the first and second grades combined and the third and fourth grades combined, in separate screenings, in the Schoenhausen Grundschule. These are the same films that the teachers and administrators viewed. The Schoenhausen first and second graders seem barely able to control their enthusiasm at the prospect of spending an hour looking at films from America. The teachers keep saying "still!" and "ssshhh!" and "*wieder-still!*" The noise level is very high and one has the impression of tremendous vitality. The teacher and then George Spindler describe the kinds of films they are going to see and what we would like the children to do. The first film shown is of a first and second grade class in Roseville on the history of exploration in the United States. Some of the children are seated at a table in the front of the room with the teacher discussing the exploration of the Mississippi River Valley, while other children are seated at their desks or moving quietly about the classroom as they pursue individual tasks. After the film is shown the Schoenhausen children bounce up and down on their seats, snap their fingers, and shout for attention. "What did you notice?" says the teacher. The children respond, "Some of them could work at a table with a teacher and others could sit alone." "They could work with another person if they wanted to." "They could go to the closet and get things to use if they wanted to and there were some of them listening to tape recorders." The teacher admonished them, "I can't hear unless you're a little more quiet!"—but the noise level continues at what to us seems a very high level. The second film is shown, also of a first and second grade classroom in Roseville. The children are shown working on preparations for Thanksgiving, so they are moving about the classroom a great deal but in the subdued way in which children move in Roseville classrooms. The Schoenhausen children are beside themselves! "Waaagh!" "Wooooo!" "Huhuhuuuuuu!" They are shouting, jumping up and down, and snapping their fingers. The teacher again attempts to still them, but with only moderate success. "Some of them are black-haired!" "The children are not fighting with each other!" "There's nobody tripping anybody else when they move around!" "There's *keine Streiten*" (no fighting). "The teacher stays up front with the group." "She doesn't even look at the others!" "Doch, dock!" "The seats are all rooted to the floor!" "They could run around anytime they wanted to!" "They were at various places." "They were *rühig* (quiet) even though they run from place to place (*verscheidene Zonen*)." "What were they doing with the paper?" "What's in those bags?" (We explained that the film had been taken on "popcorn day," when children could buy popcorn for ten cents a bag if they wanted to and that the colored paper being cut up was in order to make tails for Thanksgiving turkeys that would be put up on the bulletin board). "They picked up all the paper that they dropped on the floor!" "They were quiet in the classroom all the time." "They talked only in English." "They didn't fight at all." "They weren't loud."

Films of comparable classrooms in Roseville were shown to the Schoenhausen third and fourth grade classes. We went through the same procedure of explanation and then showed the first film. The reactions to the films were very similar to those furnished by the first and second grade children, although the older children were somewhat more reflective. They felt that the Roseville system would not work for them because there would be "too much fighting" in the Schoenhausen school. They would not learn as much without a teacher present to help them "at all times." "Learning with a teacher is much simpler than having to learn by yourself." "You couldn't have somebody walking around the classroom anytime they felt like it because somebody would be sure to trip them."

Roseville

We followed the same procedure in the Roseville school, showing the children films of their grade counterparts in Schoenhausen. We had already showed them films of their own classrooms. The children filed into the gymnasium where the film showing was to take place and where bleachers had been set up for grades 3 through 6. They took their places quietly and talked to each other in whispers. The teachers did not have to call upon them to be quiet or to focus their attention on the films. We showed three films in sequence, and we present here only a few of their comments. "I'd rather live away from school. I like riding on the bus!" "We have more recesses and they are a lot of fun and we have a gym—did they have a gym?" "I like having desks like ours where there is a special place to keep one's own things. I wouldn't like to get a table with other kids." "I like being in school a long time each day." (We had explained that the German school day was much shorter than theirs). "We like staying in school for lunch, it's fun." "It's too noisy in those (Schoenhausen) classrooms. How could you learn anything if it was so noisy?" "I couldn't work by myself if there was so much noise all the time." (A few said that they would like to be able to talk out loud and run around the room sometimes and make more noise in general but the consensus was that the Schoenhausen classrooms were too noisy). "I like being able to choose things that I want to do." "The teacher isn't always telling us what we have to do." "None of them wore hats!" "Two of them looked like Bernie and Travis (children in Roseville)." "The top of their desk was messy, there were markers lying all over." "The moving chalkboard is really neat." "I wouldn't want to live so close to the school. I like to ride on the bus." "It would be nice to have sinks in the classroom like that." (The Schoenhausen classrooms all have sinks towards the front.) "Our school is more modern and has a nice gym." "The town is very old." (We had showed one film of the Schoenhausen environment.) "I like modern buildings." "I'd like to be able to make all the noise I want!" (chorus) "No way!" "My ears would go woof woof!" "There is just too much noise."

Interpretation

Children notice the same features that adults notice, but from a different perspective, quite naturally, since they are children, but they are natives of the same system that the teachers are. The Roseville children perceive the noise level and activity of the Schoenhausen children as greater than in their own classroom, and most place a negative value on it. They appreciate the long school day, the lunch period, and living out in the country, not "packed in" with other families in houses. They also recognize the facilities such as the gymnasium and the modern school building as being positive attributes. They are, surprisingly, not particularly attracted by the route of apparent freedom to talk out loud or to engage in vigorous physical activity at times and felt that this could actually be injurious to learning. They do not reflect in the same way that the teachers do on the significance of these differences but merely accept them as given. They are much more attentive to details of the environment and details of behavior. Schoenhausen children attend to the popcorn day, the black hair, the desks, picking up paper, and not fighting when they move around. They perceive the quiet order of the Roseville classrooms and feel that it would not work that way in their own school.

These are the real conditions of the children's lives in the school. These conditions are perceived through cultural screens provided by life in Roseville and life in Schoenhausen. How far this goes into what we could think of as "American" culture or "German" culture is beyond the scope of our intent at the present. What is most important for our purposes is that there is, as will be seen, considerable similarity in teacher perceptions, administrative perceptions, and those of children of the same situations, but there are important differences that reflect the positions of the teachers, administrator, and the children respectively.

The reflections of the *Schulamtdirektor* (superintendent of schools) follow.

The Schulamtdirektor Speaks

We showed the films we have described to the *Schulamtdirektor*, his staff and the Schoenhausen teachers the third evening that we were in Germany in 1985. The *Schulamtdirektor* had expressed his strong interest in seeing the films when we explained our mission on the first day of our presence in Germany. We excerpt, following, a few translated statements from his much longer reaction.

It is difficult for me to see whether these films (of either Roseville or Schoenhausen) are typical of either the school or of other schools in a broader area. If they are typical we come to a situation. I must say that there is between the school in Roseville and that in Schoenhausen a clear difference. A decisive difference. Our teachers, our understanding about school, are situated in a specific system. This system is influenced directly from above, from the school system viewpoint. One always understands that there is a curriculum plan prepared beforehand from above that is binding. And it gives a clear statement of what instruction means. A very clear statement. Instruction is, as we understand it, as a rule joined with a certain theme. Instruction is joined with a certain class. Instruction is linked to a certain preparation, a certain goal and a certain realization of these goals. Indeed there are always variations, but these variations are always within the framework of these intentions. It binds the teachers and the school children in their relationship. The teacher is always at the front. The children sit before him. That can vary, of course, but as a rule that's the way it goes. The teacher instructs everyone at the same time. There are certain themes that can be followed in groups, but these are brought together in a successive sequence. One hears what has been done and what will be done. It is the art of the teacher to bring together these results in order to bring all of the children along, insofar as possible, in the same way. The teacher brings everything together under the same label, tries to reach the same goal, so that in every hour a little piece of the mosaic (of learning) is laid down. And so goes the work in a given hour and in the next hour, week for week until finally the teacher with the children reaches a specific goal. This is characteristic for German instruction and for our understanding of instruction. If I am to take these pictures of (Roseville) that we have seen as typical, and you say that they are, then it is very difficult for me to understand how instruction and progress can move together. There are many questions, many. For example, are the children able to reach, to proceed in similar steps towards learning goals? We have certain disciplines, as in *Deutsch*, in *Mathematik*, in *Sachunttericht*. Is there something like that comparable here? How does the teacher handle the problem of having one group further along and the other hanging along behind? I am not one to think that there is only one way to get to Rome. But without doubt, for us a goal (*Ziel*) is a goal, and without doubt a goal is to be attained. The overall goal is to maintain regular progress in the class. When a child, for example, cannot reach the goal then there is a possibility to repeat or to go to a special school. Naturally one will in instruction always seek to stimulate and follow children's personal motivation, but *Leistungsfihigkeit* (productive efficiency) for the group is the purpose—not the self-purpose of the individual. Everything goes back again into the group. This is certainly the art of the teacher.

The *Schulamtdirektor* goes on at length about the relationship of goals for the school, for instruction, for each hour of instruction. He points out that there have been changes in this curriculum plan through the years in Germany but that there always is a plan, and it is given to the teachers. He feels, paradoxically, that he had greater freedom as a younger teacher than teachers have today. He is particularly impressed with the apparent freedom of the teachers in the Roseville school to teach at their own pace and manner and that the curriculum plan is generated by the teachers themselves.

It is clear that the *Schulamtdirektor* perceives the Roseville classrooms in ways parallel to the way the Schoenhausen children do and in the same general frame of reference as Frau Wanzer does in the following interview (and Frau Wanzer represents quite well the other teachers in the Schoenhausen school). This convergence of perceptions from children, teachers and the higher administration impresses us. If we think of culture as a screen through which one perceives "reality," then a part of this screen is shared by these participants in the Schoenhausen and Roseville process. At the same time, however, it is important to recognize that the teachers, children, and the administrator are each speaking from their particular positions. Their perceptions converge, but they are not identical. The positions, and the perceptions flowing from them, are also culture. Diversity and commonality are both subsumed by cultural structure and process.

Our next step is to present the text from interviews of two teachers, one from Roseville, the other from Schoenhausen.

Two Teachers
Mrs. Schiller, Roseville Elementary School

The interview begins with a summary, by us (GLS) of what we had seen and filmed in Mrs. Schiller's classroom yesterday (and later showed in Germany). As usual, there were a group of children (twelve) at the big table at the front of the room, in this instance learning how to tell time. Mrs. Schiller seemed completely absorbed in this activity and didn't even glance at the children in the back of the room working at their desks or moving quietly about the room to get materials or books from the big closet or shelves lining the walls. Four children, in two pairs, were using flash cards for drill in arithmetic; two others had headsets on and were listening to tapes. Some were pasting paper "feathers" on the tails of paper turkeys (it is close to Thanksgiving). Yet others appear to be working on workbook lessons.

Mrs. Schiller has seen some of the same films of Schoenhausen and Roseville as the children, other teachers, and the *Schulamtdirektor* had.

GLS: It's remarkable that the children work on their own as they do. How do you prepare them to do this?

Mrs. Schiller: I'm not sure I do prepare them. They have to trust me. We try to develop a relationship, that has to happen first. Then I try to figure out which kids won't get along—there are some I would never put next to each other. I separate those—but basically we have really good kids.

GLS: How do they know what to do?

Mrs. Schiller: Well, you're probably thinking of the silent reading period that is never silent at this grade level. They want to share. They can move around, use the flashcards, whatever. I'm just glad they want to come to school and share in the activities like that.

GLS: They seem so, so independent. They are teaching each other! How do they know how to do that?

Mrs. Schiller: I suppose some need help and others know when they need it so they just do it.

GLS: It's not something you establish?

Mrs. Schiller: No, I don't. It begins as soon as they grow up a little (in first grade). This one needs math, this one reading. You know, we're pretty high in math here, but low on reading pretty much in the whole area. Jack (the principal) has ten of his students (from the seventh and eighth grades) come in and each one takes one of my children and reads a story to them, and the little ones read back, too. It is a great help. I can tell when we discuss the readings later. They are well informed. (Mrs. Schiller spoke at length about one problem child and his mother who won't come to school to consult with her.)

GLS: Now, with respect to your underlying objectives as a teacher, that is Linda Schiller as a teacher, not necessarily what you get in the education courses, what would you say your basic purpose is?

Mrs. Schiller: To teach them to be an individual, to be all they can, to the limits of their abilities; and if I can get them to be a happy person, as well as get them to do their best, then I think I have done my job. (Mrs. Schiller talks more about the problem child and his mother. The mother was going to sue because Mrs. Schiller had him repeat the first grade. What she tried to do was to help the child to learn all he could in order to overcome his reading difficulty.)

GLS: Now let's go back a little to this management process. It strikes me (GS) as rather incredible that you have some kind of understanding that they are supposed to go about their activities on their own—individually—and pick up on the things they do without wasting a great deal of time or being disruptive in the class. It seems to me that there's something pretty deep going on here. It doesn't work that way in Schoenhausen.

Mrs. Schiller: You don't feel that if I went to Germany I could operate a classroom the way I do now here? If I got them at the same age level?

GLS: It would be remarkable experiment! The kids tend to act up when adults are not around. But here in Roseville wouldn't you be able to walk out of the classroom, go down to the office, leave your class for five minutes or more?

Mrs. Schiller: Well, yes. I left the first graders alone up in front without any assignment just the other day and Jeremy grabbed the pointer and started "A,B,C,D," etc. and the whole class repeated, and then went on through the alphabet several times. And I said, "That was so nice. You did not waste time!" And then I had to go to the art room and Christopher, my repeater (a child who was "held back" a year), called all the children in the first grade to the desk to get their math books out and be ready; and he stood at the board to write names down if they were talking, so they were all ready, waiting for the class to get started. When they do things like that, I praise. We don't have any time to waste and so I was happy to have the first graders ready to go when the bell rang.

GLS: There were so many different things going on in the class we observed yesterday. It was fascinating to try and film them—this little group here, this one here, another some place else. I (GS) have a logistics question. How do the children know when and how to find what they need?

Mrs. Schiller: Well, it would be great if we could do more of this kind of free choice, but a lot of it is more structured. The head office would like us to do more of the things the kids want to do themselves.

GLS: But how do they know, when they do, what they do?

Mrs. Schiller: Well, it's just the choice. The flashcards are there somewhere, the charts, the tape recorders—you know they're, they're really all little teachers, it's just built in. They come up and ask, "Can I do the flash cards? Can I use the charts? Can I use the tape recorder?" Especially if it's a first grader that needs help and then a second grader can teach them. They love to do that.

GLS: But you arrange the materials for their use somehow?

Mrs. Schiller: Well, they ask if they can do it.

GLS: But you keep the materials in the classroom and they know where they are? Access to them is just them asking you?

Mrs. Schiller: Yes, and it's their choice of friends that they want to work with or whoever they want to share with.

GLS: Where have you taught before? (Mrs. Schiller named several places—all larger and more urban than Roseville.) Do you think it was this way in those communities also?

Mrs. Schiller: Yes, I really do. I have a lot of faith in kids. I think kids are neat! If you have high expectations, 98 percent of the time they will fulfill your expectations.

GLS: What would you feel like if you went out in the hall or someone called you to the phone and you came back after five minutes and found things in considerable disorder?

Mrs. Schiller: Well, I would tell them right out, "I am *very* disappointed! I had this important phone call and you couldn't sit for five minutes while I answered it." I would let them know it hurt me personally. It's a kind of personal thing. Oh, yes! You start building that up the first day of school. Then they feel "we can't hurt our teacher." Oh, yes, that happened today! I had to take a workbook to a parent who was taking her little girl to the dentist so she could work on it if she had to wait, and the class had the same assignment. When I came back to my room they had all finished that page that was assigned and they went right on to the next one. I praised them again, "It was *really* nice that I could count on you, and I could come back to a nice quiet class." And of course they all beamed. They just love praise!

GLS: Do you think you are different than other teachers here or elsewhere?

Mrs. Schiller: Perhaps. I have so many sisters that are all teachers and my mom is a teacher. I have my own philosophy. I don't think children need to finish every page of the workbooks, etc. It's so important for these children living in a rural area to socialize with each other, so I try never to keep a child in during recess or after school to do make-up work on a workbook. They need socialization. And I will *not* be a grouch. I'm not really strict. Some people would probably say that I was lax.

GLS: Were you struck with any special feature when you looked at the German films?

Mrs. Schiller: Well, one thing was the discipline. When they were running around the room and making a lot of noise, it was going further than it would here. But I do feel like we can learn even though we're a little noisy.

GLS: You know, we found that each of the teachers in the Schoenhausen school had a regular sequence of operations that they planned out in every classroom and every hour. Would you say that there was a sequence here and in your classroom?

Mrs. Schiller: Well, we have a curriculum, but we can handle it any way we want. I don't go through the same sequence every day. It would be too boring!

GLS: You mentioned a "curriculum"—in Germany the teachers have a "*Lehrplan*" that defines subjects and sequences and amount of time that should be spent on certain themes. Is that what you mean by curriculum?

Mrs. Schiller: There is a little book here on the shelf that happens to be for the third and fourth grade (she hands it to us).

GLS: Where does this come from?

Mrs. Schiller: The teachers put it out.

GLS: You mean—the teachers here?

Mrs. Schiller: The whole district of Arcadia (the larger area around Roseville)—teachers from Roseville had input.

GLS: Does it tell you how to teach?

Mrs. Schiller: No, it doesn't tell you that. We are still queens in our own classrooms, and there's plenty of freedom.

GLS: Now we have seen a number of reading books and some periodicals that are used in your classes. Where do these materials come from?

Mrs. Schiller: One is the *Weekly Reader*, and there's *Sprint*, and we pick our own books—there's a Reading Committee, a Math Committee, and so forth, appointed from teachers. We look over the books that the various publishers furnish and pick out the ones we want. We pick, say, three books. They are sent out to schools and then the teachers all vote on them. The ones that get the most votes are the books that we use.

GLS: Well, thank you very much for your time and all the insight you've given us. It's been a real pleasure to talk with you and we'll be doing it again, we hope.

Mrs. Schiller: It's been very enjoyable for me, and I've learned a lot looking back on my own teaching practices and classroom management. Looking at the Germans, at the films from Germany, really stirred up my thinking.

Frau Wanzer, Schoenhausen Grundschule

For the first few minutes we talked about what we wanted to do in her classroom, indicating that we would like to present a systematic view of her classroom on film, to the Roseville teachers, in our exchange activity. To help do this, we suggested that she spend some twenty minutes before the class that we were to film explaining her procedures and goals, and that we, in turn, would explain this to the Roseville teachers. She had seen the Roseville films at the same time as the *Schulamtdirektor*.

> **Frau Wanzer**: Ja! It would perhaps have been good if for the films you showed us (of the Roseville classrooms) they had this introduction. *Für mich in jeden Fall* (for me in any case), it was really difficult to see what was intended. Perhaps that was also the ground for the feeling that many of us had, "*Was lernen sie eigentlich?* (What are they learning really?)"

> **GLS**: We explained that the films shown were typical for this class and that the *friewillig* (free will) character of the classroom activity was indeed characteristic.

> **Frau Wanzer**: I can scarcely understand how the teacher working at the table with some of the children would work on without looking to see what the other children were doing in the rest of the room. How do the children working alone know what they are supposed to do? But it had to function well—they were seemingly satisfied and they weren't causing any difficulties. *Bei uns gibt es* (with us there are) *Schwierigkeiten* (difficulties) *und Streiten* (strife or fighting). This was apparently not the case (in the Roseville school)! Probably they (the children) are accustomed to this.

> **GLS**: "Frau Schiller is very proud that her classroom is productive. The *friewillig* character also impressed us." "How do the children know exactly what there is for them to do?" we asked Frau Schiller. She answered, "I do nothing—the materials are there and the children seek them out for themselves, but they usually ask me if they can use them." "Naturally, the children have specific lessons, but when they are finished—they can do what they will."

> **Frau Wanzer**: *Sie konnen tuen was sie wollen!* (They can do what they want!)

> **GLS**: They have various opportunities—such as tapes, computers, the library, flash cards, charts and posters, etc.

> **Frau Wanzer**: *Da ist naturlich ein grosser Unterschied* (There is naturally a great difference) to our school. They (Roseville) have much more time to work, much more. With us one hour equals forty-five minutes and one must in this time reach a goal. In America they have so much time and so when they are finished with their lessons they can do what they want, but with us there is no time. The more gifted children finish, but many do not and then

they must be helped to reach the goal for the lesson. (She talks about helping the slower children and how the more gifted children get less attention than they deserve. She also talks about the learning-disabled children—how some of them can reach only minimum goals defined in the curriculum plan [*Lehrplan*]).

GLS: To go back a little, so there is for every hour a specific goal you must reach?

Frau Wanzer: *Ich babe in mein Lehrplan* (I have in my curriculum plan) the goal that I must reach—the goals that I must reach. Every hour has a part goal. I must find out as the hour progresses if I'm going to have enough time to reach that goal. It depends on whether the hour goes well or badly—how much time I will spend. For example, there is the topic of "Where do we get our water?" It's fascinating. In the *Lehrplan* there are ten hours given for this subject, but the children are so *begeistert* (enthusiastic), they want to know so much! It takes much more time than the ten hours foreseen in the *Lehrplan*. Then I must narrow down the amount of time spent on other subjects such as plants or animals, all within the *Sachunterricht* (home, community, civic affairs, etc.) curriculum.

GLS: You speak of a *Lehrplan*. Is that local or Baden Württemberg?

Frau Wanzer: *Ja*, the Baden Württemburg plan.

GLS: The *Lehrplan* appears to be very tight. If you had more time would you have *freiwillig* (free-choice) periods?

Frau Wanzer: *Ja*, *bestimmt* (Yes, certainly).

GLS: How would you handle it?

Frau Wanzer: I would arrange materials beforehand that *zu eine bestimmten Thema gehört* (that belong to a specific theme). But in the framework of this theme, the children could do what they wanted. But I wouldn't just leave it up to them to choose from unorganized material. I would have the fear that they would choose things that were just play. And I have the impression that the children are so *müde* (tired), so *lustlos* (without drive) that they wouldn't do anything strenuous. They spend all afternoon and evening before the TV. This is very practical for the parents, but not good for the children. I am afraid that if I ask them to do whatever they wanted they would do *gar nichts* (nothing at all)! For instance, I told them, "Everyone bring a favorite book and we'll make a big library and we'll have a free reading period." Well, two-thirds of them read with pleasure and one-third did nothing at all and disturbed the others.

GLS: So how would you proceed? Would you have them work in groups?

Frau Wanzer: *Ja*, for example, with respect to animals that we don't have in Germany, such as camels and lions, etc., I would have four tables arranged and I would furnish each of them with books and materials, such as pictures, before the children arrive. And then they could work on whatever they chose—a lion or a camel or whatever—of the four possibilities. And then ten minutes before the end of the period I would have them report, each group, to another group. This kind of procedure will work, but *völlig frei* (fully free)? *Das macht nichts* (that makes nothing—that's of no use)! We have a time problem, and when I only have three hours per week for *Sachunterricht*, there is simply too little time for this kind of free-choice situation.

GLS: We would like to ask another kind of question. We have the impression that here in the Schoenhausen Grundschule, or for that matter in any of the schools in the nearby towns that we have visited, when you leave the classroom, *Sie erwarten class die Kinder unrühig und eben chaotic werden* (that you expect that the children will become restless and even chaotic).

Frau Wanzer: *Erwartet* (expect)! *Ich hoffe sie bleiben rühig!* (I hope they remain quiet!). But there are always those two or three children that are poorly socialized and get everyone else stirred up. There is, for example, in my class, a child that has terrible personal problems. He strikes out and shouts at other children and they tell him he's crazy and, he's very sensitive. He comes from a family with no father—a damaged home environment—he is terribly sensitive and disruptive.

GLS: Would you expect the children to work on their lessons when you leave them?

Frau Wanzer: This is my goal!

GLS: How often is it reached?

Frau Wanzer: In the course of the school year—in the first grade—hardly. In the second year it goes somewhat better. By the fourth year they can work for longer periods. You have to handle this sort of thing in little doses.

GLS: What would you do if you heard a disturbance in the room when you returned?

Frau Wanzer: I would talk to the class. I would attempt to reach an understanding. Scolding does no good. Sometimes I have said that I am *traurig* (sad).

GLS: Would you say you were *beleidigt* (hurt)?

Frau Wanzer: No, never *beleidigt*, *nur* (only) *traurig*.

GLS: Do you make the children feel guilty (*schuldig*)?

Frau Wanzer: I feel that guilt is not understandable for children of this age. How can they understand who is guilty, the one who started the trouble or the one who responded to the trouble and carried it on further?

(We carried on discussions of this kind with Frau Wanzer several times, and her interpretation of her own behavior in the classroom and that of the Roseville teachers that she had seen on film was consistent. She saw the Roseville classrooms, as did the other teachers, as tending towards being directionless, without specific goals, and not organized for the attainment of whatever goals existed. She did find the quiet orderliness of the Roseville schools impressive and as exhibiting good "teamwork.")

Interpretation

Frau Wanzer and Mrs. Schiller are two experienced teachers of about the same age, teaching the same grades, about many of the same things, in quite similar schools in parallel communities in Germany and in the United States; yet their handling of their classrooms and the assumptions that guide their behavior are significantly different at some critical points. Their perceptions of each other's classrooms reflect these differences. Mrs. Schiller's classroom is relaxed, quiet, low-keyed, and diverse. Children carry out various activities on their own, in addition to those carried out by the teacher and the small group she is leading through a specific learning task. There is little or no disruptive behavior. These qualities, confirmed in many sessions of observation by us, are apparent in the films we showed to all of the Schoenhausen teachers, the principal, the *Schulamtdirektor* (superintendent of schools) and his assistants.

Frau Wanzer perceives Mrs. Schiller's classroom as undirected, as almost goalless. At the same time, she acknowledges that there appears to be good "teamwork" but that this method would be unlikely to work this well in Schoenhausen Grundschule.

These perceptions are apparent in the interview. Frau Wanzer's assumptions are apparent: that if children are undirected they, or at least a significant proportion of them, will do nothing at all, become disruptive, or will choose to play rather than work. She also reports that when children have clear directions on an interesting topic they can become very enthusiastic about learning and will work hard at it.

Frau Wanzer explains the differences observed in terms of time, which is short in Schoenhausen, and the fact that the curriculum plan there defines the goals to be reached quite precisely. She does not see these as *cultural* attributes but as given, practical, preconditions to whatever she does, and the children do, in her classroom.

The differences run deep. Mrs. Schiller assumes that her goal is to help each individual develop to his or her fullest degree—to the limit of each one's individual capacities. Frau Wanzer assumes, as does the *Schulamtdirektor*, that her purpose is to help each child attain the standards set forth in the *Lehrplan*—that some will meet them fully and others only minimally. Frau Wanzer takes for granted the existence of a *Lehrplan* and that it is furnished to the school by the state school system, and that it will guide her management of her instruction directly. Mrs. Schiller takes for granted the fact that teachers from the school district develop their own curriculum and that it is only an approximate guide. Frau Wanzer assumes that the children eventually learn to continue working when she leaves the classroom, but that one can't expect too much of the younger first and second graders. Mrs. Schiller expects her first and second graders to be responsible for keeping a quiet, on-task classroom when she is gone for a few minutes. Frau Wanzer would "talk" to her class if there were a disruption, but she would not act "hurt," only "sad," and she would not try to make her children feel "guilty." Mrs. Schiller would develop personal liking and trust with her children, would be "hurt" if they misbehaved, and would leave them all feeling guilty if they did. The two teachers have quite different conceptions of guilt. For Frau Wanzer guilt has to be established—there is a perpetrator, a reinforcer, and perhaps a victim. For Mrs. Schiller there is a feeling state—guilt is internalized. The children feel guilty about their irresponsible behavior and hurting their teacher.

These are the assumptions, as we see them, that lie behind both the behaviors of the two teachers in their classroom, and their perception of each other's behaviors *in situ.* These are cultural differences, we believe, that are expressed in and derived from the German and American historical experience, respectively. The case for this extension would have to extend substantially beyond the scope of this chapter. We therefore confine ourselves to the observation that in Schoenhausen and Roseville, respectively, these are assumptions that we regard as cultural, in the sense that they are pervasive within the dialogue of the school and school system and antecedent to the operations of the specific teachers and children we have observed.

Conclusion

The cross-cultural comparative reflective interview procedure furnishes clear evidence that the various audiences viewing the action all saw the same things in the films of classrooms. The children and teachers in Roseville saw the children in the Schoenhausen classrooms as noisy and enthusiastic. The children and teachers in Schoenhausen saw the Roseville classrooms as quiet and orderly. Each acknowledged that their own classrooms were more "noisy" or more "quiet," as well as seeing the other in those terms.

The crosscultural comparative reflective interviews also gave us clear evidence of the ways in which position affects perceptions. The *Schulamtdirektor*, the children, and the teachers "saw" the same features of behavior in the "others'" setting, but emphasized these features differently, and the children actually "saw" some things the adults did not. The *Schulamtdirektor* viewed the action from the top down, from the perspective of a system. The children interpreted the classroom action and setting from their perspective—desks, lunch, clothes, popcorn day, teacher's position in the classroom, blackboards, and so forth, but still "saw" the quiet and order in the Roseville classroom and the noise level and boisterous activity in the Schoenhausen classrooms. The teachers, represented by Mrs. Schiller and Frau Wanzer, interpreted behavior in their own and the other's classroom with clearly different assumptions about what each expected of children and what their purposes as teachers were. These assumptions, we hold, are cultural.

All of the principals cited above are "natives," and they tell their "story" in their own way. The foreign observers, ourselves, the ethnographers, also "saw" and "interpreted." We "saw" the same features of classroom activity and our interpretations are not wildly different from those of the natives at any point, but they are influenced by our anthropological goals, our persistent search for "culture," in its various expressions. The interested reader may find confirmation of the above in our publications (Spindler, 1987a and 1987b).

What we have presented in this chapter is, in contrast to a "realistic" text, a modernist text. Modernist texts are designed to feature the eliciting discourse between ethnographer and subject or to involve the reader in the work of analysis. "The experience represented in the ethnography must be that of the dialogue between ethnographer and informants, where textual space is arranged for informants to have their own voices" (Marcus and Fischer, 1986, p. 67). We have featured both the eliciting discourse and involved the reader in the work of analysis.

Doing this (above) is regarded by Marcus (and others) as a "radical shift" in perspective—as a "derailment of the traditional object of ethnography." Part of its challenge to traditional ethnographic realism is that it avoids the assumption of shared cultural coherence. The texts we have presented in this chapter demonstrate both shared culture and culture differentiated by position. We believe that an adequate ethnography must represent both. We do not feel, however, that this "derails" ethnography, but, rather, enhances it, by making ethnography a more accurate representation of social and psychocultural reality.

In all of our ethnographic work we have paid attention to differences in culture in relation to gender (Spindler, 1990), sociocultural adaptation (Spindler, 1978), social class and ethnicity and cosmopolitan/hinterland differences (Spindler, Trueba and Williams, 1990) and we have consistently tried to let the voices of informants, of the "natives," be heard. What we have done differently in the research leading to this chapter is to place the dialogue between informant and ethnographer in the framework of an "own" and "other" reflection upon audiovisual representations of similar situations (classrooms) in our two field sites. The dialogue is thus culturally bracketed and the conversation becomes reflective, but the reflectivity is not focussed on the ethnographer, as it often is in the "new" ethnography, but on the informant. The "native" is doing his/her own cultural analysis by engaging in discourse about the self and other. Under ideal conditions the ethnographer is almost a bystander.

What is left unresolved for us is how the elicited dialogues represent "German" culture and "American" culture. We have recently represented the latter as a "cultural dialogue" (Spindler et al., 1990) and we can understand certain of Mrs. Schiller's interpretations as expressions of (for instance) individualism, achievement and internalization of authority and guilt, that are a part of this dialogue. We can understand some of Frau Wanzer's discourse, and that of the *Schulamtdirektor*, as expressing certain aspects of a long-term German dialogue about authority, efficiency, collective effort and the attainment of standards. To claim that the little elementary schools in Roseville and Schoenhausen somehow express that the national *Zeitgeist* goes further than most of us want to go, and yet there are some tantalizing connections. The action in these classrooms and the interpretations by the "native" seem to be the "tip of the iceberg." The part of the iceberg under the water is the enormous complexity of the national whole and its history. Just how to make the analytic connections remains unresolved. Neither our concepts, nor our vocabulary are sufficient. However, the value of methodology we have presented here does not rest on being able to solve this problem.

The results of our research also have some implications for the debate swirling in anthropological circles about objectivity, positivism, humanism, and the effect of the position of the ethnographer on observation and interpretation (O'Meara, 1989; Spaulding, 1988; Rosaldo, 1989; Marcus and Fischer, 1986; Clifford and Marcus, 1986). The agreement about what is observed ("seen") is greater than one would presume from the doubts cast on the possibility of objectivity in ethnography. Irrespective of position in the situation (for example, child, teacher, administrator, or anthropologist) we all "saw" the same basic features of action and setting. At the same time it is important to acknowledge that position of the observer vis à vis the action, actors, and setting, as well as training and personal experience, do affect the interpretation (and cultural translation) represented in the writing of ethnography.

Notes

[1] We used super 8 mm sound and color film rather than video and, although we have converted some of the films to video cassettes, we still use film for most viewings in our own classroom, since resolution and screen size are so much better.

[2] In some recent reading in education we found to our surprise that there is a well developed "reflective teaching" orientation that has developed in educationist circles (Ross and Weade, 1989). As we briefly explored this literature we had the feeling that one way of enhancing the desired reflective process on the part of teachers would be to create cultural "brackets" for the reflection in some manner similar to the procedure we carried out for Schoenhausen/Roseville. Even the relatively small differences in classroom management between Germany and the United States caused teachers to "stand on their heads" to look again at their own practice. In both of our research sites it was rewarding to hear teachers say that they felt that they had gained insight into their own practice as a consequence of this crosscultural reflective activity. Although improvements in practice were not one of our explicit objectives, it is always good to feel that beyond merely not doing harm one may be doing some good with one's research activity. Another effort to help teachers to reflect on their own activity in the classroom is represented by "cultural therapy," as conducted with individual teachers in conjunction with ethnographic studies of their classroom (Spindler, 1989).

[3] Our first reflective interviews were conducted in Schoenhausen in 1985 and had been preceded by interviews in Roseville, before we had read Marcus, Clifford, or others engaged in "post-modernist" criticism of traditional positivist realist ethnography. We have been influenced, however, by our recent reading of their critical writings in the interpretation of what we were doing.

References

Clifford, J., and G. Marcus, eds., 1986. *Writing Culture: The Poetics and Politics of Ethnography*. Berkeley: University of California Press.

Collier, J., Jr., and M. Collier, 1986. *Visual Anthropology*. Albuquerque: University of New Mexico Press.

Fujita, M., and T. Sano, 1988. Children in American and Japanese Day-care Centers: Ethnography and Reflective Cross-cultural Interviewing. In *School and Society: Learning Content Through Culture*, H. Trueba and C. Delgado-Gaitan, eds., pp. 73-97. New York: Praeger. (A revised version of this article appears as chapter 20 of this book.)

Marcus, G. E., and M. Fischer, eds., 1986. *Anthropology as Cultural Critique: An Experimental Movement in the Human Sciences*, Chicago: University of Chicago Press.

O'Meara, T., 1989. Anthropology as Empirical Science. *American Anthropologist*, 91:354–69.

Rosaldo, R., 1989. *Culture and Truth: The Remaking of Social Analysis*. Boston, MA: Beacon Press.

Ross, D., and G. Weade, eds., 1989. The Context of Reflection. *International Journal of Qualitative Studies in Education*, 2:273–75 (special issue on reflective teaching).

Spaulding, A. C., 1988. Distinguished Lecture: Archaeology and Anthropology. *American Anthropologist*, 90:263–71.

Spindler, G., 1973. *Burybach: Urbanization and Identity in a German Village*. New York: Holt, Rinehart & Winston.

_____, 1974. Schooling in Schoenhausen: A Study of Cultural Transmission and Instrumental Adaptation in an Urbanizing German Village. In *Education and Cultural Process: Toward an Anthropology of Education*, G. Spindler, ed., pp. 230–73. New York: Holt Rinehart & Winston.

Spindler, G., and L. Spindler, 1987a. Schoenhausen Revisited and the Discovery of Culture. In *Interpretive Ethnography of Education at Home and Abroad*, Spindler and Spindler, eds., pp. 143-67. Hillsdale, NJ: Lawrence Erlbaum Assoc.

_____, 1987b. In Prospect for a Controlled Cross-cultural Comparison of Schooling: Schoenhausen and Roseville. In *Education and Cultural Process: Anthropological Approaches*, Spindler and Spindler, eds., pp. 389–400. Prospect Heights, IL: Waveland Press.

_____, 1988. Roger Harker and Schoenhausen: From the Familiar to the Strange and Back Again. In *Doing the Ethnography of Schooling: Educational Anthropology in Action*, G. Spindler, ed., pp. 20–46. Prospect Heights, IL: Waveland Press (first published in 1982 by Holt, Rinehart & Winston).

_____, 1989. Instrumental Competence, Self-efficacy, Linguistic Minorities, and Cultural Therapy. *Anthropology and Education Quarterly*, 20:36–50.

_____, 1990. Male and Female in Four Changing Cultures. In *Personality and the Cultural Construction of Society*, D. Jordan and M. Schwartz, eds., pp. 182–200. Tuscaloosa: University of Alabama Press.

Spindler, G., and L. Spindler, with H. Trueba and M. Williams, 1990. *The American Cultural Dialogue and its Transmission*. London: Falmer Press.

Spindler, L., 1978. Researching the Psychology of Culture Change and Modernization. In *The Making of Psychological Anthropology*, G. Spindler, ed., pp. 174–98. Berkeley: University of California Press.

Stocking, G. W., 1983. *Observers Observed: Essays on Ethnographic Fieldwork*. Madison: University of Wisconsin Press.

Acknowledgments

We wish to thank the faculty and staff of both Roseville and Schoenhausen Elementary Schools and the *Schulamtdirektor* and his staff, of the Schoenhausen area. They could not have been more gracious or more helpful. We also wish to thank Mimi Navarro and Diane Johnson for their indispensable help in the development of the article from a voice on tape to a finished product. We are grateful to Hector Mendez, University of California at Santa Barbara, for his expert use of the computer in producing figure 22.1. We appreciate the perceptive readings of the first drafts of this chapter by Christine Finnan, Ray McDermott, and Bernard Siegel, and the responses of the many who attended a conference on education in a multicultural world sponsored by the Division of Education at the University of California at Davis, organized by Marcelo Suarez-Orozco and Henry Trueba, where we first presented this paper on 12 October 1990. And we are beholden to the Spencer Foundation and the Center for Educational Research at the University of Wisconsin, Madison, for crucial funding.

Part VI

TEACHING CULTURE

Preview

In 1963 *The Teaching of Anthropology*, edited by David Mandelbaum, Gabriel Lasker, and Ethel Albert, was published with the support and approval of the American Anthropological Association. In 1997 *The Teaching of Anthropology* was produced through the collaboration of the American Anthropological Association and the Mayfield Publishing Company. It is instructive to compare the emphasis and coverage of the two volumes, but to do so would take us well beyond the scope of our interests of the moment. Chapter 25 in this section, Louise Spindler's and my article on teaching culture with case studies, appeared in a shortened version in that volume. However, the version that we have published in this third edition of *Education and Cultural Process* goes well beyond the scope of the previously published version to criticize the context of the teaching of anthropology in the universities. We are sure that readers will find parallels to their own situations.

In chapter 23, "Transcultural Sensitization," I present a technique that I have used in nearly all of my courses at Stanford, in Wisconsin, or at the Universities of California during the past two decades. In it I try to describe how students can be shown, through their own responses to visual material, that their observations and interpretations of other cultures are likely to be distorted unless they have some special training. The kind of transcultural perceptual distortions that are analyzed operate wherever teachers and students are of different cultural or social classes. It would seem important that some transcultural sensitization experience be built into the teacher-training curriculum. I have found it to be essential in preparing Stanford students for fieldwork in German culture at the Stanford University Center in Germany. I also use the technique in the training of graduate students in education and anthropology, where objective and sensitized viewing of processes of cultural transmission in other cultural systems is imperative. The first phase of our training seminar in ethnographic methodology, wherever we have taught it, has always begun with this technique.

I call attention here to the fact that this procedure stimulates a form of cultural self-reflectivity. Rather than simply—even blindly at times—laying out one's own personal experience, the purpose here is showing how one's personal culture and cultural knowledge directly influence one's perception of "others'" cultures. It is surprising that graduate students in anthropology do not receive more direct training in the process of cultural self-examination.

In chapter 24, "Anthropology in a Zuni High School Classroom," Clifford Barnett and John Rick describe their experiences in working with Zuni high school students as they organized and taught a course in anthropology revamped to fit Zuni needs. They were assisted in this program by a small number of Stanford students, who worked with small groups of Zuni students. These groups concentrated on reading and discussing class materials, writing projects, and hands-on activities such as training with survey instruments, stone tool making, examination of artifacts or crafts and, later, the making of short videos. The exigencies of classroom teaching in this situation and the resulting relationships with the Zuni community make for interesting and instructive reading.

Chapter 26 by Mica Pollock compares Hutterite and inner-city school education. The two books assigned to his class for reading and discussion were *Hutterites of North America*, by John Hostetler and Gertrude Huntington (a case study in cultural anthropology published by Harcourt Brace, 1996, revised edition), and *"Shut Those Thick Lips": the Ethnography of a Slum School* by Gerry Rosenfeld (first published as a case study in cultural anthropology and reissued in 1984 by Waveland Press). The objective of the discussion—as Louise Spindler and I saw it as a part of the course, "Cultural Transmission: Education in Cross Cultural Perspective"—was to contrast a situation where people had control of their own educational system (the Hutterites) and a situation where people did not and were subject to the definition of schooling provided by the dominant mainstream culture (the inner-city school). Pollock extended the purpose of the discussion group, which found itself asking questions such as how a "culture" might be defined; how the charges of "essentialism" leveled by critical theorists might be handled; and how current the information about a given cultural case had to be in order to make the interpretations appropriate. As a transcript of the discussion shows, in comparing the Hutterite school (where a community almost completely controlled the formal education of its children) to the Harlem school (where a community had almost no control over its children's formal education), the students in the discussion group arrived at a critical discussion of culture and power in contemporary American schools. They concluded by asking whether American schooling can be "successful" in places where powerful "outsiders" are the enforcers of formal education. The enlargement of the scope of the discussion brought about by Pollock's contemporary experience proved to be very useful.

The Editor

23

Transcultural Sensitization

George D. Spindler
Stanford University

This chapter discusses the ways common errors in transcultural observation and interpretation can be anticipated and how sensitivity concerning them can be acquired. The source of data for this discussion is a sensitization technique first administered in the winter of 1968 to Stanford undergraduate students at one of the university's overseas centers, Stanford in Germany. The same technique has been used in advanced education classes at Stanford University on the home campus during most years since 1970. I am not concerned in this chapter with the differences between groups, but rather with the educational purpose of the technique and the kinds of perceptual distortions consistently revealed by it. Whether applied at Stanford in Germany or Stanford in California, the technique has been used in my classes as a way of sensitizing students to the kinds of errors one is likely to make when perceiving and interpreting behavior in cultural contexts other than one's own. Some 800 students have responded to the technique to date. The perceptual/interpretive errors they make are remarkably consistent from group to group.

There is a substantial literature in psychology, and some in anthropology, concerned with cultural variability in perception. Very little, however, has been written about the very complex process of perceiving and interpreting culturally relevant material across cultural boundaries in the manner described here. The interpretive principles applied in this chapter are implicit in much of the reported experience of anthropologists in the field (Spindler 1987), but they have not, to my knowledge, been explicitly stated or applied in the specific ways developed here.

At Stanford in Germany there were usually about eighty students, mostly sophomores, in attendance at any given time. For six months they carried on with their regular academic work while learning the language of and becoming exposed to the history, politics, and economics

Source: Written especially for *Education and Cultural Process*.

498

of their host country. The program was designed to enable nearly all interested Stanford students to have an overseas experience irrespective of their major concentrations or future professional plans. The students live together in the various centers (there are also centers in France, Italy, England, and Austria), but do a great deal of traveling and are in constant contact with the population of the areas in which the centers are located.

Whenever I have been in residence, students at Stanford in Germany have done field research in the Remstal, the area near the study center, on the continuity of the folk culture in the small villages and on the urbanization and industrialization overtaking these villages. This field research has, in turn, been related through classroom discussions and lectures to basic generalizations and interpretive principles in cultural anthropology. The purpose of my courses in anthropology as I taught them at Stanford in Germany has been to help develop a cognitive organization for observation and participation in a culture foreign to the student.[1]

German culture cannot be considered, from the anthropological point of view, to be radically divergent from North American culture. Though there are substantial cultural differences between the various European countries and North America, in the larger sense they must all be seen as versions of the same general culture. There are, however, sufficient differences to make the deeper adjustment and accurate perceptions of the European culture problematic for North Americans unless they have systematic help. Contact, even prolonged, does not necessarily result in adjustment on this deeper level. Learning to speak the language is a major step in this direction but does not guarantee accurate perceptions and understandings. Human beings tend to interpret new experience in the light of past experience unless there is decisive intervention in the interpretive process. The anthropology instruction at Stanford in Germany was designed as such an intervention.

The first step in this intervention, as I came to understand and practice it in my instruction, was to alert students to the types of perceptual distortions to which they would be subject and which could be corrected in some degree by transcultural sensitization. The specific way in which we went about this, and some general conclusions concerning the major types of distortions, are the subject of this chapter.

The Technique and Its Results

The technique consists of the administration of ten 35 mm. color slides selected from several hundred I had taken of the Remstal and its internal cultural variations. During the first week overseas the slides are shown and the students are asked to write their responses to each of the pictures and turn them in to me. I use those responses in a simple inductive content analysis, the results of which I utilize in class discussions. A description of the pictures—several of which are included in this text—and their culturally appropriate interpretation, together with the major categories of student reaction to them, follows.

Picture No. 1

The first slide is of a small area of vineyards (*Weinberge*) near the Stanford in Germany center. This area is subdivided into many small plots, most of which are not larger than a tenth of an acre. Each plot is terraced and there are poles and wires for the support of the grape vines.

The picture is very clear and presents no structural or spatial ambiguities. Students are asked to describe what they see in the picture, what it is used for, and what its possible significance might be in the cultural system of the Remstal.

The slide shows very clearly the small, terraced plots of vineyard characteristic of the area. The important point is that the plots are so small and their distribution so fragmented that mechanized cultivation is impossible. Consequently, traditional labor methods are still used for cultivation of the crop and upkeep of the poles and wires. This is a significant support, though one of several, for the entire traditional complex of viniculture and the way of life associated with it.

Students see a very wide range of possibilities in this picture. The majority see it as connected with agriculture, though usually not as vineyard plots but as an irrigation project, feeding troughs for cattle or pigs, a soil conservation project, erosion control, or cribs for grain storage. A sizable minority (about 35 percent) see it as something entirely unrelated to an agricultural operation, such as Roman ruins, rows of chairs for a mass audience, a religious congregation, a guarded border, fields destroyed by war, or gun emplacements.

The problem in accurate perception seems to be that there is no exact counterpart in the culture of the viewers for what is seen on the screen. Though vineyards are known in California, hilly, small, terraced plots of this kind are unknown. Further, there is no functional complex in the culture of the viewers into which this perception fits, even if the perception is accurate. The small size and fragmented distribution of the plots of vineyard have no meaning. Consequently, students seldom see the plots as vineyards, and only a few perceive their functional relevance. In general, the range of interpretations is wide and the level of inaccuracy high. Only about 10 percent of the students grasp the cultural significance of what is observed.

Picture No. 2

This is a picture of a middle-aged woman in dark clothing bending over and tying grapevines onto a wire trellis on a sunny, early spring day. Students are asked to describe what the subject is doing and why her activity might be functionally significant. They are also asked to indicate what they think the subject is thinking and feeling. The type of labor performed here is skilled labor which frequently is obtained, within the traditional economic framework, from the membership of the extended family. This validates these relationships, thus helping to maintain the family and values associated with it. The necessity of such intensive hand labor in the small distributed plots is one factor that has kept traditional folk-oriented adaptation intact up to the present time in this area of Germany.

Most students see that some form of agricultural activity is involved in this picture. Only a small proportion (5–15 percent) expressed an understanding of the significance of the intensive hand labor. Again, as there is no functional counterpart for this kind of work in North American culture, few students can see its cultural or economic significance.

The interpretations of what the subject is thinking and feeling run through a wide gamut, but the modalities that appear have mostly to

Picture No. 2

do with fairly grim states of mind. "Tired," "old," "tedious," "boring," "aching back," "aching bones," "tired muscles," are the responses that predominate. Though the bones and muscles of German women who work in the Weinberge do ache, the interpretation of this sensation is quite different in the traditional subculture of the Remstal than in middle-class America. Labor and its discomforts are regarded as positive, and old women complain about no longer being able to work in the Weinberge.[2] Students project from their own culture the meaning of experience appropriate to the activity as perceived.

Picture No. 3

This is a visually ambiguous picture. It shows an older female teacher helping a child of about nine years of age into an old church tower where they are to examine four very large cast bells about which she had lectured in *Heimatkunde* (homeland) just before the trip to the tower. There are heavy beams in the picture and the surroundings are generally dark and dusty looking. Students are asked to indicate what is "going on" in the picture. Actually, all that is happening is that the teacher is helping the child off the top rung of the ladder into the upper part of the tower where the bells are. Cultural significance is not in question here.

About one-third of the students see the teacher as assisting the child in some way, and about one-third see her as punishing the child. The other third of the responses are distributed over a wide range. Those who see the teacher as assisting the child refer to help given in going under a fence, coming out of a mine shaft, a cave, an earthquake-stricken building, or a collapsed basement in a deteriorated slum, or out of a bomb shelter; or in entirely different directions, as assisting her to go to the toilet or even as preventing suicide. Those who see the teacher as punishing the child usually refer to whipping in a woodshed, spanking because the child had gone some place where she should not have gone, or being caught because she tried to run away. The interpretations in the third category are too variegated to sample adequately. Most of the interpretations in all categories are irrelevant to the actual situation as it occurred.

It seems clear that the range of possible perceptions and interpretations increases as the situation observed becomes more ambiguous. Ambiguity may be either a product of cultural irrelevance or lack of clarity in spatial or structural relations. Both forms of ambiguity enter into the interpretation of this picture, but the latter are probably most important in this case. Spatial and structural relations are not clear, which is why this picture was selected. The act of climbing into an old church tower to examine bells that have been discussed in class is uncommon in both American and German culture, so the spatial and structural ambiguity is compounded. Perceptions and interpretations, therefore, tend to be fanciful and more or less irrelevant to reality. In actual fieldwork, or in ordinary contact within a foreign culture, situations where ambiguity prevails abound.

Picture No. 4

This slide shows a small bake house (*Backhaus*) in which shifts of several village women bake bread and *Kuchen*[3] together at certain hours each week. The small brick building is technically clear, as is the fire in the furnace inside. A woman is standing by the door with the long ash stirrer in her hand. Students are asked to indicate what it is they are seeing and what its significance could be in the culture of the Remstal. The significance of the Backhaus is not only in the fact that women bake their weekly bread there but in that it is a social-gathering and gossip center for the more conservative women of the village. It thus is a

Picture No. 4

contributing element of social control, as everyone is talked about there and judgments are passed on their behavior.

About 30 percent of the students see this as a Backhaus, but virtually none have ever perceived the function of this place as a communication and social-control center. The range of interpretations for the other 70 percent of the students is quite wide, including such perceptions as small-town industry, refinery, one-room house with a coal fireplace, fireplace in an inn, a kiln for making pots, an incinerator, and so forth.

Again, there is no exact cultural counterpart to the Backhaus in U.S. culture, though the general form of the structure and even its purpose may not be unknown. The picture is technically clear. The only ambiguity is the cultural one, which seems to produce a wide range of interpretations as to what is in the picture, and the absence of a cultural counterpart in the culture of the viewer leads to interpretations of significance irrelevant to the local situation.

Picture No. 5

This picture shows a man pumping a liquid of some sort into a trough which empties into a long barrellike container laid lengthwise on a trailer hauled by a small tractor. The man is actually pumping liquid from a pit under the manure pile which is found in front of each *Bauernhäus*.[4] The liquid is then taken in the barrel up to the Weinberge and distributed between the rows of grapevines. This is a substantial contribution to the enrichment of the soil, made possible by the total economic-ecological unit represented by the Bauernhäus. The animals live on the ground floor and the people above them. There is a functional interdependence between the Bauernhäus and the Weinberge other than that created by the activities of the people themselves.

Only 5 percent of the students in any of the samples have ever seen this as a pump for liquified manure or anything like it. Interpretations range widely: a cement mixer for fixing broken sidewalks or for building houses, crushed grapes being pumped into a container, water for spraying, loading coal, delivery of a pillar, tar for street repairs, pumping insecticide into barrels, filling old barrels with new wine, washing gravel, loading pipe onto a truck, erecting the base for a monument, rinsing off a grinding stone, locating a plumbing fixture, and so forth.

Again, the picture is very clear technically. There is no visual ambiguity because of structural or spatial relationships. The ambiguity is culturally introduced. There is no counterpart for the pump or for the use of liquid manure in agricultural operations in the experience of the majority of American students. They produce, therefore, a wide variety of interpretations.

Picture No. 6

Picture No. 6

This is a picture of a small boy helping his father pick black currants. It is a pleasant picture filled with sunshine, green leaves, bursting clusters of currants, and a basket heaped with the fruit. Students were asked to indicate what is going on in the picture and how the boy feels and thinks about it. Children in this area of Germany are not required to work until they are ready to do so because their parents want them to enjoy working in the fields and the Weinberge. Most children enjoy helping their parents and older siblings in this way.

About 90 percent of the students see this as an activity connected with the harvesting of grapes or currants. Most, however, see the boy as wishing he could join his comrades in play, hoping that the work will be finished so he can leave, wondering if he is going to grow up to do a tedious and boring job like his father, restive under his father's hand, wishing the sun were not so hot, resigned to the work, feeling hot and scratchy, wishing there were an easier way to do it, feeling restless, resenting the drudgery, and so forth.

Again, students tend to project their own experience or the stereotype of that experience within American culture into the perception and interpretation of events or situations in another culture. Working in the field under the hot sun, perhaps especially with one's father, is perceived as boring, tiresome, and so on. "Naturally" wanting to escape to play with one's peers is a projection, it appears, of attitudes common in U.S. culture. Though it is likely that some Remstal children feel this

way, it is doubtful that many do, given the particular cultural antecedents to the event and its interpretation in this culture.

It is clear in responses to this and other pictures that when motivations and feelings are identified, the range of perceptions and interpretations increases and the potential irrelevancy of these perceptions
likewise increases, irrespective of the technical clarity of the stimulus.

Picture No. 7

This slide shows a not atypical Bauernhaus with large double
doors through which animals and hay pass through to the ground floor
where the animals are kept, the manure pile surrounded by its square
concrete retaining wall in front with the pump in the center, and two
stories and attic under a heavy tiled roof. The Bauernhäus is the traditional structure housing the extended family and livestock and is an
especially significant representation of the traditional agricultural "folk"
adaptation. People live in these houses within the villages and farm the
many scattered strips of flatland and small plots of Weinberge from it.
The Bauernhaus, small plots, Weinberge, manure pile, and so forth,
constitute a whole functioning culture complex. It is a way of life that is
disappearing but still very much in evidence.

Students see the Bauernhaus as a warehouse, a gasoline station,
a tavern, combined hotel and restaurant, a shop or general store, a feed
store, suburban home with a two-stall garage, factory of some kind,

Picture No. 7

store with a loading platform, cheese factory, a garage where cars are fixed, a house of prostitution, a winery, an apartment house, a bakery and family home combined, and an equipment repair shop. Only about 10 percent of the students in the various groups ever saw this structure as a regular domicile, and only about half of those saw it as a structure sheltering both man and beast within the general complex described.

As in the other cases, the responses to this picture contained a wide variety of culturally ready categories imposed from the perceiver's culture upon the situation presented from another culture. Ambiguity is created not because of lack of clarity in spatial or structural relations (the picture is clear and focused), but rather because there is no specific cultural category in the perceiver's culture for the perceived event, object, or situation. Nor is there any functional complex in which the perceived situation would fit even if it were perceived relevantly.

Picture No. 8

This slide shows a male German teacher of about forty years of age standing before a fourth-grade class in the *Grundschule* (elementary school). He is standing in a more-or-less relaxed posture with his hands behind his back, looking at the class. The children are grouped around the tables, facing him. The classroom is entirely ordinary. Specific clues to the effect that this is a German classroom are lacking, so students are told that it is. The students are asked to indicate what kind of a classroom atmosphere probably exists here and what kind of a teacher this man is. The teacher, Herr Steinhardt from the Schoenhausen School, is not a "permissive" teacher but certainly is not an authoritarian one. I have observed many American classrooms that were much more strictly run than his. The nature of the school and educational philosophy are described in chapter 22. The children were allowed considerable freedom of movement and expression. Their grouping at tables rather than in traditional, formal rows of stationary seats is symptomatic of this freedom.

The student respondents saw Herr Steinhardt as formal, strict, orderly, authoritarian, austere, autocratic, dominating, arrogant, stern, meticulous, demanding, stiff, detailed, traditional, old-fashioned, "uptight," and as a "pompous authoritarian" in about 80 percent of all responses to this picture. The classroom was seen consistently in the same framework—that is, one demanding submission from the children, as having an orderly, "didactic," rigid, "alienating," highly disciplined atmosphere.

It is apparent that students responding to this picture have projected a stereotype that is patterned in their own culture about a situation in another culture. American students have stereotypes about how German classrooms are run and what German teachers are like. These stereotypes are projected. The range of perceptions and interpretations is not broad, but the irrelevancy of those offered is marked.

Picture No. 9

This slide shows the same classroom ten seconds after the slide in Picture No. 8 was taken. The teacher is in a more dynamic posture, with hand raised and a lively expression on his face, and the children are raising their hands; some are half risen from their seats. Students are asked to indicate whether this slide causes them to change their interpretation of the first picture of this classroom.

About 50 percent of the respondents say that the second picture does not cause them to modify their first perceptions significantly. The other 50 percent describe the classroom as less autocratic than they had thought, less rigid, more free, and more democratic.

It is significant that approximately one half of the students modify their interpretations in the direction of greater freedom in the classroom. This illustrates the importance of time sampling in any particular sequence of behavior and is also an important element in transcultural sensitization.

Picture No. 10

This slide shows several boys walking into the Schoenhausen School, with Herr Steinhardt standing out in the school yard with one hand raised pointing toward the door. His posture is rather relaxed and his hand and arm are not in a stiff position. Students are asked to indicate what they think the boys are thinking and feeling as they enter the classroom and school.

About one-half of the students in the various groups to which these pictures have been shown see the boys as feeling reluctant, fearful, anxious, resigned, and resentful. About one-third see the boys as eager to enter, excited, anticipatory, wanting to get started, happy, and fascinated. The rest produce a fairly wide range of responses, including "not rushing but O.K.," "amenable but not eager," "not thinking or feeling very much," being rewarded for obedience, feeling cheated because the recess break has been cut short, and so forth.

A substantial number of American student respondents appear to draw from their own experience with school. They are probably not only drawing directly from this experience but also from stereotypes about what this experience is like, particularly for boys in U.S. culture. Stereotypes of German classrooms and teachers and American student responses to these stereotypes, as well as the influence of one's school experience and stereotypes relating to that experience in U.S. culture, are intermingled. This happens frequently in transcultural perception and interpretation.

Picture No. 10

Conclusions

It should be remembered that the procedures described above are carried out as a part of an instructional program and not primarily for purposes of research on perceptual distortion. With the exception of the groups at Stanford in California, all of the students were at Stanford in Germany and were about to enter or had already entered into fairly intensive contact with German people and German culture.[5] The cultural sensitization procedure was carried out in order to enrich their overseas experience by making them more sensitive and acute observers, and also to increase the probability of success in fieldwork in the Remstal area.

The pictures were all presented on a large screen with a 35 mm. projector. The responses, as stated, were written by each student and collected at the end of the period. The instructor did a content analysis, resulting in the categories of response described above. These results were presented to each class in two fifty-minute discussion periods during which the pictures were again shown and considerable detail presented by the instructor about the content and significance of each slide. Certain general principles of perceptual distortion in transcultural observation and interpretation were derived inductively in these discussions. I will summarize these general principles briefly, as they have already been anticipated in the discussion of the pictures and student responses to them.

It appears that perceptual distortion in transcultural observation increases when:

1. There is no clear counterpart for the perceived object or event in the observer's culture. Responses to the picture of the Bauernhäus, the liquid manure wagon, and the Weinberge all fall into this category. None of these objects, events, or situations occur in North American culture.

2. There is no functional complex into which the object, event, or situation, even if accurately perceived, fits, so the significance is lost or skewed. This applies clearly to the Weinberge and the Backhaus and, to some degree, to most of the rest of the presented pictures. The Weinberge cannot be understood, even if seen as Weinberge, unless one understands that the size and distribution of the plots as well as their terracing prevents the application of large-scale mechanical power to their maintenance—and that this in turn is related to the necessity for intensive hand labor, in turn related to the extended family as a source of labor, and eventually to the utility of the Bauernhaus and the whole traditional complex. Neither can the Backhaus be understood, even if perceived as a house where bread and cakes are baked, unless it is seen as a communication and gossip center. This same line of reasoning can be applied to a number of the other pictures and responses.

3. There is a stereotype of experience related to the event, object, or situation patterned in the observer's own culture. This seems clear in the interpretation of the boys' feelings as they leave the schoolyard to go into the school. Boys would rather play, it is said; the school is confining. This is an image of school in American culture, according to the respondents themselves as they retrospected about their reactions to the pictures and their own experience. The same principle applies to the projection of aching backs and bones, the tediousness of labor, and the desire to escape from it in the interpretation of the picture of the women working in the vineyards and the picture of the small boy helping his father pick currants.

4. There is a stereotype of the experience or meaning of the event, object, or situation as it is presumed to exist in another culture. German teachers and classrooms are believed, in American culture, to be authoritarian, strict, and disciplined. This stereotype is applied to the picture of Herr Steinhardt, with the result that the responses are largely irrelevant to the actual situation portrayed in the picture.

5. There is ambiguity due to lack of clarity in the structural or spatial relations surrounding or involved in the event, object, or situation. This applies particularly to the situation where the teacher is helping a child up the last part of the ladder into the loft of the church to see the bells. The range and irrelevancy of responses is great and seems to be a function of the fact that no one understands exactly what is being seen. Potentially meaningful cues are seized upon, such as the heavy structural beams in the tower, the general dinginess of the surroundings, or the white bandage on the child's hand. There is not only spatial and structural ambiguity involved here but also cultural ambiguity, because the situation is unfamiliar in American culture.

6. There is projection of emotional states ascribed to subjects in another culture. This applies to all situations in which student respondents were asked to indicate what they thought people in the pictures might be thinking or feeling. The emotional states projected are clearly functions of the patterning of experience and beliefs about experience in North American culture. They tend to be quite irrelevant to the specific situations represented in the pictures.

7. There is a single-time sample of the action. This applies most directly to the two pictures of the classroom, but it could apply to any of the situations. In order for interpretations to be relevant (i.e., accurate), they must be based upon a sampling of parts of the whole cycle of activity, whatever it is.

Implications

The processes engaged in by students responding to the pictures described above are similar to those experienced by the field anthropologist. They are also similar to those experienced by the teacher faced with a classroom full of children, particularly when they are from different social classes or ethnic groups than his or her own. Furthermore, the children also represent a youth subculture different from that of the teacher. Teachers make the same types of errors described in this analysis, and for the same reasons the Stanford students made them. Some of these errors are mainly humorous, others suggest why there is constant, serious, often tragic, misinterpretation and noncommunication in classrooms where cultural differences are sharp.

By applying what we know about culture and about the problems of the anthropologist in the field to the analysis of materials that may be brought into the classroom from another culture, such as the slides I used, we may anticipate the kinds of errors that are likely to occur in transcultural perception and interpretation, control them better, and develop some relevant skills in observation. I have called this a transcultural sensitization process. Something similar, I suggest, should be a part of all teacher-training programs. It is one way that an anthropological perspective may help improve teaching.

Notes

[1] The fieldwork was of such high quality that I was able to utilize it extensively in a Case Study in Cultural Anthropology (G. Spindler and student collaborators, 1973).

[2] Case endings are not observed in the use of German terms in order to avoid confusing the reader who does not know German.

[3] Various kinds of baked sweet dough, usually served with fruit toppings and whipped cream.

[4] The traditional structure is quite large, housing humans, cows, pigs, and chickens, hay, and implements used in maintaining agricultural activity.

[5] Two of the Stanford in Germany groups had actually been in Germany for one academic quarter at the time the technique was administered. It is interesting that the same types of perceptual errors were displayed by these groups as by the others. The students had no anthropological training during the first quarter.

References

Spindler, George, ed. [1970], 1987. *Being an Anthropologist: Fieldwork in Eleven Cultures.* Prospect Heights, IL: Waveland Press.

Spindler, George D., and student collaboration, 1973. *Burgbach: Urbanization and Identity in a German Village.* CSCA. New York: Holt, Rinehart and Winston.

24

Anthropology in a Zuni High School Classroom

The Zuni-Stanford Program

Clifford Barnett and John Rick
Stanford University

Every other year since the spring of 1987 the co-authors of this chapter (respectively, a cultural anthropologist and an archaeologist) have been teaching a high school course on the Anthropology of the Southwest at the invitation of the Zuni Public School District and the Zuni Tribe. Each of us, teaching separate quarters of the year, have taken Stanford University students with us to serve as classroom assistants and to lead small discussion and tutoring groups during the class periods.

Zuni Pueblo, on the Zuni Reservation, is a Native American community founded more than six hundred years ago. It is located in northwestern New Mexico, near the Arizona state line, about forty-five minutes from the town of Gallup, New Mexico. While adopting many of the modern conveniences of Western culture, the majority of the approximately eight thousand Zunis retain their language and many other significant aspects of their culture.

This chapter recounts the history of this Zuni Pueblo-Stanford University Program; describes the adaptation of anthropological materials and concepts for classroom use; delineates the goals of the program as envisioned by the University group and our Zuni hosts; and relates some of the experiences of the program participants—teachers, Stanford students and Zuni students. As will become evident, this is a multifaceted service program attempting to meet the sometimes disparate needs of two very different communities. It was not designed with research or systematic evaluation in mind. It can be declared a "success" to the extent that the two authors continue to lead the program—and the Zuni school personnel, when given the option, have

Written especially for *Education and Cultural Process*, 3rd Edition.

513

enthusiastically requested that we continue. For those readers who might want to consider developing such a program, we offer our candid insights on what it takes to carry out the program. For those concerned with "multiculturalism" and how diverse cultural groups can interact, learn from each other and still maintain their own core values and culture, the program offers one model of an approach that may be generalizable to other situations.

The Stanford Teachers: Experience, Inexperience and Motivation

At the beginning of the program neither of us had any extensive formal experience working with high school students, except for occasional guest lectures at local high schools. One of us (Clifford Barnett) had worked extensively with the Navajo (Adair, Deuschle, and Barnett, 1988) and had assisted in editing a book on Zuni (Leighton and Adair, 1963), but neither of us had worked as anthropologists at Zuni. John Rick had worked in the Southwest as an undergraduate archaeology student, and both of us had working contacts over the years with the increasing number of Native American graduate and undergraduates at Stanford.

So why were we willing to step into the unknown world of high school teaching in a Native American community at a time when our own institution, and many others like it, were barely paying lip-service to teaching and giving no "points" for public service except for high-profile public positions? At a time when "publish or perish" was the rule, why would we develop a program for which we had no underlying research agenda?

The event most important to both of us was that the community leaders came to us for assistance. How many times had the shoe been on the other foot for us and our colleagues in anthropology as we sought out the help and permission of those "others" to carry out research that had little immediate significance for them? Here was a way to repay not only any personal debts, but a debt that is owed by all of us in the profession.

With our teaching experience at Stanford and our position on the faculty we felt we could accomplish something that would benefit Zuni students as well as Stanford students accompanying us to Zuni. We felt that we could help Zuni students develop academic skills appropriate to the university environment and, through the mastery of both skills and subject matter, to reinforce their academic self-confidence. Further, given our general knowledge of the incidence of alcohol, suicide and family dysfunction in Native American communities, the cultural anthropologist in the program thought that some of the conceptual tools of anthropology would be of assistance to high school students in making life-course decisions regarding continued schooling, careers and their degree of multicultural participation.

While the latter considerations were also important to the archaeologist in the program, he had an additional, more immediate goal in mind. For a number of years the Zuni Tribe had been sponsoring the Zuni Archaeology Program as a tribal enterprise. This successful program engaged in contract research both on and off the reservation. Most of the professional staff were non-Zuni, in spite of the program's goal of hiring Zunis, because there were few Zunis with appropriate academic backgrounds to occupy supervisory positions. Further, at the time there was a possibility that the Zuni Tribe would establish a Zuni cultural park, jointly with the National Park Service. Since the majority of students express and act on the strong desire to return to Zuni after leaving it for military service or to continue their education, training in archaeology would make them eligible for paying jobs in these two programs, right in their own community.

Finally, in thinking about the needs of Stanford students, we noted that Stanford had a long tradition of maintaining an overseas campus program, with a very large proportion of undergraduates spending at least one quarter at one of the European Stanford campuses. But there was no "overseas campus" option that provided the students with an intensive experience with a non-Western culture.

To the best of our understanding these were the principal, but clearly not the only, reasons for embarking on this program. Certainly, down the list was the thought that at some point research opportunities might arise that were pertinent to our respective interests in medical anthropology or archaeology, but this would be a welcome, serendipitous increment to the program.

History and Evolution of the Program

The teaching program that is the subject of this chapter had its ultimate origin in a request for assistance from the Zuni Tribal Council to Stanford University. The tribe was hopeful that Stanford might be able to provide expertise on a variety of topics, including education, medicine, administration, and communications. At Stanford, a group of faculty formed an ongoing seminar to better acquaint themselves with Zuni and to envision a response to the request. A number of projects have emerged from that context, although our teaching program has involved the most Stanford personnel and has been underway the longest of those projects.

Our initial idea was to contribute to the curriculum of the Zuni high schools by teaching our own areas of expertise in cultural anthropology and archaeology. While Zuni needs little introduction to the anthropological world, outsiders are less familiar with the Zuni Public School District. Because the context in which we have taught heavily conditioned our program, a short synopsis of the history of this school system is relevant. One of our Stanford students has written an Honors thesis which goes into much greater depth on this subject (Boyce, 1991).

Until 1980 the Zuni public schools were part of the predominantly non-Indian Gallup-McKinley County School District. The Zuni community felt they could provide better education for their youth through a locally run district, and with the concurrence of the Gallup-McKinley County School District and the State of New Mexico they were able to establish one of the few existing independent reservation public school districts. Zuni High School, as part of that system, enrolls about 450 students in grades nine to twelve and has a structure and curriculum not unlike high schools in general. Twin Buttes High School, an alternative school with a more flexible program, serves 50 to 100 students who are not easily integrated into the educational program at Zuni High School.

In the spring quarter of 1987 one of us (John Rick) decided to run a pilot project, teaching a course on the archaeology of the Southwest in the high schools. Since that initial experience, we have now taught eleven classes and two field schools over eight academic terms, the most recent ending in 1993. This teaching program has evolved considerably since its inception, and a few of the more important features and changes will be mentioned here.

Our initial goals were to provide curriculum enrichment in social sciences, but more importantly to offer a college preparatory experience in the classroom. The Zuni community looks favorably towards college education, but its students are faced with uneven prospects for admission and survival in higher education. We, and the then school superintendent, Hayes Lewis, felt a course that simulated a college experience would help to develop relevant academic skills and attract students to the idea of higher education. The entry of Zuni students into the profession of archaeology—in part through an articulation with the cultural resource management enterprise, the Zuni Archaeology Program—was seen as an additional goal. Stanford was also seen as benefitting from the teaching program, chiefly through the experience it would offer to Stanford students.

Rick's 1987 spring class was experimental, and involved a great deal of learning and adjustment to the Zuni context. He arrived in Zuni with a box of college-level Southwestern archaeology textbooks, two undergraduates, a family, and little else. Finding housing proved difficult, and foraging for utensils, food, and furniture for the ten-week stay was demanding. We had conferred and corresponded extensively with school officials, but our actual arrival was still a surprise. The assembly of a class of students was hurried and largely consisted of assigning to Rick an already existing class in world history. He was unexpectedly urged to teach a second course at Twin Buttes High School, adding further complexity to the situation.

The pilot program was made possible through minor research innovation funds provided by Stanford and, most importantly, by Stanford's willingness to consider Rick to be on duty (and thus on salary) while teaching at Zuni. The transfer of a quarter of Rick's teaching time every year was not feasible, and thus Barnett agreed to teach cultural anthropology of the Southwest in the alternate years. The program followed this pattern of spring-quarter teaching for the four years from 1987 to 1990. We were able to refine and expand our program considerably during this period. By the fourth year of the program we were also able to stimulate the interest of a number of Stanford alumni, who contributed to the financial support of the program.

At Zuni, administrators and teachers anticipated our arrival, and Zuni students were recruited and selected in advance by the faculty. We established a stockpile of household equipment, graciously stored in interim periods by the school district.

Starting in the second year of the program each Stanford student lived with a Zuni family (paying them a moderate amount for room and board) recruited by school teachers and staff. This proved a key element of the Stanford student experience and helped integrate them into the community outside of the school. They found the experience both rewarding and challenging culturally.

In the classroom, our program emphasized a mix of collegelike lectures and small-group sessions led by Stanford students. Small groups of one undergraduate and two to six Zuni students concentrated on reading and discussing the class materials and writing projects, as well as hands-on activities such as training with survey instruments, stone toolmaking, examination of artifacts or crafts and, later, the making of short videos. We found that a group of six undergraduates, sometimes aided by a graduate student, worked very well in a classroom setting of 18 to 25 high school students. Outside the classroom we emphasized field trips. The archaeology classes regularly visited local sites, as well as Chaco Canyon, Mesa Verde and Crow Canyon, on weekend field trips. For cultural anthropology, visits were paid to the Hopi and Navajo reservations, where students met with tribal officials, craftsworkers and students. We also visited the Santa Fe area, where, in addition to the museums and the American Indian Art Institute, students saw for the first time the end point of sale of work produced at Zuni.

Over these years we taught a variety of classes, with students ranging from ninth through twelfth grades (often all in the same class). As we became more experienced and the demand for our classes increased, we planned our classes for maximum effectiveness. We found that it was best to have students who elected to take our specific course, and that we could do our best teaching with eleventh and twelfth graders. By 1990, however, it was apparent that other changes were needed in the program's design. Two major changes were enacted: a change to same-year classes by Barnett and Rick, and the addition of an archaeology field school.

We found that teaching alternating subject matter every spring quarter had serious drawbacks. First, the Zuni school system starts more than a month before the regular Stanford academic year, and by the time the short "spring quarter" is underway (the Zuni school year is not divided into quarters) both students and staff are tired. Spring brings many distractions, including graduation, the school prom (which involves both the seniors and the juniors we teach), and many competitive team sports events, all of which draw students away from the classroom. Second, our presence during a short spring term fit poorly into the school schedule, and many Zuni students had credit setbacks from taking our courses. Third, Barnett and Rick were each teaching a different student group each year, because a minority of the high school students were able to enroll in both courses over two years. Finally, we had no prolonged contact or possibility of teamwork with the social science teachers in the schools and, therefore, little chance of the transfer of materials, methods, or other information in either direction.

To resolve these shortcomings, over the interim period of fall 1990 to summer 1992, we reorganized the program with the help and approval of Zuni school administrators and teachers. We arranged to collaborate with a teacher in each high school in the production of a full-year course on the anthropology, archaeology, and history of the Southwest. Rick and Barnett would thus teach archaeology and cultural anthropology in the fall and winter quarters, respectively, and the final short "spring quarter" term in the spring would be handled by our high school colleagues. By doing this we were limited to teaching every other year at Zuni, but we judged that the improved fit into students' schedules and the organization and coherency possible within a full-year course would more than compensate for the year-long break in continuity.

A second major change to the program was the addition of an archaeology field school. Rick had not initially anticipated a major fieldwork focus in the archaeology segment of the program beyond that undertaken in the course for the high school students. It became clear, however, that graduating high school students not only needed class work in archaeology to be competitive for contract archaeology positions, but that significant field experience was also required. The fortuitous discovery of a heavily eroding Basketmaker III site near Zuni crystallized the plan for student-oriented field research. The site was mapped, research problems identified, funds were secured, and tribal permission obtained to undertake surface work and excavations. Seven-week field seasons were conducted in the summers of 1990 and 1992, resulting in highly controlled surface collections and the excavation of a number of eroding storage and pit structures.

Although most easily termed a field school, the research was not designed to be a self-funding program serving the needs of researchers and a wide spectrum of college students. Rather, it was first and foremost a chance for Zuni students to gain a maximum amount of field and lab experience in legitimate research, working in close conjunction with Stanford students and staff. Thus, for each season we accepted applications from seven to eight Zuni students and an equal number of Stanford undergraduates. Zuni and Stanford students worked in pairs as micro-teams, sharing and learning a great deal from each other. A surprising number of skills were touched on, ranging from the more rote excavation techniques through trigonometric aspects of electronic theodolite use to writing skills emphasized in records and field notes.

In the fall of 1992, following the second summer field school, we began the above-mentioned, year-long teaching session. The fall class began in late August, with Stanford students arriving in mid-September. By its end in December, we had taught for eighteen weeks, in contrast to the eight weeks usually available in the spring quarter. This additional time, plus the fully functional ten-week winter segment led by Barnett, allowed a much wider range of classroom and field activities. As expected, the continuous intensive classroom experience led to much greater advances in basic academic skills, and our presence during college application preparation allowed us to aid Zuni students to move towards higher education.

This second major version of the Zuni program was designed to run for four years, including two rounds of the full-year program. Due to scheduling conflicts, however, we anticipated Barnett teaching a one-quarter course in the fall of 1994, and then Rick and Barnett would teach in sequence in the fall and winter of 1995–96. We feel that our close working relationship with ongoing Zuni school faculty will allow many aspects of our courses to continue, even in our absence. Eventually we hope, of course, that our presence will be no longer needed and that the program will establish itself in the school, perhaps in a Zuni-modified, culturally adapted form. At Twin Buttes we are already beginning to see some of these changes and adaptations, as the science and social science faculty have developed integrated units to focus on the Southwest.

Conceptual Issues and Course Content

Given the goals described above, the approach to anthropology in the classroom was intended to provide some of the substantive material that would be offered in a university course and at the same time to help students develop skills in reading, note-taking, report writing and critical thinking. We also felt that if any of these goals were to be accomplished, it was necessary to make the material reasonably relevant to the lives of the students, most of whom would not go on to college or become anthropologists.

Therefore, when the concept of culture was introduced, the functions of culture as a problem-solving and maintenance mechanism were emphasized. This enabled us to discuss some of the traditions at Zuni (and other Southwestern cultures) as solutions to problems faced by their ancestors. The mechanism of problem solving naturally led to a consideration of choices faced by society in solving problems as well as the role of other social actions directed toward maintenance of societies and cultures. Underlying both of these issues of choice and maintenance is the recognition of the fact that cultures are not static. For students brought up in a relatively isolated culture and living in a basically theocratic society, these can be potentially revolutionary concepts.

Some specific examples of this approach and the student reactions to it will illustrate how powerful these concepts can be. One of the readings for the course was an article by John Adair and Evon Vogt (1949), contrasting the Zuni and Navajo responses to their returning veterans from World War II. Basically, the Navajo welcomed back the veterans as returning warriors while the Zuni looked upon them with great suspicion as having been contaminated by their experience in the outside world. Students were asked to write comments on this and all of the articles they were assigned, and the commentaries were later discussed in class.

Typical of the responses to this article was the following:

I . . . found it explanatory for the behaviors I sometimes observe from my people even today. For example, a Zuni goes off to another place, either to go to school, or to permanently live there. They decide to visit their hometown and so they come back. What I often observe is the ridicule and name calling of the person upon returning home. I see this behavior mostly among kids my age. They think the person who has returned acts "big" and snobby and all that stuff, just because of mainly the change in dress, hair style, accent, or other. And it occurs to me that, just like the villagers back in WW II thought the returning veterans had picked up the white way, today's young people also think that whoever has left Zuni and comes back, that they have adapted into the white way, also. I especially enjoyed the contrasts in this article because it helped me to understand more thoroughly how my culture really differs from others.

The reading and presentation of this article accomplished a number of things, both for the teacher and the students. For the teacher it became clear that the students were relating the material in the class to their everyday lives and to their identity as Zunis. It was a reminder, if one was needed, that constant, careful thought was required to anticipate the potential consequences of the material that was introduced. For the students it provided an avenue to critical learning on their own. At the time this article was introduced in the spring of 1988, the librarian at Zuni High School, with the support of the school principal, had arranged a week of talks at the school by Zuni Vietnam veterans. The students were able to contrast the stories these veterans told about their homecoming with the very different circumstances faced by the World War II veterans and to discover for themselves that the cultural response had changed over time. They were also able to raise questions about the reasons for the change and discovered that the teacher did not have definitive answers. We could only propose hypotheses about why a different cultural choice had been made.

This theme of choice and change was followed by other contrasting examples in class and reading. The Zuni, who over a long historical period have had a tendency to coalesce or fuse their communities into one tight-knit settlement in response to outside threats and divisive pressures, were contrasted to the Hopi, where divisions and pressures have led to the to groups breaking away and establishing new communities. Again, the students could see that "choices" were made, and we could discuss the consequences of these two different responses.

The recognition of change was not easily accepted in other areas of culture, such as religion. Only Zuni males are initiated into the religious organizations, and, once initiated, they are proscribed from divulging what they learn. Nevertheless a number of the public religious ceremonies involved dances and costumes derived from other tribes, such as the Navajo and the Comanche. One day Barnett opened the class with a comment on the previous evening's presentation of the Comanche dance in the plaza and noted that it had come into use at Zuni early in this century. There was an audible intake of breath from many of the students, and he suggested that they consult the sources set aside in the library for them. He also suggested that they look at some of the later sources to see how the paraphernalia used in the dance had changed over time. Many students did check those sources and often utilized them in their art work.

Religion is always present as an underlying leitmotif in Zuni academia, as it is in the culture. On field trips to sites such as Chaco or Bandelier, for example, many of the female students would not enter the ancient kivas, since women at Zuni are not allowed into the kivas. When certain dances were being rehearsed the male students who were members of those kivas often would be up for many hours at night rehearsing and could not do their assignments. At times this can be used as an excuse for the unsuspecting teacher, but after rapport and trust are developed the use of a "religious excuse" sometimes is a source of humor. Near the close of one spring quarter, when a number of the seniors were at a graduation rehearsal, Barnett asked some of the male students to move up into the vacant front seats of the classroom. None of the students moved and one of the students said, "I can't." Barnett asked, "Why not?" and the student, barely able to keep from laughing, responded with the explanation, "Religious reasons!"

Reading some of the older ethnographic material on Zuni also brought to the fore that there had been many changes at Zuni and, from the point of view of the students, not all for the better. In response to a reading which described Zuni around the 1930s (Goldman, 1937), one of the students wrote: "This reading described what a wonderful, happy place Zuni used to be." This reading provided a springboard for class discussion of the kinds of changes that have occurred in cooperative activities as the Zuni economy and lifestyle became less dependent upon agriculture, and it allowed us to examine the effects of changing economic bases in other Southwestern cultures.

While all the details of their past history may not be known to the students, history is all around them and permeates their lives. Corn Mountain, which dominates the Zuni landscape, was a place of retreat for the Zuni in pre-contact and post-contact times. History also very much colors their views of other Southwestern peoples, particularly their nearest neighbors, the Navajo. Stories of early Navajo incursions against the Zuni fuel contemporary negative feelings about the Navajo. Some of these feelings were also evident in attitudes toward students in the classroom who came from Zuni-Navajo families.

One of the classroom goals stemming from these observations was our desire for the students to recognize that Zunis and Navajos had common problems and that the stereotypes they held about the Navajo were just that—stereotypes. To this end, Barnett pointed out the role of the Navajo in joining with the Zuni against the Spanish and in providing refuge to many of the Pueblo peoples who fled after the Pueblo Revolt in 1690. It was also pointed out that the Zuni provided food to the U.S. troops at Fort Defiance during the military campaign in 1861 to subdue the Navajo.

Nevertheless, the first field trip to the Navajo Reservation was one of the most poorly attended excursions. During the visit to Canyon de Chelly we heard of an evening "social dance" being held at the nearby Chinle Community Center. This was a secular event with couples competing for prizes in costume and with a number of different singing groups. The students were very reluctant to go, explaining, "There will be a lot of drinking and they will beat up on us." The compromise was to park the school bus at the community center while Barnett and his wife assessed the dance situation, with the promise that if it was not a good "scene" we would return to the campground. Our report was positive, and the students had a long, enjoyable evening.

The following day, back in class at Zuni, when one of our male Stanford students got up from where he was sitting, Barnett exclaimed in surprise, "Ray, how come you are wearing a skirt today?" He replied to the class:

> Lots of students have asked me that today. Ordinarily, if they didn't know me they might not have asked, but would have thought different things about me. But because they knew me, they didn't think those things. I think that is what our trip this week-end was all about and the students who didn't go should know that. If you know somebody, or know what people are like, you think differently about them.

We do not have measurable attitudinal change, but over time we noted that the Zuni students began to ask the non-Zuni and part-Zuni students in the class about their cultural beliefs and practices.

Rick taught what is known about ancestral Puebloan culture (and methods of knowing) predominantly from the vantage of archaeology. However, wherever Zuni culture had a known traditional viewpoint differing from the archaeological viewpoint, the attempt was made to bring in the Zuni knowledge[1] as well. A case in point was a local field trip to Hardscrabble Wash, west of Zuni. There, Alex Seowtewa, a Zuni artist and cultural consultant to the school district, presented a relevant segment of Zuni origin knowledge, describing the Wash as the origin place of the Zuni clans when it was a stopping place in the travels of the Zuni people to find the center place (Ferguson and Hart 1985). The petroglyphs covering the canyon walls were a clear affirmation of the actions Seowtewa described. Although the Zuni information about their origins contrasts with archaeological viewpoints on Native American origins, Rick did not try to avoid the contradictions between the viewpoints. Rather, he attempted to promote an understanding of the different ways in which the past can be known. At times the two sets of knowledge can be made compatible, at times it can coexist, and at times a choice will be made. Our position is to give voice to the various positions and allow our students to construct their own position.

In light of the Zuni knowledge about their past, we felt awkward teaching Zuni students cultural material about which they were already knowledgeable. We found, however, that many Zuni students did not feel well informed about their cultural past, even in the areas of traditional knowledge. To our surprise, in our first questionnaire about Zuni student interest in our course, we even had requests to teach Zuni culture!

As many Zunis feel a close relationship to the sites of Chaco Canyon, a major section of the archaeology course focused on preparing research papers on aspects of the "Chaco Phenomenon." In our most recent round of teaching we took a weekend field trip to the canyon and divided the class into research teams focused on individual sites. Each team was armed with cameras with slide film, and a variety of forms on which to record details unavailable from published sources. Within the teams each student had a special aspect of the site to investigate, working within the limitations of national park visitors' rules. An abundance of data were collected and combined with published information. Individual papers were written through multiple graded drafts, and the entire project culminated in an evening-long, slide-illustrated presentation to students' parents. This type of goal-oriented project, working with tangible evidence on culturally relevant subject matter, seemed to work the best.

We also found that prehistoric materials were often subjects for worthwhile inquiry by Zuni students within their own community. A particular case arose during the first season of fieldwork, when a partially eroded burial was encountered in the excavation of a pithouse entranceway. Our excavations were planned to avoid likely burial areas within the site, and generally we would not expose remains when discovered. In this case, however, erosion had already damaged part of the remains and threatened to expose and destroy the rest. Excavation and subsequent reburial in the Zuni cemetery was the official policy of the tribe, corresponding to cultural resource-management procedures appropriate to impending construction projects. The Zuni students felt it more appropriate that this individual be reburied in a deeper pit at the same spot, alleviating the threat of erosion in the foreseeable future. The Zuni Archaeology Program approved the request—on the condition that the Zuni students carry out the reburial in a culturally appropriate manner. To do this, they consulted with their oldest relatives about proper burial procedures and, at the end of the excavation, privately carried out the reinterment. In this way the human remains became the vehicle for the transfer of information across generations, on a subject that otherwise might never have been broached among them.

Approaches in the Classroom

Throughout both the archeological and cultural anthropological parts of our classes we have found that visual materials or presentations are very effective, particularly when they are produced by the students themselves. One way of making archeological subject matter come alive was what Rick titled "The Zuni Eleven O'Clock News," a student-designed TV news program reporting from different archeological time periods. Stanford students teamed up with a number of Zuni students to report on a different time period each week, complete with field reports, interviews with early agriculturalists, and commercials. One particularly creative Zuni student presented a memorable want ad for tree beams for Chacoan great kivas, which very neatly highlighted the difficulty involved in the procurement of the massive amount of wood these structures demanded. The entire series of news shows was filmed on video by the students themselves, providing a useful visual record of the class, reinforcing the newsroom atmosphere, and encouraging students to be creative and effective in their presentations.

In the cultural anthropology segment of the program students were given a variety of options for meeting the term-paper requirement, allowing them to utilize their graphic skills. Some students produced illustrated books about Zuni life, past and present, based on their reading of the literature or interviews with their elders. Other students chose the option of producing a five-minute video based on some aspect of Zuni life and culture. Working individually or in groups of two or three, in addition to the logistic support provided by the Stanford students, they were given basic instruction in video techniques and editing and were required to develop storyboards and an appropriate narration for the soundtrack. One student, stimulated by the previous archaeology course segment, produced a video of the archeological site of Hawikuh, taping on site and utilizing the published excavation maps and reports. Another student, using old drawings of Zuni life, contrasted these with a narrative about destructive changes being wrought on the contemporary Zuni culture by alcohol. Two male students produced a video depicting the preparation of traditional Zuni foods, such as bread and tamales, complete with a final scene of a beautifully set table suitable to the feast.

The very successful short videos were the result of a very unsuccessful attempt on Barnett's part to get each class to produce a full-length video on Zuni culture to be shown to visitors to the Pueblo at the new museum at Zuni. After a long series of class discussions about what should be included in the video, it became clear that there was insufficient consensus on what should be included and on how the work should be divided for the project to be completed in the time available to the class.

But the overall key to whatever success we can claim in the classroom is due to the work of the Stanford undergraduates as small-group leaders. As has been mentioned, lecturing has limited success in Zuni classrooms, and the high-school ambience does not permit extensive interaction between single instructors and a sizeable class. A natural rapport between undergraduates and Zuni high school students developed very quickly and provided a learning context we could not otherwise achieve. In part this was due to the small, discussion-group context, which was naturally more friendly, less inhibiting, and allowed individuals to join friends in a supportive milieu. But undoubtedly the closeness in age (some of our undergraduates were younger than their Zuni group members and some of the Zuni students were parents), along with the reduced sense of hierarchy, spurred conversation and interaction.

Each year we seemed to forget the impact of the small groups on the classroom. In 1992, however, Rick started the classes before the Stanford students arrived and was able to consciously note the differences that occurred on the first day of small-group activity. Zuni students who had been tense, bored, watching the clock, yawning (sometimes with a loud vocalization), became relaxed, smiling, interactive, and attentive to the same material in a group session. The rarely broken pattern for the lecture classroom was silence on the part of students, even when questions were asked. Starting with the first day of small-group activities, a soft buzz of conversation predominated.

The actual activities carried out in the small groups were varied and ever-expanding as we gained experience. We do some reading, both silent and aloud in the groups. Certainly all our students read, but often this is not easy for them. Coverage of basic vocabulary is important, since even a popular article can have many words unfamiliar to our Zuni students. Vocabulary breadth is probably the most limited skill. As a result, over the years we have retained the complex reading material but have decreased the amount of reading required so as to insure depth of understanding. Once the text is understood, the small groups concentrate on discussion of the implications of the salient points in the text.

Stanford undergraduates are often helpful in providing techniques to Zuni students for approaching an article or chapter that their professors never learned or have long forgotten. We rarely would suggest, for example, that a student first read the introduction to an article to get a sense what it is about and then jump to the conclusions at the end to know where the author is going to end up, before sitting down to read the entire article.

More and more we have come to emphasize written skills—taking notes, and the various stages of writing papers. Here the small group becomes a virtual tutorial session, with the Stanford students helping intensively with outlines, drafts, bibliographic sources, or figures. Stanford students serve as moderators and facilitators for group-project planning and discussion, and brainstorming is a productive activity they encourage for getting Zuni students involved with their own education.

While discussion in small groups is often very free flowing, in the larger classroom environment even students who clearly know answers or have ideas to contribute are systematically reluctant to speak up in class. This could be due to a number of causes, including simple shyness, feeling awkward in a somewhat foreign environment, or feeling inferior about their English skills. We have become convinced, however, that a deeply rooted cultural factor is involved—the desire to avoid standing out, being unique, or setting oneself apart through exhibition. The concept of peer pressure, properly interpreted in the Zuni setting, is very valuable in understanding this attitude.

There is a strong value placed on being one of a group of equals, in which no one is set apart by status, possessions, or behavior. While we often associate peer pressure with advocacy of aberrant behavior, in the Zuni case peer pressure is usually conservative, seeking the security of being nonthreatening to each other—a social collective in which strength comes from similarity. To participate in classroom interaction, with the rules defined by the teacher, sets the individual apart, stresses his or her knowledge and conversational dexterity, and is rewarded by the teacher with approval, grades, or privilege. Being rewarded in this way is apparently seen (or perhaps "felt" is better, since we are unsure how much this is explicitly recognized by Zuni students) as generating a situation of inequality that could cause a distancing from the group in general—an unsettling "unlikeness."

A shift in structure or classroom "rules" often can produce dramatic contrasts to the behavior described above. In our regular course-planning meeting (attended by Barnett, the two Zuni social studies teachers and the Stanford students), we discussed ways of reviewing the course material in preparation for the examination. The Stanford students suggested that we divide the class into teams and reproduce the format of the popular television game "Jeopardy." The Stanford students, unlike the teachers, were very familiar with the format and it became obvious the next day that the Zuni students did not need to have the rules explained to them. Students waved their arms to indicate they knew the answers and often could not resist calling out. While they were competing in teams, two students, each on a different team, took the lead in answering; it clearly became a duel between the two students. One of these students previously had been a silent presence in the class. It was clear that as avid television watchers, the students were familiar with the competitive rules of the game. On the other hand, it could be argued that the individual could put him- or herself forward so long as he or she was representing a team of which he or she was a member.

There are other exceptions to the phenomenon of peer pressure. One is that questions of a pragmatic nature are easily asked or answered—for example, how do we go about doing something, what time does the field trip leave, how do we get this computer program to work. Another context is in one-to-one teaching situations, in which Zuni students will often flood an instructor with an endless series of questions. The most common classroom responses are humorous answers to questions, but answers that do not betray any special understanding of the question. In these situations students run no risk of setting themselves apart.

Another mode of interaction that clearly does occur is that of single Zuni students instructing a small group. An example of this would be when an instructor's question to one student (on a bus travelling to a field site) is referred to another nearby student, who then answers the question at great length, seemingly speaking to the local group and the instructor, with a feeling of being a spokesperson for the group in general. Only a few people seemed selected for this role, and it usually came up in response to questions about traditional Zuni matters.

Enrollments

A brief analysis of our enrollments will provide a sense of the scale and the pattern of the program. Table 1 shows both the students in each class, and also how many returned from our prior classes or later chose to take courses again with us. There were limitations to student enrollment: we were unwilling to have class sizes much over 25 students; and there was a break in continuity between the summer field schools of 1990 and 1992. Still, in the first four years of the program a pattern of increasing interest in the program can be seen in the steadily increasing

Table 1   Enrollment Figures for Zuni Teaching Program

Year	Zuni High School # In Class		Twin Buttes High School # In Class	
	Pre[1]	Post[2]	Pre[1]	Post[2]
1987	17	(2)	4	(1)
1988	(2) 20	(3)	Not offered	
1989	(2) 26	(5)	(2) 14	(2)
1990	(4) 39[3]	(5)	Not offered	
1990 summer	(4) 4	(0)	(1) 4	(1)
1992 summer	(1) 4	(2)	(1) 3	(1)
1992–1993[4]	(3) 21		(1) 16	
Totals:				
Student enrollments[5]	145		54	
Students taking courses[6]	117		37	

[1]Number of students entering class from previous Stanford classes
[2]Number of students in this class continuing on to subsequent Stanford classes
[3]Two classes taught at Zuni High School, one of 17 and one of 22 students
[4]Fall and winter quarters (2 sequential courses)
[5]Total numbers of students in all courses within each school
[6]Distinct individuals taught, eliminating repeated enrollments

enrollment at both schools. The subsequent summer field schools were filled to capacity, and the 1992–93 teaching program was effectively at capacity, keeping in mind that the total students enrolled in all class years at Twin Buttes was in the range of 80–90.

It was reasonably common for our Zuni students to take more than one course with us. Overall, about 30 percent of the students in all our courses were with us for more than one session, but this includes the students who merely remained in the same course from fall to winter of 1992–93—clearly the option of least effort. Discounting these repeats, about 14 percent of our students deliberately chose to take more from us, and it should be stressed that students had to make sacrifices in their academic or summer schedules to rejoin us. There were no obvious benefits in spending more time in the Stanford programs, other than the learning experience involved. Given that a large proportion of our first-timers were graduating seniors who did not need additional credits and who could not return to take additional courses, we feel that our courses were seen as worthwhile and many students valued the experience sufficiently to continue it. Not surprisingly, the field school has an even stronger pattern of continuing involvement. Even though the 1990 and 1992 seasons bracketed a discontinuity in the program, nearly half of our Zuni field students came to us from prior course work, and more than a quarter went on to classroom experiences with us.

The Stanford Students at Zuni

As should be evident in the preceding parts of this chapter, the Stanford undergraduates (and the occasional graduate student) who worked with us in the classroom were essential to the viability of the program. The scale of the undertaking is much greater than a single faculty member could possibly hope to achieve. But beyond that, there is a qualitatively different contribution they made that must be underscored, as well as the rather unique condition in which they found themselves.

Over the years of the program, we have yet to take an undergraduate to Zuni who could not complete the program. This is largely because these students were self-selected, primarily with interests in Native Americans, education, archaeology, health (medicine or public health), political science, literature and cultural anthropology. Initially, only a small proportion were majors in anthropology, but some did become majors as a result of the experience. Others continued on to medical school with the intent of joining the Indian Health Service; turned to secondary school teaching; joined the Peace Corps; or pursued careers in public policy through law, political science, and economics. For some reasons, unknown to us and the students we have queried, male applicants were a rarity and there were years when we had only one or none with us.

Our students have to cover their own costs, including full Stanford tuition, transportation to and from Zuni, and room-and-board payments to Zuni families. The relatively lower cost of living at Zuni actually makes a quarter spent in the program slightly less expensive than being at Stanford, and the University financial aid packages treat our program as on-campus time.

In our recruitment process we quickly dispel any romantic or glamorous ideas about reservation life. We have rarely turned down any students for the program and sometimes have to actively recruit, at least in the sense of publicizing the opportunity to spend a quarter in this "overseas" location and earning a full quarter of credit. The fifteen units of credit are divided between their work in the classrooms at Zuni (the program is listed as a course in the Stanford catalog) and the other seven or eight units appear as "Independent Study" on their transcripts.

For their independent study units students worked with a number of community groups. They assisted in the Head Start Program, at the Zuni Senior Center, and in the Parenting Program (a program in the school for students who are parents). Some students catalogued archival materials held by the Zuni Museum, the Zuni Archeological Program or the Zuni High School library. Two students assisted the new tribal furniture factory to develop a brochure showing the products of the company, while others ran a weekly music program on the community FM station. Students with interests in health presented an AIDS education program at the Zuni health fair, and others made home visits with Indian Health Service personnel. About a quarter of our students have returned to Zuni (with competitive funding from the Stanford Undergraduate Research Office) to complete Master's or Honors theses related to diverse topics such as health care, the history of the school system, or aspects of Zuni archaeology.

The Stanford students keep journals of their experiences and write a final report, including recommendations for improvement of the program. Regular staff meetings allow them to compare and collate their observations and learn how varied a culture they are living in, despite the fact that it is often written about as a monolithic system.

For our undergraduates the Zuni program is influential in their outlook on Native America, education, and life in general. It allows them a very intimate and unfiltered experience in a very different culture, one in which they often participate rather fully. They often develop personal bonds with the families with whom they live. A telling example comes from one host household, which had a very close and happy relationship with a Stanford student. They declined to take another student in a subsequent quarter because they said they were still getting over the attachment they felt to the first Stanford student and did not want to allow a newcomer to compete with the positive feelings they had established.

At the same time, in the school and the community there has been an almost unavoidable ambiguity in the role of Stanford students. While Stanford students are sometimes treated as students by the Stanford and high school faculty and may be accepted to some degree as peers by Zuni students, they also are acting as professional staff within the Zuni public school system. Stanford students live with Zuni families and have thus far been presented as students, which allows their integration into the families as another student family member.

The definition of the Stanford student's role has important implications for relationships in the school and community and carries with it expected standards of behavior. Recognizing Stanford students as professional staff holds them to different standards than those to which they are accustomed at Stanford. Zuni community standards, as in part expressed by the Zuni School Board, are especially different from those experienced by most university students.

An important example of differing standards is alcohol consumption—illegal on the reservation, but a not uncommon part of high school students' social life. Alcohol is hardly unknown to university students, but how should they approach it at Zuni? Clearly they have no legal right to consume it, but they are subject to many different standards and pressures. Some of the Zuni students will encourage participation in alcohol-involved events, even though for Zuni students alcohol is doubly illegal and frowned on. High school teachers' standards are like those of Zuni adults, but with the added caveat that alcohol should be completely excluded from all staff-student contact. One inclination of Stanford students is to demonstrate responsible use of alcohol in events involving Zuni students, emphasizing their position as role models. The Zuni School Board, however, has explicitly prohibited alcohol use by our undergraduates, putting them in a studentlike position. While the situation is complex, the Stanford students are clearly responsible to the Stanford-Zuni program, itself predicated upon a guest-host relationship. Thus, in this particular example, the wishes of the school board, high school, and community must be respected, even if inconsistent with standards that apply to other parts of the system. Flexibility is required on the part of students, and as well as a special orientation for them so that they are prepared to play a number of shifting roles and keep the goals of the program in mind. Luckily, we can report that alcohol has rarely been an issue outside of discussions, and that perhaps all Stanford staff benefit from these extended alcohol-free sessions.

Community Relations

There are many roles that faculty in such a teaching program need to consider. We were working and living in the distinct subculture of the high school, and of course living and working within the culture of Zuni. As Anglo academics, both of these cultures were foreign to us.

While we had oriented our Stanford students to understanding that personal flexibility was a major prerequisite for a successful quarter at Zuni, so too it was required of us. Planning for and teaching a class or two classes every day of the week is an arduous change from the university environment. Class periods would be shortened due to special teacher in-service sessions or canceled entirely due to a "drug dog" sweep of the school or a failure of the water system. Classes would be interrupted with special messages from the public address system in every classroom, or students would be called out for other competitive programs. These events are common in many high schools, not just at Zuni, but they were new to us.

Like our Stanford students, we were in an ambiguous position. We were members of the high school faculty, but only temporarily. At the same time, we were perceived as coming from a prestigious university with the support of the school superintendent. We often were invited to attend faculty meetings, particularly at Zuni High School, and asked to express an opinion at times when changes in curriculum or procedures were being considered. During one of our quarter stays there was some faculty division over administrative issues unrelated to our program, and factions for opposing positions tried to recruit one of us to their side. In both of these situations we felt that we were transients and that at best we could only suggest approaches or alternatives that the long-term residents could consider. This position was accepted by those concerned, and we have continued to interact with a wide range of faculty.

The most rewarding aspect of faculty relationships came about when we changed the program and started to teach jointly with high school faculty. Both of the faculty with whom we taught had long experience at the schools and long-term relationships with the students. Their presence in the classroom gave a sense of continuity to the Zuni students and they provided us with a fund of knowledge for working in the high-school environment. From our side we were able to provide new materials they found useful in their own teaching. Since the two teachers were teaching at different high schools and only knew of each other, we also brought them together with our Stanford students to plan and evaluate the course on a weekly basis. Both teachers also joined us on the class field trips. These trips and the meetings also facilitated their communication about programs in their respective schools.

When we sought required permission from the Zuni School Board for our field trips, particularly those off the reservation, we appeared before them to inform them and the audience about our activities. Similarly, near the end of a quarter, before returning to Stanford, the tribal council would schedule a meeting to talk with the Stanford students about their experiences.

Although we naturally had contact with students, parents, school district staff, and tribal authorities, the Zuni community in general received little information about the Stanford Program. Occasionally there was negative misinformation about our activities and goals in the community, and we realized that we had to take responsibility to publicize our activities both within Zuni and the greater local area. One of the easiest ways to get word out is through existing media—specifically, radio stations, newspapers, and newsletters. We do not regard this type of publicity as self-glorifying, but rather as a responsibility we have to the people of Zuni and to the success of the program.

Conclusion

In conclusion we would like reflect on a few broader perspectives that we have acquired over the years of the program. As universities reach out to attract more Native American and other minority students it should be clear that they cannot hope to have qualified students delivered to their doors if they do not reach out to and become involved with those students while they are in high school. Upward Bound and summer institute programs constitute excellent approaches, but they do not provide instructors with an intensive understanding of the setting from which those students come; nor do they provide for interaction with the high school faculty, who are so significant to those students.

In addition to enrichment, these programs help to prepare the student for the transition from high school to college. Even for students who have grown up within mainstream American society, we recognize that the move to a University—away from family, familiar friends and a home community, and the need to take on more personal responsibility—is a difficult one. Based on our experience with Zuni High School students we feel that there is insufficient recognition of the fact that these students also must adjust to a totally different culture and the social system associated with it. We wonder whether these students would have a better university success rate if they could make one transition at a time instead of being faced with two major kinds of adaptations.

We have been struck by some of the basic similarities in the high-school environment across major cultural lines and hypothesize that a Zuni High School junior would find much that is familiar to him or her in a high school in a non-Indian community. The rest of the living circumstance would be far more different and daunting, particularly the separation from home and family. A student who already has experienced this separation while in the more familiar high-school environment might have a better chance of making the cultural jump in the more unfamiliar college environment later on.

Our original program goals were tightly focussed on certain types of outcomes—particularly the entry of Zuni students into higher education and anthropology-related career tracks. While we have seen positive results on these fronts, we have come to realize that a major part of our contribution has been to bring together a number of groups of people who would otherwise be unlikely to interact. It is in the interaction of these culturally divergent groups that we see much of the magic that inspires us to continue the program.

We have no doubt that this is indeed an enrichment program, but one which enriches all participants. We have seen a growth of skills on everyone's part, and it is probably safe to say that Zuni students are better prepared for further education, Stanford students have become fledgling educators, and Stanford and Zuni faculty have devised new ways of effective education. Yet it is the enrichment we have seen in people's lives that matters most, the recognition that cultures are rich resources from which we gain our greatest sense of human worth. The program was not conceived as having long-term impact on the lives of Stanford students, yet it undeniably has. While travel and cross-cultural experience have major value, teaching in another culture—living within it and struggling to come to terms with its values and priorities—seems particularly enriching. What better teaching vehicle to use for this purpose than the concepts and subject matter of anthropology?

Note

[1] We spoke of "Zuni knowledge" and "Zuni oral history" and did not use the words "myths" or "legends," since they ordinarily convey the meaning of being "untrue" in contrast to scientific findings.

References

Adair, John, Kurt Deuschle, and Clifford Barnett, 1988. *The Peoples Health: Anthropology and Medicine in a Navajo Community*. Albuquerque: University of New Mexico Press.

Adair, John, and Evon Vogt. Navaho and Zuni Veterans: A Study of Contrasting Modes of Culture Change. *American Anthropologist* 51, 4 (October-December 1949): 547–61.

Boyce, Suzanne M., 1991. *Community Control in Action: The Creation of the Zuni Public School District*. Education Honors Thesis, Stanford University School of Education, Spring.

Ferguson, T. J., and E. Richard Hart, 1985. *A Zuni Atlas*. Norman: University of Oklahoma Press.

Goldman, Irving, 1937. The Zuni Indians of New Mexico. In *Cooperation and*

Competition Among Primitive Peoples, Ruth Benedict, ed., pp. 313–53. New York: McGraw-Hill.

Leighton, Dorothea C., and John Adair, 1963. *People of the Middle Place: A Study of the Zuni Indians*. New Haven: Human Relations Area Files.

Acknowledgments

We are deeply indebted to the Zuni Tribal Council and the Zuni School Board and School Administration for their invitation to work at Zuni and for the encouragement and trust they have shown us. We also are indebted to the Zuni Archaeology Program, which has welcomed both the faculty and students. Many individuals have made significant contributions to the program, including Hayes Lewis, who, as Superintendent of the Zuni School District until 1993, initiated the idea for the program and provided the essential leadership and liaison for the program with the District and the community; Linda Belarde, Principal of Twin Buttes High School, who worked closely with us during the entire course of the program; Amy Nevitt, head of the Media Resource Center at Zuni High School, a major resource and counselor on all matters for us and for the many Zuni students she assists; our two teaching colleagues at Zuni, Richard Brough and Vince Quintero, who are friends and advisers; Roger Anyon, a valued consultant on all matters archaeological; Alex Seowtewa, who shared his cultural knowledge with us and with all of the students; Pam Mahooty, always helpful and supportive at Twin Buttes High School; and Mike Jump, who worked with us at Zuni High School. Our full thanks and appreciation is extended to the Zuni families who provided a true home away from home for the Stanford students.

We are grateful for the financial support accorded to us by the Office of the Dean of Humanities and Sciences at Stanford during the early years of the program. Our heartfelt thanks to Anne Medicine Ninham, Assistant Graduate Dean for Native American students, who was instrumental in bringing Zuni representatives and Stanford faculty together. Finally, we thank our financial donors, who by their actions not only materially contributed to the program but also provided outside validation to our efforts.

25

Teaching Culture

George Spindler and Louise Spindler
Stanford University

Introduction

We have taught introductory Anthropology 001 at Stanford University since 1953, and we have had about 14,000 students in the course during that time. We have introduced them to anthropology as we conceive of it. In this paper, we discuss the teaching of this course and undergraduate courses in general. We focus on the use of culture cases as vehicles for the understandings that we wish to stimulate. In particular, we concentrate on our series, *Case Studies in Cultural Anthropology*. This should not be taken as evidence of simple egotism or as a crass attempt to advertise the series. The series is integral to our conception of anthropology and of teaching anthropology. Our remarks are, further, intended to apply to culture cases from any source. To make our use of case materials understandable, we need to declare where we stand on larger matters concerning the purpose of doing anthropology and of doing education.

For us, the purpose of anthropology is education in the broad sense. We do research on diverse lifeways in order to understand better the human condition and communicate that understanding to the educating public. This understanding is constantly enlarging and modifying. The processes of education are likewise changing. We live, study, and teach in a state of flux, but we strive for continuity.

This position demands that we, as members of the academy and particularly as anthropologists, face our obligations as faculty squarely. Our primary obligation is to educate. We do the research, analyze, spin webs of explanation, in order to have something to say that will be worth communicating to others. As college and university faculty we have a pressing obligation to teach, and the primary focus of that teaching is the undergraduates, the young people who will be the educated citizens of our consensual republic (and who will ultimately determine whether

Source: Written especially for *Education and Cultural Process*, 3rd Edition.

there is an anthropology). All of the other activities of faculty are subsidiary to that obligation, including graduate training and research.

It is not that graduate training and research are unimportant, for what we have to communicate—to teach—is a product of our research, and who does the teaching is a product of our graduate training. But we cannot afford to get lost along the way to the attainment of the ultimate goal.

What, of our achieved knowledge, is worth communicating to undergraduates? Some anthropologists think theory should be the focus. The trouble with theory is that it is necessarily phrased in ways that are entirely out of the cultural framework of undergraduates. Theories are also inevitably precious, known to and circulated within small, esoteric, professional cliques. When theories become more widely recognized they don't last long. Witness the waves of theory such as structuralism and ethnoscience that have swept over anthropology and subsequently almost disappeared. Theories matter to us, as anthropologists, but they must be translated, and they must be widely applicable to understandable problems in human life to make a difference in undergraduate education. Usually they are not, and in introductory courses dominated by theory students are left puzzled and often hostile. The communication that makes a difference is not happening. It is our conviction that theories decontextualized from specific case studies of relevance to most undergraduates should not be taught in beginning anthropology courses.

We use "culture cases" because they are intrinsically interesting to everyone and because they can demonstrate the diversity and commonality of human lifeways on our little planet—something every educated person must understand—precisely because our planet is so little. In our decades of teaching undergraduates, we have never met a first-year student who did not need more of what these lessons have to teach. Most of these students come from culturally limited backgrounds, particularly the sons and daughters of the middle class in America. Ethnic minority students also bring their narrow convictions and identities to school with them, but they are likely to have had some significant and personally meaningful cross-cultural experience in our society, much of it negative. Well constructed culture case studies of diverse peoples and places challenge narrow personal persuasions issuing from a firm foundation of class and ethnic prejudice.

Of course, culture cases do not come ready-made out of diversity. Behavior and sentiment must be observed, recorded, and interpreted. Behavior that is understandable in a setting foreign to the reader must be made understandable in the conceptual universe of the reader, in order to be communicated. The processes involved are so subtle and complex that some of us have given up, or we strain our observations through theory that leaves the observations unrecognizable and often quite irrelevant to the enhanced understanding of human behavior for which we strive as teachers.

A useful culture case is close to the behavioral ground, observed and reported by a trained observer who can acknowledge cultural and conceptual bias but not allow that bias to bend observation totally out of shape and who sees oneself as part of the phenomenon being studied and interpreted. Reflexive ethnography is essential to useful culture cases. It always has been, but now we have a name for it.

There are other criteria for good ethnography and useful culture cases. In fact, we have developed a list of specific features of a "good ethnography" (Spindler and Spindler, 1992 [see chapter 4]). We have tried to apply relevant criteria in our selection and editorial development of the case studies in our series, but of course there are hundreds of culture case studies that are not in our series that exhibit the characteristics of a "good ethnography."

For us, culture cases are at the core of cultural anthropology and are the starting point of what we teach in all undergraduate courses. All the lessons to be learned from comprehending the diversity of human behavior, as well as its comforting commonality, are derived from culture cases—not directly from theories of human behavior, but from human behavior interpreted judiciously in the conceptual framework of anthropology and related disciplines.

Of course, there is more to anthropology that should be taught to undergraduates than cultural diversity and commonality. There are concepts, analytic procedures, and, yes, theory. But we can use culture cases as springboards to these matters. Concepts, analysis, and theory grounded on case studies can be communicated effectively. We will say more of this later.

Teaching the Course

During the 1950s we used, among other readings, Ruth Benedict's *Patterns of Culture* and Margaret Mead's *Coming of Age in Samoa*, and sometimes *Sex and Temperament*. There were solid ethnographies available and some classic ones as well, but often they killed rather than generated interest on the part of undergraduates. We have never used a textbook (with apologies to our friends and colleagues who write textbooks). For us they project an illusion of security and finality when neither is appropriate. Texts formalize when informality and flow are needed, and they make the strange all too familiar.

In the early days of our teaching, we also used Walter Goldschmidt's record album, *Ways of Mankind*. It may be unknown now to most people, but for us it was quite alive. We can hear Talestyva's soft, Spanish-accented voice in "Desert Soliloquy" telling us that a lot of things made him happy as a child in the pueblo. The voice was that of a professional actor, but the cultural materials were carefully worked out. We played those records in a hall seating over 700 students, and everyone listened with rapt attention.

We also used films. One of them we still use: *Churinga*, with C. P. Mountford's "imperialist colonialism" as well as his humanity coming through, and the scenes of digging for honey ants and witchedy grubs, and increasing kangaroos through ritual. Brief glimpses of the Churinga open the door to the wondrous world of Arunta cosmology.

In the mid-1950s it was daring to use films, or at least to use films that were even mildly interesting. As Felix Keesing, our chairman at that time, said, "You are spoon-feeding them pap." He taught a stern Anthro 001, but a good one by then-current standards. Today, we use ten films, one each week of the quarter, and require the reading of four case studies. We lecture on the emergence of culture from a primate base, kinship, rites of passage, early childhood, cultural transmission, demography and subsistence, gender identities and their construction, warfare and the regulation of violence, the moral equivalent of war, "normal" and "abnormal" seen cross-culturally, colonialism, and social and cultural adaptation. We require various other readings besides case studies.

If you were in our lecture hall, you would often hear more about cultures than about the topics listed above. Culture cases are our foundation, our springboard, our trampoline and our support system. Without culture cases we would not know how to teach. We would have little to say, and what we did say would lack reality and excitement for us and for our students. We start with cultures; we interpret and generalize from cultures; and we critique Western culture into this framework. We call this the inductive method, though at times we turn to deduction—but we start with cultures.

Our lectures are not, however, limited by or to the case studies; rather the case studies serve as points of departure and as ready sources of examples and illustrations already shared, through readings and films, with the students. For example, we start our discussion of kinship and social organization with the central and western desert aborigines of Australia (Arunta and Mardu). Students have read Tonkinson's *Mardu* (1991). We can refer to kinship among these people with confidence that some particulars are already shared. We can later go on to relationships among subsistence techniques, environment, demographics, and possible sociopolitical consequences, in a comparison of the Dani of the New Guinea Highlands (Heider 1991), and the Arunta/Mardu. We use the Hutterites and Amish (Hostetler and Huntington, 1980, 1992) as examples of enclaved, closed human communities and as examples of stabilized, institutionalized, socioreligious

movements. The Hutterites and Amish illustrate boundary maintenance and symbolic representation of identity and its reinforcement
through cultural transmission. We use the Yanomamö (Chagnon 1992),
along with the particularly rich film resources associated with that case
study (and now there is a CD ROM available), to demonstrate the genesis of control of aggression. We use the Sambia (Herdt 1986) as a
springboard for discussion of homosexuality cross-culturally and
reflect on the problem of gender identity in our own society, particularly
the historically extreme polarization of this identity in American culture. We use the Bateson and Mead films of the Balinese and draw upon
a number of sources for lectures that challenge complacency about cultural interpretation, since interpretations of the Balinese contain
remarkable contradictions. We use our own case study on the Menominee (Spindler and Spindler, 1984), accompanied by slides that we have
taken in the field, as the beginning of a discussion on adaptation to cat-
astrophic change, exploitation, and deprivation, and the psychological
concomitance of that adaptation.

We weave our way through the major problems and processes of
human existence with concepts, grounded theory, and contemporary
scholarship in anthropology, with some cross-disciplinary excursions,
but always with reference to known, communicated culture cases. No
generalizations are made without such reference. As often as possible
and reasonable, we make comparative reference to our own habitat, the
United States, and the problems of subsistence, of sexual politics, religion, social life, and education that students face in their daily lives.

Each culture case leads into certain topics, and each topic leads
to exploitation of certain, or all, cases. The course proceeds through the
academic quarter with a constant movement into and out of, and often
back into, culture cases and topics. The students seem to like this treatment. We have always enjoyed overflowing enrollments and strongly
positive end-of-course evaluations. Our current class is twice as large
as expected and strains the facilities of our department to provide the
necessary services for us.

The Case Study Series

In 1960, we published our first six case studies in cultural anthropology with Holt, Rinehart and Winston with David Boynton as our
anthropology editor. We started working on the series while we were at
the Center for Advanced Studies in Behavioral Sciences at Stanford in
1956–57. We were responding to our own need for good culture cases
to use in Anthro 001. Our first cases were *Being a Paluan*, by Barnett;
Bunyoro, by Beattie; *The Tiwi*, with Hart and Pilling; *The Cheyennes*
with Hoebel; and *Tepoztlan* with Lewis. *Vasilika* by Friedl followed

shortly. All these originals are still in print and are being used by anthropologists to teach introductory anthropology. Since then, more than 200 case studies have been published and 56 are currently in print. Many of those out of print have been reissued by Waveland Press. We are publishing new ones and have launched an ambitious program of revision. We know that the case studies have been read by literally millions of undergraduate (and graduate) students. Unfortunately, at least for us and the authors, most of them are read as secondhand books.

For us the most useful case studies for instructional purposes are those which can be combined with films. The Dani, Yanomamö, Hutterite, and Mardudjara case studies are good examples. But we always use some case studies that do not have associated films. We usually require minimally four case studies to be read, and we present at least seven culture cases through lectures, together with audiovisuals. We present no cases in lecture without them.

We will soon have 455 ten-page typed essays from our Anthropology 001 class using case studies as primary source material. Students choose questions that they have already had a chance to work on. They have been presented with ten possible questions two weeks prior to required completion of the essays.

Many of the authors of case studies are young, with still-warm dissertations. This is notably not true, however, for a number of authors in mid-career or beyond, such as Norman Chance, Walter Goldschmidt, Adamson Hoebel, Hilda Kuper, Richard Lee, John Hostetler, Napoleon Chagnon, Karl Heider, Evon Vogt, Alice Kehoe, Roger Keesing, Robert Tonkinson, and Annette Weiner.

Younger or older, we have had a persistent problem with the authors of case studies, and that is to get them to move from abstract analytical discussions to full-bodied expressions of discrete events in social life, to paraphrase George Marcus in *Anthropology as Cultural Critique.* This has always been a problem in anthropological publication, particularly in ethnography, and it has been recognized as such. When we were developing the format of the series in the 1950s, we had a number of discussions with colleagues at American Anthropological Association meetings. One, in particular, occurred when Pete Hallowell, Ad Hoebel, Ward Goodenough, Homer Barnett, Ralph Beals and Pete Murdock were gathered in a hotel room. In the middle of the discussion, Pete Murdock suddenly rose from his comfortable, prone position and shouted, "You've got to get the guts of the culture into those things!" He did not mean an inventory of traits; he meant the feeling, the meaning, the distinctiveness of the culture and the society that bore it. From Pete, this was particularly stirring.

Ethnographers in the past have consistently, with some notable exceptions, excluded subjective reactions, live dialogue and narrative engagement from their reports. They managed to take the life out of life. We have heard so many times from students and laypersons alike, "How do they (anthropologists) manage to make something so dull out of something so fascinating?" Anthropology too often has been taught like that and too many ethnographies written like that. We can thank the post-modernist critics, Marcus and Fisher, Clifford, Rabinow, Rosaldo, and Crapanzano, among others, for rubbing our noses in our collective failures to communicate. We have gained some freedom from traditional strictures on interpretation and communication.

In 1968–69, we began badgering some of our colleagues to describe their personal experiences, their feelings, and their personal interactions with the "natives," and to join this with the procedural hardware of their fieldwork. *Being an Anthropologist*, first published in 1970, was the result. The chapters in this volume also have been combined with the case studies to which they are relevant, and they have been reprinted. The badgering was productive and the more personal narratives were interesting and even useful, but they were compartmentalized. They were not a part of the ethnographic text. The efforts therefore fell short of full realization.

We will continue to work with authors to produce ethnographic texts in the format of our series and anyplace else where our help can be used so that their writings will communicate effectively to undergraduates. They must include a "self and other" human experience with its sensuous as well as intellectual and emotional consequences, in readable narrative form.

It is interesting that none of the critics of ethnographic writing mention the undergraduate reader. Specific mention is given to writing for colleagues and for that elusive multitude, the educated laity, but not for undergraduates—yet the largest, and potentially most important readership for anthropology is that of the undergraduate. There is no point in trying to make undergraduates into anthropologists, however. We do want to make them into citizens who will think "anthropologically" about cultural differences, multiculturalism, ethnicity, imperialism and oppression.

We think that the academic elitism of professional anthropologists in general, and that of the post-modernists in particular, prevents them from attending to the undergraduate readership or to the publications directed toward this readership. This elitism is pervasive in our field and is a great handicap. In all the discussion among the post- (and post-post) modernists of what ethnography might be, to our knowledge only one case study from our undergraduate series is mentioned: Chagnon's on the Yanomamö—yet the undergraduate readership for ethnographic case studies is larger than any other in anthropology. Why is this audience and a series of this sort ignored?

A former editor of *American Anthropologist*, explaining the failure of *AA* for the past five years to review case studies from our series (with a few exceptions), recently told me that they should be reviewed in more specialized area journals. The idea of an *instructional series* for undergraduates, of potential interest to any anthropologist teaching anthropology, was not understood or, perhaps, was not accepted.

As a last thought we would like to touch once again on the problems of cultural translation and representation. Ethnographies may be seen as a form of fiction. As Clifford points out, fiction in this sense does not connote falsehood but rather partiality and something made or fashioned (1986). We would say that an ethnography is a construct fashioned by the anthropologist-author that is never the whole truth and that is essentially an interpretation of a complex metaphor—the nature of things as lived, reported, and perceived by natives. In this sense, an ethnography is a complex metaphor of a complex metaphor, and a cultural translation of one. When handled with humanity and narrative skill, this is the stuff from which we can weave webs of significance and teach undergraduates. The subtle and complex ramifications of this are what make teaching Anthro 001 and other undergraduate courses the most challenging part of our professional lives.

Final Comments

The position that we have taken, that the primary purpose of anthropology is education, will not be popular or even taken seriously in many quarters of the academy. We faculty are so puffed up with the self-created importance of research and theory building that we often do not see the imperatives of our call to duty. Graduate students are taught as part of an undeclared agenda that teaching is a necessary evil, to be dispatched efficiently but not with dedication and passion, so that one can turn to the real work of writing articles and books for whatever clique is regarded as the significant readership at the time. Graduate students are admitted, in the first place, for their promise as researchers, not as teachers. Young faculty close their doors and minds to undergraduates, for they do not offer tenure. In fact, excessive attention to them and to their needs may obstruct the path to promotion and tenure. A joke making the rounds in academic circles is that junior faculty pray that they won't get a teaching award before they achieve tenure. Heavy enrollments in one's classes are unwelcome, since this may be seen as the result of "playing to the students" or a reputation for "easy" courses. Senior professors become so detached from teaching and the classroom that they become unavailable even to their younger colleagues, and some buy their way out of teaching with research funds so they can spend their time largely, or exclusively, on research. Of course there are many faculty and some departments to which these rather negative characterizations do not apply as a whole, but in all faculties in all of the institutions we have known as students or as visiting faculty there are serious tendencies in these directions.

There is hope. however, at least at Stanford, and similar moves are underway elsewhere. On April 5, 1990, then-president Donald Kennedy, in a speech to the Academic Council at Stanford (later rebroadcast over TV channel 6), said:

> . . . I conclude by citing some of the disparities we must erase to make present Stanford more like the one we have just visited (forecast for A.D. 2010, editor's note). The first disparity has to do with the attention we give to our students, and especially with the centrality of undergraduate education."

> The joint-product character of our enterprise has long been a source of strength to us: teaching and research are both important. But the relative weight has shifted over time, as the relatively new term "research facility" suggests. It is time for us to reaffirm that education—that is, teaching in all its forms is the primary task—and . . . our society will judge us in the long run on how well we do it. . . .

> Junior faculty who show outstanding teaching ability fail at the tenure line too often, to the dismay of students who understandably wonder about Stanford's values. Now in many cases these outcomes are unavoidable, or fair even though disappointing, or even correct. But when aggregated they give a picture of an institution that says one thing but does another. (Kennedy, 1990:10)

Recently a center for teaching at Stanford has been established and enjoys a substantial patronage from teaching assistants, junior faculty, and even a few senior faculty. Several highly regarded teaching awards have been established. (George Spindler received the Lloyd W. Dinkelspiel award in 1978 for outstanding contributions to undergraduate education, particularly the development of the case-study method of teaching—he already had tenure.) A commission on undergraduate education is currently reviewing such matters as distribution requirements, the constitution of majors, language requirements, and the role of technology in teaching. There have been reviews and recommendations for change on some of these same matters before.

Everyone knows that institutions of higher education—in fact, of any level of education—are difficult to change. The structures, requirements and explicit mandates for teaching, for education in general, may change, but nothing much seems to happen. The attitudes, values, criteria for performance as members of the academy, the *culture* of academia, will have to undergo a virtual revolution before the moves to reform undergraduate education at Stanford or anywhere else can prove successful. Resistance is deep, often disguised, sometimes quite unconscious. New understandings of the role of the faculty in education, the very purposes of a university education, the criteria for evaluation of student performances and products, the conception of a "proper" workload for a class, the extent to which cooperative learning is encouraged among students, and more, requires extensive rehabilitation if our universities and colleges are to perform their mandated roles in our society with distinction—or even adequately. Anthropology is no better or worse off than the other disciplines that grope their way along under the umbrella of the "liberal arts." If we can attend to the problems of undergraduate education wholeheartedly, and with a good heart (as the Hopi would say), we can make a difference.

We have found that our work with the case studies and their authors, and the use of these studies in teaching, rescues us from despair and cynicism and allows us to feed our idealism about our goals as anthropologists and members of the academy.

Appendix
Commentaries:
A Technique for Increasing Communication

Louise Spindler

The commentary technique, which I developed for use in our smaller classes—including Anthro 001 during summers when it too is small (35–40 students)—enhances our communication with students from a wide variety of social and cultural backgrounds (and yes, Stanford is multicultural today!). Students are instructed to ask questions of the material, express their feelings of objection and agreement, and critique the material read from a personal-experience point of view. The material is often a case study or short ethnographic piece about some distinctive culture. To avoid stage fright, which most students suffer, we require that it be put into written form and submitted to us. We review the commentaries, select certain of them for discussion, and use this as a basis for a part of our instructional period.

We emphasize that these are not "critical reviews" in the usual sense. We do not presume that the beginning student has enough background for this. We stress the *reactive* aspect and reinforce the validity of the students' personal experience and observation. Many of our students have an ethnic background or come from hinterland ranches or farms and are experiencing a form of culture shock from exposure to metropolitan California and Stanford. They do not understand their own confusion. They often ask questions of material, as read or heard in class, that add a fresh new dimension that has not occurred to us before. We even acquire interesting new data, as in the case of one young man from the Appalachian area who had much to offer in his discussion of George Hicks' *Appalachian Valley*.

So often we teach as though our students had no thoughts or feelings of their own and have only to accept and even internalize ours in order to learn. We feel that the commentaries permit us to move, in some degree, into the student's world. The commentaries also require us to be adaptive, and, hopefully, creative in our thinking about what students write. This is stimulating and adds vitality to our classroom interactions and communication.

Bibliography

Barnett, Homer, 1979 (fieldwork ed.). *Being A Paluan*. New York: Holt, Rinehart and Winston.

Bateson, Gregory, and Margaret Mead, 1939a. *Trance and Dance in Bali: Character Formation in Different Cultures*. New York University Film Library.

———. 1939b. *A Balinese Family*. New York University Film Library.

Beattie, John, 1960. *Bunyoro: An African Kingdom*. New York: Holt, Rinehart and Winston.

Benedict, Ruth, 1934. *Patterns of Culture*. Boston, MA: Houghton, Mifflin & Co.

Chagnon, Napoleon, 1992. *Yanomamö*, 4th ed. Forth Worth, TX: Harcourt Brace.

Clifford, James, 1986. Introduction: Partial Truths. In *Writing Culture: The Poetics and Politics of Ethnography*, by James Clifford and George Marcus. Berkeley: University of California Press.

Friedl, Ernestine, 1962. *Vasilika: A Village in Modern Greece*. New York: Holt, Rinehart and Winston.

Hart, C. W. M., Arnold Pilling and Jane Goodale, 1977. *The Tiwi of North Australia*, 3d ed. New York: Holt, Rinehart, and Winston.

Heider, Karl, 1996. *Grand Valley Dani: Peaceful Warriors*, 3rd ed. Fort Worth, TX: Harcourt Brace.

Herdt, Gilbert, 1986. *The Sambia: Ritual and Gender in New Guinea*. Fort Worth, TX: Harcourt Brace.

Hicks, George, 1976. *Appalachian Valley*. Fort Worth, TX: Harcourt Brace.

Hoebel, E. Adamson, 1977. *The Cheyennes*, 2d ed. New York: Holt, Rinehart and Winston.

Hostetler, John, and Gertrude Huntington, 1980. *The Hutterites of North America: Fieldwork Edition*. Fort Worth, TX: Harcourt, Brace, Jovanovich.

———. 1992. *Amish Children*, 2d ed. Fort Worth, TX: Harcourt Brace.

Kennedy, Donald, 1990. An address to the Stanford Community at the Meeting of the Academic Council, April 5, at Stanford University, Stanford, CA.

Lewis, Oscar, 1960. *Tepoztlan: Village in Mexico*. New York: Holt, Rinehart and Winston.

Marcus, George E., and Michael Fischer, eds., 1986. *Anthropology as Cultural Critique: An Experimental Moment in the Human Sciences.* Chicago: University of Chicago Press.

Mead, Margaret [1935], 1963. *Sex and Temperament in Three Primitive Societies.* Apollo eds. New York: William Morrow.

——— [1928], 1961. *Coming of Age in Samoa.* Apollo eds. New York: William Morrow.

Rabinow, Paul, 1977. *Reflections on Fieldwork in Morocco.* Berkeley: University of California Press.

Rosaldo, Rentao, 1989. *Culture and Truth: The Remaking of Social Analysis.* Boston: Beacon Press.

Spindler, George D., ed., 1970. *Being an Anthropologist: Fieldwork in Eleven Cultures.* New York: Holt, Rinehart and Winston.

Spindler, George, and Louise Spindler, 1984. *Dreamers With Power: The Menominee.* Prospect Heights, IL: Waveland Press.

———, 1992. *Cultural Process and Ethnography.* In *The Handbook of Qualitative Research in Education,* LeCompte, Goetz, and Millroy, eds., pp. 53–92. Hillsdale, NJ: Academic Press.

Tonkinson, Robert, 1991. *The Mardu: Living the Dream in Australia's Desert,* 2d ed. Fort Worth, TX: Harcourt, Brace, Jovanovich.

Acknowledgment

We acknowledge with gratitude the critical readings and suggestions by colleagues Ray McDermott, Bernard Siegel, Patricia Phelan, Christine Finnan, Janice Stockard, and Harumi Befu. The errors, faults, and prejudices are our own.

26

Classroom Discussion
Comparing Hutterite Education
and an Inner City School

Mica Pollock
Stanford University

In the spring of 1996 at Stanford University, I served as the teaching assistant for George and Louise Spindler's course entitled "Cultural Transmission: Education in Cross-Cultural Perspectives." The class, cross-listed in both the education and anthropology departments, advertised that it would discuss "the patterning of education" in a "variety of formal and informal educational contexts." About fifteen graduate education students enrolled, all hoping to glean tidbits of wisdom from the Spindlers, many asking for the first time what an anthropological perspective might offer them in their general studies of education. Eight undergraduate students also enrolled, all of whom were interested in children but many of whom were "studying" education for the first time.

I was curious, when the course began, about participants' own educational experiences, feeling that before we studied the "educational contexts" of others we should explore our own. We soon found that we had a surprisingly wide variety of educational backgrounds. As we described our backgrounds to each other, it seemed that we all had experienced some sort of clash of educational "cultures" in our lives: One blond undergraduate had moved from an ethnically mixed community to a primarily white high school which bused in kids from what was now "the other side." A bearded graduate student had grown up in a family of parents and siblings who were, like himself, deaf; he said that attending school, for him, was like walking onto a different planet. An Armenian masters student from Los Angeles described her attendance at Armenian culture and language schools from age five through high school; she felt that her knowledge of "U.S. education" came only

Source: Written especially for *Education and Cultural Process*, 3rd Edition.

from her college years at UCLA. A Native American graduate student had attended a different school across the country for almost every year of her life before entering a high school designed specifically for Native Americans; she went from this high school to college at Stanford. A "half-Japanese" graduate student who had felt excluded from the Asian American Students Association at Yale discussed her post-college experience teaching English in Japan; a Japanese graduate student who had hated school in Japan because it was "boring" discussed how, while in graduate school in Pittsburgh, she had experienced unfamiliar frictions between black and white students. I myself, a slightly observant Jew, had attended a very homogeneous (white and Christian) set of public schools in Iowa City, Iowa, had spent my college years at somewhat-more-diverse Harvard studying racial identity, and had moved to San Francisco to teach at an incredibly diverse low-income high school almost devoid of white students. Clearly, we were a bunch that had already experienced education "cross-culturally"; yet we had not yet learned how to compare educational experiences in systematic and useful ways.

George and Louise made it quite clear that they intended to teach us how to do this by having us read a number of ethnographic case studies of various educational settings. We were required to read two case studies together as a class, and then to read two more of our choice in writing a final comparative paper. The following section is a transcript, taken from my notes, of a discussion-section conversation had by myself and eight other members of our class (seven graduate students in education, one undergraduate in "human biology"). In this discussion, we compared our two assigned case studies: *Hutterites of North America* (new edition: 1996) by John Hostetler and Gertrude Huntington, and *"Shut Those Thick Lips!" A Study of a Slum School* (1983), Gerry Rosenfeld's work on a school in Harlem in the 1960s.[1] Hostetler and Huntington spent years in a Hutterite community in the Great Plains area to write their study (Huntington had in fact brought her whole family to live in the community). Rosenfeld wrote his ethnographic study based on several years spent teaching (while attending graduate school in anthropology) at the elementary school he calls "Harlem School."

At the point in April when this discussion took place, we had spent a lot of time discussing how "education" could be seen as the transmission of particular forms of cultural knowledge to children; in a sense, as George and Louise said, education of most kinds could be seen as an "intentional interference" in children's lives. We had discussed the Spindlers' labels for the various life stages that educational experiences—formal and informal—put children through in different cultures. For example, we had discussed the occurrence of "cultural compression," when a child's freedom is limited by newly imposed (adult) "rules." We had also discussed various rites of passage, particularly puberty rites, between life stages in different cultures (thus, note one student's reference in the transcription to "the Arunta subincision," a penile cut traditionally made in a puberty ritual among the Arunta aboriginal group of Australia). We had discussed the notion of "cultural commitment" (commitment to a "culture") resulting from periods of high stress, "cultural dissonance," and discontinuity for young people (for example, fraternity initiations, such as paddling, are intense periods of unfamiliar discomfort followed by relief, causing the frat member to become newly committed to the very system he cursed while being paddled; he returns the next year to swat the next group of initiates).

I myself, as the transcript shows, was particularly concerned with a number of issues throughout the class: how intentional and explicit was this transmission of "culture" or "knowledge" in various "cultures"? How much agency did various actors in the culture have during this process? More generally, how could we in fact define a "culture"? Contemporary cultural anthropology, with its current focus on blurred cultural boundaries, cultural "borderlands," and anti-essentialism, seemed to be looking with derision on studies entitled "the Hutterites."[2] Possible anachronisms also worried me: could we study the educational rituals of "the Arunta" of the past without updating students on how Arunta traditions were faring in the global economy of the 1990s? If we were to watch a film in class on "the Balinese" for information on forms of cultural transmission in Bali, did we need to spend time discussing the fact that the kid in the background of the traditional theater performance was wearing a Coca-Cola shirt?

Let me make my main point here: despite these problematizing questions so crucial to contemporary anthropology, I think the use of case studies in cross-cultural analyses of education is valid and necessary. If accompanied by critical discussion, the comparative use of case studies is in fact invaluable to educators, as it is invaluable to anthropologists trying to understand particular cultural practices—like schooling. Comparisons with "the unfamiliar" offer us new lenses through which to view our own educational practices. Finding such critical lenses is especially imperative for educators, since educational practices are so familiar to some of us—especially, ironically, to hypereducated scholars of education!—that it is dangerously easy to look right past our practices and consider them "natural."

The comparative use of case studies in educational anthropology helps us denaturalize. Through looking at the practices of "the Hutterites" (who in fact regulate the reproduction of their culture with such rigor that it seems, after a while, unproblematic to call them "the Hutterites") we might notice how disorganized, in comparison, are the educational or moral aims of the schools where many of us taught or attended. By reading about a Harlem school in the 1960s many of us can get a sense of what overt racism looks like, in order to better understand the covert racism many of us note or have experienced in schools of the 1990s. When we compare such case studies to each other, we end up coming to even richer realizations about ourselves in the present. As the transcript shows, in comparing the Hutterite school (where a community almost completely controlled the formal education of its children) to the Harlem one (where a community had almost no control over its children's formal education) we arrived at a critical discussion of culture and power in contemporary American schools. Can American schooling be "successful," we came to ask, in places where powerful "outsiders" are the enforcers of formal education?

Clearly, using case studies simply as multicultural "information" should not be our goal in classes on the anthropology of education. "Learning" that students of "X" culture might act in "X" sorts of ways in class too easily substitutes for critical analysis of actual "cultures" in schools. The most beneficial use of anthropological case studies for understanding educational practices comes when we bring in recent anthropology's essential insights about heterogeneity, the influence of the author/observer, and the problematics of looking at cultures as bounded or predictable—but also when we attempt to compare and analyze places considered by participants to be spaces where actual "cultures" interact. The true "multiculturalism" that anthropology can then offer education is in fact a *skill* for analyzing "cultures" and "difference" in educational settings—including the "culture" and "cultures" of and in our own classrooms. Such analyses of "difference" thus become, often, analyses of power relations.

This "multiculturalism" is a practical skill for educators, one based on the anthropological ability to compare "the familiar" with "the unfamiliar," to make "the familiar" strange, and finally to critique how "culture" and power function in "the familiar"—in our own educational practices. It is then that comparisons of case studies like the discussion which follows brings students, as happened here, to discussions of what "our" educational culture could be. This skill is, I believe, what George and Louise hoped to teach us.

Education 315/Anthropology 266

Discussion Section Field Notes Comparing the Hutterite case study to *"Shut Those Thick Lips"*

Mica: Do you see any salient differences between the Hutterite study and the Harlem study?

Becca: The Hutterite study seems updated compared to *"Shut Those Thick Lips"*; it doesn't sound as old-fashioned.

Kazi: The tone of the author is clearer in *"Shut Those Thick Lips."* Why wasn't Hostetler's [own] Amish culture reflected more?

Becca: There was a clear power imbalance between the Harlem ethnographer and his students. The Hutterite population, in contrast, was not approached as if it was at a power disadvantage.

Lon: The Hutterites are in complete control over their destiny; the kids at Harlem school are at the mercy of the world. They develop coping strategies that aren't necessary for the Hutterite kids.

Mica: Are the Hutterite *kids* really in control of their destiny? Shouldn't we be comparing the children of both cultures?

Lon: Hutterite kids are growing up in a society *created* by their parents.

Becca: A more foreign culture is being transmitted to the Harlem kids.

Lon: In Harlem, the kids are learning how to cope; the "culture" becomes "how to make do."

Mica: Are the Hutterite kids also learning "coping strategies" to deal with their culture (and not get "switched"/whipped)?

Lon: The Harlem kids are dealing with the contrast between their home world and the school world—the Hutterite parents are perhaps unconsciously transmitting the culture.

Mica: Let's get into this idea of "consciousness." How conscious is this "transmission"?

Jet: It's both conscious and unconscious.

Mica: Is any transmission in Hutterite culture really unconscious?

Becca: It's so clearly stated that hard work, for example, is community-building—they keep coming back to their basic rules. I'm not sure how much these rules are the author's construction.

Mica: How do we get these descriptions of "worldview" without stereotyping? That is, wouldn't your antenna go up if you were to see a list of the aspects of "the Harlem worldview"?

Becca: In the Hutterite culture, there's a consensus that this is the worldview.

Susan: The author did live in the community.

Mica: Is this a Hutterite *adult* "worldview"? Would a kid agree with this list?

Joby: Maybe a kid would try to articulate these, but wouldn't be able to.

Lon: It's part of the acculturation process: kids will have adopted the worldview by the time they are baptized.

Joby: Perhaps it would be more valid to try to articulate the worldview of Harlem adults rather than of the children.

Becca: For the Hutterites, this has been *defined* as their worldview—people come to *access* it.

Mica: So is a worldview only established by people who have "control"? Are we contrasting the Hutterites as people who have total control to those in Harlem as people who have no control?

Joby: The Hutterites have made an attempt to *establish* a worldview.

Jet: The Hutterites and the Arunta maybe would be a better comparison!

Cabral: The question seems to be whether the education is perpetuating the culture—or not. With the Arunta and the Hutterites, education serves to perpetuate the culture. Educating in Harlem similarly perpetuates a culture (that of the status-quo power structure and student disempowerment).

Lon: Maybe the Harlem transmission of culture is more peer-related, where the transmission with the Hutterites all comes from adults.

Becca: No, the Hutterite culture was somewhat peer-oriented.

Susan: We're talking about the perpetuation of the dominant culture in Harlem, not the kids' culture (she also asks whether the Harlem kids in some way come to perpetuate the power structure as well, by internalizing it).

Becca: Perhaps the cultural discontinuity isn't *resolved* in Harlem.

(We discussed here the issue of abuse, after Becca raised the examples of teachers who hit students in the Harlem school.)

Mica: Would you call the Hutterites' switching of their children "abuse"?

Becca: No.

Jet: Or the Arunta subincision?

Cabral: I think the difference is that if it's not rationalized, it's abuse. Maybe in Harlem, then, the lack of resolution is what's being perpetuated.

Mica: How about this rationalization of authority? Where teachers in Harlem might say "you do this because I'm the teacher and I said so," a Hutterite can say "you do this because God directs us to." This carries so much more weight!

Joby: But a *positive outcome* can be seen and experienced in Hutterite obedience—in the Harlem school, there's no sense that school pays off, or that obeying teachers gets you *ahead!*

Lon: How about being disciplined by someone "of their own kind" versus discipline by "the other"? With Harlem discipline, kids see a different motive when the teachers discipline them.

Becca: The teachers in Harlem *do* have a "rationalized" ideology for how/why they discipline the kids—after that poor kid was slapped in the face, he *was* quiet for the rest of the period!

Joby: The Harlem kids never see the *fruition* of the promises of the dominant "worldview."

Mica: A white teacher would never rationalize, or say to the researcher, that he was teaching kids to "be white," though we might say this. A Hutterite, however, would say he was teaching kids explicitly how to be Christians. Would the Harlem teachers ever be as explicit as the Hutterites?

Jet: It's not said explicitly, but it's clear to all—like the Harlem kid who bluffed about the singer coming in, he knew that *everybody* wanted to waste the rest of the day.

Mica: So you're saying it doesn't have to be explict—it's pervasive enough in the school culture that everyone knows what's going on.

David: When a teacher takes homework and dumps it in the garbage, that sends a clear message—you don't need to write it on the wall (that the school wants to perpetuate the power structure).

Cabral: There's cultural compression going on here.

Mica: OK, say you're a researcher: if you tell Harlem teachers that you've observed them and determined that they're perpetuating the power structure, they'll respond, "no, we're not!" Where if you tell a Hutterite that they're perpetuating Christianity, they'll agree. What do we do if teachers won't admit what they're doing?

Joby: It's like you said last week—we want to see specifics. Educational researchers who point out the huge points—"you're perpetuating the power structure"—won't work as well as those who cite specific instances, like throwing work into the garbage.

Cabral: These trends *can* be shown to teachers.

Lon: A lot of what teachers do in the classroom is unconscious. There's an internal conflict inside the teacher, between what's conscious and what's unconscious—like if they think they're teaching a kid to act white, but unconsciously they know the kid can't act white.

Susan: (suggests people read Lisa Delpit, on "Educating Other People's Children": white liberal educators selling kids of color short by not making the power structure explicit to them) The larger school structure sends clear messages to the kids—like if the school across town has a pool and everything.

Jet: So this raises the question of whether only people of "the same kind" as the kids can/should work with them.

Lon: Ideally, if teachers have adequate training in anthropology, maybe, they don't have to have the same culture as the kids.

Cabral: Maybe if they're of the same identity, it adds an incentive for the teacher—the feeling that "I'm making all of us better," improving the whole community.

Mica: The Hutterites are a good example of this. How about in other settings, then, where the teacher has no stake in the community—if the Harlem neighborhood exploded, many teachers would just be out of jobs, no big deal, right?

Becca: How about the black teachers at Harlem school, though? They seemed to be similar to the white teachers (in how they related to the kids).

Susan: In teacher training, how could we give teachers a sense of stake in the community?

Lon: Perhaps in the 1960s, black teachers had to buy into the power structure to get/keep their jobs.

Becca: (recommends reading Jim Marsh on women in business having to be more "like men" to succeed)

Cabral: (suggests teachers must have passion about students' welfare in order to be good at it)

Lon: It's similar to deaf culture, this notion of getting into the system—the teacher needs a belief in the good of the community.

Mica: To bring this back to the Hutterites: how about the English School on the Hutterite property? How about the issue of how much control they have over the school? (All discuss how Hutterite children have German School before and after English School; the English teachers show deference to the Hutterites by not using audiovisual equipment, etc.). Could other communities so bind their teachers?

Becca: No other communities are so cohesive.

Joby: Who gets to control their kids' education? Not just cohesive groups. The Hutterites have money to pay the teacher; they have resources to construct other institutions besides the English school.

Susan: Afro-centric schools would make an interesting comparison.

Joby: Kids in those schools aren't as isolated from the rest of the world—they watch TV, etc.

Mica: What do kids in nonisolated schools in this country get committed to then, if there is such discontinuity between "the school" and "the community"?

Becca: There doesn't have to be continuity—just resolution of dissonance.

Mica: What could the Harlem kids get committed *to* in school then?

Joby: Is the problem not simply that the culture of the school is different from the culture at home? Rather, that there's a *conflict* between the two cultures?

Mica: Can we *have* resolution within the kids while this conflict is still continuing between these two "cultures" in the society at large?

Becca: But the Harlem parents *did* emphasize education.

Lon: The parents may realize education is bettering—but they need more choices than the Harlem School. The Harlem School isn't *giving* an education to the kids.

Joby: It's giving them a *negative* education.

Isabel: I just came back from a conference on American Indian education—the issue came up that parents really want education for their kids, but it doesn't always translate into practice. We need to look at what parents *do*.

Mica: So the issue comes up again: do the parents have any control over their kids' education? We've been portraying the Harlem parents (who are absent from Rosenfeld's account) as powerless.

Becca: They don't have much control—there's a lot restricting what they can do.

David: Blaming parents is a danger we get into here!

Joby: The Hutterite influence was able to extend into the school, though—they could assert an active influence. These parents (in Harlem) *couldn't* exert real influence—the ultimate authority rests with the school officials.

Jet: Hutterite parents might actually not have control on an individual basis. Do we take the cynical view—like Ray McDermott's—that society *needs* 25% of the kids to be dropouts?

Joby: This gets into the notion of local control of schools—to what extent would the level of Hutterite control be successful in Harlem schools? Those parents right now aren't so empowered.

Becca: But it's clear what being an adult means in Hutterite culture. It's not in other societies—there's no clear preparation for adulthood in other cultures.

Lon: Does the Harlem school have better prospects, actually, than more multicultural schools? Harlem was more homogeneous—maybe it would be easier to make school more culturally resonant for the kids then.

Mica: How about Joby's point about these groups (white teachers, black students) on the large scale being in conflict? Do you agree that the school can't be fixed until this larger conflict is resolved?

Lon: We need to make the school fit the children—to start with the kids' world. But we need a community that's empowered to assume control of the school.

Joby: The reality of plurality—what does this mean in terms of educational control, or articulating a unified ideal of education for all kids? Does homogeneity lead to rallying more easily around a cultural ideal of education? The common denominator for "what education means" in the multicultural American context seems to get watered down to this "individual success and achievement" ideal, that school will get you a job to make money. Does that become the de facto subtext, the meaning of education in a multicultural context?

Lon: How do we find a richer common denominator?

Notes

[1] The title, as Rosenfeld himself explains early in his book, is supposed to be jarring and upsetting—an actual quote addressed by a teacher he worked with to some black students in the "slum school," the title is meant to convey the often overt racism exhibited by many teachers at the school.

[2] Labels like "the Hutterites" seem to many scholars to ignore cultural complexity by delineating the apparently "essential" qualities shared by the group (a practice much current anthropology openly critiques). Indeed, on a recent trip to a bookstore in San Francisco I noted that seemingly every tenth book in the "cultural studies" section had some reference to "borders" or "boundaries" in its title, suggesting that to speak of any "bounded" group seems, to many scholars, problematic to say the least (though we also, as Paul Gilroy points out, risk a naive rejection of the *realities* of "group" identities as scholars jump on this theoretical bandwagon). (See Gilroy, *The Black Atlantic*, Cambridge: Harvard University Press, 1993).

References

Hostetler, J., and G. Huntington, 1996. *The Hutterites in North America.* Ft. Worth, TX: Harcourt Brace.

Rosenfeld, G., 1983. *"Shut Those Thick Lips!" A Study of Slum School Failure.* Prospect Heights, IL: Waveland Press.

Finis

This is a book to which no conclusion can be written. It is true to its title, *Education and Cultural Process*. Educational anthropology began in the nineteenth century and will continue as long as there are schools and diverse cultures represented in them. Even if diversity diminishes, intracultural relations will provide ample opportunity for anthropological expertise to be applied and theories generated to help explain observations made.

In Part I we started with history, enriched by two versions, one anthropological and the other educationist. Part II addressed methods—including one chapter on the teacher role as enemy, a vantage point from which the author (Wolcott) wrote an ethnography of the Kwakiutl school in which he was the sole teacher. A reading of Wolcott's book (*A Kwakiutl Village and School*, Waveland Press, 1984) suggests that his role as enemy did not interfere with doing a good ethnography. In fact, it suggests that certain insights became more readily available to him as a consequence of this self-described role.

In the following section, Part III, we addressed a topic almost too encompassing to label—education and cultural process in the United States. We began with two closely linked chapters having similar outlooks. I discussed the issue of why minority groups in North America have been disadvantaged by their schools, followed by Ray McDermott's chapter on achieving school failure, an extension of his pioneering work of the same title in the second edition of *Education and Cultural Process*—this one for the years 1972–1996. The attention then shifted, in "Racing in Place," to one of the ways that failure for some students is guaranteed and the achievement of success becomes a perpetual game. The next three chapters focus on cultural transmission. Hostetler showed how communitarian societies depend on their educational system for survival in "Education in Communitarian Societies." In "The Bauer County Fair," Porter describes an institution, the county fair, that most urbanites don't know exists as a significant culture-transmitting agency in the rural Midwest. In "Teaching and Learning through Mien Culture," Hammond showed how the Mien, a horticultural and hunting group from Laos, proved to be an asset in the science program of a Sacramento elementary school and how children and their parents became a part of the school community. My case study of Beth Anne showed how the best of intentions on the part of teachers and parents can become a burden for children, making for costly, anxiety-producing adjustments. Finally, Gibson showed how Punjabi (Sikh) youngsters survive prejudice and make schooling a path to success.

In Part IV, Cultural Process Viewed Transculturally, we looked at cultures being transmitted or acquired in non-Western societies. Particular attention was given to the Hopi, Tiwi, Mistassini Cree, and the people of the Pacific island of Kosrae. The latter culture is discussed in Vera Michalchik's chapter, the most innovative piece in this section, calling attention to cultural knowledge displays—when, how, and to what effect children participate in the flow of cultural knowledge on Kosrae. This chapter is a departure from standard treatments of cultural transmission and acquisition and opens up new channels for research and praxis.

In Part V, Transcultural Comparisons, we took up the cases of Germany and Japan in comparisons to similar educational institutions in the United States—preschools in Japan and America and elementary schools in the United States and Germany. The difficulties of producing meaningful comparisons were stressed by Fujita and Sano, while divergent but comparable cultural solutions to issues in common are stressed by the Spindlers. Both chapters demonstrated new ways of interviewing—the cross-cultural reflective interview that put more responsibility on the informant for interpretation, so their voices are heard with a different emphasis than in standard ethnographic interviewing. The Spindlers also demonstrated the influence of position in the system on perceptions of behavior both in the system and cross-culturally. Both perceptions that are held in common and perceptions that differ are seen as parts of the culture of the school. In "Does Formalism Spell Failure?" Baker challenged a common shibboleth among Western critics of schools in developing countries—that of applying criteria derived from progressive, experimental schooling in Western countries to the formalistic methods that may be more appropriate to the cultural contexts of the developing countries.

In the last section, Part VI, Teaching Culture, we have replaced almost all of the previous chapters with new ones, including Barnett and Rich on teaching anthropology in a Zuni classroom, the Spindlers on teaching culture in the university context, and Pollock on a class discussion comparing Hutterite education with that of an inner-city slum school. Pollock brings up issues from critical anthropology about case studies and then answers them in terms of pedagogical values.

This book has been rewarding work, for both Louise and myself. We hope it serves the purpose we see for it—as an eclectic, nonprejudicial text for courses in the anthropology of education and related disciplines.

The Editor

George Spindler has been working on the relationship of anthropology to education since 1946 when he published his first article on the subject in *Journal of Education*. Often regarded as the father of the field, in over four decades he has published—as editor and contributor—eight major volumes on the application of anthropology to education. The present volume of *Education and Cultural Process* is the third edition, but its lineage extends all the way back to 1955 when it was called *Education and Anthropology*.

George and Louise Spindler have collaborated for many years in fieldwork and on publications concerned with educational anthropology. Together they have taught courses in ethnographic methods applicable to schools, American culture as a context for education, comparative German and American primary schooling, and issues concerning the self and adaptation. Their latest venture, cultural therapy, resulted in *Pathways to Cultural Awareness: Cultural Therapy with Teachers and Students* (Corwin Press, 1994). Together they have done field research in three Native American communities, in Germany, and in schools in Wisconsin and California.